User Perception and Influencing Factors of Technology in Everyday Life

Anabela Mesquita
ISCAP/IPP and Algoritmi Research Centre (Minho University), Portugal

Information Science
REFERENCE

Managing Director:	Lindsay Johnston
Senior Editorial Director:	Heather A. Probst
Book Production Manager:	Sean Woznicki
Development Manager:	Joel Gamon
Assistant Acquisitions Editor:	Kayla Wolfe
Typesetter:	Jennifer Romanchak
Cover Design:	Nick Newcomer

Published in the United States of America by
Information Science Reference (an imprint of IGI Global)
701 E. Chocolate Avenue
Hershey PA 17033
Tel: 717-533-8845
Fax: 717-533-8661
E-mail: cust@igi-global.com
Web site: http://www.igi-global.com

Library of Congress Cataloging-in-Publication Data

User perception and influencing factors of technology in everyday life / Anabela Mesquita, editor.
    p. cm.
  Includes bibliographical references and index.
  Summary: "This book addresses issues of human and technology interaction with coverage ranging from more technical subjects such as computer science, engineering, and information systems, to non-technical descriptions of technology and human interaction from the point of view of sociology or philosophy"--Provided by publisher.
  ISBN 978-1-4666-1954-8 (hbk.) -- ISBN 978-1-4666-1955-5 (ebook) -- ISBN 978-1-4666-1956-2 (print & perpetual access) 1. Information technology--Social aspects. 2. Information technology--Management. 3. Human-computer interaction. I. Sarmento, Anabela.
  HM851.U76 2013
  004.01'9--dc23
                                    2012009914

British Cataloguing in Publication Data
A Cataloguing in Publication record for this book is available from the British Library.

The views expressed in this book are those of the authors, but not necessarily of the publisher.

Table of Contents

Section 2
Mobile Technology and Media

Section 3
Information and Communication Technologies and E-Government

Section 4
Education, Health, and Professional Situations

Detailed Table of Contents

Section 1
Behaviour and Culture

Chapter 1

Osemeke Mosindi, Northumbria University, UK
Petia Sice, Northumbria University, UK

Recent trends in researching Information Behaviour in organisations show that the initial focus on technology has shifted to cognitive methods that take the individual into account, but more recently there has been a move to the social sciences approach. Literature shows that this approach has been informative but rather theoretic as there has been limited work using this approach to handle information problems in organisations. There is a need to develop and test theories to help understand Information Behaviour in organisations in a social science context that gives direct benefits to the organisation. It is useful to view organisations as complex social networks of interactions, where importance is put on the relationships between people in the organisations, as well as on the individual actor. A need exists to evaluate and connect insights from social sciences communities of practice, and complexity theory. This paper explores insights from these theories and develops a conceptual framework for understanding Information Behaviour in organisations. Data collection is in a preliminary stage, reflections and observations, of the researcher and a few participants. The intention is to provoke thoughts along the lines of seeking to use a synergy between theories that can offer different and useful platforms to help better understand the impact of information behaviour on organizational culture.

Chapter 2

Damian O. Eke, De Montfort University, UK

In the past few decades, there has been a lineal relationship between technology and development- the belief that availability of technology would produce development. This is evident in the advancements in Information and Communication Technologies (ICT), together with their rapid application in all spheres of mankind's life that have led many to call our society 'the information society'. It has become an important tool of governance that should be employed by every country-a tool Nigeria has failed to apply effectively. This paper discusses ICT integration in Nigeria, its relevance as a tool of development, socio-cultural factors constraining its integration, and suggests ways of eliminating these factors.

Linwu Gu, Indiana University of Pennsylvania, USA
Milam Aiken, University of Mississippi, USA
Jianfeng Wang, Indiana University of Pennsylvania, USA
Kustim Wibowo, Indiana University of Pennsylvania, USA

Previous studies have explored privacy instruments and disclosures as factors that affect on-line shopping intentions or attitudes. However, few have evaluated how information control affects this behavior. This paper draws on psychological and social justice theories to gain an understanding of how information control impacts on-line purchasing directly or indirectly through the mediation of intrinsic motivation. The resulting causal model was validated using structural equations with data from 179 respondents. Results show that perceived information control affects cognitive absorption, and users, as expected, value procedural fairness.

Jia Shen, Rider University, USA
Lauren Eder, Rider University, USA

Social commerce is the latest development in e-commerce to combine the power of online social networking with shopping. While the adoption of information technology is well studied, new theoretical development is needed to account for the specific characteristics of social commerce applications and their interactions with the user. This study examines factors that are associated with user acceptance of social shopping websites, which are sites designed specifically to support social interactions while users shop. This paper augments the Technology Acceptance Model with constructs that enhance the specificity of the model to the social shopping application of social commerce, including social comparison, social engagement, enjoyment as well as perceived ease of use and perceived usefulness. The model was empirically tested, and the results provided strong support. Implications and directions for future research are also discussed.

Andrew McDonald, Birkbeck, University of London, UK
Sven Helmer, Birkbeck, University of London, UK

Information Systems (IS) Project Management (PM) is fundamental to the modern, constantly changing and upgrading business world and is impacted by culture on many levels. This research shows the extent to which organisational culture in international IS projects is impacted by culture found on a national level. Current data contributing to IS PM knowledge is provided by investigating two Information Technology (IT) firms in the telecommunications sector based in Indonesia and the United Kingdom undergoing system upgrade projects using a survey and interviews. Differing trends between these organisational cultures are identified (and a third international control group) in regard to hierarchical structures and managing conflict employing a version of Hofstede's cultural survey as a basis.

Section 2
Mobile Technology and Media

Chapter 6

Swadesh Kumar Samanta, University of Essex, UK
John Woods, University of Essex, UK
Mohammed Ghanbari, University of Essex, UK

In this paper, the authors demonstrate that language diversity imposes a significant barrier in message communication like Short Messaging Service (SMS). SMS and other messaging services, including Multimedia Messaging Service (MMS) and e-mail, are widely used for person-to-person and Business-to-Consumer (B2C) communications due to their reach, simplicity and reliability of delivery. Reach and service delivery can be further enhanced if the message is delivered in the recipient's preferred language. Using language translation software and a database server, the authors show that the messages can be delivered as per language preference of the recipient irrespective of the language of the original message. They demonstrate the proposed mechanism can deliver a large number of services, such as education, health care management, notification in emergency situations, news and weather reports, to those who are currently not able to access them due to language barrier.

Chapter 7

Gareth Peevers, The University of Edinburgh, UK
Gary Douglas, The University of Edinburgh, UK
Mervyn A. Jack, The University of Edinburgh, UK
Diarmid Marshall, The University of Edinburgh, UK

In this paper, the authors compare the usability of SMS mobile banking and automated IVR telephone banking. Participants (N = 116) used SMS banking and IVR banking to find their account balance in a repeated-measures experiment. IVR banking scored higher for usability metrics: effectiveness, attitude, and quality. There was no clear difference in rank order of preference between the two channels. Participants gave positive comments regarding speed and efficiency with SMS banking, but had serious doubts over the security of the SMS channel, impacting consumer trust in SMS banking. The authors argue that usability problems and security concerns are a major factor in the low adoption of SMS mobile banking. Older users were less positive in general to SMS banking compared with the more established IVR banking. Older users had lower first time completion rates for SMS banking and gave IVR banking higher attitude and quality scores.

Chapter 8

Gareth Peevers, The University of Edinburgh, UK
Gary Douglas, The University of Edinburgh, UK
Mervyn A. Jack, The University of Edinburgh, UK

Participants (N=71) took part in mortgage interviews with a human agent interacting with a computer using four different communication modes: a standard video ink, a video link with video-data, the telephone and face-to-face. Video-plus-data came significantly higher in the rankings than phone. It is argued that video-plus-data was found to be more useful than phone, as it provided the participants with more feedback on their mortgage negotiation. Usability and preference were highest for face-to-face. Usability of video was significantly higher than video-plus-data. Comments made by the participants suggest that this may have been due to the split-attention effect and it is argued that this could be diminished by usability improvements. There were no significant differences in usability between the two video services and the telephone. Reasons for this are explored. Differences between genders were also discovered with the phone being judged to be less usable by male participants. If face-to-face mortgage interviews are to be supplemented by other communication channels then users would find video-plus-data the most acceptable, but there is much room for further improvements in usability.

Abram L. J. Walton, University of South Florida Polytechnic, USA
Sharon A. DeVaney, Purdue University, USA
Darrel L. Sandall, Purdue University, USA

This qualitative study used grounded theory to examine how university graduate students felt about closed circuit television (CCTV) as it relates to the privacy and safety of students on campuses. As a result of violence at a few universities, more administrators are considering the implementation of CCTV systems. Because graduate students are an important part of the university population, their views were solicited. A qualitative approach was used because of the lack of previous research on this particular topic. Themes that emerged from interviews with 10 graduate students at a large Midwestern land-grant university were identified as: right to safety, right to privacy, personal privacy responsibilities, post-CCTV sense of privacy, post-CCTV sense of safety, crime displacement, false sense of safety, and international perspectives. The findings provide insight into graduate students' perceptions of a CCTV system and have implications for implementation decisions regarding such a system. Additionally, the findings were utilized to formulate hypotheses for a larger scale research project.

Yann Truong, ESC Rennes School of Business, France

Through a questionnaire survey, this study identifies and investigates seven antecedents of consumer acceptance of mobile TV advertising. Negative factors include intrusiveness, lack of trust in the advertiser, and excessive frequency; positive influences include enjoyment, originality, value, and relevance. The study proposes and validates two measurement models of these antecedents and provides insights into the most influential factors of consumer acceptance. Excessive frequency of advertisements and lack of trust in the advertiser present the two largest obstacles to consumer acceptance of this medium, while the entertainment aspects of advertising offer the major positive factors in gaining acceptance. The study recommends that mobile TV advertising stakeholders focus on achieving appropriate frequency, overcoming lack of trust in the advertiser, and providing enjoyment and originality, as these are the largest contributors to higher consumer acceptance.

Jamie Murphy, University of Western Australia, Australia
Richard Lee, University of South Australia, Australia
Evan Swinger, University of Western Australia, Australia

This study investigated student adoption of university campus card (UCC) applications. A review of smart card, technology adoption and Unified Theory of Acceptance and Use of Technology (UTAUT) literature led to three focus groups and a survey of student perceptions and attitudes towards the university's campus card. Perceptions of 17 UCC components differed significantly across four student variables – international versus domestic, willingness to load funds, gender, and university level – supporting and extending UTAUT. Willingness to load funds on their UCC differed significantly across 16 out of 17 components, followed by domestic versus overseas students differing on 14 components, university level differing on 13 components and gender on 10. Overall, students reported that extra UCC features would enhance the university's image, improve their student experience, and encourage them to use UCCs. The results and managerial implications can help universities select and prioritise UCC functions for campus adoption and implementation.

Chapter 12

Mats Edenius, Uppsala University, Sweden
Hans Rämö, Stockholm University, Sweden

In this paper, the authors examine how senior managers, as professional workers, in a leading ICT company use smartphones, according to new configurations of time and space. Of special interest is how smartphones act as comforting handheld consoles without being rooted in physical location. Three non-physical places, as spatial nodes, are presented: pause in the temporal current, place as a function of the intensity of communication, and place in terms of becoming rooted by felt value. The authors argue that highlighting non-physical places as structures emanating from the use of smartphones is an important variable to account for when studying how professionals use smartphones, both in instrumental and non-instrumental terms.

Section 3
Information and Communication Technologies and E-Government

Chapter 13

Christine Sarah Fidler, De Montfort University, UK
Raed Kareem Kanaan, De Montfort University, UK
Simon Rogerson, De Montfort University, UK

This paper identifies and highlights the significance of Wasta as a barrier to e-government implementation within The Hashemite Kingdom of Jordan and is part of a wider qualitative research study of all barriers. A longitudinal research approach was applied to explore any dynamism within the presence of barriers over a three year study, as well as to seek a richer understanding of such barriers. Data, principally collected via interviews with relevant stakeholders, was analysed using Strauss and Corbin's variant of grounded theory. Using illustrative quotations primarily from interview transcripts, this paper enunciates the significant and persistent role that Wasta plays in hindering Jordan's e-government implementation, both as an explicitly mentioned barrier and as cause of other barriers. The paper supports the view that culture is a root cause of e-government implementation difficulty, and that barriers vary with the different country settings in which e-government systems are embedded.

The Initiative of establishing Information Technology (IT) and Community Service Centers, later renamed Knowledge Stations (KSs) was launched in 2001. The KSs initiative is intended to implement IT in local communities (LCs) and remote areas in preparation for the E-Government process. This study develops a model that explores KSs' role as a partnership in E-Government readiness in Jordan through answering the following two questions: why is a clearly comprehensive role of KSs needed for the readiness of E-Government in Jordan? How does this role take place practically? The research methodology is the case study that was applied to six KSs as a purposive sample in Amman, the capital of Jordan. Nine semi-structured interviews have been conducted with the director of KSs project, trainers, trainees and volunteers in the KSs project. The findings of the study showed that the role of KSs in E-Government readiness has four pillars: enhancement of community awareness in social and economic fields, development of Information and Communications Technology (ICT) capabilities, lessening computer illiteracy fulfillment of comprehensive development.

Section 4
Education, Health, and Professional Situations

ICT advances will bring a new generation of ubiquitous applications, opening up new possibilities for the health sector. However, the social impacts of this trend have largely remained unexplored. This study investigates the public representation of future ICT applications in the outpatient health sector in terms of their social acceptance. Mental models of ICT applications were elicited from inhabitants of Berlin, Germany, by means of qualitative interviews. The findings revealed that the interviewees felt ambivalent about anticipated changes; only if ICT use were to be voluntary and restricted to single applications and trustworthy institutions did they expect individual benefits. Concerns about data transmission to unauthorized third parties and widespread technological dissemination forcing compulsory participation led people to feel averse to such technology. Implications for potential implementation of future ICT applications in the outpatient health sector are discussed.

Chapter 16

This exploratory study examines the impact of email as a primary communication technology upon the perceptions and work behaviors of higher education professionals who support university administrative functions. Based on the interviews and observations of 23 participants, key themes emerged regarding the relationship of email to the interactions of higher education professionals. Findings are presented in three sections: (1) impact on productivity, (2) impact on social interactions, and (3) impact on well-being. The professionals who participated in this study articulated the importance of face-to-face interaction particularly in complex situations; they recognize the need to manage email sender expectations to deal with their own work stresses, and strive to temper the negative impact of constant disruption by email on workplace productivity.

Chapter 17

Chia-Wen Tsai, Ming Chuan University, Taiwan

Computing education in Taiwan is ineffective. Most teaching efforts in private vocational schools have been devoted to helping students pass tests through a "spoon-feeding" teaching method. Under such constraints, students may lose their long-term competence in practical terms. In this study, the author conducted a series of quasi-experiments to examine the long-term effects of web-mediated problem-based learning (PBL), self-regulated learning (SRL), and their combinations on students' computing skills over three years. The author re-examined students' long-term computing skills three years after the start of the related course. Results reveal that effects of web-mediated PBL, SRL, and their combinations on students' long-term computing skills are significant. The implications for scholars and teachers engaged in online learning were also discussed.

Chapter 18

Norazah Mohd Suki, Universiti Malaysia Sabah, Malaysia
T. Ramayah, Universiti Sains Malaysia, Malaysia
Michelle Kow Pei Ming, Universiti Sains Malaysia, Malaysia
Norbayah Mohd Suki, Universiti Malaysia Sabah, Malaysia

This paper explores the factors of enhancing employed job seekers intention to use social networking sites as a job search tool. 190 survey questionnaires were distributed to employed job seekers who have used social networking sites via the snowball sampling approach. The collected data were analysed using both linear and multiple regression analysis. The results showed that perceived usefulness and perceived enjoyment are positively and significantly related to the behavioural intention to use social networking sites as a job search tool, whereas perceived ease of use is not positively and significantly related. The study implies that the developers of social networking sites need to provide additional useful functionalities or tools in the social networking sites to help users of social networking sites with their job search. The paper provides an insight for employed jobseekers to find employment by using social networking sites as a job search tool.

Chapter 19

Lars Göran Wallgren, University of Gothenburg, Sweden
Svante Leijon, University of Gothenburg, Sweden
Kerstin Malm Andersson, University of Gothenburg, Sweden

Little is known about managers' perception of their subordinates' motivation, especially how this perception influences managerial behavior. This study, conducted in the growing IT consultancy sector, focuses on how IT consultancy first-line managers construct their subordinates' motivation. Since work motivation is a complex phenomenon, there is variation in how managers reduce this complexity. The empirical data was collected in semi-structured interviews with six team leaders (three female, three male) and are presented as narratives. In their narratives, the female team leaders present a more transformative view of their subordinates while the male managers present a more transactional view. The authors interpret this variation in the narrations as evidence that the issue of subordinate motivation is not seen as strategically important. This interpretation cast doubts on certain assumptions in organizational psychology theory.

Chapter 20

The Internet is an incredible technology, offering users a vast choice of new songs and catalogue that can be browsed, streamed or bought online. This paper aims to provide an explanation of factors influencing purchase intention of early adopters towards online music. An empirical survey was used to test the hypotheses. Data were collected from a total of 200 questionnaires distributed to early adopters of online music and were analysed using Structural Equation Modeling (SEM) via the Analysis of Moment Structure (AMOS 16) computer program. Results enumerate that perceived ease of use emerges as the important factor which affects perceived value among the respondents followed by perceived playfulness. Perceived value has the only significant impact on the purchase intentions towards online music. The paper rounds off with conclusions and an agenda for future research in this area.

Preface

This publication – "User Perception and Influencing Factors of Technology in Everyday Life" – comprises some of the best articles published in the *International Journal of Technology and Human Interaction* (*IJTHI*) during 2011. It is our purpose to offer the reader the most up to date research and discussions providing an overview of the trends and advances in this area.

IJTHI

The first issue of the *International Journal of Technology and Human Interaction* appeared in 2005 due to the increasing research being done in the area where technology and human meet. This area of research and practice emerged in the early 80s as a specialty area in computer science and has expanded rapidly since then, attracting professionals, researchers, and contributes from other disciplines. Till the late 70s the majority of professionals dealing with computers were information technology professionals, but this scenario has changed rapidly due to the explosion of personal computers, the challenge of personal computing, the development of the complexity of software engineering, and the application of technology in the so-called control domains (Carroll, 2009).

Originally the focus of human computer interaction was on usability mostly for productivity applications such as text editing and spreadsheets. Quickly it expanded to encompass visualization, information systems, collaborative systems, system development process, and areas of design. Nowadays it is taught in diverse departments such as psychology, design, communication studies, cognitive science, information science, geographical sciences, management information systems just to name a few.

This genesis and growth contributed to what Human-Computer Interaction (HCI) is nowadays. HCI has

grown to be broader, larger and much more diverse than computer science. It expanded from individual and generic user behaviour to include social and organizational computing, creativity and accessibility for the elderly, the cognitive impaired, and for all people. It expanded from desktop office applications to include games, e-learning, e-commerce, military systems and process control. It expanded from early graphical user interfaces to include myriad interaction techniques and devices, multi-modal interactions and host of emerging ubiquitous and context-aware interactions (Carroll, 2009).

Today, HCI is seen as the study of how people interact with computers and to what extent computers are or are not developed for successful interaction with human beings. This perspective arose from the conclusion of several studies which argue that the success or even the failure of the implementation of technologies were not due to the technology itself but to the interaction between the technology and the user. Furthermore, and as stated above, this problem of technology and human interaction covers all the fields and aspects of our lives, such as education, profession, private, or leisure time, just to mention a few.

Taking this into consideration, the journal provides a platform for leading research that addresses issues of human and technology interaction in all domains. The journal aims therefore at publishing interdisciplinary research, including aspects from a wide variety of disciplines. These disciplines may range from more technical ones such as computer science, engineering or information systems to non-technical descriptions of technology and human interaction from the point of view of sociology, psychology, education, communication, management, marketing or even philosophy. The journal also aspires to provide a publication outlet for research questions and approaches that are original and may find it difficult to be published in established journals following a rigid and exclusive structure. It is open to all research paradigms, either empirical or conceptual, but it requires them to be accessible and reflected. We also encourage the submission of high quality syntheses across research in different specialties that are interesting and comprehensible to all members of the information systems community and related disciplines.

The journal is open to several topics that may include (but are not limited to) the following:

- Experiential learning through the use of technology in organizations
- Influence of gender in the adoption and use of technology
- Interaction and conversion between technologies and their impact on society
- Intersection of humanities and sciences and its impact on technology use
- Perceptions and conceptualizations of technology
- Relationship of theory and practice with regard to technology
- Social impact of specific technologies (e.g. biometrics, SCM, PGP, etc.)
- Social shaping of technology and human interaction research
- Technological risks and their human basis
- Value of intellectual capital in knowledge management
- And all other issues related to the interaction of technology and humans, either individually or socially.

INSIDE THIS BOOK

This book was prepared in such a way that the reader could find theoretical and empirical research falling into four major topics: behaviour and culture; mobile technologies and media, ICT and e-government and education, health and professional situations.

Behaviour and Culture

Behaviour and culture has been a popular topic throughout the years and has managed to keep up to date due to the rapid changes in the field of information technologies. How do we behave with technology? What kind of behaviour changes do technologies induce? In the first paper, authors explore insights from theories to help understanding information behaviour in organisations in a social science context. The second paper discusses ICT integration in Nigeria and the role played by it. Why are there some on-line shopping websites that are so successful while others do not attract clients? What affects on-line shopping? These are some of the questions addressed in papers three and four. Finally, in paper five, authors discuss the impact of national culture impacts in international IS projects

Mobile Technologies and Media

In 2011, the journal published a considerable number of papers related to research concerning mobile phones, smart phones, mobile messaging services and other devices focusing on ubiquity and mobility. The issues addressed are related to automatic language translation, the usability of SMS and IVR as digital bank channels, the satisfaction of customer with alternatives to face-to-face interaction, the use of closed circuit television, the acceptance of mobile television advertising, the adoption of university smart card systems and the use of smart phones in a professional context.

ICT and E-Government

E-government is still an actual topic. In both papers in this section, authors discuss the barriers to e-government in Jordan as well as the role of partnership in e-government readiness. Results show the importance and influence of culture and knowledge stations as barriers or enablers to ICT implementation in e-government.

Education, Health, and Professional Situations

ICT can be implemented and used in different contexts. In this section, the reader will find researches done in the field of health, education and professional situations. What are the social impacts of ubiquitous ICT applications in the outpatient health sector in terms of social acceptance? What is the impact of email as a primary communication technology in a professional context? What is the effectiveness of computing in education? What factors can enhance employed job seekers intention to use social networking sites as a job search tool? How does subordinates' motivation influence managerial behaviour? What factors influence purchase intention of early adopters towards online music? These are some of the questions addressed and discussed in the papers in this section.

BEYOND THE BOOK

It is a fact that the population (particularly in Europe) is getting older. Low birth rates and higher life expectancy will transform the shape of the EU-27's age pyramid (Eurostat, 2012). This situation will also happen in the EUA, where life expectancy had increased by 0.1 year from 78.6 in 2009 to 78.7 in 2010 (NVSS, 2012). The share of older persons in the total population will increase in the coming decades, as a greater proportion of the post-war baby-boom generation reaches retirement. Moreover, people are getting more educated and highly educated men and women are likely to live longer (Eurostat, 2010). According to the statistics, it is possible to observe a systematic relationship between educational attainment and mortality meaning that at any age, life expectancy is lower amongst persons with a lower educational attainment and higher in better educated groups (Eurostat, 2010). In fact "mortality, health and the age that people die at are strongly influenced by socio-economic factors such as educational attainment, employment status and income level" (op.cit.).

This scenario will have a significant impact in our lives. As a matter of fact this represents an increased burden on those of working age to provide for the social expenditure required by the ageing population for a range of related services. However, one must be aware that this ageing population has specific characteristics and cannot be compared to the same kind of population at the end of the 19th century. Nowadays, someone on his/her 65 or 70, although already retired, can still be healthy, energetic, dynamic and disposed to learn and contribute to the society as someone in his/her 40's. We can say that they are still active, willing to spend their last years doing things, visiting places, meeting new people, and why not, using technology This means new challenges for those dealing with the relationship and interaction between human and technology. What are the needs of this older population? What kind of technologies and services do they need and expect? How can technologies and services be adapted to them? And how can they learn the necessary skills in order to use the technologies and services? These are some of the questions that arise when we think about this binomial. Furthermore, as people get older, the figures for digital exclusion get also higher. This means that older people do not use technologies or have access to information as much as younger people. How can this situation be reversed?

Some Projects and Initiatives

There are already some projects and initiatives in order to promote the digital inclusion of older people. The following list is not exhaustive but allows us to have a picture of the situation in Europe.

- **EU-Project "Mapping Existing Research and Identifying Knowledge Gaps – MERI" in 2003 and 2004 (Austria):** This project focus on the situation of older women in Europe: gathering more knowledge about their specific living conditions and problems, improving the empirical foundations regarding their condition for scientific works and raising awareness of their situation among a broad public.
- **The activity programme "FIT and ACTIVE in old age" - especially for older people to train their cognitive, motor and sensory competencies (Austria):** It is an accepted fact among gerontologists that active use of the body, mind and senses protects people from premature ageing, and that even very old people, whose mobility is already restricted or has been completely lost, can regain their physical mobility with appropriate activity and can also improve their mental performance and employ their senses more consciously.
- **Seniors at the computer (Austria):** This project was created in cooperation with the Hernals region. Here, pupils help seniors to get rid of worries about using the computer while learning to be patient at the same time (http://www.informatikhauptschule.at/projekte/senioren/seniormain.htm)
- **ADD LIFE (Czech Republic):** This project means ADDing quality to LIFE through inter-generational learning via universities („Den Jahren Leben geben durch intergenerationelles Lernen an Universitäten"). The partnership has been established in order to create new offers for senior learners at university level and in an intergenerational learning setting.
- **Internet connects the generations (Czech Republic):** This project is a part of an EU project that supports the active life of seniors and has been financed by the PHARE programme. It has been organised by the school in Vrane and Vlatavou. Here, pupils of this Elementary School teach older people in the computer classroom. During ten hours (ten evenings), seniors learn Email, Word and Internet use. Both pupils and older learners gain intergenerational experience (http://www.ucitel-skenoviny.cz/obsah_clanku.php?vydani=05&rok=05&odkaz=internet.htm)
- **EuCoNet Club (Spain):** *EuCoNet Club - European Computer Network Club* – this is a self-help initiative for introducing ICT skills developed at U3A University of Alicante, Spain from a Grundtvig learning partnership of the same name.

- **Teaching Basic PC Skills – an Alternative Approach (Slovakia):** *Teaching Basic PC Skills – an Alternative Approach* – is a course developed by the Library Dept. of Comenius University in Bratislava, Slovakia for teaching ICT skills to older people using open source applications and targeted training.
- **TownStories (Germany):** This is a Grundtvig learning partnership coordinated by Heimatmuseum Treptow, Germany, with self-directed virtual cooperation and face-to-face seminars aimed at enhancing creative writing, foreign language skills and cultural competence.
- **G&G - Grandparents & Grandsons (Italy):** *G&G - Grandparents & Grandsons* – is a European project from the eLearning program with an intergenerational approach to teaching ICT skills by young volunteer trainers, developing methods and materials, coordinated by the EnAIP FVG, Italy.
- **GERONET (Finland):** *GERONET* – is a project with much experience in teaching basic ICT skills in various locations in Finland, peer teaching models with target group-related methodology and tutor training, developed by UTA Jyväskylä, Finland.
- **SoLiLL – Self-organised Learning in Later Life (Germany):** *SoLiLL – Self-organised Learning in Later Life* – is a Socrates project exploring cooperative learning in virtual groups, developing methods for learning and virtual communication in international context, coordinated by ZAWiW, Ulm University, Germany.
- **TVL - Technical Basis for Virtual Learning (Germany):** *TVL - Technical Basis for Virtual Learning* – is a step-by-step moderated virtual course in online communication skills from ZAWiW, Ulm University, Germany, preparing for participation in thematic online courses *AVL – Applied Virtual learning.*

Finally, we would like to present the project

- **"Intergenerational ICT skills":** This Grundtvig partnership was a unique opportunity to discover the potential of activities which help seniors to acquire ICT skills within the context of non-formal educational activities. The aim of the project was to find good practice in ICT learning possibilities for seniors and intergenerational learning examples. In the next paragraphs the most important results obtained and lessons learned in this project will be summarized. They can serve as inspiration for future work. But before that we ask ourselves,

Why Intergenerational?

Intergenerational means a relationship between two different generations where both learn from each other. An intergenerational learning is a process of storytelling, through which individuals acquire skills and knowledge, but also attitudes and values, from daily experience, from all available resources and from all influences in their own life worlds (EAGLE, 2007). It can be described as a process of a "by the way learning" while doing interesting things with interesting people.

What are the motivations among seniors to learn ICT?

There are several reasons to start learning ICT. The reasons may be individual and they often differ very much from person to person. They can be related with everyday life, entertainment, social activity, access to information, just to name a few. This variety of needs should always be taken into consideration before designing the contents of an ICT course for senior learners. The items listed below might be helpful while creating the structure covering different topics within one course.

- Interest in new inventions and machines
- Curiosity and more free time available after retirement
- To communicate with children, other family members or friends abroad that cannot be visited so often
- To present their own products (stories, pictures, products)
- To buy (books) and sell (e-Bay)
- Forced by circumstances (left a widow or widower)
- Tragic experience – car accident, etc. - need of sharing with people with similar story
- To do administrative work avoiding personal visits and standing in a cue at the office
- Post-production of digital pictures, scanning of pictures
- Looking for new friends
- Substitute for TV, radio or newspaper – news and newest gossip
- To look for information about hobbies – discussion boards, clubs, groups of interest, etc.
- To look for a new partner on-line
- To look for everyday practical information (train departure, menu in ones favourite restaurant, etc.)
- Medical interest – doctors, alternative medicine, health care web pages, etc.
- Professional interest – research
- Self-esteem

What are the benefits that both actors (seniors and juniors) would receive while engaging in this relationship?

Assumptions of the Juniors

Strengths

Many youngsters are curious about the life stories of their parents or grandparents. They also have great knowledge about the newest technologies. And success in teaching seniors helps them raise self–confidence. Moreover, some young people already have some teaching experience which helps them to avoid mistakes and understand the needs of seniors. Additionally, one can transfer certain competences from the older technologies to the new ones. For instance, some older people know how to type quickly at a typing machine. And this technical knowledge can be used in the new learning situation. Finally, in case of "a teacher from the family" one can easily laugh about the success and mistakes without being afraid of public embarrassment.

Weaknesses

Young people are often not patient enough and this lack of patience can be perceived as arrogance. Moreover, young family members are not available all the time, in particular when seniors need their help.

Opportunities

The interest in photographs from the past can be a good base for storytelling and the learning process. The interest in "how did people handle everyday problems without ICT technologies" is another good base for the story telling and learning process. These activities raise awareness about the meaning of intergenerational learning and its benefits on both sides. Such a learning cooperation can be an interesting supplement to usual family activities (or a substitute if there are not enough activities). It might make the communication flow within the wider family work. For instance, it is common and easy to share ones' mood with the grandmother on Facebook.

Threats

The youngsters have different values which might cause misunderstandings during the ICT lessons. Many seniors have plenty of other activities which fill their time and which seem more important to them (hiking, meeting friends, etc.). There are certain family patterns which might influence the motivation and process of teaching (too honest reactions, hidden motivations projected into the lessons, power and role games, awareness of a secure relationship and therefore less motivation to hold on to the end). Another threat is the stereotypical image of "the right" role of a senior in the family and in the world (seniors should devote their energy to the needs of children and grandchildren). Finally, technologies develop faster and faster which might depress the seniors and create even bigger gap between them and the juniors.

Assumptions of the Seniors

Strengths

Affordable prizes of the computer equipment. Technologies are simpler every day. Rising offer on ICT courses for seniors. Post office services become more expensive. This means that stamps and envelops are more expensive and nobody answers a written letter; there is much more probability to get an email answered. Wide options of PCs and internet are a source of strong motivation:

- Comfort in doing diverse things at home
- Contact with people who live far away or cannot see each other
- Wide range of self-expression
- Creative satisfaction
- Possibility of sharing experience and opinions, etc.
- Experience of mastering computer makes the users more self-confident and brings a new "kick into life"

Weaknesses

The software is still not intuitively manageable. Sometimes, it is in English and seniors don´t know if it is possible to get a version in their language and how to do so. Clear guidelines with translation of the most common ICT abbreviation are missing or are not easily available. At some places there are still not enough competent and motivated trainers. Many seniors don´t know where to look for computer courses. And not all courses are for free. Also, there is a media support stereotypical image of a senior as a person who is too old and not enough skilled to manage ICT. They still present a dynamic senior who uses the mostly modern technology as an exception.

Opportunities

Many seniors don´t feel old and the stereotypes in the society are slowly changing. A friend of a neighbour who manages his or her life from the comfortable armchair at home is a motivation. It is possible to train the trainers in a better way and make it possible to avoid prejudice and anxiety of seniors. The content motivates to master the form (If I want to satisfy my needs and hobbies I have to learn how to find it). Internet and PC fulfil an important need of expressing stories and experience, which in different ways is very important for the seniors. Internet and PC is a potential tool for conservation of knowledge and life experience. Finally, internet is an anonymous place where seniors can try out completely new things or identities.

Threats

Primal demotivation (I am too old, too stupid); Family patterns (I am the one who is always right and my child won´t teach me what to do); Loss of motivation after the first unsuccessful try; Psychical barriers to bother children or grandchildren with requests; There may be arrogant or incompetent trainers; Experience of embarrassment in front of other course participants; Life bitterness in general; Internet as an anonymous space can be a source of frustration and negative experience (rude people).

Benefits of Intergenerational ICT Learning

There is a variety of positive influences intergenerational learning can have on relationships within the family and on personal development and growth as well. In the process of learning from a younger family member and, on the other hand the commitment to teach a family member are important messages on the relationship level. Both of them mean "I want to spent time with you. I want to help you or I want you to be the one to help me". These aspects should not be underestimated not only by the parents but also by teachers, trainers and all other experts involved in the educational system. Intergenerational cooperation should be more supported and included into the system of little projects and homework. The benefits can be divided into following basic levels:

Intrapersonal

The junior can experience the feeling of being useful and helpful while the senior can experience the acquaintance of new competences

Interpersonal

Primal benefits are ICT skills for the senior and life stories for the junior. Secondary benefit is consolidation and deepening of the relationship and possible motivation for other activities

Family Level

Members of different generations spend some efficient and creative time together. The family history will be conserved for next generations

Society Level

Learning from a family member composes of many emotional elements which can facilitate the learning process and be a source of additional knowledge to the facts learned at school. This way of making and preserving stories is an important way how to retain different points of view or different interpretations of a certain historical period as a source for critical discussion and broadening of one´s perspective.

Finally, I would like to leave here some recommendations to set up an ICT course for older people:

- Inform seniors about all possible benefits of the ICT education
- Hold the courses in small groups (maybe a few friends)
- The biggest competence of the trainer is patience and tolerance to different values
- Be sensitive towards to the complexes of the seniors
- Stress all immediate benefits after mastering certain competences
- Praise each new competence
- Motivate to train some skills everyday
- Create a table of important abbreviations in a practical format
- Think about the possibility of private lessons at senior´s home for disabled people
- Teach one competence from diverse points of view so that seniors can become aware of various ways of using it
- Involve the course participants into little simple projects and team work
- Let them create - seniors love to write about their life experience
- Respect the variety of different hobbies and fields of interest
- Train the trainers

Learning in Reverse – Life Stories

Intergenerational learning always means a two-way process. This is a process in which both participating parties win and learn something new. Besides the ICT profit and new skills learned by the seniors, the main benefit for the juniors of the bilateral cooperation can be cultural and social learning realised in the way of storytelling. Within the Intergenerational ICT skills partnership the seniors became special story tellers; suddenly they were not only grandmothers, aunts or mothers any more. Now they were the treasure stories which happened decades ago. The change of attitude was obvious and juniors made a unique experience as they mentioned in evaluation interviews at the end of the project. Often they joined the project out of curiosity and none of them expected so much fun and such a deep emotional journey to the past of their older relatives. The stories themselves are a part of the project website and they can be found here www.intergenerational-ictskills.eu.

CONCLUSION

The *International Journal of Technology and Human Interaction* is concerned with research that explores the link between people and technology. Being the technology present in all the dimensions of our lives, it is natural that all sorts of disciplines can contribute for this publication. Besides that, one acknowledges that intergenerational learning might be a solution to overcome some of the problems related with senior learning of ICT. Storytelling and non-formal learning contexts can be enablers of ICT learning, promoting lifelong learning and avoiding digital divide.

Anabela Mesquita
ISCAP / IPP & Algoritmi Research Centre, Minho University, Portugal

REFERENCES

Carroll, J. M. (2009). Human computer interaction (HCI). In M. Soegaard & R. F. Dam (Eds.), *Encyclopedia of human-computer interaction*. Retrieved from http://www.interaction-design.org/encyclopedia/human_computer_interaction_hci.html

Eurostat. (2010). *Highly educated men and women likely to live longer*. Retrieved March 1, 2012, from http://epp.eurostat.ec.europa.eu/cache/ity_offpub/ks-sf-10-024/en/ks-sf-10-024-en.pdf

Eurostat. (2012). *Population and population change statistics*. Retrieved March 1, 2012, from http://epp.eurostat.ec.europa.eu/statistics_explained/index.php/Population_and_population_change_statistics

Fischer, T. (2008). *Lessons in intergenerational learning*. EAGLE Consortium & Centre for Intergenerational Practice, Beth Johnson Foundation, 2007. Retrieved from http://www.epractice.eu/files/documents/workshops/13771-1208261792.pdf

Grandparents & Grandchildren Project. (n.d.). *Digital literacy training for adults: Initiatives, actors, strategies*. Retrieved from http://www.geengee.eu/

NVSS. (2012). *Deaths: Preliminary data for 2010*. Retrieved March 1, 2012, from http://www.cdc.gov/nchs/data/nvsr/nvsr60/nvsr60_04.pdf

Section 1
Behaviour and Culture

Chapter 1
An Exploratory Theoretical Framework for Understanding Information Behaviour

Osemeke Mosindi
Northumbria University, UK

Petia Sice
Northumbria University, UK

ABSTRACT

Recent trends in researching Information Behaviour in organisations show that the initial focus on technology has shifted to cognitive methods that take the individual into account, but more recently there has been a move to the social sciences approach. Literature shows that this approach has been informative but rather theoretic as there has been limited work using this approach to handle information problems in organisations. There is a need to develop and test theories to help understand Information Behaviour in organisations in a social science context that gives direct benefits to the organisation. It is useful to view organisations as complex social networks of interactions, where importance is put on the relationships between people in the organisations, as well as on the individual actor. A need exists to evaluate and connect insights from social sciences communities of practice, and complexity theory. This paper explores insights from these theories and develops a conceptual framework for understanding Information Behaviour in organisations. Data collection is in a preliminary stage, reflections and observations, of the researcher and a few participants. The intention is to provoke thoughts along the lines of seeking to use a synergy between theories that can offer different and useful platforms to help better understand the impact of information behaviour on organizational culture.

INTRODUCTION

This paper focuses on developing and exploring a conceptual framework to contribute to the understanding of Information Behaviour (IB) in organisations, by attempting to achieve a synergy between enactive cognitive science, social science research and communities of practice, and complexity theory. The need for such a framework has arisen from the necessity to adopt a holistic approach encompassing the study of individual behaviours, human interactions, and cultural

DOI: 10.4018/978-1-4666-1954-8.ch001

characteristics in diagnosing and improving the information environment in organisations. The study is grounded in the authors' experience in research and consultancy in a manufacturing company and their efforts to develop methods that deliver results in practice.

The theories are explained in later sections, to give you a good insight to what they all offer, and where there is possibility to achieve synergy between them. But first there is a discussion of research in information behaviour and factors that have been issues till date.

Interdisciplinary Nature and General Overview of Information Behaviour Research

Information behaviour (IB) has been studied in various fields most notably, psychology, sociology, information sciences, etc. The main platform of theories, which the studies have progressed from, were proposed by cognitive scientists with the focus on the characteristics of the individual human actor (Mutshewa, 2007), and social sciences with the focus on how the individual's surroundings play a part in IB (Wilson, 2000; Pettigrew, Fidel, & Bruce, 2001). The interdisciplinary nature of IB has led to various researchers having different definitions for the same terms and differing ideas, and thus, there has not been a general consensus in the study of IB. This may be a good thing considering the fact that it is a relatively new discourse, and the disparate views could be what the field needs to move forward and seek new findings to enhance understanding. A definition of IB that allows for a general description and wider focus is used in this paper: "Information Behaviour (IB) is the perceptions and actions of individuals towards approaching and handling information" (Davenport, 1997).

It is well established in literature that information behaviour is directly related to the specific situations or contexts that give rise to the information need or use (Julien & Michels, 2000;

Niedzwiedzka, 2003). Just like the context, there are other variables which Wilson (2000) calls intervening variables like the role the individual is in at the time. For example, an individual's behaviour could be, different when in a professional role, and could be different in another role for the same individual. The environment also matters as one of the intervening variables, which could be looked at on a local or organisational level.

This shows that the context in which IB is studied plays an important role in the understanding elicited from the study. In effect, the way the organisation is viewed when studying it, has an impact on the nature of understanding that we get from the study. To put this in plain terms: "What we can know is determined by the available methods of knowing" (Poole & McPhee, 1994). There are also other factors that determine the information behaviour in organisations, such as the leadership, industry, media of communication, etc.

Most of the research on Information Behaviour in organisations, have focused on information seeking behaviour (Vakkari, 2008), a single type of proactive behaviour. Though information use has been sometimes incorporated in these studies, the individual's variety of behaviours of information use, have not been looked at in detail, although these have an impact on organisational performance. For example, ignoring information, hoarding information, forwarding useful information to other actors, could be considered as part of the various dimensions of information behaviour. The involvement of the researcher in the study of the complex phenomenon of IB needs rethinking too, as the research process determines the quality of the outcomes.

Most of the research in IB has focused on studying the information behaviour of employees in organisations, but has delivered very limited results on understanding how to improve the information environment. For example, Choo, Bergerson, Detlor, and Heaton (2008) suggests three information capabilities that organisations should be strong in to realize superior performance results: Information technology practices, Information management practices Information behaviours and values; but there is no explanation as to how organisations should try to move towards achieving the third, i.e. information behaviour and values. The proposed framework seeks to offer ground for explanation of how information behaviour emerges and this provide a starting point for considering improvement.

Research and Framework Background

Organisations have been conceptualized in the past as 'machines', 'organisms', political systems, cultures, etc. (Morgan, 2006). More recent views of organisations have shifted towards using metaphors from complexity theory, cognitive science and the social sciences, and all these views seek to understand organisations as complex social networks of interactions. The way organisations have been understood as systems, and self organizing parts that make up the whole, takes away the complexity that exists in reality as humans are capable of making decisions, which parts of systems like mechanical or biological systems do not possess. So viewing organisations as complex social networks will help put into context the individuals background, group dynamics and the effects these have in shaping information culture and behaviour. One of the major concerns of organisations is to improve performance, survive, innovate and compete in an ever changing environment. So it is necessary for research in organisations to address this concern and look for result oriented methodologies. Figure 1 presents the needed link between the real world problem and a result oriented methodology, which is missing in current IB research.

The frame in Figure 1 is grounded in a real world problem. The problem is generic. It is encountered at a manufacturing company, which has a traditional organisational structure with several departments; there is lack of information sharing between these departments, and there is indifference towards using the available information systems, i.e. wherever possible, people put in the minimum effort, in maintaining the data in

Figure 1. Underlying problem background

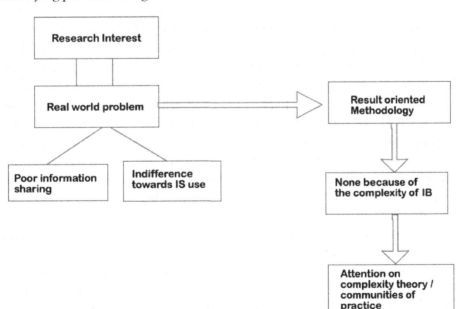

the system, which affects the generated output, and in turn affects data availability to make well informed decisions.

Through the lenses of the researchers' Worldview and research interests, it has been perceived that the underlying background of the problem is rooted in Information Behaviour.

A result oriented methodology for studying information behaviour was sought, but to no avail. This is largely due to the complex nature of the phenomenon of IB. Literature review suggests that several theories from related fields, i.e. complexity theory and communities of practice suggest an approach towards achieving practical results.

Framework for Understanding Information Behaviour: Proposed Theories

The proposed framework of understanding encompasses insights from complexity theory, communities of practice and the theory of autopoiesis.

Complexity Theory: Focuses on explaining the emergence of complex behaviour. As Mitleton-Kelly (2001) puts it: in thermodynamics the focus is on where heat comes from and goes to, complexity science is more concerned as to how the complexity comes about.

The term Complex Systems Theory is often used as a replacement of Complexity Theory. As humans we describe the world in terms of simple and composite unities, i.e. systems. Systems have become the means of understanding and explaining behaviour. The theory of complex systems is the overarching framework that is really about how systems evolve and change. The insights of complexity come from contemporary discoveries in non-linear dynamics and chaos theory and are particularly useful in understanding and analysing how complex behaviour emerges from the interactions between the systems elements.

When elements of the system interfere, or cooperate, or compete, there are non-linear interactions going on. Most of everyday life is

non-linear and thus the principle of superposition fails spectacularly. If you invest twice as much in advertising, you do not necessarily get twice as much sale. If you invest twice the effort you do not necessarily achieve twice the outcome. It is now well-recognised that people behave in a non-linear way. People have choices, they often react in ways that are stubbornly individual, even peculiar, and group behaviour is more than simply the sum of individual behaviours (Sice & French, 2006).

While it may be useful to look at human enterprises as complex systems it is important not to overlook the open nature of such systems and the continuous emergence of new interactions by way of gesture and response, that lead to further interactions which shape the power relations, norms, culture in organisations, which in turn shape those interactions (Stacey, 2001). Stacey chooses to look at organisations as Complex Responsive Processes (and not as Systems), i.e. networks of interactions, of gestures and response, and argues that these are the basis for emergence and explanation of behaviour in human enterprises.

By using metaphors from complexity theory, the reason behind the complex nature of complex phenomena can be better understood. Though we understand why a phenomenon may be complex, the causal links between the local level activities and the emerging global activities cannot be determined, because to make a causal link, there has to be a form of generalization, which is difficult as many subjective factors that influence IB cannot allow generalizations (Mitleton-Kelly, 2001). Though it sounds like this would not be of much help to the researcher, the fact that we are able to understand that these outcomes cannot be predicted, helps the researcher to set more modest objectives, and appreciate the need to get more involved in the intricate details that bring about the phenomenon on a global level. For example viewing emergence in terms of information culture, it can be perceived as generated from the interaction of different individual IB, but studying the individual IB cannot determine the information culture in the organisation, so it is an emergent property. But there have been attempts to determine an organisations information culture by using surveys on employees, and the outcome was a generalization from the responses of the employees as to what the information culture of the organisation was through their IB. So it is necessary to know if the individual behaviour actually influences the information culture or does the policies and organisational structure alone decide this? Based on emergence, the global outcomes in turn affect the local activities, so it would be useful to know if the information culture actually impacts back on the information behaviour of the individuals

Communities of Practice (COP): Was defined by Wenger (1998) as "groups of people who share a concern or a passion for something they do and learn how to do it better as they interact regularly". Like the definition suggests these people interact to learn better ways of achieving their goals, through sharing experiences, information and knowledge. The concept has been adopted most readily by organisations because of the recognition that knowledge is an asset to the organisation and as such needs to be nurtured and managed properly. Initial efforts on knowledge creation in organisations had focused mainly on information systems, but COP provides a new approach, which focuses on people and on the social structures that enable them to learn with and from each other. It is our opinion, that further development of the COP approach to information sharing and use needs to be informed by enactive cognitive science, i.e. the theory of autopoiesis. The body of knowledge known as autopoiesis was developed in 1980s by the biologists Humberto Maturana and Francisco Varela to explain the generative dynamics of living systems. The theory has found much wider application for understanding humans, organisations and communities and the impact of the human condition, i.e. wellbeing and quality of life on the effectiveness of communication and innovation in social systems (Sice & French, 2004).

Synergies of insights from complexity theory, communities of practice and autopoiesis would allow for a holistic approach to studying IB by viewing the individual, the network of interactions and the emergent properties of human enterprises as mutually determined entities.

Some Reflections on the Practical Application of the Framework in IB Research

Based on the research questions and the problem at hand, the framework suggests starting off with gathering information on individual's backgrounds, beliefs, perspectives, history, etc. On a social level, observing, studying and understanding the interactions between the individual and their immediate information environment, the people they share information with, are important. Communities of practice can be used to guide the observation of the interactions, taking into account norms and values in the organisation. The effect of these interactions on the organisation can be understood through using analogies from complex responsive processes to analyze data and emergent features in the organisation.

The metaphors used to understand organisations, play a fundamental role in how we interpret studies that are carried out in organisations. Using metaphors from complexity theory will help give new insights to studying IB in organisations. The perspective of complex responsive processes fits with the social practices suggested by communities of practice, and if the cognitive aspects of the individual are taken into account, the complexity of IB might be understood better; and this would lay a foundation for studies linking IB to organisational performance, hence the suggestion of a synergy of the theories. The researcher would also need to be involved in the everyday activities of the organisation, observing, interviewing and reflecting on issues relating the research questions, and the problem at hand.

The tool presented in Figure 2 is used to diagnose the level of complexity of different phenomena, and it can be applied to a range of fields. Looking at it from an information perspective as the diagrams shows, it gives an insight as to what the members of an organisation view as complex, and also the degree of complexity with regard to information sharing and usage in the organisation. In terms of analysis, this will serve as a starting point for breaking down information related issues in the organisation, and help to discuss what gives rise to the perceived complexity in these issues.

A brief overview of the main factors in the suggested framework, are shown in Figure 3. It shows the ground level interactions (formal and informal), information culture, organisational culture which affects the information culture, and stresses researcher involvement in the research environment.

Current Work

A research study, aiming at understanding IB by viewing organisations as complex social networks, with a view to improving organisational performance, is in the process of being carried out at a manufacturing company, as part of a global corporation, with a parent company in Germany, and other branches all over the world.

A Socratic dialogue workshop was used inquire into how people perceive information, what criteria are applied to identify information in an organisational context. Participants are also asked to fill out a diary on a bi-weekly basis, as to how they seek information when the need arises, and how they respond to information in an organisational context. Further data gathering will be informed by the framework described in this paper.

CONCLUSION

The phenomenal domain of human enterprises is realised through the network of interactions between the human actors. Such networks through the interactions of local agents are capable of spontaneous self-organisation, to produce emergent orderly, evolving patterns of behaviours of the network without any prior comprehensive blueprint for evolution. The immediate local 'intentions' of the interacting agents are continually emerging in a context. The dynamics are determined by the

Figure 2. An example of a complexity mapping tool

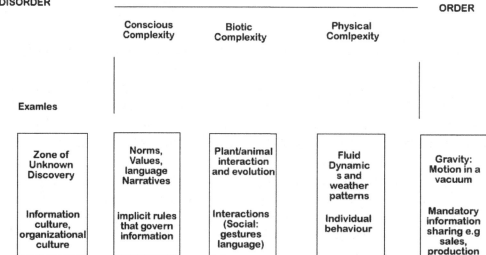

Figure 3. Framework overview

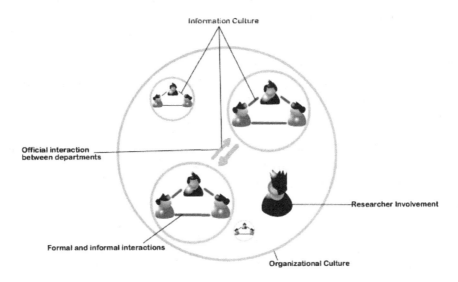

pattern and nature of the actors' relationships. Coherence is realised through communication, information sharing and use. The individual actors exhibit non-linear behaviour, i.e. their behaviour depends on their embodiment, their environment and context of activity. The understanding of the complex processes of interactions, the dynamics of gesture and response, are important pre-requisites in studying Information Behaviour in organisations. The conceptual framework for IB research proposed in this paper attempted a synergy of insights from complexity theory, communities of practice and theory of autopoiesis.

REFERENCES

Choo, C. W., Bergerson, P., Detlor, B., & Heaton, L. (2008). Information culture and information use: An exploratory study of three organizations. *Journal of the American Society for Information Science and Technology, 59*(5), 792–804. doi:10.1002/asi.20797

Julien, H., & Michels, D. (2000). Source selection among information seekers: Ideals and realities. *Canadian Journal of Information and Library Science-Revue* [Canadienne des Sciences de L 'Information et de Bibliotheconomie], *25*(1), 1-18.

Julien, H., & Michels, D. (2004). Intra-individual information behaviour in daily life. *Information Processing & Management, 40*(3), 547. doi:10.1016/S0306-4573(02)00093-6

Mitleton-Kelly, E. (2001). *Complexity science and order creation.* Retrieved from http://www2.lse. ac.uk/researchAndExpertise/Experts/e.mitleton-kelly@lse.ac.uk

Morgan, G. (2006). *Images of organization.* Thousand Oaks, CA: Sage.

Mutshewa, A. (2007). A theoretical exploration of information behaviour: A power perspective. *Aslib Proceedings: New Information Perspectives, 59*, 249–263.

Niedzwiedzka, B. (2003). Proposed general model of information behaviour. *Information Research, 9*(1).

Pettigrew, K. E., Fidel, R., & Bruce, H. (2001). Conceptual frameworks in information behavior. *Annual Review of Information Science & Technology, 35*, 43–78.

Poole, S. M., & McPhee, R. D. (1994). Methodology in interpersonal communication research. In *Handbook of interpersonal communication* (pp. 42–99). Thousand Oaks, CA: Sage.

Sice, P., & French, I. (2004). Understanding humans and organisation– philosophical implications of autopoiesis. *Journal of Philosophy of Management, 4*(1), 55–66.

Sice, P., & French, I. (2006). A holistic frame of reference for modelling social systems. *Kybernetes, 35*, 5–10. doi:10.1108/03684920610662638

Stacey, R. D. (2001). *Complex responsive processes in organizations - learning and knowledge creation*. London, UK: Routledge.

Vakkari, P. (2008). Trends and approaches in information behaviour research. *Information Research, 13*(4).

Wenger, E. (1998). *Communities of practice: Learning, meaning, and identity*. Cambridge, UK: Cambridge University Press.

Wilson, T. D. (2000). Recent trends in user studies: action research and qualitative methods. *Information Research, 5*(3).

Wilson, T. D. (2008). The information user: Past, present and future. *Journal of Information Science, 34*(4), 457–464. doi:10.1177/0165551508091309

This work was previously published in the International Journal of Technology and Human Interaction, Volume 7, Issue 2, edited by Anabela Mesquita and Chia-Wen Tsai, pp. 1-8, copyright 2011 by IGI Publishing (an imprint of IGI Global).

Chapter 2
ICT Integration in Nigeria:
The Socio-Cultural Constraints

Damian O. Eke
De Montfort University, UK

ABSTRACT

In the past few decades, there has been a lineal relationship between technology and development- the belief that availability of technology would produce development. This is evident in the advancements in Information and Communication Technologies (ICT), together with their rapid application in all spheres of mankind's life that have led many to call our society 'the information society'. It has become an important tool of governance that should be employed by every country-a tool Nigeria has failed to apply effectively. This paper discusses ICT integration in Nigeria, its relevance as a tool of development, socio-cultural factors constraining its integration, and suggests ways of eliminating these factors.

INTRODUCTION

In 2009, Nokia Siemens published a Connectivity Scorecard 2009 created by Leonard Waveman. This study shows that Nigeria has the lowest ICT penetration, potential, usage and accessibility out of 50 countries of the world sampled (Nokia Siemens Networks, 2009).

This Connectivity Scorecard measures the availability of ICTs and the extent to which people, governments and enterprise put these technologies to economically productive use. It claims to take a comprehensive look at the usage and potential of ICT in different countries of the world. Does this result mean that Nigeria has not caught up the information age? Or does it show that Nigeria has not been able to use ICTs for innovative and developmental purposes?

A few years ago, the Federal government of Nigeria (FGN) approved some IT policies for major sectors of the industry such as 'the National Telecommunications Policy' and the National Information Technology (NIT) Policy'. The IT sector was liberalized and ICT accorded priority status. And in 2001 the National Information Technology Development Agency (NITDA) was

DOI: 10.4018/978-1-4666-1954-8.ch002

established to implement the NIT policy. (Ajayi, 2003) This agency was charged with the duty of making Nigeria an IT capable country in Africa and a key player in the Information Society by the year 2005, using IT as the engine for sustainable development and global competitiveness (National Information Technology Development Agency, 2001).

Since then, some of the projects undertaken by this agency include the Public Service Network (PSNet), Mobile Internet Unit (MIU) and the Human Capacity Development (HCD). These show that the Nigerian government has not been short of effort in the integration ICT into its governance. However, Waverman's study shows that such efforts have not been enough to bridge digital divide in Nigeria. What then are the constraints on the effective integration of ICTs in Nigeria?

This paper has identified some socio-cultural constraints on the government's efforts to apply ICTs in Nigeria. Such constraints include illiteracy, corruption, lack of basic infrastructures like electricity and poverty all of which lead to what I call *digital naivety*. But before this paper continues, it will not fail to define ICT.

What is ICT?

ICT can be defined as a concept that involves the production and usage of scientific artefacts which can be used to convey or exchange information. It covers products that can store, retrieve, manipulate, transmit or receive information electronically in a digital form. For example: personal computers, network hardware and software, satellite systems digital television, radio, robots.

Therefore ICT is generally, ""concerned with the storage, retrieval, manipulation, transmission or receipt of data. Importantly, it is also concerned with the way these different uses can work with each other.""" (Stahl & Eke, 2009).

This is a concept that has blurred the lines between Information technology, computer technology and media technology. Technically, ICT

represents the convergence of these three defining technologies of our time.

This concept has been used severally in many writings in recent times. It is a concept that has been promoted strongly by the European Union (EU) and has been used so much in education within Europe. However, despite the huge role this concept plays in Europe it does not appear to have permeated the US computing parlance. The EU is indeed one of the foremost, if not the strongest, proponent of this concept ICT, the artefacts involved in it and their effective application to every sphere of life.

It is differentiated from Information Technology (IT) which concentrates more on the production of the artefacts alone and also Information Systems (IS) that finds meaning in organizations which usually refers to businesses.

ICT as a Tool of Development

The United Nations ICT Task Force posits that one of the relevant ways of measuring the differences between developed and developing countries is in the level of ICT penetration and usage. As well as having insufficient education and health care services, developing countries lack a certain level of ICT penetration and thus lag behind in development. This gap in access to ICTs is known as the "digital divide". This is a new social gap that can be external (measured between countries) or internal (measured between individuals living in the same society). It can also refer to access- based on the difference between individuals with access and those without access to ICTs; usage- based on individuals who know how to use these technologies and those who do not; or it can refer to usage quality- based on the differences between those same users (Camacho, 2006).

Digital divide is believed to be furthering the pauperization of the poor and expanding the gap between the rich and the poor parts of the world (Olubamise & Awe, 2007). With such programmes as ICT Task Force (UIT) and ICT For Development (ICT4D), the United Nations is committed to bridging this gap by creating digital opportunities. There is the belief that ICT is a powerful economic, social and political tool. This belief is shared by the European Union that sees ICTs 'as critical to improving the competitiveness of European industry and to meet the demands of its society and economy' (CORDIS, 2010).

It is true that the ICT sector in the EU represents 5.6% of EU GDP (670 Billion Euro) and 5.3% of total employment in 2007. 50% of the EU productivity growth (1.1% between 2000-2004), comes from ICT and 25% of research expenditure (2002-2003) (European Commission Enterprise and Industry, 2010). These statistics underlines the importance of ICTs to growth in Europe. The development and competitiveness of European industry and social inclusion are dependent on the effective use of ICT. For EU, ICTs not only enables development, they have great potentials to enhance the quality of life.

The European Union duly understands the importance of ICT as the very core of the knowledge based society and ultimately hopes to transform ICT progress into benefits for Europe's citizens, industry, businesses and governments. E-skills are the doorway to myriads of opportunities and this drives the EU on.

But the questions many Nigerians ask are these; does Nigeria understand the relevance of ICTs? How well is Nigeria applying ICTs for socio-economic developments? Policies have been approved but how can these policies best be used to address innovation, entrepreneurship and development problems and strategies? Lack of or poor implementations of these policies are major problems in Nigeria. In 2007, Nigeria's ICT4D annual review pointed out that the IT policy passed in 2001 was completely out of date (Olubamise & Awe, 2007). Deregulation of the telecommunications sector a few years ago led to landmark advancements in this field. This was largely successful through an active regulatory body – the Nigerian Communications Commission (NCC)

set up in 1992. It led to the arrival of major GSM providers such as MTN, Zain, Globacom, Visafone etc. Telephony has increased in both urban and rural areas with majority of the population still largely unaffected by the revolution (Olubamise & Awe, 2007).

Global brands in ICT still dominate today. Nigerian-owned companies are largely in the distributive trade except two major local brands; ZINOX Computer and OMATEK Computers. Microsoft, Hewlett Packard, Samsung, Dell, CISCO, ORACLE, SHIRON are among the leading brands with Nigerian offices. These companies have made the influx of computers possible in Nigeria. Foreign internet service providers are still key players in the provision of internet services in Nigeria. Accessibility to the internet is significantly on the rise. However, as the most populous country in Africa with the population of about 160 million, this rate of this growth is massive. But lack of adequate integration of these developments is still a cause for concern.

Nigeria's Digital Naivety

Despite the huge improvements in integrating ICT products in Nigeria, Digital naivety can be seen in every social stratum in Nigeria. A Nigerian Professor 'x' was asked to send an email to a colleague 'y' that was on sabbatical in England. He had an email account with yahoo.com and felt confident he knows how to use it. After sending the email, he duly called the colleague to inform him that he has just sent him an email but also apologised that he didn't put some information on the email because there was no more space to type. This colleague 'y' quickly logged in to read the email sent to him. Upon opening professor 'x's' email, he discovered that the entire content was typed in the 'subject' section of the email and nothing was writing in the inbox section. This was a surprise but only shows naivety and lack of digital sophistication expected from professor 'x'. Another Nigerian lecturer was having a discussion with one of his students who accidentally asked for his email (which will enable him send submit his assignment online since he will be travelling out of the state for family emergency). After a scornful look, the lecturer replied; "do you think I am a 'yahoo yahoo' member?[1] What am I going to do with an email?" These are not fairy tales. However, the fact that a few academic personnel in Nigeria exhibit such a naivety is worrying.

This type of naivety is prevalent in Nigeria's tertiary institutions and speaks volumes of the society at large. Many government parastatals still lack computerized systems of storing information and a large number of primary and secondary schools are yet to install computers. Millions of the population still lack ICT knowledge, skill and competence. This makes the usage of ICT services a practical impossibility in some sectors. A score of 1.30 on the 2009 Connectivity Scorecard demonstrates this fact. From available literature some of the socio-cultural factors that contribute to this fact include, illiteracy, corruption, lack of basic infrastructures like electricity, gender discrimination, and poverty. (Raitt, 2005; Akpan-Obong, 2009; Idowu, Ogunbodede, & Idowu, 2003)

SOCIO-CULTURAL CONSTRAINS

Corruption

Sen (2001) defined corruption as the violation of established rules for personal gain and profit. This supports the description of Nye in 1967 that corruption is the deviation from the formal duties of a public role because of private gains.(Nye, 1967) This is an anti-social behaviour that is a contributing factor to many problems in Nigeria.

Since the inception of public administration in Nigeria, cases of mis-use of public office for personal enrichment have been recorded. 29 years of military rule out of 49 years of Nigeria's statehood only exacerbated the situation even though many point to it as its chief causes. This has become one of the major problems of Nigerian polity

today. Attendant effects of corruption in Nigeria include the slow movement of files in offices, port congestion, queues at passport offices and gas stations, ghost workers syndrome, election irregularities, among others. This is a pandemic that has eaten deep into the fabrics of the Nigerian society. Without exaggeration, about 60 percent of Nigerians are corrupt. That means that in every office in Nigeria, at least two people are corrupt.

In the last decade, several state governments in Nigeria have set up at least one form of ICT resource centre. Large sums of money running into billions of dollars have been voted and spent on such projects but the only testimonies in several of these locations are "concrete halls with a mesh of wires, poorly connected dusty systems and wide expanse of space that speak of abandonment" (Oruame, 2008) Many proposed ICT projects have ended up as 'white elephants' while billions of dollars have been misappropriated. Oruame (2008) published a story on how a former Edo state governor awarded a $1 million contract for the supply of a 1.2 meter communication dish that is worth no more than $1,000. At different levels of government in Nigeria, it is hard to find a sincere ICT empowerment program effectively managed. These projects only serve as avenues of siphoning money for political officers.

Poverty

As the 6th largest oil producing country in the world, nobody expects Nigeria to be classed as a poor country. In the 1970s Nigeria had the 33rd highest per capita income in the world. Unfortunately in 1989, Nigeria became the 19th poorest country in the world and by 1997 she has slipped to the 13th position (Raji, Ayoade, & Usoro, 2006). This is poverty that is both avoidable and unfortunate, created and sustained by the Nigerian corrupt system. (United Nations Development Programme, 2000)

With the return of democracy in 1999, series of economic reforms were designed to address the structural and institutional weaknesses of the Nigerian economy. These reforms culminated in the launching of the National Economic Empowerment and Development Strategy (NEEDS) in 2004 and the subsequent development of such strategies in the 36 states known as the States Economic Empowerment and Development Strategies (SEEDS). These strategies were aimed at poverty reduction, employment generation and wealth creation (Adoghame, 2008).

These economic reforms together with the banking consolidation drive in 2006 (after which 25 banks were approved as being fit for services) have contributed to a greater economic performance. However, about 50% of the population are still living below average in Nigeria. Apparently this makes the acquisition of a computer or its knowledge practically impossible. Millions of Nigerians cannot afford a computer nor can they afford a satellite system. These are products that can only be seen in the house of the rich due to the high capital cost and also operating cost.

Children from poor families have no opportunity of garnering adequate training in computing. Numerous cyber cafes in many neighbourhoods have been immensely helpful in this area. Both staff and students are major consumers of ICT services and visit on-campus business cafes for internet usage. But many still cannot afford the 150 naira per hour charged by most cafes.

Illiteracy

A large number of the Nigerian population do not have the wherewithal to afford general education. These numbers are unable to read and write because of lack of education, are insufficiently educated or in some cases because of learning difficulties or other intellectual impairment such as brain damage. In view of this, this portion of the population is classed as illiterates or non-literates.

Also, owing to the fact that ICT has not been properly integrated in school curriculum in Nigeria, many of those who can afford education graduate without the acquisition of basic ICT knowledge and skill. These lack computer literacy and as such are non-literates in the area of computer. These two cases of non-literacy significantly affect the integration of ICT products in Nigeria.

Inadequate Power Supply

Inadequate power supply is a perennial problem that has embarrassingly crippled the Nigerian economy. Irregular supply of electrical power has hindered progress in every facet of life in Nigeria. Everybody is affected; businesses, educational institutions, government offices and homes. The average power supply in 2008 was about 4hrs per day (Iloanusi & Osuagwu, 2009). Many a time, low voltage supplies do serious damages that many rely on alternative sources of powers such as standby generators, batteries and solar energy systems. This is a problem that directly affects the use of ICT products because every artefact uses electricity.

According to Ndukwe Ernest[2], "with the present state of electricity supply in the country- the digital revolution in Nigeria cannot attain its full potential. All ICT equipment, infrastructure and terminals depend on electricity to be energised. Unless this vital source of energy is always available and reliable, the Nigerian people will not be able to fully enjoy the benefits that the digital revolution offers". Power is rarely supplied and many establishments such as universities, secondary schools and government offices cannot foot the bill maintaining standby generators, installed ICT systems waste away. Integration of ICTs in Nigeria will only remain a dream if this problem persists.

RECOMMENDATIONS

So far, this paper has explored the efforts Nigeria has made in the integration of ICT for development and innovation and the constraining factors against these efforts. It should be noted that corruption is a major factor from which other factors emanate from. Without corruption, Nigerian poverty and illiteracy levels would not be so high and also inadequate power supply is as a result of misappropriation of the funds that have been allocated for the improvement of the Power Holding Corporation of Nigeria (PHCN).

On the other hand, this paper believes that corruption is still persistent in Nigeria because, majority of Nigerians are not patriotic enough. Most Nigerians have little love for the country as a whole. Only a minority can sincerely uphold the cause of the nation. Therefore, Nigeria needs all of her citizens to love it and be committed to her cause. She needs *Collective Patriotism*. If we are collectively patriotic and committed to the needs of the nation, corruption will be combated, poverty and illiteracy levels will fall and power problems will be significantly solved.

This is a long term solution that should start in our families, schools (primary, secondary and tertiary), churches and other social groups. Step-by-step, we need to learn how to be patriotic. For the short term, the nation needs to update its ICT policies, establish an active regulatory body with more coherent planning and better strategies. NCC has done a good job in the telecommunications sector. The establishment of such active and effective body to oversee activities in the whole ICT sector would be a step in the right direction. ICTs have major roles to play in governance, and socio-economic development in Nigeria. The government should do enough to address multiple digital divides in Nigeria.

Olubamise and Awe (2007) suggested a digital solidarity as an effective way of bridging the digital divide in Nigeria. It is their belief that there should be a form of solidarity between public authorities; federal, state and local and private organisations that aims at providing ICT products, knowledge and skills to Nigerian citizens. This is a solidarity this author believes that public authorities and private companies in Nigeria ought to be committed to.

CONCLUSION

This paper has shown that a lot of efforts have been put in by the Nigerian government to integrate ICTs for development and education. Series of policies have been approved and governmental agencies established to implement these policies. But a lot of socio-cultural factors present hurdles to this endeavour. These hurdles include corruption, poverty, illiteracy and inadequate power supply. Suggestions on how these constrains could be eliminated have been made. If we could be collectively patriotic and an active regulatory body with effective planning strategies established, ICTs would be put to effective use in Nigeria.

REFERENCES

Adoghame, P. (2008). *The National Economic and Empowerment and Development Strategy (NEEDS): A critical appraisal of Nigeria's strategy for poverty reduction.* Paper presented at the 49th Annual Convention on Bridging Multiple, San Francisco, CA.

Ajayi, G. O. (2003). *NITDA and ICT in Nigeria.* Paper presented at the Abdus Salam International Centre for Theoretical Physics Round Table on Developing Countries Access to Scientific Knowledge, Trieste, Italy.

Akpan-Obong, P. I. (2009). *Information and communication technologies in Nigeria.* New York, NY: Peter Lang.

Camacho, K. (2006). *Digital divide.* Retrieved from http://vecam.org/article549.html

CORDIS. (2010). *Information and communication technologies (ICT).* Retrieved from http://cordis.europa.eu/fp7/ict/

European Commission Enterprise and Industry. (2010). *Innovation policy.* Retrieved from http://ec.europa.eu/enterprise/ict/index_en.htm

Idowu, B., Ogunbodede, E., & Idowu, B. (2003). Information and communication technology in Nigeria, the health sector experience. *Journal of Information Technology Impact*, *3*(2), 69–76.

Iloanusi, N. O., & Osuagwu, C. C. (2009). *ICT in education: Achievements so far in Nigeria.* Retrieved from http://www.formatex.org/micte2009/book/1331-1335.pdf

National Information Technology Development Agency. (2001). *The national information technology policy.* Retrieved from http://www.fs.nitda.gov.ng/index.php?option=com_content&view=article&id=65&Itemid=87

Nokia Siemens Networks. (2009). *The connectivity scorecard: Call for action to redefine connectivity.* Retrieved from http://www.nokiasiemensnetworks.com/global/Insight/ConnectivityScorecard/?languagecode=en

Nye, J. (1967). Corruption and political development: A case-benefit analysis. *The American Political Science Review*, 417–427. doi:10.2307/1953254

Olubamise, B., & Awe, J. (2007). *NIGERIA: ICT4D annual review: A synopsis of the ICT4D sector in Nigeria incorporating activities of the government, private sector and non-governmental organizations.* Retrieved from http://www.jidaw.com/itsolutions/ict4dreview2007.html

Oruame, S. (2008). *Corruption is killing ICT in Nigeria.* Retrieved from http://www.computerworldwestafrica.com/articles/2008/11/20/corruption-killing-ict-nigeria

Raitt, D. (2005). *ICT developments in Nigerian libraries* [electronic resource]. Bingley, UK: Emerald Group.

Raji, M. O., Ayoade, O. B., & Usoro, A. (2006). *The prospects and problems of adopting ICT for poverty eradication in Nigeria.* Retrieved from http://www.ejisdc.org/ojs2/index.php/ejisdc/article/viewFile/346/192

Sen, A. (2001). *Development as freedom.* New York, NY: Anchor Books.

Stahl, B., & Eke, D. (2009). *Ethical review of ICT projects across UK computing departments: The state of the art.* Paper presented at the 10th Annual Conference of the HEA, Kent, UK.

United Nations Development Programme. (2000). *Information and communications technologies for development.* Retrieved from http://www.undp.org/mlo21

ENDNOTES

[1]   A common way of referring to internet scammers in Nigeria.

[2]   Executive Vice-chairman of the Nigerian Communications Commission.

This work was previously published in the International Journal of Technology and Human Interaction, Volume 7, Issue 2, edited by Anabela Mesquita and Chia-Wen Tsai, pp. 21-27, copyright 2011 by IGI Publishing (an imprint of IGI Global).

Chapter 3

The Influence of Information Control upon On-Line Shopping Behavior

Linwu Gu
Indiana University of Pennsylvania, USA

Jianfeng Wang
Indiana University of Pennsylvania, USA

Milam Aiken
University of Mississippi, USA

Kustim Wibowo
Indiana University of Pennsylvania, USA

ABSTRACT

Previous studies have explored privacy instruments and disclosures as factors that affect on-line shopping intentions or attitudes. However, few have evaluated how information control affects this behavior. This paper draws on psychological and social justice theories to gain an understanding of how information control impacts on-line purchasing directly or indirectly through the mediation of intrinsic motivation. The resulting causal model was validated using structural equations with data from 179 respondents. Results show that perceived information control affects cognitive absorption, and users, as expected, value procedural fairness.

INTRODUCTION

Although the world economy is in recession, on-line shopping has steadily increased, e.g., 9% in 2008 (IT Facts, 2009). In addition, 48 million households in the United States paid their bills on-line in 2008, and this number is expected to increase to 63 million by 2014. However, this growth can be hindered by perceptions of a lack of information privacy on Web sites, and this

issue has been identified as one of the most important problems for e-businesses operating in our information-centric, global, and digital economy (Awad & Krishnan, 2006). Many potential on-line customers are wary of providing too much information as they can be aware that their browsing behavior might be tracked and personal data can be misused (Hann et al., 2007). Consequently, individuals want to control personal information boundaries and avoid unwanted disclosure to third

DOI: 10.4018/978-1-4666-1954-8.ch003

parties (Goodwin, 1991; Novak et al., 1999), and many visitors expect Web sites to provide a variety of information controls such as the ability for individuals to remove their names from mailing lists (Culnan & Armstrong, 1999).

Privacy, i.e., the extent to which people can control the release and dissemination of personal information (Stone & Stone, 1990), is a matter of procedural justice (Bies, 1993). In social justice theory, procedural fairness refers to an individual's perception of being treated fairly, and this perception can be positive even though there might be an unfavorable outcome (Culnan & Armstrong, 1999). However, it can become negative when consumers find increasingly invasive information collection from commercial Web sites, and therefore, they could be less willing to patronize these e-businesses (Awad & Krishnan, 2006).

Many previous studies of e-commerce have investigated antecedents of consumer satisfaction (e.g., Devaraj et al., 2002) and perceived consequences of on-line shopping behavior (e.g., Vijayasarathy, 2004). This paper explores how perceived information control relates to on-line purchase behaviors directly, and how intrinsic motivation mediates between privacy control and ultimate purchase based upon social justice and psychological theories. Individuals' perceptions that they can control their personal information influences their motivation and subsequent behavior (Alge et al., 2006), and the less control that people believe they have, the more negative psychological outcomes will arise (Stone et al., 2003).

THEORETICAL FOUNDATION

As depicted in Figure 1, theory suggests that information privacy contributes to people's intrinsic motivation that in turn influences their discretionary behavior (Hann, et al., 2007). Each of these factors is explained in more detail below.

Information Privacy

Control refers to the freedom to either accept or reject a process or decision, and according to social justice theory, control over the disclosure of information is associated with procedural justice (Alge, 2001; Hoffman et al., 1999). Stewart and Segars (2002) define information control as "the consumer's ability to control the dissemination of information related to or provided during such transactions or behaviors to those who were not present," while Westin (1967) defines privacy control as "the claim of individuals, groups, or institutions to determine for themselves when, how, and to what extent information about them is communicated to others."

Previous studies show that most consumers are willing to disclose some personal information based on their judgment of risks and benefits (Eddy et al., 1999; Woodman et al., 1982), but most consider organizations' collection of their personal information without permission to be invasive (Stone et al., 2003). Greater perceptions of privacy control result in better judgments of procedural fairness (Culnan & Armstrong, 1999), and most people don't mind negative consequences with a decision if they recognize that the procedures are fair (Miyazaki & Fernandez, 2001). People ap-

Figure 1. Information privacy and behavior model (adapted from Alge et al., 2006)

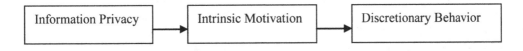

preciate the value of a system when they perceive justice (Zweig & Webster, 2002), and satisfaction with a system is enhanced when it is considered to be a less invasive (Ambrose & Alder, 2000; Kidwell & Bennett, 1994; Stanton, 2000).

Intrinsic Motivation

There are two types of motivation in cognitive research: extrinsic and intrinsic, and both are related to productivity and satisfaction (Davis et al., 1992; Kraut et al., 1989). When people are intrinsically motivated, they are entertained, and intrinsic, rather than extrinsic, motivation is the major reason why consumers shop on-line (Agarwal & Karahanna, 2000; Shang et al., 2005). That is, consumers are more willing to shop and purchase using the Web when they find the experience to be entertaining. However, if personal privacy is threatened at a Web site, there is likely to be less entertainment and less intrinsic motivation to proceed.

Discretionary Behavior

Previous research has shown that how a decision maker has been treated is related to final decision making (Sitkin et al., 1993). E-commerce customers, like any other decision makers, are

concerned about whether they are treated fairly, and this affects whether or not they make a purchase (Malhotra et al., 2004). For example, Novak et al. (1999) find that consumers do not want to engage in monetary exchanges if they think they have low information control. Potential customers might give up and not "check out" from a site, even after they have added items to their shopping cart, when they realize that their personal information could be at risk. However, greater knowledge of a Web site's information privacy procedures can increase the likelihood that a consumer will make an on-line purchase (Awad & Krishnan, 2006).

Hypotheses

Based upon this prior research, we propose the following hypotheses that are shown graphically in Figure 2:

H$_{1a}$: Perceived information gathering control positively influences on-line shopping behavior.

H$_{1b}$: Perceived information handling control positively influences on-line shopping behavior.

H$_{1c}$: Perceived general control positively influences on-line shopping behavior.

H$_{2a}$: Perceived cognitive absorption mediates the relationship between perceived information

Figure 2. Research model with hypotheses

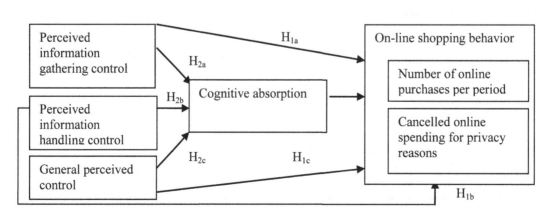

gathering control and on-line shopping behavior

H_{2b}: Perceived cognitive absorption mediates the relationship between perceived information handling control and on-line shopping behavior.

H_{2c}: Perceived cognitive absorption mediates the relationship between general perceived control and on-line shopping behavior.

The research model follows Shang et al. (2005) in operationalizing intrinsic motivation by using the construct cognitive absorption, defined as "a state of deep involvement with software," consisting of the aspects of temporal dissociation, focused immersion, and heightened enjoyment, control, and curiosity (Argarval & Karahanna, 2000). The intrinsically motivating state of cognitive absorption lowers the perceived cognitive burden associated with a satisfied shopping experience.

METHODOLOGY

Subjects and Procedures

The survey instrument shown in Appendix 1 was administered to 179 subjects, 77.1% of whom were undergraduate and graduate business students, and the remainder were students' families and friends. The mean age of the combined sample was 25.9 years, and 102 were male (56.98%). The subjects had made an average of 9.88 online purchases each over the past year, with the frequencies shown in Table 1.

All independent and mediate variables were measured by asking the subjects their perceptions using a 7-point Likert-type scale, where 1= strongly disagree and 7= strongly agree.

Table 1. Number of on-line shopping purchases in the past year

Number of participants	On-line purchases
39	More than 15
49	11-15
29	6-10
48	1-5
14	0

DATA ANALYSES

A two-step modeling approach was applied in our study (Anderson & Gerbing, 1988). The first step established the measurement model and confirmed the convergent and discriminant validities while the second applied a structural model to test the hypotheses.

Measurement Model

The measurement model was checked using confirmatory factor analysis in order to test for the reliability and the validity. The reliability (internal consistency) of items in each scale was examined using Cronbach's alpha to confirm the adequacy of the measures for testing hypotheses. As shown in Table 2, the reliabilities of all constructs are greater than 0.8 and the average variance extracted (AVE) from the constructs are greater than 0.5 (Fornell & Larcker, 1981; Nunnally, 1967). Thus, the validity test confirms results of earlier studies and provides confidence in testing the hypotheses.

Discriminant Validity

Discriminant validity is used to evaluate the extent to which constructs in a model are different from each other, and is considered fairly good if a squared correlation is less than 0.3. The squared correlation between two different measures of any two constructs should be statistically lower than

Table 2. Convergent validity test

Constructs	Construct reliability [a]	AVE
Cognitive absorption	0.928	0.750
Perceived Information gathering control	0.892	0.734
Perceived Information handling control	0.860	0.820
General perceived control	0.842	0.717
[a.] construct reliability is estimated using Cronbach's α coefficients		

the variance shared by the measures of the same construct (Fornell et al., 1982). From Table 3, we can see that the shaded values are much greater than the non-shaded ones and the non-shaded values are all less than 0.3. Therefore, the constructs of our model are confirmed with adequate discriminant validity.

STRUCTURAL MODEL

The hypotheses were tested using a structural equation model. Hypothesis 1 investigates the direct effects between the perceived information control variables and on-line shopping behavior, while Hypothesis 2 studies the mediation of cognitive absorption between the perceived information control variables and on-line shopping behavior.

Measures of the indirect effect were tested, for example, by the effect of the perceived information gathering control on cognitive absorption carried forward to the final shopping behavior.

Statistically significant relationships between the independent and mediator variables were found at $\alpha = 0.05$, as well as between the mediator and dependent variables (Figure 3).

The mediation test uses the methodology extended to structural equation modeling (Anderson & Gerbing, 1988; Grandey, 2003; Singh et al., 1994). For mediation, the first step is to test if the independent variables are related to the dependent when the mediator is absent (Figure 4). The second step is to test the indirect effects, i.e., determining whether the effects of independent variables on mediator variables are carried forward to the dependent variable (Figure 3). The third step is to test if the relationship is reduced when the mediator is added back to the structural model in the first step (Figure 5).

The three separate structural models were developed to examine the relationships between the perceived information gathering, perceived information handling, and general perceived control and on-line shopping behavior. The hypothesized mediating effect of cognitive absorption is supported when the structural model in step 3 (Figure 5) shows a significant relationship between the perceived information control variables and cognitive absorption, diminished or insignificant effects of perceived information control factors on on-line shopping behavior, and significant effects of cognitive absorption on on-line shopping behavior, compared with the effects in steps 1 and 2.

Table 3. Discriminant validity test correlations

	Perceived information gathering control	Perceived information handling control	General perceived control	Cognitive absorption
Perceived Information gathering control	0.868			
Perceived Information handling control	*0.043*	0.744		
General perceived control	*0.021*	*0.142*	0.801	
Cognitive absorption	*0.187*	*0.06*	*0.234*	0.762

Figure 3. Standardized results for the relationships among perceived information control, cognitive absorption, and on-line behavior

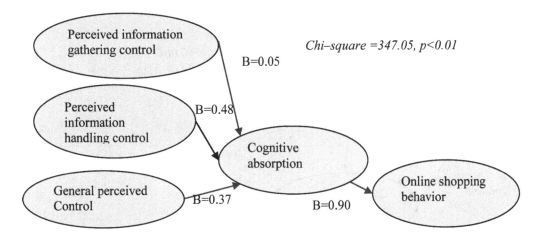

Results for Hypothesis 1

The results of the structural equation models indicate that all three hypothesized paths in Hypothesis 1 were significant at p < 0.01 (Figure 4). Thus, perceived information gathering, perceived information handling, and general perceived control all directly affect on-line shopping behavior.

Results for Hypothesis 2

All of the direct paths from the perceived information control factors to on-line shopping behavior (Figure 4) and all paths from the perceived information gathering control factors to cognitive absorption were significant (Figure 3). Figure 5 shows that the direct relationship between perceived information handling control and general

Figure 4. Effects of perceived information control factors on-line shopping behavior when the mediator is absent (step 1)

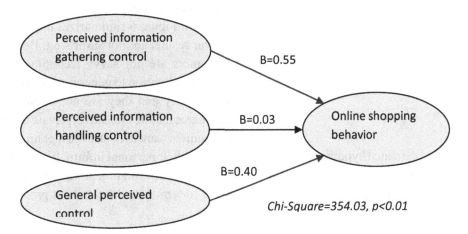

Figure 5. Effects of perceived information control factors on on-line shopping behavior after adding the mediator variable (step 3)

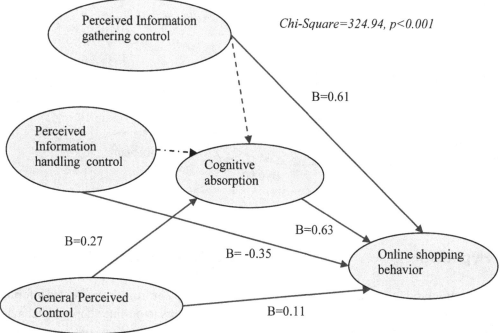

perceived control changes from significant to non-significant. However, the significant relationship between general perceived control and cognitive absorption is diminished (the coefficient drops from 0.40 to 0.11) and the relationship between cognitive absorption and on-line shopping behavior was also diminished (the coefficient drops from 0.90 to 0.63). Therefore, H_{2c} is supported.

CONCLUSION

Summary

We empirically tested the stated hypotheses based on psychological information control and social cognitive theories that show positive perceived information control increases intrinsic motivation and on-line shopping behavior. Our results show that procedural fairness is valued by users, and perceived information control affects cognitive absorption. However, cognitive absorption is a significant mediator only between general perceived information control and on-line shopping behavior. Figure 6 summarizes the results.

Our results are not surprising. Because most consumers are not savvy technologically, they pay more attention to general control of information privacy and they are not aware of how e-commerce handles sensitive, private information. Consumers want to control how commercial Web sites use their personal information, and a sudden concern for information privacy can cause a customer to terminate the checkout process.

Figure 6. The effects of perceived information control upon on-line shopping behavior

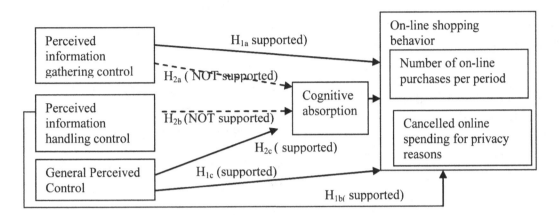

Implications

Our research implies that e-businesses should place a priority on assuring potential customers that their personal information will be protected. Most companies selling on the Web follow the applicable law (e.g., the United States' fair information practice and the European Union's safe harbor rules), but a link to a privacy policy and a statement of commitment to privacy protection might not be enough to assuage customer fears. On-line businesses might need to take additional measures to ensure a visitor's peace-of-mind. For example, providing a custom-designed frequently-asked-questions (FAQ) page about information security or a dedicated contact (email address or phone number) for questions about safety might alleviate concerns.

Limitations

Our findings are subject to a number of limitations. First, the survey relied on subjects' perceptions of what they believe to be true. However, they could be misinformed. For example, they might or might not really be able to determine the types of personal information that an organization can store. Also, the research relies on subjects'

memories of purchases, and this count could be inaccurate. We believe they were allowed enough time to review their shopping histories before they emailed their responses to ensure as accurate a count as possible, and there was no practical way to track their actual purchases besides relying on their memories.

A second potential limitation is that the vast majority of the subjects (77.1%) were undergraduate or graduate students. They are active Internet users and purchase many goods and services from e-businesses, and their on-line experiences could be rather homogeneous. Other populations, e.g., senior citizens and children, might have other perceptions of information control. Young children are likely to be very naïve about privacy, while older people could be much more cautious than the students in our survey.

A third limitation is that the survey was conducted using people from the United States. While the laws may be different, we believe privacy issues and psychological concerns are similar across the globe. In addition, potential consumers might not be aware of existing legal controls. For example, a person in the United States purchasing a product from a Web site in the United Kingdom is not likely to know the applicable information security laws for that e-business.

FUTURE RESEARCH

Because of these limitations, future research should investigate other samples of Web users with different ages, backgrounds, and geographical origins. In a more controlled study, e.g., studying those who purchased products online from Wal-Mart only, perceptions of information control could be compared to the company's actual handling of their personal data. Finally, this study was primarily concerned with purchase frequency, not the frequency of abandoning a shopping cart midway through a purchase. Another study could focus on this latter variable to confirm or refute our findings.

REFERENCES

Agarwal, R., & Karahanna, E. (2000). Time flies when you're having fun: Cognitive absorption and beliefs about information technology usage. *Management Information Systems Quarterly*, *24*(4), 665–694. doi:10.2307/3250951

Alge, B. J. (2001). Effects of computer surveillance on perceptions of privacy and procedural justice. *The Journal of Applied Psychology*, *86*(4), 797–804. doi:10.1037/0021-9010.86.4.797

Alge, B. J., Ballinger, G. A., Tangirala, S., & Oakley, J. L. (2006). Information privacy in organizations: Empowering creative and extra role performance. *The Journal of Applied Psychology*, *91*(1), 221–232. doi:10.1037/0021-9010.91.1.221

Ambrose, M. L., & Alder, G. S. (2000). Designing, implementing, and utilizing computerized performance monitoring: Enhancing organizational justice. *Research in Personnel and Human Resource Management*, *18*, 187–219.

Anderson, J. C., & Gerbing, D. W. (1988). Structural equation modeling in practice: A review and recommended two step approach. *Psychological Bulletin*, *103*(3), 411–423. doi:10.1037/0033-2909.103.3.411

Awad, N. F., & Krishnan, M. S. (2006). The personalization privacy paradox: An empirical evaluation of information transparency and the willingness to be profiled online for personalization. *Management Information Systems Quarterly*, *30*(1), 13–28.

Bies, R. J. (1993). Privacy and procedural justice in organizations. *Social Justice Research*, *6*(1), 69–86. doi:10.1007/BF01048733

Culnan, M. J., & Armstrong, P. K. (1999). Information privacy concerns, procedural fairness, and impersonal trust: An empirical investigation. *Organization Science*, *10*(1), 104–115. doi:10.1287/orsc.10.1.104

Davis, F. D., Bagozzi, R. P., & Warshaw, P. R. (1992). Extrinsic and intrinsic motivation to use computers in the workplace. *Journal of Applied Social Psychology*, *22*(14), 1111–1132. doi:10.1111/j.1559-1816.1992.tb00945.x

Devaraj, S., Fan, M., & Kohli, R. (2002). Antecedents of B2C channel satisfaction and preference: Validating e-Commerce metrics. *Information Systems Research*, *13*(3), 316–333. doi:10.1287/isre.13.3.316.77

Eddy, E. R., Stone, D. L., & Stone-Romero, E. F. (1999). The effects of information management policies on reactions to human resource information systems: An integration of privacy and procedural justice perspectives. *Personnel Psychology*, *52*(2), 335–358. doi:10.1111/j.1744-6570.1999.tb00164.x

Facts, I. T. (2009). *Online consumer spending in 2008*. Retrieved February 18, 2010, from http://www.itfacts.biz/online-consumer-spending-in-2008/12233

Fornell, C., & Larcker, D. (1981). Evaluating structural equation models with unobservable variables and measurement error. *JMR, Journal of Marketing Research, 18*(1), 39–50. doi:10.2307/3151312

Fornell, C., Tellis, G., & Zinkhan, G. (1982). Validity assessment: a structural equations approach using partial least squares. In *Proceedings of the American Marketing Association Educator's Conference*, Chicago (pp. 405-409).

Goodwin, C. (1991). Privacy: Recognition of a consumer right. *Journal of Public Policy & Marketing, 10*(1), 149–166.

Grandey, A. A. (2003). When "the show must go on": Surface acting and deep acting as determinants of emotional exhaustion and peer-rated service delivery. *Academy of Management Journal, 46*(1), 86–96. doi:10.2307/30040678

Hann, I., Hui, K., Lee, S., & Png, I. (2007). Overcoming online information privacy concerns: An information-processing theory approach. *Journal of Management Information Systems, 24*(2), 13–42. doi:10.2753/MIS0742-1222240202

Hoffman, D. L., Novak, T. P., & Peralta, M. (1999). Building consumer trust online. *Communications of the ACM, 42*(4), 80–85. doi:10.1145/299157.299175

Kidwell, R. E., & Bennett, N. (1994). Electronic surveillance as employee control: A procedural justice interpretation. *The Journal of High Technology Management, 5*(1), 39–57. doi:10.1016/1047-8310(94)90013-2

Kraut, R., Dumais, D., & Koch, S. (1989). Computerization, productivity, and quality of work-life. *Communications of the ACM, 32*(2), 220–238. doi:10.1145/63342.63347

Malhotra, N. K., Kim, S. S., & Agarwal, J. (2004). Internet users' information privacy concerns (IUIPC): The construct, the scale, and a causal model. *Information Systems Research, 15*(4), 336–355. doi:10.1287/isre.1040.0032

Miyazaki, A. D., & Fernandez, A. (2001). Consumer perceptions of privacy and security risks for online shopping. *The Journal of Consumer Affairs, 35*(1), 27–44. doi:10.1111/j.1745-6606.2001.tb00101.x

Novak, T. P., Hoffman, D. L., & Peralta, M. A. (1999). Building consumer trust online. *Communications of the ACM, 42*(4), 80–85. doi:10.1145/299157.299175

Nunnally, J. (1967). *Psychometric Theory*. New York: McGraw-Hill.

Shang, R., Chen, Y., & Shen, L. (2005). Extrinsic versus intrinsic motivations for consumers to shop on-line. *Information & Management, 42*(3), 401–413. doi:10.1016/j.im.2004.01.009

Singh, J., Goolby, J. R., & Rhoads, G. K. (1994). Behavioral and psychological consequences of boundary spanning burnout for customer service representatives. *Journal of Marketing Research, 31*(4), 558–569. doi:10.2307/3151883

Sitkin, S. B., Sutcliffe, K. M., & Reed, G. L. (1993). Prescriptions for justice: Using social accounts to legitimate the exercise of professional control. *Social Justice Research, 69*(1), 87–111. doi:10.1007/BF01048734

Stanton, J. M. (2000). Traditional and electronic monitoring from an organizational justice perspective. *Journal of Business and Psychology, 15*(1), 129–147. doi:10.1023/A:1007775020214

Stewart, K. A., & Segars, A. H. (2002). An empirical examination of the concern for information privacy instrument. *Information Systems Research, 13*(1), 36–49. doi:10.1287/isre.13.1.36.97

Stone, E. F., & Stone, D. L. (1990). Privacy in organizations: Theoretical issues, research findings, and protection mechanisms. *Research in Personnel and Human Resources Management, 8*, 349–341.

Stone-Romero, E. F., Stone, D. L., & Hyatt, D. (2003). Personnel selection procedures and invasion of privacy. *The Journal of Social Issues, 59*(2), 343–368. doi:10.1111/1540-4560.00068

Vijayasarathy, L. R. (2004). Predicting consumer intentions to use on-line shopping: The case for an augmented technology acceptance model. *Information & Management, 41*(6), 747–762. doi:10.1016/j.im.2003.08.011

Westin, A. F. (1967). *Privacy and Freedom.* New York: Atheneum.

Woodman, R. W., Ganster, D. C., Adams, J., McCuddy, M. K., Tolchinsky, P. D., & Fromkin, H. (1982). A survey of employee perceptions of information privacy in organizations. *Academy of Management Journal, 25*(3), 647–663. doi:10.2307/256087

Zweig, D., & Webster, J. (2002). Where is the line between benign and invasive? An examination of psychological barriers to the acceptance of awareness monitoring systems. *Journal of Organizational Behavior, 23*(5), 605–633. doi:10.1002/job.157

APPENDIX

Questionnaire

A. Information gathering control (Alge et al., 2006)
  1. I am able to keep my organization from collecting personal information about me that I would like to keep secret.
  2. I determine the types of information that my organization can store about me.
  3. I am completely satisfied that I am able to keep my organization from collecting personal information about me that I want to keep from them.
  4. I am satisfied in my ability to control the types of personal information that my organization collects on me.

B. Information handling control (Alge et al., 2006)
  1. Online shops always seek my approval concerning how it uses my personal information.
  2. Online shops respect my right to control who can see my personal information.
  3. Online shops allow me to decide how my personal information can be released to others.
  4. I control how my personal information is used by an online shop.

C. General Perceived Control (Malhotra et al., 2004)
  1. Consumer online privacy is really a matter of consumers' right to exercise control and autonomy over decisions about how their information is collected, used, and shared.
  2. Consumer control of personal information lies at the heart of consumer privacy.
  3. I believe that online privacy is invaded when control is lost or unwillingly reduced as a result of a marketing transaction.

D. Cognitive Absorption (modified from Shang et al., 2005)
  1. While using the Web, I am able to block out most other distractions.
  2. While on the Web, I am immersed in the task I am performing.
  3. I feel that I have control over my information control on the Web.
  4. The Web allows me to control my computer interaction.
  5. I am confident about using the Web.
  6. I am self-assured about my capabilities to use the Web.

This work was previously published in the International Journal of Technology and Human Interaction, Volume 7, Issue 1, edited by Anabela Mesquita and Chia-Wen Tsai, pp. 56-66, copyright 2011 by IGI Publishing (an imprint of IGI Global).

Chapter 4

An Examination of Factors Associated with User Acceptance of Social Shopping Websites

Jia Shen
Rider University, USA

Lauren Eder
Rider University, USA

ABSTRACT

Social commerce is the latest development in e-commerce to combine the power of online social networking with shopping. While the adoption of information technology is well studied, new theoretical development is needed to account for the specific characteristics of social commerce applications and their interactions with the user. This study examines factors that are associated with user acceptance of social shopping websites, which are sites designed specifically to support social interactions while users shop. This paper augments the Technology Acceptance Model with constructs that enhance the specificity of the model to the social shopping application of social commerce, including social comparison, social engagement, enjoyment as well as perceived ease of use and perceived usefulness. The model was empirically tested, and the results provided strong support. Implications and directions for future research are also discussed.

INTRODUCTION

Social networking and Web 2.0 technologies continue to gain popularity under the media spotlight. Seeking to tap into the potentials of such technologies for e-commerce, business managers have begun to explore ways to combine the power of social networking with online and offline shopping for better service and new business opportunities. Social commerce emerges as the latest innovation in e-commerce by combining online social networking with shopping. The distinctive feature of social commerce is its focus on supporting the social aspect of an online

DOI: 10.4018/978-1-4666-1954-8.ch004

shopping experience, although there are emerging applications that support the integration of online social networking with offline shopping as well. In contrast, traditional e-commerce technologies tend to focus exclusively on improving the efficiency of online shopping, providing features such as product search, product categorization, and personalized recommendations based on previous purchases.

In 2007, Econsultancy published its "Social Commerce Report 2007" based on an online survey to Web-based retailers (Gregoriadis, 2007). While eighty percent of the 800+ respondents stated that customer rankings and ratings of products and services were a high or medium investment priority, two thirds of the respondents also stated that investing in social networking was of equal importance. The perceived benefits associated with these online activities among consumers included greater sales and customer retention and loyalty.

A variety of social commerce applications have been developed since 2006. Companies such as Procter & Gamble began enhancing their websites to allow consumers to share their experiences of products with other consumers online, and to create online shopping communities (Vranica, 2008). Additionally, the social shopping website emerged as a new e-commerce model, designed specifically as an online social networking community devoted exclusively to online shopping. Social shopping sites such as Kaboodle and ThisNext were developed to enable consumers to share shopping advice and recommendations with likeminded individuals. Another application example included Facebook's 2007 introduction of a feature that allowed a user's purchases on a participating website, such as Overstock.com, to automatically appear as an RSS feed on the user's friends' Facebook pages. This feature was later modified due to privacy concerns (Vara, 2007). Facebook has since moved to a revised model in which users can choose to opt-in to engage in social commerce activities such as sharing RSS

feeds or purchasing recommendations with their friends on Facebook.

It is worth noting that social commerce applications have not been limited only to traditional two-dimensional websites. While outside the scope of this research, it is useful to recognize that there is also a growing commercial interest in developing social commerce applications for three-dimensional, virtual environments such as Second Life, where an avatar (virtual representation of oneself user) can shop together with other avatars for virtual or real goods (Hemp, 2006).

SOCIAL COMMERCE AND APPLICATIONS

In this study, social commerce is defined as technology-enabled shopping experiences where online consumer interactions while shopping provide the main mechanism for conducting social shopping activities. These activities may include discovering products, aggregating and sharing product information, and collaboratively making shopping decisions.

Research in the marketing literature suggests that consumers have two distinct types of orientations when visiting Business-to-Consumer (B2C) websites: transactional and social (Mathwick, 2002). The transactional orientation focuses on completing the shopping tasks, while the social orientation focuses on relationship building. The provision of customer reviews and personalized recommendations (such as on Amazon.com) has been shown to be a significant feature that improve the online shopping experience (Kumar & Benbasat, 2006). Similarly, electronic word-of-mouth websites (such as epinion.com) where consumers can read the opinions and experiences of other consumers and provide their own comments and ratings on a wide range of products online have become popular (Lee & Lee, 2009; Park, Lee, & Han, 2007). Although these technologies enhance the online shopping experience, the focus of these technologies is primarily on efficiency.

Extending the online consumer behavior typology (Mathwick, 2002), we categorize online consumer behavior into three types: transactional, informational, and social. The transactional behavior focuses on the utilitarian aspect of shopping, and the goal is to complete the shopping task in the most efficient manner. The informational behavior focuses on collecting information about products or trends, and the goal is to stay informed about products, which may lead to immediate or future purchase. The social behavior focuses on relationship building, and the goal is to develop feelings of warmth and satisfaction through the online shopping process. The three orientations tend to overlap at different stages of the online shopping process. While traditional e-commerce supports the transactional and informational aspects of online shopping, social commerce applications aim to fulfill the social aspects of shopping, and to potentially enhance the informational aspect as well. Table 1 lists the three types of consumer online behaviors, and the main e-commerce technology in support of them.

Social commerce applications employ a variety of innovative technologies. We categorize current applications into the following three categories:

1. Social Shopping Websites
2. Add-on applications to existing social networking websites
3. Mobile applications that support social retailing

Social shopping websites are designed to be online shopping communities. Examples of social shopping websites include Kaboodle.com, ShopStyle.com, ThisNext.com, and Wists.com (Steel, 2007; Tedeschi, 2006). Social shopping websites offer many unique features to facilitate online social interactions while shopping. For example, users of these sites can create rich profiles of themselves with pictures and personal information, create shopping lists to share with others, post blogs, and set up polls to collect opinions on shopping selections. In addition, the predominant method for product organization on social shopping websites is user-driven, in contrast to the conventional product categorization used by traditional retail websites (e.g., shopping.com). Social shopping websites are not retail websites where consumers can make purchases, although they can provide access to retail sites.

Add-on programs to existing online social networking sites include applications such as Beacon and Stylefeeder (Vara, 2007). For example, StyleFeeder is a social bookmarking service that allows users to browse the Web and add items they find to their RSS StyleFeeds, which they can then share with friends on social networks such as Facebook or blogs. The technology analyzes what the user adds, creating dynamically updated personalized recommendations as well as an improved shopping search engine. Add-on programs provide some of the same features as the social shopping websites, but appear on existing

Table 1. Online consumer behavior orientation and e-commerce technology support

Online Consumer Behavior Orientation	Description	E-commerce Technology Support
Transactional	Complete shopping tasks efficiently	Search, Product Categorization, Shopping Cart, Online payment
Informational	Keep informed about products and trends	Consumer Review, Product Rating, Personalized Recommendations, Opinion Forum, eWOM
Social	Develop feelings of warmth and satisfaction	Social Commerce (such as sharing information about products, comparing finds with others, asking others' opinions, and collaboratively making shopping decisions)

social networks that are not designed exclusive for shopping.

Mobile applications that support social retailing make up the third category of emerging social commerce applications. Using online social networking applications, short-range communications technologies such as RFID and Bluetooth, and mobile phone technologies, shoppers can share information synchronously or asynchronously online as they shop offline (Zaino, 2008). For example, in a 2007 retail industry expo, product developers collaborated with a New York designer to demonstrate how dressing rooms equipped with technology-enabled interactive mirrors communicated with a consumer's mobile phone to send videos and images of apparel to her friends and family for recommendations. The technology had the capability to capture the live pictures of the consumer wearing the clothes and also provide video and image recommendations, in addition to details such as pricing and sizes of similar or related items that the person could buy.

Despite the tremendous business interest and potential, it is not clear how early investments in social commerce applications have met business expectations. Advantages such as customer conversions are noted, but outcome data has not been readily available. Similarly, the true potential value of social commerce applications, which involves integrating online social networking with shopping, may not be clearly understood. Although technology adoption in general and e-commerce adoption in particular is well studied, the specificity of social commerce clearly calls for further theoretical development. For example, to date there is little if any research that has attempted to categorize social commerce applications. Additionally, Griffiths and Howard (2008) discuss the importance of understanding the effects of social networking and shopping and suggest that retailers should aim to create a seamless integration of five themes in their marketing strategy: pricing, online strategy, new media, online transactional barriers and social commerce; however, there

does not appear to be research that has tested this notion. Furthermore, there is no empirical work that examines the user's or consumer's intentions to adopt and use social commerce applications. Such understanding will add value for business managers making strategic decisions regarding the integration of social networking and online commerce, as well as for system designers who create the functionality, design, and application of such systems. In this study, we aim to provide an initial understanding of the prospective online shopper, or user, of online shopping websites. The specific focus is on what factors are likely to be associated with a user's intention to use this kind of application for online shopping.

CONCEPTUAL BACKGROUND

This research incorporates a number of well-grounded theories and factors that may affect adoption of social shopping sites. Widely used for examining user acceptance of a new information technology, the Technology Acceptance Model (TAM) has been recognized as one of the most powerful models in the information systems literature (Davis, 1989). To extend TAM to social shopping websites, three additional theories are adopted to enhance the specificity of the model to account for the social and hedonic nature of social shopping applications, including social comparison theory, social presence theory, and the flow theory.

Social Comparison

Social comparison is an essential social phenomenon where human beings compare themselves with others for self evaluation and information seeking. While the original theory of social comparison (Festinger, 1954) treated social comparison as a secondary choice when objective information to evaluate oneself is not available, subsequent research suggests that social comparison is a central feature of human social life (Buunk & Gibbons, 2007). The theory has also been extended to different types of opinion comparison, including preference assessment, belief assessment, and preference prediction (Suls, Martin, & Wheeler, 2000). The realm of social comparison theory continues to expand into new areas, including the study of economic behavior (Karlsson, Dellgran, Klingander, & Garling, 2004).

In this study, *tendency to social comparison online* (TSCO) is defined as the degree to which an individual tends to compare his or her opinions with others, and be influenced by others, particularly when shopping online. Recent studies have found that individuals differ quite a bit in their tendency to compare themselves with others (Buunk & Gibbons, 2007; Gibbons & Buunk, 1999). A related yet different construct that has been studied in extended TAM research is social influence (Hsu & Lu, 2004), which is defined as the degree to which an individual perceives that important others believe he or she should use the new system. The social influence construct is related to the external pressure the person perceives to use or not to use a system, and the pressure comes from important people in the person's life, such like family, friends, and supervisors at work. Kelman (1961) suggests that social influence operates through three processes: internalization, identification, and compliance. Internalization results from accepting information from expert sources as evidence of reality and integrating it into one's own cognitive system. Identification results from feeling some bond with a likable source and persists for as long as the likable source is still salient. Compliance results from a powerful source that has control over the message recipient. While social influence measures individual's compliance with social norms under pressure, the tendency to social comparison factor operates through the internalization and identification mechanisms. Another important difference is that social influence is significant only in mandatory settings, and not in voluntary context as in the case of online shopping (Song & Kim, 2006). Few studies have examined technology acceptance from the social comparison perspective, yet the increasing interests in information systems for voluntary use and social interactions warrant such an investigation.

Social Presence

A central difference between B2C e-commerce and the traditional brick and mortar commerce is that retail websites frequently lack the social appeal or human warmth of a face-to-face shopping experience. Online shopping is primarily geared towards reducing the user's cognitive burden, and is characterized as impersonal, anonymous, and automated compared with traditional face-to-face commerce. Some researchers have indicated that the lack of social presence may impede the growth of B2C e-commerce because of the lack of human interactions and thus trust (Gefen & Straub, 2003).

Previous research has been drawn to the concept of social presence to explore the lack of human warmth online (e.g. Chen, Olfman, & Harris, 2005). Rooted in information richness theory (Daft & Lengel, 1984), *social presence* (SP) is defined as the extent to which a medium allows a user to experience others as being psychologically present (Fulk, Steinfield, Schmitz, & Power, 1987). Bare-bone e-commerce websites that only support the transactional aspect of online shopping are considered information-lean. Research has shown that increased sense of social presence can be achieved through stimulating the imagination of interaction with other humans (e.g., through socially rich text and picture content, personalized greetings, human audio and video, intelligent agents), or by providing means for actual interaction with other humans (Hassanein & Head, 2006). Studies have shown that technologies such as personalization, recommendation, and consumer reviews can enable the feeling of a place where people interact, thus increasing the social presence of websites (Kumar & Benbasat, 2006). Increased social presence can in turn affect other factors such as perceived usefulness of the website (Gefen & Straub, 2003)

Enjoyment

Online shopping is a voluntary and hedonic activity, and users participate because they are intrinsically motivated. The experience often offers entertainment and fun, which users have been found to appreciate (Mathwick, 2002). Developed in the psychology literature, flow theory describes a state in which people are so involved in an activity that nothing else seems to matter (Csíkszentmihályi, 1990). Adapted into studies of technology adoption, the concept of perceived enjoyment (PE) has been defined and measured as the extent to which the activity of using a specific system is perceived to be enjoyable in it's own right, aside from any performance consequences resulting from system use (Davis, Bagozzi, & Warshaw, 1992).

It has been suggested that traditional usability approaches are too limited to fully explore user technology adoption and should be extended to encompass enjoyment (Blythe, Overbeeke, Monk, & Wright, 2003). In this study we postulated that the experience of being engaged or simply having fun can have an impact on intentions to adopt social shopping sites. Studies have found perceived enjoyment to be a significant antecedents to users' intentions to adopt technologies for activities such as web browsing (Novak, Hoffman, & Yung, 2000), and instant messaging (Lu, Zhou, & Wang, 2008).

Perceived Ease of Use and Perceived Usefulness

Adapted from the Theory of Reasoned Action (TRA) model, TAM posits that two beliefs – perceived ease of use (PEOU) and perceived usefulness (PU) are significant antecedents to one's behavioral intention to use a technology. PU is the degree to which a person believes that using a particular system would enhance his or her performance, and PEOU is the degree to which a person believes that using a particular system would be free of effort (Davis, 1989). Studies have shown the PU directly affects behavioral intentions to use a system (BI), and PEOU affects BI through PU (e.g., Gefen & Straub, 2003). Subsequent studies have applied TAM to a wide range of information systems and technologies (Davis & Venkatesh, 1996; Fang, Chan, Brzezinski, & Xu, 2006; McGill & Bax, 2007), including e-commerce (Gefen & Straub, 2003). Given that the social shopping website is an emerging e-commerce technology, this research study uses TAM as the base model to investigate the factors associated with the intention to use such websites.

While the parsimony of TAM makes it easy to apply to a variety of situations, the leanness of the model is also considered as one of its key limitations. The model lacks the ability to help business managers or system designers to understand the factors that contribute to the adoption or abandonment of new IT. A number of studies have been conducted to examine additional antecedents to IT use, such as positive image (Moore & Benbasat, 1996), cultural dimensions (Mao & Palvia, 2006; Straub, Keil, & Brenner, 1997), and computer playfulness (Venkatesh, 2000). Similarly, this research aims to extend the model with additional relevant constructs.

RESEARCH MODEL AND HYPOTHESES

Based on social comparison theory, social presence theory, flow theory, and TAM, the research model is proposed with six variables: Tendency to Social Comparison Online (TSCO), Social Presence (SP), Perceived Enjoyment (PE), Perceived Ease of Use (PEOU), Perceived Usefulness (PU), and Behavioral Intention to use social shopping sites (BI). Figure 1 shows the research model.

According to TAM, IT adoption is affected by prior user-related beliefs. Studies have shown the direct effect of PU on BI, and the indirect effect of PEOU on BI through PU (e.g., Gefen & Straub, 2003). Thus the hypothesized relationship among PEOU, PU, and BI are specified in H1-H2:

Figure 1. Research model

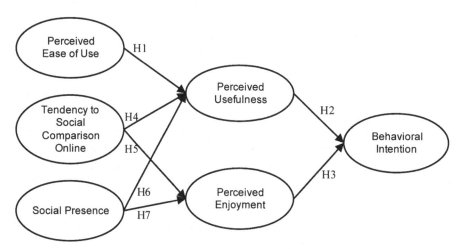

H1: Perceived Ease of Use (PEOU) will positively affect PU of social shopping websites.

H2: Perceived Usefulness (PU) will positively affect BI to use social shopping websites.

Incorporating flow theory and the results of subsequent studies of enjoyment and technology adoption (Novak, et al., 2000), it is postulated that the more the users perceive the site to be enjoyable, the more likely they will adopt the site. Thus H3 is:

H3: Perceived Enjoyment (PE) will positively affect BI to use social shopping websites.

Given the social nature of shopping, tendency to social comparison online is postulated to have an effect on one's intention to use a social shopping website. Empirical studies of online shopping revealed that the provision of recommendations and consumer reviews increase the perceived usefulness of the website (Kumar & Benbasat, 2006). These findings are consistent with marketing research indicating that consumers are influenced by other consumers in their decision making process, such as information seeking, alternative evaluation, and choice (Duhan,

Johnson, Wilcox, & Harrell, 1997; Friedman & Fireworker, 1977). In technology adoption, Song and Kim (Song & Kim, 2006) found that the users' tendency to compare their avatars with users' is an significant antecedent to users' adoption and use of an avatar-based virtual community system. Hennig-Thurau and Walsh (Hennig-Thurau & Walsh, 2003) conducted an empirical study of about 2,900 German consumers of eWOM websites, and found that people use such sites to function as "social positioners" which allow them to compare their shopping experience with other shoppers, in addition to obtaining product-related information to reduce the time in information gathering. The social positioning function significantly affected whether users planned to purchase the product (buying behavior) and whether they shared the product information with family and friends (communication behavior). Given the social nature of shopping and the specific features of social shopping websites, it is postulated that people who are more likely to compare and be influenced by others when shopping online are more likely to find the social shopping websites useful (H4), and find the sites enjoyable (H5). Thus the hypotheses are:

H4: Tendency to Social Comparison Online (TSCO) will positively affect PU of social shopping websites.

H5: Tendency to Social Comparison Online (TSCO) will positively affect PE of social shopping websites.

Finally, based on studies on social presence and the adoption of e-commerce systems (Gefen, Karahanna, & Straub, 2002; Suh & Han, 2002), it is hypothesized that the stronger the social presence of the shopping site, the more useful and enjoyable users will perceive it to be. Thus:

H6: Social Presence (SP) will positively affect PU of social shopping websites.

H7: Social Presence (SP) will positively affect PE of social shopping websites.

DATA COLLECTION

Data were collected through a survey in fall 2008 and spring 2009. The survey was given to undergraduate business students at a university in the northeastern region of United States. The participating students were from junior-level Electronic Commerce classes and senior-level Management Information Systems classes.

Kaboodle.com was chosen in this study for subjects to explore various shopping site features. Kaboodle was selected because it was the leading social shopping site at the time of the research, with about 2.5 million visitors each month as of June 2009 (Kasteler, 2009). The website offers a number of features to support social interactions while shopping online. For example, the user can select the "Join Now" function to create a rich personal profile including pictures, blogs, shopping lists, and style boards. The user can also take a compatibility test and find his or her "shopping soul mate" with similar shopping tastes. The "Community" feature allows users to create polls to gather other users' feedback, see profiles of other users, and add them as friends. The "Features Kaboodlers" function further promotes a sense of an online shopping community by featuring selected users on the home page, with links to their rich personal profiles on the site. To view the Kaboodle website, visit www.kaboodle.com.

In this study, subjects were asked to assume that they have some extra money, and they want to spend it by buying something online for themselves. They were instructed to explore the various features on the Kaboodle site including both traditional e-commerce functions, such as browsing by brands and searching, and features unique to social shopping websites such as shopping soul mates and compatibility tests, community, and featured shoppers. Subjects were then asked to write up and submit a short essay reflecting on the features provided on the website. The precise purpose of the study and the research model were neither discussed nor alluded to. After completing the assignment, students were given the URL to participate in the online survey. The survey was available online for one week. Students provided their names at the end of the survey for the sole purpose of obtaining extra credits, which was an incentive for survey participation. Students' names were deleted from the survey database as soon as extra credits were awarded.

In constructing the questionnaire, the Perceived Ease of Use, Perceived Usefulness, and Behavioral Intentions items were adapted from Davis (Davis, 1989). Items for the Tendency to Social Comparison Online scale were adapted from Gibbons and Buunk (Gibbons & Buunk, 1999) study, and were modified for the online shopping context. While some previous studies have treated Perceived Enjoyment as a multidimensional concept, the three-item scale of PE is considered to be most robust and widely used, and thus adopted in our study (Novak, et al., 2000). The Social Presence items were adapted from Gefen and Straub (Gefen & Straub, 2003). All items were measured on a seven-point scale ranging from strongly disagree (1) to strongly agree (7). The questionnaire also collected user information such as demographics, current use of online shopping and social networking websites, previous knowledge of social shopping sites, as well as open-ended questions.

The appendix lists the main constructs measured in the questionnaire.

DATA ANALYSIS AND RESULTS

The data were analyzed using Structural Equation Modeling (SEM) and SmartPLS software (Ringle, Wende, & Will, 2005). This approach allows for simultaneous analysis of the measurement model (factors) and the structural model (path analysis), and is widely used. The sections below provide the results of respondents' demographics, measurement model, and structural model.

Demographic Statistics

Among a total of 154 students, 99 responses were collected, resulting in a response rate of 64.3%. The response rate reflects the number of students who chose the extra credit assignment. 56% were male (n=55) and 44% were female (n=44). The majority of the respondents were between 20-24 years old (n=81, 82%). The respondents reported very experienced in using a PC (Mean=6.29, SD=1.00), and very experienced in using the Internet (Mean=6.76, SD=.70).

When asked about their online shopping frequency, the majority (68.7%) reported that they shop online from time to time (every few months), followed by 27.3% who shop online regularly (every month), and 4.0% who had never shopped online before. In terms of their use of social networking sites, the top site that subjects have an account and use regularly is Facebook. Table 2 lists respondents' current use of social networking sites.

Respondents were also asked about their use of the social shopping site Kaboodle before the

Table 2. Use of social networking sites

Social Networking Sites	No. of Subjects Use the Site Daily or Weekly	Percent
Facebook	81	81.8%
MySpace	20	20.2%
LinkedIn	2	2.0%
Flickr	2	2.0%

study. The great majority had never heard of Kaboodle before (84.8%), or had heard about Kaboodle but did not have a user account (12.1%). This finding reinforces the statistics (Kasteler, 2009) about monthly visits to traditional e-commerce site such as Amazon (about 51 million) vs. social shopping site such like Kaboodle (about 2.5 million), and suggests that social shopping sites are an emerging field that needs further exploration.

Measurement Model and Means of Constructs

The reliability of the constructs is reported in Table 3. As shown, the composite reliabilities of the different measures all exceed the recommended 0.70 level as well as the Chronbach's Alpha. The results indicate that the measures are robust in terms of their internal consistency reliability.

Table 4 lists the mean and standard deviation for each of the main constructs in the model. As shown, overall subjects reported positive attitude towards the social shopping site, and found it easy to use, useful, enjoyable, and are likely to use it in their shopping tasks in the future.

Convergent validity was examined using the factor loadings and cross loadings of the items to all the constructs. All items loaded on their respective constructs from a lower bound of .78 to a higher bound of .95, and they loaded more highly on their respective constructs than others. In addition, all of the items' loadings onto their respective constructs are significant at the .001

Table 3. PLS results of the measurement model

	Composite Reliability	Cronbach's Alpha
Behavioral Intention	0.93	0.89
Perceived Enjoyment	0.90	0.78
Perceived Ease of Use	0.93	0.91
Perceived Usefulness	0.94	0.88
Social Presence	0.93	0.90
Tendency to Social Comparison Online	0.87	0.80

Table 4. Means and standard deviations of the constructs

Construct	Mean	Standard Deviation (SD)
Behavioral Intention	4.66	1.45
Perceived Enjoyment	5.29	1.11
Perceived Ease of Use	5.17	1.14
Perceived Usefulness	5.14	1.31
Tendency to Social Comparison Online	4.70	1.16
Social Presence	5.13	1.11

level, as indicated by the T-statistics of the outer model loadings ranging from 11.02 to 87.15. The result confirms the convergent validity of the indicators as representing distinct latent constructs. Table 5 provides factors loadings of all the items.

Table 6 reports the discriminant validity of the measurement model. The elements in the matrix diagonals represent the square roots of the AVEs, and they are all greater than the off-diagonal elements in the corresponding rows and columns. This supports the discriminant validity of the scales.

Structural Model and Hypothesis Testing

Figure 2 shows the results of the structural model. The test yields results of path coefficients (β), which indicates the positive and negative relationships between the constructs, the strength of the relationships, and their statistical significance. The test also yields squared multiple correlations (R2) values, which indicate the amount of variance of the dependent construct that can be explained by the independent constructs.

Overall the model accounts for 66% of variance in behavioral intention, 48% in PU, and 45% in PE. PEOU is an antecedent to PU ($\beta= .33$, $p<.001$). PU has a strong effect on BI ($\beta= .52$, $p<.001$). PE also affects BI significantly ($\beta=.36$, $p<.001$). TSCO has an effect on PE ($\beta= .31$ $p<.001$)

and on PU ($\beta= .18$ $p<.01$). SP has a strong effect on PE ($\beta= .50$, $p<.001$), and a modest one on PU ($\beta= .34$, $p<.01$).

Thus the hypotheses testing results are:

H1: Perceived Ease of Use (PEOU) will positively affect PU of social shopping websites. **Supported**

H2: Perceived Usefulness (PU) will positively affect BI to use social shopping websites. **Supported**

H3: Perceived Enjoyment (PE) will positively affect BI to use social shopping websites. **Supported**

H4: Tendency to Social Comparison Online (TSCO) will positively affect PU of social shopping websites.
Supported

H5: Tendency to Social Comparison Online (TSCO) will positively affect PE of social shopping websites.
Supported

H6: Social Presence (SP) will positively affect PU of social shopping websites. **Supported**

H7: Social Presence (SP) will positively affect PE of social shopping websites. **Supported**

DISCUSSION

This study examined factors associated with a user's intention to use a social shopping website.

Table 5. Convergent validity and factor loadings (bolded)

	Behavioral Intention	Perceived Enjoyment	Perceived Ease of Use	Perceived Usefulness	Tendency to SC Online	Social Presence
BI1	**0.93**	0.68	0.52	0.76	0.61	0.48
BI2	**0.90**	0.61	0.43	0.65	0.48	0.42
BI3	**0.88**	0.67	0.55	0.69	0.50	0.57
PE1	0.76	**0.93**	0.52	0.74	0.44	0.59
PE2	0.53	**0.88**	0.50	0.51	0.44	0.50
PEOU1	0.54	0.51	**0.92**	0.57	0.44	0.48
PEOU2	0.47	0.51	**0.83**	0.54	0.34	0.41
PEOU3	0.43	0.44	**0.89**	0.43	0.36	0.49
PEOU4	0.50	0.52	**0.88**	0.54	0.37	0.54
PU1	0.72	0.68	0.55	**0.95**	0.46	0.59
PU2	0.75	0.66	0.58	**0.95**	0.37	0.51
TSCO1	0.52	0.35	0.42	0.32	**0.81**	0.25
TSCO2	0.43	0.31	0.41	0.35	**0.79**	0.23
TSCO3	0.41	0.41	0.30	0.38	**0.78**	0.38
TSCO4	0.49	0.45	0.25	0.34	**0.78**	0.24
SP1	0.46	0.52	0.49	0.49	0.28	**0.87**
SP2	0.43	0.51	0.48	0.48	0.43	**0.84**
SP3	0.50	0.54	0.46	0.52	0.28	**0.90**
SP4	0.52	0.56	0.48	0.55	0.25	**0.90**

A research model with six factors was proposed and analyzed. Using PLS, the results reveal that individual user's tendency to social comparison in online shopping affected how much they enjoyed using the website (with a coefficient of .31), and how useful they felt about the website (with a coefficient of .18). Social presence conveyed through the website affected PE (with a coefficient of .50), and PU (with a coefficient of .34). Enjoyment perceived by the users affected BI (with a coefficient of .36), suggesting the importance of engaging users and providing an enjoyable experience in designing such website. The results also supported the causal path from PEOU to PU (with a coefficient of .33), and from

Table 6. Discriminant validity of measurement model

.	BI	PEOU	PE	PU	SP	TSCO
BI	**0.90**					
PEOU	0.55	**0.88**				
Perceived Enjoyment (PE)	0.73	0.56	**0.90**			
PU	0.78	0.60	0.71	**0.95**		
Social Presence (SP)	0.54	0.54	0.61	0.58	**0.88**	
Tendency to Social Comparison Online (TSCO)	0.59	0.43	0.49	0.44	0.35	**0.79**

Figure 2. Research model results

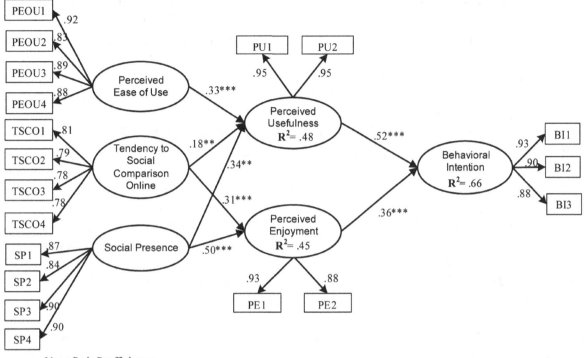

Note: Path Coefficients:
*** path is significant at the .001 level;   ** path is significant at the .01 level

PU to BI (with a coefficient of .52), as suggested in the TAM.

These results suggest that features that promoting the sense of personal presence and facilitating comparisons and sharing during the online shopping experience are critical to the adoption of such technology. In the open-ended questions, students reported that one of the main reasons they would use these websites for future shopping activities is because of the sense that they are shopping with others online: "I would use Kaboodle over other online shopping sites because it has a more personable feel and the recommendations for other products come from people instead of computer generated outputs." "What I liked best was the ability to meet people. It allowed for a more personal connection and a more trusted opinion." "Amazon is more of an individual experience while shopping online. Kaboodle,

(as a) social shopping website makes shopping a little bit more fun." These findings reinforce the importance of supporting the social aspects of shopping in e-commerce applications. While current e-commerce technology tend to focus on supporting the transactional and informational aspects of shopping more, emerging technologies that provide specific support for social interactions among shoppers and the sense of an online community are more likely to be embraced by online shoppers.

The social features of the website not only makes online shopping more enjoyable, but can also serve additional purposes such as making new discoveries of products online. Given the significant effect of social comparison on perceived usefulness and enjoyment, features that promote easy sharing and comparing of shopping ideas and experiences are likely to be important to the adoption and use of such sites. "I find the people functions of Kaboodle the most useful. The shopping soul-mates and compatibility test really helped me discover new gift ideas and it was neat to see other people's profile lists and similar tastes that they had to me." "I would (use the website in the future) because it would allow me to see what people with shopping habits similar to mine like and purchase, and because it could help me decide on gifts and purchases in the future." These social features stood out even more when students were asked to compare their experiences of using social shopping sites versus... traditional sites. Some indicated that "Other sites such as BlueFly.com and Overstock.com allow you to narrow your search according to category, price range, and gender, but Kaboodle.com made searching more enjoyable." This also reinforces the relationship between social interactions and the sense of enjoyment in online shopping activities as empirically tested in our research.

When asked about concerns that might prevent them from using the social shopping website in the future, privacy concerns topped the list. Among the concerns were issues like "I believe (such a site) could create easier access for other to hack into my account and learn about my information." "I am not able to limit what others see on my profile." Some also mentioned that while social shopping can be fun and helpful in discovering new products, it can be more time consuming too. "If I don't have a lot of time to look around online then this may not be the ideal way to go." Another issue that was pointed out was the trust placed on otherwise unknown online shoppers. "For me, shopping has always been a social activity. I go with my family or my friends to get their input on certain items. I found it difficult to trust the opinions of the other online shoppers at Kaboodle.com simply because I did not know them." This suggests that there may be individual differences in terms of the level of trust with the information provided by other online shoppers, and the strength of the relationship (family and friends

vs. unknown shoppers) may have an impact too. While the social aspect of the site was generally found to be a positive attribute, these comments suggest additional research is necessary to better understand the potential value of social shopping websites in the future.

CONTRIBUTIONS AND IMPLICATIONS

This research contributes to existing information systems theory by extending the Technology Acceptance Model with factors extracted from social comparison theory, social presence theory, and flow theory. First, three new factors: tendency to social comparison, social engagement, and perceived enjoyment were all found to be significant antecedents to intention to adoption, in addition to perceived ease of use and perceived usefulness. Second, a new scale, tendency to social comparison, was developed and empirically tested as reliable. The scale measured items such like sharing with other online shoppers about mutual opinions and experiences, finding online product reviews helpful, being affected by others' opinions, etc. All of the hypotheses were supported. Finally, our results extend prior research on user acceptance of technology by linking key social variables from the social science and management information systems literature to the well-known TAM variables, and empirically validating the relationship in the context of social commerce applications.

The findings of the study provide potential practical implications for the strategic investment and the design of social shopping sites. While our study is exploratory in nature, as it examined a relatively narrow sample population of college students, it does suggest that the attributes unique to social shopping sites may affect user acceptance and use of these sites for online shopping. Within this population, our research model reveals that in addition to ease of use and usefulness, social shopping sites will most likely be used when they (1) enable users to easily compare their shopping experiences and opinions with others, (2) foster a sense of community, and (3) are designed to make the entire process feel enjoyable.

This study is among the first to propose a framework of online consumer behaviors associated with social commerce and the technologies that support them (see Table 1). The study results provide empirical evidence to support the importance of distinguishing the social aspect of shopping from the information and transactional aspects, as well as the potential advantage to using technology to promote social interactions on e-commerce sites. The overall favorable attitudes towards adoption of such sites suggest that users embrace the idea of websites that go beyond consumer reviews and enable them to enjoy the social aspects of shopping online. These findings provide a signal to business practitioners designing and/ or managing online shopping websites that there is a noteworthy difference between the value of customer-generated reviews alone and the value of integrating these reviews with the powerful capabilities of social networking.

LIMITATIONS AND FUTURE RESEARCH

As previously noted, a limitation of this exploratory study is its focus on a particular population of online users. The sample size and the use of students as subjects in this study may both be considered limitations; however, the value of students as surrogates in TAM studies has been confirmed by previous meta-analysis of TAM (King & He, 2006). Although popular press claims suggest that this user group is among the primary target users of these kinds of sites, further research that examines perceptions across multiple age-groups and professions would be necessary to confirm and broaden our results.

Additional research to extend the findings of this study should consider the type of online shopping tasks that may be most suitable for social shopping websites. While social networking websites such as Facebook are integrating social commerce add-on applications, what, if any, is the particular market space online for social shopping websites? Similarly, what is the perceived added value of social shopping websites versus other sites that add social shopping features as an add-on, without being the primary focus of the site? Moreover, research that examines whether users prefer social shopping sites over traditional e-commerce sites for certain kinds shopping activities, such as browsing or searching (Hong, Thong, & Tam, 2004) can provide retailers with meaningful information about how best to market and sell their products or services online. An additional consideration is whether the benefits of social shopping sites could maximized when users are shopping for particular types of products, such as quality vs. preference products (Lee & Lee, 2009). That is, would users prefer sites that are more general in nature or more product-specific, i.e., when the product is more relevant to them (Park et al., 2007)? Complementary empirical investigations in these areas may provide valuable information about user perceptions that could improve the potential of social shopping technology investments by online retailers.

This study focused specifically on social shopping websites. Additional social commerce applications should be examined in order to broaden our understanding of the rapid growth and potentials for integration among social networking and online shopping activities. Furthermore, there is an opportunity for in-depth research regarding the relationship between privacy and trust and the acceptance and use of social shopping sites. For example, what is the difference, if any, in the strength of the social ties that affect users' trust of such shopping sites, such as family and friends versus other online shoppers? Early finding suggest that common online shopper attributes and interests appear to positively affect user acceptance of social shopping sites. As an emerging area in e-commerce, additional research that addresses the potential power and limitations associated with integrating social networking features with online shopping is timely and important.

REFERENCES

Blythe, M. A., Overbeeke, K., Monk, A. F., & Wright, P. C. (Eds.). (2003). *Funology: From Usability to Enjoyment*. Dordrecht, The Netherlands: Kluwer Academic Publishers.

Buunk, A. P., & Gibbons, F. X. (2007). Social Comparison: The End of A Theory and The Emergence of A Field. *Organizational Behavior and Human Decision Processes, 102*(1), 3–21. doi:10.1016/j.obhdp.2006.09.007

Chen, C. C., Olfman, L., & Harris, A. (2005). Differential Impacts of Social Presence on the Behavior Modeling Approach. *International Journal of Technology and Human Interaction, 1*(2), 64–84.

Csíkszentmihályi, M. (1990). *Flow: The Psychology of Optimal Experience*. New York: Harper and Row.

Daft, R. L., & Lengel, R. H. (1984). Information Richness: A New Approach to Managerial Behavior and Organizational Design. In L. L. C. & B. M. Staw (Eds.), *Research in Organizational Behavior* (pp. 191-233). Homewood, IL: JAI Press.

Davis, F. D. (1989). Perceived Usefulness, Perceived Ease of Use and User Acceptance of Information Technology. *Management Information Systems Quarterly, 13*(3), 319–340. doi:10.2307/249008

Davis, F. D., Bagozzi, R. P., & Warshaw, P. R. (1992). Extrinsic and Intrinsic Motivation to Use Computers in the Workplace. *Journal of Applied Social Psychology, 22*(14), 1111–1132. doi:10.1111/j.1559-1816.1992.tb00945.x

Davis, F. D., & Venkatesh, V. (1996). A Critical Assessment of Potential Measurement Biases in the Technology Acceptance Model: Three Experiments. *International Journal of Human-Computer Studies, 45*(1), 19–45. doi:10.1006/ijhc.1996.0040

Duhan, D. F., Johnson, S. D., Wilcox, J. B., & Harrell, G. D. (1997). Influences on Consumer Use of Word-of-Mouth Recommendation Sources. *Journal of the Academy of Marketing Science, 25*(4), 283–295. doi:10.1177/0092070397254001

Fang, X., Chan, S., Brzezinski, J., & Xu, S. (2006). Moderating Effects of Task Type on Wireless Technology Acceptance. *Journal of Management Information Systems, 22*(3), 123–157. doi:10.2753/MIS0742-1222220305

Festinger, L. (1954). A Theory of Social Comparison Processes. *Human Relations, 7*, 117–140. doi:10.1177/001872675400700202

Friedman, H. H., & Fireworker, R. B. (1977). The Susceptibility of Consumers to Unseen Group Influence. *The Journal of Social Psychology, 102*(1), 155–156. doi:10.1080/00224545.1977.9713254

Fulk, J., Steinfield, C. W., Schmitz, J., & Power, J. G. (1987). A Social Information Processing Model of Media Use in Organizations. *Communication Research, 14*, 529–552. doi:10.1177/009365087014005005

Gefen, D., Karahanna, E., & Straub, D. (2002). *Building Consumer Trust in Online Shopping and TAM: An Integrated Model*. Philadelphia: Drexel University.

Gefen, D., & Straub, D. (2003). Managing User Trust in B2C e-Services. *E-Service Journal, 2*(2), 7–24. doi:10.2979/ESJ.2003.2.2.7

Gibbons, F. X., & Buunk, B. P. (1999). Individual Differences in Social Comparison: Development of a Scale of Social Comparison Orientation. *Journal of Personality and Social Psychology, 76*(1), 129–142. doi:10.1037/0022-3514.76.1.129

Gregoriadis, L. (2007). *Social Commerce Report 2007*. Retrieved from http://econsultancy.com/reports/social-commerce-report-2007

Griffiths, G., & Howard, A. (2008). Balancing Clicks and Bricks - Strategies for Multichannel Retailers. *Journal of Global Business Issues, 2*(1), 69–75.

Hassanein, K., & Head, M. (2006). The Impact of Infusing Social Presence in the Web Interface: An Investigation Across Product Types. *International Journal of Electronic Commerce, 10*(2), 31–55. doi:10.2753/JEC1086-4415100202

Hemp, P. (2006). Avatar-based Marketing. *Harvard Business Review, 84*(6), 48–57.

Hennig-Thurau, T., & Walsh, G. (2003). Electronic Word-of-Mouth: Motives for and Consequences of Reading Customer Articulations on the Internet. *International Journal of Electronic Commerce, 8*(2), 51–74.

Hong, W., Thong, J. Y. L., & Tam, K. Y. (2004). The Effects of Information Format and Shopping Task on Consumers' Online Shopping Behavior: A Cognitive Fit Perspective. *Journal of Management Information Systems, 21*(3), 149–184.

Hsu, C. L., & Lu, H. P. (2004). Why Do People Play On-line Games? An Extended TAM with Social Influences and Flow Experience. *Information & Management, 41*(7), 853–868. doi:10.1016/j.im.2003.08.014

Karlsson, N., Dellgran, P., Klingander, B., & Garling, T. (2004). Household Consumption: Influences of Aspiration Level, Social Comparison, and Money Management. *Journal of Economic Psychology, 25*, 753–769.

Kasteler, J. (2009). *Why You Should Get Involved With Social Shopping: E-commerce 2.0*. Retrieved from http://searchengineland.com/why-you-should-get-involved-with-social-shopping-e-commerce-20-22995

Kelman, H. C. (1961). Processes of Opinion Change. *Public Opinion Quarterly, 25*, 57–78. doi:10.1086/266996

King, W. R., & He, J. (2006). A Meta-analysis of the Technology Acceptance Model. *Information & Management, 43*(6), 740–755. doi:10.1016/j.im.2006.05.003

Kumar, N., & Benbasat, I. (2006). The Influence of Recommendations and Consumer Reviews on Evaluations of Websites. *Information Systems Research, 17*(4), 425–439. doi:10.1287/isre.1060.0107

Lee, J., & Lee, J. N. (2009). Understanding the Product Information Inference Process in Electronic Word-of-Mouth: An Objectivity–Subjectivity Dichotomy Perspective. *Information & Management, 46*(5), 302–311. doi:10.1016/j.im.2009.05.004

Lu, Y., Zhou, T., & Wang, B. (2008). Exploring Chinese Users' Acceptance of Instant Messaging Using the Theory of Planned Behavior, the Technology Acceptance Model, and the Flow Theory. *Computers in Human Behavior, 6*(2), 1–11.

Mao, E., & Palvia, P. (2006). Testing an Extended Model of IT Acceptance in the Chinese Cultural Context. *ACM SIGMIS Database, 37*(2-3), 20–32. doi:10.1145/1161345.1161351

Mathwick, C. (2002). Understanding the Online Consumer: A Typology of Online Relational Norms and Behavior. *Journal of Interactive Marketing, 16*(1), 40–55. doi:10.1002/dir.10003

McGill, T., & Bax, S. (2007). From Beliefs to Success: Utilizing an Expanded TAM to Predict Web Page Development Success. *International Journal of Technology and Human Interaction, 3*(3), 36–53.

Moore, G. C., & Benbasat, I. (1996). Integrating Diffusion of Innovations and Theory of Reasoned Action Models to Predict Utilization of Information Technology by End-users. In Kautz, K., & Pries-Heje, J. (Eds.), *Diffusion and Aadoption of Iinformation Technology* (pp. 132–146). London: Chapman and Hall.

Novak, T. P., Hoffman, D. L., & Yung, Y.-F. (2000). Measuring the Customer Experience in Online Environments: A Structural Modeling Approach. *Marketing Science, 19*, 22–42. doi:10.1287/mksc.19.1.22.15184

Park, D. H., Lee, J., & Han, I. (2007). The Effect of On-Line Consumer Reviews on Consumer Purchasing Intention: The Moderating Role of Involvement. *International Journal of Electronic Commerce, 11*(4), 125–148. doi:10.2753/JEC1086-4415110405

Ringle, C. M., Wende, S., & Will, A. (2005). *SmartPLS (Version 2.0 (beta))*. Hamburg, Germany: University of Hamburg.

Song, J., & Kim, Y. J. (2006). Social Influence Process in the Acceptance of a Virtual Community Service. *Information Systems Frontiers, 8*(3), 241–252. doi:10.1007/s10796-006-8782-0

Steel, E. S. (2007, November 27). Where E-Commerce Meets Chat, Social Retailing Gains Traction. *The Wall Street Journal*, B8.

Straub, D., Keil, M., & Brenner, W. (1997). Testing the Technology Acceptance Model Across Cultures: A three country study. *Information & Management, 33*(1), 1–11. doi:10.1016/S0378-7206(97)00026-8

Suh, B., & Han, I. (2002). Effect of Trust on Customer Acceptance of Internet Banking. *Electronic Commerce Research and Applications, 1*(3-4), 247–263. doi:10.1016/S1567-4223(02)00017-0

Suls, J., Martin, R., & Wheeler, L. (2000). Three Kinds of Opinion Comparison: The Triadic Model. *Personality and Social Psychology Review, 4*(3), 219–237. doi:10.1207/S15327957PSPR0403_2

Tedeschi, B. (2006, September 11). Like Shopping? Social Networking? Try Social Shopping. *The New York Times*.

Vara, V. (2007). Facebook Rethinks Tracking: Site Apologizes, Makes It Easier To Retain Privacy. *The Wall Street Journal*.

Venkatesh, V. (2000). Determinants of Perceived Ease of Use: Integrating Control, Intrinsic Motivation, and Emotion into the Technology Acceptance Model. *Information Systems Research, 11*(4), 342–365. doi:10.1287/isre.11.4.342.11872

Vranica, S. (2008, April 10). Can Dove Promote a Cause and Sell Soap? *The Wall Street Journal*, B6.

Zaino, J. (2008). Tag Sale. *RFID Journal*. Retrieved from http://www.rfidjournal.com/

APPENDIX

Table A1. Items for the latent constructs

Construct		Items
Perceived Ease of Use (PEOU)	PEOU1	Kaboodle is easy to use.
	PEOU2	My interaction with Kaboodle is clear and understandable.
	PEOU3	Learning to use Kaboodle is easy.
	PEOU4	It is easy to get Kaboodle to do what I want it to do.
Perceived Usefulness (PU)	PU1	Kaboodle enables me to discover new products and get shopping idea more quickly.
	PU2	Kaboodle increases my productivity in discovering products and getting shopping ideas.
Perceived Enjoyment (PE)	PE1	I had fun using Kaboodle.
	PE2	I found my visit to the website interesting.
Behavioral Intention (BI)	BI1	I am very likely to use Kaboodle in the future to discover new products.
	BI2	I am likely to actually purchase products I found on Kaboodle.
	BI3	I will recommend Kaboodle to others.
Social Presence (SP)	SP1	There is a sense of human contact in the website.
	SP2	There is a sense of sociability in the website.
	SP3	There is a sense of human warmth in the website.
	SP4	There is a sense of human sensitivity in the website.
Tendency to Social Comparison Online (TSCO)	TSCO1	I often like to talk with other online shoppers about mutual opinions and experiences.
	TSCO2	I often try to find out what other online shoppers think who face similar problems as I face.
	TSCO3	I find online product reviews helpful.
	TSCO4	Other people's opinions tend to affect my decisions.

This work was previously published in the International Journal of Technology and Human Interaction, Volume 7, Issue 1, edited by Anabela Mesquita and Chia-Wen Tsai, pp. 19-36, copyright 2011 by IGI Publishing (an imprint of IGI Global).

Chapter 5

A Comparative Case Study of Indonesian and UK Organisational Culture Differences in IS Project Management

Andrew McDonald
Birkbeck, University of London, UK

Sven Helmer
Birkbeck, University of London, UK

ABSTRACT

Information Systems (IS) Project Management (PM) is fundamental to the modern, constantly changing and upgrading business world and is impacted by culture on many levels. This research shows the extent to which organisational culture in international IS projects is impacted by culture found on a national level. Current data contributing to IS PM knowledge is provided by investigating two Information Technology (IT) firms in the telecommunications sector based in Indonesia and the United Kingdom undergoing system upgrade projects using a survey and interviews. Differing trends between these organisational cultures are identified (and a third international control group) in regard to hierarchical structures and managing conflict employing a version of Hofstede's cultural survey as a basis.

INTRODUCTION

Information Systems (IS) Project Management (PM) is fundamental to the modern, constantly changing and globalised business world. It is no longer unusual for an IS project to span multiple geographies, be delivered using diversified human resource, or feel pressures from differing cultures and norms. Modern internationalisation is fusing different 'national' values into one international set (Warner, 1996b) - yet this is not managed, metered, or normalised and global IS PM must still be mindful of organisational cultural differences in order to deliver value in an evolving industry.

DOI: 10.4018/978-1-4666-1954-8.ch005

As organisations launch, and have launched, projects on an international level, managers already run projects according to different methods and priorities. This is due to differences in management style, project management understanding, and, last but not least, culture (Igbaria & Zviran, 1996; Zwikael et al., 2005; Karahanna et al., 2005). However, Redding and Baldwin found organisations operating in a single-culture context are ill-equipped to meet the demands of a globalised world (Redding & Baldwin, 1991). Managers can work more successfully if they understand their cultural biases and assumptions, consider the reasons why people from other cultures do things differently (and not only see irreconcilable differences) (Hoecklin, 1994). Forming strategic alliances has also become a high priority for organisations. However, Buchanan and Berman concluded cross-border corporate alliances have a high probability of failure (Buchanan & Berman, 1992), so managers need to be aware of the problems they might be facing in terms of cultural differences.

With increasing geographical divide inside modern organisations the factors affecting IS project success have been identified as the widening of management responsibility, globalisation of project teams, and understanding of specific IS cultural differences (Chauvet & Gallivan, 2007; Ailon, 2008). In this paper we show findings from a comparison of organisational cultural differences for IS projects delivered in Indonesia and the United Kingdom (UK). The research uses primary data from a study conducted in 2007/08 involving 90 IS project members. The study used a semi-structured questionnaire to deliver initial data on which further detail was gathered with interviews giving depth to the research. The aims are to present recent findings from a real project base to promote the need to understand and consider organisational culture in terms of managing conflict and ambiguity within a project. In particular we focus on the impact of other levels of culture, especially national culture, on organisational culture.

The remainder of this paper is organised as follows; a literature review section summarises relevant papers to this area; a section describing our methodology follows this; the next section presents the findings of our research; a final summary concludes our paper.

LITERATURE REVIEW

It is very difficult to provide a clear-cut definition of the term "culture"; Hoecklin lists ten different concepts from as many sources (Hoecklin, 1994), while Olie discusses over 160 different definitions (Olie, 1994). Our focus is not to further define "culture", but to provide definitions that mirror our interpretation before delving into the details of our findings.

Culture, to us, is well defined as "a collective programming of the mind which distinguishes one group from another" (Hofstede, 1980). Culture is classified using national culture, organisational culture and individual culture or behaviour (Hampden-Turner & Trompenaars, 1997; Schneider & Barsoux, 2003; Hofstede & Hofstede, 2005). Hofstede (1985) describes national culture, using his "ecological analysis", noting organisations have unique small-scale cultures and value systems with a traceable link between the founding individual and residual organisational culture. A link can also be seen between national and organisational cultures, as an organisation is typically founded inside one nation. The concept of organisational culture was first pioneered by Peters and Waterman (1982). They used a prescriptive approach to define organisational culture, classifying eight themes common to high-performing organisations. However, one of the shortcomings of their method is an oversimplification of the facts, as they pursue a 'one size fits all' approach. Another important line of research (originally inspired by Hofstede) was done by Trompenaars and Hampden-Turner (1997). Similar to Hofstede, they identified several bipolar dimensions to describe cultural aspects. Although there has been criticism of Hofstede's and Trompenaars' and Hampden-Turner's work, according to Hoecklin (1994), they "have promoted the most expressive and popular of cultural surveys/studies."

National level cultural analysis and empirical data should not be simply transferred to the organisation or individual cultural level without verification (McCoy et al., 2005). Additionally, they argue that in the wake of globalisation, one must look at both national and individual cultural levels, comparing data with theoretical models used in order to present findings of significance to organisations (McCoy et al, 2005). Tricker (1988) found that cultural dimensions affected differences between Asian and Western management of IS, and concluded national generalisations are not valid, while Kumar and Bjom-Andersen's (1990) research provides a backwards-traced link between organisation and individual culture from decisions by IS members stemming from socio-cultural background. Karahanna et al. (2005) provide insight into culture hierarchies, specifically group culture situated below organisational culture, and the make-up of organisational culture, which they see as a sum of individual cultural beliefs. Group culture shows greater detail of the organisational cultural effects on managerial behaviour, specifically decision-making preferences and influences, and Karahanna et al. (2005) research approaches aligns with ours in viewing organisational culture as a 'sum of parts' not in isolation from individuals. Ali and Brooks pick up these arguments in their literature survey when investigating the interaction of cultural levels, i.e. in an organisational setting, behaviour is influenced by the national level as well as the group level (Ali & Brooks, 2008).

Chauvet and Gallivan's (2007) research addresses national culture impacting modern IS project adoption focusing on project members for understanding the key to increasing value in IS/IT. Understanding the cultural implications of project groups in the context of cross-cultural

IS PM is imperative to improving IS projects. (This is very similar to the approach taken by us.) Although some researchers support the view that cross-cultural issues are converging (Igbaria & Zviran, 1996; Chauvet & Gallivan, 2007), our opinion is that currently differing cultural impacts to IS PM require understanding and management in order for projects to have a good chance of success. Perhaps even a new level of culture needs analysis, the project level (similar to subgroup culture in Karahanna et al (2005)), as in modern business this often involves teams from varying organisations and nations bringing together a mix of cultural views for a specific purpose and time.

Although the impact of organisational culture on IS project success and end-user acceptance has been identified as significant (Igbaria & Zviran, 1996; Chauvet & Gallivan, 2007), the attention given to cross-cultural issues within the IS and IT fields is low (Straub et al, 2002). We want to start filling this gap by providing empirical research findings from a recent examination of organisational culture; one in the UK and one in Indonesia. Hofstede (1985) found that organisations have "prevalent value systems which are part of their organisational cultures", and that research into national value systems can suggest the likely influence exerted onto organisations. Our paper argues that IS PM communities need to understand this likely influence; thus we provide empirical data from two organisational projects.

There has also been research on cultural issues in management regarding Indonesia. Indonesian society is composed of about 200 ethnic groups, with cultural impacts from Malay, Dutch, Arab and Japanese occupation plus in more modern times (since independence) westernised influence, as well as multiple religions (Warner, 1996b). Managers protect through "elder paternalism", and neither appreciate aggressive or loud behaviour, nor bad news or saying 'no' directly to any demand (Warner, 1996b).

Research Methodology

The aim of our research was not to tackle this subject in its entirety, but to look at a specific subtopic: how do PM practices differ between Indonesia and the UK? In particular we were interested in the tolerance for ambiguity, as depending on the level that is tolerated, different management styles will be more effective. In the case of low tolerance, a more supportive, clear-cut stance is appropriate, while in the case of high tolerance a manager can grant more individual freedom.

The basis for our work comes from Hofstede's (1980) work on cultural differences in the workplace. Among the different dimensions provided by Hofstede, his "Certainty Dimension" is of particular interest to us. We chose six of Hofstede's high-level questions concerning uncertainty avoidance as basis for a questionnaire, which we used to conduct a study among 90 randomly selected IS project contacts across different sample groups (61 of which returned the survey). The first two groups came from two IT firms in the UK and Indonesia), while a third control group was chosen among European and Australasian participants (to give a median indicator for comparison). The questionnaire was designed to utilise local determinants of any definitions used since creating a shared, cross-cultural vocabulary would have made the tool unwieldy. The questionnaire was complemented by interview sessions, which took place after the questionnaires had been evaluated. The purpose of the interviews was to clarify and confirm our findings from the questionnaire evaluation.

The research focused on six lines of questioning utilising Hofstede's methodology for the survey direction, namely:

1. The role of conflict within organisations
2. The need for managers to provide precise answers
3. The importance of matrix structures in organisations

4. The role of hierarchies
5. The importance of strict rules
6. Resolving conflicts through mutual compromise.

Hofstede's methodology has been widely cited in IT or IS culture research (Dorfman & Howell, 1988; Igbaria & Zviran, 1996; McCoy et al., 2005; Jones, 2007), and supported by various cross-methodology studies (Hofstede & Bond, 1984; Straub et al., 2002). Although there are various criticisms to Hofstede's methodology (Davis, 1989; McSweeney, 2002; Ailon, 2008) we continued with this as the basis for our survey in order to start from a well-known vantage point, not comment on Hofstede's overall applicability.

MAIN FINDINGS

The study compares cultural differences of the two nations and utilises Hofstede's (2005) framework to identify differences regarding specific IS PM behaviours in each geography. The following findings can influence the way in which IS PM is approached through having a clear understanding of organisational cultural differences and associated impact. These results are then compared to findings from earlier, more general research, of different 'management cultures' (Schneider & Barsoux, 2003; Warner, 1996a, 1996b).

The opening two survey questions (Tables 1 and 2) covered the IS and IS PM experience of respondents. Our findings seem to confirm those found by Warner (Warner, 1996a) about training/experience of British staff, and showed a mature workforce with standard distributed PM experience. Usually short-term projects, such as typically found within IS, lead to problems of joiners from different cultures (Hofstede, 1985).

The main survey section addressed the six questions on cultural classification. The first question (Table 3) asked respondents to give their opinion on whether organisations are better with-

Table 1. Raw and analysed data (in percentage) for responses regarding project experience by geography

	Country			
IS Experience Level	**UK**	**Indonesia**	**Control Group**	**Total**
Less than 1 year	2 / 6%			**2**
1 to 2 years	1 / 3%		1 / 7%	**2**
2 to 5 years	7 / 24%			**7**
5 to 10 years	13 / 43%	7 / 41%	5 / 35%	**25**
Above 10 years	7 / 24%	10 / 59%	8 / 58%	**25**
Total	**30 / 100%**	**17 / 100%**	**14 / 100%**	

out conflict. The research showed the UK tending to disagree (47% 'tend to disagree'), and Indonesia tending to agree (35% 'tend to agree') that removing conflict from an organisation is beneficial. Indonesian respondents tending to agree with the statement shows consistency with Schneider and Barsoux's (2003) research where a top Indonesian management culture was "decisions based on compromise – 'keep everyone happy'". On the other hand, in the UK opportunities for independent thought and action are valued personally (Warner, 1996a) meaning that controversial opinions are less likely to be subdued by organisational gain.

The second question gathered respondents' views on whether managers need precise answers (Table 4). A large proportion of the UK respondents agreed that precise answers are not always needed. The Indonesian group was divided on this question without a clear majority for or against

the statement. This is in contrast to the findings of Warner, who argued the UK's hierarchical leadership style (Warner, 1996a), and Indonesian's parental style authority allows managers to be unquestionable (Warner, 1996b).

On the third survey question (Table 5), Indonesia supported the concept of matrix-structured organisations more than the UK. Warner's research shows UK management to be a formal discipline, highly esteemed and requiring education and leadership (Warner, 1996a). Therefore having 'two bosses' is culturally less palatable for UK project members than Indonesians governed by a family-oriented management style (Warner, 1996b). Another reason Indonesia agrees with a matrix structure is its common occurrence locally for IS projects; the survey project utilised a solid reporting line for project responsibilities and dotted-line for line-management responsibilities. At first glance Indonesian agreement with a ma-

Table 2. Raw and analysed data for responses regarding IS PM experience

	Country			
IS PM Experience Level	**UK**	**Indonesia**	**Control Group**	**Total**
Less than 1 year	5 / 17%	1 / 6%	2 / 14%	**8**
1 to 2 years	5 / 17%	2 / 12%	1 / 7%	**8**
2 to 5 years	12 / 39%	8 / 47%	5 / 35%	**25**
5 to 10 years	5 / 17%	5 / 29%	3 / 22%	**13**
Above 10 years	3 / 10%	1 / 6%	3 / 22%	**7**
Total	**30 / 100%**	**17 / 100%**	**14 / 100%**	

Table 3. Raw and analysed data for responses regarding the statement: "organisations are better without conflict"

	Country			
Ranking	**UK**	**Indonesia**	**Control Group**	**Total**
Strongly Disagree	3 / 10%	2 / 12%	2 / 14%	7
Tend to Disagree	14 / 47%	4 / 24%	8 / 57%	**26**
Undecided	2 / 7%			**2**
Tend to Agree	8 / 27%	6 / 35%	3 / 21%	**17**
Strongly Agree	3 / 10%	5 / 29%	1 / 7%	**9**
Total	**30 / 100%**	**17 / 100%**	**14 / 100%**	

trix culture might seem like a contradiction with their parental leadership style, however, this ties in with decision-making based on compromise, also a cultural aspect of Indonesia, or the esteem placed on leadership (Warner, 1996b).

Indonesian respondents were divided about bypassing hierarchies to achieve results, whilst the UK agreed this could add value to IS projects (Table 6). The high level of Indonesian votes for bypassing hierarchy (18% 'strongly agree' and 47% 'tend to agree') is surprising, given Schneider and Barsoux's (2003) research showing the top Indonesian management culture as "respect for hierarchy and elders". Our findings suggest an organisational level deviation from national culture norms as theorised by Karahanna et al. (2005). This impact can be seen in IS projects in Indonesia with project groups granted high decision-making power by senior managers to bypass administrative blocks.

The UK respondents were undecided (30% tend to disagree and 30% tend to agree) on the issue of an organisation's rules not being broken (Table 7). This is explained by the UK's culture of seeing management and their decision-making authority as prestigious, so to break rules goes against tradition. Previous findings for Indonesia, however, seem to suggest a parental-style management utilising a pragmatic and revered habit of problem solving (Warner, 1996a), which would fail if trust and lines of command were broken. Our findings seem to suggest otherwise, as the result was not that clear-cut: 41% tended to disagree with the above statement, while another 41% tended to agree or agree strongly.

Table 4. Raw and analysed data for responses on the statement: "a good manager does not always need precise answers to work-related questions from subordinates"

	Country			
Ranking	**UK**	**Indonesia**	**Control Group**	**Total**
Strongly Disagree	2 / 7%	2 / 12%	2 / 14%	**6**
Tend to Disagree	9 / 30%	6 / 35%	1 / 7%	**16**
Undecided	1 / 3%	1 / 6%	1 / 7%	**3**
Tend to Agree	13 / 43%	7 / 41%	9 / 64%	**29**
Strongly Agree	5 / 17%	1 / 6%	1 / 7%	**7**
Total	**30 / 100%**	**17 / 100%**	**14 / 100%**	

Table 5. Raw and analysed data for responses on the statement: "a matrix structure organisation should be avoided"

Country				
Ranking	UK	Indonesia	Control Group	Total
Strongly Disagree	1 / 3%	1 / 6%		**2**
Tend to Disagree	9 / 30%	6 / 35%	3 / 21%	**18**
Undecided	3 / 10%	3 / 18%	5 / 36%	**11**
Tend to Agree	10 / 33%	3 / 18%	2 / 14%	**15**
Strongly Agree	7 / 23%	4 / 24%	4 / 29%	**15**
Total	**30 / 100%**	**17 / 100%**	**14 / 100%**	

Table 6. Raw and analysed data for responses on the statement: "work relationships sometimes bypassing hierarchical lines can add value"

Country				
Ranking	UK	Indonesia	Control Group	Total
Strongly Disagree	1 / 3%			**1**
Tend to Disagree	3 / 10%	6 / 35%	4 / 29%	**13**
Undecided	5 / 17%		3 / 21%	**8**
Tend to Agree	13 / 43%	8 / 47%	4 / 29%	**25**
Strongly Agree	8 / 27%	3 / 18%	3 / 21%	**14**
Total	**30 / 100%**	**17 / 100%**	**14 / 100%**	

Finally, resolving conflicts through mutual compromise (Table 8) was favoured slightly more by Indonesia than the UK. Again this resonates with Schneider and Barsoux's (2003) 'keep everyone happy' finding. Interviews provided insight into the drivers behind Indonesian respondent's strong stance uncovering IS project end-users as the main local influence on IT project acceptance and the need for all levels of IS project teams to satisfy end-user demands.

Table 7. Raw and analysed data for responses on the statement: "an organisation's rules should not be broken – not even in the organisation's perceived best interest"

Country				
Ranking	UK	Indonesia	Control Group	Total
Strongly Disagree	3 / 10%			**3**
Tend to Disagree	9 / 30%	7 / 41%	8 / 57%	**24**
Undecided	7 / 23%	3 / 18%	3 / 21%	**13**
Tend to Agree	9 / 30%	5 / 29%	1 / 7%	**15**
Strongly Agree	2 / 7%	2 / 12%	2 / 14%	**6**
Total	**30 / 100%**	**17 / 100%**	**14 / 100%**	

Table 8. Raw and analysed data for responses on the statement: "conflicts should be resolved with mutual compromise"

	Country			
Ranking	**UK**	**Indonesia**	**Control Group**	**Total**
Strongly Disagree		1 / 6%		1
Tend to Disagree	3 / 10%		2 / 14%	5
Undecided	3 / 10%		1 / 7%	4
Tend to Agree	14 / 47%	10 / 59%	8 / 57%	32
Strongly Agree	10 / 33%	6 / 35%	3 / 21%	19
Total	**30 / 100%**	**17 / 100%**	**14 / 100%**	

DISCUSSION AND CONCLUSION

Let us summarise the main findings in terms of suggestions for project managers working in certain cultural settings. We highlight the influence of national culture on the organisational culture of IT firms. Unsurprisingly, the findings from our research show that cultures in UK and Indonesian organisations differ and are likely to react differently to IS PM styles. However, the important aspect, having acknowledged the differences, is to understand how the differences can be managed.

We were able to confirm some findings of earlier studies, such as the lower tolerance for conflict within an organisation in Indonesia. IS project managers should be aware that a confrontational behaviour in an Indonesian environment may be culturally out of place and cause difficulty, yet in a UK environment an appropriate level would be tolerated. Resolving any existing conflicts through mutual compromise is also more important in Indonesia than in the UK. This is mainly due to Indonesia's cultural standpoint that organisations are seen as 'families' with protection by elders in exchange for loyalty. Compromise is seen as the primary choice for decision-making and is preferred to a win/lose outcome. The UK sample company's mission on the other hand, is more aggressive relying on relationships to resolve conflicts, and building on the fact that the resolution of conflicts will strengthen these relationships.

Some of our findings were surprising, though, showing organisational culture was influenced by more than just national culture. For example, there was an unexpectedly high proportion among the Indonesian participants who agreed with the statement that a manager does not have to have all the answers. So in both investigated organisational cultures, a management style deviating from guiding employees on every step they make is acceptable. The results for the question on a matrix-based organisation were also surprising. Judging from the Indonesian preference for a parental style of management, we would have expected more resistance to such a structure. According to our findings, the resistance against this kind of structure was much greater in the UK. Another surprise was the Indonesian group agreeing that bypassing hierarchical lines can add value and not outright rejecting that breaking rules can have a positive effect. However, this should not be seen as a carte blanche. As we have found out, the management style in Indonesia can be quite pragmatic, so if it is in the best interest for the project to break rules and bypass hierarchies, then this can be done. Nevertheless, this is limited to situations where an agreement has been reached by consensus or a group has been empowered by senior management to do so.

Project managers operating on a global scale need to be aware of cultural differences in the environment of IS development projects. We have investigated how people involved in IS projects in Indonesia and the UK think about hierarchical structures and managing conflict. We believe this is important to highlight relevant points for ongoing globalisation of IS PM that can be used by firms to normalise or understand different behaviour in future projects. Our hope is that this paper provides valuable insight into cultural patterns of IS PM and sparks further interest in the area of studying the cultural aspects of project management.

REFERENCES

Ailon, G. (2008). Mirror, mirror on the wall: Culture's consequences in a value test of its own design. *Academy of Management Review, 33*(4), 885–904.

Ali, M., & Brooks, L. (2008). Culture and IS: National cultural dimensions within IS discipline. In *Proceedings of the UK Academy for Information Systems*, Bournemouth, UK.

Buchanan, R., & Berman, T. (1992). *Building successful partnerships*. Acquisitions Monthly.

Chauvet, M., & Gallivan, M. (2007). A cross-continent comparison of IS research on IT and culture. In *Proceedings of the 15th Annual Cross-Cultural Research in Information Systems Meeting.*

Davis, F. D. (1989). Perceived usefulness, perceived ease of use and user acceptance of information technology. *Management Information Systems Quarterly, 13*(3), 319–340. doi:10.2307/249008

Dorfman, P. W., & Howell, J. P. (1988). Dimensions of national culture and effective leadership patterns: Hofstede revisited. *Advances in International Comparative Management, 3*, 127–150.

Hampden-Turner, C., & Trompenaars, F. (1997). Response to Geert Hofstede. *International Journal of Intercultural Relations, 21*(1), 49–159. doi:10.1016/S0147-1767(96)00042-9

Hoecklin, L. (1994). *Managing cultural differences - strategies for competitive advantage.* Reading, MA: Addison-Wesley.

Hofstede, G. (1980). *Culture's consequences: International differences in work related values.* Thousand Oaks, CA: Sage.

Hofstede, G. (1985). The interaction between national and organisational value systems. *Journal of Management Studies, 23*(4), 347–357. doi:10.1111/j.1467-6486.1985.tb00001.x

Hofstede, G., & Bond, M. H. (1984). Hofstede's culture dimensions: An independent validation using Rokeach's value survey. *Journal of Cross-Cultural Psychology, 15*(4), 417–433. doi:10.1177/0022002184015004003

Hofstede, G., & Hofstede, G. J. (2005). *Cultures and organisations: Software of the mind* (2nd ed.). New York, NY: McGraw-Hill.

Igbaria, M., & Zviran, M. (1996). Comparison of end-user computing characteristics in the U.S., Israel, and Taiwan. *Information & Management, 30*(1), 1–13. doi:10.1016/0378-7206(95)00044-5

ITAP. (2005). *The culture in the workplace questionnaire.* Retrieved from www.itapintl.com/ITAPCWQuestionnaire.htm

Jones, M., & Alony, I. (2007). The cultural impact of information systems – through the eyes of Hofstede – a critical journey. *Issues in Informing Science and Information Technology, 4.*

Jones, M. L. (2007, June 24-26). *Hofstede - culturally questionable?* Paper presented at the Oxford Business & Economics Conference, Oxford, UK.

Karahanna, E., Evaristo, J. R., & Srite, M. (2005). Levels of culture and individual behavior: An integrative perspective. *Journal of Global Information Management, 13*(2), 1–20. doi:10.4018/jgim.2005040101

Kumar, K., & Bjorn-Anderson, N. (1990). A cross-cultural comparison of IS designer values. *Information Systems, 33*(5), 528–538.

McCoy, S., Galletta, D. F., & King, W. R. (2005). Integrating national culture into IS research: The need for current individual-level measures. *Communications of the Association for Information Systems, 15*, 211–224.

McSweeney, B. (2002). Hofstede's model of national cultural differences and their consequences: A triumph of faith - a failure of analysis. *Human Relations, 55*(1), 89–118.

Olie, R. (1994). The culture factor in personnel and organisation policies. In Harzing, A. W., & Van Ruysseveldt, J. (Eds.), *International human resource management: An integrated approach* (pp. 124–143). London, UK: Sage.

Peters, T. J., & Waterman, R. H. J. (1982). *In search of excellence*. New York, NY: Harper & Row.

Redding, S. G., & Baldwin, E. (1991). Managers for Asia/Pacific: Recruitment and development strategies. *Hong Kong Business International*, 74-77.

Schneider, S. C., & Barsoux, J. L. (2003). *Managing across cultures* (2nd ed.). Upper Saddle River, NJ: Prentice Hall.

Steensma, H. K., Marino, L., Weaver, K. M., & Dickson, P. H. (2000). The influence of national culture on the formation of technology alliances by entrepreneurial firms. *Academy of Management Journal, 43*(5), 951–973. doi:10.2307/1556421

Straub, D., Loch, K., Evaristo, R., Karahanna, E., & Strite, M. (2002). Toward a theory-based measurement of culture. *Journal of Global Information Management, 10*(1), 13–23. doi:10.4018/jgim.2002010102

Tricker, R. I. (1988). Information resource management: A cross-cultural perspective. *Information & Management, 15*(2), 37–46. doi:10.1016/0378-7206(88)90028-6

Trompenaars, F., & Hampden-Turner, C. (1997). *Riding the waves of culture: Understanding cultural diversity in business*. London, UK: Nicholas Brealey Publishing.

Warner, M. (Ed.). (1996a). Management in the United Kingdom. In M. Warner (Ed.), *International Encyclopaedia of Business & Management* (Vol. 4, pp. 3085-3099). London, UK: Thomson Business Press.

Warner, M. (Ed.). (1996b). Management in Indonesia. In M. Warner (Ed.), *International Encyclopaedia of Business & Management* (Vol. 3, pp. 2881-2887). London, UK: Thomson Business Press.

Zwikael, O., Shimizu, K., & Globerson, S. (2005). Cultural differences in project management capabilities: A field study. *International Journal of Project Management, 23*(6), 454–462. doi:10.1016/j.ijproman.2005.04.003

This work was previously published in the International Journal of Technology and Human Interaction, Volume 7, Issue 2, edited by Anabela Mesquita and Chia-Wen Tsai, pp. 28-37, copyright 2011 by IGI Publishing (an imprint of IGI Global).

Section 2
Mobile Technology and Media

Chapter 6
Automatic Language Translation:
An Enhancement to the Mobile Messaging Services

Swadesh Kumar Samanta
University of Essex, UK

John Woods
University of Essex, UK

Mohammed Ghanbari
University of Essex, UK

ABSTRACT

In this paper, the authors demonstrate that language diversity imposes a significant barrier in message communication like Short Messaging Service (SMS). SMS and other messaging services, including Multimedia Messaging Service (MMS) and e-mail, are widely used for person-to-person and Business-to-Consumer (B2C) communications due to their reach, simplicity and reliability of delivery. Reach and service delivery can be further enhanced if the message is delivered in the recipient's preferred language. Using language translation software and a database server, the authors show that the messages can be delivered as per language preference of the recipient irrespective of the language of the original message. They demonstrate the proposed mechanism can deliver a large number of services, such as education, health care management, notification in emergency situations, news and weather reports, to those who are currently not able to access them due to language barrier.

INTRODUCTION

Messaging services currently contribute a significant proportion of the mobile operator's revenue worldwide; 5-15% for developing and 10-20% for developed countries (Grzybowski & Pereira, 2008). The messaging service can be broadly classified into two categories; textual and multimedia messages (e.g. Multimedia Messaging Service-MMS). Textual messages can be further divided into; 1) short messages such as Short Messaging Service (SMS), Enhanced Messaging

DOI: 10.4018/978-1-4666-1954-8.ch006

Service (EMS) and Instant Messaging (IM), and 2) e-mail. SMS is widely used due to its simplicity, interoperability, accessibility and reliability in delivery. SMS services can be accessed with a PC connected to the internet as well as with a mobile phone. Currently more than half of world's population has access to mobile phones and global facilities (ITU, 2009). An SMS between users who are connected to different service providers will be delivered even though they may be using different technologies (e.g. GSM, CDMA, 2.5G or 3G). In a similar way SMS from computer systems to individual users (e.g. news, weather reports and commerce application) and individual users to computer systems (e.g. voting) are used on a wide scale.

SMS subscription (i.e. the number of people who use SMS) and usage intensity varies widely across countries but little research has been done in identifying the cause of dissimilar growth among countries of similar economic and social background. One possible reason could be that data related to the SMS subscription and usage is not readily available. A large number of organizations (e.g. ITU) publish data on fixed phones, mobile phones and internet for different countries but no such data exists for SMS subscription and use. The data published by mobile operators is also not consistent since most operators do not provide the data related to usage volume. Some operators provide bulk usage volume and others provide bulk revenue from all messaging services (i.e. SMS, IM and MMS) and therefore analysis becomes complex and results may be inconclusive. In the past, researches have investigated the factors affecting the growth of SMS mostly based on survey conducted by face-to-face or telephonic interview. These surveys indicate that the charge and charging mechanism (He, 2008; Turel et al., 2007), social influence (Lopez-Nicolas et al., 2008), entertainment (Kim et al., 2008; Leung, 2007; Li et al., 2005; Wei, 2008), commerce applications (Kong & Luo, 2006) and discursive use

(He, 2008) of the service are the major factors affecting the growth of SMS.

The SMS is used for person-to-person (P2P) communications, entertainment (e.g. news, jokes), health care management (Fjeldsoe et al., 2009), education, vehicular traffic management and notification during extreme situations e.g. SARS in China and Tsunami in South East Asia (Gordon, 2007). A large number of commerce applications such as banking, sale of goods and services (Merisavo et al., 2006), advertisement and auction are regularly delivered using SMS. Due to its wide accessibility and applications both for person-to-person (P2P) and business-to-consumer (B2C) messaging, communication through SMS can potentially surpass all other modes of communication. This can be possible if all people can communicate to each other without any barrier. However, not all people understand the same language; a message delivery in the wrong language may be meaningless. To make it acceptable to the recipient, the message should be delivered in a language which the recipient can understand.

Based on case study past researches indicate that language diversity has a significant negative impact on the growth of SMS. Yan et al. (2006) observed that language diversity is one of the factors behind the dissimilar SMS usage between the China mainland and Hong Kong. Zainudeen et al. (2006) observed that lower SMS use in India and Sri Lanka compared to Indonesia and Philippines could be due to fact that most people (in low income groups) in India and Sri Lanka are not familiar with the Latin Script (i.e. English) used in SMS communication.

We compiled data about SMS usage (Table 2) as of December 2008 for a few selected countries to investigate whether language is a barrier for the growth of SMS. The data indicates that SMS usage is greater for those countries where most of the people speak the same language (e.g. the UK, USA and China) compared to those countries where people speak different languages (e.g. Switzerland,

Austria and India). We find that both private (e.g. Google) and governmental organizations (e.g. US department of defense) (DARPA, 2009) currently undertake a large volume of research to address the problem of effective communication in a multilingual society.

In this paper we first empirically establish that language diversity imposes significant barrier in message communication and also demonstrate a mechanism where users send messages in their preferred language and the system (before delivery) automatically translates the message to the preferred language of the recipient. The mechanism can be applied to multimedia communications e.g. MMS, e-mail and internet. We expect that our mechanism will increase use of messaging services as part of a multilingual society.

The rest of the paper is organized as follows: In the next section, we review previous work which aims at analyzing the factors affecting the adoption and use of messaging services. We then discuss the background and motivation for automatic language translation for messaging services and present the drawbacks of existing translation mechanisms. We also demonstrate our implementation using an open source language translation package and a database. We provide some of the applications of our implementation and concluding remarks are given.

FACTORS AFFECTING THE ADOPTION AND USE OF MESSAGING SERVICES

Most research on messaging service adoption has been done based on surveys (e.g. telephonic interview) on young users such as college students. Past research has identified that factors such as 1) charge for SMS and the underlying charging mechanism (He, 2008; Turel et al., 2007), 2) influence of family and friends (Lopez-Nicolas et al., 2008), 3) perceived entertainment from using the service (Kim et al., 2008; Leung, 2007; Li

et al., 2005; Wei, 2008), 4) commerce application (Kong & Luo, 2006), and 5) discursive use e.g. disseminating time critical emergency and administrative information (Gordon, 2007), and organizing political campaigns (He, 2008) are the major factors for the adoption and the use of SMS.

Andersson et al. (2006) were first to quantitatively analyze the effects of charges on the use of SMS. Based on billing data for the period of 1996 to 2004 for mobile users of Norway, they found that the charges for SMS and calls have a significant impact on the SMS usage. They observed that calls were a substitute to text messaging at the initial stage of the development of the mobile service, but evolved into a complement as the network size became larger. There analysis indicates that feedback effects (i.e. incoming calls and messages) are important to the demand for text messaging services. Grzybowski and Pereira (2008) investigated the impact of call charge on SMS usage. Based on monthly telephone bills for the period of April 2003 to March 2004 from the consumers of Portugal they observed that calls and messages complement one another. They also found that call and message use are determined by consumer characteristics, such as age and gender e.g. young consumers send significantly more messages than older people but make fewer calls.

Turel et al. (2007) studied the factors affecting the adoption of SMS based on a survey conducted on 222 SMS users (undergraduate students) in North America. They observed that the adoption and intensity of usage varies according to the charging scheme i.e. flat rate or pay-per-use. They found that charges for using SMS which is generally based on pay-per-use is a significant factor which gives rise to the use of SMS. Based on face-to-face interviews conducted on 3199 people (of low income group) in India and Sri Lanka (in April and May of 2005), Zainudeen et al. (2006) found that a major proportion (80%) of mobile population use the SMS for person-to-person communication in order to minimize their expenditure. Zainudeen (2007) observed that SMS usage is not dependent on the actual charge of an SMS message but the relative charge, i.e. the ratio between per SMS charge and per-minute call charge. Based on a survey conducted on mobile users of India, Pakistan, Sri Lanka, Thailand and the Philippines, she estimated the SMS usage in those countries. She found a very strong correlation between the SMS usage and the relative charge.

He (2008) indicated that low SMS charges compared to the call is a major factor behind the rapid growth of SMS usage in China. The charge for sending SMS in mainland China is 0.1 Yuan (1.2 US cents) which is much less compared to the per-minute call charge of 0.4 Yuan. Additionally, there is no charge to receive an SMS in China even though there are charges for receiving the calls. Yan et al. (2006) studied the factors behind the dissimilarity in SMS acceptance in China mainland and Hong Kong. They found that less availability of wire line internet for sending e-mail, cultural difference (e.g. preference to use SMS rather than voice mail) and lower SMS charges (e.g. SMS charge is $0.012 and $.13 in mainland and Hong Kong) are major factors behind higher SMS use in mainland China than that of Hong Kong.

Based on telephonic interviews conducted on 542 Dutch consumers, Lopez-Nicolas et al. (2008) found that social factor such as opinion of friends and relatives exert major influence on people's decision to adopt advanced mobile services i.e. SMS, MMS and other services through mobile internet. In contrast, Turel et al. (2007) found that perceived social value attached to an SMS service has no impact on the future use.

Li et al. (2005) studied the adoption of Instant Messaging (IM) and they found that the intention to continue using IM is dependent on perceived usefulness and perceived enjoyment from the service. The result of their survey among 273 students imply that IM is a useful and fun tool for fulfilling one's need for attachment and commitment and for meeting online with one's friends, family members, and others. Based on a survey

conducted on 532 college students in Korea, Leung (2007) showed that entertainment among other factors such as affection, fashion, convenience, low cost and coordination were a strong motive for SMS usage. Kim et al. (2008) similarly studied the effect of monetary value, enjoyment, usefulness and ease of use on the SMS adoption among Korean users. They found that users derive value from SMS entertainment services such as news, weather reports and jokes. They indicated that the capability of SMS in delivering entertainment services enhances SMS adoption.

Kong and Luo (2006) investigated the factors behind the rapid growth of SMS in China. During the period of 2000 to 2003, yearly SMS usage in China increased from 18.9 to 200 billion messages representing an average yearly growth of 241%. They observed that even though the SMS service was available since 1995, people seldom used it. During the period of 2000 to 2003 internet service providers and mobile operators entered into agreement for providing entertainment related service (e.g. news, weather report and jokes) using SMS which resulted in the explosive growth.

Based on telephonic interview conducted on 208 users in the US, Wei (2008) studied the factors behind the use of the mobile phone for mass communications and entertainment. He found that the most popular non-voice use of mobile phones is playing games, surfing the internet and news-seeking. Users employ mobiles not only as an interpersonal communication, but also as a source of mass communication to keep up with news and events, to find information, and to entertain. He also found that a user who spends a lot of time using a voice service is more likely to spend time in news-seeking, web surfing, and playing video games. He (2008) found that the discursive functions of SMS such as mass mobilization (e.g. disseminating time critical emergency and administrative information and organizing political campaign) are major factors behind the rapid growth of SMS in China.

BACKGROUND AND MOTIVATION

Research based on surveys provides some indication of the different factors affecting the use of SMS but they cannot explain the dissimilarity in usage between countries. As an example, SMS use per user per month in the UK in 2008 was 101 (MDA, 2009) messages compared to 38 messages in Austria (Mobilcom Austria, 2008) even though voice call usage is the same in both countries. Other dissimilarities have been observed between China and India with SMS usage of 110 (China Mobile, 2009) and 40 messages per user per month respectively.

Published research pays attention to the person-to-person communication and tends to ignore factors affecting the growth of messaging services from applications i.e. those are delivered from computer systems. A large volume of research has focused on SMS delivery from computer systems for different services such as health care management (Fjeldsoe et al., 2009; Langer et al., 2009), education (Saran et al., 2008; Song, 2008), road

traffic information (Shahjahan et al., 2008) and commerce applications such as advertising (Wei et al., 2010), auction, mobile banking (Peevers et al., 2008), sale of goods and services (Kumar et al., 2008; Merisavo et al, 2006). A simple internet search with the keyword "SMS" lists 753 publications from IEEE Explore and 499 from Science Direct. Most of this research indicates that SMS has a potential application as a notification service, be it in health care management (e.g. reminding a patient to take a medicine or stop smoking) or commerce application (e.g. advertisement, banking, news and weather report). Considering the large volume of research in this area it is not possible to review the individual findings and therefore we group them according to the service in Table 1.

The use of SMS for the delivery of a large number of applications is due to its wide reach and accessibility. The notification through SMS is assured since communication takes place even when the user is engaged in a voice call. As per the annual financial report of a leading mobile service provider in the Ukraine (MTS Ukraine,

Table 1. Research on the use of SMS for business to consumer communications

Service	Study by	Use of SMS
Health Care Management	Jiang et al. (2008); Langer et al. (2009); Mitra et al. (2008)	Both way communications between patient and computer system.
	Mohammad et al. (2006); Rahman et al. (2007); Sagahyroon et al. (2009) ; Scanaill et al. (2006); Tahat (2009); Thulasi Bai and Srivatsa (2008)	Remote patient monitoring by collecting health status at a centralized monitoring point
	Fjeldsoe et al. (2009) reviewed 33 research articles on the use of SMS in health behavior change.	Both way communication between participants (who are intending to change health behavior) and the researcher.
Education	Jiao and Zhao (2007)	Information exchange between home and School
	Mermelstein and Tal (2005)	Information delivery to students
	Saran et al., (2008); Song (2008)	SMS used in second language learning.
	Ford and Botha (2007)	SMS is used for searching in Wikipedia
Road Traffic Information	Hapsari et al. (2005)	SMS is used for sending the location of a vehicle.
	Shahjahan et al. (2008)	Vehicular traffic information is delivered using SMS
Mobile Commerce	Okazaki and Taylor (2008); Wei et al. (2010); Xu et al. (2009); Zhang and Mao (2008)	Use of SMS for advertisement delivery
	Jamil and Mousumi (2008); Kumar et al. (2008); MTS Ukraine (2009); Peevers et al. (2008)	Interchange of SMS for banking

2009) we find that 25 banks used SMS for banking services. In 2008 these banks exchanged 57 millions SMS messages with 18 million mobile users; this equates to an average yearly 3 SMS's per user. In the Ukraine people speak Ukranian, Russian and 11 other languages. It follows that the banking service will be accessible by more people if the message is delivered in recipient's preferred language.

In recent past, researches paid attention to analyse the impacts of the language on the growth of the messaging services. Lin and Sears (2005) argued that the ability to send and receive text messages in Chinese language could be useful for many people in China. Based on survey, Zainudeen et al. (2006) observed that lower SMS use in India and Sri Lanka compared to Indonesia and the Philippines could be due to the fact that the Latin Script (i.e. English) used in SMS communication is alien to them. A similar survey (CKS Consulting, 2009) reveals that low SMS use in South Asian countries such as Bangladesh, India and Pakistan is due to non availability of a local language interface for SMS messaging. Yan et al. (2006) observed that language is one of the factors behind the dissimilar SMS use on the Chinese mainland and Hong Kong. They show that for people in mainland China, it is easy to enter the Chinese language into the mobile using "Pinyin"; a way of entering the Chinese language using the English alphabet. Since "Pinyin" has been taught in all Chinese primary schools from the 1950s, Chinese people can type messages just as easily as English people. In contrast, Hong Kong, being a multilingual society, the population uses a different way of entering SMS characters which is not as easy as "Pinyin". It can be assumed that if English speaking people in Hong Kong could send messages in English which are automatically translated into Chinese and other languages before delivery then the use of SMS in Hong Kong may increase.

Industry has paid much attention to the issue of automatic language translation but research-

ers in academic institutions have tended to pay little attention to it. We find that, Climent et al. (2007) was the first to study the impact of an online language translation in cross-linguistic communication on the internet (i.e. e-mail). They argued that the existence of a machine translation system that could automatically translate e-mails into the language of the recipient would make communication much easier. Accordingly they implemented automatic translation for e-mails between Spanish and Catalan. They analyzed exchange of e-mail messages between students of a university in Spain where 97% of the students understand Catalan and 43% use Spanish. Even though the official communication language was Catalan they found that 74% of the messages were exchanged in Catalan and 24% in Spanish. They also observed that 57.1% of the messages which were written in Spanish were replied to in Catalan and 84.6% of the messages which were written in Catalan were replied to in Spanish. They observed that given the choice, the users will generally prefer to communicate in their preferred tongue.

Danet and Herring (2007) studied language preferences in the European Union (EU) which currently has 27 member states and 23 official languages. They indicated that with so many languages spoken among the member countries, the EU has to be committed to the principle of multilingualism. This implies, in particular, equal rights for information and access to legal documents in their national languages. In order to achieve this, the EU maintains a veritable army of translators for all the written documents. Similar situations exist for countries like India which have twice the population of the EU and 23 officially recognized languages. The EU example and the research of the previous scholars give an indication that the language barrier could impact SMS usage.

We compiled data about SMS usage as of December 2008 for six countries to establish whether language is a barrier for the growth of SMS. In Table 2 we provide data about monthly SMS use (i.e. the number of SMS's per user per month), charge for single SMS, monthly call usage volume (in minutes) and per-minute call charge for six countries. Additional country specific parameters such as the income of the individual (per capita GDP) and language diversity are also taken into consideration. The data is based on our own collection from sources such as annual financial reports of major operators, regulatory authorities and the internet. The data indicates that SMS usage is greater for those countries where most of the people speak the same language (e.g. the UK, USA and China) compared to those countries where people speak different languages (e.g. Austria, Switzerland and India). To investigate the impact of language diversity on the use of SMS we used language diversity index (LDI) for the respective countries from Ethnologue (Ethnologue, 2009).

The income is tabulated in American dollar and also in currency of the respective country. The charges for SMS and call are in respective currencies. In order to compare the data across the countries the charge as a percentage of income has been taken into consideration for the regression analysis (shown in Table 3). If we compare data between the UK and Austria then it appears that lower SMS usage in Austria compared to the UK is due to the greater language diversity and higher SMS charges, since other factors such as income, call charge and call usage are comparable. In order to investigate the impact of the language diversity on the use of SMS, the impacts from other parameters such as income, SMS charge as a % of income, call charge as a % of income and call usage volume are considered together.

It is assumed that the SMS usage volume is dependent on parameters such as income (in $), SMS charge as a % of income, call charge as a % of income, call usage volume, and language diversity. A country with high income and where people speak mainly one language is likely to have high SMS usage. SMS charges will have a negative impact on SMS usage; the higher the charges the lower the usage. However call charges can have a positive or negative impact depending on whether the SMS service is considered as a complement or a substitute to a voice call. Grzybowski and Pereira (2008) investigated the impact of call charges on SMS usage. Based on monthly telephone bills for the period of April 2003 to March 2004 for the consumers of Portugal they observed that calls and messages complement one another. To investigate the impact from the different parameters we perform a linear regression with different combinations of the above five parameters. In the regression analysis it is considered that the SMS usage is dependent variable and parameters such as income, SMS charge, call charge, call usage and language diversity are controlled variable. In Table 3 we provide the regression results for seven different combinations.

In combination I, the relationship between SMS usage and income has been investigated. It is found that income has a positive impact (since

Table 2. Income, SMS & call usage, SMS & call charge and language diversity index in six countries

Country	Per Capita Income		Language Diversity Index	SMS Charge	Call Usage	Call Charge	SMS Usage
	In $	In Own Currency					
UK	42,740	22,945	0.133	0.1	166	0.20	101
Austria	42,700	33,736	0.535	0.2	168	0.20	43
USA	46,040	46,040	0.319	0.2	345	0.25	200
Switzerland	59,880	70,430	0.577	0.2	114	0.27	38
China	2,360	22,760	0.509	0.1	246	0.60	110
India	950	38,084	0.940	0.6	485	0.60	40

Table 3. Impacts of the different parameters on the use of SMS

Combination	Parameters	Coefficients	t-stats	p-values	Correlation Coefficient
I	**Income**	0.0002	0.17	0.871	**0.0860**
II	Income	0.0002	0.128	0.905	0.0863
	SMS Charge as a % of Income	73388.7	0.007	0.994	
III	Income	0.0005	0.32	0.766	0.3693
	SMS Charge & Call Charge Ratio	-73.2	-0.66	0.551	
IV	Income	-0.003	-0.928	0.450	**0.6104**
	SMS Charge as a % of Income	7689456	0.669	0.571	
	Call Charge as a % of Income	-487029	-1.078	0.393	
V	Income	-0.0008	-0.636	0.569	**0.6593**
	Language Diversity Index	-180.323	-1.505	0.229	
VI	Income	0.001868	1.693376	0.232	0.9008
	SMS Charge as a % of Income	-3.6E+07	-2.7017	0.114	
	Call Usage Volume	1.458254	2.921555	0.099	
VII	Income	0.001122	1.382	0.398	0.9800
	SMS Charge as a % of Income	-2.4E+07	-2.256	0.265	
	Call Usage Volume	1.134647	3.118	0.197	
	Language Diversity Index	-137.677	-1.940	0.302	

the coefficient is positive) but the relationship is not significant since the correlation coefficient is negligible. In combination III we consider two parameters i.e. income and the ratio between the SMS charge and call charge. It is observed that the ratio between SMS charge and call charge has a negative impact on the SMS usage. This conforms to the observation of Zainudeen (2007) who found a strong correlation between the SMS usage and the relative charge for countries such as India, Pakistan, Sri Lanka, Thailand and the Philippines.

Results from combinations VI and VII indicate that SMS and voice calls are complementary to each other, which agree with earlier scholars (Andersson et al., 2006; Grzybowski & Pereira, 2008) for countries such as Norway and Portugal. However, a closer look reveals that the impact of call usage volume is higher than that of call charge since the correlation coefficient with call usage volume is greater than that for call charge.

By comparing the results from combinations V and VII it is found that income and call usage volume have a positive impact on the SMS usage. In combination VII the impact of income, SMS charge, call volume and language has been considered together and we find that all the parameters have appropriate impact i.e. impact from income and call usage volume is positive and as expected impact from language diversity and SMS charge is negative. The value of the correlation coefficient is close to one which indicates that the four parameters i.e. income, SMS charge, call usage volume and language diversity can explain the difference in SMS usage in most countries. The t-stat and p-values for language diversity and income indicate that use of SMS in a country has a greater dependency on language diversity than that of income.

Even though the sample size is small, the regression results give an indication that language is a barrier for communication in a multi-lingual society. We find that both private (e.g. Google) and governmental organizations (e.g. US department of defense) are currently undertaking a large volume of research to address the problem of effective communication in a multilingual society. Google is currently testing the implementation of language translation for Google e-mail where users can read the e-mail in their preferred language. Similar applications for the translation of the web page content are available from Google and other providers. Google Inc. is pursuing research to deliver information such as web content in the recipient's preferred language. However, the translation is performed at Google's server which increases the load on the network. If users want to view the web content in their preferred language then they need to send the web page content to Google's server which translates and send it back to the user. This increases the telecom operator's traffic three folds and therefore is not economically efficient for some technologies such as wireless. Ideally the translation can be done on the fly compared to translation outside the network by a third party as done by Google.

We may assume there is a potential demand for a service where the user can read a message in their preferred language irrespective of the language of the source material. The need for language translation began when people started travelling from place to place and the first documented cases are between the 3rd and 1st centuries b.c. In modern times, telecommunications have allowed global interaction without the need to travel at all. Currently more than half of world's population has a mobile phone and access to the global facilities (ITU, 2009). In some countries people use messaging services (e.g. short message and e-mail) more than the conventional voice calls. The mobile messaging services such as SMS and MMS provide a convenient platform where the information can be efficiently delivered off-line.

Clearly not all people understand the same language and a message in the wrong language may be meaningless (CKS Consulting, 2009).

Some messages are generated automatically and generally sent in one language, so many of the recipients may not understand. What is needed is a service that performs language translation according to the preferred language of the recipient, without them even knowing. The literature has focused on SMS language translation; where the service is implemented either in the mobile device (Agrawal & Chandak, 2007) or in the network (Chava et al., 2007; Moka LLC, 2009). There are numbers of drawbacks for translation at end devices or translation outside the telecom operator's network which has been demonstrated in our previous work (Samanta et al., 2010). In the next sections we highlight some of the drawbacks and demonstrate our mechanism which will allow seamless communication between people who speak different languages. The mechanism works for e-mail, SMS, MMS and the internet.

DRAWBACKS OF EXISTING TRANSLATION MECHANISMS

The importance of delivering information as per the end user's requirement has long been recognised. Liu et al. (2004) demonstrated a system which allows visually impaired people to enlarge the text, change colour contrast and convert text-to-speech and hence improve their information access. They argued that implementation of these facilities at the end user's device is costly which most people cannot afford. In addition, installation at the end user's device restricts access only from the device which has the required interface installed. Therefore they implemented the functionalities at the server end which improved the information access since users were not only freed from the burden of the cost but were able to get the information from any device connected to the network. Lavie et al. (2006) similarly designed a system to allow speech communication between people who speak different languages. The system was aimed at allowing anyone to interact with the human agent of the provider of an e-commerce service (i.e. tourism) using the internet. Their system provides both way automatic speech-to-speech translation and therefore enhances the interaction between the multilingual consumers and the agent who speaks a single language. The system also additionally translates the speech of one language to the text in another language.

A decision on the positioning of the translator which can facilitate communications between people who speak different language is a difficult task to make. While positioning a translator at the user's end imposes additional cost to the user, its placement at the server end increases cost to the information provider and limits access to the users. Users have access to those information where providers have the translation facility. The problems associated with the translation at either end can be eliminated if the translation is provided at the middle of the network. Ocenasek (2008) presented a similar framework using a proxy server between the user and the information provider in order to modify the information content as per requirement of the visually impaired people. This section demonstrates some of the drawbacks of mobile SMS language translation if performed at end user devices or by a third party service provider.

In a mobile network an SMS is delivered using a store and forward mechanism. When a mobile user sends a text message, the network first transfers the message to a Short Message Service Centre (SMSC) which stores it for delivery to the recipient. In a similar way, application providers deliver value-added content (e.g. ring tone, news and weather reports) to the mobile users. The header of the message contains information such as the sender and recipient's phone number. The SMSC stores the message and after collecting the routing information and status of the recipient's handset (e.g. eligible to receive SMS), it forwards the message to the mobile network which delivers to the recipient (Brown et al., 2007).

In the process of delivery from the sender to the recipient the message content (e.g. text) transpar-

ently passes through the mobile network and the SMSC. If two people speak the same language (e.g. English) then they can exchange messages in their native language. If one speaks English and other German then there are two ways they could communicate: 1) one could have a phone which converts from one language to another, and 2) one of them could employ a third party translator.

If the conversion is done on the phone then it must have the capability to translate many languages if it is to be truly international. For translation in mobile devices an appropriate software interface such as Java Micro Edition (J2ME) is needed. Therefore devices with larger memory and high processing capability are required (e.g. phones with Symbian or Windows Mobile operating systems) which tend to be costly and can be a barrier to some people. In the absence of a high end handset either the sender or the recipient can engage a third party to provide the translation service.

Mobile users can avail the translation service without a costly handset if the translation is performed in the network (Chava et al., 2007; Moka LLC, 2009). Mobile users who do not have a compatible handset can engage the services of a third party provider to translate an SMS text into a different language (Moka LLC, 2009). The existing services of the third party have a number of drawbacks e.g. high cost to the user, they reduce the message space, and are inefficient. To communicate with a foreign person the sender must know the recipients preferred language and device display capability. Mobile users who want to use the translation service indicate the source and target language (e.g. German to English) along with the actual text and then send the message to the service provider as an SMS message. After receiving the message the service provider translates the message and sends it back to the sender. This translation service is used for learning foreign languages and person-to-person communication; where the sender resends the translated message to the recipient.

The current implementation has a number of drawbacks and makes it difficult to deliver the messages which are automatically generated from applications (e.g. mobile commerce). In the current implementation the sender (e.g. mobile user) must have prior knowledge about the recipient's preferred language and or language display capability of the recipient's mobile phone. This increases the complexity if application generated messages are to be delivered in the recipient's preferred language.

Figure 1 shows the existing translation mechanism which is done by third party service providers outside the mobile network. Users connect to the service provider through the mobile network and SMSC. The translation service is used for learning foreign languages and for person-to-person communication. Users, who learn foreign languages, indicate the source and target languages (e.g. English and German) along with the word or the sentence they wish to convert, this is then sent to the translation service provider as an SMS message. The service provider translates the message and sends it back to the sender.

For person-to-person communication the sender send the message indicating their language and the recipient's language in a similar way to the language learning. The service provider translates and sends the message back to the sender who resends the translated message to the recipient. Third party translation has a number of drawbacks such as users need to indicate the source and target language along with the actual text for each translation. The mechanism is not efficient since it reduces the space available for the actual message and increases the traffic in SMSC and mobile network. For person-to-person communication there is a threefold increase in SMSC traffic and a two fold increase in network traffic. The traffic can be reduced if the sender supplies the recipient's number along with the source and target language within the text. This has additional drawback since it further reduces the available character space. As a result of including the recipient's number, the mobile network traffic does not increase, but the SMSC traffic still increases two fold. Increased SMSC traffic leads to higher cost for the mobile operator and

Figure 1. Current implementation for SMS language translation

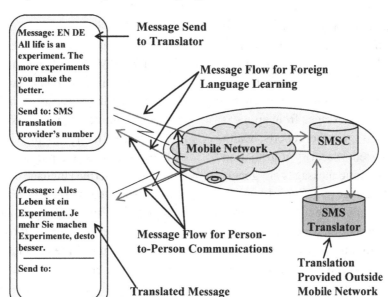

the accompanying higher service charges. The main drawbacks of SMS language translation in current implementations are listed below:

1. High cost to the user; users need to pay a premium fee for each translation request (e.g. Lingtastic LLC, one such service provider charges $1.00 per SMS).The cost can be prohibitively high and therefore can create a barrier for the growth of the translation service.
2. Not user friendly; users need to indicate the source and target languages for each translation request. Also users need to remember the set of codes for source and target language pairs. It would be better if the user could notify the language preference once and send messages without having to do it for every message.
3. Reduction of character space; less characters are available for the actual message since the source/ target language code, and the recipient's number are included in the text.
4. Inefficient; the traffic (i.e. traffic on SMSC) is increased two fold.

Under the current implementations the sender must have prior knowledge of the recipient's language and/or language display capability of the recipient's mobile phone. As an example a sender may know the recipient's language but may not know whether the phone can display the language (i.e. character set). This is a problem for automatically generated messages from application servers such as news, weather reports, health care management system, security information and notification. Automatic messages are generally sent in a single language (e.g. English) which creates a large barrier in message communication.

What is needed is a service which can deliver the message to the individual recipient in his/her language of preference. If this were the case, the application provider (e.g. governmental agencies providing emergency notification) could com-municate with any individual regardless of their native tongue. If the provider wished to perform the translation themselves at the source they would need a database containing the language preferences for all users. This would significantly increase the complexity to the sender. In order to send a message in recipient's language each message has to be sent separately after translation. This increases the cost (i.e. cost for additional software and hardware) for the application provider.

Using an open source language translation package and a database server we show that a mobile operator can provide a transparent service where the text part of the messages (both from mobile users and application providers) are automatically converted to the recipients preferred language. We show that in comparison to the existing system our implementation is efficient and cost effective and has large implications for commerce, language learning and person-to-person communication.

OUR IMPLEMENTATION

We show that the mobile operator can perform the language translation automatically by adding a standard language translation software package and a database in the network. By adding an Automatic Language Translator (ALT) in between the SMSC/MMSC and the mobile network as shown in Figure 2 we demonstrate that a mobile user can send the message in their preferred language without needing to consider the language preferences of the recipient. The ALT automatically translates the text part of the message to the recipient's preferred language before delivery. The mobile user needs to once only notify the mobile operator as to the language of preference. The message content will pass through the translation process only if the recipient has subscribed to the service, otherwise it will be transparently forwarded. In the event the translation is required, the content language is identified automatically and translated as per the language preference of the recipient. Our implementation solves many of the current problems.

In Figure 2 we show the architecture of ALT where a box (containing language translation software and a database server) is inserted in the message delivery path from SMSC/MMSC and e-mail server to mobile users. Mobile users who want to receive their communications in their preferred (e.g. native) language indicate their preferences once only by sending an SMS which is stored in the database of the ALT. When a message is received (from a mobile user or an application server), the ALT manager searches the recipient's number in the database. If the entry is not found, the message is transparently delivered. If the number is available in the database, the language preference along with the text content is forwarded to the translator. The translator automatically detects the source language and performs the translation. The translated content is forwarded to the mobile network for ultimate delivery to the recipient. Figure 2 indicates that in our implementation there is no increase in the traffic in SMSC/MMSC.

We simulated the functionality of the ALT on a PC using: The Google Translate java API, database and our own software also in java. Using J2ME (Java Micro Edition) we simulated the origin and reception of the message. In Figure 3 we show the screenshot of our simulation. A text message: "All life is an experiment. The more experiments you make the better." is sent to the recipient (number "8888888") whose language preference is German. The message is automatically translated to "Alles Leben ist ein Experiment. Je mehr Sie machen Experimente, desto besser." in German and delivered to the recipient's phone. The implementation in a real world network is relatively straightforward; it works as a relay box and therefore can work independently of other units. It can scale with the network since multiple threads allow translations in parallel.

We acknowledge that there will be a slight delay in searching the recipient's number and to perform the translation. However the delay is reduced if the ALT is integrated within the SMSC/MMSC. The ALT software package can be incorporated easily between the relay and the storage of the SMSC/MMSC.

Figure 2. Implementation of ALT in real network

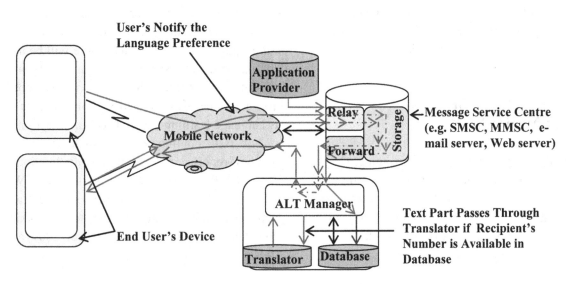

Figure 3. Screenshot of ALT simulation

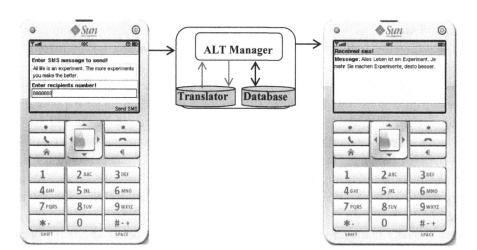

There are obvious drawbacks of automatic translation since there are difficulties with abbreviations and euphemisms (e.g. u instead of you) frequently used in SMS messages. Research on SMS texting for 11 European Union countries indicates that even though abbreviations such as "lol," "u," "brb," and "gr8," are frequently used they make up only 10% of the total words (Crystal, 2008). Therefore abbreviations may not pose as big limitation to SMS translation as first apparent. Using artificial intelligence and neural network technology (Khalilov et al., 2008) it is possible to improve translation accuracy. Some developers (Moka LLC, 2009) currently implement commercial products which translate abbreviations from Chinese to English and vice versa.

APPLICATIONS OF OUR IMPLEMENTATION

In addition to person-to-person messaging, a large number of applications such as tourism, international business communication, foreign language learning and Business to Consumer (B2C) communications will benefit from our work.

For person-to-person communication, our implementation allows the sender to input the message in their preferred language (e.g. English) and simply sends the message to the recipient (see Figure 3). There is no need to indicate the source and target language and no requirement to know the preferred language of the recipient; the recipient automatically receives the message in their preferred language (e.g. German). The communication is seamless and unobtrusive. Our implementation is efficient since there is no reduction of character space for the actual message and no increase in the SMSC traffic. Mobile operators themselves can provide the translation service using our mechanism without the need for a third party service provider. There will be additional financial cost for the translation software and database server but the cost can be recovered from additional use generated by applications such as language learning and B2C communications.

For B2C communications such as: news, weather reports, and commerce applications, messages often come from application servers. We have shown that a large number of services such as: health care management, advertisement, auctions, sale of goods and services (CellBazzar, 2009) are currently provided using SMS. Our implementation will facilitate the message delivery from applications according to the preferred language of the recipient without them even knowing and without the need to change the necessary hardware and software in each individual application server. Application providers gain benefit from by connecting to a large population who are currently not accessible to them.

CONCLUSION

In this paper we first empirically establish that language diversity imposes a significant barrier in message communication such as the Short Messaging Service (SMS). In addition to person-to-person communication people use messaging services (e.g. SMS, MMS and e-mail) for a large number of applications such as health care management, education, entertainment, news and weather and traffic reports. Similarly organizations employ the messaging service for Business-to-Consumer (B2C) communications such as banking, advertisements, auctions, sale of goods and services. Due to its wide reach and capability to deliver a large number of services, mobile operators currently generate a large proportion of their revenue from messaging services.

We demonstrate that the reach and service delivery can be further enhanced if the message is delivered in recipient's preferred language. Using an open source language translation package and a database server we implemented automatic language translation for mobile messaging services. We show that our mechanism will allow mobile operators to provide message delivery in a user's native language without the need for a third party service provider. We show that in comparison to the third party provider our mechanism is user friendly and efficient. We demonstrate that using our mechanism a large number of services

such as education, health care services, news and weather reports, advertisements, auctions and sale of goods and services can be delivered to those who are currently not able to access them due to the language barrier. This contribution represents a new trend in SMS technology and it is likely that language translation will find widespread use in mobile computing applications in the future.

ACKNOWLEDGMENT

The authors acknowledge the constructive and helpful comments and suggestions of the reviewers which have resulted in substantial improvements of this paper. This research could have not been completed without the continued help from the officers of BSNL and Department of Telecommunication, government of India. The first author thanks both Govt. of India and British Govt. for providing the financial support for this work under UK-India Education and Research Initiative scheme.

REFERENCES

Agrawal, A. J., & Chandak, M. B. (2007, April 2-4). Mobile Interface for Domain Specific Machine Translation Using Short Messaging Service. In *Proceedings of the 4th International Conference on Information Technology* (pp. 957-958).

Andersson, K., Foros, O., & Steen, F. (2006). *Text and voice: complements, substitutes or both? (CEPR Discussion Papers – Industrial Organization No. 5780)*. London: CEPR.

Brown, J., Shipman, B., & Vetter, R. (2007). SMS: The Short Message Service. *Computer, 40*(12), 106–110. doi:10.1109/MC.2007.440

CellBazzar. (2009). *SMS Buy/SMS Sell*. Retrieved from http://corp.cellbazaar.com/sms.html

Chava, V., Smith, M. R., & Dudley, W. H. (2007). *System and method for in-transit SMS language translation* (United States Patent No. 7272406). Washington, DC: U.S. Patent and Trademark Office.

China Mobile. (2009). *2008 Annual Report, page 19*. Retrieved from http://www.chinamobileltd.com/images/pdf/2009/ar/ar_2008_e_full.pdf

Climent, S., More, J., Oliver, A., Salvatierra, M., Sanchez, I., & Taule, M. (2007). Enhancing the status of Catalan versus Spanish in online Academic Forums. In Danet, B., & Herring, S. C. (Eds.), *The Multilingual Internet* (pp. 87–111). New York: Oxford University Press.

Consulting, C. K. S. (2009). *Teleuse@BOP3: A Qualitative Study, Colombo: LIRNEasia*. Retrieved from http://lirneasia.net/wp-content/uploads/2008/04/qualitativereport.pdf

Crystal, D. (2008). *Txtng: the Gr8 Db8*. New York: Oxford University Press.

Danet, B., & Herring, S. C. (2007). Language Choice in Europe: Introduction. In Danet, B., & Herring, S. C. (Eds.), *The Multilingual Internet* (p. 18). New York: Oxford University Press.

DARPA. (2009). *Multilingual Automatic Document Classification Analysis and Translation (MADCAT)*. Retrieved from http://www.darpa.mil/ipto/programs/madcat/madcat.asp

Ethnologue. (2009). *Languages of the World*. Retrieved from http://www.ethnologue.com/ethno_docs/distribution.asp?by=country#6

European Commission. (2006). *Europeans and their languages*. Retrieved from http://ec.europa.eu/public_opinion/archives/ebs/ebs_243_en.pdf

Fjeldsoe, B. S., Marshall, A. L., & Miller, Y. D. (2009). Behavior Change Interventions Delivered by Mobile Telephone Short-Message Service. *American Journal of Preventive Medicine, 36*(2), 165–173. doi:10.1016/j.amepre.2008.09.040

Ford, M., & Botha, A. (2007, May 9-11). *MobilED - an accessible mobile learning platform for Africa*. Paper presented at the IST Africa 2007 Conference, Maputo, Mozambique.

Gordon, J. (2007). The Mobile Phone and the Public Sphere: Mobile Phone Usage in Three Critical Situations. *Convergence: The International Journal of Research into New Media Technologies, 13*(3), 307–319. doi:10.1177/1354856507079181

Grzybowski, L., & Pereira, P. (2008). The complementarity between calls and messages in mobile telephony. *Information Economics and Policy, 20*(3), 279–287. doi:10.1016/j.infoecopol.2008.06.005

Hapsari, A. T., Syamsudin, E. Y., & Pramana, I. (2005, January 18-21). *Design of vehicle position tracking system using short message services and its implementation on FPGA*. Paper presented at the Asia and South Pacific Design Automation Conference.

He, Z. (2008). SMS in China: A Major Carrier of the Nonofficial Discourse Universe. *The Information Society, 24*(3), 182–190. doi:10.1080/01972240802020101

ITU. (2009). *Measuring the Information Society - The ICT Development Index, 2009 Edition*. Retrieved from http://www.itu.int/ITU-D/ict/publications/idi/2009/index.html

Jamil, S., & Mousumi, F. A. (2008, December 24-27). Short messaging service (SMS) based m-banking system in context of Bangladesh. In *Proceedings of the 11th International Conference on Computer and Information Technology*, Khulna, Bangladesh (pp. 599-604).

Jiang, J., Yan, Z., Shi, J., & Kandachar, P. (2008, May 30-31). Design of wireless mobile monitoring of blood pressure for underserved in China by using short messaging service. In *Proceedings of the International Conference on Technology and Applications in Biomedicine*, Shenzhen, China (pp. 319-322).

Jiao, W., & Zhao, J. (2007, November 23-25). Study on Communication between Home and School System Based on Mobile Education Platform. In *Proceedings of the First IEEE International Symposium on Information Technologies and Applications in Education*, Kunming, China (pp. 478-482).

Khalilov, M., Fonollosa, J. A. R., Zamora-Martinez, F., Castro-Bleda, M. J., & Espaa-Boquera, S. (2008, November 3-5). Neural Network Language Models for Translation with Limited Data. In *Proceedings of the 20th IEEE International Conference on Tools with Artificial Intelligence*, Dayton. *OH. Osteopathic Hospitals*, *2*, 445–451.

Kim, G. S., Park, S.-B., & Oh, J. (2008). An examination of factors influencing consumer adoption of short message service (SMS). *Psychology and Marketing*, *25*(8), 769–786. doi:10.1002/mar.20238

Kong, J., & Luo, J. (2006, October 25-27). The Innovative Business Model behind the Rapid Growth of SMS in China. In *Proceedings of the International Conference on Service Systems and Service Management*, *2*, 1472–1477. doi:10.1109/ICSSSM.2006.320741

Kumar, S. B. R., Raj, A. A. G., & Rabara, S. A. A. (2008, December 12-14). Framework for Mobile Payment Consortia System (MPCS). In *Proceedings of the International Conference on Computer Science and Software Engineering* (pp. 43-47).

Langer, A., Kumar, B., Mittal, A., & Subramaniam, L. V. (2009, March 6-7). Mobile Medicine: Providing Drug Related Information through Natural Language Queries via SMS. In *Proceedings of the IEEE International Advance Computing Conference*.

Lavie, A., Pianesi, F., & Levin, L. (2006). The NESPOLE! System for Multilingual Speech Communication Over the Internet. *IEEE Transactions on Audio, Speech and Language Processing*, *14*(5), 1664–1673. doi:10.1109/TSA.2005.858520

Leung, L. (2007). Unwillingness-to-communicate and college students' motives in SMS mobile messaging. *Telematics and Informatics*, *24*(2), 115–129. doi:10.1016/j.tele.2006.01.002

Li, D., Chau, P. Y. K., & Lou, H. (2005). Understanding Individual Adoption of Instant Messaging: An Empirical Investigation. *Journal of the Association for Information Systems*, *6*(4), 102–129.

Lin, M., & Sears, A. (2005). Chinese character entry for mobile phones: a longitudinal investigation. *Interacting with Computers*, *17*(2), 121–146. doi:10.1016/j.intcom.2004.11.003

Liu, S., Ma, W., Schalow, D., & Spruill, K. (2004). Improving Web access for visually impaired users. *IT Professional*, *6*(4), 28–33. doi:10.1109/MITP.2004.36

Lopez-Nicolas, C., Molina-Castillo, F. J., & Bouwman, H. (2008). An assessment of advanced mobile services acceptance: Contributions from TAM and diffusion theory models. *Information & Management*, *45*(6), 359–364. doi:10.1016/j.im.2008.05.001

MDA. (2009). *Text IT, Mobile Data Association*. Retrieved from http://www.text.it/mediacentre/sms_figures.cfm

Merisavo, M., Vesanen, J., Arponen, A., Kajalo, S., & Raulas, M. (2006). The effectiveness of targeted mobile advertising in selling mobile services: an empirical study. *International Journal of Mobile Communications, 4*(2), 119–127.

Mermelstein, B., & Tal, E. (2005, November 28-30). Using cellular phones in higher education: mobile access to online course materials. In *Proceedings of the IEEE International Workshop on Wireless and Mobile Technologies in Education*.

Mitra, S., Mitra, M., & Chaudhuri, B. B. (2008, November 19-21). Rural cardiac healthcare system-A scheme for developing countries. In *Proceedings of the IEEE Region 10 Conference* (pp. 1-5).

Mobilcom Austria. (2008). *Annual Report Year Ending December 2008*. Retrieved from http://www.telekomaustria.com/ir/annual-reports.php

Mohammad, A.-R., Al-Ali, A. R., & Eberlein, A. (2006). Remote patient monitoring and information system. *International Journal of Electronic Healthcare, 2*(3), 231–249.

Moka, L. L. C. (2009). *Moka Partners with China Mobile for Mobile Chinese to English Language Translation and Language Learning*. Retrieved from http://www.moka.com/en/news/news-1.htm

Ocenasek, P. (2008). Modification of Web Content According to the User Requirements. In *Edutainment 2008* (LNCS 5093, pp. 324-327).

Okazaki, S., & Taylor, C. R. (2008). What is SMS advertising and why do multinationals adopt it? Answers from an empirical study in European markets. *Journal of Business Research, 61*(1), 4–12. doi:10.1016/j.jbusres.2006.05.003

Peevers, G., Douglas, G., & Jack, M. A. (2008). A usability comparison of three alternative message formats for an SMS banking service. *International Journal of Human-Computer Studies, 66*(2), 113–123. doi:10.1016/j.ijhcs.2007.09.005

Rahman, F., Kumar, A., Shabana, N., & Srinivasan, S. (2007, November 27-29). Design of a wireless physiological parameter measurement and monitoring system. In *Proceedings of the International Conference on Computer Engineering & Systems*, Cairo, Egypt (pp. 401-405).

Rownok, T., Islam, M. Z., & Khan, M. (2006, December). Bangla Text Input and Rendering Support for Short Message Service on Mobile Devices. In *Proceedings of 9th International Conference on Computer and Information Technology*, Dhaka, Bangladesh.

Sagahyroon, A., Raddy, M., Ghazy, A., & Suleman, U. (2009). Design and implementation of a wearable healthcare monitoring system. *International Journal of Electronic Healthcare, 5*(1), 68–86. doi:10.1504/IJEH.2009.026273

Samanta, S. K., Achilleos, A., Moiron, S. R. F., Woods, J., & Ghanbari, M. (2010). Automatic language translation for mobile SMS. *International Journal of Information Communication Technologies and Human Development, 2*(1), 43–58.

Saran, M., Cagiltay, K., & Seferoglu, G. (2008, March 23-26). Use of Mobile Phones in Language Learning: Developing Effective Instructional Materials. In *Proceedings of the Fifth IEEE International Conference on Wireless, Mobile, and Ubiquitous Technology in Education*, Beijing, China (pp. 39-43).

Scanaill, C. N., Ahearne, B., & Lyons, G. M. (2006). Long-term telemonitoring of mobility trends of elderly people using SMS messaging. *IEEE Transactions on Information Technology in Biomedicine, 10*(2), 412–413. doi:10.1109/TITB.2005.859890

Shahjahan, M., Nahin, K. M., Uddin, M. M., Ahsan, M. S., & Murase, K. (2008, June 1-8). An implementation of on-line traffic information system via short message service (SMS) for Bangladesh. In *Proceedings of the IEEE International Joint Conference on Neural Networks*, Hong Kong (pp. 2612-2618).

Song, Y. (2008). SMS enhanced vocabulary learning for mobile audiences. *International Journal of Mobile Learning and Organisation, 2*(1), 81–98. doi:10.1504/IJMLO.2008.018719

Tahat, A. A. (2009, February 11-13). Body Temperature and Electrocardiogram Monitoring Using an SMS-Based Telemedicine System. In *Proceedings of the 4th International Symposium on Wireless Pervasive Computing*, Melbourne, Australia (pp. 1-5).

Thulasi Bai, V., & Srivatsa, S. K. (2008). Portable telecardiac system for arrhythmia monitoring and alerting. *International Journal of Healthcare Technology and Management, 9*(5/6), 517–525. doi:10.1504/IJHTM.2008.020202

Turel, O., Serenko, A., & Bontis, N. (2007). User acceptance of wireless short messaging services: Deconstructing perceived value. *Information & Management, 44*(1), 63–73. doi:10.1016/j.im.2006.10.005

MTS Ukraine. (2009). *MTS Group financial results for the fourth quarter and full year 2008.*

Wei, R. (2008). Motivations for using the mobile phone for mass communications and entertainment. *Telematics and Informatics, 25*(1), 36–46. doi:10.1016/j.tele.2006.03.001

Wei, R., Xiaoming, H., & Pan, J. (2010). Examining user behavioral response to SMS ads: Implications for the evolution of the mobile phone as a bona-fide medium. *Telematics and Informatics, 27*(1), 32–41. doi:10.1016/j.tele.2009.03.005

Xu, H., Oh, L.-B., & Teo, H.-H. (2009). Perceived effectiveness of text vs. multimedia Location-Based Advertising messaging. *International Journal of Mobile Communications, 7*(2), 154–177. doi:10.1504/IJMC.2009.022440

Yan, X., Gong, M., & Thong, J. Y. L. (2006). Two tales of one service: User acceptance of short message service (SMS) in Hong Kong and China. *INFO: The Journal of Policy, Regulation and Strategy, 8*(1), 16–28.

Zainudeen, A. (2007). *Proof that cost differentials drive SMS usage.* Retrieved from http://blogs.dialogic.com/2007/06/proof-that-cost.html

Zhang, J., & Mao, E. (2008). Understanding the acceptance of mobile SMS advertising among young Chinese consumers. *Psychology and Marketing, 25*(8), 787–805. doi:10.1002/mar.20239

This work was previously published in the International Journal of Technology and Human Interaction, Volume 7, Issue 1, edited by Anabela Mesquita and Chia-Wen Tsai, pp. 1-18, copyright 2011 by IGI Publishing (an imprint of IGI Global).

Chapter 7
A Usability Comparison of SMS and IVR as Digital Banking Channels

Gareth Peevers
The University of Edinburgh, UK

Mervyn A. Jack
The University of Edinburgh, UK

Gary Douglas
The University of Edinburgh, UK

Diarmid Marshall
The University of Edinburgh, UK

ABSTRACT

In this paper, the authors compare the usability of SMS mobile banking and automated IVR telephone banking. Participants (N = 116) used SMS banking and IVR banking to find their account balance in a repeated-measures experiment. IVR banking scored higher for usability metrics: effectiveness, attitude, and quality. There was no clear difference in rank order of preference between the two channels. Participants gave positive comments regarding speed and efficiency with SMS banking, but had serious doubts over the security of the SMS channel, impacting consumer trust in SMS banking. The authors argue that usability problems and security concerns are a major factor in the low adoption of SMS mobile banking. Older users were less positive in general to SMS banking compared with the more established IVR banking. Older users had lower first time completion rates for SMS banking and gave IVR banking higher attitude and quality scores.

1. INTRODUCTION

Internationally, banks are investing considerable sums of money into mobile phone banking (mBanking) services (Lee & Chung, 2009; Laukkanen, 2007; Luarn & Lin, 2005), but the uptake by customers has been disappointingly low (Laukkanen, 2007; Pousttchi & Schurig, 2004; Suoranta & Mattila, 2004). Many of the advantages of Internet banking are shared by mBanking, e.g., convenience and time saving. The most optimistic supporters of mBanking claim it is cheaper, safer and more convenient compared with Internet banking (Lee & Chung, 2009; Luarn & Lin, 2005). The appeal of mBanking lies in the fact that the customer can access their account on

DOI: 10.4018/978-1-4666-1954-8.ch007

the move, regardless of time or place. A major factor in the success of Internet banking is its ease of use (Hudson, 2002; Karagaluoto, 2002). In contrast, a major factor in the low adoption of mBanking applications relates to the usability problems inherent with these smaller devices.

This paper is concerned with one application of mBanking: Short Message Service (SMS) banking. It compares the usability of SMS banking to the more established Interactive Voice Response (IVR) automated banking. The paper describes the results of an empirical investigation into the integration of an SMS banking channel into a bank's multichannel environment[1]. The paper compares the usability of an SMS banking channel with an IVR banking channel for balance requests. The aim of the experiment was to inform the practical application of SMS banking in order to maximise customer acceptance and adoption, and to contribute to better understanding of the reasons for the low adoption of SMS banking. The usability methodology was based on previous work in SMS banking (Peevers & McInnes, 2009; Peevers et al., 2008).

1.1. Background

SMS, or text messaging, as it is more commonly known, is still a tremendous growth area in mobile communications. It is estimated (Martin, 2010) that worldwide some 4.1 trillion text messages were sent in 2008: the Mobile Data Association (MDA) reports that in 2008 a total of 78.9 billion text messages were sent in the UK alone (MDA, 2009), 216 million per day, and this was an increase of 22 billion on the annual total in 2007. Research has found that text messaging is most commonly used as an effective one-to-one method of communication between friends (Sillence & Baber, 2004), but businesses have also realised that there is huge potential in SMS for carrying out business activities, and for individual communication with customers. The market research group Radicati estimated that in 2004, 55% of

text messaging was for business use, with much further growth to come (Faulkner & Culwin, 2005). SMS banking services have already been successfully implemented by banks in Asia, the Middle East and South Africa, with both *Push* (automatic) and *Pull* (customer initiated) services offered to customers (Rumpa, 2005). At the time of writing the services offered by banks in the UK are limited to *Push* only, such as the bank sending the customer a weekly account balance, and basic *Pull* services such as ordering a new cheque book. The popularity of SMS banking in markets such as India (Ahmed, 2004; BBC News, 2005a) is due in part to the low cost of mobile handsets compared to desktop computers.

The popularity of SMS messaging has led to a body of usability research on text entry methods (Curran et al., 2006; Friedman et al., 2001; James & Reischel, 2001), and on mobile phone ergonomics (Balakrish et al., 2005; Soriano et al., 2005) and there has been general research on mobile phone user interfaces (Lee et al., 2006). The small keypads used on mobile phones have been found to pose usability problems (Kurniawan, Nugroho, & Mahmud, 2006; Soriano et al., 2005). Thumb size has been shown to cause usability problems with texting (Balakrishnan & Yeow, 2008). It has been found that older users have usability problems with texting on mobile phones (Kurniawan, 2008; Peevers et al., 2008), and there has been research into producing mobile phones aimed at the older generation (BBC News, 2005b). One study (Ornellan & Stephanie, 2006) showed that when keys are placed too close together they cause problems for older users. Older users have also been found to be passive users of mobile phones, and can find the process of text messaging intimidating (Kurniawan, 2008).

1.2. Low Adoption of Mobile Banking

The advantages of mBanking are convenience, access to banking no matter the time or place and efficiency (Laukkanen, 2007; Jarvenpaa et al.,

2003; Suoranta, 2003; Tiwari et al., 2007). In spite of these advantages there has been a continued, if slow, development of mBanking services (Lee & Chung, 2009; Pousttchi & Schurig, 2004), yet in countries such as Korea, Finland, and Taiwan studies have shown the usage levels of mBanking remain small (Laukkanen, 2007; Lee & Chung, 2009; Luarn & Lin, 2005). What are the factors preventing more wide scale adoption of mBanking services? Research has shown that customers worry about how much it will cost (Luarn & Lin, 2005), along with the security of the service (Brown et al., 2003; Luarn & Lin, 2005), although some researchers (Laukkanen, 2007; Laukkanen & Lauronen, 2005; Suoranta, 2003) have argued that security concerns are not a barrier. Users' perceived complexity of mBanking is also argued to be a cause of low usage levels (Lee at al., 2003). Research (Lee & Chung, 2009) has also argued that trust is one of the most important factors in the low adoption of mBanking, and is the factor that most impacts on customer satisfaction with this banking channel. Trust has an impact on level of adoption in all forms of digital banking (Aladwani, 2001), and has been researched extensively (Grabner-Krauter & Kaluscha, 2003; Kim & Prabhakar, 2000; Kim & Moon, 1998; Suh & Han, 2002).

A survey study on mBanking in Taiwan (Lee & Chung, 2009) used a research model based on Delone and Mclean's (1992) information system (IS) success model with the three quality measures of system quality, information quality and interface design quality. They found that system quality and information quality affected trust more than user satisfaction, and argue that these factors are important in building trust in an mBanking channel. System quality is defined as the quality manifested in the system's overall performance (Delone & McLean, 1992) as measured by a customer's perception. Information quality, including accuracy, is of major importance to any digital banking channel and will influence customer satisfaction (Kim et al., 2008). Lee and

Chung argue that interface design quality may be an important factor in building trust, but it is not as important as system quality and information quality. For a bank offering an SMS banking channel, interface design is something that cannot ultimately be controlled, as it is dependent on the type of mobile phone the customer owns. With many of the studies described above there are still questions over how generalizable the findings are, because they are specific to individual countries and cultural factors may play a part.

Another major factor in the slow adoption of mBanking is the number of limitations of mobile devices: small screen size, small keypads, reception and network problems and slow connection speeds. Writing a text message is still not the easiest thing to do due to the methods of text entry available on mobile devices, and the lack of a standard user interface, or even a standard layout of the keypad. The usability of mobile devices is therefore seen as an important factor in the low adoption of mBanking (Laukkanen, 2007). The distinct lack of empirical research evaluating the usability issues surrounding implementing SMS banking inspired studies in this topic (Peevers & McInnes, 2009; Peevers et al., 2008).

1.3. Context of Research

Much of the previous research in mBanking has been based on surveys. Usability studies emphasise hands-on usage and the collection of performance and qualitative data, and there are actually few studies (Hyvarinen et al., 2005; Peevers et al., 2008) in which observations of actual user performance with mBanking services have been conducted, and SMS banking in particular. It is argued (Laukkanen, 2007) that to bring more understanding to the low adoption of mBanking services, the usability issues surrounding this channel need to be more fully understood.

Usability, along with functionality, both influence real world usage of technology (Whiteside et al., 1988). It is important that any new product or service is based on user needs and requirements rather than being driven by technology. This is an important issue to consider with SMS banking. Research related to the usability design issues surrounding Internet banking is relevant to SMS banking. Customers want digital banking designs that are secure (Furnell, 2004) and have good error prevention functionality (Liao & Chung, 2002). They also want user-friendliness, speed, accuracy and control (Jayawardhena & Foley, 2000). If a new digital banking channel such as SMS banking is to succeed it must also be satisfying to the user, because as has been pointed out (Anderson et al., 1996) if the user's first experience of a new service is unsatisfactory they may revert to the use of a more traditional channel.

There has been little research into comparisons of the usability of mobile banking and competing (digital) banking channels. One survey study (Laukkanen, 2007) compared customer value perceptions of Internet banking and mBanking for bill payments. The study found that customers' value perceptions differed between the two channels. The differences were based on efficiency, convenience and safety, with a marked perceived difference in usability between the two channels due to the smaller screen size of the mobile phone. Other research (Peevers et al., 2008) has identified that an SMS balance on-demand service was the one most likely to be used by customers. The capability to provide balance on-demand initiated by *Pull* SMS message requests from customers would remove the need for the customer to call telephone banking for a balance, and could offer potential cost reductions and improved customer experience.

1.4. Hypotheses

The experiment investigated usability and user preferences for an SMS banking channel when compared with an existing IVR telephone banking channel in the context of checking an account balance.

H1: There will be differences in the two banking channels based on completion rates.

H2: There will be differences in the two channels based on the results of a usability attitude questionnaire.

H3: There will be differences in the two channels based on the quality measure and preferences.

H4: The usability measurements will differ between age groups.

2. METHOD

2.1. Experiment Design

The method used for this research was based on previous studies on SMS banking usability and eBanking (Peevers et al., 2008, 2009; Peevers & McInnes, 2009). To enable experiment participants to compare the two different digital banking channels (SMS and IVR) they were given simple background scenarios and the task of enquiring about their account balance. A working version of a *Pull* SMS banking application in the style and livery of the case bank was created for use with a Sony Ericsson K800i handset. Participants received realistic confirmation messages back when using the service. For the IVR banking service a stand-alone copy of the case bank's automated telephone banking service was used.

The experiment was conducted in a usability laboratory, and not in the field. In conducting such laboratory research it is understood that there will be some limitations, but these can be minimised by recruiting target users by means of appropriate screening questions and by offering realistic scenarios with the designs under study. For the purposes of gaining control over variables and gathering observation and empirical data, studies in the laboratory are very useful. Of course mobile devices are used on the move and in various locations so laboratory tests do not simulate the context where mobile devices would be used in the real world. Given the large numbers (116) of participants recruited for this experiment, practical and time constraints precluded a field study. Further to this, studies (Kaikkonen et al., 2005) comparing a mobile application in a laboratory test and in a field test found the same problems in both environments: the only difference was in the frequency of the occurrence, concluding that that field testing may not be worthwhile when searching for interface flaws. However, research in real world settings is also required to complement this work, and studies designed to investigate longitudinal learning and usage issues, which were not specifically tested here, would also be beneficial.

The experiment reported here had one within-participant independent variable: SMS banking versus IVR banking. The participant factors controlled for in the experiment were age group (median age 45) and gender. The repeated-measures experiment was designed to have the order of experience of the independent variable (SMS, IVR) balanced across the participants of differing age groups and genders.

2.2. Dependent Variables

2.2.1 Usability Metrics

The usability of each version of the service was measured using a combination of task completion observation and attitude questions. The usability attitude questionnaire was modified from previous research (Frokjaer et al., 2000; Peevers & McInnes, 2009; Peevers et al., 2008, 2009). Its design followed best practice (Root & Draper, 1983) by using an equal number of negative and positive statements presented in a randomised order. The questionnaire used a 7-point Likert (Likert, 1932) format that ranged from "Strongly Agree" (1) to "Strongly Disagree" (7). Following reversal of the polarity of negative questionnaire statements, a score of 7 indicates a positive attitude to the usability attribute. The questionnaire used consisted of 17 statements that address a range of

usability attributes pertaining to human-computer interaction (HCI): *cognitive attributes* (level of concentration and degree of confusion), *the fluency and transparency of the service* (knowledge about what is expected, ease of use, degree of complication), and *quality attributes* (efficiency of service, amount of improvement service is felt to require, reliability of service). The 17 questionnaire items are shown in Table 1.

For this experiment it was not deemed appropriate to time the participants' performance as a measure of efficiency since in completing the tasks there would invariably be differences in time taken using the IVR banking service compared to the SMS service due to the nature of the two types of interaction. Indicators of efficiency were be measured by verbal reports and perceptions of efficiency as measured in the usability questionnaire. Usability was measured objectively by the ability to successfully request an account balance and subjectively using the mean of the usability attitude questionnaire, and by examining the individual questionnaire items.

The quality metric has been used in previous research (Peevers et al., 2008; Weir, Douglas, Carruthers, & Jack, 2009; Weir, Douglas, Richardson, & Jack, 2009) and involves participants making a quality rating, recorded as a value on a 0-30 linear scale. This quality rating involved evaluating both services against each other on the linear scale, and was also used to indicate an explicit preference, or no preference. The quality rating is a subjective measurement, but unlike the attitude questionnaire a participant is specifically asked to compare both services against each other, which can be a useful result to compare with the questionnaire scores. If there is a discrepancy between the two, then the qualitative data from the one-to-one structured interviews can be consulted for an explanation.

2.2.2 Post-Experiment Questionnaire

A structured set of open and closed questions concluded the experiment session. Participants

Table 1. Usability attitude questionnaire items

1	I thought this service was too complicated
2	When using this service I didn't always know what I was expected to do
3	I thought the service was efficient
4	I would be happy to use this service again
5	I found this service confusing
6	The service was friendly
7	I felt under stress using this service
8	I thought the service was polite
9	I enjoyed using this service
10	I found this service frustrating to use
11	I felt flustered using this service
12	The service was easy to use
13	Using the service took a lot of concentration
14	I did not feel in control using this service
15	I feel this service needs a lot of improvement
16	I felt confident in the security of this service
17	I felt that the service was reliable

were asked what they liked, disliked and suggestions for improvements; and were given an opportunity to comment on their experiences and give their opinions.

2.3. Participants

The number of participants needed depends upon the amount of segmentation required in the population, for robust statistical testing, larger numbers are needed in each key demographic group, e.g., differing age groups and genders (Landauer, 1988), to lessen the impact of individual differences. A cohort of 116 participants was recruited in Edinburgh. They were all customers of the case bank and were all mobile phone owners. There were 53 male participants and 63 female participants (Table 2). The age range of the participants was 20 to 76 and the median age was 46.

A total of 82% of the cohort had sent a text message prior to the experiment. Those who used text messaging were asked about their frequency

of use (Table 3) and whether they used predictive text. Some 52% of participants used predictive text (T9), while 42% did not, and 6% sometimes made use of predictive text when writing SMS messages.

2.4. SMS Banking Service Used in the experiment

The SMS service used in the experiment was designed to exactly match the functionality of the case bank's existing SMS *Pull* service for new PIN and cheque/pay-in books, requiring the user to simply send a text message, Text BAL 6439 to 61119. The SMS banking service worked with abbreviations following published research findings (Peevers et al., 2008). The last 4 digits of the customer's account number are included in the text message sent to the bank, as a method of identifying for which account the customer wants a balance'. The functionality of SMS banking services (as modeled in this experiment) are currently limited by the absence of secure log-in to non-secure activities such as account balance, recent transactions and cheque book requests.

In order that all participants received the same experience during each session, it was vital that each text message reply sent from the bank was delivered with the constant time delay. Thus, in order to guarantee this, an emulator was used to recreate the required network environment. A J2ME application using MIDP2.0 was created for the Sony Ericsson K800i handsets used in the experiment. For the purposes of experimental control it was decided to restrict the participants to the use of the default Multi-tap text entry method following the method employed in Peevers et al. (2008). An example SMS balance is shown in Figure 1.

In the experiment, to ensure experiment control, participants were all provided by the researchers with the same mobile phone type (Sony Ericsson K800i) to use in the experiment and allowed time to become familiar with the operation of this

Table 2. Participant demographics

	Age 18 – 45	Age 46 and over	Total
Males	26 (22.4%)	27 (23.3%)	53 (45.7%)
Females	29 (25.0%)	34 (29.3%)	63 (54.3%)
Total	55 (47.4%)	61 (52.6%)	116 (100%)

Table 3. Participants' SMS usage levels

Frequency	Number (Percentage)	Age 18 – 45	Age 46 and over
A few times a day or more	42 (44%)	28 (56%)	14 (31%)
Daily	22 (23%)	14 (28%)	8 (18%)
A few times a week	20 (21%)	7 (14%)	13 (29%)
Weekly	5 (5%)	0 (0%)	5 (11%)
Monthly	0 (0%)	0 (0%)	0 (0%)
Less often	6 (6%)	1 (2%)	5 (11%)

Figure 1. Example SMS balance message format

phone before their experiment session started. They used this mobile phone for access to the SMS banking service. They used a push-button and line phone for (local number) calls to the IVR service. Use of the two phone types was considered appropriate in the experiment since the SMS service would normally be accessed from a mobile phone and the IVR service accessed from a landline phone.

2.5. IVR Telephone Banking Service Used in the Experiment

The service used in the experiment was a replica of the commercial service offered by the case bank (Wilkie et al., 2005). To access the service the participants first had to go through an authentication stage were they were asked to enter their account details (account number and sort code) and their (secret) security details. The service then offered them the option to hear the balance for that account, or continue in the IVR to transact for other services and other accounts.

2.6. Experiment Scenarios and Tasks

The participants were asked to imagine that they were customers of the case bank. In Scenario 1 participants were told to find out the balance of their account by sending a text message to the bank using the SMS banking service. In scenario 2 participants were told to find out the balance of their account by phoning the bank. The participants were given all of the (fictitious) account details and information they would need to complete the tasks via fictitious persona details.

For SMS banking, the participants were given an A4 blow-up diagram of the layout of the keypad on the handset to demonstrate the use of the buttons and their mapping. They were given a demonstration of how to use the keypad to get a desired character by repeated pressing of a key. They were also specifically shown that if they held down the desired key, rather than repeatedly pressing it, they could get the number assigned to that key. They were then given two practice tasks. The first was to write their own name and the second was to write the message '12345', send it and then open and read the reply message. The participant was then given a task sheet with the scenario instructions, which the researcher also read out aloud to them. They were allowed three attempts to complete the task. If they failed three times the researcher stepped in and helped them to complete the task.

For IVR banking the participant was given a scenario sheet with the instructions on, which the researcher also read out aloud to them. They were allowed three attempts to complete the task. If they failed three times the researcher stepped in and helped them to complete the task.

3. RESULTS

3.1. Completion Rates

The software used for each version of the service was used to log if the participants completed each task. Table 4 shows the completion rates (not taking into account the number of attempts). Using the Adjusted Wald method (Lewis & Sauro, 2006; Sauro & Lewis, 2005) the confidence intervals for each completion rate were calculated. These are also shown in Table 3. Further analysis was not carried out on this data due to the ceiling effects caused by the lack of variability in scores.

3.1.1. First Time Completion Rates

Table 5 shows the successful first time completion rates with their confidence intervals.

A repeated measures analysis of variance (ANOVA) was performed on the overall first time completion rates, with banking channel as the within-participant factor, and age group and gender as between-participant factors. The analysis showed a significant difference between channels (d.f. =1.0, $F = 5.15$, $p = 0.025$). There was also a within-participants interaction between SMS and age group (d.f. =1.0, $F = 7.61$, $p = 0.007$) with the older age group having a lower overall completion rate using the SMS channel compared to the younger group. The data also revealed a between-participant effect for age group (d.f. =1.0, $F = 10.45$, $p = 0.002$) with older participants having a lower overall completion rate across both banking channels.

3.2. Attitude Scores

The scores for the 17 usability attributes were averaged to obtain an overall usability score for each channel: SMS banking and IVR banking. The mean overall usability attitude scores for both channels were SMS banking: 5.36 (SD=0.90) and IVR banking: 5.78 (SD=0.82). Results of a repeated measures ANOVA (d.f. = 1.0, $F = 24.25$, $p < 0.001$) indicate significant differences overall in the attitude to IVR banking compared to SMS banking, in favour of IVR banking. A significant age group interaction was found (d.f. = 1.0, $F = 5.02$, $p < 0.05$) where younger participants scored the two channels similarly, while older customers gave much higher scores to IVR banking. A between-participants gender effect was also noted ($p < 0.05$) where male participants gave lower scores to both channels compared with their female counterparts.

Statistical analysis on the individual questionnaire attributes revealed differences between IVR and SMS for 11 of the 17 usability attributes: *confusion, flustered, stress, knew what to do next* at $p < 0.05$, and *concentration, would use again, reliability, improvement needed, friendly, polite* and *confidence in security* at $p < 0.01$, with IVR scoring higher for all 11 of these attributes.

To test for a relationship between the usability attitude scores and participant age group, correlation analysis was carried out. Pearson's correlation coefficient (r) was used to analyse the overall mean for SMS and the overall mean for IVR banking. The analysis showed there was a weak but significant relationship for SMS banking by age group ($r = -0.247$, $p < 0.01$). This was a negative relationship, suggesting that attitude decreased with the age of the participant. There was no significant relationship between age group and attitude scores for IVR banking ($r = -0.055$, $p < 0.56$).

Table 4. Completion rates with confidence intervals for participants completing the tasks within three attempts

	SMS banking		IVR banking	
Task	Mean	Confidence Interval	Mean	Confidence Interval
Balance	91.5%	85.7% - 96.0%	100%	97.3% - 100%

Table 5. Successful first time completion rates with confidence intervals

	SMS banking		IVR banking	
Task	Mean	Confidence Interval	Mean	Confidence Interval
Balance	85.6%	78.7% - 91.4%	94.1%	88.9% - 97.8%

3.3. Quality and Preference

To collect a quality rating for each version participants were asked to order and rate each version by preference by placing magnetic markers on metal scale marked from 0 (worst) to 30 (best). The overall mean scores for each channel were IVR banking 22.54 (SD=5.44) and SMS banking 20.82 (SD=6.88).

Results of a repeated measures ANOVA who the SMS channel as scoring significantly lower than the IVR channel, $p = 0.036$. There was also an interaction ($p < 0.05$) for age group with younger customers scoring both channels equally, but older customers giving higher scores to the IVR channel.

To test if there was a relationship between the quality metric and the age group of the participants, correlation analysis was carried out. Pearson's correlation coefficient (r) was used to analyse the mean score for SMS and mean score for the telephone. The analysis showed there was no significant relationship for SMS banking quality and age group ($r = -0.138$, $p = 0.144$). But there was a weak significant relationship between age group and quality scores for IVR banking ($r = 0.230$, $p = 0.014$). This was a positive relationship, with quality rating increasing with age of the participant.

3.3.1 Rank Order of Preference

Converting the quality rating data into a rank order results in the data presented in Table 6.

3.4. Qualitative Analysis

3.4.1 SMS Banking Channel

Asked about what they *liked*, 88% of the participants gave positive comments about the experience of using SMS to get their account balance. Others either did not mention any particular likes, or made neutral remarks. 54% of comments related to the speed of the service, as mainly "very quick" or "quick". Another 38% referred to the ease of use, simplicity or how straightforward the service was; and 27% mentioned that the process could be used anytime, anywhere, whilst away or "on the move". Other comments included that the service was perfect or impressive (5%); had a quick response (4%); was convenient (4%); private (27%); helpful (2%); avoids eavesdropping (2%); uncomplicated (2%) and informative (2%). When it came to *dislikes*, 57% of the participants gave negative comments regarding aspects of the channel; the most frequent concern was the security of the SMS channel (45%). The most often mentioned improvement concerned either making the service more secure by using some password or similar system. Others simply questioned the security, wanting more information.

Table 6. Rank order for banking channels

Rank	N	%
SMS best	47	40.5%
IVR best	54	46.6%
Equal Rank	14	12.1%
TOTAL	114	98.3%*

3.4.2. IVR Banking Channel

Asked about what they *liked*, 85% of participants gave positive comments about the experience of using the IVR channel to get their balance. Others either did not mention any particular likes, or made neutral remarks. 31% of comments were about the ease of use, simplicity or how straightforward the service was. Also, often mentioned was how quick or efficient the service was to use (29%) and 27% of comments mentioned that the process felt secure, private and safe. Other comments included that is was familiar (20%) being the current service many participants chose to use. When it came to *dislikes*, 37% of the participants made negative comments regarding aspects of the service. The most frequent concern was the how long the call took, including the length of the security process (12%), a few found the service confusing or frustrating (5%). The most often mentioned improvement concerned making the call quicker.

4. DISCUSSION

This paper has reported empirical results on usability issues in a comparison between SMS banking and IVR banking channels derived from an experiment with a controlled sample of 116 banking customer. There were differences in completion rates between the two banking channels with IVR banking having a significantly higher first time completion rate, though completion rates overall (three attempts) were high for both channels. It

should also be noted that these participants had prior experience of IVR banking, and in this regard the completion rates for the SMS channel can be judged comparable. There was also a difference in attitude to usability, and again, overall, the IVR channel was rated significantly higher and also higher with the quality metric. IVR had lowers scores for *confusion, flustered, stress, concentration* and *improvement needed*, higher scores for *knew what to do next, would use again, reliability, user-friendly, polite* and *confidence in security*. Converting the quality rating into a rank order preference did not indicate a clear customer preference between the IVR or SMS channels. Regarding the efficiency of the channels, a large percentage of the positive comments regarding the SMS channel focussed on the (fast) speed of the service.

That the IVR channel scored higher for usability for a balance request should not be too surprising. Automated (IVR) telephony services are a familiar and mature technology in the banking sector, while the use of SMS is relatively new in banking. Reviewing the qualitative data indicates that the most frequent concern about an SMS banking service was perceived security, one of the main obstacles to overcome in widespread customer acceptance of SMS banking. Security has been shown to be a key factor in customer acceptance (O'Gorman, 2003; Schultz et al., 2001) in electronic banking, and particularly in mobile banking (Brown et al., 2003; Luarn & Lin, 2005), though it has been argued that security concerns (Laukkanen, 2007; Laukkanen & Lauronen, 2005; Suoranta, 2003) are not a reason for low adoption of mobile banking, but rather (Laukkanen, 2007) that it is a feeling of uncertainty about making errors due to the small size of the screen and slowness of access rather than the actual data security of the system, which related more to the usability of mobile phones. In contrast, to that work, the results reported in this paper suggest that with SMS banking concern with the actual security of the medium (data security) is indeed a major customer concern. SMS banking is more convenient than telephone banking, but it seems that a combination of usability problems and security concerns are significant factors in the low adoption of SMS banking.

A concept tied to security is trust, and participants may place more trust in an IVR telephone banking service because it is more established. Trust (Kim et al., 2008; Lee & Chung, 2009) is an important factor in usage intentions of mBanking, seen as the variable that most affects customer satisfaction with mobile banking, and that interface design quality is not as important a factor in building trust compared to information quality and system quality. As discussed previously, interface design quality for SMS banking is beyond the control of the bank and is dependent on the model of mobile phone the customer owns. Interface design quality is obviously an aspect of usability, but most users will be experts in writing text messages on their own mobile phones. In this study where a generic mobile phone was used, the process of using SMS banking to get an account balance was found to score lower in usability compared to IVR banking. The participants in this study appeared to be relatively happy with the information quality of the SMS service but not the security, which is considered to be an aspect of system quality (Lee & Chung, 2009; Delone & Mclean, 1992). Also the study reported here only looked at first time use of the SMS banking service for requesting a balance request, whilst the participants had used IVR services before, so with extended use of the SMS service it could be argued that trust in the service would increase, which could impact on satisfaction, and usability. This may lead to SMS banking comparing more favourably towards an IVR service, which should be investigated in a more longitudinal study investigating user behaviour over an extended period.

Only one type of form factor was used in this experiment for the mobile device, along with the commonest text input method for mobile phones. Performance with SMS banking could vary slightly with different types of handheld devices, and with different text input methods.

As in previous research (Peevers et al., 2008) differences between the age groups were discovered. The older age group had lower first time completion rates with SMS banking, and gave the IVR banking significantly higher scores for attitude and quality compared to the SMS service. Older users can suffer from visual, cognitive and motor impairments to varying degrees (Christopher, 1999; Jagaacinski et al., 1995; Krampe & Ericsson, 1996; Kurniawan, King, Evans, & Blenkhorn, 2006; Walker et al., 1997), and have been shown to have problems with mobile phones (Ornella & Stephanie, 2006). It is argued these factors would impact on the usability of an SMS banking service for older users. This is due to the fact that mobile phones are not generally designed specifically with the older user in mind. The difference in results here can also be attributed to these usability problems, and a negative relationship was discovered between overall usability attitude score for the SMS service and age.

SMS usage patterns and experience levels are also a probable factor in the differences in scores (Peevers et al., 2008). The older age group in general were found to send SMS less frequently than the younger (Table 3). There was a positive relationship between age group and quality rating of IVR banking found in the experiment, and it is plausible that older users are more positive towards IVR banking, as it has been argued that older users are less positive in general to mobile phones (Ling, 2007). Older people are active users of the landline telephone, and older people also value personal contact highly (Blythe et al., 2005). It is also argued that older people do perceive the main function of a mobile phone as being a communication device (Kurniawan, 2008), a safety line. The study reported here was concerned only with balance requests via SMS banking compared to IVR banking. If other types of transactions were compared, such as funds transfers, it is arguable that the differences between age groups would be even more pronounced.

REFERENCES

Ahmed, Z. (2004). *Youth drives India's mobile phone revolution.* Retrieved from http://news.bbc.co.uk/1/hi/business/3585257.stm

Aladwani, A. M. (2001). Online banking: a field study of drivers, development challenges, and expectations. *International Journal of Information Management, 21*(3), 213–225. doi:10.1016/S0268-4012(01)00011-1

Anderson, A. H., Newlands, A., Mullin, J., Fleming, A. M., Doherty-Sneddon, G., & Van der Velden, J. (1996). Impact of video-mediated communication on simulated service encounters. *Interacting with Computers, 8*(2), 193–206. doi:10.1016/0953-5438(96)01025-9

Balakrishnan, V., & Yeow, H. P. (2008). A study of the effect of thumb sizes on mobile phone texting satisfaction. *Journal of Usability Studies, 3*(3), 118–128.

Balakrishnan, V., Yeow, H. P., & Ngo, D. C. L. (2005). An investigation on the ergonomic problems of using mobile phones to send SMS. In P. D. Bust & P. T. McCabe (Eds.), *Proceedings of the Contemporary Ergonomics 2005 Conference* (pp. 195-199). London, UK: Taylor & Francis.

Blythe, M. A., Monk, A. F., & Doughty, K. (2005). Socially dependable design: The challenge of aging populations for HCI. *Interacting with Computers, 17,* 672–689. doi:10.1016/j.intcom.2005.09.005

Brown, I., Cajee, Z., Davies, D., & Stroebel, S. (2003). Cell phone banking: predictors of adoption in South Africa – an exploratory study. *International Journal of Information Management, 23*(5), 381–394. doi:10.1016/S0268-4012(03)00065-3

Christopher, P. (1999). *Older adults – Special considerations for special people.* Retrieved from http://www.gsu.ed/~mstswh/course/it7000/papers/newpage31.htm

Curran, K., Woods, D., & Riordan, O, B. (2006). Investigating text input methods for mobile phones. *Telematics and Informatics, 23,* 1–21. doi:10.1016/j.tele.2004.12.001

Delone, W. H., & McLean, E. R. (1992). Information systems success: The quest for the dependent variable. *Information Systems Research, 3*(1), 60–95. doi:10.1287/isre.3.1.60

Faulkner, X., & Culwin, F. (2005). When fingers do the talking: a study of text messaging. *Interacting with Computers, 17,* 167–185. doi:10.1016/j.intcom.2004.11.002

Friedman, Z., Mukherji, S., Roeum, G. K., & Ruchir, R. (2001). *Data input into mobile phones: T9 or keypad?* Retrieved June 10, 2006, from http://www.otal.umd.edu./SHORE2001/mobilePhone/index.html

Frokjaer, E., Hertzum, M., & Hornbaek, K. (2000). Measuring usability: are effectiveness, efficiency and satisfaction really correlated? *CHI Letters, 2*(1), 345–352.

Furnell, S. (2005). Why users cannot use security. *Computers & Security, 24,* 274–279. doi:10.1016/j.cose.2005.04.003

Grabner-Krauter, S., & Kaluscha, E. A. (2003). Empirical research in on-line trust: a review and critical assessment. *International Journal of Human-Computer Studies, 58*(6), 783–812. doi:10.1016/S1071-5819(03)00043-0

Hudson, W. (2002). The lost world of e-banking. *ACM SIGCHI Bulletin, 34*(5).

Hyvarinen, T., Kaikkonen, A., & Hiltunen, M. (2005). Placing links in mobile banking applications. In *Proceedings of the 7th International Conference on Human Computer Interaction with Mobile Devices and Services*, Salzburg, Austria (pp. 63-68). New York, NY: ACM.

Jagacinski, R. J., Liao, M. J., & Fayyad, E. A. (1995). Generalized slowing in sinusoidal tracking in older adults. *Psychology and Aging, 9*, 103–112.

James, C. L., & Reischel, K. M. (2001, March 31-April 5). Text input for mobile devices: Comparing model prediction to actual performance. In *Proceedings of CHI'01: Human Factors in Computing Systems*, Seattle, WA (pp. 365-371). New York, NY: ACM Press.

Jarvenpaa, S., Lang, K. R., Takeda, Y., & Tuunainen, V. K. (2003). Mobile commerce at crossroads: An international focus group study of users of mobile handheld devices and services. *Communications of the ACM, 46*(12), 41–44. doi:10.1145/953460.953485

Jayawardhena, C., & Foley, P. (2000). Changes in the Banking Sector - the case of Internet Banking in the UK. *Internet Research: Electronic Networking, Applications and Policy, 10*(1), 19–30.

Kaikkonen, A., Kallio, T., Kekalainen, A., Kankainen, A., & Cankar, M. (2005). Usability testing of mobile application: A comparison between laboratory and field testing. *Journal of Usability Studies, 1*(1), 4–16.

Karajaluoto, H. (2002). Selection criteria for a mode of bill payment: empirical investigation among Finnish bank customers. *International Journal of Retail & Distribution Management, 30*(6), 331–339. doi:10.1108/09590550210429540

Kim, G., Shin, B., & Lee, H. G. (2008). Understanding dynamics between initial trust and usage intention of mobile banking. *Information Systems Journal, 19*(3), 283–311. doi:10.1111/j.1365-2575.2007.00269.x

Kim, J., & Moon, J. Y. (1998). Designing emotional usability in customer interfaces trustworthiness of cyber-banking system interfaces. *Interacting with Computers, 10*, 1–29. doi:10.1016/S0953-5438(97)00037-4

Kim, K., & Prabhakar, B. (2000, December 10-13). Initial trust, perceived risk, and the adoption of internet banking. In *Proceedings of the 21st International Conference on Information Systems*, Brisbane, QLD, Australia (pp. 537-543).

Krampe, R. T., & Ericsson, K. A. (1996). Maintaining excellence: deliberate practice and elite performance in young and older pianists. *Journal of Experimental Psychology. General, 125*, 331–359. doi:10.1037/0096-3445.125.4.331

Kurniawan, S. H. (2008). Older people and mobile phones: A multi-method investigation. *International Journal of Human-Computer Studies, 66*(12), 889–901. doi:10.1016/j.ijhcs.2008.03.002

Kurniawan, S. H., King, A., Evans, D. G., & Blenkhorn, P. L. (2006). Personalising web page presentation for older people. *Interacting with Computers, 18*(3), 457–477. doi:10.1016/j.intcom.2005.11.006

Kurniawan, S. H., Nugroho, Y., & Mahmud, M. (2006). A study of the use of mobile phones by older persons. In *Proceedings of CHI'06: Human Factors in Computing Systems*, Montreal, QC, Canada (pp. 989-994). New York, NY: ACM Press.

Landauer, T. K. (1988). Research methods in human-computer interaction. In Helenader, M. (Ed.), *Handbook of Human-Computer Interaction* (pp. 905–928). Amsterdam, The Netherlands: North-Holland.

Laukkanen, T. (2007). Internet vs mobile banking: comparing customer value perceptions. *Business Process Management Journal*, *13*(6), 788–797. doi:10.1108/14637150710834550

Laukkanen, T., & Lauronen, J. (2005). Consumer value creation in mobile banking services. *International Journal of Mobile Communications*, *3*(4), 325–328. doi:10.1504/IJMC.2005.007021

Lee, K. C., & Chung, N. (2009). Understanding factors affecting trust in and satisfaction with mobile banking in Korea: A modified Delone and Mclean's model perspective. *Interacting with Computers*, *21*(5-6), 385–392. doi:10.1016/j. intcom.2009.06.004

Lee, M. S. Y., McGoldrick, P. F., Keeling, K. A., & Doherty, J. (2003). Using ZMET to explore barriers to the adoption of 3G mobile banking services. *International Journal of Retail & Distribution Management*, *31*(6), 340–348. doi:10.1108/09590550310476079

Lee, Y. S., Hong, S. W., Smith-Jackson, T. L., Nussbaum, M. A., & Tomioka, K. (2006). Systematic evaluation methodology for cell phone user interfaces. *Interacting with Computers*, *18*, 304–325. doi:10.1016/j.intcom.2005.04.002

Lewis, J. R., & Sauro, J. (2006). When 100% really isn't 100%: Improving the accuracy of small-sample estimates of completion rates. *Journal of Usability Studies*, *3*(1), 136–150.

Liao, Z., & Cheung, M. T. (2002). Internet based e-banking and consumer attitudes: an empirical study. *Information & Management*, *39*, 283–295. doi:10.1016/S0378-7206(01)00097-0

Likert, R. (1932). A technique for the measurement of attitudes. *Archives de Psychologie*, 140.

Ling, R. (2007). SMS og hvordan elder blir utestengt. In Proitz, L., Luders, M., & Rasmussen, T. (Eds.), *Livet I og utenfor skjermene*. Oslo, Norway: Uniersitetetsforlaget.

Luarn, P., & Lin, H. H. (2005). Toward an understanding of the behavioral intention to use mobile banking. *Computers in Human Behavior*, *21*(6), 873–891. doi:10.1016/j.chb.2004.03.003

Martin, O. (2010). Texting was never actually designed for the consumer market. *The Guardian*. Retrieved from http://www.guardian.co.uk/business/2010/jan/01/texting-never-designed-for-consumers

News, B. B. C. (2005a, October 28). *Vodafone buys into India's Bharti*. Retrieved from http://news.bbc.co.uk/1/hi/business/4384258.stm

News, B. B. C. (2005b, May 21). *A back-to-basics mobile launched*. Retrieved from http://news.bbc.co.uk/1/hi/technology/4566809.stm

O'Gorman, L. (2003). Comparing passwords, tokens and biometrics for user authentication. *Proceedings of the IEEE*, *91*(12), 2021–2040. doi:10.1109/JPROC.2003.819611

Ornella, P., & Stephanie, B. (2006). Universal Designs for Mobile Phones: A Case Study. In *Proceedings of the Computer Human Interaction 2006 Conference*.

Peevers, G., Douglas, G., & Jack, M. A. (2008). A usability comparison of three alternative message formats for an SMS banking service. *International Journal of Human-Computer Studies*, *66*(2), 113–123. doi:10.1016/j.ijhcs.2007.09.005

Peevers, G., & McInnes, F. (2009). Laboratory studies. In Love, S. (Ed.), *Handbook of Mobile Technology Research Methods*. Hauppauge, NY: Nova.

Peevers, G., McInnes, F., Morton, H., Matthews, A., & Jack, M. A. (2009). The mediating effects of brand music and waiting time updates on customers' satisfaction with a telephone service when put on-hold. *International Journal of Bank Marketing, 27*(2-3), 202–217. doi:10.1108/02652320910950196

Pousttchi, K., & Schurig, M. (2004, January 5-8). Assessment of today's mobile banking applications from the view of customer requirements. In *Proceedings of the 37ᵗʰ Hawaii International Conference on System Sciences*, Big Island, HI. Washington, DC: IEEE Computer Society.

Root, R. W., & Draper, S. (1983, December 12-15). Questionnaires as a software evaluation tool. In *Proceedings of the CHI 83 Conference*, Boston, MA. New York, NY: ACM.

Rumpa, G. (2005, February 6). Are you banking more on your mobile? *The Times of India*. Retrieved from http://timesofindia.indiatimes.com/articleshow/1013140.cms

Sauro, J., & Lewis, J. R. (2005). Estimating completion rates from small samples using binomial confidence intervals: comparisons and recommendations. In *Proceedings of the Human Factors and Ergonomics Society Annual Meeting (HFES 2005)*, Orlando, FL.

Schultz, E. E., Proctor, R. W., Lien, M. C., & Savendy, G. (2001). Usability and security: an appraisal of usability issues in information security methods. *Computers & Security, 20*(7), 620–634. doi:10.1016/S0167-4048(01)00712-X

Sillence, E., & Barber, C. (2004). Integrated digital communities: combining and competition. *Interacting with Computers, 16*(1), 93–113. doi:10.1016/j.intcom.2003.11.007

Soriano, C., Raikundalia, G. K., & Szajman, J. (2005). A usability study of short message service on middle-aged users. In *Proceedings of the OZCHI 2005 Conferece*, Canberra, ACT, Australia.

Suh, B., & Han, I. (2002). Effect of trust on customer acceptance of internet banking. *Electronic Commerce Research and Applications, 1*(3), 247–263. doi:10.1016/S1567-4223(02)00017-0

Suoranta, M. (2003). Adoption of mobile banking in Finland. *Studies in Business and Management, 28*.

Suoranta, M., & Mattila, M. (2004). Mobile banking and consumer behaviour: new insights into the diffusion pattern. *Journal of Financial Services Marketing, 8*(4), 354–366. doi:10.1057/palgrave.fsm.4770132

The Mobile Data Association. (2009). *The Q4 2008 UK mobile report*. Retrieved from http://www.themda.org/mda-press-releases/the-q4-2008-uk-mobile-trends-report.php

Tiwari, R., Buse, S., & Herstatt, C. (2007). Mobile services in banking sector. The role of innovative business solutions in generating competitive advantage. In *Proceedings of the 8ᵗʰ International Research Conference on Quality, Innovation and Knowledge Management*.

Walker, N., Philbin, D. A., & Fisk, A. D. (1997). Age-related differences in movement control: adjusting submovement structure to optimise performance. *The Journals of Gerontology. Series B, Psychological Sciences and Social Sciences, 52B*(1), 40–52. doi:10.1093/geronb/52B.1.P40

Ward, L. (2004, December 23). Texting 'is no bar to literacy'. *Guardian Unlimited*. Retrieved from http://education.guardian.co.uk/schools/story/0,5500,1378951,00.html

Weir, C. S., Douglas, G., Carruthers, M., & Jack, M. (2009). User perceptions of security, convenience and usability for eBanking authentication tokens. *Journal of Computers and Security*, *28*(1), 47–62. doi:10.1016/j.cose.2008.09.008

Weir, C. S., Douglas, G., Richardson, T., & Jack, M. (2009). Usable Security: User Preferences for authentication methods in eBanking and the effects of experience. *Interacting with Computers.*

Whiteside, J., Bennett, J., & Holzblatt, K. (1988). Usability engineering: Our experience and evolution. In Helander, M. (Ed.), *Handbook of human computer interaction* (pp. 91–817). New York, NY: North-Holland.

Wilkie, J., Jack, M. A., & Littlewood, P. (2005). System-initiated digressive proposals in automated human-computer telephone dialogues: the use of contrasting politeness strategies. *International Journal of Human-Computer Studies*, *62*, 41–71. doi:10.1016/j.ijhcs.2004.08.001

ENDNOTE

[1] The case bank for this research is one of the UK's High Street banks.

This work was previously published in the International Journal of Technology and Human Interaction, Volume 7, Issue 4, edited by Anabela Mesquita and Chia-Wen Tsai, pp. 1-16, copyright 2011 by IGI Publishing (an imprint of IGI Global).

Chapter 8

Multimedia Technology in the Financial Services Sector:
Customer Satisfaction with Alternatives to Face-to-Face Interaction in Mortgage Sales

Gareth Peevers
The University of Edinburgh, UK

Gary Douglas
The University of Edinburgh, UK

Mervyn A. Jack
The University of Edinburgh, UK

ABSTRACT

Participants (N=71) took part in mortgage interviews with a human agent interacting with a computer using four different communication modes: a standard video ink, a video link with video-data, the telephone and face-to-face. Video-plus-data came significantly higher in the rankings than phone. It is argued that video-plus-data was found to be more useful than phone, as it provided the participants with more feedback on their mortgage negotiation. Usability and preference were highest for face-to-face. Usability of video was significantly higher than video-plus-data. Comments made by the participants suggest that this may have been due to the split-attention effect and it is argued that this could be diminished by usability improvements. There were no significant differences in usability between the two video services and the telephone. Reasons for this are explored. Differences between genders were also discovered with the phone being judged to be less usable by male participants. If face-to-face mortgage interviews are to be supplemented by other communication channels then users would find video-plus-data the most acceptable, but there is much room for further improvements in usability.

DOI: 10.4018/978-1-4666-1954-8.ch008

1. INTRODUCTION

The continual widespread advances in computer technologies have encouraged many banks to adopt new methods of interacting with customers to in an attempt to lower costs and to maintain competitive advantage, whilst creating more convenient methods of banking for the customer. Banks are now committed to transferring many customer services that have traditionally involved interacting with staff in branches to different technology channels such as the telephone, email or the Internet. One such technology channel is Video-Mediated Communication (VMC), and multimedia contact centres offering video conferencing are already being developed by financial services.

Offering customer services over the telephone, or via VMC, will involve a customer representative working in front of a computer, and interacting with the computer on the customer's behalf. This type of interactive process has been referred to as customer-agent computer interaction (CACI) (Kira, Nichols, & Apperley, 2009), and is typical in many types of business communication, not just in the financial services sector (the typically cited example is a travel agency). In all of these settings the agent/advisor acts as an interface between the customer and organisation (Randall & Hughes, 1995).

The introduction of any new banking channel will require research to compare it with available services in terms of usability and customer satisfaction with the service, because as has been pointed out (Anderson et al., 1996) if a user's first experience of a new service is unsatisfactory they may revert to the use of a more traditional form of service. It may also result in loss of business to competitors. This paper describes research with customers of a UK bank (here termed the Case Bank) on the CACI scenario of introducing alternative channels for mortgage application interviews. The aim was to deliver empirical data to compare customer attitude to the alternatives to face-to-face communication: VMC and the telephone. The findings would inform and guide the future deployment of the technology. This work builds on previous research (Anderson et al., 1996; Fish et al., 1990; Sellen, 1992; Tang & Isaacs, 1993; Watts & Monk, 1996) that has already reported user preference for richer media, such as video conferencing.

Customer-Agent Computer Interaction (CACI)

CACI requires three entities: one or more customers, a representative for the organisation (the agent) and the agent's computer. In addition, the customer will have specific details relating to the task, and the agent will have domain expertise. The agent's role is one of mediation between the customer and the organisation's information system accessed via the computer. The customer does not directly interact with the computer. Research on CACI is limited but work carried out by Kira et al., (2009) is relevant to this paper. The aim was to investigate how two people interact over face-to-face and telephone communication modes where there is also a computer involved in the interactions. The scenario was travel planning and booking a flight. The major findings were that task completion rates were significantly faster and more task-focused with telephone interactions, that with the telephone there was more doubling up of activities and that the subjective satisfaction rating was only slightly more favourable for the face-to-face condition, but not significantly so. Kira et al. (2009) argue that the telephone is not necessarily an impoverished communication mode and suggest call centres are efficient in providing customer service.

Video-Mediated Communication (VMC)

Much previous research on video-mediated communication (VMC) has produced little evidence to show that it can confer comparable benefits to face-to-face interaction, or show benefits over audio-only communication on task performance (Anderson et al., 1996; Boyle, Anderson & Newlands, 1994; Chapanis, 1975; O'Malley et al., 1996; Whittaker, 2003). It has been argued (Reid, 1977; Short, Williams & Christie, 1976; Williams, 1977) that tasks that involve a larger social element have revealed more of the benefits of using VMC. This forms one point of departure in motivating the experiment reported here since the mortgage / insurance interview involves a large degree of social interaction. Research (Damian et al., 2000) on groups using VMC, and more longitudinal studies (Isaacs & Tang, 1994; Van der Kleig et al., 2005) have had more positive results. It has also been argued (Isaacs & Tang, 1994) that the benefit of video will not be revealed in interactions between strangers, or in artificial experimental sessions. But Rutter et al. (1981) argue that face-to-face is more time-consuming and less efficient, and others (Ochsman & Chapanis, 1974; Orvis et al., 2002) argue that a non-visual communication mode may not result in a less satisfactory outcome. It has been suggested though, that people prefer face-to-face interactions (Fletcher & Major, 2006; Masoodian & Apperley, 1995; Masoodian et al., 1995), and, historically, this is the method of communication most used in customer services.

'Video-as-data' (Gaver et al., 1993; Nardi et al., 1997; Whittaker, 1995, 2003) is a more recent application of VMC where video is used to transmit information (documents, or a drawing) about the shared objects involved in an interaction along with, or rather than, an image of the participants themselves. Where some research (Chapanis et al., 1972; Gale, 1991; Ochsman & Chapanis, 1974) suggests that adding visual communication to verbal communication does not improve interaction, studies on shared workspaces showed that adding video-as-data improved the efficiency of speech communication (Bly, 1998; Whittaker et al., 1991; Whittaker et al., 1993). It has been

argued (Whittaker et al., 1991, 1993) that this type of research provides unambiguous support for the importance of certain *types* of 'video-as-data' in communication. Participants in one study (Anderson et al., 2000) judged video data to be generally more useful and important than a plain video link (head and shoulders). Such a preference for the use of video data may not be so surprising because it has been argued (Greenspan et al., 2000; Whittaker, 1995, 2003) that it is often more important to be able to share video images, maps, drawings, and text than to be able to see the face of a collaborator. It is generally concluded (Anderson et al., 2000; Whittaker, 1995, 2003) that the nature of the task will impact on the usefulness of 'video-as-data'. This forms the second motivation for investigation of video-plus-data in the experiment reported here.

Context for Research

The objective of this research was to derive objective, empirical data on the impact on the customer experience of introducing alternative channels for a mortgage application interview. A typical mortgage interview is conducted at a bank in a face-to-face situation with a mortgage advisor and their desktop computer, and is mostly arranged by appointment. Mortgage interviews can also be conducted via an arranged phone call, but this is less common. The mortgage service scenario envisioned here is that a customer will be able to gain instant access to a mortgage advisor via video conferencing at their local branch. The advisor will communicate with the customer while also interacting with a computer. In this kind of context (Muller et al., 1995) the agent is a kind of knowledge worker, and a mortgage interview involves a large amount of information exchange, a type of task which has been argued (Anderson et al., 2000) will not generally reveal the benefits of normal video links, but which is typical in CACI (Kira et al., 2008).

Hypotheses for this Research

The null hypotheses were:

H1: The four channels used for a mortgage application interview will not differ in terms of customer attitude.

H2: The four channels used for a mortgage application will not differ in terms of quality metric.

H3: The attitude and quality metrics for the channels will not differ between customer groups (age, gender).

2. METHOD

Experiment Design, Independent Variables

The experiment focused on customers experiencing realistic mortgage application interviews with experienced banking staff using fully realistic copies of their bank's software applications. The main experimental variable was communication channel (four treatments). The four treatments were: (1) face-to-face, (2) phone, (3) video, and (4) video-plus-data. Participants experienced all four treatments in a repeated-measures design. A repeated-measures design uses the same participants for each treatment. Its advantage is that it diminishes the influence of individual differences. Counterbalancing was used to avoid possible carry over effects between treatments such as novelty, learning and fatigue. With counterbalancing participants are placed in groups and the presentation order of the treatments is randomly assigned to each participant within the group. It was ensured that each group experienced all possible orders of treatments equal amounts of time.

There were two other (participant) variables included in the analysis and these were gender and age group (39 years and under versus 40 years

and over). It would be interesting to compare a further age group of 60 years and over, as it could be hypothesised that this group may react differently yet again, but a larger sample size would be needed to assess this. The age groups used here were based on the median age of the Case Bank's customer sample.

The participants completed two mortgage application interviews. Each was split into two sections at a natural point in the process - after the mortgage application had been completed with the associated home insurance and life cover discussions to be completed in the second section. In each section the participants experienced a different condition (face-to-face, phone, video, video-plus-data), so over their two different mortgage interviews the participants experienced all four treatments randomised across the sample. The participants were given different personae and mortgage scenarios for each of the two interviews.

Dependent Variables

Customer satisfaction with the four banking channels was measured using an attitude questionnaire, and customer preference using a quality metric with preference scores.

Experiment Participants

The number of participants needed depends upon the degree of segmentation planned in the cohort. For robust statistical testing, larger numbers are needed in each key demographic group, in for example, different age groupings and genders (Landauer, 1998) to lessen the impact of individual differences. A cohort of 75 participants was recruited in Edinburgh. They were all customers of the Case Bank. In total, 71 complete participant data sets were obtained and used in the statistical analysis. There were 34 male participants and 37 female participants (Table 1). The percentage of participants recruited who currently held a mortgage was 57%.

Experiment Tasks

Two different fictitious personae were created, each with a male and female version available. The two persona/scenario sheets used by each participant contained different personal, health, contact, employment, financial and property details. The participants role-played customers who had gone into their local branch to attend a pre-arranged interview with a mortgage advisor. The two scenarios used were refined to allow completion of both interviews in a single experiment session that lasted some 90 minutes. Both scenarios therefore assumed that the customer had "already been into a branch" and been through the early stages of a mortgage interview process with the mortgage advisor - in which they discussed their general financial situation and their lending requirements. It was assumed that the mortgage advisor had subsequently partially completed the mortgage application up to the point where lending details were required. In the scenarios, the applicant then had supposedly left for a prior (dentist / doctor) appointment. Hence for both scenarios in the experiment the effective starting point was defined conveniently as a follow-on interview leading on from an initial meeting in the bank.

The participants were given some latitude to use their own imagination. However, participants were made aware by the researcher that for the success of the experiment they must get the 'best deal', as specified in the scenario sheet. The participants were told that the mortgage advisor might advise them on different mortgage products, but that they must negotiate the mortgage detailed in the scenario. It was observed by the authors that many of the participants actively engaged in the role-play during the interviews, by adding their own embellishments to the scenarios. Indeed, some of those participants with mortgages were personally interested in the deals on offer and

Table 1. Participant demographics

	Age 18-39	Age 40 and over	Total
Males	18 (25.4%)	16 (22.5%)	34 (47.9%)
Females	22 (31.0%)	15 (21.1%)	37 (52.1%)
Total	40 (56.4%)	31 (43.6%)	71 (100%)

indicated that they would probably look into the matter further.

Mortgage Advisors

Five experienced mortgage advisors were recruited to take part in the experiment. There were three female advisors and two male advisors. All five advisors were fully versed in the range of mortgage products used in the scenarios. The assignment of mortgage advisor to participant was random. The mortgage advisors were used in sequence during the day to ensure that they did not become fatigued. Each of the advisors had prior training with the technology in pilot studies.

Video Conferencing Technology

In the experiment, two video-conferencing 'studios' were set-up and were configured according to the recommendations for lighting, layout and furnishings made in The Video Technology Advisory Services (VTAS) guidelines. Digital video cameras were used to film the mortgage advisor and transmit the images to the participant's screen, which was a 42-inch plasma screen, to achieve broadcast quality frame rate with no appreciable audio lag, similar to the methodologies used in other studies (Grayson & Coventry, 1998; Huang, Wei, & Olsen, 2002; Van der Kleij et al., 2005). In this way deleterious effects caused by poor frame rate and audio lag would be controlled for. The mortgage advisors used desktop PCs with 17 inch TFT monitors. The mortgage advisor was able to see (and hear) a live image of the participant on their PCs using a standard webcam via Microsoft NetMeeting video-conferencing. Technological limitations meant that the video preview of a participant's own image could not be displayed on the customer's plasma screen alongside the image of the mortgage advisor, so the practical decision was made to allow the participant to view their video preview before the start of the interview on a PC monitor.

In the video-plus-data condition the application sharing was achieved by using the capabilities of Microsoft NetMeeting. The mortgage application package was displayed full screen on a 17 inch TFT desktop PC monitor for the participant to view. In the video-plus-data condition participants had two separate screens to attend to, one displaying the video image of the advisor, and one displaying the application data. Whilst the participants could see the mortgage advisor entering data in real time, the control of the application was solely with the mortgage advisor. The participants could not type or navigate in the shared application.

The large plasma screens used in the experiment were placed on desks giving the participants the impression that the mortgage advisor was sitting facing them at relatively the same height since it has been shown (Huang et al., 2002) that physical context cues can be distorted through camera angle and the position of the monitor or screen, such that setting the camera angle and monitor high in one room and low in another can give the artificially tall person more influence in a group decision making.

Face-to-Face Scenario

For the face-to-face scenario current practice was followed and the participant sat next to the advisor as they completed the application process. This set-up would enable the participant to see what the advisor was typing if they so wished.

Questionnaires

The design of the attitude questionnaire used for this experiment followed standard practice (Likert, 1932) by using an equal number of negative and positive statements presented in a randomised order. The use of questionnaires to evaluate services and user interfaces has a long history (LaLomia & Sidowski, 1990; Root & Draper, 1983). The attitude questionnaire was modified from previous research (Peevers et al., 2008, 2009; Weir et al., 2006, 2007, 2009). The questionnaire used a 7-point Likert format that ranged from "Strongly Agree" (1) to "Strongly Disagree" (7). Following reversal of the polarity of positive questionnaire statements, a score of 7 consistently indicates a strongly positive attitude and 1 a strongly negative attitude. The questionnaire used consisted of 28 statements that address a range of cognitive and affective attributes relating to the user experience: *cognitive attributes* (level of concentration and degree of confusion), *the fluency and transparency of the service* (knowledge about what is expected, ease of use, degree of complication), and *quality attributes* (efficiency of service, amount of improvement service is felt to require, reliability of service) plus statements relating to customer perception of the mortgage advisors (friendliness, politeness, trustworthiness, helpfulness).

All participants ($N = 71$) completed the questionnaire following exposure to each of the four experiment conditions. An overall attitude score was determined by determining the overall mean for all of the attributes by all participants. Individual attributes were also analysed separately to analyse any specific issues that arose.

Quality and Post Experiment Questionnaire

At the end of the session the participants were asked which channel they preferred, and by rating the four channels on a 0-30 linear scale they provided an overall rating as well as a rank order of preference. This type of quality metric has been used in previous research (Peevers et al., 2008; Weir et al., 2009a, 2009b). Participants also completed a structured exit interview composed of a set of open and closed questions. Participants were asked about their reactions to the different channels and their likes and dislikes.

Experiment Procedure

The participant was taken into the experiment room and given a brief explanation of the structure of the session. The participant was then introduced to the first of their two fictitious personae – these were pre-allocated to ensure balance across the cohort. The participant was given time to familiarise themselves with the persona details. The experimenter then asked them a few questions about their persona to help them immerse themselves in the scenario. The participant then experienced the first of the four channels (face-to-face, phone, video or video-plus-data) in the first part of their first mortgage application interview. After the mortgage advisor had completed the mortgage application the participant was asked to complete the attitude questionnaire. The participant then experienced another of the four channels in the second part of their interview - where the mortgage advisor completed home insurance and life cover for the participant. Again, after the channel was experienced the participant completed a questionnaire. After a short break the participant was then introduced to the second of the two fictitious personae. The participant repeated the same two-part procedure for their second mortgage interview with the remaining two channels.

3. RESULTS

Preference Results

Participants were asked to rate the quality of the four services on a 0-30 point rating scale between "poor" and "excellent". The overall means of the ratings measurements for the alternative ser-

vices were face-to-face: 24.76, video-plus-data: 19.25, video: 17.75 and phone: 16.13. A repeated measures analysis of variance (ANOVA) was performed on the mean scores to test for effects of the main experimental variable, with age group and gender as between-participant factors. With a within-participants design, a repeated measures ANOVA is used. The null hypothesis is that there is no difference, on the population, between the mean values of the dependent variable (e.g. usability score) for different levels of the experimental variable (e.g. different treatments – experienced by the same participants in the experiment). The hypothesis is tested using *within-participants* differences in the dependent variable between treatments. The results of the analyses revealed a highly significant difference in the ratings of the four channels [$df = 2.3$, $F = 23.012$, $p < 0.001$].

A significant main effect for gender was found ($p = 0.037$). There were two noticeable differences between the genders regarding their preference rating (Table 2). The first was that for the male participants the mean score (taken from the preference data) achieved by phone was much lower than for the females (13.69 compared to 18.59), and the second was that for the female participants phone, video and video-plus-data achieved very similar mean scores (18.59, 18.18 and 18.42, respectively). For males the ratings scores were more diverse (13.69, 17.32, and 20.09). The male participants had stronger feelings regarding the four channels and phone was their least favourite. The female participants' preferences were not as strong and they considered phone, video and video-plus-data to be similar. Face-to-face though achieved the same highest score for both genders (males: 24.75, females: 24.77).

Further pair-wise tests on the data revealed that the differences between the ratings for face-to-face and each of the other three services was statistically significant ($p < 0.001$ for all three). The difference between video-plus-data and phone was statistically significant ($p = 0.026$). The differences between video-plus data and video and

Table 2. Comparison of male and female mean ratings of services (30-point scale)

Service	Overall mean	Males	Females
Face-to-Face	24.76	24.75	24.77
Video-plus-data	19.26	20.09	18.42
Video	17.75	17.32	18.18
Phone	16.14	13.69	18.59

Table 3. Preference rankings

	Face-to-Face	Telephone	Video	Video-plus-data
1st	47	8	5	20
2nd	16	15	19	16
3rd	6	12	33	19
4th	2	36	14	16

between video and phone were not statistically significant.

For each participant a ranking of the four channels by perceived quality was derived from the four ratings. From this an overall picture of preference for each channel was collected. The rankings are given in Table 3.

It can be seen from Table 3 that face-to-face received the top rating with video-plus-data second, and the telephone receiving the most last place ratings.

The participants were also explicitly asked which channel they would choose if they required a mortgage interview in the future. The vast majority (70%) stated face-to-face, with 17% picking video-plus-data, 10% the telephone and 3% video.

Customer Attitude

Overall Results by Channel

The mean overall attitude scores, computed over the 28 statements in the questionnaire, for each of the four treatments were face-to-face 5.98 (SD=0.61), video 5.45 (SD=0.87), phone 5.39 (SD=0.94) and video-plus-data 5.20 (SD=1.02).

Statistical Analysis of Mean Scores

A repeated measures ANOVA with the between-participant factors of age group and gender was performed on the mean scores. The main effect of channel was found to be highly significant [$df = 2,3$,

$F = 18.32, p < 0.001$]. There were no significant effects for interactions between channel and age or channel and gender. There were no significant between-participant effects found.

Further pair-wise statistical analysis on the overall means revealed that the difference between the mean attitude score for face-to-face and the three other channels was statistically significant ($p < 0.001$). The difference between the attitude score for video-only and the score for video-plus-data was statistically significant ($p < 0.01$). There were no significant differences found in overall mean scores between video and phone, and between video-plus-data and phone.

Statistical Analysis of Individual Attribute Scores

A repeated measures ANOVA was performed on the scores for each of the 28 attributes separately, with the same factors as the overall scores. In contrast to a multivariate analysis approach, the separate analysis per attribute has the benefit that the results relate directly to specific attributes mentioned in the questionnaire. When read in conjunction with the results above on the mean scores, therefore, these results indicate which particular aspects of user satisfaction show the strongest evidence of being affected by the factors under consideration.

Data for the individual attributes are listed in Table 4. Analysis of mean score differences for individual attributes revealed that for 21 of the 28 items face-to-face was rated significantly more positively than each of the other three channels ($p<0.005$). The analysis revealed that in six of the 28 usability attributes video was rated significantly ($p<0.05$) more positively than video-plus-data. Participants found video more *enjoyable*, they were less *confused*, *flustered*, and *frustrated*, they had to *concentrate* less and the service met their *expectations* more. The results also showed that in three of the attributes phone was rated significantly ($p<0.05$) more positively than video-plus-data. Participants found phone less *confusing*, they also felt less *flustered* and *self-conscious*. Only two significant effects ($p<0.05$) were found between video and phone. Participants judged that phone made them feel less *self-conscious*, but they found the mortgage advisor *easier to understand* with the video-only service.

The analysis also revealed a number of significant ($p<0.05$) main effects for gender. The males found the phone more *confusing* and *frustrating*, they felt the mortgage advisor was less *reliable* on the phone and they felt they knew less about what they were *expected to do* during a mortgage interview conducted on the phone. But males did find video-plus-data less *confusing* and they were more aware of what they were *expected to do* using the video and video-plus-data channels compared to females, though they did find video more *frustrating*.

It should be noted that with over 20 attributes some combinations could be expected to give statistically significant results by chance, but it is argued that results at p<0.01 should be considered to be valid.

Qualitative Analysis

The participants were also asked if there was anything in particular they liked or disliked about their experiences with the different channels. For face-to-face there were 41 responses for likes and 22 for dislikes, for phone 18 for likes and 28 for dislikes, for video 23 likes and 28 dislikes, and finally for video-plus-data, 27 likes and 34 dislikes. It should be noted that the likes and dislikes encompassed every facet of the participants' experience with the channels. Further analysis discovered an interesting finding within the negative comments for phone and video. A factor common to both of these services that provoked a substantial negative reaction among the participants was the factor of not being able to "see" what the mortgage advisor was typing on their behalf: 32% of the negative comments for phone could be attributed to this factor, 36% for video. This seemed to be due to security issues and confusion.

4. DISCUSSION

The results on customer attitude show that they rate face-to-face highest for satisfaction in a banking CACI context, and it is their preferred channel for mortgage application interviews. This result confirms the findings of Fletcher and Major (2006), Masoodian and Apperley (1995) and Masoodian et al. (1995), and in regard to customer satisfaction it is a stronger finding than Kira et al. (2009). Previous research (Kira et al., 2009; Rutter et al., 1981) has found that telephone interaction is less time-consuming and more efficient. The results here, based on attitude and preference, show that even though this might be the case customers can be significantly less satisfied with the telephone. It can be argued also that telephone is the least preferred mode of communication. This effect could be due to the context and the nature of the task. The task in Kira et al., (2009) was to book a flight, a substantially different task to applying for a mortgage. Also, this study used actual customers of the bank who therefore should have been more engaged. Further work should be carried out to investigate if these findings can be generalised, or are specific to this banking domain.

There was no difference in customer attitude towards both video channel and the telephone. This result is consistent with much previous re-

*Table 4. Means scores for usability attributes. Attributes where face-to-face was rated significantly higher than all of the other three services are indicated (*p<0.05; **p<0.01; ***p<0.001)*

	Attribute	Face-to-Face	Phone	Video-plus-data	Video only
1.	Confusion	6.1**	5.6	5.1	5.7
2.	Concentration	5.0*	3.9	3.7	4.3
3.	Flustered	6.0**	5.5	4.9	5.3
4.	Stress	6.0***	5.2	4.9	5.2
5.	Frustration	6.2**	5.6	5.3	5.7
6.	Complication	6.1**	5.6	5.5	5.8
7.	Competency	5.9**	5.3	5.1	5.3
8.	In control	6.0**	5.4	5.0	5.2
9.	Speed	5.5	5.3	5.0	5.3
10.	Easy to understand	6.2**	5.7	5.6	5.8
11.	Use again	6.2***	5.1	5.0	5.4
12.	Reliable	6.0	5.8	5.8	5.7
13.	Efficient	6.5**	5.6	5.5	5.8
14.	Needs improvement	5.9***	4.8	4.7	5.0
15.	Friendly	6.4	6.2	6.1	6.2
16.	Liked	6.1***	5.2	5.0	5.3
17.	Enjoyment	6.0***	5.0	4.8	5.3
18.	Polite	6.4	6.2	6.3	6.3
19.	Helpful	6.2	6.0	6.1	6.1
20.	Trustworthy	6.0	5.7	5.8	5.9
21.	Understand advisor speaking	6.2	5.8	5.7	5.9
22.	Engaged in conversation	5.7**	5.3	5.1	5.3
23.	Felt free to speak	5.3**	4.7	4.6	4.6
24.	Self-conscious	5.5*	5.1	4.3	4.5
25.	Conversation was easy	6.2***	5.4	5.2	5.6
26.	Clear when to speak	6.0*	5.6	5.3	5.5
27.	Met expectations	6.0***	5.4	5.1	5.5
28.	Security confident	6.2***	5.1	5.4	5.4
	Overall mean scores	5.98	5.39	5.45	5.20

search (Anderson et al., 1996; Boyle et al., 1994; Chapanis, 1975; O'Malley et al., 1996) on VMC that has found little benefit for video over audio-only. It had also been expected that the two video channels would have advantages over the phone because they would let customers see the face of the mortgage advisor, which should be important in a financial setting, but this expectation was

not confirmed in the attitude data. In previous research (Anderson et al., 2000; Gaver et al., 1993), participants found video data more useful than an image showing the face of the person they were talking to. The results from the quality and preference metric showed that video-plus-data was rated significantly higher than phone. Many of the negative comments made regarding phone and the plain video link focussed on the inability to 'see' what the advisor was filling in. The issues raised by participants focussed on security, or transparency, and the confusion caused by not being able to see for themselves what information was required for the application. Trust will play an important role in financial situations and customers must be able to trust that the advisor will enter the correct details on their behalf. When the customer can see the form, or application, while it is being completed they can correct any mistakes. They can also see, and read, for themselves, which could make them feel more in control and reduce confusion. Even though video-plus-data had the lowest attitude score, the quality and deduced preference results showed that customers would prefer it to the telephone.

The reason for the absence of stronger support for the value of the simple video link over telephone and towards face-to-face could be due to the interactions studied here having a limited social engagement dynamic (Isaac & Tang, 1994). This may be unrealistic for the specific banking context addressed in this paper. The reason is that a mortgage interview would occur one-to-one between people who might only share one or two interactions.

The simple video link was deemed more *enjoyable* to use, the participants were less *confused*, *flustered* and *frustrated*, they had to *concentrate* less, and the service met their *expectations* more when compared with video-plus-data. Reasons for the difference between customer attitudes to the two video channels may be found in the comments made by the customers. When analysing the negative comments made by the participants regarding video-plus-data it was found that 50% made reference to the confusion of having to attend to two distinct screens and the physical set-up of the VMC technology. The process of attending to two separate sources of information can cause a higher cognitive load, which is referred to as the split-attention effect (Chandler & Sweller, 1991, 1992; Yeung, Jin, & Sweller, 1997). This effect may have impacted on the user experience with video-plus-data.

Usability and usefulness can be two different things. A highly usable channel will not appeal to people if they can find no use for it, and maybe a channel that is judged to be less usable than another can still be preferred if it has a higher utility. Video-plus-data may be more useful precisely because participants could see what the mortgage advisor was filling in on their behalf. They have access to more information and receive more feedback with the video data. If video-plus-data's usability problems are addressed then customer attitude towards this channel could be more positive compared with face-to-face.

Research on the social use of telephones has shown similar gender differences (Chabrol & Périn, 1993; Claisse & Rowe, 1993; Dordick & LaRose, 1992; Ling, 1998; Lacohee & Anderson, 2001; Moyal, 1992; Smoreda & Licoppe, 2000) to those discovered in this study, but these differences may be culture specific. A wide study of the use of the telephone, (Lacochee & Anderson, 2001) found significant gender differences that may be relevant in the context of the present findings in that women agreed more strongly that they enjoy speaking on the phone and that they could spend hours on the phone given the chance. Results on telephone usage in the USA (Tannen, 1992) attributes the gender differences to the fact that men and women have differing attitudes towards the purpose of communication. Lacochee and Anderson (2001) found a clear difference between what men and woman think the telephone should be used for. Reviewing the literature on gender differences in telephone usage it seems that the findings in the experiment reported here could be due to a combination of factors. These are the different views held by the genders on the purposes of communication in general, and their different views of what the telephone should be used for. These are offered as interesting findings for telephone service managers in the financial services sectors.

REFERENCES

Anderson, A. H., Newlands, A., Mullin, J., Fleming, A. M., Doherty-Sneddon, G., & Van der Velden, J. (1996). Impact of video-mediated communication on simulated service encounters. *Interacting with Computers*, *8*(2), 193–206. doi:10.1016/0953-5438(96)01025-9

Anderson, A. H., Smallwood, L., MacDonald, R., Mullin, J., & Fleming, A. (2000). Video data and video links in mediated communication: what do users value? *International Journal of Human-Computer Studies*, *52*, 165–187. doi:10.1006/ijhc.1999.0335

Bly, S. A. (1988, September 26-28). A use of drawing surfaces in different collaborative settings. In *Proceedings of the Conference on Computer-Supported Cooperative Work (CSCW '88)*, Portland, OR (pp. 250-256). New York, NY: ACM Press.

Boyle, E. A., Anderson, A. H., & Newlands, A. (1994). The effects of eye contact on dialogue and performance in a co-operative problem solving task. *Language and Speech*, *37*(1), 1–20.

Brown, G., Anderson, A. H., Yule, G., & Shillcock, R. (1984). *Teaching Talk*. Cambridge, UK: Cambridge University Press.

Bruce, V. (1996). The Role of the face in communication: implications for video-phone design. *Interacting with Computers*, *8*(2), 166–176. doi:10.1016/0953-5438(96)01026-0

Chabrol, J. L., & Périn, P. (1993). *Les pratiques de communication des Français*. Paris, France: Télécom/DPS.

Chandler, P., & Sweller, J. (1991). Cognitive load theory and the format of instruction. *Cognition and Instruction*, *8*(4), 293–332. doi:10.1207/s1532690xci0804_2

Chandler, P., & Sweller, J. (1992). The split-attention effect as a factor in the design of instruction. *The British Journal of Educational Psychology*, *62*, 233–246. doi:10.1111/j.2044-8279.1992.tb01017.x

Chapanis, A. (1975). Interactive human communication. *Scientific American*, *232*, 36–42. doi:10.1038/scientificamerican0375-36

Chapanis, A., Ochsman, R. B., Parrish, R. N., & Weeks, G. D. (1972). Studies in interactive communication: the effect of four communication modes on the behaviour of teams during co-operative problem-solving. *Human Factors*, *14*, 487–509.

Claisse, G., & Rowe, F. (1993). Téléphone, communications et sociabilité: des pratiques résidentielles différenciées. *Sociétés Contemporaines*, *14*(15), 165–189. doi:10.3406/socco.1993.1133

Damian, D. E., Eberlein, A., Shaw, M. L. G., & Gaines, B. R. (2000). Using different communication media in requirements negotiation. *IEEE Software*, *17*(3), 28–36. doi:10.1109/52.896247

Dordick, H. S., & LaRose, R. (1992, June 14-17). The telephone in daily life. In *Proceedings of the International Conference of the International Telecommunication Society*, Sydney, NSW, Australia.

Fish, R., Kraut, R., Root, R., & Rice, R. (1992). Evaluating video as a technology for informal communication. In *Proceedings of Conference on Computer Supported Co-operative Work*, Toronto, ON, Canada (pp. 1-12). New York, NY: ACM Press.

Fletcher, T. D., & Major, D. A. (2006). The effect of communication modality on performance and self-rating of teamwork components. *Journal of Computer-Mediated Communication, 11*(2), 557–576. doi:10.1111/j.1083-6101.2006.00027.x

Gaver, W., Sellen, A., Heath, C., & Luff, P. (1993). One is not enough: multiple views in a media space. In *Proceedings of CHI'94: Human factors in Computing Systems (CSCW '00),* Boston, MA (pp. 335-341). New York, NY: ACM Press.

Grayson, D., & Coventry, L. (1998). The effects of visual proxemic information in video mediated communication. *SIGCHI Bulletin, 30*(3), 30–39. doi:10.1145/565711.565713

Greenspan, S., Goldberg, D., Weimer, D., & Basso, A. (2000, December 2-6). Interpersonal Trust and Common Ground in Electronically Mediated Communication. In *Proceedings of the Conference on Computer Supported Co-operative Work (CSCW '00),* Philadelphia, PA (pp. 251-260). New York, NY: ACM Press.

Huang, W., Olson, J., & Olson, G. (2002, November 16-20). Camera angle affects dominate in video-mediated communication. In *Proceedings of the Conference on Computer Supported Co-operative Work (CSCW '02),* New Orleans, LA. New York, NY: ACM Press.

Isaacs, E., & Tang, J. C. (1994). What video can and cannot do for collaboration: A case study. *Multimedia Systems, 2*(2), 63–73. doi:10.1007/BF01274181

Kira, A., Nichols, D. M., & Apperley, M. (2009). Human communication in customer-agent-computer interaction: Face-to-face versus over telephone. *Computers in Human Behavior, 25,* 8–20. doi:10.1016/j.chb.2008.05.013

LaLomia, M. J., & Sidowski, J. B. (1990). Measurements of computer satisfaction, literacy, and aptitudes: A review. *International Journal of Human-Computer Interaction, 2*(3), 231–253. doi:10.1080/10447319009525982

Likert, R. (1932). A technique for the measurement of attitudes. *Archives de Psychologie,* 140.

Ling, R. (1999). Traditional and fixed and mobile telephony for social networking among Norwegian parents. In L. Elstrom (Ed.), *Human Factors in Telecommunication: 17th International Symposium* (pp. 209-256).

Locohee, H., & Anderson, B. (2001). Interacting with the telephone. *International Journal of Human-Computer Studies, 54,* 665–699. doi:10.1006/ijhc.2000.0439

Mantei, M. M., Baecker, R. M., Sellen, A. J., Buxton, W. A. S., Milligan, T., & Wellman, B. (1991, April 28-June 5). Experiences in the use of a media space. In *Proceedings of CHI'91: Conference on Human Factors in Computing Systems,* New Orleans, LA (pp. 203-208). New York, NY: ACM Press.

Masoodian, M., & Apperley, M. (1995). User perceptions of human-to-human communication modes in CSCW environments. In *Proceedings of ED-MEDIA'95: World Conference on Educational Multimedia and Hypermedia,* Graz, Austria (pp. 430-435). Chesapeake, VA: AACE.

Masoodian, M., Apperley, M., & Frederikson, L. (1995). Video support for shared work-space interaction: An empirical study. *Interacting with Computers, 7*(3), 237–253. doi:10.1016/0953-5438(95)93603-3

Moyal, A. (1992). The gendered use of the telephone: an Australian case study. *Media Culture & Society, 14,* 51–72. doi:10.1177/016344392014001004

Muller, M. J., Carr, R., Ashworth, C., Diekmann, B., Wharton, C., Eickstaedt, C., & Clonts, J. (1995). Telephone operators as knowledge workers: consultants who meet customer needs. In *Proceedings of the SIGCHI Conference on Human Factors in Computing System (CHI'95),* Denver, CO (pp. 130-137). New York, NY: ACM Press/ Addison-Wesley Publishing Co.

Nardi, B., Huchinsky, A., Whittaker, S., Leichner, R., & Schwarz, H. (1997). Video-as-data: technical and social aspects of a collaborative multimedia application. In Finn, K., Sellen, S., & Wilbur, S. (Eds.), *Video-Mediated Communication*. Hillsdale, NJ: Lawrence Erlbaum.

O'Malley, C., Langton, S., Anderson, A., Doherty-Sneddon, G., & Bruce, V. (1996). Comparison of face-to-face and video-mediated interaction. *Interacting with Computers*, *8*(2), 177–192. doi:10.1016/0953-5438(96)01027-2

Ochsman, R. B., & Chapanis, A. (1974). The effect of 10 communication modes on the behavior of teams during cooperative problems solving. *International Journal of Man-Machine Studies*, *6*(5), 579–619. doi:10.1016/S0020-7373(74)80019-2

Orvis, K. L., Wisher, R. A., Bonk, C. J., & Olson, T. M. (2002). Communication patterns during synchronous Web-based military training in problem solving. *Computers in Human Behavior*, *18*(6), 782–795. doi:10.1016/S0747-5632(02)00018-3

Peevers, G., Douglas, G., & Jack, M. A. (2008). A usability comparison of three alternative message formats for an SMS banking service. *International Journal of Human-Computer Studies*, *66*(2), 113–123. doi:10.1016/j.ijhcs.2007.09.005

Peevers, G., McInnes, F., Morton, H., Matthews, A., & Jack, M. A. (2009). The mediating effects of brand music and waiting time updates on customers' satisfaction with a telephone service when put on-hold. *International Journal of Bank Marketing*, *27*(2-3), 202–217. doi:10.1108/02652320910950196

Randall, D., & Hughes, J. A. (1995). Sociology CSCW and working with customers. In Thomas, P. J. (Ed.), *The Social and Interactional Dimensions of Human-Computer Interfaces*. New York, NY: Cambridge University Press.

Reid, A. (1977). Comparing the telephone with face-to-face interaction. In Pool, I. (Ed.), *The Social Impact of the Telephone*. Cambridge, MA: MIT Press.

Root, R. W., & Draper, S. (1983). Questionnaires as a software evaluation tool. In *Proceedings of the CHI 83 Conference*. New York, NY: ACM, New York.

Rutter, D. R., Stephenson, G. M., & Dewey, M. E. (1981). Visual communication and the content and style of conversation. *The British Journal of Social Psychology*, *20*(1), 41–52. doi:10.1111/j.2044-8309.1981.tb00472.x

Sellen, A. J. (1992, May 3-7). Speech patterns in video-mediated conversations. In *Proceedings of the CHI 92 Conference,* Monterey, CA (pp. 49-59). New York, NY: ACM Press.

Short, J. (1974). Effects of medium of communication on experimental negotiation. *Human Relations*, *27*, 225–243. doi:10.1177/001872677402700303

Short, J., Williams, E., & Christie, B. (1976). *The Social Psychology of Telecommunications*. New York, NY: Wiley.

Smoreda, Z., & Licoppe, C. (2000). Gender-specific use of the domestic telephone. *Social Psychology Quarterly*, *63*(3), 238–252. doi:10.2307/2695871

Tang, J., & Isaacs, E. (1993). Why do users like video? Studies of multimedia supported collaboration. *Computer Supported Collaborative Work: An International Journal*, *1*, 163–196. doi:10.1007/BF00752437

Tannen, D. (1992). *You Just Don't Understand: Women and Men in Conversation*. London, UK: Virago Press.

Van der Kleij, R., Paashuis, R., & Schraagen, J. M. C. (2005). On the passage of time: temporal differences in video-mediated and face-to-face interaction. *International Journal of Human-Computer Studies*, *62*, 521–542. doi:10.1016/j.ijhcs.2005.01.003

Watts, L., & Monk, A. (1996). Remote assistance: a view of the work and a view of the face. In M. Tauber (Ed.), *Proceedings of CHI 96: Conference on Human Factors in Computing Systems,* Vancouver, BC, Canada (pp. 101-102). New York, NY: ACM Press.

Weir, C. S., Anderson, J. N., & Jack, M. A. (2006). On the role of metaphor and language in design of third party payment in eBanking: Usability and quality. *International Journal of Human-Computer Studies*, *64*, 770–784. doi:10.1016/j.ijhcs.2006.03.003

Weir, C. S., Douglas, G., Richardson, T., & Jack, M. (2009). Usable Security: User Preferences for authentication methods in eBanking and the effects of experience. *Interacting with Computers*, *22*(3), 153–164. doi:10.1016/j.intcom.2009.10.001

Weir, C. S., McKay, I., & Jack, M. A. (2007). Functionality and usability in design for eStatements in eBanking services. *Interacting with Computers*, *19*(2), 241–256. doi:10.1016/j.intcom.2006.08.010

Whittaker, S. (1995). Rethinking video as a technology for interpersonal communication: theory and design implications. *International Journal of Human-Computer Studies*, *42*, 501–529. doi:10.1006/ijhc.1995.1022

Whittaker, S. (2003). Things to talk about when talking about things. *Human-Computer Interaction*, *18*, 149–170. doi:10.1207/S15327051HCI1812_6

Whittaker, S., Brennan, S., & Clark, H. (1991). Coordinating activity: an analysis of computer supported co-operative work. In *Proceedings of CHI'91: Human Factors in Computing Systems,* New Orleans, LA (pp. 361-367). New York, NY: ACM Press.

Whittaker, S., Geelhoed, E., & Robinson, E. (1993). Shared workspaces: how do they work and when are they useful? *International Journal of Man-Machine Studies*, *39*, 813–842. doi:10.1006/imms.1993.1085

Williams, E. (1977). Experimental comparisons of face-to-face and video-mediated communication. *Psychological Bulletin*, *84*, 963–976. doi:10.1037/0033-2909.84.5.963

Yeung, A. S., Jin, P., & Sweller, J. (1998). Cognitive Load and Learner Expertise: Split-Attention and Redundancy Effects in Reading with Explanatory Notes. *Contemporary Educational Psychology*, *23*(1), 1–21. doi:10.1006/ceps.1997.0951

This work was previously published in the International Journal of Technology and Human Interaction, Volume 7, Issue 4, edited by Anabela Mesquita and Chia-Wen Tsai, pp. 17-30, copyright 2011 by IGI Publishing (an imprint of IGI Global).

Chapter 9
Graduate Students' Perceptions of Privacy and Closed Circuit Television Systems in Public Settings

Abram L. J. Walton
University of South Florida Polytechnic, USA

Sharon A. DeVaney
Purdue University, USA

Darrel L. Sandall
Purdue University, USA

ABSTRACT

This qualitative study used grounded theory to examine how university graduate students felt about closed circuit television (CCTV) as it relates to the privacy and safety of students on campuses. As a result of violence at a few universities, more administrators are considering the implementation of CCTV systems. Because graduate students are an important part of the university population, their views were solicited. A qualitative approach was used because of the lack of previous research on this particular topic. Themes that emerged from interviews with 10 graduate students at a large Midwestern land-grant university were identified as: right to safety, right to privacy, personal privacy responsibilities, post-CCTV sense of privacy, post-CCTV sense of safety, crime displacement, false sense of safety, and international perspectives. The findings provide insight into graduate students' perceptions of a CCTV system and have implications for implementation decisions regarding such a system. Additionally, the findings were utilized to formulate hypotheses for a larger scale research project.

INTRODUCTION

Public universities in the United States are entrusted with maintaining the safety and well-being of students (Griffin, 2007). Undergraduate students represent the majority of the population on most university campuses, and their concerns regarding safety and privacy have been studied (Griffin, 2007). Graduate students are an important

DOI: 10.4018/978-1-4666-1954-8.ch009

constituency-group at universities because they provide a significant source of revenue, are critical to both the research and teaching functions of the university, and will be the professors, administrators, and researchers of the future. Their attitudes and beliefs about safety and privacy should be explored and considered in decisions regarding efforts to protect students, faculty, and staff on university campuses. Although graduate students are a critical part of the university population, no literature was identified which involved graduate students and their concerns regarding safety and privacy.

The right to privacy in the United States has been the subject of widespread debate and invasions of privacy have been the focus of an increase in the number of lawsuits (Nieto, 1997; Nissenbaum, 1998). Furthermore, the current legal foundation of the surveillance-privacy debate rests on only a few Supreme Court decisions and amendments to the Bill of Rights. The first major electronic surveillance act (Omnibus Crime Control and Safe Street Act) was passed in 1968 and it was not changed until the 1986 Electronic Communications Privacy Act (Schlosberg & Ozer, 2007; Spencer, 2000). These two Acts form the underpinnings of the American government's core policies regarding an individual's right-to-privacy, especially with regard to electronic data capture and use. Together these Acts played a major role in establishing boundaries for the 1994 Violent Crime Control and Law Enforcement Act, as well as for organizations that utilize surveillance systems (Spencer, 2000; Taylor, 2002).

In the United States, an increase in surveillance for security purposes is often perceived as leading to a decrease in privacy of individuals in the areas being monitored. The debate over security versus privacy has ensued for the last 50 years. During this time constituents from legislative bodies, law enforcement agencies, courts, businesses and industry, as well as the general public, have each sought to legitimatize their interpretation of the Fourth Amendment of

the U.S. Constitution. Government and others concerned with safety or security are naturally on one side of the surveillance debate due to their organizational agenda and desire to maintain the social order (Armitage, 2002; Goold, 2004; Lyon, 2001, 2002; Nieto, 1997).

It should be noted that there are significant differences in legal protections and allowances between the U.S. and other westernized-countries; including, but not limited to the U.K., Canada, and the European Union. Much effort has been given in researching issues related to security, surveillance, privacy, and their respective laws in these countries (Armitage, 2002; Goold, 2004; Lyon, 2001; Tavani, 2008). However, this paper will focus instead of perceptions of individuals within the U.S., regardless of their international background, but within the context of U.S. culture. More importantly, however, regardless of culture or national law, it appears that surveillance and privacy issues and the research thereof are ultimately reduced to a study of both the intended and unintended social consequences their impact on law and society.

In fact, many organizations and law enforcement agencies have implemented surveillance systems, much to the dismay of civil-rights privacy advocates (Bellovin, 2005; Caloyannides, 2003). Although surveillance is a legally sanctioned activity, some who practice it have exceeded their legal boundaries (Brey, 2006; Gelbord & Roelofsen, 2002; Griffin, 2007). While technology and digital recording capabilities evolve exponentially, government and civil-rights advocates struggle to reach agreement on the privacy implications of technology (Gelbord & Roelofsen, 2002).

Recent deadly shootings such as those at Virginia State University and Polytechnic Institute in 2006, at Delaware State University in 2007, and at Northern Illinois University in 2008 have shaken students, parents, and administrators with the realization that similar events could happen on any university campus (Lipka, 2007; Hoover & Lipka, 2007). Likewise, "several tacks have been taken to try to plug the gaps in intelligence and security" related to issues of national security, such as 911; the attacks of which, have only served to also heighten the perceived need for surveillance nationwide (Lyon, 2002, p. 3). Furthermore, due to these unexpected and extremely violent incidents, universities are searching for remedies, such as the use of surveillance technology (e.g. CCTV), which can be installed rather quickly. However, in their haste to find a solution to the problem, university administrators might move to install CCTV systems without considering the full social consequences and effects on students, faculty, and staff. These examples serve to support Lyon's statement that whether national, regional, or local issues are at hand, "surveillance of all became routine during the twentieth century" (Lyon, 2002, p. 2).

Lyon (2002, p. 3) suggests that, "privacy can no longer refer to fixed spaces. Both privacy and surveillance now exist in a world of *flows*" (italics added by Lyon) (Castells, 1996). He goes on to suggest that since so many people travel through so many different and open settings, that people can no longer hope to avoid surveillance; as is the case with a University's public setting. Furthermore, these conclusions support the inclusion of Floridi's 2P2Q theoretical framework delineated below. In that, as people are increasingly transient, and move between or in and out of regions of surveillance, their individual infosphere-based ontological friction should contract and expand accordingly. Therefore, the purpose of this study was to explore graduate students' views on privacy and safety, involving the use of CCTV in a public setting. To accomplish this purpose, the following research questions were addressed:

- What are the perceived rights regarding privacy and safety at a large, public, Land-grant University?
- What is the University's role and responsibility to provide a safe environment that also respects individuals' privacy?

- How do perceptions of privacy and security change with the implementation of a CCTV system?

The research questions were examined using a Piagetian constructivist epistemological framework, which holds that knowledge is objective and can be validated through various forms of exploratory experimentation. In this research, interviews were used to query the beliefs and perceptions of the participants. The sample was drawn from a large land-grant research university that had recently decided to install CCTV. The ultimate intent of the research was to provide a framework for understanding perceptions regarding privacy concerns and CCTV. The findings from this research could enable the university's administrators to respond to the safety and privacy needs of graduate students, and it could provide other universities with a framework for the decision to implement a CCTV system. Also, if universities decide to implement CCTV, future research based on this study's findings could help establish guidelines for promoting awareness of the pros and cons of a CCTV system.

Conceptual Framework

Several literature-based theories were reviewed and considered as frameworks for this study, the two main theories of which included Floridi (2005) and Tavani (2008). This paper does not attempt to delineate between the various theories or purposefully build upon the theories in the field of Privacy, Security, and Surveillance. Admittedly, there is much debate in this field of inquiry regarding which theory is most philosophically correct. Instead of yet another philosophical argument, it was a tertiary intent of this study to attempt to apply the chosen theory (Floridi, 2005) to an actual, exploratory study based on the grounded theory methodology. Floridi's 2p2q was chosen based on a review of the associated literature, a comparison with other theories in this field, and ultimately through a determination that Floridi's theory appeared most axiomatic and pragmatically applicable to the study in question. Therefore, this study was not an attempt to validate Floridi's theory, but rather used this model to inform the interpretations and outcomes of the data. Moreover, the limitations of using only one theory are acknowledged; and therefore, it may be prudent and feasible, given the data presented herein, to reinterpret this study's findings using yet a different theory. However, for the sake of time and space, those efforts are best left for future research.

Floridi's theory (2005) introduced the concept of an infosphere, in which 'ontological friction' becomes a measure or metric of informational privacy; or, an individual's perception of privacy (or lack thereof). The underpinnings of Floridi's theory are based on a widely accepted informational privacy hypothesis known as 2P2Q (Floridi, 2005). The precepts for this hypothesis address the issue of Informational and Communication Technology's (ICTs) ability to aggravate privacy concerns. Due to increasing technological advancements, globalization through computerized applications, and instant communicative capabilities, the 2P2Q hypothesis suggests that the ever increasing data *Processing (P)* capabilities (e.g., increased computer power) and the *Pace (P)* at which data can be processed (e.g., increased global bandwidth capabilities and computer-processing sharing capabilities), coupled with the data *Quantity (Q)* (e.g., sheer file size increases and storage capabilities) and data *Quality (Q)* (e.g., less data loss over networks, such as clearer internet-video conference capabilities) that can be assimilated, increasingly exacerbate informational privacy concerns (Floridi, 2005).

Floridi (2005) suggested that ontological friction in any infosphere can be represented by identifying the 1) region of the infosphere (e.g., the location of concern, such as a university); 2) informational agents (e.g. the constituents or participants in question, such as students, or visitors of the university, as well as those monitoring the

video feeds); and 3) the limited environment (e.g., limited by only focusing on the areas of campus that are monitored by CCTV cameras). When considered together, these three coefficients establish the 'informational gap' between the agents, or in other words, their ontological friction. When the informational gap between agents decreases, their level of information privacy decreases; likewise, as the informational gap increases, privacy increases as well.

For example, in small infospheres (or small/close physical spaces such as in a small classroom), where the information gap is small since constituents can likely see, hear, or otherwise sense the other agents in the region, the presence of CCTV does not necessarily change the ontological friction in such an environment (i.e., in this example, even without CCTV, there is little expectation of privacy; thus, with CCTV, there is still only a low expectation of privacy). Although as in the previous example, the ontological friction caused by a CCTV system can be represented using the infosphere model, this theory alone may not entirely represent the privacy issues related to CCTV.

Speculatively, CCTV has only a passive effect on an individual's infosphere. The effect is passive since all other individuals in the infosphere do not necessarily have an active role in creating or limiting the information gap (i.e., other constituents in the limited environment do not have access to the video tapes and those types of items that would limit privacy, other than the fact that they too are being monitored). With this in mind, constituents are negligibly aware that the only individuals that are monitoring or reviewing the videotapes (i.e., the agents) will have influenced or decreased their informational gap. In other words, since no one is actively walking around videotaping constituents, constituents are theoretically much less aware of the informational gap, and thus the ontological friction (or perception of a lack of privacy) is diminished. The agents (those monitoring the video tapes) are only symbolized and represented to the other constituents in the limited environment by the mere presence of the CCTV system, or camera, which may be easily disregarded. With this passive exposure to the agents of friction, constituents may or may not actually perceive the ontological friction created by the informational gap caused by the CCTV system.

Since no research was identified regarding graduate students' perceptions of privacy and safety involving CCTV systems, it is unknown if participants will perceive CCTV as having a positive or negative effect on their infosphere. Thus, the 2P2Q theory might help to interpret the findings of this research by enabling researchers to understand participants' perceptions regarding their personal level of privacy in relation to their perceptions of CCTV and safety.

REVIEW OF LITERATURE

The literature review begins by describing the historical uses of CCTV systems, purported effects of CCTV systems, public responses to the systems, and governmental positions regarding the systems. This background is followed by a brief discussion of privacy and legality questions of such systems, especially in the electronic environment of the 20th and 21st century. Finally, more recent trends in CCTV system implementation efforts are described, especially in light of increased occurrences of campus violence. The literature review thus explains the history and current trends of CCTV systems, including questions as to their legality and the perceived need in order to provide a safe environment to faculty, staff and students of university campuses.

Historical Use of CCTV

The chronological origins of CCTV are inexact. However, it is known that various countries had accepted and adopted surveillance technologies in the early 20th century. In 1949, George Orwell published his novel, *Nineteen Eighty-Four*. The novel introduced the concept of an Orwellian society in which its members have no right to privacy, and whose members' movements and daily actions are recorded by the government (Taylor, 2002).

While this book was not the cause of the fear CCTV may espouse, it exemplifies a historical paradigm attributed to the initial concept and fear of government watching every action of the public; which in turn, may have prompted privacy advocates to pursue enhanced legal protections for individual privacy (Schlosberg & Ozer, 2007; Taylor, 2002). While the initial uses of surveillance technologies had little to do with limiting privacy, but rather protecting human, independent organizational, or national interests, privacy advocates argued that privacy was invaded nonetheless (Nieto, 1997; Privacy International, 2007; Schlosberg & Ozer, 2007).

In addition to the CCTV implementations by independent organizations in the 1960s and 1970s, governments began to experiment with CCTV systems to protect national security. They began to expand their use of CCTV systems when experiments showed that CCTV systems might be able to reduce crime and aid in the investigation of suspected criminals (Nieto, 1997). Private companies adopted this idea and it aided them in their goal of reducing crime in corporate complexes and shopping malls. To preemptively address and overcome any potential public reluctance and fears of privacy invasion, governments and security-sensitive organizations promoted the social acceptance of CCTV surveillance through campaigns such as "CCTV: Looking out for you" (Wikipedia, 2007).

With the increase in CCTV usage, crime rates appeared to decline at significant rates, and the benefits of CCTV were widespread and relatively inexpensive (Chace, 2001; NIJ, 2003; Schlosberg & Ozer, 2007). Cities could 'patrol' multiple public areas without having to place an officer in the vicinity. CCTV recordings have been used to identify, capture, and convict countless criminals.

Moreover, the presence of CCTV systems were a deterrent for crime, decreasing burglaries by 56%, property damage by 34%, and vehicle theft by 11% (NIJ, 2003). However, while most of the advertising or promotion of CCTV was conducted by politicians, media, and other governmental regulation agencies, CCTV success as a surveillance technology was highly dependent on each individual implementation, whether governmental or by a private organization. Failed implementations were often highlighted by media, and it was possible that one or two unsuccessful implementations could derail the entire effort.

It is not surprising that these government promotions worried privacy advocates (Brey, 2006; Gelbord & Roelofsen, 2002; Schlosberg & Ozer, 2007). If, as a result of the government promotions, society gave up its collective right to privacy, privacy advocates believed that an unrelenting invasion of privacy might be close at hand. Despite these concerns, the use of CCTV continued to increase. For example, in 2003, it was determined that British citizens living in mid-to-high density cities have their picture taken, or are video recorded, an average of 300 times per day (NIJ, 2003). While there are large-scale CCTV implementations, most CCTV systems are used in a small or limited environment, and are hosted by independent organizations versus the government. The data or video collections from these environments or organizations are usually not shared, with the exception of law enforcement or other necessary entities.

While an attempt has been made to justify the increased use of CCTV through a crime reduction campaign, anti-CCTV campaigns have also been launched to expose the unintended and potentially negative consequences of CCTV. Aside from concerns regarding the vast number of times an individual is video-recorded, privacy advocates cite misuse of CCTV systems; to include a complete lack of standard operating procedures and training, misuse of video tapes or other digital data, as well as a sheer lack of regulatory enforcement (Chace,

2001). There are five concerns that represent the issues that most privacy scholars agree must be addressed prior to any, especially large-scale, or national CCTV system being implemented.

1. **Proportionality:** does the level of risk or safety threat to society warrant the use of CCTV?
2. **Legality:** all operators of CCTV systems must be trained according to the new standard operating procedures, and they must sign a code-of-conduct.
3. **Accountability:** CCTV users must ensure that usage adheres to the codes set forth in the new laws.
4. **Necessity/compulsion:** is CCTV the only way to accomplish the crime prevention goals?
5. **Subsidiarity:** the CCTV system must operate in a way that creates minimal interference with an individual's right to privacy (Armitage, 2002).

While the boundaries provided by new laws have enabled CCTV users to legally implement their crime prevention systems, many concerns are still raised about the enforcement and follow-through on any privacy laws and CCTV implementations (Armitage, 2002). If strict legal standards are not followed, the potential legal value of a CCTV system, or value as evidence can be diminished or eliminated.

In many cases, if an organization, whether private, public, governmental, or otherwise, implements a CCTV system, it is usually with the intent to decrease, deter or prevent crime, and ensure the security of organizational assets and human capital. If crimes are committed, most organizations prosecute offenders. Therefore, it is believed that those with CCTV systems have an advantage in prosecuting offenders as the systems may have captured video footage of the offense. However, if the video system is not maintained with videos being recorded and stored appropriately and with strict security controls over who has access to the videos, the video's value and creditability as evidence dissolves, and would be useless in court. Therefore, as organizations continue to implement CCTV to prevent crime; serious deliberation should also be given to the maintenance and security of the CCTV system, recordings, and storage, which has significant implications for privacy of individuals.

Legal Right to Privacy

There has been a long debate as to whether the Bill of Rights to the U.S. Constitution formally affords all persons in the U.S. with a right to privacy. While the U.S. Constitution does not specifically explicate an individual's right to privacy, it is believed by many to be inherent in a number of the decisions issued by the Supreme Court of the United States, and in many of the amendments in the Bill of Rights (Nieto, 1997; Nissenbaum, 1998). Because a right to privacy has not been clearly established, the debate continues. Additionally, cultural differences of what constitutes privacy and what aspects of a person's life are legally protected are central to this study, as 42% of the graduate students at the university in this study are international graduate students.

In most developed countries, there are many facets of privacy. However, most current privacy laws can be categorized into a few main types. The aim of most developed-nations' governments is to protect the individual's privacy through health, financial, online, communication, international, and general privacy laws (Nieto, 1997; Nissenbaum, 1998; Spencer, 2000).

The U.S. and other developed nations have become increasingly digitized. This creates increased opportunity for a change in an individual's informational gap. Part of the privacy debate is whether an individual's right to privacy, and the laws protecting privacy, have expanded enough or representatively, as new technology emerges. One of the newest, yet not comprehensive, areas

of law regarding privacy is the area of law protecting digital information (Nissenbaum, 1998; Schlosberg & Ozer, 2007). Digital information includes areas such as online or internet actions, certain subscription information, as well as videos or transcripts that may contain personally identifiable information or data. It is under this set of laws that arguments surrounding the installation and employment of closed circuit television (CCTV) systems have escalated (Chace, 2001). In some instances, CCTV is simply an analog video recording system that captures images of people and areas. However, in many new CCTV systems, digital versions of the video are being recorded as video files on hard-drives and in databases, and technologies such as facial recognition are being utilized. Therefore, as technology continues to advance, the newest CCTV systems are increasingly digitized. To further understand issues leading to the digital advancements of CCTV and the laws that address privacy, a brief overview of the historical use of CCTV is discussed.

Recent Trends in CCTV

Regardless of the lack of standardization of privacy protection laws and CCTV operating procedures, the number of CCTV implementations has continued to increase. Moreover, technology has enabled more efficient and effective surveillance systems at ever decreasing prices. Since September 11, 2001, there has been a significant increase in CCTV use (Bellovin, 2005; Brey, 2006; Griffin, 2007). Surveillance systems have become so inexpensive, that nearly any individual, organization, or institution can afford to implement a CCTV system. In theory, all CCTV systems are only legal as long as their procedures adhere to the legal standards. However, no documentation was identified that explicated the true state of CCTV use (Chace, 2001). Additionally, although it may be inexpensive to implement a CCTV system, the ongoing cost of maintaining and securing the system to the levels required for use as evidence are increasingly hard to measure and sustain. Furthermore, while the U.K. has laws that are moderately applicable to CCTV systems, with the lack of strict and directly applicable laws in the U.S., most CCTV operators are completely unaware of any necessary security (Chace, 2001).

New technological advancements are helping to enable more accurate, stable, and secure video privacy systems. While video surveillance is becoming omni-present, especially in city life, new technological advancements show promise in their ability to provide the safety aspects of surveillance systems, when combined with the video data and storage requirements needed for legal use (e.g., evidence in a legal case), while limiting privacy intrusions (Senior et al., 2005). Yet within each CCTV installation there may be a lack of U.S. governmental and legal support to verify its legality, security, and value. Without proper regulation and licensing of CCTV systems, and without governmental support to enforce the regulations and licensing, a law in and of itself would not be enough. Again, this is due to the increasing number of CCTV systems that are being privately installed, and thus need oversight and require enforcement. In addition to a lack of regulation, there is no official licensing arm of the government to continually enforce privacy standards. This suggests that until there is proper enforcement, there will be little, if any, impact on the actual practices used with CCTV systems.

Institutions of higher education are no exception regarding the increased use of CCTV (Griffin, 2007). For example, the University of Iowa implemented a campus-wide CCTV system shortly after September 11, 2001. With continued campus security and safety problems, such as the shootings at Virginia Tech, more higher education institutions are implementing CCTV, with hopes of deterring or eliminating criminal activity on campus (Griffin, 2007). Similar to many other higher education institutions, the university in this study has been studying these trends in CCTV, weighing the crime prevention benefits, and the costs to the institution, as well as to individual privacy. After much deliberation as to whether or not to implement a CCTV system, in September 2007, the university decided that it would invest $6 million to implement a campus-wide CCTV system. The captain of the university Police Department stated that he believed the CCTV system would help to deter crimes and aid in investigations (Thomas, 2007). Normally, it would be suggested that research efforts focus on studying whether or not to pursue a CCTV implementation. Since the university has already formally approved the implementation of a campus-wide CCTV system, this study sought to examine graduate students' perceptions of the forthcoming installment.

METHODOLOGY

Grounded Theory

For exploratory research questions that have limited empirical support, qualitative methods are the most appropriate means for data collection. Grounded theory provides a framework to examine new phenomena. Due to the emergent nature of concepts, the researcher conducts data collection parallel to the data analysis process, and uses the constant-comparative method of inquiry (Corbin & Strauss, 1990; Creswell, 2003). As concepts emerge from the interviews and data analysis, researchers codify them into concepts, which are then classified into themes that are fundamental to the research outcomes. Moreover, as research progresses and new themes are identified, the constant-comparative method of inquiry allows for an adaptation of the interview questions that will be better suited to investigate the new phenomena. Finally, a narrative interpretation of the findings is presented.

This qualitative study used grounded theory to examine graduate students' perceptions of privacy and safety as they relate to closed circuit television systems (CCTV). When considering grounded theory, one can take approaches as described by Glaser or Straus. Because of the nature of this research and the differences between the two approaches, aspects of each approach were included in this research study. This research used the inductive and emergent Glaserian approach while using the theoretical sensitive coding, theoretical sampling and the contextually relevant comparative analysis of Straus (1987). Since this research was an exploratory examination of graduate students' perceptions, interviews were determined to be the most effective method for data collection (Borg & Gall, 1989; Corbin & Strauss, 1990; Creswell, 2003).

Sample

The population for this study consisted of all current graduate students at a large Midwestern research university. Since this was an exploratory study of a qualitative nature, a small sample was adequate to address the research questions (Creswell, 2007, 2009; Creswell & Clark, 2007). Because the university has one of the nation's highest percentages of international graduate students and a growing population of nontraditional graduate students, it was desired that these demographic segments be represented in the sample. In fact, the percentage of international students represented in the sample is commensurate with the number of international students at the university in this study. Nontraditional graduate students were defined as individuals who had been separated from formal education for at least ten years prior to becoming graduate students. The international and nontraditional segments were included due to the fact that their backgrounds might lead them to hold different perceptions regarding privacy, technology, safety, and CCTV systems. In addition to these attributes, graduate students in general have more and different life experiences than undergraduate students, and thus have a broader basis of experiences upon which to base an understanding of the privacy concerns and

implications of a CCTV system. Finally, in addition to the above reasons, graduate students were selected as the sample for this study as they are an under-studied group of individuals on university campuses as compared to undergraduate students.

Participants were recruited by word-of-mouth. This is a non-probability convenience sampling technique that is sometimes referred to as snowball sampling (Crewswell, 1998; Portney & Watkins, 2000). The interviews were conducted in a location of the participant's choice, usually in their office or the researcher's office. When conducting interviews as a research technique, a narrow range of questions can be asked of a larger number of people or a larger and more in-depth set of questions can be asked of a smaller number of people (Creswell & Clark, 2007; Patton, 2002). Therefore, as is common with qualitative, exploratory research (Creswell & Clark, 2007, p. 112), a small sample size of 10 graduate students was obtained. The sample size was limited as recommended by Creswell (1998, 2003, 2007, 2009) and Creswell and Clark (2007 p. 112), leading the researchers to stop soliciting participants when the same themes arose repeatedly and no new themes or information were disclosed in the interviews, a point known as saturation.

The saturation technique was utilized to limit the number of extraneous interviews, when it was determined the interviews were no longer providing new information that added to new knowledge or understanding; hence the sample size of 10 participants. Specifically, it was determined that at the conclusion of the 7th interview (which consisted of 5 U.S., and 2 International students), no new information had been received. Accordingly, and in keeping with the respective sample percentages, two more U.S. graduate students were interviewed (one traditional graduate student and one non-traditional), and one more international graduate student was interviewed. None of these three additional interviews uncovered new knowledge, and thus saturation was ensured. Each interview lasted approximately

45-60 minutes. Table 1 displays the demographics of the participants. The questions used in the interviews are shown in the Appendix.

It should be noted however that a limitation and strength of qualitative research exists in the exploratory nature and the ordered and structured delivery of the interview questions. A limitation of interviewing is that in responding, the participants engage their unique mental models, schema, pre-conceptions, experiences and biases, which are unknown to the interviewer. These may significantly influence a participant's response to a question (Creswell, 2009). However, using the constant comparative method of inquiry allows the interviewer to explore these schema using follow-up questions, thus providing a greater benefit to the interview and study overall.

Analysis of Data

Qualitative research requires that specific data collection, data recording, data analysis, and interpretation procedures be followed for valid qualitative research (Creswell, 2003; Corbin & Strauss, 1990; Goulding, 2005). Validity, sometimes referred to as authenticity, credibility, or trustworthiness, is a strength of qualitative research (Cresswell & Miller, 2000). There are a number of procedures to help ensure validity in qualitative research

(Cresswell, 2003), and this study employed two: triangulation and member-checking. To ensure the quality of the data analysis performed in this study, the research followed the six data analysis steps established by Creswell (2003), Corbin and Strauss (1990), and Goulding (2005) as effective methods for conducting valid qualitative research. In general, the steps are: 1) to organize and prepare data for analysis by transcribing interviews; 2) to become familiar with data transcripts by reading through them and reflecting on their overall meaning; 3) to begin detailed analysis by coding data into related sections, reviewing sections for consistency and similarity, and then labeling each section with a distinguishable code; 4) to create general descriptions and categories for the explanations of the emergent themes in the data; 5) to analyze and discuss the emergent themes and develop a narrative that will represent the data; 6) to bring meaning to the data, and providing an interpretation of the data, in light of any narrative that was derived in step five. In step 3, the data can be coded by hand or by using a qualitative software program. The researchers coded the data by hand and followed the previous six steps in performing the data analysis for this effort. In performing the steps, the researchers ensured credibility, dependability, and conformability of the research. To ensure transferability, during

Table 1. Sample Demographics

Number	Gender	Major	Graduate Year	Nationality
1	Female	Developmental Psychology	3rd yr PhD	American
2	Male	International Business and Manufacturing	2nd yr MS	Nigerian
3	Female	Technology	2nd yr MS	Polish
4	Male	Child Development and Family Studies	1st yr PhD	American
5	Female	Developmental Studies	4th yr PhD	American
6	Female	Psychology	1st yr PhD	American
7	Male	Industrial Engineering	4th yr PhD	Colombian
8	Female	Conflict Management	4th yr PhD	American
9	Female	Engineering Education	5th yr PhD	American
10	Male	Lean Healthcare	2nd yr MS	American

the data analysis process, quotations from the interviews were selected to support the emergent themes from the research. The emergent themes and the selected quotes from the interviews are presented below.

Upon completing these steps, it was necessary for researchers to validate their findings to ensure accuracy and representativeness of their interpretations. This research established validity by using member-checking (Creswell, 2003). After each interview was transcribed, researchers reviewed the transcription with the participant to ensure both accurate representations of their perceptions as well as a verbatim transcription of the interview. Themes, and participant specific quotes identified from the interview transcriptions, were also reviewed with the interviewee as part of the member-checking process. Upon review, the interviewee was then asked if they had any other comments regarding the interview questions. Each interview was concluded only after the participant reviewed their transcript. Triangulation of sources (Patton, 1999) was utilized to examine the consistency of the information provided by the interviewees.

Emergent Themes

The data from the interviews were coded into themes based on the emergent groupings of comments and concerns made by participants. No preconceived groupings were used; rather the emergent themes were a direct result of participants' comments in response to the interview questions. While the interviews followed a similar pattern of questioning for each participant, since this study employed the constant comparative method of inquiry, each interview was unique. Thus, while the emergent theme-titles appear to closely represent the main questions from the interviews; these themes were only identified post-hoc. Although saturation was met, due to the

small sample size, and the nature of exploratory, grounded theory research, the data and implications presented herein are only transferable to those individuals who participated in the study, and not to the population at-large.

The emergent themes from this research were identified as: right to safety, right to privacy, personal privacy responsibilities, post-CCTV sense of privacy, post-CCTV sense of safety, crime displacement, false sense of safety, and international perspectives. There was a slight difference in perceptions between men and women regarding participants' initial perceptions of safety, post-CCTV implementation. The themes presented here are representative of only those students who participated in the research. In the following sections, each theme is presented along with supporting quotations. The age and gender of the participants who provided the quotes are provided to help understand the meaning of the quotes.

Right to Safety

Participants were asked to discuss what they perceived as their right to safety as a graduate student at the university. Most participants discussed the open nature of the University; it's buildings, classrooms, and even some offices. Although the university has a relatively dense campus, where no external or third-party businesses reside, the campus is not a closed campus to persons or vehicles. However, most participants felt they had a greater right to safety as a student on campus than the average citizen, mostly since they were paying the University.

A 23 year old male said:

I think the University does have to enforce things, and I'm paying money to be here, so I feel they should foster an environment where I feel safe, but at the same time, where I don't feel invaded.

A 25 year old female said:

As a student, I have the right to feel safe in my working environment; I should be able to feel safe without worrying about whether I'm going to get hurt or something. Like to know that there's at least some measures put in place to help keep me safe, such as the police department and public services like that.

A 33 year old male said:

I think the University should look to provide all the appropriate safeguards to provide safety for all of its constituents. Have a set of procedures, tools, equipment, staff, and so on, that enable the university to oversee what happens on campus.

Right to Privacy

Participants were asked to discuss what they perceived as their right to privacy as a graduate student at the university. Initially, participants began by discussing what they perceived as their universal right to privacy. However, since universities have more access to private information about students, participants also mentioned specific areas for which universities need to have privacy protection rules, such as one's health, financial, and educational records. In general though, participants described their right to privacy in an all-inclusive manner.

A 27 year old female said:

Privacy is the right to keep my personal life secret, and if anybody needs any kind of information about me personally, I have a right to refuse to give this kind of information.

A 25 year old female said:

I think that the university is responsible for keeping private information within the University system.

I think they're responsible for making sure that the people that they employ at the University are aware of our rights.

A 26 year old male said:

I feel that it's the University's responsibility to monitor and evaluate the safety of the campus, therefore privacy on the campus is not as critical in my opinion. I would rather have a safe campus environment than a private campus environment.

Personal Privacy Responsibility

While discussing their perceptions regarding privacy as a graduate student, all participants commented that they felt maintaining and securing their privacy was predominantly their individual responsibility. While there are certain aspects of privacy that they cannot manage or ensure, such as who has access to their health or educational records, participants acknowledged that their actions, while in public, are their responsibility.

A 24 year old female said:

What I choose to do outside, if that violates my privacy, then, I violated it myself. You put yourself out there, so it's your responsibility

A 23 year old male said:

I think it's the University's responsibility to ensure that students know about their policies regarding privacy, that way student can act accordingly.

A 29 year old female said:

[CCTV] will be in a public space, so if you're doing anything wrong in a public space, then you're doing something you shouldn't be doing!

A 26 year old male said:

When you're on campus, you're not in private.

Post-CCTV Sense of Privacy

Participants were told that the university would be implementing a CCTV system, and were asked to think about how their perceptions of privacy would change after the CCTV implementation. Most participants had little, if any, reservations or negative perceptions regarding the CCTV privacy implications. Their perceptions may be tied to their initial feelings towards earlier questions; resulting in their belief that it is the University's responsibility to secure the campus, and that it is the student's responsibility to maintain their privacy when in public. Thus, if students were already likely to self govern their actions while in public, the implementation of a CCTV system was not likely to influence their behavior. Overall, the participants were most concerned with how the system or CCTV data would be used. However, they all agreed that there needs to be a standard set of operating procedures to oversee the CCTV implementation, operation, and security.

A 24 year old male said:

I don't think it's wrong to monitor at all, if it's done in an ethical way; if there's some kind of system in place to monitor who has access to the tapes and what they're used for, that's ok.

A 33 year old male said:

I don't have a problem with [CCTV] as long as when that information is stored or used, it is used for the right reasons... as long as those videos or that feedback remains private or with access to only those people that have authority to view it; for example, the police.

A 48 year old female said:

We're allowing anybody else to become more knowledgeable, more a part of our lives than

maybe we want them to be. This sounds extreme, but stalkers, people stealing identities; there's lots of ways to become a victim because your privacy is invaded, by cameras or other means.

Post-CCTV Sense of Safety

Participants were asked to discuss what they perceived their level of safety would be as a graduate student at the university, following a campus wide CCTV implementation. Women participants were more likely to have an initial perception of increased safety due to the CCTV system. However, it became apparent that the more the participant thought about the new safety environment, the more they became aware of their initial misperceptions. Participants realized that the video cameras may not actually be monitored 24/7/365. And thus, they were still vulnerable to be attacked with no guarantee of a monitoring agent that could alert authorities. However, besides the perceived deterrent effect on crime, and despite the lack of constant monitoring, participants still felt that the campus would be safer. Moreover, participants felt that the CCTV system would provide police an extra investigatory tool for trying to identify perpetrators.

A 23 year old male said:

[Dissenters] don't want anyone to know anything about them and are pessimistic, and are afraid of [CCTV] being used against them, when in fact it's trying to help their safety.

A 29 year old female said:

I think I'd feel a little more secure if they did it. I would know that someone was watching for us, and that if something horrific was going on, they could pinpoint the problem more quickly or catch it before it happens. Like if someone has a gun or is getting assaulted. I think it will streamline the way emergencies are handled.

A 25 year old female said:

I think in general [CCTV] is a good idea, because... if there was a crime, there could be at least some kind of video evidence.

Crime Displacement

While participants were discussing their perceptions of safety in a post-CCTV environment, most participants began to consider and deliberate another possible, yet unintended consequence of CCTV systems; possible crime displacement. Participants commented that the university would need to ensure that the entire campus is covered with CCTV cameras. Participants' perceptions were that if the entire campus was not monitored, criminals may move to the unprotected or unmonitored areas. Moreover, participants worried that even if all of the university was under surveillance, crimes may be displaced to neighboring communities. The perception was that participants were or would be cognizant of where the crimes may be displaced to and would thus be more careful when traveling to those areas or communities, regardless of whether or not there was a real or measurable displacement of crimes.

A 24 year old female said:

If they're going to implement it, they have to go full force; if not, then the criminals will just spread out to the areas where there aren't cameras. They're not going to stop, just go somewhere else.

A 23 year old male said:

Other major cities in the world already have this system in place and still have pretty sizable crime rates, respectably.

A 27 year old female said:

If there is someone doing something bad, then knowing that there's surveillance, they might move somewhere else.

False Sense of Safety

During the interview, while participants were being asked about their post-CCTV sense of safety, many participants began to modify their assumptions regarding the specific uses of the CCTV system. Their initial assumptions were that they were going to be monitored 24/7/365. However, it was evident that after pondering the safety implications of CCTV, participants began to realize that their initial perceptions of safety may be inaccurate. The discussion turned from participants feeling safer, to participants feeling like they still needed to take all necessary safety precautions regardless of CCTV, and not let their guard down. Most of the participants came to the conclusion, that while CCTV may deter or prevent some crimes, there are some types of crimes that are not as easily preventable. Participants gave examples of crimes they perceived as possibly unpreventable, such as those committed as an act of rage or passion, those from the drunk and disorderly, and those that may be expertly planned to avoid or mitigate CCTV surveillance. In these circumstances, participants felt that regardless of safety measure in place, criminals would be likely to commit crimes.

A 23 year old male said:

I do feel [CCTV] will create this certain sense of safety within the campus. Just a sense; it doesn't mean it will be a safe campus.

A 23 year old female said:

I don't think that [CCTV] would change my feeling of safety. If something were to happen to me and they do have the CCTV, they might be able to get some sort of evidence from that, but at the moment, that's not going to help me. Because that's not going to be monitored 24/7, so anything that's going to happen is going to happen, whether there is video or not.

A 48 year old female said:

I think that it gives people, students, a perception of safety that's not there, and that's even worse, because people perceive it's a safe environment, but it's not really safer. Then people don't take the precautions, because they have this wrong perception.

International Perspectives

In 2007 through 2009, the university was ranked as one of the top three universities in the U.S. in the number of enrolled international students. With a substantial number of international graduate students at the university, researchers felt it was vital to include their perspectives about privacy and safety within the context of U.S. culture, law, and society. This theme represents their general perceptions of privacy and safety at the university. All the international participants had been enrolled at the university between one and six years. The international educational experiences of participants are important because it provides the participants with a longitudinal mindset with which to compare their perceptions of the university in this research versus those from their home country. Overall, participants felt that the university was safer and more private than both their home country and other institutions of higher education abroad. They contended that this perception would only be increased with the implementation of a CCTV system.

A 23 year old male said:

I never feel my privacy is being violated. Compared to my home country, [the university] is a few generations ahead with regards to respecting people's privacy and providing safety for people.

A 27 year old female said:

This is the first campus actually that is being secured so much; because I'm an international student. I don't know any university in Europe providing police, so I think that the security here is on a high, high level, but I think that the CCTV would help.

A 33 year old male said:

Coming from a country like Colombia, where I could never leave my computer on a table, then coming here where I could leave it on the table for hours, that means that whatever procedures or whatever are implemented are working.

FINDING, IMPLICATIONS, AND FUTURE RESEARCH

Findings

As the interviews progressed, the graduate students seemed to reevaluate their perceptions of privacy and safety, both pre- and post- CCTV implementation. For the most part, initial perceptions were positive, and the graduate students perceived CCTV as being an effective means for creating a safer campus. As the interview progressed, participants began to alter their perceptions, from CCTV actually creating a safer environment, to CCTV simply providing and increasing their 'sense' of safety, not necessarily their actual safety. As the interviews continued, the participants seemed to become more cognizant of potentially unintended, yet significant consequences, hence the emergence of the themes dealing with 'crime displacement' and a 'false sense of safety'. While most graduate students still agreed that CCTV would be an effective means to increase safety, or at least a sense of safety, they began to comment on how not all crimes would be prevented. Ultimately, the interviews changed from the 'system' being responsible for the participants' safety, to how people need to still be aware of their surroundings and take all necessary safety precautions.

The participants' perceptions and emergent themes are consistent with the literature review. The literature suggests that initial perceptions toward the CCTV surveillance systems effects on privacy and safety are positive (Spencer, 2000). Moreover, while most constituents and institutions initially implement CCTV for safety reasons, most privacy, safety, and crime displacement concerns are not addressed nor realized until after the CCTV surveillance system has been implemented. Finally, the literature suggests that there is still a need to study the unintended consequences of CCTV on privacy, safety, and crime displacement, and the students' comments reflected this need as well (Armitage, 2002; Nieto, 1997). While the literature provides no consensus on crime displacement, future research could further investigate constituents' perceptions and possible reactions to the idea of crime displacement. For instance, if participants felt that crime was being displaced, would they be more or less likely to travel to those new locations?

The findings from this study, specifically, the ontological transformation of participants' perceptions, are also comparable to Floridi's (2005) 2P2Q theoretical 'infosphere' model. Since the CCTV surveillance cameras are slightly out of sight, and those monitoring the system are completely out of sight, participants' initial perceptions regarding privacy are unchanged. However, upon further reflection, participants began to become more aware of the other possible agents in their infosphere (i.e., the presence of signs demarcating the existence of CCTV cameras, thus bringing to

mind those monitoring the video feeds). After consciously paying attention to these agents, which in turn decreases the informational gap (i.e., the gap decrease since the monitoring agents can active monitor the constituents), the participants are thus more likely to sense the theoretically-supported increase in ontological friction (the friction that occurs when the informational gap is decreased); or, in other words, the participants are more likely to perceive a decrease in privacy. This finding supports the concerns of perceived and actual loss of privacy as raised by privacy advocates in the literature (Brey, 2006; Gelbord & Roelofsen, 2002; Schlosberg & Ozer, 2007).

Implications

This research could help institutions of higher education decide if they should implement a CCTV system; and, if so, how to implement such a system so as to maximize its efficiency, while minimizing the impact of constituents' privacy. While there is no clear consensus in the literature regarding the crime preventing effectiveness of CCTV, it appears that the participants perceive CCTV to posses such attributes. However, while CCTV may be perceived to be an effective way to prevent, if not deter crime, this research has provided the framework to investigate some of the unintended consequences. Specifically, participants felt that they were unsure as to whether or not there would be crime displacement, and whether or not they perceived a false sense of security. Accordingly, not only do legislative bodies need to pass laws standardizing CCTV installations, participants feel that there needs to be a strong and supporting body that can both regulate, enforce, and oversee the licensing of CCTV systems. Participants feel that standard operating procedures for who controls, monitors, and has access to videotapes or video feeds need to be established.

Although a broad concept of transferability is a limitation of qualitative research as compared to generalizability in quantitative research, the participants' perceptions can aid future researchers in developing a research effort that would further delineate and justify policy recommendations. The participants identified several policy concerns and implications including researching procedures regarding the most effective means of using CCTV for investigatory purposes; so as to ensure accurate representation of the event in question. Participants felt that research should be conducted on developing an oversight committee to monitor and oversee the operation of the CCTV system in order to ensure legal viability. Moreover, participants felt that an awareness campaign could aid in informing constituents as to the benefits of a CCTV system, and how to adjust their actions to maximize the effects of such a system.

This research was conducted at a university that had already decided to implement a CCTV system, hence the pre- and post- CCTV implementation question. Nonetheless, research should be conducted that evaluates at the pre- and post- CCTV implementation timeframe, to assess possible crime displacement issues, safety issues, and privacy concerns. Although some institutions and organizations implement CCTV under the assumption of increased safety and decreased crime, there is still debate in the literature as to which situations, locations, and specific factors make a CCTV campaign successful. A CCTV safety and privacy awareness research campaign could raise awareness about issues relating to CCTV systems. Students, staff, and faculty should be informed of the intended uses of the CCTV system, and how to maximize its effectiveness. Additionally, this education provided to faculty, staff and students could inform them about the purposes, pervasiveness, and limitations of the CCTV system, as well as how privacy is addressed by the organization's policies related to the CCTV system. It may be effective for organizations to intermittently collect data regarding the crime reduction and prevention, evidentiary uses, and crime displacement effects of the CCTV system for dissemination to constituents.

Limitations and Future Research

The themes from this research are applicable only to the students who were interviewed, and to the university setting in which this research was conducted. However, the emergent themes provide insight and a framework for the development of further research. This future research could help institutions of higher education decide if they should implement a CCTV system; and, if so, how to implement such a system so as to maximize its efficiency while minimizing the impact of constituents' privacy.

Future research could address the question: what are the perceived safety and privacy implications relating to CCTV for undergraduate students (and perhaps faculty and staff) at higher education institutions? The themes from this research provide a foundation for several hypotheses that could be used to examine the research question. Some suggested hypotheses are as follows:

H_1: Constituents believe that implementing a campus-wide CCTV system will better enable the university to fulfill its responsibility of providing a safe campus environment.

H_2: Constituents believe that implementing a campus-wide CCTV system will not decrease their level of privacy.

H_3: Constituents believe that implementing a campus-wide CCTV system will create a false sense of safety.

H_4: Constituents believe that implementing a campus-wide CCTV system will displace some crime to neighboring communities.

For each of these hypotheses, the common denominator is the implementation of a campus-wide CCTV system. For H_1 the focus would be perceptions of participants of the ability of the university to fulfill its responsibility to provide a safe campus environment. For H_2 the focus would be the constituent's perceived level of privacy. For H_3 the focus would be the participant's belief that

CCTV will provide a false sense of safety to other constituents. For H_4, the focus would be the displacement of crime to neighboring communities. This future research could be performed using a quantitative or mixed-methods approach based on the findings of this qualitative exploratory study.

The difference in findings between the groups could provide insight into the value of possible CCTV implementations and possible awareness campaigns about CCTV systems for university constituents. Several other research questions could then be addressed.

Example 1: Is CCTV the most effective way to ensure safety on a university campus?

Example 2: Does an awareness campaign further increase a university constituent's perceptions of the CCTV system's safety effects?

Example 3: Are university constituents more or less likely to perceive CCTV to violate their right to privacy after an awareness campaign?

These issues could be addressed through either qualitative or potentially quantitative research, and possibly transferred or generalized to an entire university population, if not institutions of higher education in general, depending on the research type and design. These future studies are important, because institutions of higher education are rapidly embracing the use of CCTV as a means to further secure their campuses. Researching university constituents' perceptions towards CCTV is important, as it may provide universities and society with a better understanding of how to best implement a CCTV system, and possibly awareness campaigns.

REFERENCES

Armitage, R. (2002). *To CCTV or not to CCTV? A review of current research into the effectiveness of CCTV systems in reducing crime.* Retrieved from http://www.nacro.org.uk

Bellovin, S. (2005). Security and privacy: Enemies or allies? *IEEE Security & Privacy*, *3*(3), 92. doi:10.1109/MSP.2005.80

Borg, W. R., & Gall, M. D. (1989). *Educational research*. White Plains, NY: Longman.

Brey, P. (2006). Surveillance and privacy. *Ethics and Information Technology*, *7*, 183–184. doi:10.1007/s10676-006-0015-1

Caloyannides, M. (2003). Society cannot function without privacy. *IEEE Security & Privacy*, *1*(3), 84–86. doi:10.1109/MSECP.2003.1203230

Chace, R. W. (2001). *An overview on the guidelines for closed circuit television (CCTV) for public safety and community policing*: *CCTV for Public Safety and Community Policing Guidelines and Supplemental Information*. Alexandria, VA: Security Industry Association.

Corbin, J., & Strauss, A. (1990). Grounded theory research: Procedures, canons, and evaluative criteria. *Qualitative Sociology*, *13*(1), 3–21. doi:10.1007/BF00988593

Creswell, J. W. (1998). *Qualitative inquiry and research design: Choosing among five traditions.* Thousand Oaks, CA: Sage.

Creswell, J. W. (2003). *Research design: Qualitative, quantitative, and mixed methods approaches* (2nd ed.). Thousand Oaks, CA: Sage.

Creswell, J. W. (2007). *Qualitative inquiry & research design: Choosing among five approaches* (2nd ed.). Thousand Oaks, CA: Sage.

Creswell, J. W. (2009). *Research design: Qualitative, quantitative, and mixed methods approaches* (3rd ed.). Thousand Oaks, CA: Sage.

Creswell, J. W., & Clark, V. L. P. (2007). *Designing and conducting mixed methods research.* Thousand Oaks, CA: Sage.

Creswell, J. W., & Miller, D. L. (2000). Determining validity in qualitative inquiry. *Theory into Practice, 39*(3), 124–130. doi:10.1207/s15430421tip3903_2

Floridi, L. (2005). The ontological interpretation of information privacy. *Ethics and Information Technology, 7*, 185–200. doi:10.1007/s10676-006-0001-7

Gelbord, B., & Roelofsen, G. (2002). New surveillance techniques raise privacy concerns. *Communications of the ACM, 45*(11), 23–24. doi:10.1145/581571.581586

Goold, B. J. (2004). *CCTV and policing: Public area surveillance and police practices in Britain.* New York, NY: Oxford University Press.

Goulding, C. (2005). Grounded theory, ethnography, and phenomenology: A comparative analysis of three qualitative strategies for marketing research. *European Journal of Marketing, 39*(3-4), 294–308. doi:10.1108/03090560510581782

Griffin, O. R. (2007). The evolving safety and security challenge. *Pierce Law Review, 5*(3), 413–432.

Hoover, E., & Lipka, S. (2007). Colleges weigh when to alert students to danger. *The Chronicle of Higher Education, 54*(15), 1.

Lipka, S. (2007). Lessons from a tragedy. *The Chronicle of Higher Education, 53*(34), 12.

Lyon, D. (2001). *Surveillance society: Monitoring everyday life.* Buckingham, UK: Open University Press.

Lyon, D. (2002). Surveillance studies: Understanding visibility, mobility and the phenetic fix. *Surveillance & Society, 1*(1), 1–7.

National Institute of Justice. (2003). *CCTV: Constant cameras track violators.* Retrieved from http://www.cops.usdoj.gov/html/cd_rom/tech_docs/pubs/CCTVConstantCamerasTrack-Violators.pdf

Nieto, M. (1997). *Public video surveillance: Is it an effective crime prevention tool?* Retrieved from http://www.library.ca.gov/CRB/97/05

Nissenbaum, H. (1998). Protecting privacy in an information age: The problem of privacy in public. *Law and Philosophy, 17*, 559–596.

Patton, M. (2002). *Qualitative research and evaluation methods* (3rd ed.). Thousand Oaks, CA: Sage.

Patton, M. Q. (1999). Enhancing the quality and credibility of qualitative analysis. *HSR: Health Services Research Part II, 34*(5), 1189–1208.

Portney, L. G., & Watkins, M. P. (2000). *Foundations of clinical research: Applications to practice.* Upper Saddle River, NJ: Prentice-Hall.

Privacy International. (2007). *CCTV frequently asked questions.* Retrieved from https://www.privacyinternational.org/article/cctv-frequently-asked-questions

Schlosberg, M., & Ozer, N. A. (2007). *Under the watchful eye: The proliferation of video surveillance systems in California.* Retrieved from http://www.aclunc.org/docs/criminal_justice/police_practices/Under_the_Watchful_Eye_The_Proliferation_of_Video_Surveillance_Systems_in_California.pdf

Senior, A., Pankanti, S., Hampapur, A., Brown, L., Tian, Y., & Ekin, A. (2005). Enabling video privacy through computer vision. *IEEE Security & Privacy, 3*(3), 50–57. doi:10.1109/MSP.2005.65

Spencer, M. (2000). *CCTV and the protection of privacy: A tale of two cultures.* Retrieved from http://www.worldlii.org/int/journals/PLBIN/2000/43.html

Strauss, A. (1987). *Qualitative analysis for social scientists*. Cambridge, UK: Cambridge University Press. doi:10.1017/CBO9780511557842

Tavani, H. (2008). Informational privacy: Concepts, theories and controversies. In Hoven, J. V. D., & Weckert, J. (Eds.), *Information technology and moral philosophy* (pp. 131–164). Cambridge, UK: Cambridge University Press.

Taylor, N. (2002). State surveillance and the right to privacy. *Surveillance & Society, 1*(1), 66–85.

Thomas, A. (2007, September 12). Plan introduces safety cameras. *The Exponent*, p. A1.

Wikipedia. (2007). *Closed-circuit television.* Retrieved from http://en.wikipedia.org/wiki/Closed-circuit_television

APPENDIX

Interview Questions

1. How do you define privacy?
2. What do you believe your rights are as a student regarding safety?
3. What do you believe your rights are as a student regarding privacy?
4. What is your perception of the University's responsibility regarding student/campus safety?
5. What is your perception of the University's responsibility regarding student/campus privacy?
6. How do you feel about the University implementing a closed-circuit television (CCTV) system? (how would that change your feeling of safety?)
7. What would your perception of privacy be if the University implemented a closed-circuit television (CCTV) system?
8. What is your current perception regarding privacy at the University?
9. What is your current perception regarding safety at the University?

This work was previously published in the International Journal of Technology and Human Interaction, Volume 7, Issue 3, edited by Anabela Mesquita and Chia-Wen Tsai, pp.50-69, copyright 2011 by IGI Publishing (an imprint of IGI Global).

Chapter 10
Antecedents of Consumer Acceptance of Mobile Television Advertising

Yann Truong
ESC Rennes School of Business, France

ABSTRACT

Through a questionnaire survey, this study identifies and investigates seven antecedents of consumer acceptance of mobile TV advertising. Negative factors include intrusiveness, lack of trust in the advertiser, and excessive frequency; positive influences include enjoyment, originality, value, and relevance. The study proposes and validates two measurement models of these antecedents and provides insights into the most influential factors of consumer acceptance. Excessive frequency of advertisements and lack of trust in the advertiser present the two largest obstacles to consumer acceptance of this medium, while the entertainment aspects of advertising offer the major positive factors in gaining acceptance. The study recommends that mobile TV advertising stakeholders focus on achieving appropriate frequency, overcoming lack of trust in the advertiser, and providing enjoyment and originality, as these are the largest contributors to higher consumer acceptance.

INTRODUCTION

In this highly competitive environment, marketers also have little information about consumers' acceptance of mobile TV advertising, or even about mobile marketing in general (Hanley, Becker, & Martinsen, 2006). Yet the personal nature of mobile phones requires marketers to gain consumer acceptance for any form of marketing activities (du Pre Gauntt, 2008; Merisavo et al., 2007; Ranch-

hod, 2007). This study addresses the research inadequacies by examining the most important factors influencing consumer acceptance of mobile TV advertising. On the basis of a review of the nascent literature, this study tests a series of hypotheses using confirmatory factor analysis (CFA) and structural equation modeling (SEM). The results validate an exhaustive and robust measurement model for consumer acceptance of mobile TV advertising and increase understand-

DOI: 10.4018/978-1-4666-1954-8.ch010

Copyright © 2013, IGI Global. Copying or distributing in print or electronic forms without written permission of IGI Global is prohibited.

ing of the factors that most influence consumer acceptance of this rapidly growing form of mobile advertising.

The rise of mobile TV, which will soon rival traditional TV in terms of viewing time and occasions (Andersen, Jakobsen, & Nilsen, 2007; Rappaport, 2007), is generating intense competition within the industry to capture a portion of the growing revenues from both TV services and advertising. The latest estimates show that mobile television revenues will increase eight-fold between 2008 and 2012, reaching $10 billion worldwide (White, 2008), but these figures do not take into account the potential advertising revenues that will accompany the development of mobile TV. Mobile advertising allows advertisers to connect directly with individual consumers through a mobile phone, personal digital assistant (PDA), or laptop computer in real time, without spatial or wiring constraints (Frolick & Chen, 2004). In 2008, mobile phone sales alone reached 1.25 billion mobile phones worldwide, and several countries in Europe and Asia had penetration rates above 100% (Idate, 2008a, 2008b, 2009). Media applications on mobile phones are also expected to become mainstream in the near future (Repo, Hyvonen, Pantzar, & Timonen, 2006). Therefore, given the substantial potential of mobile phones in terms of audience reach, mobile advertising offers one of the most promising media for marketers and advertisers within the near future (Buellingen & Woerter, 2004; Ferris, 2007; Okazaki, 2006).

Advertisers are enthusiastic about mobile advertising's potential for many reasons. Mobile phones offer considerable potential for marketers in forging brand–consumer connections especially with teenagers and young adults. Since each mobile phone number represents a unique individual, one of the main advantages mobile advertising offers is the possibility of identifying and reaching specific consumers. This capability permits more personalized messages and more precisely targeted mobile advertising campaigns (Ranchhod, 2007). Additionally, mobile technologies

provide real-time performance metrics for measuring the effectiveness of a campaign (Vollmer, 2008). For example, advertisers can determine the exact number of users who actually open and read text messages during a campaign. Several studies demonstrate that mobile advertising increases consumer involvement, recall, and attitude in general (Okazaki, Katsukura, & Nishiyama, 2007; Trappey III & Woodside, 2005). Other potential advantages of mobile services include better customer relationships and additional revenues generated by new services (Merisavo, Vesanen, Arponen, Kajalo, & Raulas, 2006; Steinbock, 2006).

However, even though mobile advertising is likely to be the next big thing in marketing, few researchers have yet written on this topic because of its rapid development. Given the promising potential effects of mobile advertising on consumer behavior, empirical evidence of its effectiveness would significantly further academic knowledge in this new area of advertising. More particularly, one important area to focus on is the antecedents to consumer acceptance of advertising on mobile phones as this is a pre-requisite to any marketing activities on this medium.

MOBILE ADVERTISING

Advertising is used by marketers to build long-term brand image and maintain or increase sales (Zhou, Zhou, & Ouyang, 2003). Television is often considered as a traditional media vs. new media such as the Internet (Nagar, 2009). One of the main characteristics of television advertising is its ability to reach a mass audience and therefore maximize awareness of a product or brand (Wilbur, 2008). Even though advertising revenues from television has been transferring to new media, television advertising is still capturing the largest market share in the industry (Wilbur, 2008). Nevertheless, the extensive exposure time of advertising on television has led to an increasing negative opinion of advertising from viewers who often switch channels when advertisements interrupt the content (Alwitt & Prabhaker, 1994). Given the growing negative public opinion of advertising on traditional media, marketers seem to agree that advertising on new media should adopt a radically different approach (Nagar, 2009). For example, recent studies suggest that advertising on mobile phones should focus on consumer opt-in, avoid intrusive formats and propose exclusive and personalized contents (Andersen et al., 2007; Choi, Kim, & McMillan, 2009; Hanley et al., 2006; Merisavo et al., 2007; Okazaki et al., 2007; Shim, Park, & Shim, 2008).

Mobile advertising is a recent phenomenon that investigators predict will yield substantial revenues for mobile operators and technology enablers in the future (DeZoysa, 2002). Most published work on this topic is less than five years old and usually focuses on basic text advertising formats, such as short message service (SMS, or text messaging) and multimedia message service (MMS, or picture-based messaging). Studies so far reveal promising findings on the positive effects of mobile advertising on consumer behavior. For example, compared to traditional advertising (except cinema), mobile advertising effects included improved attitudes and better recall (Okazaki et al., 2007; Okazaki & Taylor, 2008), higher levels of consumer acceptance and responsiveness (Barwise & Strong, 2002), and increased purchase intent for mobile services (Nysveen, Pedersen, & Thorbjørnsen, 2005). However, consumers hold a very personal relationship with their mobile phones which accompany them everywhere and connect them to their community (Li & Stoller, 2007). For this reason, consumers can easily find irritating any advertising that appears on their mobile phones without their express consent (Heinonen & Strandvik, 2003).

Consumer acceptance of mobile advertising defines the willingness of the users to receive advertisements on their mobile phones (Bauer, Barnes, Reichardt, & Neumann, 2005). Acceptance depends on both negative and positive effects of that advertising. Negative effects relate to any issue that creates unfavorable attitudes or poor evaluations of advertisements (Eagly & Chaiken, 1993). The literature suggests three important negative factors: intrusiveness, undesirable frequency of advertisements, and lack of trust in the advertiser. Advertisements are perceived as intrusive when they are unsolicited and incongruent with the current task of the user and provoke irritation (Hernandez, Chapa, Minor, Maldonado, & Barranzuela, 2004). Given consumers' personal relationship with their mobile phones, perceived intrusiveness is perhaps the highest concern for advertisers (Li & Stoller, 2007), with the result that permission-based marketing is a critical prerequisite to effective mobile advertising (Ranchhod, 2007). Consumers also resist frequent solicitations on their mobile phones. One study finds that the optimal level of brand recall was five advertisements per day, although a slightly higher frequency seems to be acceptable if the advertisements provide a tangible value such as personalized promotional discounts (Li & Stoller, 2007). In general, consumers expect advertisements to be less frequent on mobiles than on other mass media (Haghirian & Madlberger, 2005). The third negative factor relates to lack of trust, which is associated with the users' fear that advertisers would infringe privacy laws (Merisavo et al., 2007). Though, lack of trust seems to be less critical than the two previous factors but may be one element that could radically repulse consumers who are sensitive to the source of the advertisements (Merisavo et al., 2007; Okazaki et al., 2007). For example, lack of trust in a brand would lead to rejection of the associated advertisement.

H₁: Perceived intrusiveness has a negative effect on consumer acceptance of mobile TV advertising.

H₂: Higher exposure frequency has a negative effect on consumer acceptance of mobile TV advertising.

H₃: Lack of trust in the advertiser has a negative effect on consumer acceptance of mobile TV advertising.

Positive factors of consumer acceptance of mobile TV advertising relate to the perceived value of exposure to advertisements and include relevance, value, enjoyment, and originality. Research regarding text- and picture-based mobile advertising suggests that the personal nature of mobile phones requires that any form of advertising should be relevant to the consumer, that is, personalized to the consumer's needs and presented at an opportune time and in an appropriate space (Merisavo et al., 2007; Xu, Liao, & Li, 2007). Consumers also expect advertising on mobile phones to be informative and to help them save time and money. Thus, the informative value of mobile advertisements seems to be an important factor (Haghirian & Madlberger, 2005; Xu et al., 2007). The third factor relates to the level of enjoyment, that is the extent to which viewing a particular advertisement lead to positive affect and mood of the consumer (Hoffman & Novak, 1996). Mobile devices provide extensive rich media applications to consumers (Lin & Hsu, 2009), who are used to interactive services and therefore expect advertising to be entertaining (Hanley et al., 2006). Moreover, consumers often view mobile TV on a "snacking" basis—that is, they access content for short periods of time to fill an empty or idle time slots (Andersen et al., 2007). This consumption pattern implies that consumer attention is more difficult to capture using a traditional TV advertising spot (Idate, 2008b), and suggests that mobile TV advertising may require special attention to both format and content. Mobile advertising in general differs from mass media advertising in that it is more suitable for pull rather than push campaigns (Leppäniemi, Karjaluoto, & Salo, 2004), and interactive advertising campaigns can contribute more toward more positive consumer experience than simple

push videos can. The last positive factor is the perceived originality of advertisements. Some industry reports posit that consumers are more willing to view advertising on their mobile phone if the advertisements are more creative and less common than those broadcast on traditional mass media (TNS, 2008).

H₄: Relevant advertising has a positive effect on consumer acceptance of mobile TV advertising.

H₅: Higher perceived tangible value has a positive effect on consumer acceptance of mobile TV advertising.

H₆: Higher perceived enjoyment has a positive effect on consumer acceptance of mobile TV advertising.

H₇: Higher perceived originality has a positive effect on consumer acceptance of mobile TV advertising.

Past studies have investigated some of these factors in the context of simple mobile advertising which mostly consists of text-based and image-based messages (Carroll, Barnes, Scornavacca, & Fletcher, 2007; Lin & Hsu, 2009; Okazaki & Taylor, 2008). However, mobile television advertising is more sophisticated because it is associated with short video contents on a small screen. Therefore, it is expected that consumers hold different expectations from advertisements that are shown when viewing broadcast contents. This study proposes to investigate the differences in consumer expectations in the case of mobile television advertising.

METHOD

The study tested the seven hypotheses using a two-stage process. The first stage consisted of building and validating two measurement models for the positive and negative factors using confirmatory factor analysis (with SPSS) and structural equation modeling (with AMOS). Hypothesis testing began once the two measurement models produced acceptable fit statistics.

Item Generation

The measurement model for negative factors included "trust" (perceived trust in the advertiser), "intrusiveness" (perceived intrusiveness of the ads) and "frequency" (frequency of the ads). The five items for trust followed Okazaki et al. (2007), and those for intrusiveness and frequency followed Merisavo et al. (2007) and Xu et al. (2007). All items used a seven-point Likert scale (1= strongly disagree, 7 = strongly agree), which includes a neutral point (Albaum, 1997; Garland, 1991).

The measurement model for the four positive factors that increase consumer acceptance of mobile TV advertising comprised "relevance" (personalized and contextualized ads), "value" (perceived value in being exposed to ads), "enjoyment" (perceived enjoyment of watching ads), and "originality" (perceived originality of ads). Past empirical studies on consumer acceptance of mobile advertising provided the basis for five items for each of the four factors. Items for relevance and value were modifications from Merisavo et al. (2007) and Haghirian and Madlberger (2005); those for enjoyment and originality were adaptations from Haghirian and Madlberger (2005) and Xu et al. (2007).

Item Translation and Purification

In preparation for a pilot study to test the questionnaire, two bilingual professors of marketing translated the 35 items (7x5) from English to French. Two different professors then back-translated the items. A professor of linguistics then reviewed the back-translated and original items to verify that the two sets of items still held similar semantic meanings. After verification of consistency, a con-

venience sample of 100 consumers in France and another 100 in the UK received the questionnaire in a pilot test. Recruitment of the consumers in the samples took place through online forums that discuss mobile television and videos. Confirmatory factor analysis of the data collected from the two samples produced consistent results for the two samples. Kaiser-Meyer-Olkin tests (>0.80) and Bartlett tests of sphericity (p<0.01) confirmed that the data were appropriate for factor analysis (Schumacker & Lomax, 2004). After removal of items that did not load with the expected factor with a loading of greater than 0.5 or that loaded on two different factors, the final set of 23 items generated satisfactory reliability scores. As SEM procedure recommends, at least three items measured each factor to ensure sufficient homogeneity and validity (Byrne, 2001),. Table 1 shows the final set of items with their corresponding factors.

Data Collection

Online posts in relevant mobile television and 3G video discussion forums in France recruited 361 consumers (after removal of 17 responses owing to missing data) who received the final questionnaire containing 23 items. The same recruitment method resulted in a smaller sample of 105 consumers in the UK, who received the English version of the questionnaire (after removal of four responses owing to missing data). The English sample served not as a dataset for an extensive comparative study as a point of comparison for validating the measurement instrument. For example, comparison of factor loadings and reliability scores verified that the two samples would produce similar results with the same measurement instruments. Similar results from the two samples, even with a smaller English sample, would strengthen the validation of the measurement instruments.

A message in the online post stated that all participants must have had prior 3G video or mobile TV experience, and an appropriate demographic

Table 1. Final set of items

Model 1: Negative Factors	
Trust (α = 0.78)	(N1) I think ads on mobile TV should provide objective information on the advertised brand. (N2) I think ads on mobile TV should be strictly compliant with privacy laws and regulations. (N3) I think ads on mobile TV should only contain trustworthy content.
Frequency (α = 0.72)	(N4) I think too many ads on mobile TV would make it less enjoyable (RC). (N5) I think I would be bothered if there are too many ads on mobile TV (RC). (N6) I think there should not be any ads on mobile TV (RC).
Intrusive (α = 0.80)	(N7) If I am watching TV on my mobile, advertising would be annoying. (N8) Advertising on mobile TV would get in the way of enjoying the program. (N9) I think mobile TV advertising would waste my time.
Model 2: Positive Factors	
Enjoyment (α = 0.85)	(P1) I would be prepared to view ads on mobile TV if they are amusing. (P2) I would be prepared to view ads on mobile TV if they are fun. (P3) I would be prepared to view ads on mobile TV if they are entertaining. (P4) I would be prepared to view ads on mobile TV if they are enjoyable.
Originality (α = 0.86)	(P5) I would be prepared to view ads on mobile TV if they are creative. (P6) I would be prepared to view ads on mobile TV if they are original. (P7) I would be prepared to view ads on mobile TV if they are innovative.
Value (α = 0.90)	(P8) I would be prepared to view ads on mobile TV if they are associated with some sort of promotions. (P9) I would be prepared to view ads on mobile TV if they inform me of good deals. (P10) I would be prepared to view ads on mobile TV if they provide me with useful information. (P11) I would be prepared to view ads on mobile TV if they help me save time.
Relevance (α = 0.85)	(P12) I would be prepared to view ads on mobile TV if they suit my lifestyle. (P13) I would be prepared to view ads on mobile TV if they suit my current needs. (P14) I would be prepared to view ads on mobile TV if they are about brands that interest me.

representation of the targeted population was a primary objective. The TeleAnalytics Mobile TV Highlights (2008) characterize the typical mobile TV user to be an educated younger person (mid-20s to mid-30s) with an above average income, living in an urban area and holding a higher degree. To avoid community biases, a variety of carefully selected forums carried the posts advertising the study. Both the French and English samples were reasonably representative of the targeted population in terms of gender (France: 55% males, UK: 47%), average age (France: 28, UK: 27), average income (France: 15% above average, UK: 10%), and education (France: 70% hold higher degrees, UK: 62%). All participants had prior experience with either mobile TV or 3G video, and 70% had experienced both.

MODEL VALIDATION

Fit tests, convergent validity tests, and discriminant validity tests, which are the most common tests for validating measurement instruments (Schumacker & Lomax, 2004), validated the two measurement models (positive and negative factors). Satisfactory results on all three tests indicate that the models are acceptable as measurement instruments for positive and negative factors affecting mobile TV acceptance.

Fit Tests

The results for Model 1, which measures the negative factors, produced higher indices than Model 1, with NFI (0.97), TLI (0.98), CFI (0.99), and RMSEA (0.38). All results from the fit tests indicate that both models are acceptable. Model

2, which measures the positive factors, produced relatively high fit indices. The NFI (0.94), TLI (0.95) and CFI (0.96) indices were above the recommended 0.90 cutoff, and RMSEA (0.78) was below 0.80 (Garson, 2006). These indices are preferable to the popular GFI and AGFI indices, which some researchers consider to be sample-biased (Garson, 2006).

Convergent Validity

Convergent validity verifies that the actual test results confirm the expected relationships between the items and factors. Observations of factor loadings and squared multiple correlations (SMC) of the items tested convergent validity. Table 2 reports the results of the CFA tests for the two models. Overall, the results confirmed convergent validity

of the two measurement instruments. All but two loadings scored well above 0.70 and all but three SMC scores exceeded 0.50. A deeper analysis of the scores indicates that Model 2 is more solid on convergent validity than Model 1.

Discriminant Validity

The discriminant validity test verifies that the factors of a model are not overly intercorrelated and thus seem to represent distinct factors. Figures 1 and 2 report the interconstruct correlation coefficients between the factors. Correlations that are significantly less than 1 demonstrate discriminant validity. In both figures, all correlations but frequency-intrusiveness (0.86) confirmed discriminant validity. The higher correlation between frequency and intrusiveness may indicate

Table 2. CFA results for models 1 and 2

Model 1: Negative Factors			
Factors/items		Loadings	SMC
Trust	N1	0.84	0.48
	N2	0.83	0.59
	N3	0.81	0.54
Frequency	N4	0.73	0.33
	N5	0.72	0.63
	N6	0.53	0.50
Intrusiveness	N7	0.84	0.57
	N8	0.75	0.48
	N9	0.74	0.69
Model 2: Positive Factors			
Factors/items		Loadings	SMC
Enjoyment	P1	0.84	0.67
	P2	0.82	0.63
	P3	0.80	0.75
	P4	0.75	0.57
Originality	P5	0.87	0.56
	P6	0.82	0.70
	P7	0.77	0.76
Value	P8	0.91	0.54
	P9	0.85	0.76
	P10	0.84	0.81
	P11	0.63	0.69
Relevance	P12	0.76	0.65
	P13	0.75	0.76
	P14	0.70	0.66

that the two constructs share confounding items that need to be clarified. The implications section discusses this possibility.

HYPOTHESIS TESTING

Tests of the seven hypotheses consisted of analyzing the means and standard deviations of the relevant item scores of each factor for the entire sample. Since "four" represents the neutral point on a seven-point Likert scale, any score higher than four would signify an expression of agreement from the respondents. Therefore, a mean (AVE) of the related factor of above 4 and a standard deviation (SD) of less than 1.50 indicated confirmation of a hypothesis.

Perceived intrusiveness, higher exposure frequency, and lack of trust in the advertiser were all detrimental to consumer acceptance of mobile TV advertising, confirming H_1, H_2, and H_3. The highest rated factor was high exposure frequency (AVE=5.48, SD=1.12), followed by lack of trust (AVE=5.25, SD=1.11) and perceived intrusiveness (AVE=4.52, SD=1.13). Research in the area rarely

Figure 1. Model 1 inter-construct correlations

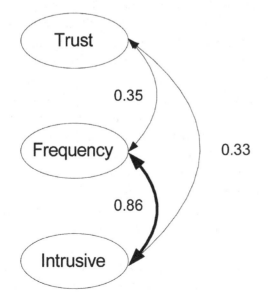

conceptualizes exposure frequency as a distinct latent variable. Haghirian and Madlberger (2005) integrate exposure frequency in their study of consumer acceptance of mobile advertising in Austria, but represent the construct by a unique item. This study proposes a different approach by conceptualizing exposure frequency as a latent construct measured by three items that compare the ideal exposure frequency of consumers with actual exposure frequency on traditional media. The results of the CFA as illustrated in Figure 1 also show that exposure frequency and perceived intrusiveness were highly correlated but very distinct from lack of trust. Higher frequency of advertising exposure may lead to increased perceived intrusiveness, resulting in the higher correlation between the two constructs. Lack of trust is conceptually different from exposure and intrusiveness as it relates to the consumer's attitude toward the advertised brand or the medium rather than to the advertising format.

The results show that perceived enjoyment (AVE=4.99, SD=1.41) is the highest contributor to consumer acceptance, followed by perceived originality (AVE=4.53, SD=1.19) and perceived relevance (AVE=4.25, SD=1.18), confirming H_4, H_6, and H_7. However, perceived value (AVE=3.97, SD=1.53) failed to meet the requirements, and H_5 could not be confirmed. With perceived enjoyment and perceived originality being ranked at the top, the results suggest that mobile TV users value the entertaining aspects of advertisements rather than more tangible aspects such as level of personalization or perceived tangible value.

Table 3 lists the means and standard deviations of each factor in order of importance. The overall ranking of the means suggests that negative factors are more influential with respect to consumers' acceptance of mobile TV advertising, as frequency and lack of trust are the only factors to surpass five on a seven-point scale. Additionally, intangible aspects of mobile TV advertising seem to prevail over more tangible aspects such as relevance and value.

Figure 2. Model 2 inter-construct correlations

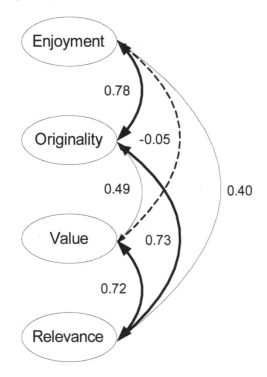

DISCUSSION

Theoretical Implications

The nascent field of research in mobile advertising focuses on basic advertising formats of text-based messages (SMS) or sometimes picture-based messages (MMS) (Carroll et al., 2007; Ferris, 2007; Haghirian & Madlberger, 2005; Haghirian, Madlberger, & Tanuskova, 2005; Merisavo et al., 2007; Okazaki, 2006; Okazaki et al., 2007; Xu et al., 2007). Although researchers predict that text- and picture-based messages will grow at a rapid pace in the next decade, mainly owing to diminishing costs for mobile users (Carroll et al., 2007), the potential revenue from these advertising formats for broadcasters, advertising agencies, and content aggregators may be far less important than future revenue from the mobile TV market (Holland, 2006; White, 2008). However, little research to date has examined mobile TV advertising.

The main contribution of the present study is the validation of two measurement models that are more exhaustive than previous models which do not consider all the positive and negative factors in a single study. In fact, past research has rarely even considered a typology of antecedents for consumer acceptance in mobile advertising. The results of this study suggest that satisfactorily addressing negative factors is an essential prerequisite to advertising on mobile TV. Conceptually, negative factors do not increase the perceived benefits of advertising exposure; rather, they relate to consumers' initial reluctance to receive advertisements. Much of this reluctance relates to privacy issues. Consequently, advertisers must plan campaigns to be nonintrusive, to be of acceptable frequency, and to promote trust in the source of the advertisements.

On the other hand, positive factors—particularly those related to entertainment—act as enhancers of consumer acceptance of mobile TV advertising. Positive factors are the true contributors toward increasing acceptance, but only if advertisers first address the negative factors in order to lower the initial reluctance. As the results of this study show, advertisers and researchers may consider negative and positive factors to be overarching dimensions of influence that produce different effects on consumer acceptance, but investigators of mobile advertising must study them conjointly.

Although past research indicates that the entertainment aspect of mobile advertising is one of the most important drivers of consumer acceptance (Carroll et al., 2007), no prior research seems to support the importance of this factor in mobile TV advertising. The present study shows that a two-factor approach to measuring entertainment (perceived enjoyment and perceived originality) is more effective than a single-factor approach suggested by past studies (Haghirian & Madlberger, 2005; Haghirian et al., 2005; Xu et al., 2007). Finally, the results indicated that the degree of personalization and the tangible value of the advertisements were less important

Table 3. Means and standard deviations of the factors

Factor	AVE	SD
Frequency	5.48	1.12
Trust (lack of)	5.25	1.11
Enjoyment	4.99	1.41
Originality	4.53	1.19
Intrusiveness	4.52	1.13
Relevance	4.25	1.18
Value	3.97	1.53

to consumers than other factors, suggesting a revision of the prevailing assumption that mobile advertising should be systematically personalized and contextualized. Mobile TV advertising differs from other forms of mobile advertising in that the contents are broadcast on a one-to-many system rather than one-to-one, such as text- or picture-based messages. Consequently, study of mobile TV advertising should avoid a strict application of existing models of consumer acceptance of text- and picture-based advertising (SMS and MMS). Researchers can apply the two validated models in this paper for future empirical studies specific to mobile TV advertising.

Practical Implications

Stakeholders in the mobile industry (mostly telcos and broadcasters) have invested massive sums of money in building adequate infrastructure for broadcasting mobile TV without a clear view on how to amortize these costs (Holland, 2006), and advertising-based revenues could become a principal source of funding for these investors. Therefore, research in mobile TV advertising is critical to helping advertisers build successful strategies. Investigating the topic from the perspective of consumer acceptance may be one of the most fruitful approaches, as many practitioners indicate that the new digital economy inevitably results in a shift of control from advertisers to

consumers because digital media offer consumers the choice of where, when, and how they want to see advertisements (Berman, Abraham, Battino, Shipnuck, & Neus, 2007; IBM, 2007; Nelson, Kline, & Van Dem Dam, 2007). Within this evolving context, advertisers and marketers must understand how to optimize consumer acceptance for a given campaign.

The implications of this study for practitioners lie in two aspects of the mobile consumer's behavior: reluctance and enjoyment. The personal nature of mobile phones implies that consumers tend to perceive any form of advertising as being intrusive, making them reluctant to attend to advertisements that appear without their permission. Moreover, contextual issues can increase perceived intrusiveness. Past research shows that consumers view mobile TV mostly on a snacking basis, accessing content for short periods of time (Andersen et al., 2007). The snacking consumption pattern leads to aversion to viewing advertisements during these moments. Successful advertising campaigns may overcome this initial reluctance by presenting less frequent and less interruptive advertisements in a trustworthy environment for consumers and by using appropriate ad formats. More specifically, displaying advertisements during programs would be highly undesirable, whereas presenting them before or after may be more effective. Broadcast mobile TV relies on splicing time, which is the waiting time between two programs. Customarily, splicing time is filled with a unicolor screen displaying a loading counter, but one could easily imagine replacing the screen with a discrete and static advertisement while the viewer is waiting for the next program to load. As a general rule of thumb, the advertisements should be discretely integrated within the programming with few or no perceived interruptions.

This study also reveals that enjoyment is the most important advertising factor for consumers. Snacking behavior implies that any form of advertising on mobile TV must be original and entertaining to catch attention and sustain interest.

Advertisers may capture attention with interactive and exclusive contents that engage consumers when they are being exposed to advertisements. In contrast to text- and picture-based advertisements, which must be targeted and value-centered to get consumers to open and read messages (e.g., promotional offers), mobile TV advertisements are broadcasted to a wider audience and therefore need to focus on enjoyment rather than pure tangible value such as traditional couponing. Another notable difference between text- and picture-based advertisements and mobile TV advertising is that broadcast advertisements can be less personalized and contextualized. Mobile TV advertisements will likely need to be consistent with both the broadcast content (the show) and the profile of the consumer, requiring less personalization than text-based advertisements which are not content-relevant. Consumers may be annoyed by irrelevant text messages, but viewing a broadcast advertisement before or after a TV show can be enjoyable even if the advertised product does not totally fit the profile of the consumer. To capture consumer attention with enjoyable and original advertisements, advertisers must find the optimal level of consistency between the broadcast content and the advertising content. Practitioners must acknowledge these fundamental differences between mobile TV advertising and text-based advertising or online advertising.

LIMITATIONS AND FUTURE RESEARCH

Although the study followed a rigorous research design, it has some limitations. First, both the French and English samples were mainly composed of younger consumers, thus limiting the generalizability of the findings to the entire population. Second, the negative factors of intrusiveness and frequency were closely correlated, indicating that the two factors may have confounding items. Future investigations should optimize the discrimi-

nant validity of these two factors or determine whether they make up a single broader factor.

Future research should attempt to validate the measurement models in several countries. Although cultural differences are important influences in consumer behavior, mobile TV consumption patterns do not seem to vary much across countries (Andersen et al., 2007). For example, most current consumers watch mobile TV during commuting time. Further, research is generally lacking on mobile use among older consumers, as investigators believe that many models appearing in the mobile commerce and mobile advertising literature apply only to a younger population. Consequently, future studies might expand the applicability of the constructs to a wider population. Finally, future research should extend the use of experimental design to confirm the viability of the constructs. Such experimentation would help verify whether the proposed constructs and recommendations translate into causal effects on consumer behavior.

CONCLUSION

So far, little is known on consumer acceptance of advertising on mobile television as most studies on mobile marketing have been conducted in the context of simple text- or image-based messages. The objective of this study is to test seven antecedents of consumer acceptance of mobile television advertising. The current research shows evidence that frequency of advertisements and lack of trust are inhibitors that reinforce consumers' reluctance to advertising exposure on this medium, whereas originality and personal enjoyment are found to be the highest contributors to acceptance. The findings suggest that practitioners should first focus on aspects that lower the negative effects of excessive advertising exposure and trust issues. Then, they should ensure that advertisements are original and entertaining.

REFERENCES

Albaum, G. (1997). The Likert scale revisited: An alternate version. *Journal of the Market Research Society. Market Research Society, 39*(2), 331–342.

Alwitt, L. F., & Prabhaker, P. R. (1994). Identifying who dislikes television advertising: Not by demographics alone. *Journal of Advertising Research, 34*(6), 17–29.

Andersen, H., Jakobsen, M. H., & Nilsen, S. (2007). *Mobile-TV usage - customer insights.* Oslo, Norway: Telenor R&I.

Barwise, P., & Strong, C. (2002). Permission-based mobile advertising. *Journal of Interactive Marketing, 16*(1), 14–24. doi:10.1002/dir.10000

Bauer, H. H., Barnes, S. J., Reichardt, T., & Neumann, M. M. (2005). Driving consumer acceptance of mobile marketing. *Journal of Electronic Commerce Research, 6*(3), 181–192.

Berman, S. J., Abraham, S., Battino, B., Shipnuck, L., & Neus, A. (2007). *Navigating the media divide.* Armonk, NY: IBM Institute for Business Value.

Berman, S. J., Battino, B., Shipnuck, L., & Neus, A. (2007). *The end of advertising as we know it.* Armonk, NY: IBM Institute for Business Value.

Buellingen, F., & Woerter, M. (2004). Development perspectives, firm strategies and applications in mobile commerce. *Journal of Business Research, 57*(12), 1402–1408. doi:10.1016/S0148-2963(02)00429-0

Byrne, B. M. (2001). *Structural equation modeling with AMOS: Basic concepts, applications, and programming.* Mahwah, NJ: Lawrence Erlbaum.

Carroll, A., Barnes, S. J., Scornavacca, E., & Fletcher, K. (2007). Consumer perceptions and attitudes towards SMS advertising: Recent evidence from New Zealand. *International Journal of Advertising, 26*(1), 79–98.

Choi, Y. K., Kim, J., & McMillan, S. J. (2009). Motivators for the intention to use mobile TV: A comparison of South-Korean males and females. *International Journal of Advertising, 28*(1), 147–167. doi:10.2501/S0265048709090477

DeZoysa, S. (2002). Mobile advertising needs to get personal. *Telecommunications, 36*, 8.

du Pre Gauntt, J. (2008). *Mobile advertising: After the growing pains.* New York, NY: eMarketer.

Eagly, A., & Chaiken, S. (1993). *Psychology of attitudes.* New York, NY: Harcourt.

Ferris, M. (2007). Insights on mobile advertising, promotion, and research. *Journal of Advertising Research, 47*(1), 28–37. doi:10.2501/S0021849907070043

Frolick, M. N., & Chen, L. (2004). Assessing m-commerce opportunities. *Information Systems Management, 21*(2), 53–62. doi:10.1201/1078/44118.21.2.20040301/80422.8

Garland, R. (1991). The mid-point on a rating scale: Is it desirable? *Marketing Bulletin, 2*, 66–70.

Garson, G. D. (2006). *Structural equation modeling.* Retrieved from http://www2.chass.ncsu.edu/garson/pa765/structur.htm

Haghirian, P., & Madlberger, M. (2005, May 26-28). *Consumer attitude toward advertising via mobile devices - an empirical investigation among Austrian users.* Paper presented at the 13th European Conference on Information Systems, Regensburg, Germany.

Haghirian, P., Madlberger, M., & Tanuskova, A. (2005, January 3-6). Increasing advertising value of mobile marketing - an empirical study of antecedents. In *Proceedings of the 38th Hawaii International Conference on System Sciences*, Big Island, HI (p. 32).

Hanley, M., Becker, M., & Martinsen, J. (2006). Factor influencing mobile advertising acceptance: Will incentives motivate college students to accept mobile advertisements? *International Journal of Mobile Marketing, 1*(1), 50–58.

Heinonen, K., & Strandvik, T. (2003). *Consumer responsiveness to mobile marketing.* Paper presented at the Stockholm Mobility Roundtable, Stockholm, Sweden.

Hernandez, M. D., Chapa, S., Minor, M. S., Maldonado, C., & Barranzuela, F. (2004). Hispanic attitudes toward advergames: A proposed model of their antecedents. *Journal of Interactive Advertising, 5*(1), 74–83.

Hoffman, D. L., & Novak, T. P. (1996). Marketing in hypermedia computer-mediated environments: Conceptual foundations. *Journal of Marketing, 60*, 50–68. doi:10.2307/1251841

Holland, N. (2006). *Rescuing 3G with mobile TV: Business models and monetizing 3G.* Cambridge, UK: Pyramid Research.

IBM. (2007). *IBM 2007 digital consumer study.* Armonk, NY: IBM.

Idate. (2008a). *DigiWorld yearbook 2008.* Montpellier, VT: Idate.

Idate. (2008b). *Mobile 2008: Markets and trends.* Montpellier, VT: Idate.

Idate. (2009). *Mobile 2009: Markets and trends.* Montpellier, VT: Idate.

Leppäniemi, M., Karjaluoto, H., & Salo, J. (2004). The success factors of mobile advertising value chain. *E-Business Review, 4*, 93–97.

Li, H., & Stoller, B. (2007). Parameters of mobile advertising: A field experiment. *International Journal of Mobile Marketing, 2*(1), 4–11.

Lin, J. C.-C., & Hsu, C.-L. (2009). A multi-facet analysis of factors affecting the adoption of multimedia messaging service (MMS). *International Journal of Technology and Human Interaction, 5*(4), 18–36. doi:10.4018/jthi.2009062502

Merisavo, M., Kajalo, S., Karjaluoto, H., Virtanen, V., Salmenkivi, S., & Raulas, M. (2007). An empirical study of the drivers of consumer acceptance of mobile advertising. *Journal of Interactive Advertising, 7*(2), 1–19.

Merisavo, M., Vesanen, J., Arponen, A., Kajalo, S., & Raulas, M. (2006). The effectiveness of targeted mobile advertising in selling mobile services: An empirical study. *International Journal of Mobile Communications, 4*(2), 119–127.

Nagar, K. (2009). Advertising effectiveness in different media: A comparison of web and television advertising. *IIMB Management Review, 21*(3), 245–260.

Nelson, E., Kline, H., & Van Dem Dam, R. (2007). *A future in content(ion).* Armonk, NY: IBM Institute for Business Value.

Nysveen, H., Pedersen, P. E., & Thorbjørnsen, H. (2005). Intentions to use mobile services: Antecedents and cross-service comparisons. *Journal of the Academy of Marketing Science, 33*(3), 330–346. doi:10.1177/0092070305276149

Okazaki, S. (2006). What do we know about mobile internet adopters? A cluster analysis. *Information & Management, 43*(2), 127–141. doi:10.1016/j.im.2005.05.001

Okazaki, S., Katsukura, A., & Nishiyama, M. (2007). How mobile advertising works: The role of trust in improving attitudes and recall. *Journal of Advertising Research, 47*(2), 165–178. doi:10.2501/S0021849907070195

Okazaki, S., & Taylor, C. R. (2008). What is SMS advertising and why do multinationals adopt it? Answers from an empirical study in European markets. *Journal of Business Research*, *61*(1), 4–12. doi:10.1016/j.jbusres.2006.05.003

Ranchhod, A. (2007). Developing mobile marketing strategies. *International Journal of Mobile Advertising*, *2*(1), 76–83.

Rappaport, S. D. (2007). Lessons from online practice: New advertising models. *Journal of Advertising Research*, *2*, 135–141. doi:10.2501/S0021849907070158

Repo, P., Hyvonen, K., Pantzar, M., & Timonen, P. (2006). Inventing use for a novel mobile service. *International Journal of Technology and Human Interaction*, *2*(2), 49–64. doi:10.4018/jthi.2006040103

Schumacker, R. E., & Lomax, R. G. (2004). *A beginner's guide to structural equation modeling* (2nd ed.). Mahwah, NJ: Lawrence Erlbaum.

Shim, J. P., Park, S., & Shim, J. M. (2008). Mobile TV phone: Current usage, issues, and strategic implications. *Industrial Management & Data Systems*, *108*(9), 1269–1282. doi:10.1108/02635570810914937

Steinbock, D. (2006). The missing link why mobile marketing is different. *International Journal of Mobile Marketing*, *1*(1), 83–94.

TeleAnalytics. (2008). *The quarterly TeleAnalytics mobile TV tracking service 5*. Toronto, ON, Canada: TeleAnalytics.

TNS. (2008). *Baromètre on-off-mobile*. Paris, France: TNS Sofres.

Trappey, R. J. III, & Woodside, A. G. (2005). Consumer responses to interactive advertising campaigns coupling short-message-service direct marketing and TV commercials. *Journal of Advertising Research*, *45*(4), 382–401.

Vollmer, C. (2008). *Always on: Advertising, marketing and media in an era of consumer control*. New York, NY: McGraw-Hill.

White, C. (2008). *Mobile TV: Strategies, business models & technologies*. London, UK: Informa Telecoms & Media.

Wilbur, K. C. (2008). How the digital video recorder (DVR) changes traditional television advertising. *Journal of Advertising*, *37*(1), 143–149. doi:10.2753/JOA0091-3367370111

Xu, D. J., Liao, S. S., & Li, Q. (2007). Combining empirical experimentation and modeling techniques: A design research approach for personalized mobile advertising applications. *Decision Support Systems*, *44*(2008), 710-724.

Zhou, N., Zhou, D., & Ouyang, M. (2003). Long-term effects of television advertising on sales of consumer durables and nondurables. *Journal of Advertising*, *32*(2), 45–54.

This work was previously published in the International Journal of Technology and Human Interaction, Volume 7, Issue 3, edited by Anabela Mesquita and Chia-Wen Tsai, pp. 70-83, copyright 2011 by IGI Publishing (an imprint of IGI Global).

Chapter 11
Student Perceptions and Adoption of University Smart Card Systems

Jamie Murphy
University of Western Australia, Australia

Richard Lee
University of South Australia, Australia

Evan Swinger
University of Western Australia, Australia

ABSTRACT

This study investigated student adoption of university campus card (UCC) applications. A review of smart card, technology adoption and Unified Theory of Acceptance and Use of Technology (UTAUT) literature led to three focus groups and a survey of student perceptions and attitudes towards the university's campus card. Perceptions of 17 UCC components differed significantly across four student variables – international versus domestic, willingness to load funds, gender, and university level – supporting and extending UTAUT. Willingness to load funds on their UCC differed significantly across 16 out of 17 components, followed by domestic versus overseas students differing on 14 components, university level differing on 13 components and gender on 10. Overall, students reported that extra UCC features would enhance the university's image, improve their student experience, and encourage them to use UCCs. The results and managerial implications can help universities select and prioritise UCC functions for campus adoption and implementation.

INTRODUCTION

Smart cards exemplify an intermediating technology, which requires a critical mass of adopting groups for the technology to succeed (Plouffe, Vandenbosch, & Hulland, 2001). Electronic customer relationship systems, for example, need adoption by both individuals and organisations (Jones, 2009; Wu & Wu, 2005). In a tertiary environment, successful smart card applications depend on students as individual adopters and organisational adoption by the university and campus merchants such as cafeterias, vending machines and bookshops. Successful implementation of smart cards requires

DOI: 10.4018/978-1-4666-1954-8.ch011

acceptance by all these parties, particularly the end users. As such, this study focuses on University Campus Card (UCC) adoption at the individual level, by students.

About the size and shape of a credit card, UCCs integrate well into student life on campus (Rochet & Tirole, 2003). A dynamic platform rather than a plastic card, the applications on a UCC may depend on university funding and usually require widespread acceptance by students, merchants and the university. Among other things, these smart cards can incorporate student photos, authenticate memberships or building access, facilitate library borrowing, store homework and pay for purchases such as photocopying, food and drink.

In part due to UCCs' rapidly evolving and growing role in student experiences, there seems little research of smart cards in tertiary education. Yet as UCC technology evolves, universities grapple with issues such as what smart card applications to implement, encouraging student use and successful UCC implementation across myriad departments and organisations. Universities also need to identify and prioritise UCC functions that improve student experiences, university investments and merchant relationships. Business such as bookshops, cafeterias, bank ATM machines and vending machines are woven into the campus tapestry. Finally, universities must gauge external partnerships. Collaborating with public transport, for example, would add a UCC function and reduce the need for a card.

To help address the questions above, this paper draws upon technology adoption literature and an Australian university's UCC challenges. Unlike adoption research that assumes a single adopting group (Plouffe et al., 2001; Wu & Wu, 2005), this paper treats UCCs as an intermediating technology with three adopting groups – merchants, students and the university. The Unified Theory of Acceptance and Use of Technology (UTAUT) (Venkatesh, Morris, Davis, & Davis, 2003) helps frame two qualitative and one quantitative investigation of student UCC adoption.

As individual differences, such as gender, relate to technology acceptance (Sun & Zhang, 2006; Wu & Wu, 2005), this study investigated how four variables – gender, university level, willingness to load fund, and student status – relate to student attitudes towards and use of UCCs.

Besides applying and extending UTAUT to campus cards, the study helps university administrators understand short to medium term implications of UCC systems, including key drivers for increasing UCC use. Understanding these drivers would help universities plan and manage their ongoing UCC investment decisions.

This study starts with a review of smart card technology and its applications in tertiary institutions. Next, technology acceptance literature and the results of two exploratory focus groups lead to a modified UTAUT model and subsequent quantitative survey. After highlighting the quantitative results, the paper concludes with implications, limitations and future research.

LITERATURE REVIEW

Smart Card Review

Compared with traditional magnetic strip cards, smart cards – plastic cards resembling credit cards – have increased storage capacity, security, and application capabilities (Ma et al., 2008; Omar & Djuhari, 2004). Of the two smart card types, memory cards store limited information on a basic chip, usually for a single application such as credit for telephones, vending machines or public transport. Intelligent cards contain microprocessors that can read, write and calculate data (Anderson, 2009; Turban & McElroy, 1998).

Contact-cards contain a metal antenna that must contact a card reader. Contactless cards communicate via a Radio Frequency Identification Device (RFID) and are optimal in areas such as public transport, which have a high volume of rapid transactions (Bain, 1995; Turban & McElroy, 1998).

Smart cards in the mid 1990s had a single function such as storing credit or controlling access (Elliot & Loebbecke, 1998). Increased storage capacity and transfer rates led to contactless intelligent cards with multiple applications (Anderson, 2009; Omar & Djuhari, 2004). Smart card advantages include fast transactions, convenience, reduced cost of fund collections, and reduced transaction errors (Truman, Sandow, & Rifkin, 2003). These technological advances and consumer confidence continue to yield several smart card applications.

Smart Card Applications

E-purses, which store prepaid cash on smart cards, suit micropayments; transaction charges for small items render credit cards impractical and unprofitable (Ching et al., 2009; M'Chirgui, 2003). E-purses fit tertiary environments, as many transactions are high volume, small cost products. E-purses can also automate discounts, such as for public transport or campus cafeterias. Smart cards fit public transport as they can reduce fare skipping, save fiddling with cash, and track transactions efficiently (Attoh-Okine & Shen, 1995). Smart cards give consumers convenience, flexibility and personalisation, while allowing transport companies to automate data collection and improve services (Fleshman, Schweiger, Lott, & Peirlott, 1998).

Smart card parking in the US West Coast improved revenues, management of parking services through interlinked pay stations, landscape aesthetics due to removing older pay-stations, and user convenience (McCourt, 2006). Smart card parking can increase consumer satisfaction, revenue, security, and transaction monitoring (SCA, 2006).

The digital nature of smart cards provides the capability to integrate with other technologies and go beyond payment systems. For example, researchers combined smart cards and related technologies to monitor the eating habits of chil-

dren (Lambert et al., 2005). The system provided nutrient analyses for the foods each student chose.

The forecasted next wave of smart card technology, High Density Smart Cards (HDSCs), have up to 1000 times the memory and 100 times the data transfer rate of conventional smart cards (Mayes & Markantonakis, 2006). Up to a gigabyte of data storage gives HDSCs potential applications in industries such as healthcare and entertainment. For tertiary education, HDSCs may resemble flash memory, allowing students to store notes, assignments and lecture recordings on their cards. Yet due to high costs, difficulty developing a standardised transfer rate and lack of trial outcomes, this technology is in its infancy (Mayes & Markantonakis, 2006). Smart cards can store biometric data such as fingerprints, for use as health cards or drivers licenses (Anderson, 2009). Yet as an intermediation technology, the relevant organisations must have biometric card readers. Biometric application increase security and user convenience, and could control access in tertiary institutions (Kumar & Ganesh, 2005).

Two other developments, however, threaten the future of traditional swipe cards. Following successful trials, credit card companies such as MasterCard and American Express produced composite smart cards – contactless debit cards – with an RFID and magnetic strip (Noe, 2005). A phased implementation of these contactless debit cards let consumers adapt to the new uses while keeping traditional swipe card uses. A second development, smart cards in mobile phones, would alter payment practices whereby phones serve as debit cards (Ondrus & Pigneur, 2006).

Smart Cards in Tertiary Institutions

Smart card technologies benefit students, staff and educational institutions through automated, convenient and cost-saving applications (Ching et al., 2009; Materka, Strzelecki, & Debiec, 2009; Rastogi & Das, 2002; Turban & McElroy, 1998).

Georgia Perimeter College in Atlanta, for example, integrated energy and UCCs with magnetic locks in exterior doors, and interior motion detectors (White, 2001). The combined system automatically adjusts lights and temperatures when students or employees enter or leave a room. Similar to most UCCs, the card stores credit for vending machines and other inexpensive purchases.

Sydney's Deakin University introduced smart cards in July 1999, for students and staff to pay for campus meals, library printing, Internet access, and retail items (CBORD, 2006). Users can check their balances online, view transaction histories, and deactivate lost cards. In 2002, Deakin initiated a program to improve card awareness and use. Promotions such as "buy 5, get 1 free" on vending machines and 10% drink discounts during happy hour spurred card use.

Edith Cowan University launched a contactless intelligent card in January 2007 (http://www.ecu.edu.au/fas/sts/access_cards.php). Besides identity with the Australian university, students can use the cards on Perth's public transport network, Transperth, pay for photocopying, and load funds on their cards via the Internet.

Tertiary institutions are moving towards multiple application smart cards (Materka, Strzelecki, & Debiec, 2009; Omar & Djuhari, 2004) that eventually replace other campus cards such as for fees, examinations, attendance, health, academic records, canteens and debits (Rastogi & Das, 2002). Smart cards may also facilitate students' e-learning by improving access to the Internet and universities' computer systems (Rastogi & Das, 2002).

Despite the sanguine scenarios, few studies examine tertiary student perceptions and acceptance of smart cards. Particularly for an intermediating technology such as smart cards, addressing the student needs is critical (Plouffe, Vandenbosch, & Hulland, 2000). For example, e-purses are useful only if consumers use the smart card regularly (Ching et al., 2009; Rochet & Tirole, 2003). It is essential to investigate consumer UCC acceptance,

leading to repeated use and increasing returns on university investments.

Technology Acceptance Literature

For over half a century, scholars have built on the Diffusion of Innovations (DOI) theory to explain and predict individual and organisational adoption of technologies (Rogers, 2003). Probably the most popular theoretical approach to information technology adoption, the Technology Acceptance Model (TAM) built on DOI as well as the Theory of Reasoned Action and Theory of Planned Behaviour (Lee, Kozar, & Larsen, 2003). TAM's parsimony and subsequent lack of predictive or explanatory ability, however, has led researchers to compare (Jen, Lu, & Liu, 2009; Plouffe, Hulland, & Vandenbosch, 2001) and integrate (Wixon & Todd, 2005; Wu & Wu, 2005) other models with TAM.

Striking a balance between parsimony and predictive ability, Figure 1 shows the Unified Theory of Acceptance and Use of Technology (UTAUT). User intentions and behaviours towards a new technology stem from four determinants (Venkatesh et al., 2003). *Performance expectancy* is user perceptions that a technology will improve task performance. *Effort expectancy* is a technology's perceived ease of use. *Social influence* is beliefs that important others approve of using a technology. Finally, *facilitating conditions* are how users perceive organisational and technical infrastructures support using the technology.

In addition, and important for organisations to accelerate the adoption of a intermediating technology, UTAUT incorporates four individual variables – age, gender, experience, and voluntariness of use – to moderate determinant relationships with behavioural intentions. For example, Sun and Yang (2006) proposed that age amplified the effect of effort expectancy but attenuated the performance expectancy and subjective norm effects. The authors argued that compared to women, the performance expectancy effect was

Figure 1. The Unified Theory of Acceptance and Use of Technology Model (Venkatesh et al., 2003, p. 447)

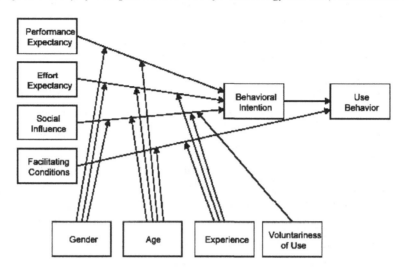

stronger for men but the effects for social influence and effort expectancy were weaker. Understanding the role of moderating variables helps examine adoption by the individual (Birch & Irvine, 2009; Cheng et al., 2009).

FOCUS GROUP

As a preliminary, exploratory step, three focus groups discussed how UTAUT's four determinants related to student UCC use. The first focus group comprised six UCC Steering Committee members, four Information technology staff members and two full-time academics. A key aim was to solidify questions for a subsequent quantitative survey that would help clarify actionable items for the steering committee. An author of this paper facilitated the focus group and aligned some discussion with UTAUT determinants and moderators.

The focus group discussions suggested using *undergraduate versus graduate students* as a proxy for age. Since students had no smart card option other than the UCC, *willingness to load funds* replaced UTAUT's voluntariness of use. *International versus national students* substituted for UTAUT's moderating variable of experience.

Results gleaned from this variable could help university organisations who deal with students, international and local. The fourth UTAUT variable, *gender*, remained.

The same facilitator ran two subsequent focus groups – convenience samples of local undergraduate students or overseas graduate students – on UCC perceptions. The steering committee helped recruit eight Australian undergraduates, and the authors recruited four graduate students from Australia, Germany, China and Taiwan. During the 45-minute sessions, participants ranked and discussed existing and potential UCC applications such as public transport, cafeterias, bookstores, parking, vending machines and online access. The focus groups sought to identify issues related to the four UTAUT determinants: performance expectancy, effort expectancy, facilitating conditions, and social influence.

Performance Expectancy

The focus groups discussed and ranked seven proposed UCC services. Relative to undergrads, graduate students perceived integration with local transport three ranks lower than parking (Table 1). They said smart card parking would be convenient, reduce how often they skipped payment and help avoid fines. Graduate students wanted an online record of smart parking activities, which could simplify tax auditing. Undergraduate students had similar rankings on all services except for integration with local transport; they used public transport regularly.

Vending machine payment was the second option for both groups. It was convenient for after hours purchases, reduced the need to carry cash and students seemed comfortable buying low-cost items. Cafeteria payments ranked third for both groups. Graduate students used the cafe primarily in the evenings and perceived less risk with small UCC payments. Undergraduates also noted small payments, as well as automating student union discounts.

The graduate students thought local transport integration would reduce how many cards they carried, encourage public transport use, and automate student discounts. However, the accessible personal information concerned them. The undergraduates said transport integration would be convenient, they would use it regularly, and possible discounts were appealing. The undergraduates were unconcerned about storing their personal information, but wanted to know why the transport company collected this information. Though it rated fifth, both groups said online access to add funds and monitor transactions was essential.

Both groups thought little of integrating the sport centre card; few students used the centre. Finally, neither group favoured off campus payments with the UCC. In particular, undergraduates noted off-campus products were expensive and would have little purchasing interest without sufficient discounts. A subsequent quantitative survey excluded these two applications.

Effort Expectancy

Students perceived some UCC aspects as unfriendly. Focus group participants knew current

Table 1. Ranking of UCC services

UCC Service	Graduate rank	Undergraduate rank
Local transport integration	4	1
Vending machine payment	2	2
Cafeteria payment	3	3
Parking integration	1	4
Online monitoring	5	5
Sport Centre integration	6	6
Off campus payments	7	7

UCC uses, but felt the university should simplify learning these functions. They disliked the procedures for reporting and replacing lost or stolen cards. Participants were unaware of an available online reporting facility and expected an email alert for UCCs handed in. Finally, going to separate buildings to pay for and collect replacement cards was an inconvenient and unwarranted annoyance.

Graduate students had problems knowing where and how to load money on their UCCs. As they accessed computer laboratories predominantly after hours, they had to withdraw funds from an ATM machine and then locate an afterhours machine to recharge their cards. These late night hassles raised student safety and security concerns. As the graduate students spent little time on campus, adding funds online was a priority. The graduates also hated no online access to audit or withdraw UCC funds at the end of semester.

Facilitating Conditions

The graduate group used the UCC for photocopying, student identification, library borrowing and building access, but wanted more UCC information available. As they were on campus less than undergraduate students, more online information seemed particularly beneficial for them. Suggestions on website content included adding loading station locations, a list of UCC functions and procedural guides.

Graduate students wanted to submit a digital photo for their UCC, rather than sitting for a photo. They argued that adding new functions and funds to the card highlighted the need to improve processes for reporting lost cards, and verifying and cancelling UCC funds. They would load little money on their cards if they could not recoup funds from lost or stolen cards easily.

Undergraduates voiced concerns over recording personal information. They wanted a privacy policy detailing the use of their personal information in order to make informed decisions on new services. One student wanted online access to any information stored on their card. Graduates saw online records as positive; they would simplify organizing tax deductions. Both groups envisaged no problems with non-intrusive banner advertisements on UCC web pages as long as the banner content was relevant and the revenue subsidised UCC functions.

Similar to Noe (2005), graduate students said implementing UCC services should be incremental and undergo systematic trials to gauge student acceptance. Both groups emphasised that the process of adding funds to the card must improve, such as online access to add funds or automated direct debit to restock their cards, to support new functions.

Social Influence

Finally, the focus group discussions highlighted the importance of social influence on students' learning and using UCCs. The participants had similar UCC knowledge but complained they had to learn UCC uses, and its website and content, through peers.

In summary, the focus group outcomes helped adapt UTUAT with relevant moderating variables for UCCs. The focus groups also identified 17 components for UTAUT's performance expectancy (six components), effort expectancy (five),

facilitating conditions (three) and social influence (three). Table 2 lists these 17 components.

Yet this study differed from typical UTAUT applications in that students had access to some UCC functions, such as borrowing books and accessing facilities, and other functions were hypothetical. Typical UTAUT applications gauge participant intentions to adopt a technology. Hence, instead of behavioural intentions as the dependent variable, this study adapted the model to investigate how each determinant component differed across the four moderating variables. As well, behavioural intentions are implicit in many of the 17 components identified through the focus groups (e.g., "I would like to use UCC for campus vending machines"). Figure 2 shows the adapted research model.

SURVEY

Questionnaire development stemmed from UTAUT, focus group findings and the UCC steering committee's interests in actionable items. Distributing draft questionnaires to a few students and the steering committee for feedback, helped reconcile differing organisational expectations and clarify questions. The final questionnaire tapped perceptions of the 17 components using 5-point Likert scales, anchored on strongly disagree and strongly agree. The final section contained student willingness to load funds on their UCC, the amount they were willing to load on each occasion, and three demographic variables – gender, university level as undergraduate or graduate, and student status as international or domestic.

An email with brief study information and noting a random draw for one of two iPod Nanos, invited about 15,000 students to complete an online questionnaire. After data cleaning, the final sample comprised 3,307 responses, over a 20% response rate. Albeit, the actual response rate was higher as many students rarely check their university email accounts.

Table 2. Relating the Four Independent Variables and 17 Dependent Components

Independent Variables	17 Components	Spearman's rho (2- tailed)		Kruskal Wallis Test		
		Willingness to Load Funds		University Level*	Gender**	International vs Domestic***
Performance Expectancy	Would like to use UCC for campus vending machines.	0.351	χ^2	14.119 U	7.422 M	26.502 I
		< 0.001	p	< 0.001	0.006	< 0.001
	Would like to use the UCC to top up print quotas online.	0.228	χ^2	7.265 U	1.288 M	4.282 I
		< 0.001	p	0.007	0.256	0.039
	Would like to use the UCC to top up internet quotas online.	0.233	χ^2	8.091 U	13.281 M	25.000 I
		< 0.001	p	0.004	< 0.001	< 0.001
	Would like to use the UCC at campus cafeterias.	0.368	χ^2	2.193 U	0.271 M	25.919 I
		< 0.001	p	0.139	0.603	< 0.001
	Would like to use the UCC to pay for campus parking.	0.285	χ^2	1.63 U	0.013 M	1.315 D
		< 0.001	p	.202	0.908	0.251
	Would like to use the UCC to purchase at the campus bookshop.	.178	χ^2	6.324 G	.298 F	72.053 I
		< 0.001	p	0.012	.585	< 0.001
Facilitating Conditions	Would like online access to add money to UCC.	0.297	χ^2	0.814 G	3.968 M	0.151 I
		< 0.001	p	0.367	0.046	0.698
	Would like the UCC to combine university cards.	0.239	χ^2	0.172 U	24.796 M	4.585 I
		< 0.001	p	0.679	< 0.001	0.032
	Would like to combine the UCC with local transport.	0.238	χ^2	13.146 U	12.955 M	6.196 D
		< 0.001	p	< 0.001	< 0.001	0.013
Effort Expectancy	Aware of current UCC uses.	0.064	χ^2	42.824 U	8.665 F	21.229 I
		< 0.001	p	< 0.001	0.003	< 0.001
	Would like detailed online guides on using the UCC.	0.105	χ^2	6 G	0.781 M	85.301 I
		< 0.001	p	0.014	0.377	< 0.001
	Extra UCC features would encourage me to use the UCC more.	0.347	χ^2	16.654 U	18.480 M	15.046 I
		< 0.001	p	< 0.001	< 0.001	< 0.001
	Satisfied with the current use of the UCC.	-0.241	χ^2	7.633 U	17.963 F	1.278 D
		< 0.001	p	0.006	< 0.001	0.258
	Know where to access the UCC website.	0.017	χ^2	7.962 G	0.003 F	46.500 D
		0.319	p	0.005	0.957	< 0.001

continued on following page

Although a convenience sample, the respondent and student populations were similar. Compared to the student population, slightly more female (57% versus 51%) and international students (18% versus 15%), and less graduate students (14% versus 24%) completed the survey.

Just 3% of the students never used the UCC and 77% used their UCC at least weekly. Over half (54%) the respondents were satisfied with current UCC uses.

Given the ordinal nature of Likert scales, Kruskal-Wallis tests investigated significant

Table 2. Continued

Independent Variables	17 Components	Spearman's rho (2- tailed)		Kruskal Wallis Test		
		Willingness to Load Funds		University Level*	Gender**	International vs Domestic***
Social Influence	Would like access to a privacy policy.	0.04A6	χ^2	23.457 G	3.696 M	82.696 I
		0.008	p	**< 0.001**	0.055	**< 0.001**
	Extra UCC features would improve the university image.	0.251	χ^2	10.488 U	44.664 M	111.595 I
		< 0.001	p	**0.001**	**< 0.001**	**< 0.001**
	Extra UCC features would improve my student experience.	0.350	χ^2	8.99 U	32.069 M	38.484 I
		< 0.001	p	**0.003**	**< 0.001**	**< 0.001**

* Undergraduate or Graduate students rated the measure higher.

** Male or Female students rated the measure higher.

*** Domestic or International Students rated the measure higher.

differences with the 17 components across three nominal variables – gender, university level and international/domestic students – and correlation tests using Spearman's rho related willingness to load funds with the components. Table 2 contains the test results.

RESULTS AND DISCUSSIONS

Willingness to load funds showed significant differences on all but one – where to access the UCC website – of the 17 dependent variables. The strongest relationships was student perceptions that adding extra UCC features would encourage them to use the card (rho =.47). Adding proposed services changed students' willingness to load funds on their UCC dramatically. On average, students were willing to load about $10 on each occasion. Only 13% of the students would load over $20 on their UCC with current services. Students willing to load over $20 quadrupled to 56% with additional UCC services. The weakest correlations were for topping up print (rho =.228) and Internet (rho =.233) quotas online. The only negative relationship, satisfaction with willingness

to load funds (rho = -.241), may suggest frustration by those keen to use the UCC.

Comparing undergraduate versus postgraduate students, 13 out of 17 components differed significantly. Except for knowledge on UCC website access and access to privacy policy, undergraduate students reported stronger views on the components than the undergraduates did. Undergraduate students were particularly significant and strong for internet and print quota top-up, vending machines and local transport integration. They also had stronger UCC awareness and sought more detailed online guide and access to privacy policy.

For gender, 10 components differed significantly, and males tended to express stronger views of the components than females were. Males had more interest in additional UCC services, felt stronger about these services improving their student experience and leading them to use the UCC more often. However, female students were more satisfied with the UCC and more aware of the UCC website than their male colleagues were.

Finally, international and domestic students differed significantly on 14 of the 17 components. Except for local transport integration, UCC website knowledge, and campus parking, international

Figure 2. The research model

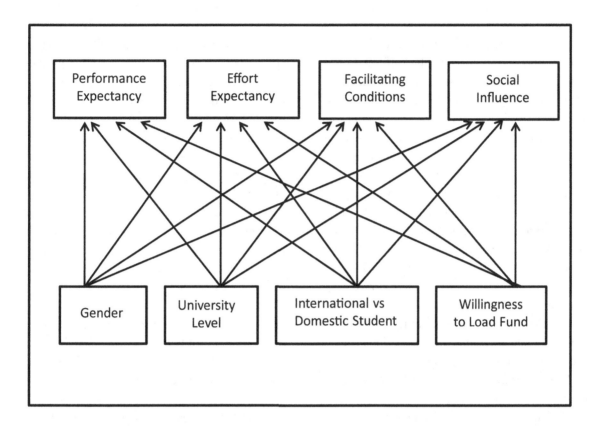

students rated the components higher than domestic students did. There was no significant difference between the groups on satisfaction with the UCC. The international students felt particularly strong that extra UCC features would improve the university's image.

Regarding the results of individual components, over half (54%) the students were satisfied with UCC services, while the same percentage of students (54%) did not know of the UCC website. This lack of knowledge about the UCC website highlighted poor awareness of a valuable information source. Furthermore, about two of three students (65%) agreed that extra UCC features would improve their student experiences and the university's image. Most students may underutilise the UCC because of their perceived lack of features on the UCC.

Collectively, the above results suggests adding information, such as photos of and maps to recharging stations, and greater visibility of lost/stolen card reporting procedures to the UCC website may help increase UCC awareness and satisfaction. Particularly with international students, dissatisfaction probably stemmed from interest in UCC services, but poor online information hampered their use. Universities marketing goods and services to current and potential international students must make UCC information easily available.

All but one proposed UCC extension had support from two-thirds of the respondents. The proposed option with mediocre support, bookstore payments, resonated with focus group findings that bookstore goods were costly and impractical for e-purses, which suit high volume micro payments (M'Chirgui, 2003).

Seventy percent of the respondents knew current UCC uses, but the focus group results suggested students learned from experience and peers. This finding helps explain why undergraduate students rated additional online information as important. Compared with senior students, new students might have fewer peers – who were also new – or experiences to rely on for information.

About half the students wanted a privacy policy concerning their personal information. This finding should become increasingly important with additional services' potential to collect additional personal information. Seven of ten students wanted to merge individual cards. International students sought to merge individual university cards, such as bookstore and residence hall cards into the UCC. In contrast, domestic students were keen to combine the UCC with the local transport card. With their new contactless intelligent UCC, the university can integrate these functions, hence catering to both student groups.

An encouraging result for UCC implementation was 85% agreement that additional services would increase UCC use. Furthermore, thanks to new services, students would load more funds on their UCC fourfold. This dramatic rise in willingness to load funds supports adding new UCC functions. However as the focus groups suggested, to facilitate this willingness to load funds students expected online access for adding funds and improved services to cancel and recoup funds in the event of lost or stolen cards.

Academic Implications

Smart cards facilitate student campus activities such as library loans, building access, and vending machine purchases, as well as off-campus functions such as public transport. Successful implementation of intermediating technologies, such as smart cards, necessitates investigating consumer perspectives (Plouffe et al., 2001). Thus, this study drew upon complementary qualitative and quantitative techniques to gauge consumer

insights. The results add to the limited research of smart cards in tertiary institutions.

The Unified Theory of User Acceptance of Technology (Venkatesh et al., 2003) provided a structure to identify perceptions of and problems with existing and future smart card uses. One contribution of this study is the role of demographic variables in UTAUT. Albeit exploratory, the results showed the importance of one UTAUT variable, gender, as well as two new demographic variables, educational level and international versus domestic students.

Of the ten components that related significantly to gender, males rated eight measures higher than females did. The females showed significantly stronger answers to awareness of UCC uses and, perhaps subsequently, stronger UCC satisfaction. This finding resonates with research indicating that attitude is a key in driving technology adoption for males, but not for females (Venkatesh, Morris, & Ackerman, 2000). Similarly, Sun and Yang (2006) suggest that males are more likely than females to adopt a technology they perceive as useful.

Thirteen components significantly related to university level. Undergraduate students generally rated the measures higher than graduates did. The measures reflect the undergraduate students' perceived usefulness of and desires for extra UCC services. Extra UCC services would encourage undergraduates to increase their use of the services. These results align with Sun and Yang (2006), who proposed that compared with older users, younger users who perceive a technology as useful or easy to use are more likely to adopt the technology. That age relates negatively with technology adoption, complements and extends a rich stream of research in innovation diffusion (Rogers, 2003).

Similarly, domestic students and their international counterparts differed significantly in perceptions. International students rated 12 components higher than domestic students did. Yet domestic students were more satisfied with their UCC experience and more knowledgeable on where to access the UCC website. These findings highlight the importance of a possible new variable, domestic versus international student status, when applying UTAUT for technology adoption studies in tertiary institutions.

Furthermore, this study found significant results based on a behavioural variable, the willingness to load fund. The willingness to load funds was strongest with intentions to use UCCs in campus cafeterias and weakest with print quota top-ups. Universities could use this knowledge to guide their choice of new services. Research of smart cards, and similar intermediating technologies, should capture the willingness to spend. The role of these and other possible UTAUT variables is one of several promising future research areas.

CONCLUSION

In conclusion, this study offers a series of short- and mid-term managerial recommendations, followed by suggestions for future research. Although the suggestions – which incorporate feasibility and observable results – apply to the university in this study, the suggestions should help other tertiary institutions improve their current and future smart card systems. Overall, universities should note that student perceptions of UCCs changed with year level. Hence, universities might differentiate their UCC offerings depending on undergraduates or graduates as the intended users.

Short Term Recommendations

In line with UTAUT's facilitating conditions, an improved website and promoting that website are critical to UCC adoption. Students, particularly new and international students, learned how to use the UCC from peers. They desired detailed UCC information online. The revised website should provide guides with pictures and maps of reloading stations, information about UCC services and a finely crafted privacy policy to inform students

on use of their personal information. Website redevelopment could be immediate as the university can decide autonomously without consulting external organisations such as the local transport company. Redevelopment aside, the site needs improved promotion and awareness.

Given the strong interest towards smart card vending machines, phased trials of vending machine payments is a second short term recommendation. To align the phased trials with UTAUT's effort expectancy and facilitating conditions, the vending machines should be hybrid cash and smart card to avoid alienating current users. Collaborating with vendors underscores the requisite multiple group adoption for an intermediating technology to succeed (Plouffe et al., 2001) and would give universities actual results to assess goals for future UCC services.

Mid Term Recommendations

The medium term recommendations highlight multiple group adoption of UCCs. The students perceived online access to add funds and monitor transactions as integral to successful expansion of UCC capabilities. The university could also merge online access with facilities to top up internet or print quotas. Yet online access requires additional investment, collaboration with an external financial provider and collaboration with other university entities. There are also concerns over the immediacy of online recharging, as students may top-up online but the university system may not credit the account for up to 24 hours.

Cafeteria payment is another mid-term opportunity. Complementary success factors include online access to add funds, investments in smart card readers and integrating student union discounts into the card. A final mid-term recommendation is local transport integration, the most popular proposed services. Given the overwhelming support, a dialogue should commence to reconcile differing organisational requirements and plan implementation.

Although there was moderate support for smart card parking, this recommendation requires large financial investments to purchase, convert and integrate campus smart card parking systems. Also due to the lack of successful implementation in tertiary institutions, the benefits of smart card parking are unknown. Perhaps UCC parking could be trialed in a small parking lot to assess student acceptance. This would provide observable results and cost effectiveness without the financial risk of a failed campus wide smart card parking system. Similar to the phased trials of smart card vending machines, this suggestion aligns with UTAUT's effort expectancy and facilitating conditions as well as multiple group adoption of an intermediating technology.

Future Research

There are several limitations to these results, which future research could address. For example, the study failed to consider if students acted on their intentions. Although intentions may predict behaviour, a longitudinal approach to relate actual behaviour to intentions would shed more light on student UCC adoption. Future research could analyze actual use versus intended use of new services, such as vending machine payments.

Future analysis of student UCC acceptance could investigate the role of social influence. Sun and Zhang (2006) propose that compared with experienced users, novice users are more prone to social influence when adopting a technology. Similarly, this study found students learned UCC use from peers. Future research could assess how to leverage peer groups to improve the frequency and satisfaction with using UCCs. Moreover, social influence might be *injunctive* compliance with others to obtain rewards and avoid punishments, or *descriptive* acceptance of others' opinions and behaviours as evidences of truth (Rivis & Sheeran, 2003; Sheeran & Orbell, 1999).

In addition to how injunctive and descriptive sources relate to student UCC adoption, at least one study using UTAUT found culture as a social influence dimension (Bandyopadhyay & Fraccastoro, 2007). Thus, future research could also examine culture, such as collectivism versus individualism (Hofstede, 2001), as this study found significant differences between domestic and international students.

Although this study did not examine how variables moderated UTAUT's four determinants of behavioural intentions, it did explore how these variables related to components of these. Given the many significant results, future research could use these results to develop an appropriate survey instrument to test UTAUT with Structural Equation Modelling.

Future research could also assess how university faculties differ in their UCC needs. Faculties could play a mediating role in the success of UCCs and at the student level, the student discipline or faculty be a UTUAT moderator. This analysis could also examine departmental or faculty problems administering UCCs, such as replacing cards or inter-faculty authentication of lab access.

Finally, future research could examine the effect of incentives (Ross, 1976) and behavioural learning (Rothschild & Gaidis, 1981) on the adoption and use of UCC services. For example, what incentives switch students from cash to smart card e-purses? This analysis could focus on whether cashless systems attract new consumers, or simply convert students from cash to cashless transactions. Answers to these questions would help address issues related to multiple groups adopting the innovation in order for the technology to succeed (Plouffe et al., 2001).

In conclusion, this study provides insights into the challenges and benefits of smart card implementations in tertiary institutions. Outcomes from this study should help universities planning to implement or already using smart cards. As the technology evolves, research must continually investigate the implications of new UCC services in order to ensure that universities derive maximum benefits for themselves as well as for the other users – students and merchants.

REFERENCES

Andersson, J. (2009). SIM cards–the new frontier for biometrics. *Card Technology Today*, *21*(4), 10–11. doi:10.1016/S0965-2590(09)70095-7

Attoh-Okine, N., & Shen, L. (1995). *Security issues of emerging smart cards fare collection application in mass transit*. Paper presented at the Vehicle Navigation and Information Systems Conference.

Bain, D. (1995). *Smart cards: Implications for privacy*. Sydney, Australia: Australian Privacy Commissioner.

Bandyopadhyay, K., & Fraccastoro, K. A. (2007). The effect of culture on user acceptance of information technology. *Communications of the Association for Information Systems*, *19*(23), 522–543.

Birch, A., & Irvine, V. (2009). Preservice teachers' acceptance of ICT integration in the classroom: Applying the UTAUT model. *Educational Media International*, *46*(4), 295–315. doi:10.1080/09523980903387506

CBORD. (2006). *Client successful story- Deakin University*. Retrieved from http://www.cbord.com/news/success/profile_82.htm

Cheng, D., Liu, G., Qian, C., & Song, Y. (2009). User acceptance of internet banking: An extension of the UTAUT model with trust and quality constructs. *International Journal of Services Operations and Informatics*, *4*(4), 378–393. doi:10.1504/IJSOI.2009.029186

Ching, S., Tai, A., Pong, J., & Cheng, M. (2009). Don't let micropayments penalize you—experience from the city University Of Hong Kong. *Journal of Academic Librarianship*, *35*(1), 86–97. doi:10.1016/j.acalib.2008.10.018

Elliot, S., & Loebbecke, C. (1998). Smart-card based electronic commerce: Characteristics and roles. In *Proceedings of the IEEE 31st Hawaii International Conference on System Sciences* (Vol. 4, pp. 242-250).

Fleshman, D., Schweiger, C., Lott, D., & Peirlott, G. (1998). *Multipurpose transit payment media*. Retrieved from http://onlinepubs.trb.org/onlinepubs/tcrp/tcrp_rpt_32.pdf

Hofstede, G. (2001). *Culture's consequences: Comparing values, behaviors, institutions and organizations across nations*. Thousand Oaks, CA: Sage.

Jen, W., Lu, T., & Liu, P. (2009). An integrated analysis of technology acceptance behaviour models: Comparison of three major models. *MIS Review*, *15*(1), 89–121.

Jones, D. (2009). Viewpoint a role for the smart card industry in 'social banking'. *Card Technology Today*, *21*(5), 16. doi:10.1016/S0965-2590(09)70082-9

Kumar, Y., & Ganesh, S. (2005). Integration of smart card and gabor filter method based fingerprint matching for faster verification. In *Proceedings of the IEEE Annual Indicon Conference* (p. 526).

Lambert, N., Plumb, J., Looise, B., Johnson, I. T., Harvey, I., & Wheeler, C. (2005). Using smart card technology to monitor the eating habits of children in a school cafeteria. *Journal of Human Nutrition and Dietetics*, *18*(4), 243–254. doi:10.1111/j.1365-277X.2005.00617.x

Lee, Y., Kozar, K. A., & Larsen, K. R. T. (2003). The technology acceptance model: Past, present and future. *Communications of the Association for Information Systems, 12*, 752–780.

M'Chirgui, Z. (2003). *An empirical evidence of the electronic purse's adoption: The case of Moneo*. Aix-en-Provence, France: Universite de la Mediterranee.

Ma, L., Banerjee, P., Lai, J., & Shroff, R. (2008). Diffusion of the 'Octopus' smart card e-payment system. *International Journal of Business and Information, 3*(1), 115–128.

Materka, A., Strzelecki, M., & Debiec, P. (2009). Student's electronic card: A secure Internet database system for university management support. *Internet-Technical Development and Applications, 64*, 59–72. doi:10.1007/978-3-642-05019-0_8

Mayes, K., & Markantonakis, K. (2006). On the potential of high density smart cards. *Information Security Technical Report, 11*, 147–154. doi:10.1016/j.istr.2006.05.002

McCourt, R. S. (2006). *Smart parking meters take over the west*. Retrieved from http://www.dksassociates.com/admin/paperfile/Smart_Parking_Meters_Take_Over_the_West.pdf

Noe, J. (2005). Contactless cards: The next best thing? *ABA Banking Journal, 97*(9), 42–46.

Omar, S., & Djuhari, H. (2004). Multi-purpose student card system using smart card technology. In *Proceedings of the Fifth International Conference of Information Technology Based Higher Education and Training* (pp. 527-532).

Ondrus, J., & Pigneur, Y. (2006). Towards a holistic analysis of mobile payments: A multiple perspectives approach. *Journal Electronic Commerce Research and Applications, 5*, 246–257. doi:10.1016/j.elerap.2005.09.003

Plouffe, C. R., Hulland, J. S., & Vandenbosch, M. (2001). Richness versus parsimony in modeling technology adoption decisions--understanding merchant adoption of a smart card-based payment system. *Information Systems Research, 12*(2), 208–222. doi:10.1287/isre.12.2.208.9697

Plouffe, C. R., Vandenbosch, M., & Hulland, J. S. (2000). Why smart cards have failed: Looking to consumer and merchant reactions to a new payment technology. *International Journal of Bank Marketing, 18*(3), 112–124. doi:10.1108/02652320010339662

Plouffe, C. R., Vandenbosch, M., & Hulland, J. S. (2001). Intermediating technologies and multi-group adoption: A comparison of consumer and merchant adoption intentions toward a new electronic payment system. *Product Innovation Management, 18*(2), 65–81. doi:10.1016/S0737-6782(00)00072-2

Rastogi, L., & Das, P. (2002). *Re-engineering educational institutions through smart cards*. Retrieved from http://www.au-kbc.org/bpmain1/Security/smartcardwp.pdf

Rivis, A., & Sheeran, P. (2003). Descriptive norms as an additional predictor in the theory of planned behaviour: A meta-analysis. *Current Psychology (New Brunswick, N.J.), 22*(3), 218–223. doi:10.1007/s12144-003-1018-2

Rochet, J., & Tirole, J. (2003). An economic analysis of the determination of interchange fees in payment card systems. *Review of Network Economics, 2*(2), 69–79. doi:10.2202/1446-9022.1019

Rogers, E. M. (2003). *Diffusion of innovations* (5th ed.). New York, NY: Free Press.

Ross, C. A. (1976). The effects of trial and incentives on repeat purchase behavior. *JMR, Journal of Marketing Research, 13*(3), 263–269. doi:10.2307/3150736

Rothschild, M. L., & Gaidis, W. C. (1981). Behavioral learning theory: Its relevance to marketing and promotions. *Journal of Marketing*, *45*(2), 70–78. doi:10.2307/1251666

SCA. (2006). *Smart cards and parking*. Princeton, NJ: Smart Card Alliance.

Sheeran, P., & Orbell, S. (1999). Augmenting the theory of planned behavior: Roles for anticipated regret and descriptive norms. *Journal of Applied Social Psychology*, *29*(10), 2107–2142. doi:10.1111/j.1559-1816.1999.tb02298.x

Sun, H., & Zhang, P. (2006). The role of moderating factors in user technology acceptance. *International Journal of Human-Computer Studies*, *64*(2), 53–78. doi:10.1016/j.ijhcs.2005.04.013

Truman, G., Sandow, K., & Rifkin, T. (2003). An empirical study of smart card technology. *Information & Management*, *40*, 591–606. doi:10.1016/S0378-7206(02)00046-0

Turban, E., & McElroy, D. (1998). Using smart cards in electronic commerce. In *Proceedings of the 31st Annual Hawaii International Conference on System Sciences* (pp. 62-69).

Venkatesh, V., Morris, M. G., & Ackerman, P. L. (2000). A longitudinal field investigation of gender differences in individual technology adoption decision-making processes. *Organizational Behavior and Human Decision Processes*, *83*, 33–60. doi:10.1006/obhd.2000.2896

Venkatesh, V., Morris, M. G., Davis, G. B., & Davis, F. D. (2003). User acceptance of information technology: Toward a unified view. *Management Information Systems Quarterly*, *27*(3), 425–478.

White, L. (2001). Internet security is the killer application for campus card. *Card Technology Today*, *13*(10), 13–14.

Wixon, B. H., & Todd, P. A. (2005). A theoretical integration of user satisfaction and technology acceptance. *Information Systems Research*, *16*(1), 85–102. doi:10.1287/isre.1050.0042

Wu, I. L., & Wu, K. W. (2005). A hybrid technology acceptance approach for exploring E-Crm adoption in organisations. *Behaviour & Information Technology*, *24*(4), 303–316. doi:10.1080/0144929042000320027

This work was previously published in the International Journal of Technology and Human Interaction, Volume 7, Issue 3, edited by Anabela Mesquita and Chia-Wen Tsai, pp. 1-15, copyright 2011 by IGI Publishing (an imprint of IGI Global).

Chapter 12
An Office on the Go:
Professional Workers, Smartphones and the Return of Place

Mats Edenius
Uppsala University, Sweden

Hans Rämö
Stockholm University, Sweden

ABSTRACT

In this paper, the authors examine how senior managers, as professional workers, in a leading ICT company use smartphones, according to new configurations of time and space. Of special interest is how smartphones act as comforting handheld consoles without being rooted in physical location. Three non-physical places, as spatial nodes, are presented: pause in the temporal current, place as a function of the intensity of communication, and place in terms of becoming rooted by felt value. The authors argue that highlighting non-physical places as structures emanating from the use of smartphones is an important variable to account for when studying how professionals use smartphones, both in instrumental and non-instrumental terms.

INTRODUCTION

Mobile phones have evolved from being used largely for oral communication and information transfer, to handheld personal devices also used for accessing emails and Internet sites, as well as retrieving and storing all kinds of digital data. Expanding from being a mobile phone to becoming an integrated handheld wireless digital service provider – a smartphone. In line with other ICT-

applications, smartphones let us move away from traditional office structures towards increasingly mobile and flexible management and workforce (Wellman, 2001; Kakihara & Sorensen, 2002) where multiple tasks are engaged simultaneously, practices coordinated and synchronized in new ways, and performed at higher speed (Townsend, 2000).

Mobile computing activities facilitate information management on the move (Wiredu, 2007,

DOI: 10.4018/978-1-4666-1954-8.ch012

p. 123; Kakihara et al., 2004; Cousins & Robey, 2005). The conventional argument is that mobile phones are no longer telephones linked to a certain place (in an office, a house, etc; cf. García-Montes, 2006) in which a person is inserted. For that reason, place has been argued as becoming less relevant when social and work-related transactions can be carried out in spaces. Harvey (1989) even argues that communication technologies "compress" time and space with the potential to eliminate characteristics of place. However, even if Alfred Marshall asserted already in his 1890 treatise, *The Principles of Economics*, that in economic life the influence of time is more fundamental than the influence of space, time still needs to be understood together with human notions of space and place.

Spatiotemporal configurations and their applications are well studied areas. This study follows the approach that temporal issues does not mean that place loses its meaning and vanishes into thin air in an accelerating flow of events (e.g. Giddens, 1990, p. 18). Rather the opposite; previous research about mobile computing noticably accentuates the importance of spatial dimensions and their close affinity to time. Cousins and Robey (2005), for example, not only show that agency in organizations is affected by physical locations (e.g. home, road, office etc.), but also that different boundaries are quite clear for the (nomadic) agents, which allowed them to use segments of time in a wide range of spaces more productively. Furthermore, Sørensen and Pica (2005) stress the need to study the relationships between the situational aspects of work, the institutional context of work and the use of mobile technologies supporting work (see also Lee, 1999; Mazmanian, Yates & Orlikowski, 2006; Prasopoulou, Pouloudi & Panteli, 2006; Wiberg & Ljungberg, 2001; Wireu & Sørensen, 2006). While these studies have yielded important insights about place relatedness in virtual work, few have explicitly addressed human time and space configurations in professional mobile communication, and studies of time-space con-

figurations that highlight spatial aspects of mobile organizing are particularly scant (cf. Lee & Whietley 2002; Schultze & Boland, 2000; Wiberg & Ljungberg, 2001).

What is undeveloped and somewhat neglected in previous discussions on mobile phone use is not only that ICT build relationships between places through processes of time and space compression, but that these mobile influences also tend to undermine singular stable and unitary conceptions of place. This study therefore argues that patterns of smartphone use should not only be described in terms of explicating different dimensions of physical places, and their relation to temporal, and contextual properties (e.g., office, road, home, etc., cf. Cousins & Robey, 2005). Instead, in the spirit of Jacussi et al.'s (2006) headline plea "…taking complexity seriously in IS research" a theoretical approach is proposed in this study that highlights how different physical, as well as non-physical, nodal places, may be manifested in contemporary smartphone use as emergent structures enacted by professionals' daily use of smartphones. This is the first aim of this paper. The second aim is then to explore how nodal places as theoretical categories can be incorporated into the analysis of time-space configurations of mobile technology use in a professional context.

This paper's empirical material is primarily based on a qualitative and interpretative investigation of how managers as professional workers in a world-leading Nordic ICT company adopt and incorporate smartphones in their daily life. By professional workers we mean actors that have to deal with increasingly complex work and are able to flexibly make decisions and interact with a large number of people (cf. Kakihara & Sørensen, 2002; Sørensen & Gibson, 2004; Schön, 1983).

The paper is organized in the following way: The next section will further exploit how time-space can be configured in human place and space, and how these socially-constructed concepts are employed in this paper. The following section addresses methodological issues. There subsequently follows an empirical investigation that gives several viewpoints and illustrative examples of how professional workers use smartphones, and how smartphones act as comforting consoles without being rooted in physical location. The paper ends with a discussion and concluding results.

SMARTPHONES AND THE CONSTRUCTION OF TIME AND PLACE

The relationship between technology and organizing processes in general and outcomes in particular has long been of interest in scholarly literature (for an overview, see Robey, Boudreau & Rose, 2000). However, the interest during the last decades has moved from understandings of technology as a determinant of organizational structures, to perspectives where researchers apply notions to social phenomena such as innovations, learning and improvisation to account both for more dynamic perspectives, as well as to understand organizational implications of new technologies (Ciborra, 2000; Cook & Brown, 1999; Orlikowski, 1996, 2000). Such perspectives give the potential to find a number of theories emphasizing different structures, structural properties and their relation to human agency, ICT, and action. Within such focus on the individual professional worker in an organizational context, time-space configurations are understood as socially constructed entities.

This paper follow a vein that has become commonplace in social theory; namely that time and space are always contextually interlinked and that place and space are the two central spatial aspects in human time-space configurations (Giddens, 1990; Urry, 1985, 1991). The starting point is that 'place' could fruitfully be regarded as safety and security of dwelling, whereas space is freedom, and "that we are attached to the one and long for the other" (Tuan, 1977, p. 3; see also Gregory, 1994; Normark & Esbjörnsson, 2004; Schultze & Boland, 2000; for partly contrasting defini-

tions: Massey, 1988; Gieryn, 2000). Thus, the two human spatial entities of space and place are interlocked into a contextual duality whereby the one meaning constitutes the other. However, human time-space configurations are unfolding into different meanings in the various social, cultural and political contexts where they are mediated. It is, for example, a well-established premise in social thought that the dominant technologies of a particular period define temporal and cultural understandings of it (e.g. Harvey, 1989). Concepts ranging from "labor time" (Rifkin, 1987) to the more recent "Internet time" (Lee & Liebenau, 2000) are just two time-related illustrations of development and progress over the last centuries. Recent examples of empirically oriented elaborations with time and space configurations in ICT studies include, for example, Lee and Liebenau's (2000) finding that to grasp how time is perceived and organized, a conceptual guide is needed to access where new ICT (i.e. Internet) makes a real difference to temporality. Lee and Liebenau (ibid.) propose, for example, that features like duration, sequence and deadlines are important concepts to scrutinize in this context. Green (2002, p. 284), among others, also illuminates that ICT in general and mobile phones in particular increase the communication activities carried out, while at the same time fragmenting that communication into more numerous communications of shorter duration. Green (ibid.) also argues that mobile phones seem to intensify the extent that the subjective experience, the feeling of time, is accelerating. It must be kept in mind, however, that smartphones are just one communication technology among others, and furthermore, as been put forth by Virilio (1986; Harvey, 1989), speed and time-space compression could even be regarded as a generic trait of contemporary society.

However, as already been noticed, time needs to be understood together with spatial aspects in human time-space configurations, and as noted by Casey (1993, 1997), Gieryn (2000: 472), Tuan (1977) and others – a sense of place is not only the ability to locate things, but also the attribution of meaning. Places are constructed as people ascribe qualities to the attributes gathered there. To identify how smartphones in use can generate nodal places, without being rooted in physical locations, a further discussion is needed about what is meant by nodal places. A sense of place implies that people and things are implaced, i.e. present and engaged in communication. Being, rather than becoming, is then a characteristic of place (cf. Harvey, 1989). It is this boundedness, and this recurrence of events that fill place not only with feelings of pause, safety and stability, etc., but also with restricted movement and limited change (Casey, 1993, 1997; Giddens, 1991; Harvey, 1989; Schultze & Boland, 2000). However, this restrictiveness in place would be unthinkable without space that "raises" the social life above here and now. In contrast to the boundedness of place, space embodies an image of a uniform and infinite expanse, through which people and ideas can move freely (Casey, 1993, 1997; Tuan, 1977).

It is within such a background Tuan elaborates his analytical framework in the book *Space and Place: The Perspective of Experience* (1977), in which he postulates that that a space requires a movement from a place to another place. Similarly, a place requires a space to be a place. Hence, the two notions form a duality and that we are "attached to the one and long for the other" (ibid: 3).

Adam (in Rettie 2005, p. 18) concurs "there is no single time, only a multitude of time which interpenetrate and permeate our daily lifes". This study sheds light on that there are – to paraphrase Adam – no single places, only a multitude of places which interpenetrate and permeate our daily lives. This may be obvious in phone conversations that occur simultaneously and remotely in two or more physical places. The participants are on the phone, the meeting is real, but there is no common meeting place or concrete shared location. The phone call occurs in a space, but not in place. A deeper analysis of the extremely complex rela-

tion between place and space – matters addressed already by the ancient Greeks – is far beyond the scope of this article.

Thus, following Tuan (1977), we suggest a differentiation into three sets of time-space configurations in terms of nodal places that permeates the professionals' daily working lives:

Firstly, place as a pause in the temporal current when the professional workers are on the move to different meetings; Secondly, attachment to a place when the professional are in meetings (in communication with others), captured in the following quotation: "While it takes time to form an attachment to place, the quality and intensity of experience matters more than simple duration" (Tuan, 1977, p. 198), and; Thirdly, place in terms of becoming rooted and related to how information is represented in the smartphone. The above viewpoints will be further specified and empirically exemplified in this paper.

METHODOLOGY AND THE EMPIRICAL ARENA

The perspective employed in this article is based upon what Orlikowski (1992, 2000) has coined as "a practice lens for understanding technology use". Employing such a practice draws attention to emergent structures enacted in practice when a technique is used in different milieus in recurrent ways in everyday situated activities. For example, some properties that are provided by the artifact do not exist for the user as a part of their technology in practices, while some others do. This practice lens approach ameliorates appreciation of the lived complexities of human organization in terms of what Schatzki et al. (2001) called a "practice turn", where the social is a field of embodied, materially interwoven practices centrally organized around shared practical understandings where the action is. Research based on such a practice lens approach has received support in many different studies in the proposed research field (cf. Boudreau & Robey, 2005; Cousins & Robey, 2005; Schultze & Orlikowski, 2004; Sørensen & Pica, 2005).

In order to explore how professional workers perceive their daily use of smartphones at their work, information has been collected from people in their context of use, naturally buttressed by other studies' empirical results. The empirical approach is closely linked to what has been called making ethnographic interviews, where interviews (sessions) are conducted in work environments, where people can act more naturally, and where the researcher can take into account and explore surroundings and settings (Barley & Kunda, 2004; Spradley, 1979; Taylor & Bogdan, 1984).

A series of interview questions was developed to explore mobile communication strategies and techniques with the help of smartphones when used by professional workers in their everyday managerial work. In this explorative study, interviews with 15 managers in a world-leading Nordic ICT company were conducted by 3 interviewers. All of the managers were selected from the top management level in different departments of the company (e.g., Finance, Legal department, Marketing, Production, R&D, etc). The managers' work, and the reason why we picked them out, correspond very much to what we see encapsulating professional workers - their job was complex and they had to be able to make decisions flexibly and interact with a large number of people. Given the small group of interviewees, the discussions were intended to shed light on key issues of smartphone use, rather than to collect generalizable data. Working in a leading ICT company also means that these persons are familiar with using smartphones in their jobs. Each person was contacted by phone to set up a time to conduct the interview in their offices. Each *in situ* interview took from 50 to 100 minutes. The survey questions were used as a guide for the conversation, rather than as a strict question-and-answer tool.[1] In this way, the interviewers were able to structure the conversation in a way that obtained the most

relevant information about the respondent's use of smartphones. The respondents were asked to tell us about and describe their work and how they used their smartphones. We let them make comments about the most typical functions they used, step by step, and where they used these functions. We also let them describe their thoughts and experiences about using smartphones related to specific work tasks and work environments.

Initially, a theoretically grounded inquiry was set out that related to how new configurations of time and space appeared in different context to the managers' daily activities. Interviews constituted the modes of the investigation. Each interview was recorded and each of these was later transcribed verbatim. In addition, notes were taken throughout each interview. During the interview with the various representatives, the discussions were substantially richer in content than the following text and summary depict. The aim of the interviews was to generate to a degree a general picture of how different time and space aspects are experienced and dealt with in the managers' daily lives. Parallel with the empirical fieldwork a thematic analysis was conducted. Different data was identified and put into different sub-themes of classified patterns in line with Constas' (1992, p. 258) note that that the interpretative approach should be considered as a "distinct point of origination". By doing this, a more comprehensive picture was reached of how the managers as professionals use smartphones as part of their collective experiences.

The presentation of our empirical material is divided according to different aspects and foci of the study. In some instances the respondents provide the best picture of the circumstances that are thought to prevail. Consequently, to a certain extent examples are given from the transcribed interview text. All the interviews and the current workplaces are anonymous. The reason for the anonymity is that information was not collected in order to comment on the advantages or drawbacks of any particular workplace; rather, the aim was exclusively to illustrate place and space of everyday use of smartphones.

However, it must be noticed that in spirit with the explorative approach of this paper all the empirical material is not to be regarded as an endeavor to conceive of a clear order from different observations, like a "pure" induction or a complete "case study". Verifying clear theories or hypotheses is not the primary goal of this paper. The approach is thus based on an *abductive method* (Hanson, 1958). The abductive method encapsulates the kind of uncertainty that is present in the research strategy. In line with such a method the empirical material speaks as if it solves the question at stake, equivalent to the propositions we make up in the beginning of this article. The explorative approach of this paper follows the vein of Charles Sanders Peirce (1992; see also Tsoukas, 1989) suggesting that making a reasonable guess is the only way of getting closer to attaining new and fruitful knowledge.

THE EMPIRICAL ARENA

When asking managers at the IT company how they internalize new forms of ICT in their everyday management practice, all stressed the dependency (or even symbiosis) they have with their smartphones – and the aspiration to eventually replace laptops with a fully integrated PC smartphone unit, that can be linked with any full size keyboard and monitor (when improved ergonomics and interfaces can match the need). Almost all the managers have their smartphones switched on day and night, though on silent mode during the night.

The managers use the smartphones to communicate, to receive information, to improve their knowledge and manage different activities. Roughly speaking, the professional workers receive 20-70 mails and make at least 10-50 phone calls a day. Frequent traveling and extensive

meetings are scheduled and coordinated by using the smartphone, rather than with the help of a secretary. As one manager said:

I think we can increase doing things more efficiently due to the mobile phones. I can receive a question at 10 pm and respond to it immediately. Otherwise we have to stretch the time... I can work at airports and I can get information about when my plane departs and from which gate... I can get information about everything... and I got all my days planned out thanks to the calendar in my mobile phone.

However, by using the smartphone, the managers not only stretch out their working days, but also change the rhythm of their work. Much of the managers' work can also be described in terms of unpredictable sequences, which existed in the flux of unfolding activities related to both personal meetings and not at least the smartphone:

I'm always on duty; my phone is always on duty; I always answer when it rings. I check emails constantly; as a key account manager, you've got to be reachable all the time. Anything might happen anytime. To fix something, to read emails, SMS can be used anytime, with the phone on silent mode. You could say that for 5 years now, I've been online all the time...

One manager explains how he acts during a meeting in following way:

This afternoon I will participate in a meeting that will take 3 hours. However, just about half of the time is about issues that I am interested in. The rest of the time I will do something else. I cannot run out of the meeting and come back, because I never know when my issues will pop up on the agenda or just be discussed. ...We do work with a lot of complex issues and it is hard not to have meetings like this because things have to be dis-

cussed, but in my world is it perfectly alright to read your mail or to write instant messaging when there are tasks that are being discussed that do not belong to your field.

Both the statement that smartphones "speed up" different processes, and that using smartphones changes the rhythm in their daily work, were common among the interviewees. These statements are closely linked to conventional variables representing areas of temporal studies, like identifying activities of time and how actors relate themselves to time etc. (cf. Ancona et al., 2001). The empirical investigation in this study is also congruent with the argument that mobile phones both conserve and consume time. The managers as professional workers improve time management, but they also increase availability and impromptu meetings, calls etc, so that more time is used for communication (see also Rettie, 2005). Starting from Tuan's (1977) framework of nodal places, the focus will now turn towards the question how smartphones in use can generate nodal places and explore how patterns of professional smartphone use can be explained by the suggested nodal places.

THREE VIGNETTES

1. To be Implaced by a Pause

Parallel with different impromptu situations, the managers are almost fully occupied with participation in meetings. One manager alluded humorously to John Cleese's words, when saying: "I can't go to meetings 'cause I'm always in meetings!". Another manager explained the situation in the following way:

I had a meeting in the morning and then a second one, followed by discussion about our forthcoming financial report, and then I'd a meeting downtown with some bank representatives, because we're

dealing with M/A issues too [mergers & acquisitions], and then I'd had four more meetings, and...

The numbers of meetings differ of course, but it is not unusual to participate in 6-10 meetings a day. It could be said that the smartphones both are related to generating impromptu meetings, and to administrating and coordinating different meetings. Some managers' even said that they primarily used their smartphones to administrate meetings.

I would say that the most important contacts are calls for meetings; acceptance of appointments, or rescheduling appointments; there are lots of such issues. That's the most important, I would say, because when I travel, it's a question of attending meetings, and you need to know details about the meetings; that's what this tool has done for me.

A frequent problem is, however, that one meeting might end at the same time as the next meeting starts in a different part of the company's premises. Hence, a need to SMS delay notices. The number of meetings seems to have become too many, frequently grouped too closely together and sometimes quite unnecessary according to the managers' working tasks. Some of the interviewees express this phenomenon by saying that they felt bustled about, but the smartphone, partly, helped them out of this dilemma, as in the following case:

Before, you needed to be there on time, otherwise the work couldn't be started. And then you went home when the rest went home, because there was no point in staying. That's not the situation today. This new mobile technology has wiped out much of the traditional office hours. You can start before anyone else has arrived, because you can call them up and discuss over the phone.

There are so many meetings to participate in, at the same time you have to spend time on management...When I'm on the way to different meetings,

I usually take the opportunity to sit down and clean up my inbox or to make some phone calls, it a nice way to spend your time when you're on your way somewhere.

Isn't it clever to be able to communicate when you are on the move, sitting in a gate in an airport, or just in the bus on the way to the offices...it may just take a few minutes, but it will let you to look for what is new in the inbox and things like that.

These illustrations show that the managers seem rather to be "on the move", occupied in a lot of meetings, and filling their working time with supposedly productive time. Yet, at the same time the managers are finding "gaps" as pauses for handling all sorts of tasks with the smartphone acting as a nodal platform.

It has become accepted to be in constant state of "on the move" between different more or less planned meetings and being in different impromptu meetings (cf. Townsend, 2000; Green, 2002). The smartphone seems, in this context, to give the user a feeling of control, to reach security, to limit the range of activities. It has become a place to slow down a bit, to be able to just sit down making phone calls or administrate the mail. Smartphones' are thus acting as platforms – creating a sense of nodal place. Quite paradoxically then, using the smartphone has become a pause in the managers' work – a place to be at, in a race for time that is running non-stop. The pause understood as a place was also made explicit in several cases by the managers. They expressed it that they had "killed time" when using the smartphones.

2. To be Implaced by the Intensity of Communication

It is getting to be a common occurrence at meetings to leave the smartphone turned on, but turned to the silent mode during presentations. Nowadays, interrupting meetings by smartphones (or mobile phones) going off is still an offence (at least in the company we studied), but having it on silent mode – or even checking and writing messages at a meeting – is no longer impolite or rude.

In terms of space and place configurations this means it does not matter if you are not listening while being present at the meeting, since you are at least attending, but you are not supposed to interfere or interrupt your colleagues at the meeting.

When we're having our executive meetings, our phones are silent, not switched off. If someone says "let's switch off our phones", then I'll switch mine onto silent mode, because I want to see if, for instance, my kids are calling – if something's happening.

What's happening in the meeting room depends on who's receiving the call. If it's someone important for the meeting, everything stops. If it's someone less important, then the meeting goes on (but phone calls will still be taken individually).

Multitasking during meetings is a really good thing; it has become possible thanks to the mobile phones and computers... You can do so many more things at a meeting today by killing silent moments [by using their smartphones] or moments where irrelevant issues are discussed.

The managers are also aware that the receiver of a call might be sitting in a meeting but they still send an SMS and more or less expect that it will be read:

I would say that SMS is a sort of non-intrusive way of communicating something of importance, when I know the other party's having a meeting, and then I'll send him an SMS, which can be read during a meeting

It is also something you might do to people sitting in the same meeting:

When you're in negotiations you might send a message to each other in the same room asking, for instance: "shall we accept this", and sometimes I contact people outside the room to check up important issues.

These examples illustrate that different institutionalized virtues are still important to follow. You should not speak loudly when taking a phone call in a meeting, you rather prefer to put it into silent mode or communicate via SMS. The compression of time and space would largely not be possible if it were not possible to communicate during meetings. However, managers' participation in different meetings does not have to be very much engaged in the meeting conversations as such. Instead, the managers can always be connected and compress their time by multitasking with their smartphones at the meeting.

Consequently, the managers attend numerous meetings, planned and unplanned. However, physical presence in a meeting includes not only temporary mental absence – when dealing with other matters on the smartphone – but also informal, under the tabletop, electronic conferencing with other participants over details in the meeting, etc.

You can see that there is a lot of multitasking going on at the company...if there are meetings with different issues on the agenda and not all the issues are closely linked to you, and then it is absolutely alright to do something else during the meetings.

Attachment is seldom acquired in passing. Instead, as Tuan (1977, p. 184) so aptly put it by quoting the philosopher James K. Feibleman "the importance of events in any life is more directly proportionate to their intensity than to their extensity." What seems most at issue for the managers is not to be inserted in different extensive meetings, but to be implaced in a scheme of intensity of different communication acts, to

"kill silent moments". Occasionally the speaker of the meeting can be the place to attach to, but the attachment to the smartphone as a comforting nodal platform – becoming an eye in an intense working environment – seems frequently to be of more importance.

3. To be Implaced by Felt Value

The third vignette theme is that the speed of information exchange today seems to drive a nonstop mentality, which demands multitasking. The managers could find themselves in a multitude of physical and mental spaces and times which interpenetrate and permeate their daily lives. The smartphone seems indeed to have increased the communication activities carried out, while at the same time fragmenting that communication into more numerous communications of shorter duration (cf. Green, 2002). Today's managers have become, at the same time, increasingly involved in frequent browsing of the inbox and incoming phone calls in a constant evaluation and classification of the incoming messages.

It's about everyday decisions. A decision could be to inform someone that you're 15 minutes late for a meeting, or that you can't attend, because you're caught in another meeting. Such information makes things roll.

To be a professional worker in general is to be almost fully occupied with making judgments and making evaluations. It could be said that different managers' cognitive capacities are highlighted according to new time and space configurations. The professional workers have learned to evaluate in an instant, in both space and time. However, this seems not to be an uncomplicated process. As described by one manager:

The drawback is that you've to take the active decision not to check incoming messages. On average, I receive 70 mails a day and if my computer is switched off, they all come to my mobile. It's convenient when you're traveling, when making an intermediate landing, you can check your important e-mails. In that situation, I can call or reply to an email, that's a good function. Otherwise, you just are postponing your problems. The numbers of email you receive each day will not disappear, but stacks up, and you'll get twice as much to do the next day.

The managers have to make their own decisions about whether they should answer a phone call and if and when they should respond to an incoming mail immediately or not. Nobody else makes the decision for them. This situation differs from what it used to be. As a manager said by evoking an idealized and stable past:

Some years ago, you wrote a draft, which you gave to a secretary, who wrote and corrected the text, and it came back and you read it, corrected it, well it was a pretty long process before that letter was sent to someone outside and formulations were altered. Today it's an email; and Beep, it's away without anyone seeing it, perhaps even to an external party.

The number of phone calls and incoming mail is large. The managers are forced to prioritize, but how do they prioritize?

When my boss calls, then you take the call, always. You know it's pretty important and you take the call. Otherwise calls go to your voice-mail and you sort them out.

I always take calls from my boss. It's our way of prioritizing. She's top priority. My wife is the second highest priority during office-hours, and on weekends there're some other people.

Sorry, but I have to answer this phone call – it is the fifth time it's ringing, yes, I suspect it must be something important...

By splitting the world into swift prioritizing of "this and that"; by doing this the managers bring into consciousness the constituent parts of the phenomenon they are interested in. In other words, getting to know how to handle smartphones entails knowledge to make competent use of the categories and the distinctions in that domain (cf. Townley, 2002). By dividing their incoming calls and messages the managers can maintain a vision, get a feeling of control, and ascribe significance to certain aspects of the world (cf. Foucault, 1983). The managers seem to urge for security by getting in an analytical space of colleagues and family members and friends. It is at the same time a space of ranks and a place of potential comparisons. It renders a sense of stability in an unruly world.

However, what happens if the prioritizing division is lost? Then also vision, control, and security are jeopardized or lost. When a manager gets an anonymous phone call or mail, they got confused and said that they did not answer such a message or phone call.

It is always possible to see who is calling, you get a kind of ranking list according to your phone book, but there are also some calls where I can't see who is calling, people with a hidden number... usually I don't bother to answer such calls at all.

The managers have learned to be in a steady mode of instant evaluations. They will find themselves oriented in an analytical space of distinctions (like the intensity of communication acts), generating compression of time and space, but attached to and rooted in different social relations. What began as undifferentiated spaces have become familiar places when the users get to know them as either a function of pure time urgency (the boss is calling, or the fifth time it rings) or finding a time-place slot, both rendered visible on the screen of smartphones.

EXPLORING SMARTPHONE USE IN TERMS OF NODAL PLACES

What does it mean in terms of time-space configurations to be accessible online all the time by having the smartphone switched on? The interviewees point out that their smartphones have made them more independent of time and place. Several of the interviewees' pointed out a rapid development in the way they communicate and the coordinative capability of smartphones. Daily routines have been radically shifted by using smartphones in the company. Now they could, for example, come late to meetings. These results may not appear to be surprising. Nevertheless, if smartphone usage evokes a feeling of a pause in the intensity in working life communication, and security in terms of being rooted, then they are also structural entities (enacted in the professionals' daily use of their smartphones) to take into account when managing and analyzing spatial and temporal effects of using smartphones.

However, smartphones, like technologies in general, are designed to achieve particular tasks. They are by definition purposeful, instrumental, directed at achieving a particular end (cf. Arnold, 2003). Modern reason speaks of means. It is the matching of means efficiently to ends. "Action is judged in relation to consequences as compared with alternative, possible courses of action and their consequences" (Townley, 2002, p. 557). Optimization of a deployed mobile application, for example to reach the highest speed of business processes, lies in mobile activities at specific time and places and for particular purposes. However, the use of smartphones – and technology in general – can at the same time, undermine such target-oriented approaches. Professionals' use of smartphones has, for example, speeded up different business processes, but professionals can also find themselves interrupted by taking phone calls and messages all the time (cf. Davis 2002). The supposedly rational and goal-directed instrumental focus of our will sometimes acts in other directions

too[2]. The introduction of the theoretical concept of nodal place offers a potentially productive way forward – not only to explorations of smartphone usage in general – but also to discussions about both the coordinative possibilities as well as the failed promises of smartphones.

We start this discussion by focusing on the three sets of time-space configurations in our empirical material in terms of the nodal places presented above in terms of a pause, intensity and felt value. In the subsequent part we will extend our explorative study by also putting our analytical categories – nodal places – into play in other studies about new technologies and time-space configurations.

As highlighted by e.g. Plant (2002), the personal and social consequences of the mobile workforces show how mobile phones may result in a loss of "commitment to appointment"; something that is discernible in the empirical material. Meetings could easily be postponed just by sending an SMS and subsequently transferring to another day. This may be part of a ambition to reach highest efficiency by prioritizing different activities. However, by regarding the place of pause as an important place for professional workers, gives a possible explanation or even a rudimentary theory that goes beyond more conventional reasons of postponing a meeting or theories posited. The professional workers might just search for a quiet moment – a pause in their hasty life. This opens up a discussion about sustainable communication, and how to balance, a hasty life of always being in communication mode. It also shed light on the complexity of managing professional workers' smartphone use, because the illustrations go in another direction beyond a conventional rational discourse of optimizing organizational processes; the users seem to struggle for nodal place havens, and they are occupied of taking breaks and pauses.

The professional workers are also Implaced by the Intensity of Communication. Information is not only designative, but works in terms of topography. Consequently, to represent the act of representing cannot be done (cf. Derrida, 1997; Foucault, 1983). By illuminating how the smartphone use is linked to structures of the intensity of communication shows that the topography of information is of major importance in professional workers' daily work. The professional workers are surrounded by different information sources all day long. Should they, for instance, continue listening to a presentation at a meeting or should they start handling their messages? However, pre-planned topics at a meeting do not follow a controllable schedule, rendering multitasking a necessity in many meetings, which frequently are arranged impromptu. As a consequence, the professional workers are working in less predictable sequences. Different stages of intensity – which correlate to nodal places – makes it possible for the managers to work with different things in non-directed ways. They follow the pre-planned assignments in their Outlook calendars, as well as constantly rearranging assignments. They plan different meetings, but are always ready to rearrange them. The smartphone has helped them with this process. The manager's are thus acting both in monochronic (when work goes according to the daily schedule) and a polychronic environment (where a number of discrete events over the working day happen in unpredictable sequences, cf. Barley, 1988; Zerubavel, 1979). This process of managing and synchronizing lies at the heart of optimizing organizational processes.

However, by alluding to the words of Castells (1996), the promised coordinative possibilities of creating a space of flows by using mobile technology are somewhat offset by smartphones' coordinating capacity of arranging an increasing number of physical (impromptu) meetings in not only physical places, but also non-physical, nodal places. The managers' working days have thus become less clear than they were some years ago. This is rather opposite to the slogan that smartphones are in the hands of managers to control their work. The nodal place as intensity might, for example, draw attention to how new networks may appears or even how new knowledge is generated at the boundaries between unforeseen disciplines or specializations.

When the two former nodal places (i.e. to be implace by a pause, and to be implaced by the intensity of communication) are linked to multitasking, the third (to be implaced by felt value) is more related to the network that is potentially maintained by the smartphone. The expectation, and sometime compulsive nature, of constantly being online means that situations of not being connected create feelings of anxiety and confinement.

The mistrust and the tensions are there for sound reasons. The contemporary mobile phone user seems to reduce the number of activities he or she is capable of doing without the phone at hand (cf. Garcia-Montes, 2006, p. 77). As Plant (2002) points out: mobile users will feel more isolated and vulnerable than if they had never used a mobile phone. As one of the managers said:

Mobiles are a necessity for traveling. If I'm in Korea, not reachable on the phone, that's scary.

However, storing the phone calls, the e-mail, the SMS text, etc. makes it possible to get a feeling of order and control of the agenda. It becomes easy to pick up relevant addresses and find out who in the network it is worth spending time to send e-mail to. The number of times someone is trying to reach somebody might give a sense of being in touch with others or identity (cf. Mello & Sahay, 2007). The interviewees also glance through their e-mail inboxes and make similar decisions about who to call, or look at the calendar to make a reservation, etc. However, these practices also limit the range of the network. Gieryn (2000, p. 481) writes that place attachment results from accumulated biographical experiences: we associate places with the fulfilling (secret) events that happened there. "The longer people have lived in a place, the more rooted they feel, and the greater their attachment to it." While social practices and "bodies" may be geographically disembedded, the associated social and existential separation is far more complex to achieve (cf. Mello & Sahay, 2007).

In times when mobility is embraced, new forms of placial interconnectedness are still needed. For the urban flaneurs it is the café with WiFi access; for adolescents it is the social network website; and for the iterant professional worker it is the smartphone that becomes a nodal place. Managers that were once motivated and disciplined to a place of work are now striving for semi-private space outside the cubicle; because a loss of space may have devastating implications for any individual. As Gieryn (2000, p. 482) writes "To be without a place of one's own – persona non locata – is to be almost non-existent." Smartphones acting as nodal places creates comfort in working environments characterized by mobility and always being on the move – somewhat substituting yesterday's security of being implaced in an office room at a desk.

Is seems like the users attempt to construct a sense of rootedness and security, or what might also be said to be a "psychic place" (cf. Knigths & Murray, 1994). However, the connected and flexible workers seem at the same time be stuck in the same place, limited to her or his phonebook and calendar. The sense of belonging to a place could be transformed into the sense of belonging to one's communicative network (cf. Fourtinati, 2000, in Rettie, 2005, p. 19). Unfortunately, however, the communicative network seems paradoxically to be limited to the smartphone's telephone book or outlook-calendar. This might work in a contrary direction for a professional worker struggling with being open-minded, ready for impromptu meetings, and open-minded in a connected world. It also stresses the importance of managing knowledge processes that have been made possible by smartphones, because independence of time and space does not mean that the professional workers do not get stuck in their independence.

To sum up; The former sections have shown that by disaggregating managers' use of smartphones into nodal places, this might extend our understanding of the professional workers' response to

their diverse and shifting environments, and even though mobile activities are carried out at specific times and places and for particular purposes, the use of smartphones can at the same time undermine such processes.

However, with the second aim of this study in mind; to explore how nodal places as theoretical categories can be incorporated into the analysis of time-space configurations of mobile technology, nodal places can also serve as a springboard for an extended analysis of current studies of smartphone use in the light of time and space. Three prominent and frequently-quoted empirical-based studies about mobile ICT, mobile work and time-space configurations are put forward as example. Even though these three related studies have contributed with insightful analyses about time-space configurations and mobile work, they have not made nodal-places explicit in their analyses.

The first study serving as a springboard is Cousins and Robey's (2005) article that focuses on how nomadic computing workers manage the boundaries between business and personal activities through technology use. Three related dimension of nomadic computing are examined by Cousins and Robey; temporal, spatial (home, road, office) and contextual (business and personal) dimensions. These three dimensions are proposed to be regarded as closely interconnected suggesting that their effects be examined together empirically. One of the results put forth by Cousins and Robey is their questioning of the common interpretation that different boundaries may become blurred in nomadic computing and that blurred boundaries are associated with greater ambiguity and lack of control (cf. Davis, 2002). Cousins and Robey's data propose that nomads are in control of their working processes rather than overwhelmed and confused. The boundaries between business and personal contexts appeared clear, not blurred. This allowed the nomadic workers to use, for example, segments of time in a wide range of spaces (like homes, automobiles and offices) which even made them more productive.

The empirical material in our study shows that smartphone users' seem to work within rather clear boundaries too. The professional workers are, for example, aware of when to switch the smartphone off and on. The users are also aware of the boundaries between different nodal places (as expressed, for example, when managers' are taking breaks by making a phone calls or getting stucked into their smartphones' phone books). However, what seems less clear is whether they are aware about how different nodal places are interrelated with different physical spaces? Even though making a phone call or administrating mails could be seen as pauses for managers on the move in their job, it may also be contextually dependent, as for example when the professional is at home with their family. The professional workers are moving back and forth across different places, physical as well as non-physical, implying potential identification with multiplicity of places. Despite the managers being keen on being accessible, they also make it clear that they have to set limits. As mentioned by one professional worker:

With this kind of job, I would say it is alright to be disturbed occasionally at nights as well. There is always a possibility to switch off the phone… firstly you think you can handle all your work the whole day long, but now I have got a family with children and you start to prioritize. Most of the time you can answer that call at another time. Before, you answer that call when dinner was finished. But is has changed…

The pause seems to take a twist, and become something demanding instead of releasing. The intensity of the communication in this example may still be of importance. However, to come through with a call because it is the fifth time you ring seems not to be a successful formula among professional workers having dinner with their families. They will still find themselves oriented in an analytical space of distinctions, but attached to and rooted in one dominant social relation: the

family. The above example not only shows the importance of incorporation nodal places into the analysis, but also addresses the importance of understanding the multitude of different places, physical as well as non-physical, and the contextuality that impinges upon the feelings and actions of using smartphones.

The second study is Orlikowski and Yates' (2002) insights into how time is instantiated in organizational life through the process of temporal structuring. Orlikowski and Yates focus on time and space from primarily a managerial perspective and they argue that temporal structures with a broader scope are more persistent and more difficult to change than those with narrower scope. Size, penetration, dispersion, embeddedness, and extent are proposed as dimensions to the notion of scope. Orlikowski and Yates propose, for example, that within a firm, temporal structures are expected to be enacted by most or all organizational members, and that is more difficult to change than temporal structures enacted by a specific group of staff/workers.

By incorporating different nodal places into the analysis of temporal structuring demonstrates that striving for security in term of different nodal places might be as important to reach changes. Managing changes in the intensity of communication, finding places for pauses, and the need for well structured phone books, might be as efficient to reach change as are the impact of the scope of size and penetration. As been shown in the previous sections, participants are both implaced in communities as well as implaced in the intensity of a communication act.

The last study is Green's (2002) investigation of rhythms salient to "mobile time", which proposes three interconnected domains in "mobile time" in everyday life: rhythm of mobile use, rhythms of uses in everyday life, and rhythms of mobility and institutional change. Green (ibid.) shows, in opposition to thoughts about "timeless time" and "instantaneous time", how many temporalities can be demonstrated to be relatively enduring. Green admits that the quest for "speed" in modern life and potential fragmentation in social relationships via temporal changes are visible in the empirical material. However, Green also argues that mobile technologies introduce opportunities for new continuities across space and time. What has been shown in our empirical material – in addition to the previous study by Green – is that continuities across space and time might also be regarded as a matter of non-physical (nodal) places. For example, managers' search for a quiet moment – a pause in their hasty life – might be one way to further explore enduring places and enduring temporalities beyond the concepts put forth by Green.

CONCLUSION

This study complements and expands on previous work by addressing more specific instances in which smartphone use undermines singular and stable conceptions of place. The increasing use of mobile ICT not only builds relationships between places through time and space compression, but also alters how spatiality is conceived in terms of space-time and formed through social relations and interactions – in this study by focusing on managers as professional workers. What has been proposed is that the handheld platform of ICT services is also creating a handheld spatial center of activity, which is increasingly replacing the office desk with its PC and phone (with a secretary at the other end of the line) as the primary management attributes. Acting as a nodal handheld place, without being fixed to a certain place, will also (re)construct the relation in which a manager is embedded, which in turn affects managerial work. When the center of managerial practice is increasingly coordinated from a mobile handheld device, then not only the promises of increasing productivity and revenue potential should be analyzed, but also some of the more subtle twists and effects of mobile ICT.

The themes in this paper therefore suggest a figurative reverse – a return of the importance of place in order to understand the professionals' daily practice with their handy smartphones. Previously unstudied spatial aspects of smartphone use have been brought to the fore. The investigation of professional workers' use of smartphones put forth in this paper might not at the first glance reveal much that is surprising. However, our theoretical exploration of nodal places put into a more or less familiar context of professional workers' use of smartphones has provided a new context to the observation described. This new context encompasses both generic categories of nodal places that might contribute to further understanding of smartphone usage, and new entities to focus on and manage. An organization can incorporate these categories in its plans, procedures, management programs, etc., not only because there are different non-physical places to relate to, but also how different places might be interrelated and interpenetrate.

This paper's focus on spatio-temporality in emerging mobile management practice has been driven by a recognition of the necessity to move beyond more or less uniform and unproblematic understandings of spatiality in human action. More studies, however, are needed in order to better specify the spatial implications of smartphone use. Questions that arise are, for example: 'What are the losses and gains with controlling and managing different nodal places that are unfolding from the use of smartphones?', and; 'How can different spaces evoke different feelings of the security of places, in situations when traditional place consciousness at the workplace in the office is lost?' To answer these questions, richer and more perceptually-enhancing empirical material would be required.

Managers acting in demanding environments of goal-directed spaces – in fast-moving environments boosted by increasingly sophisticated ICT systems – eventually create needs for timely nodal places that are more non-directed and humanly paced; be it then a place for moments of reflection and contemplation, working from distance or be it just a private moment when making a phone call. These problems are not unique to top managers as professional workers. Most organizations will face similar problems when smartphones are introduced on a wider scale. Top managers in a leading ICT company are thus only the (technophile) avant-garde in designing, promoting and using such mobile devices, from whose experience others can learn.

The supposed liberating potential of ICT, to free us from traditional spatial boundaries, has consequently created an increased demand for nodes acting as havens – being non-directed spaces in ever-increasing and fast-moving goal-directed spaces. Smartphones can be seen as such nodes, creating virtual sites as a form of remedy against possible feelings of estrangement and being lost in high-paced management roles. Increasing goal-directedness also increases our need for non-directed spaces that act as virtual and/or physical nodes in the communication network; the smartphone's display being the virtual node, and the meeting and the office being the physical nodes. The need for place is sometimes manifested in an unexpected guise. Sending redundant information to our peers' smartphones or arranging (more) physical meetings with the smartphone's coordinative capacity serves as comforting reassurance and balances daily work in the emerging new form of mobile practice. The need for nodes in a mobile network is not decreasing. Instead, the numbers of virtual-place nodes are increasing, but traditional physical meetings remain ubiquitous.

These new emerging spatio-temporal forms of fast-changing mobile management practice are based on ongoing learning processes that have yet to be implemented. Managing the dualism between fast moving goal-directed spaces enhanced by ICT, and the need for non-directed nodes in timely places will however remain a necessity, not only for professional workers but for all of us.

ACKNOWLEDGMENT

We are very grateful for insightful comments made by the reviewers and the Editor on previous versions of the paper. We are also indebted to those who helped us generate the empirical material.

REFERENCES

Ancona, D., Okhuysen, G., & Perlow, L. (2001). Taking Time to Integrate Temporal Research. *Academy of Management Review, 28*(4), 512–529. doi:10.2307/3560239

Arnold, M. (2003). On the Phenomenology of Technology: The 'Janus-faces' of Mobile Phones. *Information and Organization, 13*(4), 231–256. doi:10.1016/S1471-7727(03)00013-7

Barley, S. (1988). On Technology, Time, and Social Order: Technologically Induced Change in the Temporal Organization of Radiological Work. In Dubinskas, F. (Ed.), *Making Time: Ethnographies of High-Technology Organizations* (pp. 123–169). Philadelphia: Temple University Press.

Barley, S., & Kunda, G. (2004). Gurus, Hired Guns, and Warm Bodies. In *Itinerant Experts in a Knowledge Economy*. Princeton, NJ: Princeton University Press.

Boudreau, M.-C., & Robey, D. (2005). Enacting Integrated Information Technology: A Human Agency Perspective. *Organization Science, 16*(1), 3–18. doi:10.1287/orsc.1040.0103

Casey, E. (1993). *Getting Back Into Place: Toward a Renewed Understanding of the Place-world*. Bloomington, IN: Indiana University Press.

Casey, E. (1997). *The Fate of Place: A Philosophical History*. Berkeley, CA: University of California Press.

Castells, M. (1996). The Information Age: Economy, Society and Culture: *Vol. 1. The Rise of the Network Society*. Oxford, UK: Blackwell.

Ciborra, C. (Ed.). (2000). *From Control to Drift -The Dynamics of Corporate Information Infrastructures*. Oxford, UK: Oxford University Press.

Constas, M. (1992). Qualitative Analysis as a Public Event: The Documentation of Category Development Procedures. *American Educational Research Journal, 29*(2), 253–266.

Cook, S., & Brown, J. (1999). Bridging epistemologies: The generative dance between organizational knowledge and organizational knowing. *Organization Science, 10*(4), 381–400. doi:10.1287/orsc.10.4.381

Cousins, K., & Robey, D. (2005). Human Agency in a Wireless World: Patterns of Technology Use in Nomadic Computing Environments. *Information and Organization, 15*(2), 151–180. doi:10.1016/j. infoandorg.2005.02.008

Davis, G. (2002). Anytime/anyplace computing and the future of knowledge work. *Communications of the ACM, 45*(12), 67–73. doi:10.1145/585597.585617

Derrida, J. (1997). *Of Grammatology*. Baltimore, MD: The John Hopkins University Press.

Foucault, M. (1983). *This is Not a Pipe*. Berkeley, CA: University of California Press.

García-Montes, J., Caballero-Munoz, D., & Pérrz-Álvarez, M. (2006). Changes in the Self Resulting from the Use of Mobile Phones. *Media Culture & Society, 28*(1), 67–82. doi:10.1177/0163443706059287

Giddens, A. (1990). *The Consequences of Modernity*. Stanford, CA: Stanford University Press.

Giddens, A. (1991). *Modernity and Self-identity: Self and Society in the Late Modern Age*. Stanford, CA: Stanford University Press.

Gieryn, T. (2000). A Space for Place in Sociology. *Annual Review of Sociology, 26*, 463–496. doi:10.1146/annurev.soc.26.1.463

Green, N. (2002). On the Move: Technology, Mobility and Mediation of Social Time and Space. *The Information Society, 18*(4), 281–292. doi:10.1080/01972240290075129

Gregory, D. (1994). *Geographical Imaginations*. Cambridge, UK: Blackwell.

Hanson, N. (1958). *Patterns of Discovery. An Inquiry into the Foundation of Science*. Cambridge, UK: Cambridge University Press.

Harvey, D. (1989). *The Condition of Postmodernity*. Oxford, UK: Basil Blackwell.

Heidegger, M. (1977). *The question concerning technology and other essays*. New York: Harper and Row.

Jacussi, E., Hanseth, O., & Lyytinen, K. (2006). Introduction: Taking Complexity Seriously in IS Research. *Information Technology & People, 19*(1), 5–11. doi:10.1108/09593840610649943

Kakihara, M., & Sørensen, C. (2002). Post-Modern Professionals' Work and Mobile Technology, New Ways of Working in IS. In *Proceedings of the 25th Information Systems Seminar in Scandinavia (IRIS25)*. Copenhagen, Denmark: Copenhagen Business School.

Kakihara, M., Sørensen, C., & Wiberg, M. (2004). Negotiating the Fluidity of Mobile Work. In Wiberg, M. (Ed.), *The Interaction Society: Practice, Theories, and Supportive Technologies*. Hershey, PA: Idea Group.

Knigths, D., & Murray, F. (1994). *Managers Divided-organizational Politics and Information Technology Management*. London: Wiley.

Lee, H. (1999). Time and Information Technology: Monochronicity, Polychronicity and Temporal Symmetry. *European Journal of Information Systems*, *8*(1), 16–26. doi:10.1057/palgrave.ejis.3000318

Lee, H., & Liebenau, J. (2000). Temporal Effects of Information Systems on Business Processes: Focusing on the Dimensions of Temporality. *Accounting, Management & Information Technologies*, *10*(3), 157–185. doi:10.1016/S0959-8022(00)00003-5

Lee, H., & Whitley, E. (2002). Time and Information Technology: Temporal Impacts on Individuals, Organizations, and Society. *The Information Society*, *18*(4), 235–240. doi:10.1080/01972240290075084

Massey, D. (1998). *Space, Place and Gender*. Cambridge, UK: Polity Press.

Mazmanian, M., Yates, J., & Orlikowski, W. (2006, July). Ubiquitous Email: Individual Experiences and Organizational Consequences of Blackberry. In *Proceedings of the IFIP 8.2 Working Conference on Ubiquitous Computing*, Cleveland, OH.

Mello, M., & Sahay, S. (2007). "I am Kind of Nomad Where I have to Go Places and Places"… Understanding Mobility, Place and Identity in Global Software Work from India. *Information and Organization*, *17*(3), 162–192. doi:10.1016/j.infoandorg.2007.04.001

Normark, D., & Esbjörnsson, M. (2004). The Mobile Workplace – Collaboration in a Vast Setting. In Wiberg, M. (Ed.), *The Interaction Society: Practice, Theories and Supportive Technologies* (pp. 251–270). Hershey, PA: Information Science Publishing.

Orlikowski, W. (1992). The Duality of Technology: Rethinking the Concept of Technology in Organizations. *Organization Science*, *3*(3), 398–427. doi:10.1287/orsc.3.3.398

Orlikowski, W. (1996). Improvising Organizational Transformation over Time: A Situated Change Perspective. *Information Systems Research*, *7*(1), 63–92. doi:10.1287/isre.7.1.63

Orlikowski, W. (2000). Using Technology and Constituting Structures: A Practice Lens for Studying Technology in Organizations. *Organization Science*, *11*(4), 404–428. doi:10.1287/orsc.11.4.404.14600

Orlikowski, W., & Yates, J. (2002). It's About Time: Temporal Structuring in Organizations. *Organization Science*, *13*(6), 684–700. doi:10.1287/orsc.13.6.684.501

Peirce, C. S. (1976). *Collected Papers of Charles Sanders Peirce*. Cambridge, MA: Harvard University Press.

Plant, S. (2002). *On the Mobile: The Effects of Mobile Telephones on Social and Individual*. Retrieved from http://www.motorola.com/mot/doc/0/234_MotDoc.pdf

Prasopoulou, E., Pouloudi, A., & Panteli, N. (2006). Enacting New Temporal Boundaries: The Role of Mobile Phones. *European Journal of Information Systems*, *15*(3), 277–284. doi:10.1057/palgrave.ejis.3000617

Robey, D., & Bourdreau, M.-C. (1999). Accounting for the Contradictory Organizational Consequences of Information Technology: Theoretical Directions and Methodological Implication. *Information Systems Research*, *10*(2), 167–185. doi:10.1287/isre.10.2.167

Sahay, S., & Walshm, G. (1977). Social Structure and Managerial Agency in India. *Organization Studies*, *18*(3), 415–444. doi:10.1177/017084069701800304

Schatzki, T., Knorr-Cetina, K., & von Savigny, E. (Eds.). (2001). *The Practice Turn in Contemporary Theory*. London: Routledge.

Schön, D. (1983). *The Reflective Practitioner: How Professionals Think in Action*. London: Temple Smith.

Schultze, U., & Boland, R. (2000). Place, Space and Knowledge Work: A Study of Outsourced Computer Systems Administrators. *Accounting, Management and Information Technologies, 10*, 187–219. doi:10.1016/S0959-8022(00)00006-0

Schultze, U., & Orlikowski, W. (2004). A Practice Perspective on Technology-mediated Relations: The Use of Internet-based Self-service Technologies. *Information Systems Research, 15*(1), 87–106. doi:10.1287/isre.1030.0016

Sørensen, C., & Gibson, D. (2004). Ubiquitous Visions and Opaque Realities: Professional Talking About Mobile Technologies. *Info, 6*(3), 188–196. doi:10.1108/14636690410549516

Sørensen, C., & Pica, D. (2005). Tales from the Police: Rhythms of Interaction with Mobile Technologies. *Information and Organization, 15*(2), 125–149. doi:10.1016/j.infoandorg.2005.02.007

Spradley, J. (1979). *The Ethnographic Interview*. New York: Holt, Rinehart and Winston.

Taylor, S., & Bogdan, R. (1984). *Introduction to Qualitative Research Methods: The Search for Meanings*. New York: John Wiley & Sons.

Townley, B. (2002). Managing with Modernity. *Organization, 9*(4), 549–573. doi:10.1177/135050840294003

Townsend, A. (2000). Life in the Real-time City: Mobile Telephones and Urban Metabolism. *Journal of Urban Technology, 7*(2), 85–104. doi:10.1080/713684114

Tsoukas, H. (1989). The Validity of Ideographic Research Explanations. *Academy of Management Review, 14*(4), 551–561. doi:10.2307/258558

Tuan, Y.-F. (1977). *Space and Place: The Perspective of Experience*. Minneapolis, MN: University of Minnesota Press.

Urry, J. (1985). Social Relations, Space and Time. In Gregory, D., & Urry, J. (Eds.), *Social Relations and Spatial Structures* (pp. 20–45). London: Macmillan.

Urry, J. (1991). Time and Space in Social Theory. In Bryant, C., & Jarry, D. (Eds.), *Theory of Structuration: A Critical Appreciation* (pp. 160–176). London: Routledge.

Virilio, P. (1991). *The Aesthetics of Disappearance*. New York: Semiotext(e).

Wiberg, M., & Ljungberg, F. (2001). Exploring the Vision of "Anytime, Anywhere" in the Context of Mobile Work. In Y. Malhotra (Ed.), *Knowledge Management and Business Model Innovation* (pp. 153-165). Hershey, PA: IGI Publishing.

Wiredu, G. (2007). User Appropriation of Mobile Technologies: Motives Condition and Design Properties. *Information and Organization, 17*(2), 110–129. doi:10.1016/j.infoandorg.2007.03.002

Zerubavel, E. (1979). *Patterns of Time in Hospital Life: A Sociological Perspective*. Chicago: University of Chicago Press.

ENDNOTES

[1] The questionnaire can be found in appendix.

[2] This perspective is put forth by Heidegger (1977) and others and is elegantly encapsulated in what Arnold (2003: 236) calls a Substantive Approach, i.e. technology "… enframes the world such that the question is changed along with the answer, the need is changed along with its gratification, and direction is changed along with the mechanism."

APPENDIX

Questionnaire

1. Respondent's name and background
2. Describe "your" normal" work day or work week (if there are normal days).
3. Describe your mobile phone and how you're using it; which functions are you using / do not use. Give examples.
4. When are you not using your mobile phone? In how many occasions, situations, do you turn off your phone? Give examples.
5. Time aspects – how fast do you / your colleagues expect to get feedback on SMS, mails, calls? Any changes (in time/speed) over the last couple of years? Expectations over the coming years? Stress? Information overload?
6. Face-2-face meetings: when do you travel for meetings; when do you choose mail, SMS, phone, video? Give examples, and pros and cons. What kind of information / knowledge transfer is suitable in each case?
7. Communication between colleagues and / or clients / customers: which channel is best suited?
8. What do you do with the information you're getting over the mobile phone? Describe and give examples of different applications.
9. What triggers information exchange via the mobile phone. Describe and give examples.
10. Security – limiting mobile phone use. Which communication channel for different forms of communication.
11. PDA telephone vs. Laptop: pros / cons; please motivate.
12. Changes in your work from your use of mobile phone. Describe before and after the introduction of mobile phones. How do you plan your work; predictability and structure of working day?
13. Leadership and technology (push calls? – push mail: mail from pc to mobile phone).
14. Has your work as a manager changed in relation to your colleagues? Has your way of managing changed?; (if yes: How?)
15. Has your mobile phone provided new useful functions? Any function missing? What is expected from new functions; can these new functions improve your working situation?
16. Conference calls – using the mobile phone when in conference?
17. Hierarchies and priorities – how to screen out calls? Private vs. Internal vs. External / Clients / Customers? Multiple lines. Different cultures?
18. Any additional question I should have asked? Thank you very much!

This work was previously published in the International Journal of Technology and Human Interaction, Volume 7, Issue 1, edited by Anabela Mesquita and Chia-Wen Tsai, pp. 37-55, copyright 2011 by IGI Publishing (an imprint of IGI Global).

Section 3
Information and Communication Technologies and E-Government

Chapter 13
Barriers to E–Government Implementation in Jordan:
The Role of Wasta

Christine Sarah Fidler
De Montfort University, UK

Raed Kareem Kanaan
De Montfort University, UK

Simon Rogerson
De Montfort University, UK

ABSTRACT

This paper identifies and highlights the significance of Wasta as a barrier to e-government implementation within The Hashemite Kingdom of Jordan and is part of a wider qualitative research study of all barriers. A longitudinal research approach was applied to explore any dynamism within the presence of barriers over a three year study, as well as to seek a richer understanding of such barriers. Data, principally collected via interviews with relevant stakeholders, was analysed using Strauss and Corbin's variant of grounded theory. Using illustrative quotations primarily from interview transcripts, this paper enunciates the significant and persistent role that Wasta plays in hindering Jordan's e-government implementation, both as an explicitly mentioned barrier and as cause of other barriers. The paper supports the view that culture is a root cause of e-government implementation difficulty, and that barriers vary with the different country settings in which e-government systems are embedded.

1. INTRODUCTION

Wasta is a custom that is prevalent within Arab societies, including the Lebanon (Makhoul & Harrison, 2004), Saudi Arabia (Faisla & Abdella, 1993) and Egypt (Mohamad & Hamdy, 2008). It has even been identified, albeit under the pseudonym of Guanxi, as a practice within China (Hutching & Weir, 2006). Cunningham and Sarayrah (1994) define Wasta as "either mediation or intercession. It denotes the person who mediates/intercedes as well as the act of mediation/intercession"(p.

DOI: 10.4018/978-1-4666-1954-8.ch013

1). Wasta is a way of life for Jordanian citizens (Cunningham & Sarayrah, 1994). It originates from tribal traditions, where one tribe would use a Wasta to intercede with another tribe to resolve any inter-tribal conflict and unrest. Nowadays, Wasta is most often associated with the act of one person interceding on behalf of another for financial/status gain. The Wasta has the same tribal origins to the person for whom s/he is interceding and is either a close friend or someone from within the extended family network. Performing the Wasta role is a way of gaining the respect of the network.

Although Wasta has similarity in meaning to several English terms, there is no wholly equivalent English concept. For instance, the activity of Wasta requires the presence of three roles; the role requiring Wasta to occur, the Wasta role per se, and the role that is the target of the Wasta (Kilani & Sakijha, 2002). In contrast, terms such as favouritism and nepotism (i.e., a special kind of favouritism shown to relatives when one is in a position of power, particularly with regard to job recruitment (Wong & Kleiner, 1994; Arasli et al., 2006) require only two of the three roles to be present within the act; namely, the receiver and the giver of the favouritism. Neither does Wasta equate to bribery, as the latter involves something to be given (often money) in exchange for 'the favour' received (Noonan, 1984) whereas the former relies on the strength of obligation of the Wasta to his/her network. Wasta could be classed as a form of corruption (Klitgaard, 1991), given that it is a behaviour that could be seen as corrupt, i.e., deviant from that which is ethically and/or morally correct (although, as Hooker (2009) explains, what might be considered ethically correct or incorrect may differ between cultures on the basis of their underlying traditions and values). However, corruption takes many forms than just Wasta, bribery being one other of these. Wasta appears to resemble aspects of the Freemason concept (which is more fully described in both Jones (1970) and Kameron (2008)), where gaining

membership is at least enhanced via the intercession of an existing member and that membership comes with obligations to other members to secure required ends (although it is formally stated that a Freemason should never use "his membership to promote his own or anyone else's business, professional or personal interests" (Mole, 2007)) However, unlike freemasons, Jordanian tribes do not have any written 'codes of conduct', and citizens have no choice as to which tribe they belong and whether or not they remain a member of the tribe.

In Jordan, Wasta is acknowledged publicly and formally supported (Kilani & Sakijha, 2002). Here, "senior members of the extended family intercede on behalf of younger or less privileged members in making arrangements for employment, overseas travel, business partnerships, university admissions, bank loans, marriages, and most other out-of-the-ordinary forms of negotiation" (Cunningham & Sarayrah, 1993, p. 1). Wasta is considered to have a major impact on decision making and any political change (Schlumberger, 2002; Cunningham & Sarayrah, 2004)). Yet and rather surprisingly, Wasta has not figured as a significant barrier to e-government implementations in any of the existing literature based on countries in which such practices are prevalent, despite the fact that e-government implementation is employed as a instrument for political reform/change.

This paper describes the identification and justification of Wasta as a significant and persistent factor in impeding the e-government implementation within Jordan. Identification of this factor occurred as a result of analysing fieldwork data collected as part of a wider-ranging, qualitative research project exploring the nature and interrelationships between any factors that were found to influence Jordan's e-government implementation over time (as detailed in Kanaan, 2009). After a general review of the existing literature concerning barriers to e-government implementations, this paper provides an overview of the research methodology that was employed within the larger project, and how factors, such as Wasta, were identified. Quotations principally from interview transcripts are used to illustrate the significant effects of Wasta on Jordan's e-government implementation process, both as an explicitly mentioned barrier and as an underlying cause of other explicitly mentioned barriers. The identification of Wasta provides further support to the view that culture is at the root of many of the the difficulties faced in e-government implementations, and also that the barriers found in different country settings reflect the differing cultural contexts within which the e-government systems are embedded. The paper then finishes with a summary and some concluding remarks.

2. BARRIERS TO E-GOVERNMENT IMPLEMENTATIONS: AN OVERVIEW OF EXISTING RESEARCH

Many previous researchers have explored the barriers that effect e-government implementations within developed societies[1], including Lambrinoudakis et al. (2003), Mullen and Horner (2004), Choudrie et al. (2005) and Lam (2005). More recently, research attention has been placed on e-government implementations within less developed settings (as exemplified by United Nations Conference on Trade and Development (2001), Schware and Deane (2003), United Nations (2003), Ndou (2004) and United Nations (2008a)). This is as a consequence of the upsurge in e-government implementation projects within developing countries (including Arab ones such as Dubai, Jordan, Egypt, Kuwait, Bahrain and Saudi Arabia), coupled with the recognition that although some of these projects are successful (such as India's property tax payment and issue of land registration certificates systems (Schware & Deane, 2003), Kuwait's civil service recruitment portal, and Bahrain's Internet election system

(Moores, 2003)), most projects fail to achieve their planned goals (Heeks, 2003).

Table 1 provides a summary of the e-government implementation barriers that have been found to exist within a developed country environment by previous researchers. It also provides a comparison to those found to exist within a less developed society context. Although recognising that several barriers could fit into more than one category, each barrier has been classed according to its principal focus, thus highlighting the multidimensional nature of the difficulties faced by e-government implementations.

As shown in Table 1, several barriers (e.g., resistance to change, absence of leadership) are common to both developing and developed societies (although the underlying causes of the factor may differ). There are also some differences in the barriers faced by developed and developing societies; a fact which Schware (2000) and NDou (2004) also acknowledge. For instance, the list of barriers for each context reflects the relative maturity of the said context to embrace e-government. For instance, in the developed countries, the majority of adopters and users of any new technology (in this case, e-government) already possess the fundamental knowledge and skills that are pre-requisite to the use of that technology (e.g., how to perform basic operations on a client PC). However, in developing countries, these skills will typically have to be accumulated first before the full benefits from the technology can be realised (Bell & Pavitt, 1993). Furthermore, a number of studies within developed country situations identify privacy and security to be key barriers (Layne & Lee, 2001; OECD, 2003), yet these issues are not considered mainstream concerns within the studies concerning developing countries, probably because the latter countries are still grappling with the fundamental issues regarding access to e-government (e.g, lack of education, lack of road and rail network, women access to technology, the language barrier, and

Table 1. Barriers to e-government implementation mentioned within existing literature: developed versus developing societies (adapted from Kanaan, 2009)

Category	Barriers identified from existing literature	
	Developed Society	Developing Society
Technical	• Lack of technical infrastructure • Inflexibility of legacy systems • Lack of shared standards • Differences in the security models	• Lack of ICT skills • Penetration of Internet
Economic	• Lack of money/funding • High cost of secure solutions	• Lack of Funding
Organisational	• Resistance to change • Absence of leadership • Lack of IT training programs	• Resistance to change • Absence of leadership • Inadequate human resource training • Lack of e-readiness
Strategic	• Lack of clear guidance • Contradiction in the goals between the departments	
Political	• Departments do not share their own data with others	• Political commitment
Social	• Digital Divide • Privacy and confidentiality	• Digital divide • Lack of education • Women have less access to technology
National		• Monopolies over telecommunication sector • Lack of electricity supplies • Inadequate road and rail network • Cost of Internet and telephones

the lack of e-readiness) rather than focusing on how it is used.

Another issue that offers significant explanation as to the differences between the e-government implementation barriers within developing and developed contexts is culture; the culmination of "knowledge, experiences, beliefs, values, attitudes, meanings, hierarchies, religion, timing, roles, spatial relations, concepts of the universe, and material objects and possessions acquired by a large group of people in the course of generations through individual and group striving" (Samovar et al., 1981, p. 25). Feng (2003) considers that the principal barriers to any implementation of e-government are not technical but cultural. Different barriers have been identified in different cultures. For instance, the traditions and attitudes within a society regarding payment methods for services/goods influence the preferences regarding, and/or ability of citizens to engage in, services involving e-payment. E-payment is therefore seen

as a major barrier in some contexts such as Japan (Aoki, 2002) but not so in others such as the USA and UK. Furthermore, religious practices and/or traditions in some societies act as barriers to women's learning about, and/or access to, ICT in general and e-government in particular, leading to a gender-based 'digital divide'. This is in contrast to other societies where this form of digital divide is not prevalent (although other forms of digital divide may exist, based on issues such as language barrier, age, disability and location).

3. THE RESEARCH CONTEXT: JORDAN AND ITS E-GOVERNMENT PROGRAMME

Jordan is a relatively small country of 6,198,677 million people. The country is young, with 32.2% of the population under the age of 15, 63.7% between 15-64 years and only 4.1% over the age of

64 (Department of Statistics: Jordan, 2008; CIA, 2008). Jordan is located in the Middle East within a total area of 92,300 Square Kilometres, the vast majority of which is either desert or semi-arid. Jordan neighbours comprise Iraq, Israel, Saudi Arabia, Syria and the West Bank (CIA, 2008), and the whole area can be described as "volatile". The capital city of Jordan is Amman with a population of 2 million. Other principal cities include Irbid, Zarqa, Salt, and Aqaba.

98% of Jordanians are Arab, with some Armenian and Circassian minorities. Islam is the official religion; about 92% of the population is Muslim, with 6% being Christian. 83% of population live in urban areas of the country. Arabic is the official language, but English is widely understood among citizens. The legal system in Jordan combines Islamic and French codes of law.

Jordan's history starts around 2000 BC, when the first Semitic Amorite tribes settled near the banks of the River Jordan. It is prominent within the Bible as a region comprising three Kingdoms; Moab, Ammon and Edom. Since that time, Jordan has been occupied and controlled by several countries, the last of which was Britain. Jordan became an independent country in 1946. Its formal name, adopted in 1950, is "the Hashemite Kingdom of Jordan". The current monarchy is King Abdullah II, who succeeded his father, King Hussein, in 1999.

Modern day Jordan is still intensely tribal in nature, with the king essentially acting as a mediator between tribes to resolve any disputes and to reach consensus on matters of national significance. The tribal system is considered the fabric of Jordanian society which has to be preserved, and that any attempt to disintegrate the tribal system is considered subversive and against the good of the country (Alon, 2007).

The political structure of Jordan has both decreed and elected elements. The king appoints the prime minister, who appoints (and dismisses) cabinet members in consultation with the king. Thus, the Jordanian cabinet consists of the prime minister and however many ministers that are required to run the ministries in order to satisfy the envisaged public needs. The numbers of ministries in Jordan can vary in each cabinet depending on the public services provided by the government and their importance (PM, 2008). Current ministries include The Ministry of Information and Communications Technology (MOICT), The Ministry of Industry and Trade, and The Ministry of Finance. Any work on e-government currently falls within the domain of The MOICT.

In addition to the cabinet, Jordan has a National Assembly (Majlis al-Umma), and this has two chambers. The Upper House is the 55-member Senate, appointed for a four-year period by the king from selected categories of public figures. The Parliament (also known as The House of Representatives), which has 110 members elected directly by citizens again, for a four-year period, based on proportional representation (House of Representatives, 2008).

Jordan is poor in terms of natural resources, except for potash and phosphate (which are used in fertilisers, explosives, and in some household wares, such as glass and ceramics, and cleaning products, such as soaps). It has no oil, and its economy is built on a very narrow industrial base (CIA, 2008). Unemployment and poverty is high, and for these reasons King Abdullah II places significant emphasis on social and economic reforms. As a result of improved education and training programmes, 90% of the population aged over 15 can read and write, and the new generation of young children are equipped with at least basic computer literacy (CIA, 2008). Whilst progress is impressive, several challenges still remain for Jordan, including the reducing of dependence on foreign grants, the reducing of the budget deficit, the attracting of further investments, and the creating of new jobs (since the current unemployment rate is still high at 13.5% and inflation stands at 5.4%) (CIA, 2008). Also, over the past few years, Jordan has had to contend with a difficult external environment because of problems in the neighbouring regions such as the West Bank, Israel and Iraq.

As part of king's strategy for economic growth, the Jordanian government embarked on a major long-term e-government initiative in the year 2000. The project aimed to deliver positive change to both government and its services, by improving service delivery, improving responsiveness to customer needs, increasing transparency (and thus reducing the potential for corruption) and efficiency of operations, and by enhancing, via the use of e-government, the level of understanding of ICT in general with Jordanian society (MOICT, 2006).

At the outset of the e-government initiative, eight, so-termed "fast-track" projects were initially planned so that a range of e-government services would very quickly be implemented for business, citizens and government departments/ employees. However, nine years on and several strategy reviews/revisions later (including one conducted in 2003 by The MOICT (MOICT, 2003)), the e-government project in Jordan still falls predominantly within the informational stage of e-government evolution (Hiller & Belanger, 2001) with only just over a half of the ministries having a (frequently inadequate) web presence.

Ciborra (2005) considers the king's approach to ICT in general (which encompasses e-government) to be a "textbook case for its vision to become the Singapore or Bangalore of the Middle East" (p. 262). Given Jordan's similarities in terms of religion, language and history to other neighbouring countries, the building up of a descriptive case study of ICT/E-government development within Jordan would likely be of benefit to those countries with similar characteristics. It was this reason, coupled with recognition of Jordan's very slow progress on the e-government project (as confirmed in Belwal & Al-Zoubi, (2008)), which provided the underlying motivation for the present research.

4. RESEARCH METHODOLOGY

Wasta was one of several barriers identified by the authors as a result of a wider enquiry into the nature of, and interrelationships between, both positive and negative factors that impact on Jordan's e-government implementation; the details about which can be found in Kanaan (2009). A longitudinal, qualitative, case study approach was taken to this wider enquiry, so as to explore any dynamism within the presence of factors over a three year period (from 2006 to 2008) as well as to seek a rich understanding of such factors. A substantive theory (Glaser & Strauss, 1967) regarding the factors that were found to impact on Jordan's e-government implementation over time would then be proposed. The principal primary data collection method employed was semi-structured interviews with representatives of key stakeholder groups (covering citizen, and public and private sector employees). Secondary data sources, such as newspaper articles, were also utilised where relevant to e-government. Key public sector employees were selected initially based on the public sector roles and/or departments that were considered essential to the e-government implementation within official e-government documentation: these included the Director of E-Government and the Director of Change Management from within The MOICT. A total of seven stakeholders were identified this way, and three interviews were conducted with each; one in 2006, one in 2007 and one in 2008. A further stakeholder was added to the list before the second period of interviews, as a consequence of what was said within the first round of interviews, and another was likewise included within the third round of interviews. User representatives from both government departments and the public at large were also selected and interviewed over the three year period. In total, 42 semi-structured interviews were carried out over the three years of study.

Interview questions were open in nature, allowing each interviewee to express his/her opinions as to why s/he felt the e-government programme was not progressing effectively, with the interviewer deciding whether or not to ask one or more appropriate follow-up questions depending on the answers received. All interviews were conducted in Arabic, subsequently translated to English and checked over by two independent people with both Arabic and English proficiency to provide some degree of confidence in the researcher's translation.

Data analysis was carried out using the Strauss and Corbin variant of grounded theory (Strauss & Corbin, 1990). This variant was chosen for several reasons, including its recognition of the use and influence of existing technical literature, the availability of strong guidance in its application, that most criticisms levelled specifically at grounded theory are associated with the alternative Glaser variant (e.g., the criticisms by Hammersley (1989) and Smith & Pohland (1969)), and that it has been acknowledged as a suitable data analysis tool within the context of a case study research strategy (as formalised and discussed in Halaweh et al., 2008). Open coding was followed by axial coding which was followed by selective coding. Through this procedure a total of 18 barriers emerged (Table 2), one of which was Wasta; the principal focus of discussion within the next section of this paper.

Table 2. Barriers to e-government implementation within Jordan: results from grounded theory analysis (adapted from Kanaan, 2009)

	Barrier	Indicative Quotation
1	Changing ministers	"Notice how many ministers have been changed and the program is still stop."
2	Citizens' expectations prior to e-government	"Bedouin areas are poor and need for developmental enterprises before the E-government."
3	Complication in processes	"Procedures in Jordan overlap terribly."
4	Corruption	"We have officers taking bribes to issue work statements."
5	Cost of living and Internet	"The prices of computers and Internet subscription must be reduced."
6	Data security	"Some security departments do not want to disclose their databases."
7	Funding issues	"Without external funding, this will be extremely difficult."
8	Government's priorities	"Government has a lot to work on before taking any such initiatives."
9	Lack of e-government understanding	"Their knowledge of the E-government is almost zero."
10	Lack of IT skills	"There is tremendous lack of trained employees that are able to deal with this initiative."
11	Legacy systems	"We are used the traditional system for tens of years."
12	Parliament's priorities	"… but till now I have not heard that anything is to be formally discussed in Parliament regarding e-government."
13	Previous experience with government projects	"Many enterprises before this, failed and their files were closed."
14	Public sector weaknesses	"The infrastructures in the ministries are very weak."
15	Resistance to change	"We find strong resistance on the side of the officers."
16	Regulation and legislation	"Up to now there is no laws dealing with any e-service."
17	War in Iraq	"950,000 Iraqi citizens entered into Jordan, which costs the government too much to take care of them."
18	Wasta	"You cannot go to any department without Wasta."

5. OUTCOMES: THE ROLE OF WASTA

As shown in Table 2, Wasta emerged as an explicitly mentioned barrier from the grounded theory analysis of fieldwork data. It was also found to be a persistent barrier throughout the three year period of study (whereas others, such as the 'War in Iraq', were more dynamic in nature). The following are a sample of quotations from the interview transcripts that explicitly or implicitly refer to Wasta and its impact:

As a result of recruiting people by the way of Wasta you don't necessarily find the right people in the right place in.. government departments (public sector employee)

I was surprised by the appointment of one employee who graduated in 2005 and who is a relative of the Minister of our ministry ... he became the head of our department, he was responsible for supervising 10 employees. He is absolutely unqualified for his position (public sector IT employee)

Who will guarantee that the manager of the e-government programme was not appointed by means of Wasta? (public sector employee)

To be honest, most of our (computer) contracts go to one company. This is because the owner of this company has good connections with officials, and sometimes he uses his power to appoint people in the ministry (public sector employee)

An analysis of these and other such statements within the interview transcripts suggests that the principal impacts of Wasta on government activities associated with the e-government implementation concern (1) staff appointments and promotions, and (b) contract awarding.

The pervasiveness of Wasta throughout government departments is aptly summed up by the following two statements found within the citizens' transcripts:

As a Jordanian citizen wanting to make a government transaction, you must use Wasta so as to achieve things rapidly without delay.. only Wasta applies in government departments (citizen)

There is always Wasta in promotion in the public sector... They consider who has the Wasta not who is qualified (citizen)

Interestingly, several interview statements that explicitly refer to Wasta attempt to provide it with 'an air of legitimacy'. For instance, one citizen stated that:

You can only say that Wasta is corruption when it is connected to money (citizen)

Even the Minister of Justice within Jordan was quoted within a local newspaper article to say that:

Wasta is a social, widely acknowledged custom in which a person attempts to help someone else to get a certain right or service

This statement omits any reference to Wasta's ethical/moral position, instead creating a wholly positive and caring picture of the act.

Not only was Wasta mentioned explicitly within the fieldwork data, but also Wasta could at least partially explain the presence of several of the other emergent barriers. For instance, Wasta is seen as a key (if not the) cause of 'Corruption' (another identified barrier in Table 2), as the following quotation from one of the citizen interviews highlights:

I think that Wasta is the basis of corruption in Jordan; it exists in all government departments, where no transaction can be done or any job applied for without Wasta. It is definitely corruption

Consider, for example, the following quotation from one of the interviews conducted with the Director of Change Management within The MOICT:

If you take a look to the public sector in Jordan you will definitely realise that some offices have six employees while the job can be done with just two

Wasta within the appointments process may be the cause of there being six employees rather than two within a department. This redundancy of work within and/or between departments can lead to 'Complications in Procedures' (an explicitly identified barrier that is listed in Table 2). Employees duplicate each other's work in an effort to maintain a suitable workload to justify their position. This makes procedures for dealing with citizen issues less clear, given that several points of contact may be now available rather than just the one.

Any anticipated change to make work more streamlined and effective (as envisaged with the implementation of e-government services) may be met by those in redundant positions with 'Fear of and Resistance to Change' (another explicitly mentioned barrier in Table 2).

The promise of Wasta may lead to MPs being elected, as a citizen from the Bedouin (nomadic tribe) area of Jordan pointed out within one of his interviews:

If you want to be an MP in the Jordanian parliament, you should offer jobs or other benefits for the family members who will vote for you

The consequence of electing MPs on the expectation of Wasta was also commented on by another interviewee:

MPs in Jordan win elections because they belong to the big tribes. MPs always give commitments to their local citizens, such as finding jobs and improving the infrastructure of their areas, I cannot see them to be the right people to make the required change in the public sector (public sector employee)

In other words, 'Parliaments Priorities' (another listed barrier in Table 2) are not aligned with the effective implementation of e-government; MPs focus attention on their local tribe requirements and on acting as Wasta, rather than what is critical for Jordan's prosperity as a whole. This means that the 'Regulations and Legislation' (also found in Table 2) which are needed for more e-government to become more accepted (e.g., laws regarding e-payments and e-crimes) are not a priority for Parliament, and the lack of such regulations and legislation continues to be a major hindrance to the implementation of e-government services.

6. SUMMARY AND CONCLUSION

This paper has shown, using illustrative quotations from fieldwork data collected over a three year period, that Wasta is a significant and persistent cultural barrier to e-government implementation within Jordan. It is not only explicitly mentioned by interviewees as a barrier in its own right, but also provides an explanation for the presence of other explicitly mentioned barriers to Jordan's e-government implementation, such as "Complications in procedures', 'Fear of and resistance to change', 'Parliaments priorities' and 'Regulations and legislation'. Wasta, within the Jordanian e-government implementation context, leads to situations of:

- Over-staffing of ill-qualified people within government departments
- The wrong contractors being awarded e-government work
- People (e.g., MPs) with low e-government priority

It can be added to the list of e-government implementation barriers that have been found within one or more developing country contexts, and offers another barrier that enhances the position of Feng (2003); that culture is the principal reason for the difficulties faced in e-government implementations. Its specific presence within Jordan (but not having been identified in previous studies in other countries) also supports the view that barriers may vary due to the cultural contexts in which e-government systems are being implemented.

Having highlighted the significant role that Wasta plays within the Jordanian e-government context, then there is always the follow-on question as to whether there are any ways of lessening the effect of this factor? Although strictly beyond the remit of this current paper, Kanaan (2009) suggests several potential actions that might be undertaken in this respect. However, it must be noted that something that is so integral to Jordanian culture, such as Wasta, would be extremely difficult and slow to change. Furthermore, the e-government programme, which was initiated with an aim to reduce corruption (including Wasta) within government departments, is itself a victim of Wasta in the manner detailed within this paper. This cycle has to be broken before any significant progress on reducing the effects of Wasta on public sector activities can be achieved.

REFERENCES

Alon, Y. (2007). *The making of Jordan*. London, UK: I.B. Tauris.

Aoki, K. (2000). *Cultural differences in e-commerce: A comparison between the United States and Japan*. Retrieved from http://www.isoc.org/inet2000/cdproceedings/7d/7d_1.htm

Arasli, H., Bavik, A., & Ekiz, E. H. (2006). The effects of nepotism on human resource management. *The International Journal of Sociology and Social Policy*, 26(7-8), 295–308. doi:10.1108/01443330610680399

Bell, M., & Pavitt, K. (1993). Technological accumulation and industrial growth: Contrasts between developed and developing countries. *Industrial and Corporate Change*, 2(1), 157–210. doi:10.1093/icc/2.1.157

Belwal, R., & Al-Zoubi, K. (2008). Public-centric e-governance in Jordan: A field study of people's perception of e-governance awareness, corruption and trust. *Journal of Information. Communication and Ethics in Society*, 6(4), 317–333. doi:10.1108/14779960810921123

Choudrie, J., Weerakkody, V., & Jones, S. (2005). Realizing e-government in the UK: Rural and urban challenges. *The Journal of Enterprise Information Management*, 18(5), 568–585. doi:10.1108/17410390510624016

CIA. (2008). *The world factbook*. Retrieved from https://www.cia.gov/library/ publications/the-world-factbook/geos/jo.html

Ciborra, C. (2005). Interpreting e-government and development efficiency, transparency or governance at a distance? *Information Technology & People*, 18(3), 260–279. doi:10.1108/09593840510615879

Cunningham, R. B., & Sarayrah, Y. K. (1993). *Wasta: The hidden force in Middle Eastern society*. Seattle, WA: Greenwood Publishing.

Cunningham, R. B., & Sarayrah, Y. K. (1994). Taming Wasta to achieve development. *Arab Studies Quarterly*, 16(3), 29–39.

Department of Statistics. Jordan (2008). *Population and housing census*. Retrieved from http://www.dos.gov.jo/dos_home_a/main/index.htm

Faisal, A., & Abdella, M. (1993). A methodological analysis of Wasta: A study in Saudi Arabia. *Journal of King Saud University: Arts*, 5(1).

Feng, L. (2003). Implementing e-government strategy in Scotland: Current situation and emerging issues. *Journal of Electronic Commerce in Organizations, 1*(2), 44–65. doi:10.4018/jeco.2003040104

Glaser, B. G., & Strauss, A. L. (1967). *The discovery of grounded theory*. Chicago, IL: Aldine.

Halaweh, M., Fidler, C. S., & McRobb, S. (2008, December 14-17). Integrating the grounded theory method and case study research methodology within IS research: A possible "road map". In *Proceedings of the International Conference on Information Systems*, Paris, France.

Hammersley, M. (1989). *The dilemma of qualitative method: Herbert Blumer and the Chicago Tradition*. London, UK: Routledge.

Heeks, R. (2003). *Most e-government-for-development projects fail: How can risks be reduced*. Manchester, UK: iGovernment Working Paper Series.

Hiller, J. S., & Belanger, F. (2001). *Privacy strategies for electronic government*. Arlington, VA: PricewaterhouseCoopers Endowment for the Business of Government.

Hooker, J. (2009). Corruption from a cross-cultural perspective. *Cross Cultural Management, 16*(3), 251–267. doi:10.1108/13527600910977346

House of Representatives. (2008). *Jordanian House of Representatives-formation of the House*. Retrieved from http://www.parliament.jo/english/Fomation.shtm

Hutchings, K., & Weir, D. (2006). Guanxi and Wasta: A comparison. *Thunderbird International Business Review, 48*(1), 141–156. doi:10.1002/tie.20090

Jones, B. E. (1970). *Freemasons's guide and compendium* (2nd ed.). London, UK: Harrap.

Kameron, G. (2008). *Freemasonry - the truth*. Retrieved from http://books.google.com/books?id=3GBkhju1XZUC&dq=gordon+kameron&source=gbs_navlinks_s

Kanaan, R. K. (2009). *Making sense of e-government implementation in Jordan: A qualitative investigation*. Unpublished doctoral dissertation, De Montfort University, Leicester, UK.

Kilani, S., & Sakijha, B. (2002). *Wasta: The declared secret*. Amman, Jordan: Jordan Press Foundation.

Klitgaard, R. (1991). *Controlling corruption*. Berkeley, CA: University of California Press.

Lam, W. (2005). Barriers to e-government integration. *The Journal of Enterprise Information Management, 18*(5), 511–530. doi:10.1108/17410390510623981

Lambrinoudakis, C., Gritzalis, S., Dridi, F., & Pernul, G. (2003). Security requirements for e-government services: A methodological approach for developing a common PKI-based security policy. *Computer Communications, 26*(16), 1873–1883. doi:10.1016/S0140-3664(03)00082-3

Layne, K., & Lee, J. (2001). Developing fully functional e-government: A four stage model. *Government Information Quarterly, 18*(2), 122–136. doi:10.1016/S0740-624X(01)00066-1

Lonely Planet. (2008). *Map of Jordan*. Retrieved from http://www.lonelyplanet.com/maps/middle-east/jordan/

Makhoul, J., & Harrison, L. (2004). Intercessory Wasta and village development in Lebanon. *Arab Studies Quarterly, 26*(3), 25–41.

Mohamed, A. A., & Hamdy, H. (2008). *The stigma of Wasta: The effect of Wasta on perceived competence and morality*. Retrieved from http://mgt.guc.edu.eg/wpapers/005mohamed_hamdy2008.pdf

MOICT. (2000). *e-Government program overview.* Retrieved from http://moict.gov.jo/

MOICT. (2002). *Launching e-government in Jordan: A proposed approach.* Retrieved from http://moict.gov.jo/downloads/Jordan_E-Gov_Ch4.pdf

MOICT. (2003). *e-Government: Status update.* Retrieved from http://www.moict.gov.jo/en_index.aspx

MOICT. (2006). *e-Government program overview.* Retrieved from http://moict.gov.jo/MoICT_program_overview.aspx

Mole, E. (2007). *An explanation of freemasonry.* Retrieved from http://www.macclesfieldmasons.org/index.php?option=com_content&task=view&id=31&Itemid=36

Moores, S. (2003). *e-Government in the Middle East.* Paper presented at the Future IT Conference: Keynote Address, Bahrain.

Mullen, H., & Horner, D. S. (2004). Ethical problems for e-government: An evaluative framework. *Electronic. Journal of E-Government, 2*(3), 187–196.

Ndou, V. (2004). e-Government for developing countries: Opportunities and challenges. *The Electronic Journal on Information Systems in Developing Countries, 18*(1), 1–24.

Noonan, J. T. (1984). *Bribes: The intellectual history of a moral idea.* London, UK: Macmillan.

OECD. (2003). The e-government imperative. Paris, France: OECD. Retrieved from http://213.253.134.43/oecd/pdfs/browseit/4203071E.pdf

PM. (2008). *Prime ministry of The Hashemite Kingdom of Jordan.* Retrieved from http://www.pm.gov.jo/arabic/index.php?page_type=pages&part=1&page_id=126

Samovar, L. A., Porter, R. E., & Jain, N. C. (1981). *Understanding intercultural communication.* Belmont, CA: Wadsworth.

Schlumberger, O. (2002). Transition to development? In Joffe, G. (Ed.), *Jordan in transition* (pp. 225–253). London, UK: Hursy & Co.

Schware, R. (2000). Information technology and public sector management in developing countries: Present status and future prospects. *The Indian Journal of Public Administration, 46*(3), 411–416.

Schware, R., & Deane, A. (2003). Deploying e-government programs: The strategic importance of "I" before "E". *Info, 5*(4), 10–19. doi:10.1108/14636690310495193

Smith, L. M., & Pohland, P. A. (1969). *Grounded theory and educational ethnography: A methodological analysis and critique.* St. Ann, MO: Central Midwestern Regional Education Library.

Strauss, A., & Corbin, J. (1990). *Basics of qualitative research: Grounded theory procedures and techniques.* London, UK: Sage.

United Nations. (2008a). *e-Government survey, from e-government to connected governance.* Retrieved from http://unpan1.un.org/intradoc/groups/public/documents/un/unpan028607.pdf

United Nations. (2008b). *Handbook on the least developed country category: Inclusion, graduation and special support measures.* Retrieved from http://www.un.org/esa/policy/devplan/cdppublications/2008cdphandbook.pdf

United Nations Conference on Trade and Development. (2001). *E-commerce and development report.* Retrieved from http://www.unctad.org/Templates/Page.asp?intItemID=2629&lang=1

Wong, L. C., & Kleiner, B. H. (1994). Nepotism. *Work Study, 43*(5), 10–12. doi:10.1108/EUM0000000004002

World Bank. (2010a). *Data - a short history.* Retrieved from http://go.worldbank.org/U9B-K7IA1J0

World Bank. (2010b) *Data – country groups: Lower-middle-income economies.* Retrieved from http://go.worldbank.org/D7SN0B8YU0

ENDNOTE

[1] The criteria for judging whether or not a country or society is developed or developing are not universally agreed, and many previous papers that compare developing and developed countries offer no definition of these terms. The United Nations (as found in United Nations, 2008b) prefers to define a Least Developed Countries (LDC), based on defined levels of economic, human and industrialisation activities, allowing countries to self-assess themselves to be in this category. A developed country can therefore be seen as one that considers itself to have achieved advancements in the stated LDC criteria at least to the defined threshold level, and a developing country can be seen as one that considers itself to be working towards substantial improvements in the LDC criteria, but not yet having achieved all threshold levels. The World Bank (2010a) explains that "the term 'developing economies' has been used to denote the set of low and middle income economies". Jordan is classified as a country of lower middle income having a Gross National Income of $975 or less per capita (World Bank, 2010b).

This work was previously published in the International Journal of Technology and Human Interaction, Volume 7, Issue 2, edited by Anabela Mesquita and Chia-Wen Tsai, pp. 9-20, copyright 2011 by IGI Publishing (an imprint of IGI Global).

Chapter 14

The Role of Partnership in E-Government Readiness:
The Knowledge Stations (KSs) Initiative in Jordan

Zaid I. Al-Shqairat
Al-Hussein Bin Talal University, Jordan

Ikhlas I. Altarawneh
Al-Hussein Bin Talal University, Jordan

ABSTRACT

The Initiative of establishing Information Technology (IT) and Community Service Centers, later renamed Knowledge Stations (KSs) was launched in 2001. The KSs initiative is intended to implement IT in local communities (LCs) and remote areas in preparation for the E-Government process. This study develops a model that explores KSs' role as a partnership in E-Government readiness in Jordan through answering the following two questions: why is a clearly comprehensive role of KSs needed for the readiness of E-Government in Jordan? How does this role take place practically? The research methodology is the case study that was applied to six KSs as a purposive sample in Amman, the capital of Jordan. Nine semi-structured interviews have been conducted with the director of KSs project, trainers, trainees and volunteers in the KSs project. The findings of the study showed that the role of KSs in E-Government readiness has four pillars: enhancement of community awareness in social and economic fields, development of Information and Communications Technology (ICT) capabilities, lessening computer illiteracy fulfillment of comprehensive development.

INTRODUCTION

The partnership concept is still unclear, because most collaborative activities in social and economic areas between the public and private sector are located under the heading of partnerships (Lund-Thomsen, 2007). The partnership concept is not the only issue that has been debated between researchers, but also the advantages and disadvantages of partnership have undergone extensive debate too. Osborne (2000) explores two perspectives about this debate: The first

DOI: 10.4018/978-1-4666-1954-8.ch014

perspective believes the advantages will not be achieved without partnership, while the second believes the advantages or positive results will happen despite the partnership (collaborative) rather than because of it.

Partnership is more than outsourcing joint capital investment and project financing. It also means implementing policies that create the demand of services and conditions, a suitable return of investment in implementing and deploying government processes (Bassanini, 2002). Also, it does not mean limitation in the government's role, it means the creation of different governmental roles, since the position of the private partner is strong and this needs more skilled government participation (Jamali & Olayan, 2004). The concept of partnership is used broadly by researchers according to their perspectives about the discussed issues and the nature of the collaboration initiatives between public and private sectors in addition to the collaborative areas. Partnership has re-shaped the government's role to be able to obtain a suitable position in managing, controlling and evaluating partnership projects with private partners to accomplish its needs of financial resources and qualified people.

Osborne and Plastrik (2000), Executive Privatization Commission (2000, pp. 4-5), Campbell and Fuhr (2004), Ferlie et al. (2005), and Sharma (2007) mentioned different forms of partnership that include:

1. Build, Operate and Own (BOO) projects that means: building government projects through the private sector and subsequently operating them through the private sector for a limited time, where the private sector can own such projects by agreement with the government.
2. Build, Operate and Transfer (BOT) projects that means: the government builds the projects through the private companies and after a limited time the government retrieves the projects to transfer them to another company.

3. Build, Transfer and Operate (BTO) projects that means: building government projects through the private sector, and after that transferring them to other private sectors in order to operate them for a limited time.
4. Build, Operate, Own and Transfer (BOOT) projects that means: the private sector builds the enterprise, owns, exploits and operates it then transfers it and its ownership to the public sector.

E-Government initiatives benefited from partnership projects by following the accelerated development of E-Government implementation, since the formal relations between the government and the private sector enhances the efficiency and transparency of E-Government projects and contributes in E-Government maturity through the contribution of development social integration (Song, 2006). Therefore, the E-Government approach re-shaped the government's role and moved it from being a direct service provider to enabler and intermediary for service provision. Furthermore, with this new role, governments emphasized the importance of partnership arrangements with other sectors such as the private and voluntary sectors (Griffin & Halpin, 2002).

LITERATURE REVIEW

E-Government Initiatives

E-Government became an opportunity to rethink how the government provides services, and how it links them in a way that is convenient for a user's needs not only to put forms and services online (Davison et al., 2005). E-Government also was seen as a mean of empowering people, changing the way people access public services, by promoting transparency and accountability in governmental action of acquiring knowledge (Bassanini, 2002). Thus, E-Government is defined as creating and applying a strategy that enables a rethinking of the governments' role, its institutional structures, processes, functions and also its commitment to provide services (Al-Shqairat, 2009).

This strategy seeks to enhance participation and interaction with stakeholders (citizens, employees, clients, suppliers and donors) through developing several sub-strategies such as political initiatives, adopting different instruments, for instance e-democracy and using available ICTs tools such as the internet and media. In the 1990s, E-Government became a strategy for reform and development in public sector agencies through the rethinking of the government's role as a whole. Also, the development of E-Government followed the example of E-Commerce through the use of a business model to solve government problems that include the weakness of democracy, bureaucracy and duplication of public departments' efforts (Stahl, 2005).

Collaboration between the service provider (public sector) and its stakeholders has been seen as a way of involving the private sector in E-Government projects to meet the needs of the main stakeholders (citizens and businesses) in public services delivery. Moreover, it has been held as a manner in which to avoid the problems that appeared from the implementation from previous ways of public sector reform, such as privatization (Jamali & Olayan, 2004; Ah-Lian et al., 2006).

E-Government and Partnership

Partnership in E-Government can be defined as "all the available integrated collaborative agreements between the E-Government programme as a representative for all public sector institutions and the private sector, which is built on clear sharing of revenue and sharing of risks, such as: the high cost of the E-Government programme, the conflicting decisions and lack of skills within public sector agencies, in addition to the clear exchange of benefits such as, capacity building, information, financial and human resources with consideration of the requirements of the planning,

implementation and evaluation stages of each PPP project" (Al-Shqairat, 2009, p. 219).

There are many justifications to adopt the partnership approach in E-Government implementation (Osborne, 2000; Jamali & Olayan, 2004; Devadoss et al., 2002; Bassanini, 2002; OECD, 2004; Blundell, 2005; Rocheleau & Wu, 2005):

1. Allowing the public sector to concentrate on the administration's core business, pubic policies, planning, and business issues, while the private sector partner takes over ICT production issues.
2. Transferring the accountability towards the private sector.
3. Reducing the risks and failed transactions by a formal assessment of solutions available in the market.
4. Improving the transformation strategy for E-Government services delivery on the functions level: (e.g. customer's centric services), the processes level; (e.g. sharing) and on the capacity level; (e.g. building capacity).
5. Promoting both public and private sectors to benefit from the strengths, resources and expertise of each other.
6. Providing partnership projects, particularly in the initial stages a holistic view focusing on a comprehensive sense.

Partnership approaches lead to organizational, managerial, strategic, technical and operational benefits for both public and private sectors. For example adopting enterprise architecture integration approach in E-Government to link up separated and isolated information systems in public organizations, such as delivering business counter products/services through a complex network of partnerships between public and private organizations (Janssen & Cresswell, 2005).

Since the emergence of E-Government, most countries called for a real partnership with the private sector. So working with different private sectors was a feature of almost all E-Governments activities (OECD, 2004). For example, the UK was advanced in realizing the need of strategic partnerships and private provisions of services instead of public provisions of services, these partnerships included many sectors, such as the public, private and voluntary sectors (Osborne, 2000; Jones & Crowe, 2001). In the 1990s, the UK adopted Private Finance Initiative (PFI) as an element of the new public management strategy (Osborne, 2000). The US also underwent a long process to turn over many government functions to the private sector by abandoning some, selling others and contracting private companies to handle others (Osborne & Gaebler, 1992).

However, partnership in developing countries emerged to tackle many challenges such as lack of public sector performance, high public services costs, governments' budgets constrains, absence of required skills sets in public sector bodies and absence of incentives to reward performance (Jamali & Olayan, 2004; Sharma, 2007). Thus, developing countries have realized that partnerships between the public and private sector is one of the important solutions to increase investment in communication infrastructure, in training and learning, in addition to enabling them to increase their capabilities to deal with all problems in a stabilized way. For instance, new E-Government applications and portals, such as Electronic Service Delivery (ESD) and Central Cyber Government Office (CCGO) in Hong Kong were developed and rolled out from 2000 onwards to facilitate electronic transactions between the Hong Kong Special Administrative Region Government (HKSARG) and its external (business firms and citizens) and internal (government departments and employees) customers (Ho, 2007). In Dubai, the E-Government strategy emphasized the importance of participation with technological companies and content providers to build the programme, maintain it and enrich the portal with information and innovative eServices. This was through partnership with approximately 24 national and international organizations from the public and private sectors in the fields of IT

solutions, training and development, infrastructure software, learning solutions, finance and education (Dubai E-Government, 2008a, 2008b).

Jordan: General Background

- Jordan is a developing middle-income country located in south west Asia, with a Government type of Constitutional Monarchy, the head of state being King Abdullah II. Jordan's capital is Amman the language is Arabic and English as the second language, and the population is 5,473 million (Jordanian Department of Statistics, 2006; Jordanian E-Government, 2008). Although it has scarce natural resources, Jordan has some competitive advantageous factors, which include the following (REACH, 2000; Al-Jaghoub & Wetrup, 2003; Department of Statistics, 2006; Jordanian E-Government, 2008):
- Educated human resources
- Hard working population
- Enlightened leadership
- High youth rate of the population, which is 51.7%
- Supportive friends around the world

The rate of the diffusion of technology increased in Jordan since 2000, but it is still less than the required level for socio-economic development. Therefore, there is a low level of the ICT usage on one hand, and deficiency in the usage of ICT and obtaining the benefits from it on the other hand. Jordan has a high rate of owning and using landlines and mobile phones, but simultaneously there is a low rate in owning computers and accessing the internet. However, the aspiration for increasing the usage of ICT and enhancing the way in which people may benefit from it.

The King and the government sought to invest in the competitively advantageous factors in order to make a basic change in the investing of ICT development in the life of individuals, the public and private sectors in Jordan. In this regards, for example the King Abdullah II said: "*It is the time to widen the scope of our participation in the knowledge economy, from being mere isolated islands on the periphery of progress, to becoming an oasis of technology that can offer the prospect of economies of scale for those who venture to invest in our young available talent*" (Jordanian E-Government, 2008).

In Jordan, it was realized that without collaboration between all country sectors all lunched development initiatives particularly the ICTs initiative would not be able to achieve their objectives. Therefore, the key strategies, which aimed to ensuring a more prosperous future for Jordan, included establishing an effective partnership approach to support the economic development, and designing an E-Government initiative with clearly stated goals to create systems and enhance transparency, accountability, and efficiency for public sector agencies (Jordan Vision 2020, 1999). The initiative of establishing Knowledge Stations (KSs) came in correspondence with the vision of His Majesty Abdullah II to create a universal access to ICT for all Jordanians as part of the efforts to join global economy, promote sustainable human development, and support governments' efforts to implement E-Government, particularly in LCs and Remote Areas in Jordan.

Partnership Approach and E-Government Readiness in Jordan

The traditional public-private sector relationships in Jordan used to be described in terms of separation, and the existing element of distrust between public and private sectors, since the public sector considers the private sector as profit-hungry and driven solely by selfish motives. In addition, the private sector views the public sector as an obstacle that must be circumvented (Al-Kayed et al., 1999; Jordan Vision 2020, 1999). Partnership was defined in Jordan as "a contractual arrange-

ment between the public and private sector, with a clear agreement on mutually established objectives, for the delivery of assets and/or services by the private sector" (Executive Privatization Commission, 2008). In Jordan, it is believed that increased cooperation and interaction between the two sectors will, in turn, increase the level of confidence in the private sector. At the same time, will allow the public sector to achieve a broader perspective in its services and improve level of customer satisfaction (Al-Kayed et al., 1999). In order to adopt the partnership approach, the Jordanian government appointed Electronic Product Code (EPC) to issue the required regulations for partnership and develop, implement and manage the partnership strategy and its project pipeline, in cooperation with public and private stakeholders (Executive Privatization Commission, 2008).

Moreover, the Privatization Law was enforced in 2000 and specified the methods that can be adopted to establish specific investment enterprises pursuant to agreements between public and private sector, which include (Executive Privatization Commission, 2000, pp. 4-5):

1. The building, exploitation and operation of enterprise, by the private sector for a specific period then its transferred to the public sector at the end of the specific period (BOT)
2. The private sector builds the enterprise, transfers its ownership to the public sector while retaining the right to exploit and operate it for specific period (BTO)
3. The building of, ownership of, exploitation of the enterprise, by the private sector, which also operates it for its own account (BOO)
4. The private sector builds the enterprise, owns, exploits and operates it then transfers it and its ownership to the public sector (BOOT)

The previous methods provide the government with the options that can be followed to undertake public sector projects in Jordan. these options allowed the government to adopt a collaborated approach, since most of privatized projects as State Owned Enterprises (SOEs) were sold to the private sector, such as Jordan Telecom Company (JTC) which was sold to the private sector, with only 41.5% of the ownership being governmental (Amman Stock Exchange).

Jordan realized that there is an essential need to distribute the roles between both public and private sectors, through an integrated form that enables the public sector to carry out its roles in the regulation and supervision of development projects, at the same time, enabling the private sector to carry out its role in supporting and facilitating such projects. The partnership approach eliminated the negative points that privatization created, and attained some advantages such as the sharing of revenue, which led to its acceptance in public opinion in Jordan (Fanek, 2008b). In addition, it became a top priority of the public sector, and this required re-building the relationship between public and private sectors, particularly in the areas of private sector participation (Al-Kayed et al., 1999):

Jordan's Readiness for E-Government

The readiness for E-Government is not limited to the development and preparedness of public sector agencies for E-Government processes, but it is also important to consider human resources, existing budgetary resources, national infrastructure, economic, education, information policies, and private sector development (Al-Omari & Al-Omari, 2006). E-government readiness includes organizational readiness, governance and leadership readiness, customer readiness, competency readiness, technology readiness, and legal readiness (Mohammad et al., 2009).

The National Agenda (NA) (2006) addressed some of the important factors that prevent effective E-Government implementation, such as:

1. Low internet diffusion in Jordan, which was about 4.9%
2. Lack of IT local qualified resources
3. The weakness in public sector infrastructure
4. The absence of legislation and organizing framework
5. The lack of governmental and business sectors awareness for E-Government concept and its benefits.

The NA sought to develop a comprehensive strategy for E-Government through clear objectives and completion indicators that correspond with the public sector reform requirements. The E-Government strategy was consistent with NA, because it sought to achieve a positive impact on comprehensive development and to transfer Jordan's economy to be based on knowledge. Partnership requirements also included the country's role in creating a suitable environment for the investment from all sectors in Jordan, particularly the IT private sector, and this was one of the National Agendas' priorities, that realizes the lack of IT local qualified resources (National Agenda, 2006).

Until 2006, Jordan's E-Government achieved many projects that were related to the implementation stage of the E-Government programme, such as the Secure Government Network (SGN), training programmes for over 9000 public sector employees, the E-Government Portal, the E-Government Contact Centre, the Payment Gateway, E-Services Portfolio, and the launching of E-Government Strategy (Hourani, 2006). The need of training programmes for most public sector employees to be able to deal with E-Government requirements was one of priorities, and from the planning stage, there were many IT programmes for thousands of public sector employees (MOICT, 2006a).

Jordanian government through the MOICT, which is responsible for E-Government implementation, started establishing entities and centers to facilitate its initiatives and enhance its implementation. Such as, the National Information Technology Center (NITC) that was the implementation arm for the E-Government programme in Jordan, to facilitate the interdepartmental coordination and collaboration between government entities and to enhance the implementation level of e-government services (MOICT, 2006, 2008).

The creation of a sustained partnership is one of the supporting requirements to achieve success in the E-Government implementation strategy in Jordon, since the development and current technical support for E-Government projects through the institutions and technical employees in the public sector is not presently sufficient (Al-Azam, 2001; Shawwa, 2004). King Abdullah II encouraged the partnership with international IT companies, such as Microsoft, which has a strategic agreement with the MOICT to support the private IT sector in order to develop the country's IT industry, that undertakes an important role in E-Government Implementation.

Furthermore, the success of a long-term strategy for E-Government requires a partnership approach, because neither the public nor private sector alone can build and implement a comprehensive strategy for E-Government, since a joint strategy serves both of them and affects both of them as well. The E-Government programme in Jordan realized the need for a national partnership unit to manage and control the partnership projects, since the use of the partnership approach is increasing in Jordan, as it is for E-Government efforts in other countries (MOICT, 2006b).

Before and post the launch of the E-Government programme in Jordan in 2001, many initiatives in the ICT field were adopted as pioneer projects to facilitate and support E-Government implementation, whether from public sector, private sector, nonprofit organizations, or from international organizations. The Jordanian government and the private sector sought to establish some private and public organizations related to the ICT field, and launch many ICT initiatives to support and help

E-Government implementation. The Information Technology and Community Service Centers (later renamed Knowledge Stations) (KSs) was one of ICT initiatives which were launched in 2001 and were intended to implement IT in local communities and remote areas to prepare them for the implementation of the E-Government programme (Knowledge Stations, 2007b).

Thus, the initiative of establishing Knowledge Stations (KSs) came in correspondence with the vision of His Majesty Abdullah II to create a universal access to ICT for all Jordanians as part of the efforts to join global economy, promote sustainable human development, and support governments' efforts to implement E-Government, particularly in LCs and Remote Areas in Jordan.

Partnerships and the Knowledge Station Project

- Many partnership initiatives have been conducted in Jordan since 2004, such as Reach Initiatives from 2000 until 2004 that motivated private sector companies to take the initiative and participate as an important partner in the development of IT sector in Jordan (Jordan ICT Forum, 2002; REACH 1.0, 2000; REACH 2.0, 2001, REACH 3.0, 2002, REACH 4.0, 2004). It was one of the main efforts in the ICTs field in Jordan that came as a response to a challenge from his Majesty King Abdullah II in 1999 for a private sector companies to take the initiative and participate as an important partner in the development of the IT sector in Jordan (Jordan ICT Forum, 2002). In order to achieve its objectives, a comprehensive framework was established to develop key areas (Jordan ICT Forum, 2002a) including:
- IT industry development.
- Human resource development.
- Infrastructure development.

The REACH initiative was one of numerous examples of public–private partnerships that attracted investment particularly in ICT, through the development of laws and government policies related to MOICT investment from national and international companies. Also, as a partnership initiative, it was composed as a series of four initiatives focused on improving ICT capabilities for public sector employees and empowering the population in IT usage (REACH 1.0, 2000; REACH 2.0, 2001; REACH 3.0, 2002, REACH 4.0, 2004). The E-Village project in Jordan was another pioneer project built on a partnership approach including public and private sector organizations from local and international areas (UNIFEM, 2006). This project sought to develop the local community in different ways such as conducting IT training courses through the IT Academy Lab, which was developed in the E-Villages for local unemployed women and men to get jobs requiring IT skills and certifications. Al-Manar Project was also a live example for the importance of partnership to deliver e-services in a developed and integrated way in exchanging information and technical experiences between the partners to achieve project objectives in a way that serve all of them, which include (National Center for Human Resources Development, 2006):

1. Partnership with Aqaba Special Economic Zone Authority (ASEZA) to offer employment services by providing different labour markets services and information for investors, employers and job seekers.
2. Partnership among productive sectors, education institutions, the labour market, and local communities to enhance the learning process and to provide more jobs as well as the promotion of economic and personal development.
3. Cooperation with the National Employment Center (NEC) in the Ministry of Labour to integrate and coordinate the activities between the two projects, and exchange technical experiences

KSs were established by National Information Technology Center (NITC), financed by King Abdullah II Fund for Development, distributed throughout the Kingdom of Jordan and involved an integrated network to facilitate communication and integration among the multiple nationwide projects in the IT field in Jordan (Jordan Times, 2004). The first KS was established in October 2000 as a part of stage one that included 20 KSs. In 2003 phase, two and three were completed and included 75 KSs and in 2004, the total arrived at 100 KSs (Knowledge Stations, 2004).

By the end of 2006 there were about 130 KSs distributed throughout the different governorates. The methodology for KSs distribution in Jordan's Governorates depended on the following criteria:

1. KSs diffusion should include all Jordan regions
2. The consideration of the population, geographic, social and economic aspects
3. The avoidance of KSs duplication
4. The availability of IT services from public and private organizations in local communities (National Information Technology Centre, 2005).

KSs effectively, have a dual role as community centers to serve two primary roles; first, as training centers for IT and social programmes, second, as walk-in centers to provide services such as internet, fax machine usage and photocopiers (Knowledge Stations, 2004). The KSs initiative aims to enable all segments of the Jordanian society despite their geographical, location, or economic status to get the necessary ICT skills that will allow them to enhance their socio–economic capabilities (MOICT, 2007). Moreover, they have the following objectives (Knowledge Stations, 2007a):

1. Lessening the digital divide between the governorates and different regions in the Kingdom

2. Introducing ICT to the different localities in Jordan and encouraging the use of ICT in the day to day life of citizens
3. Reducing IT illiteracy by providing training in ICT
4. Encouraging the use of the National Information System for retrieving local information
5. Enhancing the use of the Internet for socio-economic development at the community level
6. Enhancing LC skills through ICT training
7. Enhancing competition among citizens by increasing their knowledge in ICT
8. Preparing the local communities to get involved in the e-government project

Through 132 KSs, which are distributed throughout the different governorates in 2006, 8200 training courses have been conducted for 82450 trainees, and 166450 citizens benefited from KSs services (Knowledge Stations, 2008a). Knowledge Stations (KSs), were built on the partnership approach between the government, the private sector and civic organizations in building, hosting, controlling and implementing this project (Knowledge Stations, 2004). Several organizations from the public and private sectors distributed their roles to manage and render the KSs successful, which include the following:

1. Royal committee for following the establishment of KSs
2. NITC, an exclusive institution to establish KSs and distribute them in various Jordanian areas, and control business execution for the KSs infrastructure
3. King Abdullah development fund (KADF) as the finance for KSs
4. Management unit for KSs to manage KSs under the umbrella of NITC
5. Hosting Organizations (HOs), which include a myriad of public and private organizations to provide services to the community includ-

ing city councils, the Jordan Hashemite Fund for Development, youth centers of the Higher Council for Youth, Noor al-Hussein Foundation, Jordan River Foundation, and numerous cultural centers (Knowledge Stations, 2004, 2008b).

The Study Methodology

The study methodology depended on the qualitative case study (QCS) approach. It was applied on six KSs as a purposive sample in Amman-the capital of Jordan. Yin (1994, p. 13) defines case study methodology as "*an empirical inquiry that investigates a contemporary phenomenon within its real-life context, especially when the boundaries between the phenomenon and its context are not clearly evident*". Qualitative case study research means "*a research strategy using case studies involving qualitative data collection and qualitative analysis*" (Weerd & Nederhof, 2001, p. 513). Case study methodology is useful in the areas that have little understanding of how and why processes or phenomenon occurs and when the phenomenon is dynamic and not yet mature or settled (Darke et al., 1998). Moreover, as Yin (2003) argues that the case study enables the researchers to understand the phenomenon when it is not distinguishable from its context.

This study aimed to answer two main questions. First, why a clearly comprehensive role of KSs is needed in the E-government readiness in Jordan? Second, how does this role take place in successful forms? For answering these questions, the researchers suppose that the case study methodology is one of the suitable approaches to clarify the KSs' role in E-government readiness in Jordan. That is because KSs' role needs more discussion and debates, at the same time, there is a little understanding about this role, particularly on the practical side. The researchers conducted nine semi-structured interviews with the directors of the KSs project, trainers, trainees and volunteers in KSs project and relied on the interviews and the formal and informal documents to obtain the data. Semi-structured interviews were used in order to allow the interviewees to shape the flow of information and control the discussion if it moves away from the key subject matter (Wilkinson & Birmingham, 2003).

A combination or mixed purposeful sampling were used in this research to get triangulation and flexibility (Patton, 1990), by using snowball or chain sampling according to the recommendations of the informants that were interviewed from the population, and who know other people who are involved in KSs initiative. Also, purposeful random sampling was used by selecting the other informants randomly from the population. Purposeful random sampling was selected according to particular features of the informants to increase the creditability and attain an insight about the role of partnership in KSs in terms of the justifications, requirements, fields, the progress indications and their obstacles. Purposeful random sampling allowed the researchers to increase the research credibility and reduce the suspicion about why certain informants were selected for QCS (Patton, 1990).

According to Carter (1999), analysis in qualitative research concerns the process of bringing order to the data, organizing what is there into patterns, categories, and basic descriptive units. Qualitative analysis was used to attain in depth understanding of the phenomena, and interrelationships among all its aspects (Stake, 1995). The researchers used many steps to analyze their findings, started from preparing data for analysis; making the interpretation of the finding according to the information that are gleaned from the literature review and experiences that they gained from their work experiences as government employees (Creswell, 2003).

Based on the literature review and the documents that obtained from KSs project and E-Government program in Jordan, five main issues were derived. They represented the components of unit of analysis as the main key issues of the case study. For example, King Abdullah II said: *"It is the time to widen the scope of our participation in the knowledge economy, from being mere isolated islands on the periphery of progress, to becoming an oasis of technology that can offer the prospect of economies of scale for those who venture to invest in our young available talent"* (Jordanian E-Government, 2008).

To discuss these issues some questions were created, which were derived from the research's two main questions mentioned before, which in turn, have been derived from the literature review. These questions acted as guidance for the dialogue with the informants during the interviews. These questions represented the main key issues and covered the following sub- issues

- The nature of the partnership role and the ability in adopting such role in E-Government readiness through the KSs project in Jordan.
- The reasons for the adoption of partnership role in KSs project in Jordan.
- The basic requirements for the adoption of the partnership approach in KSs project in Jordan and the current situation of the existence of partnership requirements in Jordan.
- The areas of partnership role that can be adopted in KSs project and those which can be adopted in the Jordanian situation.
- The indications for partnership progress in KSs project in Jordan.

Thus, the five key categories, which explored the aspects of KSs role in E-Government implementation involved: justifications of KSs' role, the requirements, the fields, the progress indications and obstacles of KSs' role. Figure 1 illustrates the design of the unit of analysis that involves the five key categories, mentioned by the researchers previously.

The Key Features of the Informants in the Case Study

In the case study, nine interviews were conducted with the directors of the KSs project, trainers, trainees and volunteers in KSs project. The features of those people include: their position title, location, degree, experience in years, experience field, gender, and age. These features indicate the nature of the sample in the case study, which depended on the purposive sample type and explored the extent to which this sample serves the research purposes. The informants were given numbers according to the interview time. After finishing the analysis process, as explored in Table 1, the findings showed that one of the interviewees was the director of Knowledge stations project (KSs) in the National Information Technology Centre, three were station's managers, two trainers, two trainees and one was volunteer. The table also shows that the interviewees have IT qualifications, since most of them have Bachelor degree in Computing or computer science, one has B.S.C. in Electrical & Electronics Engineering and one has Bachelor in Math. In addition, the interviewees' experience in years is shown, since the average

for the experience years was six and the experience fields included management, IT training, teaching, and computing. As the table shows, six of the interviewees were male and three female, while the average of their ages was thirty years.

Thus, the previous mentioned features in Table 1 validate the selection of a purposeful sample, which enabled the obtaining of informants with particular features in order to increase the creditability of the research findings, since most of the informants have high level qualifications (Bachelor degree), and have responsible positions in their stations. Moreover, some of them are in the top administrative level and others in the second level as trainers. The informants were distributed in different stations in Amman – the capital of Jordan. The average experience for the informants was six years and most of the experience was in computing, IT or in related fields such as management and teaching.

FINDINGS

The researchers have discussed the findings from the following aspects:

Figure 1. The unit of analysis

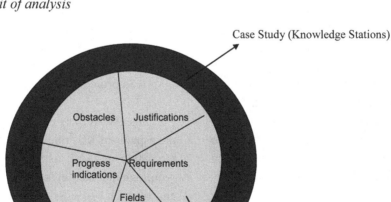

Table 1. The sample features in the case study

Interviewee code	Position title	Location	Degree	Experience years	Experience field	Gender	Age
1	Director	Knowledge stations project (KSs) in the National Information Technology Centre	B.SC. in Electrical & Electronics Engineering	23	Managing various types of National Projects Information technology & community development	Male	49
2	Trainee	Abu Nuseir Knowledge Station	Bachelor in Computing	2	Computing	Female	24
3	Station Manager	Abu Nuseir Knowledge Station	Bachelor in Computing	4	Managing training programs & Station activities	Male	28
4	Station Manager	Al Bayader Knowledge Station	B.SC. in Computer Science	7	Managing training programs & Station activities	Male	29
5	Trainer	Iraq Al amir Knowledge Station	B.SC. in Computer Science	2	IT Training	Male	27
6	Trainee	Iraq Al amir	Bachelor in Maths	3	Teaching	Female	26
7	Volunteer	Iraq Al amir	B.SC. in Computer Science	1	Computing	Male	23
8	Station Manager	Al Moaqar Knowledge Station	B.SC. in Computer Science	4	Managing training programs & Station activities	Female	32
9	Trainer	Al Moaqar Knowledge Station	Bachelor in Computing	4	IT training	Male	35

The Justifications of KSs' Role

This study displayed many justifications for KSs, as one of the country's needs to solve the deficiency in the ICT field in Jordanian communities, which include the lack of internet access in local communities, the need for ICT services and facilities in local communities, the need for presenting multiple socio-economic services in local communities and local communities' need for comprehensive development. KSs trainers emphasized the need of KSs, one of them said, *"the population in this village is about 10.000, they do not have internet services. The Ministry of Education declares General Secondary Education Certificate Examination (Tawjihi) (high school)* *results on the internet, KS is the lone place for presenting internet service, the villagers come to get the results of their children here, and we give them this service for free"*

The Requirements of KSs' Role

All the interviewees emphasized that KSs will not undertake their role successfully, without getting their basic requirements that include; providing them with a sufficient number of trainers, promotion volunteers from public and private sector to help KSs in fulfilling their activities, creating the suitable ways in marketing KSs activities, variation of their programmes and enabling them to enhance their services quality.

The Fields of KSs

The documents from NITC and KSs, and the interviews indicated many areas that can be covered by KSs. Figure 2 explores the fields that KSs concentrate on and there divisions as they have been mentioned by the informants:

These fields include social activities that include workshops and lectures, computer maintenance for LCs people, lessening the digital divide, internet services, IT training programmes, ICTs capacity building programmes (for students, teachers, unemployed people and also the volunteers), loans services for LCs, (for example, employment and development fund loans), and access points for E-government. As the researchers mentioned before, KSs (2007a) determined many objectives that represent the fields of KSs role and include lessening the digital divide between the governorates in the Kingdom. In addition, it introduced ICT to the different localities in Jordan, encouraged the use of ICT in the daily life of citizens, and enhanced the use of the Internet for socio-economic development at the community level. The trainers in KSs mentioned some of these fields, as one of them said:

Our region is an agricultural and economic one, we collaborate with the agriculture loan fund to offer loans for farmers by using the electronic applications via the internet, and at the same time we collaborate with the private companies to offer job opportunities for unemployed people.

Figure 2. KSs fields

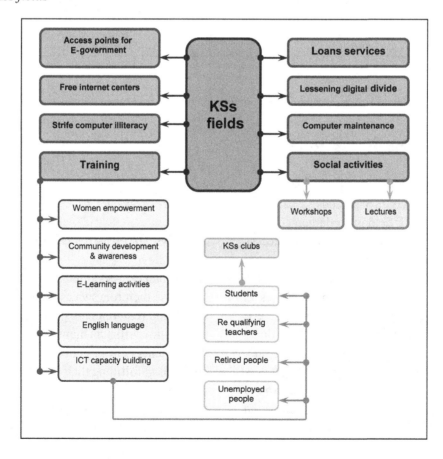

The Progress Indications for KSs Role

The informants mentioned some progress indications for KSs role that emerged from their experience. These indications include; the successful stories, housewives' employment, increasing programmes and activities, media supporting, KSs promotion for tourism activities, the collaboration with international organizations, job opportunities for unemployed people and establishing special websites for some of the LCs. One of the trainers stated: *"The youngest child who has an ICDL certificate was one of our graduates; he attained the certificate at the age of 11. This year he conducted a basic computer course for his school colleagues between 12-15 years old, and we consider that a successful story for our KS".*

Another trainer stated, *"we conducted many programmes and workshops in the coordination with non profit organizations in the fields of labour law, social insurance, child rights and health fields".*

In addition, the trainees' emphasize this progress, one of them said: *"we can now get IT training in our village, before the establishment of KS we could not travel far away from our village as girls to get such training, the fees are very low and we can pay them and after that we will get an ICDL certificate".* Another said, *"the population here is about 10.000, we have conducted 122 training courses and graduated 575 trainees since the last five years in this village, and we consider that a great success".*

The Obstacles for KSs 'Role

Despite of KSs progress, the interviewees indicated many aspects that hinder KSs role, these include:

1. The weakness of KSs revenue from their activities
2. The weakness of coordinating between KSs and LCs
3. The duplication in KSs supervision between NICT and HOs for KSs
4. The instability of KSs trainers
5. The consumption of KSs revenue from HOs
6. The weakness of LCs support for KSs activities
7. The difficulties of clarifying IT and change importance in LCs
8. Some of HOs direct KSs activities to serve their objectives
9. The weakness of contacting between KSs
10. The absence of data base about target LCs

Therefore, most of the interviewees suppose that many of the hosting organizations are not able to serve the comprehensive objectives for KSs, because HOs are specialists in their work and some of them try to direct KSs activities to serve their goals.

The Model of the Study

Through the discussion and interpretation of the previous discussed findings, the researchers found that there are two main aspects for KSs as one of the partnership projects between government private sector and non-government organizations. These aspects include the pillars of KSs role and its applications. KSs' role has four key pillars that have been derived from KSs objectives which were mentioned before in this study (Knowledge Stations, 2007a), and the collected documents such as (Knowledge Stations, 2004).

These pillars formalize E-Government readiness requirements in Jordan and include, enhancement of awareness within LCs in the social and economic aspects to increase livelihood levels for local people in both aspects (social and economic); development in ICT capabilities for LCs, because ICT services are the important tools that relate to the daily activities for individuals and organizations. In addition, the pillars include fulfillment of comprehensive development in LCs, this development includes; social, economic, culture and political sides, and strife computer illiteracy for local people as a basic element for E-government services that affects daily life needs.

The findings indicate that KSs have expressed their pillars through four applications which consist of IT training programmes such as, basic computer literacy training, programme applications and ECDL programme applications (e.g. the trained people through 132 KSs reached 82.450 and the training courses reached 8.200 by August 2007 (Knowledge Stations, 2007c). The applications also include ICT capacity building programmes that include special training courses to enhance ICT needs like (Auto CAD, computer maintenance and CISCO certificate training).

Moreover, socio economic activities are covered through KSs applications such as social programmes, which enhance people's awareness in many issues such as their rights, obligations, and the laws that arrange their life. In addition, economic activities are covered such as providing job opportunities for local people, whether from KSs themselves or from private and public organizations at the local and national level in the coordination with KSs. This will enhance the importance of knowledge economy concept in the comprehensive development of LCs.

To achieve these pillars, different applications are needed such as the internet access that is given to all people free, and the training for using the internet which is given to the local people for a small fee, (e.g. the users of KSs services reached 18.000 in 2005 (Knowledge Stations, 2007d); ICT capacity building; and socio-economic activities. Therefore, KSs role pillars and their applications are the two important aspects that should be addressed to enable the country to be ready for E-Government implementation in Jordan theoretically and practically, particularly in LCs.

Figure 3 shows the study model that illustrates the role of KSs as one of partnership projects in E-government readiness through its pillar (E-

government readiness requirements), and its applications (E-government readiness applications), and at the same time, answers the two questions that were posed by the researchers in this paper.

The previous pillars reflected the importance of the comprehensive role of KSs in E-government implementation through many applications such as IT training programmes, internet services, socio-economic activities, and ICT capacity building. Through the applications of their roles, KSs, as one of the visible examples for partnership initiatives in E-government implementation in Jordan, can build their pillars, and conversely, based on their pillars, can activate their applications to be involved in the basic requirements for E-Government implementation in Jordan.

CONCLUSION

This study aimed to develop a model that explores KSs' role as a partnership in E-Government readiness in Jordan through answering two basic questions: why is a clearly comprehensive role of KSs needed for the readiness of E-Government in Jordan? And how does this role take place practically? QCS methodology was applied to six KSs in Amman - the capital of Jordan, as one of the suitable approaches to clarify the KSs' role in E-government readiness in Jordan. A combination of mixed of random and snowball purposeful sampling were applied to select the informants according to their particular features to increase the creditability and attain an insight about the role of partnership in KSs in terms of the justifications, requirements, fields, the progress indications and their obstacles.

The discussion and interpretation of the findings indicated that there were two main aspects for KSs as one of the partnership projects, included the pillars of KSs role and its applications. KSs' role has four key pillars included, enhancement of awareness within LCs in the social and economic aspects; developing ICT capabilities for LCs; ful-

Figure 3. The model of the study (KSs role in E-government readiness)

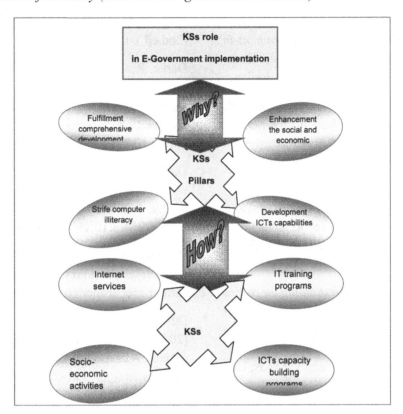

fillment of comprehensive development in LCs; and strife computer illiteracy for local people. To achieve these pillars, some applications are needed such as IT training, ICT capacity building, socio-economic activities, and internet access. Both of KSs pillars and their applications formized two important aspects for the study model and they should be addressed to enable the country to be ready for E-Government implementation in Jordan theoretically and practically, particularly in LCs.

According to the study findings and its model, the researchers clarify the following recommendations:

1. KSs should be expanded vertically through the enrichment of quality without ignoring the horizontal expansion in their numbers, because there is a need to increase the numbers of KSs and distribute them justly on

the demographic ground in Jordan. (Jordan Times, 2004)

2. KSs should vary their programmes and activities - not only IT programmes - to promote their activities and present more qualitative services and this will contribute to KSs continuity.

3. More financial support for KSs from all sectors in Jordan

4. Establishing (Mobile KSs) will help LCs to get e-services, particularly internet services.

5. Consolidation in KSs supervision to be hosted by one type of organization, such as Municipalities that have comprehensive development objectives.

6. Further research about KSs, particularly in the assessment of the successful factors for KSs role, and the relationship between the cultural factors and KSs' progress.

REFERENCES

Al-Azam, H. (2001). *Electronic government in Jordan, applying possibilities.* Unpublished master's thesis, Yarmouk University, Irbid, Jordan.

Al-Kayed, Z., Fayyad, R., & Assaf, M. (1999). *The best practices in the Jordan civil service reforms for sustainable human development in Jordan.* Amman, Jordan: Jordan Institute of Public Administration.

Al-Omari, A., & Al-Omari, H. (2006). E-Government readiness assessment model. *Journal of Computer Science, 2*(11), 841–845. doi:10.3844/jcssp.2006.841.845

Al-Shqairat, Z. (2009). *Understanding the role of public private partnership (PPP) in e-government implementation in developing countries: Case study of Jordan.* Unpublished doctoral dissertation, Leeds Metropolitan University, Leeds, UK.

Bassanini, F. (2002). *Delivering services and public: Private partnership in e-government, with a final warning about digital divide, digital opportunity and the danger of a new colonialism.* Paper presented at the 3rd High Level Forum on City Informatization in the Asia-Pacific Region, Shanghai, China.

Blundell, J. (2005, July 13). *Linking e-government with efficiency.* Paper presented at the 5th Annual London Connects Conference on Engaging London with Efficient Services, London, UK.

Campbell, T., & Fuhr, H. (2004). *Leadership and innovation in sub national government: Case studies from Latin America.* Washington, DC: World Bank.

Carter, S. (1999). Anatomy of qualitative management PhD. part two – getting finished. *Management Research News, 22*(12), 1–18. doi:10.1108/01409179910781887

Creswell, J. W. (2003). *Research design: Qualitative, quantitative, and mixed methods approaches* (2nd ed.). London, UK: Sage.

Darke, P., Graeme, S., & Broadbent, M. (1998). Successfully completing case study research: Combining rigor, relevance and pragmatism. *Information Systems Journal, 8*(4), 273–289. doi:10.1046/j.1365-2575.1998.00040.x

Davison, R., Wagner, C., & Ma, L. (2005). From government to e-government: A transition model. *Information Technology & People, 18*(3), 280–299. doi:10.1108/09593840510615888

Department of Statistics. (2006). *Employment and unemployment survey (second round).* Amman, Jordan: Department of Statistics.

Devadoss, P. R., Pan, S. L., & Huang, J. C. (2002). Structural analysis of e-government initiatives: A case study of SCO. *Decision Support Systems, 34*(3), 253–269. doi:10.1016/S0167-9236(02)00120-3

Dubai e-Government. (2008a). *e-Government core services.* Retrieved from http://egov.dubai.ae/?Services_Corp,Services_Corp,1,&_nfpb=true&_pageLabeCATindex

Dubai e-Government. (2008b). *Partner.* Retrieved from http://egov.dubai.ae/?partners_corp,partners_corp,1,&_nfpb=true&_pageLabel=i dex

Executive Privatization Commission. (2000). *Privatization law no. 25.* Retrieved from http://www.epc.gov.jo/EPC/Home/PrivateLaw/tabid/86/Default.aspx

Executive Privatization Commission. (2007). *Public private partnership in Jordan.* Retrieved from http://www.oecd.org/dataoecd/44/29/38404517.pps

Executive Privatization Commission. (2008). *Public private partnership policy for the government of Jordan.* Retrieved from http://www.epc.gov.jo/

Grunbaum, N. (2007). Identification of ambiguity in the case study research typology: What is a unit of analysis? *Qualitative Market Research: An International Journal, 10*(1), 78–97. doi:10.1108/13522750710720413

Ho, K. K. W. (2007). The e-government development, IT strategies, and portals of the Hong Kong SAR government. *International Journal of Cases on Electronic Commerce, 3*(2), 71–89.

Hourani, H. (2006, December 6-7). *e-Government: Jordan experience.* Paper presented at the Jordan ICT Forum, Dead Sea, Jordan.

Jamali, D., & Olayan, S. (2004). Success and failure mechanisms of public private partnerships (PPPs) in developing countries: Insights from the Lebanese context. *International Journal of Public Sector Management, 17*(5), 414–430. doi:10.1108/09513550410546598

Janssen, M., & Cresswell, A. (2005). Enterprise architecture integration in e-government. In *Proceedings of the 38th Hawaii International Conference on System Sciences* (p. 118).

Jones, D., & Crowe, B. (2001). *Transformation not automation: The e-government challenge.* London, UK: Demos.

Jordanian, E.-Government. (2008). *e-Government program.* Retrieved from http://www.jordan.gov.jo/wps/portal/General/?New_WCM_Context=/wps/wcm/conect/eGov/Home/&lang=en

Jordan, I. C. T. Forum. (2002, September 30-October 1). *REACH initiative.* Paper presented at the Jordan ICT Forum, Amman, Jordan.

Jordan Times. (2004, November 21). *Meeting discusses future of knowledge stations.* Amman, Jordan: Jordan Times.

Jordan Vision 2020. (1999) *JV2020 Phase I.* Retrieved from http://www.jv2020.com/Default.shtm

Knowledge Stations. (2004). *Progress report.* Retrieved from http://www.ks.gov.jo/

Knowledge Stations. (2007a). *Knowledge stations objectives, Jordan.* Retrieved from http://www.ks.jo/objectives.htm

Knowledge Stations. (2007b). *Knowledge stations: Together towards a digital economy & comprehensive development, Jordan.* Retrieved from http://www.ks.jo/default.htm

Knowledge Stations. (2008a). *Statistical data.* Retrieved from http://www.ks.gov.jo/default.htm

Knowledge Stations. (2008b). *Engaging the local community.* Retrieved from http://www.ks.jo/KS_engage.htm

Lund-Thomsen, P. (2007). *Assessing the impact of public-private partnerships in the global south: The case of the Kasur Tanneries pollution control project.* New York, NY: United Nations.

Mohammad, H., Almarabeh, T., & Abu Ali, A. (2009). e-Government in Jordan. *European Journal of Scientific Research, 35*(2), 188–197.

MOICT. (2006a). *e-Government strategy document* (06-09). Amman, Jordan: MOICT.

MOICT. (2006b). *New e-government strategy* (2007-2008-2009). Retrieved from http://www.gov.jo/en_index.aspx

MOICT. (2007) *Statement of government policy 2007 on the ICT & postal sectors.* Retrieved from http://www.moict.gov.jo/MoICT/en_index.aspx

National Agenda. (2006). *The Jordan that we want (2006-2015).* Amman, Jordan: National Agenda.

National Center for Human Resources Development. (2006). *Human resources development information system (Al-Manar).* Amman, Jordan: National Center for Human Resources Development.

National Information Technology Center. (2005). *The affection of knowledge stations in bridging digital divide*. Amman, Jordan: National Information Technology Center.

OECD. (2004). *The e-government imperative*. Paris, France: OECD.

Osborne, D., & Gaebler, T. (1992). *Reinventing government: How the entrepreneurial spirit is transforming the public sector*. Reading, MA: Addison-Wesley.

Osborne, D., & Plastrik, P. (2000). *The reinventor's field book: Tools for transforming your government*. San Francisco, CA: Jossey-Bass.

Osborne, S. (2000). *Public –private partnership: Theory and practice in international perspective*. London, UK: Routledge.

Patton, M. (1990). *Qualitative evaluation and research methods* (2nd ed.). London, UK: Sage.

REACH 1.0. (2000). *Launching Jordan's software and IT industry: A strategy and action plan*. Retrieved from http://www.reach.com.jo/

REACH 2.0. (2001). *Launching Jordan's software and IT services industry: An updated strategy and action plan*. Retrieved from http://www.reach.com.jo/

REACH 3.0. (2002). *Launching Jordan's software and ICT services: An updating strategy and action plan*. Retrieved from http://www.reach.com.jo/

REACH 4.0. (2004). *Launching Jordan's software and ICT services: An updating strategy and action plan*. Retrieved from http://www.reach.com.jo/

Rochelean, B., & Wu, L. (2005). e-Government and financial transactions: Potential versus reality. *Electronic. Journal of E-Government, 3*(4), 219–230.

Sharma, S. (2007). Exploring best practices in public–private partnership (PPP) in e government through select Asian case studies. *The International Information & Library Review, 39*, 203–210. doi:10.1016/j.iilr.2007.07.003

Shawwa, N. (2004). *Public officials' attitudes towards the implementation of e- government in Jordan: Field study*. Unpublished master's thesis, Jordan University, Amman, Jordan.

Song, H. (2006). *e-Government in developing countries: Lessons learned from republic of Korea*. Bangkok, Thailand: UNESCO.

Stahl, B. (2005). The ethical problem of framing e-government in terms of e-commerce. *Electronic. Journal of E-Government, 3*(2), 77–86.

UNIFEM. (2006). *e-Villages project*. Amman, Jordan: UNIFEM.

Weerd, D., & Nederhof, P. C. (2001). Case study research, the case of a PhD research project on organizing and managing new product development systems. *Management Decision, 39*(7), 513–538. doi:10.1108/EUM0000000005805

Wilkinson, D., & Birmingham, P. (2003). *Using research instruments: A guide for researchers*. London, UK: Routledge. doi:10.4324/9780203422991

Yin, K. (1994). *Case study research: Design and methods* (2nd ed.). London, UK: Sage.

Yin, K. (2003). *Application of case study research* (2nd ed.). London, UK: Sage.

This work was previously published in the International Journal of Technology and Human Interaction, Volume 7, Issue 3, edited by Anabela Mesquita and Chia-Wen Tsai, pp. 16-34, copyright 2011 by IGI Publishing (an imprint of IGI Global).

Section 4
Education, Health, and Professional Situations

Chapter 15
Public Representation of Ubiquitous ICT Applications in the Outpatient Health Sector

Stephanie Moser
University of Bern, Switzerland

Susanne Elisabeth Bruppacher
University of Freiburg Regina Mundi, Switzerland

Frederic de Simoni
University of Bern, Switzerland

ABSTRACT

ICT advances will bring a new generation of ubiquitous applications, opening up new possibilities for the health sector. However, the social impacts of this trend have largely remained unexplored. This study investigates the public representation of future ICT applications in the outpatient health sector in terms of their social acceptance. Mental models of ICT applications were elicited from inhabitants of Berlin, Germany, by means of qualitative interviews. The findings revealed that the interviewees felt ambivalent about anticipated changes; only if ICT use were to be voluntary and restricted to single applications and trustworthy institutions did they expect individual benefits. Concerns about data transmission to unauthorized third parties and widespread technological dissemination forcing compulsory participation led people to feel averse to such technology. Implications for potential implementation of future ICT applications in the outpatient health sector are discussed.

INTRODUCTION

Over the last few decades, advances in information and communication technologies (ICT) have been changing many aspects of modern society, including the health sector. New ICT applications, mostly subsumed under the term 'e-health', have

facilitated access to and exchange of health-related information. The diffusion of ICT into the health sector has led to, for example, changing operation processes, new forms of patient information-seeking behaviors, and changes in physician-patient relationships (Andreassen, Trondsen, Kummervold, Gammon, & Hjortdahl, 2006; Kivits, 2006;

DOI: 10.4018/978-1-4666-1954-8.ch015

Richardson, 2003; Tautz, 2002). Moreover, these changes have attracted growing scientific interest; since the turn of the millennium, the number of publications related to e-health has increased markedly (Ahern, 2007; Curry, 2007).

However, most of this research has concentrated on current ICT applications mainly based on the Internet. Only rarely has attention been paid to present and prospective technological changes, as well as to the social impacts that might accompany these changes. The enhanced power of microchips and storage devices allow ICT components to be smaller and cheaper (Mattern, 2005), and to be integrated into so-called 'smart' everyday objects. Such 'smart objects' can be identified, localized and linked to associated data records and broader sensor networks. Thereby, they are enabled to interactively explore their environment (e.g., collect and deliver environmental data such as temperature, location and speed) and to respond to other smart things or human beings. This vision of invisible, smart computers assisting individuals' everyday tasks almost anywhere and at any time, has been called 'ubiquitous computing' (Weiser, 1991).

Ubiquitous ICT offer both the in- and outpatient health sector a new application spectrum. In the outpatient health sector, i.e., in non-clinical and non-institutional care, this application spectrum ranges from smart consumer-goods packaging that might allow for diet monitoring, to clothes that might attend to physical training by recording bodily indicators such as duration and intensity, to portable devices that register bodily indicators, such as blood pressure, glucose level and substance use. Sensor networks may allow for these registered indicators to be automatically transmitted to a patient's electronic health record, with the option to generate warning signals to the patient (or directly to the corresponding medical service) if there is significant deviation from normal values. As a feature of 'smart homes', such ubiquitous ICT applications may compensate for handicaps and support convalescence or

aging (Brown, Hine, Sixsmith, & Garner, 2004; Dengler, Awad, & Dessler, 2007; IAF, 2006; The Royal Society, 2006).

Expected benefits from ubiquitous ICT applications in the outpatient health sector may be threefold. First, convenience and autonomy for those in need of care may increase, e.g., by enabling them to stay longer or come back earlier to their own home (Brown et al., 2004). Second, ubiquitous ICT may enhance efficiency in health administration and health care and thus help to reduce health costs (Hillestad et al., 2005; Tan, 2005). And third, ubiquitous ICT applications are assumed to include several features which may enhance individual preventive health behavior; they are accessible independently of time and location, and allow for a widespread dissemination of general information as well as for tailored and personalized information, feedback and interactivity (Curry, 2007; Evers, Prochaska, Driskell, Cummins, & Velicer, 2003; Fogg, 2003; Neuhauser & Kreps, 2003). Since modifiable risk factors such as smoking, alcohol or substance use, lack of physical activity, or inappropriate nutrition, are important causes of premature mortality (Mokdad, Marks, Stroup, & Gerberding, 2004), there is a growing interest in this third, preventive application of ubiquitous ICT to support and monitor health-related behavioral changes.

However, in order to establish efficient ubiquitous ICT services in the outpatient health sector, public acceptance is needed. First of all, general public agreement is needed in order to set up, convert and interconnect the health services on an electronic basis. And secondly, users have to be able and willing to apply the technology in the intended way. Public opposition could defer, or even prevent, ubiquitous ICT implementation, and incomplete or inaccurate use may obviate its potentials, or even create yet unknown risks (The Royal Society, 2006).

This study addresses the potential long-term impacts of ubiquitous ICT in the outpatient health sector from a user perspective. Its aim was to explore individual expectations and acceptance of the diffusion of ubiquitous ICT applications, and their potential to support healthy behaviors. In doing this, we focused on the following questions: What changes do individuals expect from ubiquitous ICT? Based on what notions do people arrive at their expectations? Thus, what are the attributed drivers of the expected changes? What potential for supporting users' health-related behavior do ubiquitous ICT applications offer?

To address these questions, qualitative interviews were carried out with inhabitants of Berlin, Germany. In these interviews the participants' individual mental models regarding the prospective diffusion of ubiquitous ICT in the outpatient health sector were explored.

EXPLORING INDIVIDUALS' ANTICIPATIONS WITH MENTAL MODELS

Mental models can be defined as individually held naïve theories or knowledge representations about the functioning of human interactions with or within complex systems (Doyle & Ford, 1998; Gentner & Stevens, 1983; Thüring & Jungermann, 1986). Examples of such empirically investigated systems are technological devices (e.g., pocket calculators in Young, 1983), ecological systems (e.g., global climatic change in Bostrom, Morgan, Fischhoff, & Read, 1994) or social systems (e.g., teams in Langan-Fox, Code, & Langfield-Smith, 2000). The mental models approach has a long tradition in cognitive (Gentner & Stevens, 1983; Newell & Simon, 1972) and risk psychology (Morgan, Fischhoff, Bostrom, & Atman, 2002). Mental models help individuals to describe purposes and forms of systems, to explain system functions and observed system states, as well as to predict future system states (Rouse & Morris, 1986). Thus, to shed light on people's anticipations about the diffusion of ubiquitous ICT applications in the outpatient health sector, the elicitation of mental models seems particularly suitable.

Mental models are formulated and modified through interactions with the target system. They are assumed to be found on associative networks in the memory, and to contain an individual's subjective assumptions about the causes and consequences of system changes when reasoning, i.e., when making sense of the world. Given the factual possibility of an antecedent (in our case the potential prospective diffusion of ubiquitous ICT in the outpatient health sector), mental models allow individuals to infer different possible consequences. In contrast to alternative approaches of conditional reasoning (e.g., the formal rule theory) the mental model approach accounts for the contextual meaning of the conditional, as in this approach it is assumed that the reasoning occurs against a background of previous knowledge and the interpretation of the situation (Byrne & Johnson-Laird, 2009; Johnson-Laird & Byrne, 2002).

Crucial to this investigation is the assumption that people explore the future on the basis of an underlying mental model (Rouse & Morris, 1986; Thüring & Jungermann, 1986). Thus, people let their mental model 'run' in their mind's eye if asked for a prognosis or decision, in order to anticipate the potential outcome of a certain situational constellation of their own or others' behaviors. As Böhm and Pfister argue, mental models are 'the fundamental cognitive structures on which risk perceptions ... and behavioral decisions are based' (Böhm & Pfister, 2001, p. 23). These authors demonstrated that differences in the causal structures of mental models were related to different responses, such as help, aggression, escape, political action, and self-focus (Böhm & Pfister, 2000). Thus, people consider different action alternatives, depending on the consequences they anticipate on the basis of their mental models. The investigation of these models therefore allows not only the elucidation of the causally linked knowledge structure concerning a certain scenario, but also the response tendencies they evoke.

METHOD

Methodological Approach

In view of the innovative nature of this research topic, an exploratory qualitative approach seemed appropriate, since only an open-ended method guaranteed a broad identification of contents and structures of mental models which people hold about ubiquitous ICT applications in the outpatient health sector. Therefore, an approach termed 'Cognitive Mapping' (Bryson, Ackermann, Eden, & Finn, 2004; Eden, 1992) was adopted. This method is based on Kelly's theory of personal constructs (Kelly, 1955), from which also the better known repertory grid method originates (for a comparison of the two methods cf. Brooks, Davis, & Lycett, 2005). The cognitive mapping method was originally used in operational research (Eden & Ackermann, 2004). It is designed to create visual 2-D representations of patterns of causally linked concepts. 'Concepts' are understood in a broader sense, containing not only 'knowledge units', but also constructs such as 'goals', 'values' or 'action intentions'. Concepts are represented by nodes, which contain a concept's description in note form, and are linked by arrows, which stand for positive or negative causal relationships between the corresponding concepts. To elicit an individual 'map' the interviewer tries to move up and down the chains of the interviewee's arguments. Interviewees are asked 'why' they mentioned a certain concept, i.e., what the concept's implications are (moving up to elicit the consequences), and 'how' the concept is achieved, i.e., what the concept's reasons are (moving down to elicit its causes).

The visual support of 'cognitive mapping' helps to structure, organize, and analyze complex, systemic data (Eden & Ackermann, 2004). Its implementation is facilitated by the computer software Decision Explorer®, which was specifically designed to elicit and analyze 'cognitive maps'. A further advantage of this technique is its constructivist approach; whereas in most other mental-model approaches, concepts are given to the interviewees, and/or their relations retrospectively identified by the researcher, 'cognitive mapping' is done by elaborating content and structure during the interview session, in cooperation with the interviewee (for an overview of elicitation and representation techniques of mental models, see Langan-Fox, et al., 2000).

PROCEDURE

The interviews were conducted by the first author in October 2006 in Berlin, Germany. The language of the interviews was German. Interviews were held in the interviewees' home or workplace and varied in length between one and four hours. All of them were tape-recorded with the interviewees' informed consent.

The interviews started with demographic questions and questions about their current use of ICT. Next, the cognitive-mapping method was introduced to the interviewees by demonstration with a short example how causal structures can be displayed in the desired visual form of nodes and arrows. After this, the interviewees were introduced to the topic of ubiquitous ICT in the outpatient health sector with the help of a leaflet (Figures A1 and A2 in the Appendix) that described different ubiquitous ICT applications, imitating a health insurer's advertising brochure. Interviewees were informed that this leaflet was formulated by the researcher, i.e., it was fictitious, but that the technologies mentioned are already available or in preparation. Interviewees were asked to imagine living ten to fifteen years in the future, receiving this leaflet from their health insurer.

Following the procedure recommended by Morgan et al. (2002), the interview was started with an open question by asking the interviewee if he or she could imagine participating in the health program offered. The individual maps were created on a laptop with the Decision Explorer® software directly during the interview, involving the interviewee in this task. After responding to the opening question, the interviewees were invited to comment on their decisions by explaining what they believed their participation would change. Most interviewees described their thoughts in a narrative way. Their representation in the form of nodes and arrows was then jointly developed by the interviewee and the interviewer through discussion. The emerging chains of anticipated consequences were moved up until reaching the level of general (anti)goals, such as 'data abuse', or 'healthier population'. If interviewees had already answered the entry question on this general level, they were asked to explain exactly how participation in the insurer's program would lead to this general concept. This procedure was continued until the interviewee stated that no further consequences could be drawn. Then, interviewees were asked to explain situations or conditions under which they could imagine participation or non participation (thus moving down the chain of argumentation). The detailed interview guideline (in German) is available from the first author upon request.

After completing the full interview, the interviewees received €20 in appreciation of their participation.

INTERVIEWEES

Interviewees were recruited using a snowball technique; starting with persons from the authors' circle of acquaintances, who, in turn, suggested further interview partners. Recruitment was stopped after eleven interviews. Three female and eight male interviewees took part. Interviewees' details are presented in Table 1; for reasons of anonymity fictitious names are used. Their age ranged from 26 to 42 years, with a mean of 32.2 years. Three of them were students, one employed at the university, one employed as a waiter, and

six were self-employed in a range of professions (self-employment having become increasingly common in Germany). Two had acquired professional IT skills, as they worked regularly or part-time as IT consultants. None of the interviewees had specific experience with ICT applications in the health sector; however, all mentioned using current ICT such as the Internet.

MATERIAL

In order to help the interviewees understand the topic, a leaflet was created about a health program offered by a fictitious health insurance company (Figures A1 and A2 in the Appendix).

The applications of ubiquitous ICT offered in the leaflet were taken from Neitzke et al. (2006), who formulated various scenarios about how ubiquitous ICT might pervade daily life. One of these scenarios addressed the outpatient health sector. The technologies described in the leaflet were derived from current developmental trends, although giving the interviewees the chance to base their reactions on existing technologies was stressed. Thus, some of the applications described do not correspond to the latest developments. The situation of a health insurer as supplier was chosen in order to account for the fact that, within the health sector, ICT applications have been and will be mainly driven by for-profit companies (Eng, 2004; Fogg, 2003; Neuhauser & Kreps, 2003). Health insurers may have a particular interest in implementing ubiquitous ICT applications in order to reduce the information gap about their customers (Coroama & Höckl, 2004). Pretests revealed that the original form of the input material – a narrative description of the above-mentioned scenario – evoked feelings of unreality and low involvement among the interviewees. Therefore the same content was made to look like a company leaflet, thus attaining greater credibility.

Table 1. Interviewees' details

Interviewee	Age	Profession	Previous use of Internet /ICT applications
'Anne'	28	Student	Information, e-mail, chatting, shopping
'Anthony'	28	Self-employed IT-supporter	Information, communication, downloading of updates
'Cindy'	30	Student	Information, e-mail, Internet telephoning
'Marc'	41	Self-employed photographer	Information, e-mail, shopping, providing a website
'Eric'	42	Researcher, IT-supporter	Information, communication
'Ben'	26	Student	Information, e-mail, shopping, downloading music
'Michel'	35	Self-employed (no specific declaration)	Information, e-mail
'Helen'	30	Self-employed project manager	Information, e-mail, chatting, Internet telephoning, downloading, learning languages
'Neal'	26	Self-employed author	Information, e-mail, shopping, downloading of updates and movies
'Bob'	40	Self-employed event manager	Information, e-mail (providing a newsletter), 'Skype'
'Donald'	29	Steward	E-mail, Internet telephoning, playing games, reading newspapers
Notes: To protect interviewees' anonymity, names have been changed.			

DATA ANALYSIS

The data analysis, conducted with the help of the Decision Explorer® software, was carried out in four steps:

Step One: Merging the Individual Maps. In a first step the individual maps were merged into a comprehensive 'cause map'. 'Merging' is an iterative process in which concepts within and between the individual maps are compared and put together, retaining the original causal links (Eden & Ackermann, 1998). The decision to merge two concepts depended on their content (i.e., similar contents were merged into a new unipolar concept, and differing contents into a new bipolar one) and structural position (i.e., similarity of causes and consequences). The merging process yielded a condensed 'cause map' that contained all eleven individual maps.

Step Two: Identification of Key Concepts. Second, the cause map was examined for clusters, i.e., groups of concepts on the same topic. From each cluster, the most central, i.e., the most densely linked, concept was extracted as the key concept. Decision Explorer® offers a centrality calculation (Eden & Ackermann, 1992) to determine the number of direct and indirect links of each concept, as well as their weighting according to their level (e.g., direct links were weighted with 1 and indirect links of the first level with .5). This calculation revealed high centrality scores for most of the key concepts identified. However, high centrality scores are impacted by merging, i.e., more frequent merged concepts combined more links from the individual maps and thus reached higher centrality scores. Since we were interested in a qualitative overview per se, and not in representative statements, we also accepted key concepts with lower centrality scores, but which represented an otherwise uncovered topic.

Step Three: Classification of Key Concepts. Next, according to their content, the key concepts identified were classified as 'consequences', 'causes', or 'actions'.

Step Four: Comprehension of the Linking Structure between the Key Concepts. Finally, to understand the context of the key concepts, the linking chains between the key concepts were detailed with the help of the cause map. The outcomes of this final step of analysis are different simplified representations of the cause map with the key concepts of interest, as well as their structural interconnections as the main focus.

RESULTS

In the following section we provide insights into the key concepts identified, as well as in their structural interconnections. This is done with help of a series of four simplified representations of the 'cause map'. First, Representation A in Figure 1 shows the shared aggregated basic structure of identified key consequences that resulted from the merging procedure. Next, the example of the key consequence 'loss of versus gain in control' is detailed (Representation B in Figure 2). Then, the structural embedding of the actions 'participation in the insurer's health program' (Representation C in Figure 4), and 'change or refusal to change health-related behavior' (Representation D in Figure 5) is described.

BASIC BELIEF STRUCTURE OF EXPECTED CONSEQUENCES OF UBIQUITOUS ICT APPLICATIONS IN THE OUTPATIENT HEALTH SECTOR

Key concepts categorized as 'consequences' can be arranged, as is shown in Figure 1, with the help of two identified key 'causes' (in arrows): the general 'acceptance and dissemination of ubiquitous ICT'

in society and the 'data transmission' of sensitive data from a health insurer to third parties. Depending on whether the interviewees supposed these two developments would occur, all expected key consequences could be allocated to one of four groups (shown in the 4-quadrant table in Figure 1). The groups differed first as to whether the consequences would affect the individual user only, or, in the case of widespread dissemination of ubiquitous ICT, all of society, i.e., non-users also. Second, the expected consequences varied as to whether the interviewees assumed the data-exchange to be restricted to the user and the health insurer or whether they suspected the data would be transmitted to further actors, such as the government, private industry or other individuals, due to data hacking or selling, or security deficiencies in the storage or transmission of the data.

Anticipated immediate consequences for individual users interacting exclusively with the health insurer as the only actor with access to the data (shown in the lower left quadrant in Figure 1), can be characterized by ambivalence. Interviewees anticipated losses of as well as gains in time and control, positive as well as negative impacts on their own state of health, and sanctions as well as privileges (e.g., premium discounts or increases, shorter or longer queuing time for health services, refusal of cost absorption).

Conversely, anticipated long-term consequences were judged to be negative, with the exception of the ambivalent impacts on the labor market. Increased interconnectedness of data files, due to data transmission, was seen to be accompanied by increased defective and abusive incidences (in the lower right quadrant in Figure 1). Increased diffusion of ubiquitous ICT in different life domains was perceived to provoke discrimination of people who are unwilling or unable to follow this technological trend (as shown in the upper left quadrant in Figure 1). Finally, as shown in the upper right quadrant in Figure 1, under the assumption that both developments - technology dissemination as well as transmission of data

Figure 1. Representation A: Basic belief structure of expected consequences of ubiquitous ICT applications in the outpatient health sector. Note: Key consequences (in rectangles), arranged according to two key causes (in arrows).

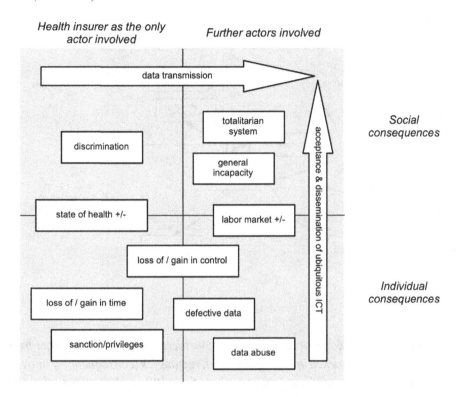

- would occur, interviewees anticipated highly undesirable social changes, such as people's increased 'general incapacity' and the emergence of a 'totalitarian system'. 'General incapacity' was referred to by expressions such as, 'stupefaction' (Michel), and 'stultification'(Helen). 'Totalitarian system' was described by expressions such as, 'total surveillance (Neal), 'enforced inspection' (Michel), or 'uniformity' (Anne).

LOSS OF VERSUS GAIN IN CONTROL

Of the key consequences identified, the concept 'loss of versus gain in control' attained the highest centrality score and will therefore be detailed in the following. Its merged original statements are listed in Table 2. Concerning the loss of control, the statements ranged from rather general ones, such as 'heteronomy / intrusion into own life' (Anne) or 'intrusion into personality' (Helen), to very specific assertions resulting from the use of ICT, such as 'restrictions of freedom to choose what to eat or drink' (Donald), or '… when to consult a doctor' (Neal). Conversely, interviewees also expected a certain gain in control due to the use of ubiquitous ICT, e.g., an 'increase in personal freedom' (Marc), or a 'gain in control over otherwise unobservable indicators' (Eric).

The embedding of the key concept 'loss of versus gain in control' into the basic structure is illustrated in Representation B (Figure 2): Attributed causes (shown by in-pointing arrows) were threefold: The first was 'insurer's data analysis and feedback'. Interviewees argued that

Figure 2. Representation B: Causal structure of the concept 'loss of versus gain in control'. Note: Causes are displayed in arrows, consequences in rectangles.

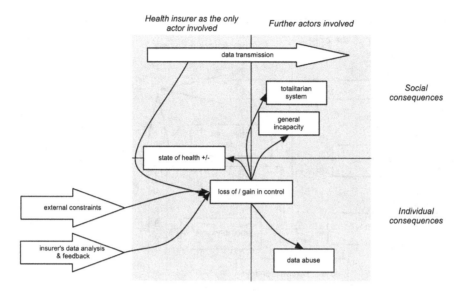

Figure 3. Merged reasons of the concept 'cost-benefits considerations'. Notes: Extract from the cause map. Identified key concepts are marked in arrows (causes), rectangles (consequences) or ovals (actions). Numbers above 2000 stand for merged concepts, numbers from 100 to 1100 refer to the corresponding interviewee. Three dots (...) divide the two poles of bipolar concepts.

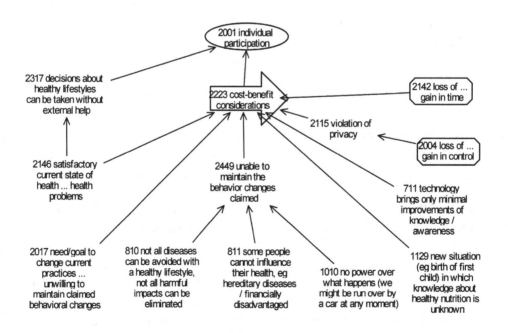

Figure 4. Representation C: Causal structure of the concept 'participation in the health insurer's program'. Note: Causes are displayed in arrows, consequences in rectangles.

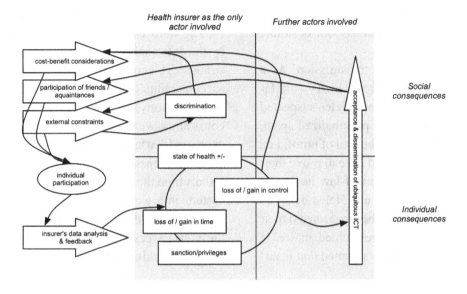

the insurer's data analysis and feedback would make people lose the ability to recognize and interpret their body's signals, or that laziness would make people delegate the responsibility over their own body to these technologies. Interviewees feared that applying ubiquitous ICT would provoke a loss of feeling for one's own body, as well as an inability to survive without technological support, and that technological dependence would be increased by the fact that complex technologies were non-transparent for most users. However, Ben, Eric, and Neal also believed that

Figure 5. Representation D: Causal structure of the concept 'change or refusal to change health-related behavior'. Note: Causes are displayed in arrows, consequences in rectangles.

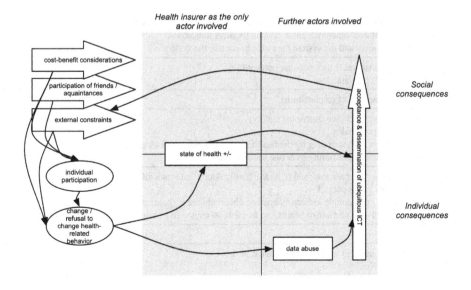

the feedback provided would allow for positive effects, such as an early diagnosis or prevention of serious diseases. External data analysis and feedback were thus regarded as both desirable and undesirable.

Interviewees saw 'data transmission' as a second cause of loss of control, which would facilitate data abuse. Anthony and Helen suspected they would be swamped by personalized spam. Eric feared a reversal of the burden of proof, i.e., that suspected persons would have to prove their innocence rather than a court of law having to prove their guilt. Eric, Ben, and Helen believed that innocent persons would be prosecuted if their data profile unfortunately resembled that of a suspect. Furthermore, Helen assumed that insur-

ers and providers of sportswear or food would enter agreements whose conditions would limit the freedom of choice between products.

The third cause of loss of control revealed by the data analysis was coded as 'external constraints'. This concept contained such expressions as 'constraints' (Marc) and 'constraining supervision' (Anthony). The reasons mentioned for such constraints were manifold. Apprehension was expressed that lack of money might force individuals to participate to get discounts, or that within a short time the insurer would convert the bonus system into a malus system, sanctioning non-participants with higher premiums. Furthermore, the interviewees assumed that a majority of health insurers would accept that trend and that no further

Table 2. Merged original statements of the concept 'loss of versus gain in control'

Interviewee	Statements (translated from German to English)
'Anne'	'Loss of self-determination / not to be the boss of one's own body anymore (e.g., how many glasses of wine to drink)' 'Food restrictions (no freedom of choice)' 'Heteronomy / intrusion into own life' 'One's own control of a healthy lifestyle is not possible anymore'
'Anthony'	'Decrease in personal freedom'
'Cindy'	'Responsibilities / decisions are relegated to the health insurer' 'Self-control is lost / is taken over by the health insurer'
'Marc'	'Increase in personal freedom'
'Eric'	'The health insurer automatically intervenes when he thinks that I need something, instead of me seeking contact when I want' 'Loss of control over different domains of one's own life (taken over by the health insurer)' 'Gain in control over otherwise unobservable (bodily) indicators' 'Few people understand the system / are able to control the system'
'Ben'	'Otherwise unobservable data become perceptible' 'Own control of the data'
'Michel'	'Disposal / avoidance of responsibility'
'Helen'	'Loss of freedom of choice (restricted supply)' 'Intrusion into personality' 'Responsibilities are taken over by the health insurer (expansion of its competences)' 'Loss of personal responsibility over one's state of health
'Neal'	'Unnecessary services are imposed (e.g., the family doctor automatically intervenes)' 'Health insurer exerts control' 'Unobservable / perceptible indicators become observable (e.g., heart attack)' 'No self-control over one's own health / no freedom of choice (e.g., when to consult a doctor)'
'Bob'	-
'Donald'	'Restriction of freedom to choose what to eat or drink' 'Feeling controlled'

technology-free alternatives would therefore be offered and that the technology would be declared legally mandatory due to the government's desire to control health expenses.

After describing the causes attributed to a loss of or gain in control, we turn now to its effects (outgoing arrows in Figure 2). According to the interviewees' anticipations, the result of a gain in control was a healthier lifestyle, and consequently an improved 'state of health'. Conversely, a loss of control was expected to lessen an individual's emotional wellbeing and thereby damage their state of health. For example, Anthony anticipated more 'stress' and Anne 'sadness about her own inability'.

An important further outcome of the above-mentioned delegation of responsibility for one's own state of health was seen by the interviewees as a 'general incapacity' of people, and they feared increased, uncontrollable data abuse and violations of privacy, fostering the emergence of a 'totalitarian system'.

PARTICIPATING IN THE INSURER'S HEALTH PROGRAM

Of further interest was the question about the circumstances under which individual use of ubiquitous ICT might be considered. The reasons identified for participating in the health program offered or for refusing to do so, were threefold: 'cost-benefit considerations', 'participation of friends/acquaintances' and 'external constraints'.

'Cost-benefit considerations' appeared in statements such as 'personal costs are not related to the benefits' (Anthony), or 'added value of participation' (Ben). Participation was only taken into consideration if anticipated benefits outweighed anticipated costs. As shown in Figure 3, these considerations occurred against the background of one's own degree of (subjective) satisfaction with the current state of health (merged concept number 2146, Figure 3), and the perceived need

to change current practices (merged concept number 2017).

A further aspect considered was the program's perceived effectiveness, depending on whether decisions about healthy lifestyles could be taken without external help (merged concept number 2317), whether the program might provide additional knowledge (concept number 711), and whether it might be helpful in new situations (concept number 1129).

Most interviewees perceived the anticipated immediate positive or negative consequences, such as a gain in or loss of time and control, as costs or benefits, respectively (illustrated in representation C in Figure 4). However, other interviewees also took long-term, social consequences into account. For instance, Helen and Bob feared that not all people would be able '...to maintain the behavioral changes claimed...' (merged concept number 2449 in Figure 3), since for some risk groups with predestined vulnerabilities, some diseases would lie beyond their control. In such a case, the interviewees expected sanctions from the insurer against those unwilling or unable to keep up a healthy lifestyle, in which case 'the insurance principle of solidarity would be driven ad absurdum' (Ben), and 'protection against control would become a luxury good' (Helen). These considerations led to negative cost-benefit considerations on their part.

The second reason to participate, the 'participation of friends/acquaintances' (Figure 4), was characterized by statements such as 'friends and acquaintances are enthusiastic about it' (Anne), 'friends and acquaintances are participating' (Cindy, Marc), 'a highly regarded person had a good experience' (Neal). And third, the 'external constraints', presented above, turned out to foster participation.

The anticipated causal relationships between the concepts involved indicated several reinforcing dynamic developments. First, the interviewees feared that participating might lead to a loss of control and thus to technological dependence, so that a satisfactory state of health could no longer be reached without technological support, which might foster participation. Second, although most of the interviewees rated costs higher than benefits, and consequently did not consider participating, they believed a majority of people positively evaluate ubiquitous ICT, and would thus accept and use it. This 'general acceptance and dissemination of ubiquitous ICT' was seen to enhance the impact resulting from friends and acquaintances as well as the external constraints, again emphasizing the reasons for individual participation and the discrimination against risk groups.

CHANGING OR REFUSING TO CHANGE HEALTH-RELATED BEHAVIOR

Furthermore, the analysis revealed that participation in the health program offered may not result in health-protecting behaviors at all. Under the term 'change or refusal to change health-related behavior', all statements were coded about behavioral adaptations due to participation in the program. Merged original statements are displayed in Table 3.

Original statements ranged from intended changes (e.g., Donald: 'stop smoking') to the maintenance of minimal requirements (Marc: 'unmotivated participation'), boycotting (Neal: 'enjoy something unhealthy'), and attempting to prevent or even manipulate the data recording (Bob: 'emigrate' or Ben: 'prevent data recording by putting aluminum foil around the chip').

The behavioral changes mentioned depended on the reasons for participation, as shown in Figure 5. If participation were to be based on positive 'cost-benefit considerations', interviewees stated that they would be motivated to improve their own state of health and to use ubiquitous ICT in the intended way. Conversely, the more the participation related solely to compliance with 'external constraints' (e.g., financial pressure), interviewees

would feel bothered by the feedback system, and consequently intend to avoid a real behavioral change, or even to manipulate data, thus provoking 'data abuse'. Needless to say, interviewees anticipated their 'state of health' would improve as a result of successful behavioral changes. However, at the same time, the interviewees indicated that unmotivated or even manipulative participation, caused by external constraints, would lead to a negative impact on people's emotional wellbeing in the form of 'emotional unease' (Michel) or 'moral conflict' (Eric). Thus, a forced behavior change was seen to harm the state of health, thereby decreasing the success of the program, slowing down technological dissemination, and, in turn, reducing the external constraints.

DISCUSSION

By eliciting the mental models of eleven interviewees, our investigation has shed light on their views about ubiquitous ICT applications in the outpatient health sector. The benefits and threats the interviewees anticipated from the diffusion of ubiquitous ICT in the health sector can be differentiated into changes concerning individual users and changes concerning the whole society. For individual users, the interviewees expected several positive impacts, such as a gain in time and control, as well as an improved personal state of health. However, these benefits were outweighed by the expected individual and social negative consequences, such as the loss of control, inherent sanctions, the potential abuse and defect of personal (health) data, as well as general incapacity and increased discrimination against citizens. These fears coincide with concerns of other researchers about ubiquitous ICT applications, for example, about growing health disparities, the emergence of digital divides, inequalities between those who will benefit and those who will bear the negative consequences, loss of control, and open questions about data

Table 3. Merged original statements of the concept 'change or refusal to change health-related behavior'

Interviewee	Statements
'Anne'	-
'Anthony'	'Inopportune behavior to the health insurer' 'Not follow the insurer's recommendations about healthy living' 'To try to avoid data transmission'
'Cindy'	'Pay attention to nutrition and exercise'
'Marc'	'Adjust own physical training' 'Unmotivated participation / refusal'
'Eric'	'Inopportune behavior, such as to drink a glass of wine' 'Cheat the system (e.g., give the sensors to my friend who is a marathon runner)' 'Found or enter an alternative social system (e.g., anarchy)'
'Ben'	'Maintain ideal bodily indicators' 'Not undertake physical training' 'Prevent data recording by putting aluminum foil around the chip'
'Michel'	'Change habits'
'Helen'	'Engaging in risky sports would no longer be possible' 'Disregard the orders (e.g., smoking)' 'Not attain the expected performance' 'Prevent data recording, boycott, cheat (e.g., not wear the bracelet)'
'Neal'	'Enjoy something unhealthy'
'Bob'	'Drop out of the system (emigrate, enter a monastery, offer armed resistance)' 'Search for a niche in the underground' 'Emigrate / found an independent commune on an island'
'Donald'	'Lose weight' 'Stop smoking'

security and privacy (Atienza et al., 2007; Eng, 2004; McLean, 2008; Pitkänen & Niemelä, 2009; Viswanath & Kreuter, 2007). Moreover, some of our interviewees' anticipation of what to expect even went beyond these predictions, such as the fear of a totalitarian system precluding all individuality or freedom, or a general incapacity on the part of citizens.

The main drivers for such an unfavorable development were said to be an abusive handling of confidential data, and the pervasion of all ubiquitous ICT into all areas of life due to improvident adoption. These concerns reflect a certain institutional distrust (Kasperson, Golding, & Tuler, 2005). For example, the interviewees mentioned a lack of trust due to insufficient technological safety, expressing concerns about data defects, abusive data intrusion by a third person (data hacking), and assumptions about the ease of unauthorized data manipulation. Concerns regarding technological trustworthiness have previously been stressed in relation to smart homes (Edenius, 2006). Additionally, a lack of trust in the provider of the program was observed; interviewees assumed that profit-driven health insurers would sell data and transform the program into a malus system as soon as the social participation was sufficiently high. Moreover, interviewees did not trust the government to enact reliable data-protection laws in time. In fact, the government was assumed to have a particular interest in an increased control of its citizens, and therefore to actively foster the diffusion of ubiquitous ICT in the health sector or to enforce legal access to citizens' data. And finally, there was no trust in a self-regulating market. On the contrary, interviewees believed that their fellow citizens would improvidently adopt new technologies, and thereby reinforce normative influence and external constraints.

As initially outlined, ubiquitous ICT applications are expected to support the maintenance of a healthy lifestyle (Neuhauser & Kreps, 2003). The results indicate that success in this domain may depend on the user's favorable evaluation of the technology; only if the expected benefits of an application outweighed anticipated costs (individual as well as societal) did interviewees intend to use the technology in an appropriate way. Interviewees made their evaluation in line with their underlying satisfaction with their own health. In other words, only if interviewees were already aware that their own state of health should be improved and were motivated to undertake the needed behavioral changes was the use of ubiquitous ICT more closely considered. Attributes of ubiquitous ICT intended to support behavioral changes, like tailored information and feedback, were perceived as annoying or even disturbing if there was no intrinsic motivation for healthier lifestyle modifications. In line with this is the assertion of Fogg (2003) that only those technologies that support people in achieving their individual goals are evaluated positively. Conversely, as the results indicate, forced diffusion by extrinsic 'motivators', such as the restriction of choice or financial or legal pressure, seem to be completely counterproductive regarding behavioral change. Forcing individuals to participate, especially if done by government or industry, may lead to reactance and unintended adverse effects, such as technological refusal or data manipulation. This is crucial because experts have agreed that ICT technologies in the health sector will only be disseminated by commercial ventures and sales or financial support from foundations (Eng, 2004).

The interpretations outlined above must be viewed with a certain degree of caution. First of all, only accessible thoughts can be acquired by exploring mental models (Doyle & Ford, 1998). Unconscious representations (implicit models)

remain beyond comprehension. Furthermore, mental models present what people think, but not why, i.e., they do not provide direct insights into mental processes (Rouse & Morris, 1986). Thus, mental processes should be investigated with other procedures. Caution is also advised as to the generalization of the findings. Despite the diversity of the concepts, we are aware that the variety of personal parameters of the sample, such as the age range, is rather low. The sample was restricted to inhabitants of Berlin, Germany. Moreover, the sample did not include any interviewees with severe health problems. Those suffering from a disease may have looked at the current development from a patient's perspective and their hope for a better future may have affected their opinion differently than those from a healthy sample.

CONCLUSION

The study of the public impacts of ubiquitous ICT in the outpatient health sector is in its infancy. Clearly, much more research needs to be conducted in this area. Nevertheless, the findings gave rise to the hypothesis that the diffusion and implementation of ubiquitous ICT will only succeed if the problems of mistrust and cost-benefit appraisal, as discussed above, are addressed. This can be accomplished by evaluation, communication, and participation (The Royal Society, 2006). The evaluation of ubiquitous ICT applications in the health sector is a widely expressed need (Glasgow, 2007). Eng et al. (1999) call for strict control mechanisms of new ICT applications similar to those for drugs and medical devices, demonstrating their safety and effectiveness before approval. Only a serious assessment of the impacts of ubiquitous ICT may guarantee quality, utility, and effectiveness. Communicating these evaluations may then promote public confidence and increase their ability to deal with risks appropriately. However, communication should not only flow from experts to citizens, but also in the reverse direction, from citizens to experts (Pidgeon & Rogers-Hayden, 2007). The early participation of user groups in the product-development life cycle may inspire trust and separate the technological wheat from the chaff, thereby maximizing the utility and usability of future ICT technologies in the outpatient health sector so as to minimize their risks.

ACKNOWLEDGMENT

This study was embedded in a broader investigation on the use and perception of current and future information and communication technologies, and was realized within the project "AAC-Crisks". This project was funded by the German Federal Ministry for Education and Research, within the research program "social-ecological research", under the thematic topic "systemic risks". We thank our project partners from the "Ecolog Institut" (www.ecolog-institut.de) and from "Sinus Sociovision" (www.sociovision.de) for their substantial help and fruitful cooperation. The writing of this paper was funded by the University of Zurich, Switzerland.

REFERENCES

Ahern, D. K. (2007). Challenges and opportunities of ehealth research. *American Journal of Preventive Medicine, 32*(5), 75–82. doi:10.1016/j.amepre.2007.01.016

Andreassen, H. K., Trondsen, M., Kummervold, P. E., Gammon, D., & Hjortdahl, P. (2006). Patients who use e-mediated communication with their doctor: New constructions of trust in the patient-doctor relationship. *Qualitative Health Research, 16*(2), 238–248. doi:10.1177/1049732305284667

Atienza, A. A., Hesse, B. W., Baker, T. B., Abrams, D. B., Rimer, B. K., & Croyle, R. T. (2007). Critical issues in ehealth research. *American Journal of Preventive Medicine, 32*(5), 71–74. doi:10.1016/j.amepre.2007.02.013

Böhm, G., & Pfister, H.-R. (2000). Action tendencies and characteristics of environmental risks. *Acta Psychologica, 104*, 317–337. doi:10.1016/S0001-6918(00)00035-4

Böhm, G., & Pfister, H.-R. (2001). Mental representation of global environmental risks. In Böhm, G., Nerb, J., McDaniels, T., & Spada, H. (Eds.), *Environmental Risks: Perception, Evaluation and Management* (pp. 1–30). Amsterdam, The Netherlands: JAI. doi:10.1016/S0196-1152(01)80022-3

Bostrom, A., Morgan, M. G., Fischhoff, B., & Read, D. (1994). What do people know about global climate change? 1. Mental models. *Risk Analysis, 14*(6), 959–970. doi:10.1111/j.1539-6924.1994.tb00065.x

Brooks, L., Davis, C. J., & Lycett, M. (2005). Organisations and information systems: Investigating their dynamic complexities using repertory grids and cognitive mapping. *International Journal of Technology and Human Interaction, 1*(4), 39–55. doi:10.4018/jthi.2005100103

Brown, S., Hine, N., Sixsmith, A., & Garner, P. (2004). Care in the community. *BT Technology Journal, 22*(3), 56–64. doi:10.1023/B:BTTJ.0000047120.60489.7a

Bryson, J. M., Ackermann, F., Eden, C., & Finn, C. B. (2004). *Visible thinking. Unlocking causal mapping for practical business results*. Chichester, UK: John Wiley & Sons.

Byrne, R. M. J., & Johnson-Laird, P. N. (2009). 'If' and problems of conditional reasoning. *Trends in Cognitive Sciences, 13*(7), 282–287. doi:10.1016/j.tics.2009.04.003

Coroama, V., & Höckl, N. (2004, April). *Pervasive insurance markets and their consequences.* Paper presented at the First International Workshop on Sustainable Pervasive Computing, Vienna, Austria.

Curry, S. J. (2007). Ehealth research and healthcare delivery: Beyond intervention effectiveness. *American Journal of Preventive Medicine, 32*(5), 127–130. doi:10.1016/j.amepre.2007.01.026

Dengler, S., Awad, A., & Dessler, F. (2007, May 21-23). Sensor/actuator networks in smart homes for supporting elderly and handicapped people. In *Proceedings of the 21st International Conference on Advanced Information Networking and Applications,* Niagara Falls, ON, Canada (pp. 863-868).

Doyle, J. K., & Ford, D. N. (1998). Mental models concepts for system dynamics research. *System Dynamics Review, 14*(1), 3–29. doi:10.1002/(SICI)1099-1727(199821)14:1<3::AID-SDR140>3.0.CO;2-K

Eden, C. (1992). On the nature of cognitive maps. *Journal of Management Studies, 29*(3), 261–265. doi:10.1111/j.1467-6486.1992.tb00664.x

Eden, C., & Ackermann, F. (1992). The analysis of cause maps. *Journal of Management Studies, 29*(3), 309–324. doi:10.1111/j.1467-6486.1992.tb00667.x

Eden, C., & Ackermann, F. (1998). Analyzing and comparing idiographic causal maps. In Eden, C., & Spender, J.-C. (Eds.), *Managerial and Organizational Cognition: Theory, Methods and Research* (pp. 192–209). London, UK: Sage.

Eden, C., & Ackermann, F. (2004). *Making strategy: The journey of strategic management.* London, UK: Sage.

Edenius, M. (2006). The function of representation in a 'smart home context'. *International Journal of Technology and Human Interaction, 2*(3), 1–15. doi:10.4018/jthi.2006070101

Eng, T. R. (2004). Population health technologies: Emerging innovations for the health of the public. *American Journal of Preventive Medicine, 26*(3), 237–242. doi:10.1016/j.amepre.2003.12.004

Eng, T. R., Gustafson, D. H., Henderson, J., Jimison, H., & Patrick, K. (1999). Introduction to evaluation of interactive health communication applications. *American Journal of Preventive Medicine, 16*(1), 10–15. doi:10.1016/S0749-3797(98)00107-X

Evers, K. E., Prochaska, J. O., Driskell, M. M., Cummins, C. O., & Velicer, W. F. (2003). Strengths and weaknesses of health behavior change programs on the Internet. *Journal of Health Psychology, 8*(1), 63–70. doi:10.1177/1359105303008001435

Fogg, B. J. (2003). *Persuasive technology: Using computers to change what we think and do.* San Francisco, CA: Morgan Kaufmann.

Gentner, D., & Stevens, A. L. (1983). *Mental models.* London, UK: Lawrence Erlbaum.

Glasgow, R. E. (2007). Ehealth evaluation and dissemination research. *American Journal of Preventive Medicine, 32*(5), 119–126. doi:10.1016/j.amepre.2007.01.023

Hillestad, R., Bigelow, J., Bower, A., Girosi, F., Meili, R., & Scoville, R. (2005). Can electronic medical record systems transform health care? Potential health benefits, savings, and costs. *Health Affairs, 24*(5), 1103–1117. doi:10.1377/hlthaff.24.5.1103

Institute for Alternative Futures (IAF). (2006). *The biomonitoring futures project: Final report and recommendations.* Princeton, NJ: Author.

Johnson-Laird, P. N., & Byrne, R. M. J. (2002). Conditionals: A Theory of Meaning, Pragmatics. and Inference. *Psychological Review, 109*(4), 646–678. doi:10.1037/0033-295X.109.4.646

Kasperson, R. E., Golding, D., & Tuler, S. (2005). Social distrust as a factor in siting hazardous facilities and communicating risks. In Kasperson, J. X., & Kasperson, R. E. (Eds.), *The Social Contours of Risk* (*Vol. 1*, pp. 29–50). London, UK: Earthscan.

Kelly, G. A. (1955). *The psychology of personal constructs*. New York, NY: Norton.

Kivits, J. (2006). Informed patients and the Internet: A mediated context for consulations with health professionals. *Journal of Health Psychology*, *11*(2), 269–282. doi:10.1177/1359105306061186

Langan-Fox, J., Code, S., & Langfield-Smith, K. (2000). Team mental models: Techniques, methods, and analytic approaches. *Human Factors*, *42*(2), 242–271. doi:10.1518/001872000779656534

Mattern, F. (2005). Ubiquitous computing: Scenarios for an informatized world. In Zerdick, A., Picot, A., Schrape, K., Burgelman, J.-C., Silverstone, R., & Feldmann, V., (Eds.), *E-Merging Media - Communication and the Media Economy of the Future* (pp. 145–163). Berlin, Germany: Springer.

McLean, R. (2008). Pixel chix and digi guys: Exploring the experiences of the 'digital citizen' in two contexts. *International Journal of Technology and Human Interaction*, *4*(2), 1–21. doi:10.4018/jthi.2008040101

Mokdad, A. H., Marks, J. S., Stroup, D. F., & Gerberding, J. L. (2004). Actual Causes of Death in the United States, 2000. *Journal of the American Medical Association*, *291*(10), 1238–1246. doi:10.1001/jama.291.10.1238

Morgan, M. G., Fischhoff, B., Bostrom, A., & Atman, C. J. (2002). *Risk communication: A mental models approach*. Cambridge, UK: Cambridge University Press.

Neitzke, H.-P., Behrendt, D., & Osterhoff, J. (2006). *Alltagsszenarien in der AACC-Welt [Scenarios of everyday living in an AACC-world]* (Tech. Rep. No. 1/2006). Hannover, Germany: Ecolog-Institut.

Neuhauser, L., & Kreps, G. L. (2003). Rethinking communication in the e-health era. *Journal of Health Psychology*, *8*(1), 7–23. doi:10.1177/1359105303008001426

Newell, A., & Simon, H. A. (1972). *Human problem solving*. Englewood Cliffs, NJ: Prentice-Hall.

Pidgeon, N., & Rogers-Hayden, T. (2007). Opening up nanotechnology dialogue with the publics: Risk communication or 'upstream engagement'? *Health Risk & Society*, *9*(2), 191–210. doi:10.1080/13698570701306906

Pitkänen, O., & Niemelä, M. (2009). Humans and emerging RFID systems: Evaluating data protection law on the user scenario basis. *International Journal of Technology and Human Interaction*, *5*(2), 85–95. doi:10.4018/jthi.2009040105

Richardson, K. P. (2003). Health risks on the internet: Establishing credibility on line. *Health Risk & Society*, *5*(2), 171–184. doi:10.1080/1369857031000123948

Rouse, W. B., & Morris, N. M. (1986). On looking into the black-box: Prospects and limits in the search for mental models. *Psychological Bulletin*, *100*(3), 349–363. doi:10.1037/0033-2909.100.3.349

Tan, J. (2005). *E-health care information systems. An introduction for students and professionals*. San Francisco, CA: Jossey-Bass.

Tautz, F. (2002). *E-Health und die Folgen. Wie das Internet die Arzt-Patienten-Beziehung und das Gesundheitssystem verändert* [E-health and its consequences. How the Internet changes the physician-patient relationship and the health system]. Frankfurt, Germany: Campus.

The Royal Society. (2006). *Digital healthcare: The impact of information and communication technologies on health and healthcare*. London, UK: The Royal Society.

Thüring, M., & Jungermann, H. (1986). Constructing and running mental models for inferences about the future. In Brehmer, B., Jungermann, H., Lourens, P., & Sevon, G. (Eds.), *New Directions in the Research on Decision Making* (pp. 163–174). Amsterdam, The Netherlands: North-Holand.

Viswanath, K., & Kreuter, M. W. (2007). Health disparities, communication inequalities, and ehealth. *American Journal of Preventive Medicine, 32*(5), 131–133. doi:10.1016/j.amepre.2007.02.012

Weiser, M. (1991). The computer for the 21st century. *Scientific American, 265*(3), 94–104. doi:10.1038/scientificamerican0991-94

Young, R. M. (1983). Surrogates and mapping: Two kinds of conceptual models for interactive devices. In Gentner, D., & Stevens, A. L. (Eds.), *Mental Models* (pp. 35–52). London, UK: Lawrence Erlbaum.

APPENDIX

Input Material for the Interviews

Figure 6. Front side of fictitious leaflet of a health insurer offering its clients technology-supported health monitoring (version translated from German to English)

Your health
is important to us

We would like to help you both to stay
healthy and also to save premiums!

Recent information and communication
technologies now allow for an individual
health monitoring.

Find out about our health program and
let us prepare your individual support
package for you.

Figure 7. Inside of fictitious leaflet of a health insurer offering its clients technology-supported health monitoring (version translated from German to English)

It takes little effort to lead a good healthy life. The key is a balance of proper nutrition and physical training. Create your own health program by choosing from our offers listed below:

	Functioning:*	Our standard offer	Options
Physical training condition	Carry our 'sports wear'. Integrated movement sensors collect data about your physical training condition and transmit them to us.	You will be given weekly feedback as to whether you've achieved your quota or how much is missing. Depending on your cooperation and success you will benefit from up to 15% premium discount!**	
Healthy nutrition	Put all your meals on the scale (even snacks!), and enter their composition into the mini computer.	We will evaluate your nutrition on a daily basis, and provide you with recommendations in the form of - recipes - menu advice Depending on your cooperation and success, you will benefit from up to 15% premium discount!**	On our website you can arrange for and order healthy recipes. The required ingredients or the complete meal is delivered to your home by our associated shops. To make manual weighing obsolete, we suggest choosing the complete menus delivered with an RFID label that can be recognized by the mini scale.
Monitoring of bodily indicators	Carry our multitask implant to monitor your pulse, blood sugar, and cholesterol level 24/7. A multitask watch informs you immediately about possible changes.	Implantation is free; we monitor your bodily indicators 24/7, and inform you immediately if a critical threshold is exceeded.	Possibility of direct transmission of critical indicators to your family doctor, so that he can attend to you immediately.
Avoidance of unhealthy lifestyles	As has been proven, smoking and excessive consumption of alcohol harms your health. Carry our implanted detectors, which alert you in the case of over-consumption via a multitask watch.	Implantation is free.	

* All data are transmitted from the sensors, via local radio network, to your mobile phone, and from there automatically to our central office.
** Our computerized monitoring program registers the discounts automatically with your account.

This work was previously published in the International Journal of Technology and Human Interaction, Volume 7, Issue 4, edited by Anabela Mesquita and Chia-Wen Tsai, pp. 62-80, copyright 2011 by IGI Publishing (an imprint of IGI Global).

Chapter 16
Effects of Email Utilization on Higher Education Professionals

Nancy M. Chase
Gonzaga University, USA

Becky Clegg
Consultant, USA

ABSTRACT

This exploratory study examines the impact of email as a primary communication technology upon the perceptions and work behaviors of higher education professionals who support university administrative functions. Based on the interviews and observations of 23 participants, key themes emerged regarding the relationship of email to the interactions of higher education professionals. Findings are presented in three sections: (1) impact on productivity, (2) impact on social interactions, and (3) impact on well-being. The professionals who participated in this study articulated the importance of face-to-face interaction particularly in complex situations; they recognize the need to manage email sender expectations to deal with their own work stresses, and strive to temper the negative impact of constant disruption by email on workplace productivity.

INTRODUCTION

The advancement of network technologies and communication applications enables individuals to connect with others regardless of location, to view information stored on servers worldwide, and to work any hours, from any where. Moreover, asynchronous communication technologies such as email and instant messaging have accelerated the exchange of information beyond what could have been imagined even ten years ago. Collie

(2005) proposed that contemporary technology tools of the Web, PDAs, laptops, pagers, cell phones, text messages, Blackberry®, and email messages can create stress in the workplace. Increasingly, knowledge workers wrestle with an overwhelming feeling of anxiety created by the communication explosion appropriately labeled email overload. Research has confirmed that excessive volumes of electronic messages can affect workers' health, emotional stability, and social interactions (Bellotti, Ducheneaut, Howard,

DOI: 10.4018/978-1-4666-1954-8.ch016

Smith, & Grinter, 2005; Dabbish & Kraut, 2006; Farhooman & Drury, 2002; Hall, 2004; Huang & Lin, 2009). Consequently, investigations based on work habits related to email usage may enable organizations to grapple with issues affecting the performance, productivity, and well-being of employees.

The purpose of this exploratory study was to investigate the use of email as a primary communication technology upon the work behaviors of higher education professionals who support university administrative functions. Although email usage has achieved ubiquitous status as a communication technology for personal use as well as for business use across a multitude of industries, relatively few studies have focused on this tool within the realm of higher education. This study, by design, sought out the perceptions of the professional staff in administrative departments. Qualitative methods typically focus on a limited number of individuals and cases, producing an abundance of in-depth information. This approach is "particularly oriented toward exploration, discovery, and inductive logic" (Patton, 1990, p. 44), beginning with specific individual data and building toward general categories and patterns. The gathering of in-depth information is seen as appropriate by sociologists when minimal empirical attention has been given to a specific group (Denzin & Lincoln, 2000)—as is the case with academic administrative workers.

LITERATURE REVIEW

Research conducted over the past 10 years focused on the overwhelming nature of electronic mail communication citing stress in the workplace, negative social behaviors, and diminished productivity among knowledge workers (Burgess, Jackson, & Edwards, 2003; Ducheneaut & Watts, 2005; Jackson, Dawson, & Wilson, 2002; Neustaedter, Bernheim Brush, Smith, & Fisher, 2005; Whittaker & Sidner, 1996). Smith (2008) reported

that the average employee spends between 90 minutes and two hours per day reading email messages. As the email inbox becomes cluttered with retained emails, incoming messages, irrelevant chain mail, and spam, workers may become victims of email overload or, at a minimum, face increasing frustration attempting to manage electronic communication in a disciplined fashion (Betts & Ouellette, 1995; Jackson, Dawson, & Wilson, 2003b).

Multiple studies relating to email overload have emerged from the U.K. (Burgess, Jackson, & Edwards, 2005; Jackson, Dawson, & Wilson, 2003a), but this topic has not generated much interest elsewhere until recently. Researchers report that the average corporate email user sends and receives approximately 156 messages per day, "and this number is expected to grow to about 233 messages a day by 2012" (Radicati Group, Inc., 2008, p. 4). One result of the explosive growth in email volume is that organizations increasingly face key decisions on how to address the monster of email (Dudman, 2003). At Loughborough University in England, Jackson conducted a series of research projects (Jackson et al., 2002; 2003a, 2003b; Jackson, Burgess, & Edwards, 2006) examining email tolerance levels, cost of email to organizations, and reduction of email defects through training of workers. Challenges identified in the studies included: poorly written email, email as a distraction, email used improperly (i.e., when face-to-face was warranted), and email carbon copy abuse. Jackson et al. (2003a) found that 65% of emails sent to recipients failed to provide enough information for the receiver to respond appropriately. Similarly, email messages may not provide the reader with enough information to accurately determine the context or tone (Whitaker, Bellotti, & Gwizdka, 2006). Consequently, the recipient faces additional pressure and frustration attempting to reach a satisfactory resolution to the communication (Burgess, Jackson, & Edwards, 2004).

Eppler and Mengis (2004) reported a variety of email stress symptoms that contribute to feelings of overload: confusion, pressure, fatigue, lack of motivation, and stress. Additionally, frustration with email technology may result in wasted time seeking lost email and delays in the completion of work tasks (Lazar, Jones, & Shneiderman, 2006; Leavitt, 2008). Several studies concluded that email not only distracts workers, but also causes them to interrupt their planned activity to respond to the incoming message before resuming work (Burgess et al., 2004; Charman-Anderson, 2008; Jackson et al., 2002, 2003a, 2003b; Renaud, Ramsay, & Hair, 2006). "Email clearly has the potential to be disruptive. The majority [of study participants], kept e-mail running in the background at work; indeed, 55% also kept e-mail running in the background at home" (Renaud et al., 2006, p. 324).

Several researchers report the potential for email to become a problem of pandemic proportions with senders of messages expecting immediate responses (Demirdjian, 2005; Renaud et al., 2006). Renaud et al. (2006) observed, "This tool... appears to have the potential to tyrannize, overload, and enslave its users" (p. 317). Demirdjian (2005) suggested that a flawed expectation has emerged in the academic setting; students believe faculty should be available 24/7 through use of email. Most importantly, employees tend to respond to email as it arrives, "taking an average of only one minute and 44 seconds to act upon a new email notification; 70% of alerts got a reaction within six seconds. That's faster than letting the phone ring three times" (Charman-Anderson, 2008). On the other hand, Tyler and Tang (2003) reported that email responsiveness is frequently negotiated between sender and receiver based upon prior email behaviors. "People project responsiveness images to each other, they use email peri-synchronously, and they calibrate their email behaviors to mirror the rhythms of their correspondents" (p. 253).

Email can elicit strong emotions from the receiver. Some researchers believe that the use of email as a channel medium for the exchange of information creates inefficient, inaccurate communication, and causes ambiguity resulting in miscommunication and misunderstanding (Eppler & Mengis, 2004; Frazee, 1996; Janssen & de Poot, 2006; Wilson, 2002). Byron (2008) states that, "whereas face-to-face communication is highest in richness, email is leaner because fewer cues are available and because feedback can be delayed and is less obtainable. With leaner media, communicators have greater difficulty resolving ambiguity and facilitating understanding" (p. 311).

Research in the area of higher education remains somewhat sparse with the majority of studies examining various aspects of faculty-student communication (Duran, Kelly, & Keaten, 2005; Salajan, Schönwetter, & Cleghorn, 2010; Waldeck, Kearney, & Plax, 2001; Weiss & Hanson-Baldauf, 2008). Salajan et al. (2010) approach the use of digital learning technologies from a generational perspective using the framework of digital natives (students) and digital immigrants (faculty). Their study focuses on an array of e-tools (including email) on one hand, and Blackboard (a learning management system utilized by many academic institutions) on the other. The e-tool data (21 items) were consolidated into one variable labeled "TechUse" and reported at an aggregate level. Consequently, specific findings do not relate directly to email usage, which is the focus of our study.

Weiss and Hanson-Baldauf (2008) explore expectations and appropriate e-mail use by both faculty and students. They reported that both students and faculty "agree that increased e-mail communication contributes to learning and teacher-student relationships" (p. 46). The Waldeck et al. (2001) study also examines attitudes toward e-mail communication by faculty and students. Interestingly, they found that "students are more likely to exchange e-mail regarding coursework with their peers than with teachers" (p. 67). On the other hand, Duran et al. (2005) focus only on faculty perspectives relative to teacher-student interactions. Not surprisingly, the study reported that utilizing e-mail can result in efficient and effective communication, but it can also be very time-consuming.

Each of the previous studies within higher education focuses on the technology that enables and enhances communication between faculty and students. On the other hand, Lindback and Fodrey (2009) examine the relationship between student applicants and a university office of admissions. This study provides insight into the technology available to the admissions office to recruit and to communicate with the current applicants as well as insight into the technology preferred by these potential students. Lindback and Fodrey (2009) report that the "highest use of technologies are associated with more established technologies such as school Web sites and email, rather than emerging technologies such as podcasts, vodcasts and virtual worlds" (p. 29).

The Recascino (2009) study examines email usage and its relationship to job satisfaction for the administrative and professional staff (not faculty) in a major metropolitan university setting. Recascino also considers how email usage varies among staff and supervisory groups. Interestingly, job satisfaction was not affected by the number of emails sent or received, and also not affected by campus location or job classification.

The limited historical perspective of studies relating to email and its effects on individuals in an academic setting, highlights the need for additional research to address email impacts and implications for higher education professional employees. Given the far-reaching consequences of the onslaught of email communication in today's world, research conducted on the influence of email and stress behaviors can add to the body of knowledge regarding this phenomenon.

METHOD

The purpose of this qualitative study was to explore the influence of email as a primary com-

munication technology upon work behaviors of higher education professionals who support administrative functions. By design, the study focused specifically on the perceptions of staff professionals within academic support areas of the university, rather than exploring the perceptions of students, faculty, or professionals from other non-administrative areas of the institution. In order to work with a manageable set of data and to gain access to higher education administrative professionals, the researchers intentionally limited the study to three academic support areas (Academic Services, Office of Admissions, and Registrar's Office) within one university. Each of these areas interacts extensively with students, faculty, and a variety of individuals and organizations both inside and outside of the university community.

The following research questions were addressed:

1. How does email activity affect productivity in the higher education workplace?
2. How does email activity impact social interactions in the workplace for higher education professionals?
3. How does email activity impact the well-being of higher education professionals?

This research employed a qualitative approach in order to focus on a limited number of individuals and to yield in-depth information. Qualitative research typically lends itself to exploration (Patton, 1990), beginning with detailed individual information, and then proceeding in an iterative fashion towards general categories and patterns. The researchers were interested in exploring human experience and meaning, which indicates the use of qualitative rather than quantitative methods (Denzin & Lincoln, 2000).

Participants in this study included staff professionals from one of three administrative areas within a small private university in the western United States. An important criterion for participation in the study was that each individual be actively involved in the daily work of an academic support area (e.g., registrar, admissions, etc.), and utilize email (minimum of 15 incoming emails per day) to communicate with parents, students, faculty, colleagues, or other constituents.

The supervisors of multiple administrative departments were contacted to determine their interest in participating in this study. A number of departments declined to allow their employees to contribute to the study due to the time commitment required (between two and four hours over three months) for each participant. Fortunately, participating supervisors agreed to allow study members to engage with the researchers during normal business hours.

An introductory information session was conducted with each of the three administrative areas expressing interest in this research and 23 individuals chose to participate. Each participant completed an informed consent agreement prior to the data gathering process, as well as an initial survey that provided the researchers with demographic data and participant perceptions of their own email usage. Every effort was made to protect the privacy, confidentiality, and anonymity of the individuals participating in this study.

The qualitative data for this study were captured using a series of informal observations and semi-structured interviews. Throughout the data gathering process both researchers paid considerable attention to developing an appropriate level of rapport with each participant based upon "respect, interest, attention, and good manners" (Seidman, 1998, p. 81). The observation approach to data gathering allowed the researchers to gain first hand knowledge of participant behaviors over an extended time (Fetterman, 2009; Merriam, 1988). Due to time constraints specified by participating departments (30 minutes per individual per week), each interview session focused on a particular topical area.

The participants were divided into two groups, which enabled each researcher to observe and interview half of the participants in any given week. By alternating groups each week, both researchers interacted with every participant at least four times during the study. A series of eight informal observations and semi-structured interviews consisting of both open-ended and close-ended questions were scheduled with each of the 23 participants (18 females and 5 males) over a three month period. By limiting the study to the three academic support areas willing to participate in the research, the mix of employees was not evenly distributed, but reflects the workplace reality at that point in time.

Each individual interview session lasted between 15 and 30 minutes; consequently, each participant spent between 2 and 4 hours talking with the researchers. Interview data were captured in a field log using pen and paper, and immediately entered into electronic files upon completion of the interview.

Data analysis involved examination and coding of participant interviews for recurring patterns, which resulted in the formation of preliminary categories. Iterative review and analysis of the data eventually led to an identification of general categories (Silverman, 2001). Subsequently, the interconnections between groupings of categories were identified and finally, explanatory and illustrative participant stories were matched to the refined categories.

Limitations on the research design included time, financial resources, and a necessarily narrowed focus. Additionally, the extent to which the findings of this study may generalize to other populations is unclear, as is the case with many qualitative studies (Maxwell, 2009).

RESULTS

Email has evolved into a multi-faceted tool used for a variety of business and personal needs. Within the higher education environment, email remains an important tool to communicate with internal and external individuals including colleagues, parents, and students. The purpose of this exploratory study was to explore the impact of email as a communication technology on the work behaviors of selected higher education professionals who support administrative functions.

An initial questionnaire captured participant demographic information as well as a snapshot in time of individual perceptions of email usage. Participants' ages ranged from 24 to 68, with a mean of 37.17 years. A majority of participants (74%) self described their level of computer use as advanced, and 78% indicated that they use email at home.

The research findings are presented in three sections: (1) impact on productivity, (2) impact on social interactions, and (3) impact on well-being.

IMPACT ON PRODUCTIVITY

As participants described their perceptions and experiences of email usage within the higher education environment, three themes emerged relating to workplace productivity: (1) the perception of email as a double-edged sword, (2) the effect of poorly constructed messages, and (3) the influence of the individual's use of email software.

Perception of Email as a Double-Edged Sword

Participants found the instant communication of email to be both a benefit and a source of irritation and frustration. Speed and convenience were identified as an advantage to both the senders and receivers of messages. Many participants reported that the immediacy of email allows for the efficient gathering of information from prospective students, current students, faculty, and others, and benefits them as receivers. On the other hand, participants also indicated that email creates additional stress and anxiety due to the perception that senders expect an immediate response to

electronic messages. One example illustrating this expectation by the sender involved a student who had sent a request to an administrative office on the weekend and expected a response by 8:00 Monday morning from a staff professional. Participant #8 articulated that people not only expect a quick response to email messages, but also assume that the priorities of the receiver match those of the sender. Participant #13 added that with email, students often want to "make their crisis my crisis". Another respondent noted that it is sometimes difficult to remain patient when waiting for an email response, particularly if the individual is a higher administrator. The dilemma then becomes whether it is more annoying to send another email message or to risk being a pest by resorting to a phone call.

Although the "Reply to All" option within email software allows wide-spread knowledge of the interactions of others within the office, this functionality can also result in voluminous amounts of email in an individual's in-box. Some university offices routinely use the "Reply to All" option in order to keep everyone in the office aware of current activity (particularly with at-risk students, probation situations, etc.), and this approach seems to work well for those offices. On the other hand, other administrative offices avoid it entirely. Several participants expressed concern that utilizing the carbon copy function of email increases the potential of an email being embedded within another message thread which may then be sent to a source that they did not intend to receive the email.

One of the strengths of today's email applications is the ability to retain, organize, and retrieve stored messages. Thus, the application provides documentation and evidence of activity with students, faculty, and other offices both inside and outside of the university. The majority of participants (78%) in this study indicated that they retain (and frequently print) email messages to document interactions with other individuals and to provide evidence (a paper trail) of task completion. Participant #1 commented, "I am extremely careful about what I put in email, particularly on tricky or political or overly complex issues, because I am constantly thinking about how it would look in black and white in court." Others indicated that the ability to organize and archive communication enables them to trust that the email system will provide the retention capabilities needed by their respective offices.

Another challenge with email communication in the higher education environment relates to messages that convey anger and frustration, or are accusatory in nature. Participants commented that some individuals within the university receive numerous email messages of this type. Most participants attribute accusatory emails to frustration on the part of the sender. For example, many students email professionals in the Registrar's Office during registration periods particularly when the servers are down and they are unable to register. Likewise, students may be frustrated and angry when they aren't able to get the classes they want because courses are full. One individual shared that "When I get a negative email, it feels like it doesn't matter whether I respond or not. People have already made up their mind to be angry and vent" (Participant #5). If this type of communication were handled face-to-face, rather than through email, negative or inflammatory statements might be avoided, and hurt feelings kept to a minimum. Participant #1 expressed concern with emails that attack the individual. "I hate the impersonal response. People would never behave this way if they were face-to-face with me." In addition, several participants admitted that when they receive an upsetting email message, they request a colleague to review both the original message and the carefully crafted response before the reply is sent. This approach provides a buffer for the individual to resolve emotional stress and obtain adequate time to respond appropriately and professionally.

Effect of Poorly Constructed Messages

Effective email communication requires a meaningful subject and well articulated message body. The preliminary email use survey found that the vast majority of the administrative professionals in this study (83%) cannot assess the importance of some email messages based upon the detail contained in the subject line. Consequently, several additional messages must be exchanged to obtain the needed information before the original message can be processed. Participants also voice frustration with messages that don't provide adequate personal contact information although the message may request a return phone call. "I am amazed at the number of messages I receive that have no greeting, no signature, no phone number and yet request a return call" (Participant #11).

The manner in which an email is worded can create a variety of reactions from anger to frustration to a neutral response. Misinterpretation of an email often occurs when poor grammar and sentence structure interferes with the smooth flow of the message. Although email may be touted as the panacea of efficiency, receiving a message that is poorly written diminishes the effectiveness of the communication. Members of the study support this observation through their comments regarding the informality of both student email as well as parent communication. "My brain stops if the email is poorly worded." (Participant #23) or "I've received some email with run on sentences and poor punctuation, which make it very difficult to read" (Participant #13).

Although most email applications have spelling and grammar check features, comments by the group members reflect the frustration with receiving email messages full of spelling errors, grammar mistakes, and informal writing. Participant #23 noted that, "I get jaded this time of year. I can't stand emails with misspelling and poor grammar. It annoys me when people don't use the tools available like spell check, grammar check, and the thesaurus." Several individuals felt that some email messages they receive elicit a strong, negative response, but that the university code of conduct and personal manners prevent them from responding in an unprofessional way. "Some students will send email that sounds like they are talking to their friends. This is a university" (Participant #18). Across the board, study respondents articulated that current modes of communication, particularly email and text messaging, do not assure adequate levels of formality for communicating with formal organizations such as a university.

Impact of the Individual's Use of Email Software

The review of the literature reveals that email not only distracts workers, but also may trigger an interruption of their work in order to respond to an incoming message (Burgess et al., 2004; Charman-Anderson, 2008; Jackson et al., 2002, 2003a, 2003b; Renaud, Ramsay, & Hair, 2006). In the preliminary survey conducted at the outset of this study, 14 of the participants agreed or strongly agreed that email "often distracts me from important work." Interestingly, the majority of participants (21 members) had the Outlook email application configured to check for arriving email every five minutes. Additionally, several group members were surprised to learn that this parameter can be adjusted by the individual.

Twelve members of the group maintain an extensive file folder structure created within the email application to store the multitude of messages received, such as college news, work communication, parent interaction, student responses, and personal email. On the other hand, others used only a few folders to store messages. Several participants do not utilize a folder structure at all, but retain all messages in the in-box until deleted. In two cases, the retention of all messages in the in-box resulted in an enormous number of messages

(11,047 and 7,552 respectively). Interestingly, four group members were more concerned about retaining the messages sent, which resulted in the "Sent" folder containing between 3,000 and 7,000 messages. In every case, participants indicated that they retain messages for documentation and historical purposes. The number of folders and/or messages utilized by the individual does not appear to hinder the ability to locate and retrieve messages when desired. Likewise, the number of folders did not appear to have an effect on stress. Participants acknowledged that over time they have developed their own strategies that enable them to quickly locate desired email message.

Another benefit provided by email applications is the ability to check for messages on any computer that has the appropriate software and access to the Internet. Eighteen of the 23 participants have email at home and are able to check messages off campus; five individuals routinely check their office email from home. For example, Participant #21 checks office email in the evening and again in the morning before leaving for work. Another study member articulated that it is less stressful to check email and know what is in the in-box than it is to be surprised when arriving at work. Several study participants commented that although email is a valuable tool to assist with workload, it can also be a drain on work time and productivity; both a time saver and a time consumer. Additionally, one study member noted that the ability to check for email messages at any time from anywhere tends to blur the line between the work environment and home.

Impact on Social Interactions

As participants described the impact of email on their social interactions, two primary themes emerged: (1) the avoidance of face-to-face conversation, and (2) the isolation of the individual.

When asked what participants believed were the key components of good conversation, the top six responses were listening, humor, eye contact, body language, open mindedness, and respect. Observations during this study revealed that individuals consistently agree that email has been used to avoid conversation. Many participants commented that email has replaced face-to-face or phone conversations as a preferred method of sharing information or requesting services from both inside and outside of the university. Thus, the pervasiveness and ease of use in instantly transmitting information has resulted in email becoming the favored way to communicate. It is worth noting that the preliminary survey revealed that 100% of the study participants agree or strongly agree that "email sent to me is often used in place of other forms of communication".

Although several participants indicated a personal preference for speaking one-on-one with another individual, most study participants admitted that they email a co-worker within the university even when it would be easier to discuss an issue face-to-face. One study member commented, "We don't get out of our holes" (Participant #2), which can result in isolation of the individual. Some of the reasons given for this approach include the desire to document the communication, the expediency of email, the lack of desire to leave the cubicle, and the sender's preference for written communication.

Impact on Well-Being

As study participants described the impact of email on their well-being, the following themes emerged: (1) anxiety, stress, and tension, (2) physical impacts, and (3) feeling enslaved by the tool.

ANXIETY, STRESS, AND TENSION

Participants in this study experience an unusually high volume of email traffic related to registration activities, admission application deadlines, and add/drop class changes, to name a few. The researchers observed that these recurring events

resulted in increased anxiety, stress, and tension in the participants. The desire to help current students, faculty, and potential students with an immediate response to questions and issues seemed prevalent throughout the study group. Consequently, these individuals feel pressured to organize and reply to emails in a timely fashion. However, many participants also commented that one of the most satisfying elements of their job is assisting students and faculty.

Although a few participants felt that using email did not directly produce a stress reaction, the initial survey found that 16 participants (70%) agreed or strongly agreed that they had experienced "tension (tightness, emotional or physical strain) due to email". An additional 61% agreed that they had "experienced anxiety (worry, nervousness, unease) due to email". Individual interviews revealed that 12 participants occasionally experienced some form of stress or anxiety from the content of an email message or a from a perceived email attack by another individual. Participant #19 observed that "the hard thing with email is that you cannot tell the tone of the message, and therefore, it's easy to jump to conclusions." One participant explained that a strongly worded email can affect interactions with others, and acknowledged that, "It can even poison relationships. It's too easy to respond with a terse email. Everyone needs to just step back before they respond. I like the phone and face-to-face [communication] because it is more personalized for contact" (Participant #23).

Additionally, in order to reduce frustration and maintain an appropriate level of professionalism, higher education professionals spend a great deal of time constructing email messages that may be going outside the university community. Participant #7 stated, "In an email, I can agonize [over] how to best state the situation, and spend a lot of time rewriting it [the message] trying to make sure that I am providing the best information, and then still have it misunderstood or misconstrued". On the other hand, when a colleague assists with crafting a response to a difficult email, the end result is a professional communication that is reflective and not reactive.

Examining the impact of email usage on the well-being of individuals revealed that keeping pace with volumes of email on a day-to-day basis causes anxiety and tension in most participants. In order to keep ahead of the incoming work, several participants routinely check emails from home. They reported that this technique allows them a feeling of peace, which was perceived to be more effective for them rather than waiting to arrive at the office only to discover the volumes of emails waiting to be handled.

PHYSICAL IMPACTS

Study respondents reported a variety of physical ailments resulting from continuous and prolonged time spent sitting in front of a computer absorbed with the details of the work, formulating messages, and solving problems. The preliminary survey discovered that 52% of respondents agreed that they had "headaches due to email". Individual interviews revealed several instances of carpal tunnel, increased blood pressure, joint pain (fingers, neck, or shoulders), and weight gain. Another seven participants (30%) reported issues with back pain, and eight individuals (35%) indicated problems with their eyes.

It is important to note that study members applauded the university's expanded efforts to provide the work environment with ergonomic chairs, keyboards, and foot rests, etc., which has improved the work environment. Several participants reports that these changes have eliminated or reduced the impact of physical issues resulting from lengthy periods in front of a computer screen.

Feeling Enslaved by the Tool

Many study respondents feel tied to email, which could be described as the perception of being a slave to the tool. Twenty-one participants (91%)

believe that their jobs could not be performed effectively today without email. One felt that, "Life is simpler with email" (Participant #19). When asked what life would be like without email, comments ranged from "It would be quiet, peaceful, and blissfully ignorant. The job would be more time consuming" to "My life would be 10 times more hectic without email. Email is a time saver", and "Without email, I'd have to have a surgical attachment of the phone" (Participants #1, 16, & 23). In short, "It would mean lots of phone calls. We'd lose the history of the email conversations and lose the ability to search electronically. We'd probably be buried" (Participant #13). The vast majority of participants could not imagine what the university environment would be like without email and that although there are issues related to email usage, this tool is essential to the effective functioning of academic support units.

DISCUSSION

This study examined the use of email as a communication tool within higher education's administrative support environment, an area that has not been extensively scrutinized by other research studies. The professionals participating in this study acknowledge the ubiquity of email, and virtually all participants believe that email will not and should not be replaced by the traditional paper and pen method of communication. Likewise, participants acknowledge that reverting back to strictly telephone communication is not a viable option. On the other hand, several study members suggested that it will be interesting to observe if and to what extent academic workplaces accept other evolving forms of electronic media such as instant messaging and text messaging. Not surprisingly, it was younger (under age 35) employees who already employ these technologies, who proposed that the future may bring a variety of alternative communication choices to higher education. Lindback and Fodrey (2009) examined a variety of technologies used by an undergraduate admissions office in communicating with prospective students, including instant messaging and text messaging, although they reported that the predominant technologies experienced by students were the school web site and email.

One significant finding from this study is the perception by participants that the university environment should be regarded with the respect and formality that many adults reserve for the corporate business environment. Several staff from each academic area reported that some individuals, including parents, alumni, and students, use email to communicate informally when formality remains a component of the institutional protocol to demonstrate respect for the individuals receiving messages. With the prevalence of modern text messaging and associated slang, many email senders do not consider the ramifications of an email sent with text style acronyms, emoticons, and poor speech patterns. Senders may craft hasty emails using a virtual memo approach rather than spending the time to create a professionally written document, and this casual approach may prove detrimental in the final analysis.

Participants indicated that they become frustrated and annoyed when they must constantly deal with messages rife with a lack of proper etiquette, with poor spelling and grammar, or with an ambiguous tone. Most of them uphold the view that email within a professional environment (such as a university) should be treated as a business communication and messages should appropriately address the recipient, and utilize proper grammar and correct spelling. Hershkowitz-Coore (2005) observed:

The details count. Proper punctuation, the right word spelled correctly, and correct grammar show respect for your reader. Writers who can't find the time to honor their readers by spell checking, proofreading, and then rereading their message for accuracy show a brazen disregard for their own reputations and that of the organization they represent. (p. 13)

In short, the participants of this study are frequently offended by the informal and careless communications of individuals both inside and outside of the institution.

Constantly checking email demonstrates the addictive nature of the email application. Jackson et al. (2003a, 2003b) discovered that individuals who configure email to refresh at a short time lapse are positioned for continual interruptions at work. Likewise, Evans and Wright (2008) maintain that an individual's "compulsion to respond and take actions relating to an email" (p. 24) not only requires time, but also distracts from other activities. The majority of participants in this study had their Outlook email application configured to check for arriving email every five minutes, and they confirmed that arriving messages frequently distract them from important work, which aligns with the findings of Jackson and also with Evans and Wright.

Additionally, participants of this study reported that responding to difficult or complex situations via email requires the focus of several individuals over time in order to craft an appropriate and professional response. All academic units involved in this research encounter these types of messages and utilize a similar procedure of review with colleagues to assure that responses are respectful and professional.

This study also confirms that one of the impacts on the professionals' social interactions is an avoidance of face-to-face conversation. Hall (2004) maintains that face-to-face communication is critical to the health of organizations even though electronic communication has permeated the workplace and become a predominant mode of communication. Unfortunately, the "normalcy of social interaction has been replaced by the unnatural rule of efficiency" (Hall, 2004, p. 43). Consequently, workers need balance between virtual communication and face-to-face interaction in order to maintain a healthy level of job satisfaction. The participants in this study admit that complex or politically-charged situations require face-to-face discussion although there is a perception by some individuals that email is more efficient than using the phone or having a face-to-face conversation. In a similar vein, Duran et al. (2005) reported that faculty members expressed concern that email negatively impacts faculty-student interaction outside of the classroom. That is, although email has the potential to enhance faculty interaction with students, the perception is that email has replaced face-to-face contact.

Renaud et al. (2006) completed a study which focused on the perceptions of email recipients and which supports this study's conclusions "... the email phenomenon is something of a puzzle - everyone is aware of its potential for enhancing and facilitating communication, but the evidence for its dark side is emerging as email becomes more widespread" (p. 318). Wojcik (2005) expands on the concept of email having a dark side with, "the growing pressure to consume more and more data and to work harder, faster, and better than ever before has a dark side…Overload in fact can jeopardize your decisions, your performance, and even the performance of others" (p. 51). Discussions with the participants of this study validate that electronic communication continues to require intense focus to remain efficient in today's workplace.

CONCLUSION

This study examines the impact of email as a primary communication technology upon higher education professionals and differs from previous studies in terms of target participants and methodology. The qualitative approach provides valuable insights into the perceptions and work behaviors of higher education staff professionals who support administrative functions of the university. Although some findings were similar to previous studies conducted within other industries, the results of this research are notable in several ways.

First, the study expands the body of research within higher education beyond the faculty-student realm and explores the effects of email usage upon three specific administrative units (Office of Admissions, Registrar's Office, and Academic Services) within a small university. These professionals articulated a desire for email communication within the higher education environment to be treated as seriously as a corporate business communication.

Secondly, each administrative unit reported cyclical volumes of email that they anticipated within the academic calendar. These recurring events included registration, admission deadline, add/drop class changes, and grade submission, and the increased volume of email correspondence often resulted in increased tensions within the group.

Thirdly, the participants of this study recognize the necessity of utilizing electronic communication within today's workplace in order to correspond with students, potential students, faculty, and other individuals both inside and outside of the academic community. Although drawn to the strengths of today's email applications, participants also emphasized the importance of initiating face-to-face interaction, particularly in complex situations; they recognize the need to manage email sender expectations in order to deal with their own work stresses, and they strive to temper the negative impact of constant disruption by email on workplace productivity.

Although careful consideration was given to the design of this research, several limitations remain. This study consisted of three administrative areas of one university. The researchers had no control over the pool of eligible participants within these academic units, and acknowledge that the disparity between males and females is a shortcoming. Future research should focus on other academic/administrative offices (e.g., Financial Aid, Residential

Life/Housing, and University Relations, to name a few) as well as expand to other institutions of higher education. With the recent rise of text messaging and instant messaging, it may be appropriate to study whether stress behaviors could be resulting from these highly popular transmission mediums. Additionally, it may be beneficial to conduct quantitative studies on institutions of higher education.

The ubiquity of email as a communication tool in today's society accentuates the need to understand how to increase the effectiveness of this tool. Gaining a better understanding of the issues related to utilizing electronic communication in the higher education environment should positively impact the effectiveness and productivity, as well as the work/life balance for individuals within these organizations.

REFERENCES

Bellotti, V., Ducheneaut, N., Howard, M., Smith, I., & Grinter, R. E. (2005). Quality versus quantity: E-mail-centric task management and its relation with overload. *Human-Computer Interaction*, *20*, 89–138. doi:10.1207/s15327051hci2001&2_4

Betts, M., & Ouellette, T. (1995, November 6). Taming the email shrew. *Computerworld*, *29*(45), 32–33.

Burgess, A., Jackson, T. W., & Edwards, J. (2003, May). Measuring electronic communication defects and their impact at 3M. In G. Ross & M. Staples (Eds.), *Proceedings of the Process Improvement and Project Management Issues Conference*, Glasgow, UK (pp. 343-353).

Burgess, A., Jackson, T. W., & Edwards, J. (2004). Email overload: Tolerance levels of employees within the workplace. In Khosrow-Pour, M. (Ed.), *Innovations through Information Technology* (pp. 205–207). Hershey, PA: Idea Group.

Burgess, A., Jackson, T. W., & Edwards, J. (2005). Email training significantly reduces email defects. *International Journal of Information Management*, *25*(1), 71–83. doi:10.1016/j.ijinfomgt.2004.10.004

Byron, K. (2008). Carrying too heavy a load? The communication and miscommunication of emotion by email. *Academy of Management Review*, *33*(2), 309–327. doi:10.5465/AMR.2008.31193163

Charman-Anderson, S. (2008, September 9). Email becomes a dangerous distraction. *The Sydney Morning Herald*. Retrieved October 31, 2008, from http://www.smh.com.au/news/biztech/youve-got-interruption/2008/09/08/1220857455459.html

Collie, D. (2005). Tame information overload to increase productivity. *Business Times*, *27*(1), 36–37.

Dabbish, L. A., & Kraut, R. E. (2006). Email overload at work: An analysis of factors associated with email strain. In *Proceedings of the 20th Anniversary Conference on Computer Supported Cooperative Work*, Banff, AB, Canada (pp. 431-440).

Demirdjian, Z. (2005). Toward taming the monster in electronic mail. *Journal of American Academy of Business*, *7*(1), i–ii.

Denzin, N. K., & Lincoln, Y. S. (2000). Introduction: The discipline and practice of qualitative research. In Denzin, N. K., & Lincoln, Y. S. (Eds.), *Handbook of qualitative research* (pp. 1–28). Thousand Oaks, CA: Sage.

Ducheneaut, N., & Watts, L. A. (2005). In search of coherence: A review of e-mail research. *Human-Computer Interaction*, *20*, 11–48. doi:10.1207/s15327051hci2001&2_2

Dudman, J. (2003, April 15). Email overload. *Computer Weekly, 36*.

Duran, R. L., Kelly, L., & Keaten, J. A. (2005). College faculty use and perceptions of electronic mail to communicate with students. *Communication Quarterly*, *53*(2), 159–176. doi:10.1080/01463370500090118

Eppler, M., & Mengis, J. (2004). The concept of information overload: A review of literature from organization science, accounting, marketing, MIS, and related disciplines. *The Information Society, 20*, 325–344. doi:10.1080/01972240490507974

Evans, C., & Wright, W. (2008). To: ALL USERS: Copy: ALL USERS. *Management Services, 52*(1), 24–27.

Farhooman, A., & Drury, D. (2002). Managerial information overload. *Communications of the ACM, 45*(10), 127–131. doi:10.1145/570907.570909

Fetterman, D. M. (2009). Ethnography. In Bickman, L., & Rog, D. J. (Eds.), *The SAGE handbook of applied social research methods* (pp. 543–588). Thousand Oaks, CA: Sage.

Frazee, V. (1996). Is email doing more harm than good? *The Personnel Journal, 23*.

Hall, H. T. (2004). The standardization of efficiency and its implications for organizations. *Journal of Critical Postmodern Organization Science, 3*(1), 42–53.

Hershkowitz-Coore, S. (2005). Email: Toxic or terrific? *Journal for Quality and Participation, 28*(2), 11–14.

Huang, E. Y., & Lin, S. W. (2009). Do knowledge workers use e-mail wisely? *Journal of Computer Information Systems, 50*(1), 65–73.

Jackson, T. W., Burgess, A., & Edwards, J. (2006). A simple approach to improving email communication. *Communications of the ACM, 49*(6), 107–109. doi:10.1145/1132469.1132493

Jackson, T. W., Dawson, R. J., & Wilson, D. (2002). Case study: Evaluating the effect of email interruptions within the workplace. In *Proceedings of the Conference on Empirical Assessment in Software Engineering,* Keele, UK (pp. 3-7).

Jackson, T. W., Dawson, R. J., & Wilson, D. (2003a). Reducing the effect of email interruptions on employees. *International Journal of Information Management, 23*(1), 55–65. doi:10.1016/S0268-4012(02)00068-3

Jackson, T. W., Dawson, R. J., & Wilson, D. (2003b). Understanding email interaction increases organizational productivity. *Communications of the ACM, 46*(8), 80–84. doi:10.1145/859670.859673

Janssen, R., & de Poot, H. (2006, October 14-18). Information overload: Why some people seem to suffer more than others. In *Proceedings of the 4th Nordic Conference on Human-Computer Interaction: Changing Roles,* Oslo, Norway (pp. 397-400).

Lazar, J., Jones, A., & Shneiderman, B. (2006). Workplace user frustration with computers: An exploratory investigation of the causes and severity. *Behaviour & Information Technology, 25*(3), 239–251. doi:10.1080/01449290500196963

Leavitt, W. (2008). The tyranny of email. *Fleet Owner, 103*(7), 20.

Lindback, R., & Fodrey, B. (2009). Using technology in undergraduate admission: Current practices and future plans. *Journal of College Admission, 204*, 25–30.

Maxwell, J. A. (2009). Designing a qualitative study. In Bickman, L., & Rog, D. J. (Eds.), *The SAGE handbook of applied social research methods* (pp. 214–253). Thousand Oaks, CA: Sage.

Merriam, S. (1988). *Case study research in education: A qualitative approach.* San Francisco, CA: Jossey-Bass.

Neustaedter, C., Bernheim Brush, A. J., Smith, M. A., & Fisher, D. (2005, April). Beyond "from" and "received": Exploring the dynamics of email triage. In *Proceedings of the CHI 2005 Conference on Human Factors in Computing Systems.* New York: ACM Press.

Patton, M. (1990). *Qualitative evaluation and research methods*. Newbury Park, CA: Sage.

Patton, M. Q. (2002). *Qualitative research and evaluation methods* (3rd ed.). Thousand Oaks, CA: Sage.

Radicati Group, Inc. (2008). *Addressing email chaos: The Email-Manager™ solution*. Retrieved February 6, 2010, from http://www.radicati.com/files/emm-final.pdf

Recascino, A. (2009). *Email utilization by university employees: Relationship to job satisfaction in higher education*. Saarbrücken, Germany: VDM Verlag.

Renaud, K., Ramsay, J., & Hair, M. (2006). You've got e-mail...shall I deal with it now? Electronic mail from the recipient's perspective. *International Journal of Human-Computer Interaction, 21*(3), 313–332. doi:10.1207/s15327590ijhc2103_3

Salajan, F. D., Schönwetter, D. J., & Cleghorn, B. M. (2010). Student and faculty inter-generational digital divide: Fact or fiction? *Computers & Education, 55*, 1393–1403. doi:10.1016/j.compedu.2010.06.017

Seidman, I. (1998). *Interviewing as qualitative research: a guide for researchers in education and the social sciences* (2nd ed.). New York, NY: Teachers College Press.

Silverman, D. (2001). *Interpreting qualitative data: Methods for analysing talk, text and interaction* (2nd ed.). Thousand Oaks, CA: Sage.

Smith, D. (2008, March 9). Email 'a broken business tool' as staff spend hours wading through inboxes. *The Observer*. Retrieved October 31, 2008, from http://www.guardian.co.uk/technology/2008/mar/09/internet/print

Tyler, J. R., & Tang, J. C. (2003, September). When can I expect an e-mail response? A study of rhythms in e-mail usage. In *Proceedings of the 2003 8th European Conference on Computer-Supported Cooperative Work*, Helsinki, Finland (pp. 239-258).

Waldeck, J. H., Kearney, P., & Plax, T. G. (2001). Teacher e-mail message strategies and students' willingness to communicate online. *Journal of Applied Communication Research, 29*(1), 54–70. doi:10.1080/00909880128099

Weiss, M., & Hanson-Baldauf, D. (2008). E-mail in academia: Expectations, use, and instructional impact. *EDUCAUSE Quarterly, 31*(1), 42–50.

Whittaker, S., Bellotti, V., & Gwizdka, J. (2006). Email in personal information management. *Communications of the ACM, 49*(1), 68–73. doi:10.1145/1107458.1107494

Whittaker, S., & Sidner, C. (1996, April). Email overload: Exploring personal information management of email. In *Proceedings of CHI 96: Conference on Human Factors in Computing Systems*, Vancouver, BC, Canada (pp. 276-283). New York, NY: ACM Press.

Wilson, E. V. (2002). Email winners and losers. *Communications of the ACM, 45*(10), 121–126. doi:10.1145/570907.570908

Wojcik, E. (2005). Full-time stress. *Electric Perspectives, 30*(4), 50–55.

This work was previously published in the International Journal of Technology and Human Interaction, Volume 7, Issue 4, edited by Anabela Mesquita and Chia-Wen Tsai, pp. 31-45, copyright 2011 by IGI Publishing (an imprint of IGI Global).

Chapter 17

How Much Can Computers and Internet Help?
A Long-Term Study of Web-Mediated Problem-Based Learning and Self-Regulated Learning

Chia-Wen Tsai
Ming Chuan University, Taiwan

ABSTRACT

Computing education in Taiwan is ineffective. Most teaching efforts in private vocational schools have been devoted to helping students pass tests through a "spoon-feeding" teaching method. Under such constraints, students may lose their long-term competence in practical terms. In this study, the author conducted a series of quasi-experiments to examine the long-term effects of web-mediated problem-based learning (PBL), self-regulated learning (SRL), and their combinations on students' computing skills over three years. The author re-examined students' long-term computing skills three years after the start of the related course. Results reveal that effects of web-mediated PBL, SRL, and their combinations on students' long-term computing skills are significant. The implications for scholars and teachers engaged in online learning were also discussed.

INTRODUCTION

The challenge of maximizing students' learning has been paramount in many nations (Sablonnière, Taylor, & Sadykova, 2009). In Taiwan, professionals with a vocational degree represent a major portion of the work force (Shen, Lee, & Tsai, 2008). It is particularly important to develop

practical skills for vocational students in Taiwan (Tai, Chen, & Lai, 2003). However, vocational school curricula in Taiwan have historically been based on the National Curriculum Guidelines. Thus, schools in this context did not have much freedom in curriculum development (Hsiao, Chen, & Yang, 2008). At the bottom tier of Taiwan's education system are newly recognized private

DOI: 10.4018/978-1-4666-1954-8.ch017

institutions that are mainly teaching-only institutes (Wu, 2009).

Most teaching efforts in private vocational schools have been devoted to helping students pass tests through a "spoon-feeding", or didactic, teaching method. This traditional teaching method puts students' attention less on mastering application software and more on preparing for tests through memorization. Consequently, a student who has passed the exam may still be unable to apply what was learned in school, and worse, lacks motivation to learn more in the future (Shen et al., 2008). In addition, the computing courses in Taiwan traditionally emphasize memorization by applying short, disjointed, lack-of-context examples. Learning from only such examples may result in uncompetitive employees. In this regard, computing education in vocational schools in Taiwan can hardly be deemed as effective (Lee, Shen, & Tsai, 2008). Students under such constraints may even lose their long-term competence and practical computing skills when they enter the workplace.

A country's national competitiveness is contingent upon the quality of its education system (Hong et al., 2008). Technical and vocational skills development should be fully utilized by all in the labour market (Palmer, 2009). The importance of employees having a substantial foundation in basic skills and the ability to use technology to solve important problems has been indicated in other research (Bottge et al., 2009). However, the application software education in vocational schools in Taiwan can hardly be regarded as practically oriented.

In order to develop students' practical and long-term computing skills, problem-based learning (PBL) is considered to be a most appropriate pedagogical choice. PBL is a method of organizing teaching by introducing relevant problems at the beginning of the instruction cycle to provide the context and motivation for the learning that follows (Barrows & Tamblyn, 1980; Hussain et al., 2007). In PBL settings, students are required to collaborate in the same way as people tend to solve problems in real life (Oliver, 2008). Therefore, PBL was applied in this study to develop students' long-term computing skills.

The topic of technology in higher education and online learning has for many years received increased attention among higher education researchers (Renn & Zeligman, 2005). However, institutions of higher education that provide online learning are currently being challenged by increasingly complex changes, including new demands for networked participation, the rapid development of new communication technologies, demand for emphasis on learning outcomes instead of teaching input and content, and postmodern ways of knowing (Kanuka et al., 2008). One major disadvantage of online learning cited by students is their sense of isolation and loss of personal interaction with instructors and peers (Billings, 2000; Buckley, 2003). In online learning environments, the physical absence of the instructor and the increased responsibility demanded of learners to effectively engage in learning tasks may present difficulties for learners, particularly those with low self-regulatory skills (Dabbagh & Kitsantas, 2005). Online learning differs from didactic presentation, where the student has few opportunities to deviate from the teacher's presentation of the material (Greene & Azevedo, 2007). Therefore, there is a continuing debate about effective design of online learning environments (Azevedo, 2005; Jacobson, 2005).

Online learning is primarily self-directed learning because the learner attends lectures only to register time, place, subject, and to alter the order of attending future lectures (Lee & Lee, 2008). Success in online courses often depends on students' abilities to successfully direct their own learning efforts (Cennamo, Ross, & Rogers, 2002). Therefore, it is suggested that students should have self-regulated learning (SRL) strategies when they study in an online learning environment because the potential for them to drop out is increased without such strategies (Kogo & Nojima, 2004). Studies examining how students learn complex and challenging tasks have suggested that successful students deploy key self-regulatory strategies and processes (Greene et al., 2008; Shen et al., 2008). In this regard, SRL was applied in this study to help students develop regular learning habits.

Solving difficult problems requires extraordinary self-management skills (e.g., metacognition and evaluation) (Bottge et al., 2009; Glasgow, 1997). It is believed that students could improve their computing skills after receiving the combined training of PBL and SRL. However, there are very few studies that discuss the simultaneous effects of PBL and SRL (Shen, Lee, & Tsai, 2008), particularly regarding long-term effects. Moreover, web-mediated learning and techniques have been receiving more attention as they suitably combine both aspects of computer-assisted learning methodologies with the anywhere, anytime access feature of the Internet at the client end (Girma, 2002). In this regard, the author redesigned a course, 'Packaged Software and Applications,' integrating web-mediated teaching methods (including PBL and SRL) and learning technologies to develop students' long-term computing skills.

In the following sections, related literature about the effects and validity of web-mediated PBL and SRL is individually reported in 'Literature Review'. Subsequently, 'The Empirical Study' describes the participants and the course involved, the experimental design and procedure, the interventions for experimental and control groups, along with how students' computing skills were evaluated. Then, the testing and analysis of data are presented in the 'Results' section. Finally, the findings in this study and possible implications for educators and schools are addressed in the sections 'Discussion and Implications' and 'Conclusion'.

LITERATURE REVIEW

Problem-Based Learning

PBL is a method of instruction that uses problems as a context for students to develop problem-solving skills and basic knowledge (Banta, Black, & Kline, 2000). It is focused, experiential learning organized around the investigation, explanation, and resolution of authentic, or contextualized problems (Barrows, 2000; Hmelo-Silver, 2004; Torp & Sage, 2002). In a PBL environment, students have opportunities to practice applying their knowledge and skills while working on meaningful problems and projects; thus, PBL helps students acquire the knowledge and skills required in the workplace (Dunlap, 2005).

PBL is also introduced to provide an education that allows students to compete successfully in a changing world (Hussain et al., 2007). Based on designed knowledge gaps in the problems and out of students' intrinsic curiosity, students set their own learning goals and decide on what they are going to study (Budé et al., 2009). This not only emphasizes the learning of the subject area, but also provides opportunities for students to practice and apply many skills and knowledge. What is learned in a meaningful context will be more easily retrieved than that which is acquired in isolation. The resemblance between the context of learning and the context of future applications facilitates the transfer of knowledge (Charlin, Mann, & Hansen, 1998).

Many researchers have examined PBL's positive impact on knowledge and skill acquisition and transfer, problem solving, attitudes and opinions about courses and programs, measures of performance, and self-directed learning (Dunlap, 2005). Moreover, Polanco, Calderón and Delgado (2004) point out that students in PBL groups attain significantly higher scores than students from a control group in a course composed of physics, mathematics and computer science. In Chanlin and Chan's (2004) study that uses PBL in web-based instruction, it was revealed that students in the PBL treatment reflected more variation in peer assessment. More commendations and criticisms in reference to peers' effort and involvement were obtained from PBL group members. Thus, it is believed that the adoption of PBL in online learning environment may contribute to students' learning of critical thinking and develop their practical skills.

Self-Regulated Learning

SRL refers to learning that results from students' self-generated thoughts and behaviors that are systematically oriented toward the attainment of their learning goals (Schunk, 1989). SRL is an active, constructive process whereby learners set goals for their learning and then attempt to monitor, regulate, and control their cognition, motivation, and behavior in the service of those goals (Winne, 2001; Winne & Hadwin, 1998; Zimmerman & Schunk, 2001). SRL emphasizes autonomy and control by the individual who monitors, directs, and regulates actions toward goals of information acquisition, expanding expertise, and self-improvement (Paris & Paris, 2001). Characteristics attributed to self-regulated persons coincide with those attributed to high-performing, high-capacity students, as opposed to those with low performance, who show deficits in metacognitive, motivational, and behavioral variables (Montalvo & Torres, 2004; Reyero & Tourón, 2003; Zimmerman, 1998). Researchers have consistently shown that self-regulation helps high achievers reach their potential (Risemberg & Zimmerman, 1992).

With regard to the effects of SRL in the online learning environment, it is indicated that successful students in an online course generally use self-regulated learning strategies and the effect of self-regulation on students' success is statistically significant (Yukselturk & Bulut, 2007). Montalvo and Torres (2004) also indicate that SRL learners show greater efforts to participate in the control and regulation of academic tasks, classroom climate and structure to the extent that the context allows. In Kramarski and Gutman's (2006) study, they compared the treatments of e-learning with and without SRL in solving mathematical problems. Their results showed that SRL students significantly outperformed non-SRL students in problem-solving procedural and transfer tasks regarding mathematical explanations in a web-based learning environment. Therefore, we believe that the adoption of SRL in this online course could help students learn, and further develop their long-term computing skills.

THE EMPIRICAL STUDY

Participants and the Course Involved

The course in the present experiment is a semester-long, 2 credit-hour class, targeting first-year students from different major fields of study. Students solve a series of authentic tasks by applying Microsoft Office (including Word, Excel, and PowerPoint). The major focus of this course is to develop students' skills in applying the functions of Microsoft Word, Excel, and PowerPoint, popular packaged software for developing and creating documents, worksheets, and visual aids with some graphs and tables.

In this study, there were 86 first-year students taking a compulsory course of 'Packaged Software and Application' in an institute of technology in Taiwan. Students in Taiwan usually take the same teacher's class with their cohort of classmates; then, they can ask questions, share course content and information, discuss and cooperate with familiar classmates. This was true for the 76 out of 86 students who were from the department of business administration. As it is very difficult to gather all participants from different departments to take a posttest in the 36th month after the course began, the author chose the students from the department of business administration for analysis, who were enrolled in another compulsory course in the 36th month. So, there were 76 students who actually completed both the pretest and posttest for the quasi-experiment over three years.

The students participating in this experiment came from two classes. The author purposely chose the first class for the experimental groups that would receive web-based teaching methods, because there were more students in this class to divide them into groups. In the first week, the lecturer declared that this class section would be partially provided with innovative instructional methods mediated by the web as an intervention. Students in the first class had the freedom to drop this class section and take another teacher's class section, if preferred. After this declaration, 45 students continued in this class section, and no student dropped this class mid term.

As for dividing students into groups, the author used Microsoft Excel to randomly select half the students from the first class and divided this class into two experimental groups (Case 1 and Case 2), while the second class served as the control group (Case 3). There were twenty-three students in Case 1 that was composed of web-mediated PBL and SRL teaching methods, twenty-two students in Case 2 that received PBL intervention only, while thirty-one students in Case 3 received traditional teaching method in the face-to-face classroom. In addition, none of the students majored in information or computer technology. There was no student who had taken a web-based course before taking this class.

Experimental Design

Case 1 and Case 2 were conducted as blended learning, while students from Case 3 learned in a traditional face-to-face classroom. In the first three weeks, the classes for Case 1 and Case 2 were conducted in a physical classroom. After three weeks, most of the coursework for Case 1 and Case 2 was moved onto the website. The

teacher audio recorded every session of his lecture and later transferred lectures into HTML files with flash, video, and voice. These HTML files were then loaded into the course website. Students from Case 1 and Case 2 could preview and review the course sessions on this course website.

The course design in the study consists of three subsequent modules: Word, Excel, and PowerPoint modules. A skill test was administered after the completion of each module. The first test was held during the midterm examination (8th week). The second test was held in the 13th week and the final one in the 16th week. Moreover, the author re-examined students' long-term computing skills 36 months after the course started.

The Experimental and Control Intervention

Intervention Concerning Web-Mediated PBL (for Case 1 and Case 2)

In PBL environments, small groups of students learn collaboratively in the context of meaningful problems that describe observable phenomena or events (Loyens, Magda, & Rikers, 2008; Schmidt, 1983), and actively participate in the learning process (Sungur & Tekkaya, 2006). Thus, the teacher in this research created interesting and challenging simulated problem situations for students in Case 1 and Case 2. At the beginning of each class period, the teacher first led students in a 10-minute warm-up activity to review the computing skills they had worked on the previous week, then introduced new material and illustrated the procedures and functions of Microsoft Office. Following, students were told about the situations and related problems that they should solve. For the remainder of class, they had to consider and discuss with their team members how to solve the problems by applying the skills and knowledge they had just learned. Some of the tasks required teamwork. Students had to collaborate and contribute their ideas to complete the tasks. Students could discuss ideas with their team members in the traditional classroom, online forums, chat rooms, or via online messengers.

In the instruction period, the teacher first demonstrated how he could approach the situation and solve the problem accordingly. In addition to the teaching of skills of application software, similar situations and related applications were also discussed in the class. In the latter, the teacher guided students in constructing their own models of problem solving.

Finally, the teacher spot-checked whether students attended the online classes and listened to the content through their login records. The teacher would remind the students who did not regularly attend the online classes and submit the assignments.

Intervention Concerning Web-Mediated SRL (for Case 1 only)

Participants in Case 1 received additional instruction in SRL strategies after school during the first week. They were gathered in a classroom and a two-hour lecture was delivered discussing how to manage study time and regulate their learning. The content of this SRL instruction was composed of the following processes (Zimmerman, Bonner, & Kovach, 1996):

a. **Self-evaluation and monitoring:** learners assess their learning effects based on self-observations of previous learning achievement.
b. **Goal-setting and strategy planning:** learners set learning goals by analyzing their learning missions, then, they plan and generate appropriate learning strategies to achieve their learning goals.
c. **Strategy implementation and monitoring:** learners implement the learning strategies and monitor the effectiveness of learning strategies via self-monitoring.

d. **Monitoring of the outcome of strategy:** learners assess the learning effects of learning strategies by observing the relationship between learning achievement and strategies.

After this lecture discussing SRL and relative learning strategies, students had to implement these four processes of SRL and strategies to manage their time, and regulate their learning. Students from Case 1 were required to take notes in class and review the notes after school. In addition, students had to regularly prepare and read the textbook before classes, and, after class, practice the skills of using application software they had learned. Students were also asked to record their learning behavior and write a reflective summary for each learning task every week. The learning journals were recorded on the course website instead of in their notebooks in order to prevent falsification of records. Based on these records, students could self-evaluate their learning according to the goals they had set in advance.

Although Case 1 and Case 2 came from the same class, the instruction for these two cases was separated in the course website in order to effectively control the intervention concerning web-mediated SRL. The requirements for Case 1 students to implement SRL and record their learning behavior were only announced in that exclusive forum. That is, students from Case 2 could neither see these extra requirements, nor have the chance to learn SRL strategies in the course website.

Teaching in the Control Group (Case 3)

Instead of focusing on web-based PBL and SRL, students from Case 3 were taught in the face-to-face classroom with traditional teaching methods. Except for the two-hour lecture of SRL for Case 1 students, the control group (Case 3) was submitted to the same number of teaching hours as the experimental groups (Case 1 and

Case 2), including both face-to-face and online classes, in order to control for unintended effects of the design. The students in the control group experienced the traditional style of teaching and did not deal with the extra requirements of SRL. Moreover, the teacher did not audio record any session of his lecture. That is, students in Case 3 were not provided with either chance or channels to review or practice after class.

Finally, they also participated in the measurements after the completion of each module and were re-examined in the 36th month after the course began. As such, this case was a so-called non-treatment group.

Interventions for the three cases are illustrated and compared in Table 1.

Evaluation

A detailed evaluation of the project was conducted. Before the experiment began, the author empirically assessed the differences of students' computing skills among the three cases. In the first week, all students were asked to complete three Microsoft Word documents as pretest. The researchers chose Word for the pretest because almost every student in Taiwan learns Word before

he/she learns other packaged software. 'One-way ANOVA' was used to test the differences of students' pretest grades among the three cases. The pretest grades showed that computer skills of almost all were similarly low. The difference of students' pretested computing skills among the three cases was not statistically significant ($p = 0.198$, see Table 2). None of the participants was able to answer any of the pretest questions completely and correctly. It was confirmed that all students in the three cases had a little knowledge or skill in packaged software. Therefore, it is assumed that the students have equally low computing skills before they took this course.

In the last week of the 36th month following the start of the course, the researcher went to another compulsory course to ask the participants in the course involved in this quasi-experiment to take the posttest. During this week, all students taking this course had to attend to check their grades in this compulsory course. Thus, the researcher could collect all students' posttest grades for analyzing students' long-term computing skills.

Students from the three cases were gathered in two classrooms to test their long-term computing skills. Before testing, students were assigned random seats. In the test, students had to complete

Table 1. Interventions concerning web-mediated PBL and SRL

Interventions / Activities	Intervention concerning PBL	Intervention concerning SRL	Teaching in the control group
Teaching Activities	A teacher... creates interesting and challenging simulated problems. demonstrates how to solve simulated problems discusses its potential applications.	A teacher... teaches SRL skills in an extra course. assigns homework for students' practice every week. urges students to study regularly.	A teacher... lectures by applying short, disjointed, lack-of-context examples. gives the same number of content teaching hours as Case 1 and Case 2.
Learning Activities	Students... discuss ideas with their team members in the traditional classroom, or via Internet. take on authentic tasks and learn by problem solving.	Students... complete teacher's assignments before the required time. implement SRL and record learning behaviors every week.	Students... are taught in the face-to-face classroom. receive traditional teaching methods.
Cases Involved	Both Case 1 and Case 2	Case 1	Case 3

Table 2. Pretest: Grades of three cases

Group	n	Mean	Std. Deviation	Std. Error	95% Confidence Interval for Mean	
					Lower Bound	Upper Bound
PBL and SRL group (Case 1)	23	11.26	7.916	1.651	7.84	14.68
PBL group (Case 2)	22	10.77	7.994	1.704	7.23	14.32
Control group (Case 3)	31	8.19	4.393	0.789	6.58	9.80

Word, Excel, and PowerPoint files, which each consisted of 5 to 8 sub-problems. The problems given on this test were taken from the Certification of Microsoft Office, which is administered by a trustworthy organization in Taiwan called the Computer Skills Foundation (CSF). For instance, students were required to build a worksheet with some tables and graphs to compare market shares with competitors. Forty minutes was given for students to complete the three files. After the test, students were required to leave this classroom. Then, the teacher used a test evaluation system provided by CSF to grade, and record the results immediately. The teacher could not recognize the identity of the students while grading and recording in a blinded condition.

This test evaluation system assigns students' scores according to the correctness and completeness of their files. Students got high grades if they completely solved the problems with appropriate processes. Then, the long-term computing skill was averaged from the scores of these three files. Finally, the author compared the differences among students' long-term computing skills (students' grade in the 36th month) under the three different cases. Furthermore, the enhancement of students' computing skills is the result of one's grade in the 36th month minus his pretest grade. The enhancement of students' computing skills after 36 months was also tested in this study.

RESULTS

The Effects of the Web-Mediated SRL

The independent samples t-test was used to compare students' long-term computing skills between Case 1 (PBL and SRL group) and Case 2 (PBL group). As shown in Table 3, the grades in Case 1 (83.91) were significantly higher than those in Case 2 (70.09). In addition, the enhancement of students' computing skills in Case 1 (72.65) was also statistically higher than that in Case 2 (59.32). That is, students who received the combined treatment of web-mediated PBL and SRL appear to gain better and more lasting long-term computing skills than those who received PBL only.

Table 3. Comparison of PBL and SRL to PBL only

Variables	Group	Mean	S. D.	F	t-value	df	p
Grades in the	PBL and SRL group	83.91	4.852	22.163	4.923	43	< 0.001
36th month	PBL group	70.09	12.524				
Enhancement	PBL and SRL group	72.65	7.952	1.542	4.852	43	< 0.001
of grades	PBL group	59.32	10.376				

The Effects of the Web-Mediated PBL

Results in Table 4 show that the average grade in Case 2 (PBL group, mean=70.09) was significantly higher than that in Case 3 (Control group, mean=38.55). Moreover, the enhancement of students' computing skills in Case 2 (59.32) was also statistically higher than that in Case 3 (30.35). Therefore, effects of web-mediated PBL on students' long-term computing skills are positive, and higher than for those who did not receive PBL.

The Effects of Combined Treatment of Web-Mediated PBL and SRL

Data from Table 5 show that the average grade in Case 1 (PBL and SRL group, mean=83.91) is significantly higher than that in Case 3 (Control group, mean=38.55). The improvement of students' computing skills in Case 1 (72.65) was very substantially higher than that in Case 3 (30.35).

Finally, students' grades among the three cases were also compared in Figure 1. Based on the data shown in Table 5 and Figure 1, it is concluded that the effects of web-mediated PBL and SRL intervention on students' long-term comput-ing skills are positive, and students' corresponding skills are higher than those of students taught by traditional methods.

DISCUSSION AND IMPLICATIONS

Many developing countries are starting to utilize the potential of educational technologies and software (Bisaso et al., 2008). The application of different parameters and technologies in online learning has been an important research topic for the last few decades in computer-based or web-based learning (Burgos, Tattersall, & Koper, 2007). Motivating students to achieve in online learning environments is of practical concern to instructional designers, and of theoretical concern to researchers (Paas et al., 2005). However, in an environment that is full of Internet allure with its array of shopping websites and free online games, it is a difficult challenge to the teachers to help students be involved in an online course (Shen et al., 2008). Teachers should adopt innovative teaching methods (e.g. web-mediated PBL, and web-mediated SRL) and apply networked technologies (e.g. course website, and audio-recorded content) to help students attain better learning ef-

Table 4. Comparison of PBL to control

Variables	Group	Mean	S. D.	F	t-value	df	p
Grades in the	PBL group	70.09	12.524	.251	9.032	51	< 0.001
36th month	Control group	38.55	12.530				
Enhancement	PBL group	59.32	10.376	.658	8.347	51	< 0.001
of grades	Control group	30.35	13.713				

Table 5. Comparison of PBL and SRL to control

Variables	Group	Mean	S. D.	F	t-value	df	p
Grades in the	PBL and SRL group	83.91	4.852	11.666	16.441	52	< 0.001
36th month	Control group	38.55	12.530				
Enhancement	PBL and SRL group	72.65	7.952	3.356	13.216	52	< 0.001
of grades	Control group	30.35	13.713				

Figure 1. Students' grades for the three cases at the first and 36th month

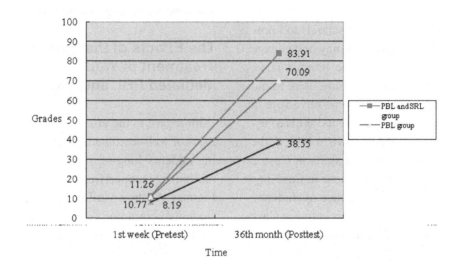

fects (Shen, Lee, & Tsai, 2007), and further lead to students' long-term competence. Therefore, we explored the effects of the combined training of PBL, SRL, and online learning on students' long-term computing skills over three years in this study.

The Effects of Web-Mediated SRL

Self-regulation is one of the issues that strike at the heart of current debates about the organization of education and the nature of the relationship between institutions and learners (Johnson & Liber, 2008). It is critical to develop students' skills of SRL to manage their learning in online learning environments (Winnips, 2000). In the implementation of web-mediated SRL in this study, students were required to regularly prepare and read the textbook before classes, and practice the skills of using application software they had learned after school. They had to record their learning behaviors on the course website weekly.

As the data shows in Table 3, it is indicated that the difference of students' computing skills in the 36th month between Case 1 and Case 2 is statistically significant ($p < 0.001$). Besides, the difference in enhancements of students' computing skills between Case 1 and Case 2 is also statistically significant ($p < 0.001$, see Table 3). The effects of web-mediated SRL can be seen since students who received the combined treatment of web-mediated PBL and SRL gained better learning effects than those who received PBL only.

This effect of web-mediated SRL is consistent with that of Yukselturk and Bulut's (2007), Montalvo and Torres's (2004), and Tsai and Shen's (2009) studies indicating that the effect of self-regulation variables on students' learning effects was statistically significant. Students experienced and developed their regular learning habits in the online learning environment. They set learning goals and controlled the different aspects influencing the learning process and evaluated their actions. Then, they became less dependent on others and on the contextual features in a learning situation (Järvelä et al., 2007). The findings of this study are similar to those that appeared in previous studies; however, this study extended the effects of SRL to the online learning environment and the field of application software education.

The Effects of Web-Mediated PBL

It is important for teachers and schools to know what kinds of learning activities may best engage students in learning through the Internet (Lee, Shen, & Tsai, 2008). In this study, it is found that web-mediated PBL plays a positive role in enhancing and maintaining students' skills of using application software. As shown in Table 4, the grades for students' computing skills in Case 2 were significantly higher than those in Case 3 ($p < 0.001$). In addition, the difference of students' enhancements in computing skills between Case 2 and Case 3 is also statistically significant ($p < 0.001$, see Table 4). Web-mediated PBL contributed to students' long-term computing skills in this study.

The shift from a product-based economy to knowledge-based economy results in an increased demand for knowledge workers who are capable of higher-order thinking and skills to solve complex problems in the workplace (Ong & Lai, 2006). In this study, the author empirically explored the effects of web-mediated PBL on developing students' practical and long-term computing skills. The findings of this research are similar to those that appeared in previous studies, which revealed that web-enabled PBL fosters problem-solving behaviors in learners (Kenny, Bullen, & Loftus, 2006). Moreover, this study extended the effects of PBL to the field of application software education over the long-term.

Students' computing skills in Case 2 being significantly higher than those in Case 3 in the 36th month may be because students who received web-mediated PBL had learned practical computing skills were willing to continually use what was learned and further contribute to their proficiency. However, students from Case 3 may not have developed practical computing skills, and suffered when they faced real problems. That is, they had less opportunity to apply and practice what they learned. In this regard, we suggest that computer teachers should adopt innovative teaching methods, such as PBL, to develop their students' thinking and practical skills.

The Effects of the Combined Treatment of Web-Mediated PBL and SRL

With regard to the effects of the combined treatment of web-mediated PBL and SRL on enhancing students' long-term computing skills, we find preliminary support from the results in Table 5 and Figure 1. As shown in Table 5, the enhancement of students' computing skills in Case 1 is statistically higher than that in Case 3 ($p < 0.001$). This finding is similar to Kramarski and Gutman's (2006), Paris and Paris's (2001), and Perels, Gürtler and Schmitz's (2005) studies, which emphasize the importance of the combination of problem-solving and self-regulation. Therefore, it is believed that the combined treatment of PBL and SRL could contribute to students' long-term computing skills in online learning environments.

Furthermore, we also found that students in Case 3 who received the traditional teaching method in the classroom exhibited the poorest grades for computing skills in the 36th month (see Figure 1). For the development of students' long-term skills and competitiveness, it is suggested that teachers should consider redesigning their courses, adopting appropriate teaching methods and technologies to help their students have better learning effects. In this study, we found that web-mediated PBL and SRL could help students achieve better computing skills and maintain their skills for several years, thus providing them the chance to train as competitive employees.

Limitations

The results of this study generally supported that there are positive effects of web-mediated PBL, web-mediated SRL and their combinations on enhancing students' long-term computing skills. However, problems of experimental validity may result from students in the comparison group being incidentally exposed to the treatment condition (Gribbons & Herman, 1997). In order to effectively prevent Case 2 students from learning SRL strategies from Case 1 students, each case had their own exclusive instruction and forum. As this experiment was conducted in two real classes, however, it was difficult to completely prevent students' interaction in the physical learning environments. Students from Case 2 may have interact with those from Case 1 in other face-to-face classes, and learned about the extra requirements for SRL and additional assignments. Thus, the author has to indicate that the experiment in this course may have unavoidable problems, for example, occurrence of students' interaction between Case 1 and Case 2 in this real class.

Furthermore, the well-known problems such as population selection, the Hawthorne effect, and match of assessment to curriculum and instruction make it difficult to conclude with certainty whether a web-mediated teaching method with SRL is the only factor responsible for improving on traditional modes of teaching (Bruce et al., 2005).

CONCLUSION

Educational development is happening in different ways outside of traditional classrooms. To increase access to education and enhance existing educational frameworks, information and communication technologies (ICTs) are being used to enhance delivery and provide more channels and flexibilities for students' learning (DeBoer, 2009). The extent to which the education field introduces teachers and educators to perspectives from those who are experts in online learning will likely result in significant implications for both research and practice (Arbaugh, 2008). In this study, we explored the potential effects of web-mediated PBL and SRL on enhancing students' long-term computing skills. The results are generally supportive. That is, the effects of

web-mediated PBL, SRL, and their combination on students' long-term skills of using application software are significant.

The results of this study emphasized the importance of course redesign and the adoption of innovative teaching methods and technologies to help students learn and develop long-term skills and competitiveness. It is believed the interventions concerning web-mediated PBL and SRL may provide reference for educators and teachers who are preparing for or presently engaged in implementing online learning. We expect that the treatments of web-mediated teaching methods and findings in this study could be helpful for teachers to assist their students in developing regular learning habits, and more importantly, possessing long-term practical computing skills. Finally, it is also suggested that the teaching methods in this study could also be simultaneously applied in traditional learning environments.

ACKNOWLEDGMENT

The author would like to express thanks for the financial support of NSC 98-2410-H-130-056- from National Science Council, Taiwan, R.O.C.

REFERENCES

Arbaugh, J. B. (2008). Introduction: Blended learning: Research and practice. *Academy of Management Learning & Education, 7*(1), 130–131.

Azevedo, R. (2005). Using hypermedia as a metacognitive tool for enhancing student learning? The role of self-regulated learning. *Educational Psychologist, 40*(4), 199–209. doi:10.1207/s15326985ep4004_2

Banta, T., Black, K., & Kline, K. (2000). PBL 2000 plenary address offers evidence for and against problem-based learning. *PBL Insight, 5*(3), 1–7.

Barrows, H. S. (2000). *Problem-Based learning applied to medical education.* Springfield, IL: Southern Illinois University Press.

Barrows, H. S., & Tamblyn, R. M. (1980). *Problem-based learning: An approach to medical education.* New York: Springer.

Billings, D. M. (2000). A framework for assessing outcomes and practices in web-based courses in nursing. *The Journal of Nursing Education, 39*(2), 60–67.

Bisaso, R., Kereteletswe, O., Selwood, I., & Visscher, A. (2008). The use of information technology for educational management in Uganda and Botswana. *International Journal of Educational Development, 28*(6), 656–668. doi:10.1016/j.ijedudev.2007.09.008

Bottge, B. A., Rueda, E., Kwon, J. M., Grant, T., & LaRoque, P. (2009). Assessing and tracking students' problem solving performances in anchored learning environments. *Educational Technology Research and Development, 54*(4), 529–552. doi:10.1007/s11423-007-9069-y

Bruce, B. C., Dowd, H., Eastburn, D. M., & D'arcy, C. J. (2005). Plants, pathogens, and people: Extending the classroom to the web. *Teachers College Record, 107*(8), 1730–1753. doi:10.1111/j.1467-9620.2005.00540.x

Buckley, K. M. (2003). Evaluation of classroom-based, web-enhanced, and web-based distance learning nutrition courses for undergraduate nursing. *The Journal of Nursing Education, 42*(8), 367–370.

Budé, L., Imbos, T., Wiel, M. W. J. V. D., Broers, N. J., & Berger, M. P. F. (2009). The effect of directive tutor guidance in problem-based learning of statistics on students' perceptions and achievement. *Higher Education, 57*(1), 23–36. doi:10.1007/s10734-008-9130-8

Burgos, D., Tattersall, C., & Koper, R. (2007). How to represent adaptation in e-learning with IMS learning design. *Interactive Learning Environments, 15*(2), 161–170. doi:10.1080/10494820701343736

Cennamo, K. S., Ross, J. D., & Rogers, C. S. (2002). Evolution of a web-enhanced course: Incorporating strategies for self-regulation. *EDUCAUSE Quarterly, 25*(1), 28–33.

Chanlin, L. J., & Chan, K. C. (2004). Assessment of PBL design approach in a dietetic web-based instruction. *Journal of Educational Computing Research, 31*(4), 437–452. doi:10.2190/UF9Y-92YM-9TUV-RJ78

Charlin, B., Mann, K., & Hansen, P. (1998). The many faces of problem-based learning: A framework for understanding and comparison. *Medical Teacher, 20*(4), 323–330. doi:10.1080/01421599880742

Dabbagh, N., & Kitsantas, K. (2005). Using web-based pedagogical tools as scaffolds for self-regulated learning. *Instructional Science, 33*(5-6), 513–540. doi:10.1007/s11251-005-1278-3

DeBoer, J. (2009). The relationship between environmental factors and usage behaviors at 'Hole-in-the-wall' computers. *International Journal of Educational Development, 29*(1), 91–98. doi:10.1016/j.ijedudev.2008.02.005

Dunlap, J. C. (2005). Problem-based learning and self-efficacy: How a capstone course prepares students for a profession. *Educational Technology Research and Development, 53*(1), 65–83. doi:10.1007/BF02504858

Girma, D. (2002). Teaching assistant portal in an engineering education: experiences with web-mediated teaching at the University of Strathclyde. In *Proceedings of the 2002 ASEE/SEFI/TUB Colloquium*. Retrieved May 11, 2010, from http://www.asee.org/conferences/international/papers/upload/Teaching-Assistant-Portal-in-Engineering-Education.pdf

Glasgow, N. (1997). *New curriculum for new times: A guide to student-centered, problem-based learning*. Thousand Oaks, CA: Corwin.

Greene, J. A., & Azevedo, R. (2007). Adolescents' use of self-regulatory processes and their relation to qualitative mental model shifts while using hypermedia. *Journal of Educational Computing Research, 36*(2), 125–148. doi:10.2190/G7M1-2734-3JRR-8033

Greene, J. A., Moos, D. C., Azevedo, R., & Winters, F. I. (2008). Exploring differences between gifted and grade-level students' use of self-regulatory learning processes with hypermedia. *Computers & Education, 50*(3), 1069–1083. doi:10.1016/j.compedu.2006.10.004

Gribbons, B., & Herman, J. (1997). True and quasi-experimental designs. *Practical Assessment, Research & Evaluation, 5*(14). Retrieved May 11, 2010, from http://PAREonline.net/getvn.asp?v=5&n=14

Hmelo-Silver, C. E. (2004). Problem-based learning: What and how do students learn? *Educational Psychology Review, 16*(3), 235–266. doi:10.1023/B:EDPR.0000034022.16470.f3

Hong, J. C., Horng, J. S., & Lin, C. L., & Chan-Lin, L. J. (2008). Competency disparity between pre-service teacher education and in-service teaching requirements in Taiwan. *International Journal of Educational Development, 28*(1), 4–20. doi:10.1016/j.ijedudev.2006.12.004

Hsiao, H. C., Chen, M. N., & Yang, H. S. (2008). Leadership of vocational high school principals in curriculum reform: A case study in Taiwan. *International Journal of Educational Development, 28*(6), 669–686. doi:10.1016/j.ijedudev.2007.12.002

Hussain, R. M. R., Mamat, W. H. W., Salleh, N., Saat, R. M., & Harland, T. (2007). Problem-based learning in Asian universities. *Studies in Higher Education, 32*(6), 761–772. doi:10.1080/03075070701685171

Jacobson, M. J. (2005). From non-adaptive to adaptive educational hypermedia: Theory, research, and design issues. In Chen, S., & Magalas, G. (Eds.), *Advances in Web-based education: Personalized learning environments* (pp. 302–330). Hershey, PA: Idea Group.

Järvelä, S., Näykki, P., Laru, J., & Luokkanen, T. (2007). Structuring and regulating collaborative learning in higher education with wireless networks and mobile tools. *Journal of Educational Technology & Society, 10*(4), 71–79.

Johnson, M., & Liber, O. (2008). The personal learning environment and the human condition: from theory to teaching practice. *Interactive Learning Environments, 16*(1), 3–15. doi:10.1080/10494820701772652

Kanuka, H., Jugdev, K., Heller, R., & West, D. (2008). The rise of the teleworker: false promises and responsive solutions. *Higher Education, 56*(2), 149–165. doi:10.1007/s10734-007-9095-z

Kenny, R. F., Bullen, M., & Loftus, J. (2006). Problem formulation and resolution in online problem-based learning. *International Review of Research in Open and Distance Learning, 7*(3). Retrieved May 11, 2010, from, http://www.irrodl.org/index.php/irrodl/article/view/248/751

Kogo, C., & Nojima, E. (2004). Student dropout in e-learning and its symptom. In *Proceedings of the 20th Annual Conference of Japan Society for Educational Technology* (pp. 997-998).

Kramarski, B., & Gutman, M. (2006). How can self-regulated learning be supported in mathematical E-learning environments? *Journal of Computer Assisted Learning, 22*(1), 24–33. doi:10.1111/j.1365-2729.2006.00157.x

Lee, J. K., & Lee, W. K. (2008). The relationship of e-Learner's self-regulatory efficacy and perception of e-Learning environmental quality. *Computers in Human Behavior, 24*(1), 32–47. doi:10.1016/j.chb.2006.12.001

Lee, T. H., Shen, P. D., & Tsai, C. W. (2008). Applying web-enabled problem-based learning and self-regulated learning to add value to computing education in Taiwan's vocational schools. *Journal of Educational Technology & Society, 11*(3), 13–25.

Loyens, S. M. M., Magda, J., & Rikers, R. M. J. P. (2008). Self-directed learning in problem-based learning and its relationships with self-regulated learning. *Educational Psychology Review, 20*(4), 411–427. doi:10.1007/s10648-008-9082-7

Montalvo, F., & Torres, R. (2004). Self-regulated learning: Current and future directions. *Electronic Journal of Research in Educational Psychology, 2*(1), 1–34.

Oliver, R. (2008). Engaging first year students using a Web-supported inquiry-based learning setting. *Higher Education, 55*(3), 285–301. doi:10.1007/s10734-007-9055-7

Ong, C. S., & Lai, J. Y. (2006). Gender differences in perceptions and relationships among dominants of e-learning acceptance. *Computers in Human Behavior, 22*(1), 816–829. doi:10.1016/j.chb.2004.03.006

Paas, F., Tuovinen, J. E., van Merrienboer, J. J. G., & Darabi, A. A. (2005). A motivational perspective on the relation between mental effort and performance: Optimizing learner involvement in instruction. *Educational Technology Research and Development, 53*(3), 25–34. doi:10.1007/BF02504795

Palmer, R. (2009). Skills development, employment and sustained growth in Ghana: Sustainability challenges. *International Journal of Educational Development, 29*(2), 133–139. doi:10.1016/j.ijedudev.2008.09.007

Paris, S. G., & Paris, A. H. (2001). Classroom applications of research in self-regulated learning. *Educational Psychologist, 36*(2), 89–101. doi:10.1207/S15326985EP3602_4

Perels, F., Gürtler, T., & Schmitz, B. (2005). Training of self-regulatory and problem-solving competence. *Learning and Instruction, 15*(2), 123–139. doi:10.1016/j.learninstruc.2005.04.010

Polanco, R., Calderón, P., & Delgado, F. (2004). Effects of a problem-based learning program on engineering students' academic achievements in a Mexican university. *Innovations in Education and Teaching International, 41*(2), 145–155. doi:10.1080/1470329042000208675

Renn, K. A., & Zeligman, D. M. (2005). Learning about Technology and Student Affairs: Outcomes of an Online Immersion. *Journal of College Student Development, 46*(5), 547–555. doi:10.1353/csd.2005.0055

Reyero, M., & Tourón, J. (2003). *El desarrollo del talento: la aceleración como estrategia educativa* [*The Development of Talent: Acceleration as An Educational Strategy*]. Coruña, Spain: Netbiblo.

Risemberg, R., & Zimmerman, B. J. (1992). Self-regulated learning in gifted students. *Roeper Review, 15*(2), 98–101. doi:10.1080/02783199209553476

Sablonnière, R. D. L., Taylor, D. M., & Sadykova, N. (2009). Challenges of applying a student-centered approach to learning in the context of education in Kyrgyzstan. *International Journal of Educational Development, 29*(6), 628–634. doi:10.1016/j.ijedudev.2009.01.001

Schmidt, H. G. (1983). Problem-based learning: Rationale and description. *Medical Education, 17*(1), 11–16. doi:10.1111/j.1365-2923.1983.tb01086.x

Schunk, D. H. (1989). Social cognitive theory and self-regulated learning. In Zimmerman, B. J., & Schunk, D. H. (Eds.), *Self-regulated learning and academic achievement: Theory, research, and practice* (pp. 83–110). New York: Springer-Verlag.

Shen, P. D., Lee, T. H., & Tsai, C. W. (2007). Applying web-enabled problem-based learning and self-regulated learning to enhance computing skills of Taiwan's vocational students: a quasi-experimental study of a short-term module. *Electronic Journal of e-Learning, 5*(2), 147-156.

Shen, P. D., Lee, T. H., & Tsai, C. W. (2008). Enhancing skills of application software via web-enabled problem-based learning and self-regulated learning: An exploratory study. *International Journal of Distance Education Technologies, 6*(3), 69–84.

Shen, P. D., Lee, T. H., Tsai, C. W., & Ting, C. J. (2008). Exploring the effects of web-enabled problem-based learning and self-regulated learning on vocational students' involvement in learning. *European Journal of Open, Distance and E-Learning*. Retrieved May 11, 2010, from, http://www.eurodl.org/materials/contrib/2008/Shen_Lee_Tsai_Ting.htm

Sungur, S., & Tekkaya, C. (2006). Effects of problem-based learning and traditional instruction on self-regulated learning. *The Journal of Educational Research, 99*(5), 307–320. doi:10.3200/JOER.99.5.307-320

Tai, C. F., Chen, R. J., & Lai, J. L. (2003). How technological and vocational education can prosper in the 21st century? *IEEE Circuits & Devices Magazine, 19*(2), 15–51. doi:10.1109/MCD.2003.1191433

Torp, L., & Sage, S. (2002). *Problems as possibilities: Problem-based learning for K–12 education* (2nd ed.). Alexandria, VA: ASCD.

Tsai, C. W., & Shen, P. D. (2009). Applying web-enabled self-regulated learning and problem-based learning with initiation to involve low-achieving students in learning. *Computers in Human Behavior, 25*(6), 1189–1194. doi:10.1016/j.chb.2009.05.013

Winne, P. H. (2001). Self-regulated learning viewed from models of information processing. In Zimmerman, B. J., & Schunk, D. H. (Eds.), *Self-Regulated Learning and Academic Achievement: Theoretical Perspectives* (pp. 153–189). Mahwah, NJ: Erlbaum.

Winne, P. H., & Hadwin, A. (1998). Studying as self-regulated learning. In Hacker, D. J., Dunlosky, J., & Graesser, A. (Eds.), *Metacognition in Educational Theory and Practice* (pp. 277–304). Hillsdale, NJ: Erlbaum.

Winnips, K. (2000). *Scaffolding-by-Design: A Model for WWW-based Learner Support*. Enschede, The Netherlands: University of Twente Press.

Wu, C. C. (2009). Higher education expansion and low-income students in Taiwan. *International Journal of Educational Development, 29*(4), 399–405. doi:10.1016/j.ijedudev.2009.01.006

Yukselturk, E., & Bulut, S. (2007). Predictors for student success in an online course. *Journal of Educational Technology & Society, 10*(2), 71–83.

Zimmerman, B. J. (1998). Developing self-regulation cycles of academic regulation: An analysis of exemplary instructional model. In Schunk, D. H., & Zimmerman, B. J. (Eds.), *Self-regulated learning: From teaching to self-reflective practice* (pp. 1–19). New York: Guilford.

Zimmerman, B. J., Bonner, S., & Kovach, R. (1996). *Developing self-regulated learners: Beyond achievement to self-efficacy*. Washington, DC: American Psychological Association. doi:10.1037/10213-000

Zimmerman, B. J., & Schunk, D. H. (2001). *Self-Regulated learning and academic achievement: Theoretical perspectives*. Mahwah, NJ: Erlbaum.

This work was previously published in the International Journal of Technology and Human Interaction, Volume 7, Issue 1, edited by Anabela Mesquita and Chia-Wen Tsai, pp. 67-81, copyright 2011 by IGI Publishing (an imprint of IGI Global).

Chapter 18

Factors Enhancing Employed Job Seekers Intentions to Use Social Networking Sites as a Job Search Tool

Norazah Mohd Suki
Universiti Malaysia Sabah, Malaysia

Michelle Kow Pei Ming
Universiti Sains Malaysia, Malaysia

T. Ramayah
Universiti Sains Malaysia, Malaysia

Norbayah Mohd Suki
Universiti Malaysia Sabah, Malaysia

ABSTRACT

This paper explores the factors of enhancing employed job seekers intention to use social networking sites as a job search tool. 190 survey questionnaires were distributed to employed job seekers who have used social networking sites via the snowball sampling approach. The collected data were analysed using both linear and multiple regression analysis. The results showed that perceived usefulness and perceived enjoyment are positively and significantly related to the behavioural intention to use social networking sites as a job search tool, whereas perceived ease of use is not positively and significantly related. The study implies that the developers of social networking sites need to provide additional useful functionalities or tools in the social networking sites to help users of social networking sites with their job search. The paper provides an insight for employed jobseekers to find employment by using social networking sites as a job search tool.

INTRODUCTION

Social networking sites are a type of virtual community (Murray & Waller, 2007). Virtual community consists of a group of people who communicates via electronic means such as the Internet. They share interest without physical contact or the need to be in the same place or belong to the same ethnic group (Kardaras, Karakostas, & Papathanassiou, 2003). Users of social networking sites will create their own profile with their personal information and will usually add their friends, friends of friends or new friends. Social networking sites are usually used to keep in touch with friends and families by posting their updates, photos, blogs, and chatting,

DOI: 10.4018/978-1-4666-1954-8.ch018

apart from enjoyment and relaxation. There are many consumer-networking sites available such as Facebook, MySpace, Friendster, Hi5, Bebo and Multiply. Facebook claims that it has 200 million active users who have returned to the site in the last 30 days (as of April 2009) (Facebook, 2009). According to Warr, 2008, as of March 2008, Facebook claimed that there were 66 million active users. Within a year, from 2008 to 2009, Facebook's active users increased by 134 million.

A study was conducted on passive job seekers (employed job seekers) adoption of e-recruitment technology in Malaysia by Tong (2009). The passive candidates are of higher quality when compared to the active candidates (Tong, 2009). For this empirical study, the questionnaire was distributed to employed job seekers with experience in using third parties' e-recruitment web sites. The author conducted a mini survey among the industries in Malaysia and India to understand how companies use social media technologies for sourcing of passive candidates. Out of the nine respondent companies in Malaysia and India, only one company uses social networking sites for recruitment. The social networking sites used for sourcing of candidates are LinkedIn and Facebook. The author's employer uses LinkedIn to source for candidates in the US (Kow, 2009). The author's employer with headquarters located in the U.S. had successfully hired some key positions via LinkedIn, which attracted a sizable pool of applicants. From the research conducted, the author recommended to the HR management team that LinkedIn and Facebook should be used as one of the sourcing methods. The recruiters of the author's company with plants and offices in Asia (Thailand, Singapore, China, and Malaysia), US and Europe have been using Facebook and LinkedIn to source for candidates since November 2008. However, the author did not conduct a research on the Employed Job Seekers' acceptance of the social networking sites as a Job Search tool. This research will cover this gap since the author will obtain the employed job seekers' view, on their intentions to use of social networking sites as a job search tool. Since most of the researches were conducted on the third party e-recruitment web sites and corporate career web sites, the author seeks to examine this alternative recruitment source that is social networking sites.

LITERATURE REVIEW

Conceptual Model and Hypotheses

The Technology Acceptance Model is a highly validated model and was tested by many researchers in their study (Figure 1). This research also bases its model on the extended TAM model by Tong (2009) but introduces an intrinsic motivation variable which is perceived enjoyment (Figure 2).

Perceived Ease of Use (PEOU)

Perceived ease of use is defined as "the degree to which a person believes that using a particular system would be free from effort" (Davis, 1989). All else being equal, an application perceived to be easier to use is more likely to be accepted by the users (Davis, 1989). In majority of the research conducted using the TAM model, perceived ease of use was found to have positively influenced the behavioural intention to use a system (Fagan, Wooldridge, & Neill, 2008; Guriting & Ndubisi, 2006; Hsu, Wang, & Chiu, 2009; Huang, 2008; Ramayah, Chin, Norazah, & Amlus, 2005). However, it is also found in other research that perceived ease of use is found to have not directly influenced the behavioural intention to use a system (Ruiz-Mafé', Sanz-Blas, & Aldas-Manzano, 2009). Generally, when a system is found to be easy to use, users will have the intention to use the system. In this research, the author will examine the relationship between perceived ease of use and the behavioural intention to use online social networking sites as a job search tool. The first hypothesis is therefore constructed as follows:

Figure 1. Technology Acceptance Model (TAM)

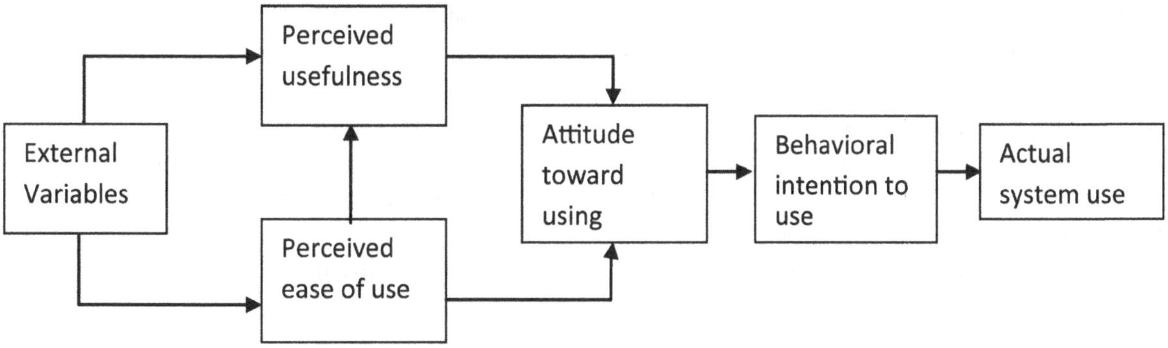

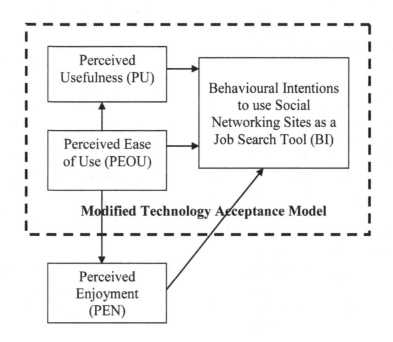

H1: There is a positive influence of perceived ease of use on the behavioural intention to use online social networking sites for job search.

Perceived ease of use has also been found to influence behavioural intention to use indirectly through perceived usefulness (Davis, 1989; Ha & Stoel, 2009; Norazah, Ramayah & Norbayah, 2008; Oh, Ahn, & Kim, 2003; Ruiz-Mafe´ et al., 2009). According to Venkatesh and Davis (2000), the less effort a system is to use, the more using

it can increase job performance. This means that when a system is easy to use, users will perceive that the system is more useful. Systems that are difficult to use are less likely to be perceived as useful and thus lead to decreased usage. In general, if a system is easy to use, less effort is required by the users, therefore increasing the likelihood of usage.

Particularly in e-recruitment, Tong (2009) discovered that perceived ease of use is not positively related to perceive usefulness in e-recruitment

Figure 2. Proposed research framework

adoption. This indicates that even though the system is easy to use, it is not necessary that it is perceived as useful by the users. However, in this research, the author would like to re-examine the relationship between perceived ease of use and perceived usefulness. Thus it is hypothesized that:

H2: There is a positive influence of perceived ease of use on perceived usefulness of online social networking sites for job search.

Perceived Usefulness (PU)

Perceived usefulness is defined as "the degree to which a person believes that using a particular system would enhance his or her job performance" (Davis, 1989). Within the organisational context, a system that is high in perceived usefulness is one that the user believes will have a positive use-performance relationship. Previous researches have shown that perceived usefulness influences computer usage directly. In general, when the users found that the system is useful for them, then they will have the intention to use it and lead to the actual usage of the system. Based on previous research using the TAM model, it is found that perceived usefulness is the primary antecedent that determines the behavioural intention to use a computer system (Davis, 1989; Venkatesh & Davis, 2000).

Perceived usefulness was found to have positively influenced the behavioural intention to use a computer system (Fagan et al., 2008; Guriting & Ndubisi, 2006; Ha & Stoel, 2009; Hsu et al., 2009; Huang, 2008; Norazah et al., 2008; Ruiz-Mafe´ et al., 2009; Seyal & Rahman, 2007; Tong, 2009). However, in some other research conducted based on the TAM model in a mandated environment. Instead, it is found that perceived usefulness does not directly influence the behavioural intention to use a computer system (Brown, Massey, Montoya-Weiss, & Burkman, 2002). In e-recruitment context, Tong (2009) discovered that perceived usefulness is positively related to behavioural

intention to use e-recruitment for job search. In this research, the author seeks to re-examine this relationship. The third hypothesis therefore states:

H3: There is a positive influence of perceived usefulness on the behavioural intention to use online social networking sites for job search.

Perceived Enjoyment (PENJOY)

Perceived enjoyment is a type of intrinsic psychological motivation (Davis, Bagozzi, & Warshaw, 1989). Perceived enjoyment is defined as "the extent to which the activity of using the computer is perceived to be enjoyable in its own right, apart from any performance consequences that may be anticipated" (Davis, Bagozzi, & Warshaw, 1992). Social networking site is a new method for people to socialise with one another. Through this method, people will feel that they are having fun while enjoying the rich features provided in the social networking sites. When they perceive these social networking sites as enjoyable, they will use it more frequently and spend more time on it (Rouibah, 2008). Perceived enjoyment was found to be positively influenced by behavioural intention to use a computer system (Davis et al., 1992; Lee, Cheung, & Chen, 2007; Teo, Lim, & Lai, 1999). According to Van der Heijden (2004) "for hedonic systems, perceived enjoyment (a dimension of perceived playfulness) is a stronger predictor of behavioural intention to use than is perceived usefulness." However, there are other researches suggesting that perceived enjoyment does not positively influenced the behavioural intention to use a computer system (Fagan et al., 2008; Shin & Kim, 2008; Venkatesh, Speier, & Morris, 2002). The fourth hypothesis is thus created:

H4: There is a positive influence of perceived enjoyment on the behavioural intention to use online social networking sites for job search.

Perceived enjoyment was found to be related to perceived ease of use. Some studies have shown that the perceived enjoyment influence the perceived ease of use of a computer system or application (Fagan et al., 2008; Kim, Oh & Park, 2008; Yi & Hwang, 2003) whereas some studies have shown that the perceived ease of use influenced the perceive enjoyment of the computer system or application (Igbaria, Parasuraman, & Baroudi, 1996; Liao, Tsou, & Huang, 2007; Rouibah, 2008). Common sense predicts that when a computer system or technology is perceived to be easy to use, it will lead to perceived enjoyment. However, this may not always be true. For example, for the case of wired voice telephony, it is very easy to use, however it is not perceived as enjoyable as compared to short message service (SMS), where Korean users find it very enjoyable to send short messages to friends (Kim et al., 2008).

For this research, the relationship used is the perceived ease of use influences the perceived enjoyment of social networking sites. This relationship is chosen because when users perceive that the online social networking sites are easy to use and user friendly, they will then be able to enjoy using the social networking sites. If the online social networking sites are found to be not user friendly or difficult to use then the users will not enjoy using the social networking sites. The next hypothesis states therefore:

H5: There is a positive influence of perceived ease of use on perceived enjoyment of online social networking sites.

Behavioral Intention (BI)

According to Warshaw and Davis (1985), behavioural intention is defined as "the degree to which a person has formulated conscious plans to perform or not to perform some specified future behaviour". This is in line with the Theory of Reasoned Action (Fishbein & Ajzen, 1975) and its successor the Theory of Planned Behaviour (Ajzen, 1985), where it is stated that behavioural intention is a strong predictor of actual behaviour. Intention is defined as "the cognitive representation of a person's readiness to perform a given behaviour, and it is considered to be the immediate antecedent of behaviour" in Theory of Planned Behaviour (Ajzen, 1991).

Studies on intention to use a computer system is mostly for the new technologies and studies on the actual usage is usually conducted on the computer systems that have already been used for long (Ramayah & Ignatius, 2005). Since online social networking sites as a job search tool is a new technology, this study investigates the factors that influence the behavioural intention to use the online social networking sites as a job search tool.

Methodology

190 survey questionnaires were distributed to employed job seekers who have used social networking sites via the snowball sampling approach. This sampling method is useful when researchers are trying to reach populations that are inaccessible or hard to find (Trochim, 2005). The collected data were analysed using both multiple regression analysis and linear regression analysis via the Statistical Packages for Social Sciences (SPSS version 16 for Windows computer program) with the aims to study on the relationships between the external variables on independent variables and the dependent variable. The questionnaire comprises three sections with fifty-six questions in total (socio-demographic and economic profile of the respondents, characteristics of social networking sites users, and the variables used in the study. Summary of variables, operation definition and measurement sources are presented in Table 1.

Table 1. Summary of variables, operation definition and measurement sources

Variable	Operation Definition	Measurement Sources
Behavioural Intention to Use	The cognitive representation of a person's readiness to perform a given behaviour, and it is considered to be the immediate antecedent of behaviour.	Warshaw & Davis (1985)
Perceived Enjoyment	Perceived enjoyment is a type of intrinsic psychological motivation.	Davis et al. (1989)
Perceived Ease of Use	The degree to which a person believes that using a particular system would be free of effort.	Davis et al. (1989)
Perceived Usefulness	The degree to which a person believes that using a particular system would enhance his or her job performance.	Davis (1989)

RESULTS

Profile of Respondents

A total of two hundred and fifty questionnaires were distributed to employed job seekers in Malaysia. Over a period of three weeks, only 210 respondents responded. However, 20 of the respondents indicated that they do not use social networking sites. Therefore, only 190 data samples are used for this study with 82.6% response rate. Table 2 describes personal profile of the respondents. There were 64.7% female respondents and 35.3% were male respondents. The average ages of the respondents were 31 years old with the youngest respondent aged 22 years old and oldest respondent aged 49 years old. As for the ethnic distribution, 117 respondents were Chinese (61.6%). Majority of the respondents hold a Bachelors Degree (66.3%) as the highest level of education, earns an annual income of RM30,000 to RM60,000.

The nature of the current job of the respondents varies as they come from different business functions. The majority of the respondents' nature of the current job are from Information Technology (19.5%), followed by Human Resource (14.2%). The majority of the respondents access the Internet from their home and private room (88.4%) followed by accessing the Internet from the office (47.9%), Internet cafes (8.4%), others (3.2%) and libraries/community centres (2.1%).

The average number of years of working experience in the current company for the respondents is 3.98 years, with the least working experience at 0.08 years and the most at 19.17 years. The average number of years of overall working experience for the respondents is 7.96 years, with the least overall working experience at 0.08 years and the most at 30 years. The average number of years using social networking sites by the respondents is 3.09 years, with the least number of years using social networking sites at 0.08 years and the most at 11 years. The average number of years using the Internet by the respondents is 10.55 years, with the least number of years using the Internet at 1 year and the most at 24 years.

As stated in Table 3, Facebook is the most popular social networking sites (91.6%), followed by Friendster (52.1%), LinkedIn (15.3%), MySpace (7.9%) and others (6.3%). Out of one hundred and ninety respondents, thirty five respondents (18.4%) used Social Networking Sites for Job Search. The rest of the respondents have not used social networking sites for job search. This result shows that using social networking sites as a job search tool is not a common trend in Malaysia. Many users of the social networking sites do not use these social networking sites as a job search tool yet. Over the past one month, the majority of the respondents used social networking sites a few times a week (25.8%). They spent 10 to 20 minutes (28.4%) each time using social networking sites.

Table 2. Personal profile of respondents

Variable	Frequency	Percentage (%)
Gender		
Female	123	64.7
Male	67	35.3
Race		
Malay	32	16.8
Indian	37	19.5
Chinese	117	61.6
Others	4	2.1
Marital Status		
Single	108	56.8
Married	77	40.5
Divorced	5	2.6
Education Level		
High School and below	1	.5
Certificate/Diploma	32	16.8
Bachelors Degree	126	66.3
Masters Degree	29	15.3
Others	2	1.1
Annual Income		
RM30K and below	45	23.7
RM30,001 to RM60K	99	52.1
RM60,001 to RM90K	26	13.7
RM90,001 to RM120K	8	4.2
Over RM120K	12	6.3
Job Level		
Top Management	10	5.3
Middle Management	34	17.9
Professional Staff/Leader/Supervisor/Engineer	106	55.8
Support Staff/Non-Executive Staff/Administrative	33	17.4
Others	7	3.7
Nature of Current Job		
Engineering	23	12.1
Production	10	5.3
Information Technology	37	19.5
Finance/Accounting	15	7.9
Sales/Marketing	17	8.9
Human Resource	27	14.2
Education	19	10.0
Consultancy	12	6.3
Customer Service/Administration/Business Support	17	8.9
Others	13	6.8

GOODNESS OF MEASURE

Since each variable was measured by multiple items, factor analysis with varimax rotation was conducted to identify sets of related variables into separate dimensions to achieve summarisation and data reduction. The results show that the Bartlett's test of Sphericity is significant where p-value is less than 0.05 with Kaiser-Meyer-Olking (KMO) measure of sampling adequacy at 0.895, which is above the acceptable level of 0.50. The anti image correlation matrix values of MSA of all items are above 0.50. The cumulative total variance explained is 81.24. The rotated component matrix was reviewed to assign uniquely one variable to only one factor. Table 4 shows that most items are

Table 3. Social networking sites usage

Variable	Frequency	Percentage (%)
Access Internet		
Home/Private Room	168	88.4
Office	91	47.9
Internet Cafe	16	8.4
Libraries/Community Centres	4	2.1
Others	6	3.2
Used Social Networking Sites		
Facebook	174	91.6
Friendster	99	52.1
LinkedIn	29	15.3
MySpace	15	7.9
Others	12	6.3
Used Social Networking Sites for Job Search		
Yes	35	18.4
No	155	81.6
Frequency using social networking sites over the past one month		
Less than once a week	29	15.3
Once a week	27	14.2
2 or 3 times a week	27	14.2
A few times a week	49	25.8
About once a day	33	17.4
Several times a day	25	13.2
Time spend each time using social networking sites over the past one month		
Less than 10 minutes	27	14.2
10 - 20 minutes	54	28.4
20 - 30 minutes	28	14.7
30 minutes - 1 hr	35	18.4
1 - 1.5 hrs	14	7.4
1.5 - 2 hrs	19	10.0
2 hrs or more	13	6.8

loaded properly on the expected factors with three factors extracted. Factor 1 defines the perceived usefulness, factor 2 consists of items measuring perceived ease of use, and factor 3 measures the items for perceived enjoyment.

Reliability Analysis

In order to test the internal consistency of the items in the survey instrument, reliability analysis was conducted on all variables before forming composite index of each variable. According to Nunnally and Bernstein (1994) and Hair et al. (2005), the minimum acceptable value of Cronbach's Alpha is between 0.60 to 0.70. Table 5 lists the summary of reliability analysis. The Cronbach's Alpha values for all the external variables, independent variables

and the dependent variable range from 0.84 to 0.97 which is within the acceptable limit. None of the items was dropped from the reliability analysis.

Correlations Analysis

Correlation analysis was conducted on the external variables, independent variables and the dependent variable. According to Sekaran (2000), although correlation analysis does not prove causation, it can be a predictor of causation. The intercorrelation analysis adopted the level of p value criteria of less than 0.01 and 0.05. The correlation analysis and descriptive statistics of the variables results are shown in Table 6.

It was found that perceived ease of use correlates with behavioural intention at $r=0.12$,

Table 4. Results of factor analysis for perceived usefulness, perceived ease of use, perceived enjoyment

	Factor			Communalities
	1	**2**	**3**	
PU1: Using social networking sites enabled me to look for job quickly	.909			.842
PU2: Using social networking sites improved my job searches	.949			.905
PU3: Using social networking sites to look for job was very effective	.940			.893
PU4: Using social networking sites made it easier for me to look for jobs	.968			.940
PU5: Overall, social networking sites were useful for me for job searching.	.946			.898
PEOU1: Learning to use social networking sites was easy for me		.873		.803
PEOU2: I found it easy to do what I want to do in social networking sites		.869		.817
PEOU3: My interaction with social networking sites was clear and understandable		.823		.740
PEOU4: It was easy for me to become skillful at using a social networking sites		.810		.734
PEOU5: Overall, I found social networking sites easy to use		.854		.823
PENJOY1: Using social networking sites is fun			.833	.746
PENJOY2: Using social networking sites is pleasant			.856	.808
PENJOY3: Using social networking sites is positive			.792	.663
PENJOY4: Using social networking sites is exciting			.863	.812
PENJOY5: Overall, I enjoyed using social networking sites			.818	.764
Eigenvalue	4.49	3.91	3.79	
Percentage Variance (81.24)	29.92	26.04	25.29	

$p<0.05$. This indicates that the variables would explain the variance in one another to the extent of 3.61% (0.12^2). This shows that although the social networking sites may be easy to use, it does not necessarily lead to the behavioural intention to use it as a job search tool. Perceived enjoyment correlates with behavioural intention at $r=0.19$, $p<0.01$. This indicates that the variables would explain the variance in one another to the extent of 1.44% (0.19^2). This shows that although the social networking sites may be enjoyable, it does not necessarily lead to the behavioural intention to use it as a job search tool.

Hypotheses Testing

Multiple regression analysis is employed to test the hypotheses. It is applied to analyse the relationship between a single dependent variable and several independent variables (Hair et al., 2005). Multiple regression analysis is therefore selected as it is viewed as an appropriate method for this study. The summary of result analysis is shown

Table 5. Summary of reliability analysis

Variable	Number of items	Items dropped	Cronbach Alpha
Perceived Ease of Use	5	-	0.93
Perceived Usefulness	5	-	0.97
Perceived Enjoyment	5	-	0.92
Behavioural Intention to use	4	-	0.90

Table 6. Correlation analysis among variables

Variables	Perceived Ease of Use	Perceived Usefulness	Perceived Enjoyment	Behavioural Intention
Perceived Ease of Use	1.00			
Perceived Usefulness	0.13*	1.00		
Perceived Enjoyment	0.54**	0.13*	1.00	
Behavioural Intention	0.12*	0.58**	0.19**	1.00
Mean	3.83	2.55	3.88	2.69
Standard Deviation	0.72	0.90	0.66	0.96

** $p < 0.01$, * $p < 0.05$

in Table 7 where it can be observed that the R^2 value of 0.35 suggests that 35% of the variance in behavioural intention to use social networking sites as a job search tool is explained by the independent variables (perceived usefulness, perceived ease of use and perceived enjoyment). The Durbin Watson value is within the range of 1.50 to 2.50, thus representing no serious autocorrelation problem. The standardised beta value of 0.56 ($p < 0.10$) for perceived usefulness and 0.13 ($p < 0.10$) for perceived enjoyment suggests that perceived usefulness and perceived enjoyment directly influence behavioural intention to use social networking sites as a job search tool, whereas perceived ease of use does not significantly influence behavioural intention to use social networking sites as a job search tool. Thus, H1 is not supported and H3 and H4 are supported.

In Table 8, R^2 value of 0.27 suggests that 27% of the variance in perceived enjoyment of social networking sites is explained by perceived ease of use. The low value of R^2 indicates that the variance in perceived enjoyment is not highly explained by perceived ease of use. This indicates that there are other factors that can join with perceived ease of use to influence the perceived enjoyment of social networking sites. The Durbin Watson value is within the range of 1.50 to 2.50 thus representing no serious autocorrelation prob-

lem. The standardized beta value of 0.52 ($p < 0.01$) suggests that perceived ease of use directly and significantly influences perceived enjoyment of social networking sites. Therefore, H5 is supported.

It can be seen in Table 9 that the R^2 value of 0.04 suggests that 4% of the variance in perceived usefulness of social networking sites is explained by perceived ease of use. The low value of R^2 indicates that the variance in perceived usefulness is not highly explained by perceived ease of use. This indicates that there are other factors that can join with the perceived ease of use to influence the perceived usefulness of social networking sites. The Durbin Watson value is within the range of 1.50 to 2.50 thus representing no serious autocorrelation problem. The standardised beta value of 0.20 ($p < 0.05$) suggests that perceived ease of use directly and significantly influences perceived usefulness of social networking sites as a job search tool. Hence, H2 is supported.

DISCUSSIONS AND IMPLICATIONS

Results confirmed that perceived ease of use is not positively and not significantly related to the behavioural intention to use social networking sites as a job search tool. Thus, the hypotheses

Table 7. Results of multiple regressions: PU, PEOU, PENJOY on BI

	Dependent variable Behavioural intention
Independent variables	
Perceived usefulness	0.56***
Perceived ease of use	-0.02
Perceived enjoyment	0.13*
F value	32.94***
R²	0.35
Adjusted R²	0.34
Durbin Watson	1.83

*** p<0.01, ** p<0.05, * p<0.10

Table 8. Results of Linear Regression: PEOU on PENJOY

	Dependent variable Perceived enjoyment
Independent variable	
Perceived ease of use	0.52***
F value	69.89***
R²	0.27
Adjusted R²	0.27
Durbin Watson	1.89

*** p<0.01, ** p<0.05, * p<0.10

of perceived ease of use positively influences the behavioural intention to use social networking sites as a job search tool is rejected. This finding is consistent with the findings of other studies where perceived ease of use is not positively related to the behavioural intention to use a computer system or application (Ramayah & Bushra, 2004; Ruiz-Mafe' et al., 2009). In most of the research conducted based on TAM in Malaysia, perceived ease of use was found to be directly related to perceived usefulness but not so much of the direct influence of perceived ease of use on behavioural intention to use or actual usage. This finding is not consistent with majority of the research conducted using the TAM model, where perceived ease of use was found to have positively influenced the behavioural intention to use a system (Fagan et al., 2008; Guriting & Ndubisi, 2006; Hsu et al., 2009; Huang, 2008; Ramayah et al., 2005; Wang, Wang, Lin, & Tang, 2003).

From the findings of other research conducted based on the TAM model, it is found that users who have familiarised with the computer system and have used it for long time, their perceived ease of use of the computer system has a lower effect on behavioural intention to use the computer system (Venkatesh, Morris, Davis, & Davis, 2003). The average number of years of using the social networking sites by the respondents in this

research is about three years. They are familiar in using the social networking sites since they have used it averagely for three years. From the finding, it shows that they do not have the intention to use the social networking sites as a job search tool. Only 18.4% of the respondents used social networking sites as a job search tool. The majority of the respondents used the social networking sites to connect with friends, relatives, and business contacts. Therefore, this finding shows that if an application is easy to use, it may not necessarily lead to the intention to use the application. Although the social networking sites are easy to use and user friendly, this does not influence the users' intention to use social networking sites as a job search tool.

However, this study has also found that perceived ease of use is positively related to perceived usefulness of social networking sites as a job search tool. Thus, the hypotheses of perceived ease of use positively influence the perceived usefulness of social networking sites as a job search tool is accepted. This relationship between perceived ease of use and perceived usefulness has been proven by many studies (Davis, 1989; Ha & Stoel, 2009; Liao et al., 2007; Oh et al., 2003; Ramayah et al., 2005; Ruiz-Mafe' et al., 2009; Seyal & Rahman, 2007; Wang et al., 2003). This finding is not the same as the findings from Tong (2009), where perceived ease of use was found to be not positively related to perceive usefulness in e-recruitment adoption.

Table 9. Results of linear regression: PEOU on PU

	Dependent variable Perceived usefulness
Independent variable Perceived ease of use	0.20**
F value	7.9**
R^2	0.04
Adjusted R^2	0.04
Durbin Watson	1.74

*** $p<0.01$, ** $p<0.05$, * $p<0.10$

This research has proven that perceived ease of use positively influenced perceive usefulness of social networking sites as a job search tool. When the application is perceived to be easy to use and user friendly, it will lead to the users perceiving that the application is useful. Therefore, in the case of social networking sites as a job search tool, users perceive the application to be easy to use and will continue to use the application and eventually find that the application is useful as a job search tool.

In this research, it is found that perceived ease of use is also found to be positively related to perceived enjoyment. Thus the hypotheses of perceived ease of use positively influence the perceived enjoyment of social networking sites is accepted. Other studies which have also found this similar relationship between perceived ease of use and perceived enjoyment (Igbaria et al., 1996; Liao et al., 2007; Rouibah, 2008). Since the social networking sites are found to be easy to use and user friendly, the users found that the social networking sites to be enjoyable, pleasant, fun and positive. If an application or computer system is difficult to use and not user friendly, the users will find difficulty in using it and will not find the application or computer system as enjoyable.

Next, it is found that perceived usefulness is positively related to the behavioural intention to use social networking sites as a job search tool. This is in line with the majority of the researches conducted on the Technology Acceptance Model,

where perceived usefulness is found to be positively related to the behavioural intention to use or actual usage of a computer system or application (Fagan et al., 2008; Guriting & Ndubisi, 2006; Ha & Stoel, 2009; Hsu et al., 2009; Huang, 2008; Ramayah et al., 2005; Ramayah & Bushra, 2004; Seyal & Rahman, 2007; Ruiz-Mafe´ et al., 2009; Tong, 2009; Wang et al., 2003). Hence, the hypotheses of perceived usefulness positively influence the behavioural intention to use social networking sites as a job search tool is accepted.

In the context of social networking sites as a job search tool, this means that the users of social networking sites found that social networking sites are useful as a job search tool. Therefore users of social networking sites can look for job using the social networking sites. They can view the listings of the jobs posted via the social networking sites and apply directly from the social networking sites. They can also contact the recruiters directly via the social networking sites as well as contact their friends who are in their list of connections to enquire regarding the job openings posted in the social networking sites. The users' profiles in the social networking sites can also act as their resume as recruiters can view the information provided and contact them directly. Users of social networking sites can also post their status in the social networking sites to show that they are currently looking for a new job. There are a variety of ways to use social networking sites and these are just some of them. For example in Facebook, there are many applications available which are related to job search. Users can utilise these applications for free.

Employers who intend to use social networking sites as a recruitment tool should design their recruitment strategy in the social networking sites to be easy to use and user friendly. Employers can create their own Facebook page or LinkedIn group. They can post the jobs listing in these pages or have an automated feed of the jobs listing in these pages. The email address or the contact information of the recruiter should be made available so that the users can easily get this information and send in their resumes or contact the recruiter for more information. The links to the company's corporate recruitment application should also be provided so that the user can immediately submit their application into the company's corporate recruitment websites. Users should not need to click many times to get to the page that they need. Using the applications or features provided by the social networking sites, companies can sent invitation to invite potential candidates for a career fair or walk in interview. Users will receive the invitation and be notified with an email notification. Recruiters can also use the chat feature available to chat with the potential candidates and build their networks. In case there are any job vacancies available and suitable for this particular candidate, the recruiter can contact the candidate immediately. Developers of social networking sites should develop the social networking sites to be as user friendly as possible.

Similarly, perceived enjoyment is also positively related to the behavioural intention to use social networking sites as a job search tool. This finding is consistent with the findings of many other studies where perceived enjoyment is positively related to the behavioural intention to use a computer system or application (Liao et al., 2007; Ramayah & Ignatius, 2005; Rouibah, 2008). This finding is not consistent with the other research that found that perceived enjoyment do not positively influenced the behavioural intention to use a computer system (Fagan et al., 2008; Shin & Kim, 2008; Venkatesh et al., 2002). Therefore, the hypotheses of perceived enjoyment positively influence the behavioural intention to use social networking sites as a job search tool is accepted.

Users of social networking sites find social networking sites as fun, enjoyable, pleasant, positive and exciting. Social networking sites are easy to use and they provide many enjoyable features and applications where users can play games, quizzes, hug a friend virtually, write on the friend's wall, send messages, and many more.

These enjoyable features and applications, makes the users addicted to the social networking sites and they will go into the application frequently. 25.8% of the respondents for this research logs in to the social networking sites a few times a week and about 17.4% logs in to the social networking sites about once a day. Whilst in the social networking sites, 28.4% of the respondents spent 10 to 20 minutes and 18.4% of the respondents spent about 30 minutes to 1 hour using the social networking sites. Since the users perceived social networking sites to be enjoyable, they will spend a lot of time using it and eventually find that the social networking sites is useful for job search.

Recruiters who use the social networking sites as a recruitment tool should try to include the element of fun in the recruitment strategy. Recruiters can make the pages or groups in the social networking sites more interesting by adding videos that show the work life balance of the employees, the nice working environment in the company, or employees' video or photo competition. Recruiters can also make the pages or the groups in the social networking sites to be more interactive, where employed job seekers' can post discussions, and have real-time chat.

Limitations

This study was conducted only in Malaysia and does not cover other countries. Therefore, the findings are only applicable in Malaysia and cannot be generalised for the other countries. Furthermore, this study is only conducted on the acceptance of social networking sites as a job search tool and does not include the other new job search tools using social media technologies such as blogs, podcasts, video sharing web sites such as YouTube.com and etc.

The sample size of 190 respondents is relatively small for the population in Malaysia. The majority of the respondents are female (64.7%) and majority from Professional Staff/Leader/Supervisor/Engineer job level (55.8%). There should be more balance in the demographic aspect of the respondents. There is no indication of which states in Malaysia do the respondents come from. Therefore, we are not able to know where most of them come from.

CONCLUSION AND RECOMMENDATION

Having a social networking sites account is a norm for most Internet users. Social networking sites are mostly used for connecting and keeping in touch with friends and families. Social networking sites can also be used as a job search tool. Using social networking sites as a job search tool is still a very new way of looking for jobs and not many people are aware of this. This research was conducted to explore the factors enhancing employed job seekers intention to use social networking sites as a job search tool. The variables studied were Perceived Ease of Use, Perceived Usefulness, and Perceived Enjoyment. The findings from this study indicated that Perceived Usefulness, Perceived Enjoyment had significant effect on the behavioural intention to use social networking sites as a job search tool. Perceived ease of use was found to be not significant and does not influence the behavioural intention to use social networking sites as a job search tool.

From this study, it is found that social networking sites are accepted by employed job seekers' as a job search tool. Therefore, employers can include social networking sites as part of their recruitment strategy especially during the economic meltdown where cost cutting is required as the use of social networking sites are free and require minimal cost as compared to the third parties' e-recruitment web sites such as Jobstreet.com, JobsDB.com, Monster.com and etc.

It is recommended to future researches to conduct a study on the active job seekers such as fresh graduates' and final year students' acceptance of social networking sites as a job search

tool and expand this research to other countries as currently this study is limited to employed job seekers in Malaysia. Other social media technologies such as blogs, podcasts, and video sharing web sites such as YouTube.com should also be studied as they can also be used for recruitment and job search purposes. Future researchers should also increase the sample size and to have a more balanced demographic of the respondents. A longitudinal approach can be taken to study the effect of increased experience in using social networking sites that could influence the intention to use social networking sites as a job search tool.

REFERENCES

Ajzen, I. (1985). From intentions to actions: A theory of planned behaviour. In Kuhl, J., & Beckman, J. (Eds.), *Action-control: From cognition to behavior* (pp. 11–39). Berlin, Germany: Springer-Verlag.

Ajzen, I. (1991). The theory of planned behavior. *Organizational Behavior and Human Decision Processes*, *50*(2), 179–211. doi:10.1016/0749-5978(91)90020-T

Brown, S. A., Massey, A. P., Montoya-Weiss, M. M., & Burkman, J. R. (2002). Do I really have to? User acceptance of mandated technology. *European Journal of Information Systems*, *11*(4), 283–295. doi:10.1057/palgrave.ejis.3000438

Davis, F. D. (1989). Perceived usefulness, perceived ease of use, and user acceptance of information technology. *Management Information Systems Quarterly*, *13*(3), 319–340. doi:10.2307/249008

Davis, F. D., Bagozzi, R. P., & Warshaw, P. R. (1989). User acceptance of computer technology: A comparison of two theoretical models. *Management Science*, *35*(8), 982–1003. doi:10.1287/mnsc.35.8.982

Davis, F. D., Bagozzi, R. P., & Warshaw, P. R. (1992). Extrinsic and intrinsic motivation to use computers in the workplace. *Journal of Applied Social Psychology, 24*(14), 1111–1132. doi:10.1111/j.1559-1816.1992.tb00945.x

Facebook. (2009). *The facebook network.* Retrieved from http://www.facebook.com

Fagan, M. H., Wooldridge, B. R., & Neill, S. (2008). Exploring the intention to use computers: An empirical investigation of the role of intrinsic motivation, extrinsic motivation, and perceived ease of use. *Journal of Computer Information Systems*, 31–37.

Fishbein, M., & Ajzen, I. (1975). *Belief, attitude, intention and behavior: An introduction to theory and research.* Reading, MA: Addison-Wesley.

Guriting, P., & Ndubisi, N. O. (2006). Borneo online banking: Evaluating customer perceptions and behavioural intention. *Management Research News, 29*(12), 6–15. doi:10.1108/01409170610645402

Ha, S., & Stoel, L. (2009). Consumer e-shopping acceptance: Antecedents in a technology acceptance model. *Journal of Business Research, 62*, 565–571. doi:10.1016/j.jbusres.2008.06.016

Hsu, M. K., Wang, S. W., & Chiu, K. K. (2009). Computer attitude, statistics anxiety and self-efficacy on statistical software adoption behavior: An empirical study of online MBA learners. *Computers in Human Behavior, 25*, 412–420. doi:10.1016/j.chb.2008.10.003

Huang, E. (2008). Use and gratification in e-consumers. *Internet Research, 18*(4), 405–426. doi:10.1108/10662240810897817

Igbaria, M., Parasuraman, S., & Baroudi, J. (1996). A motivational model of microcomputer usage. *Journal of Management Information Systems, 13*(1), 127–143.

Kardaras, D., Karakostas, B., & Papathanassiou, E. (2003). The potential of virtual communities in the insurance industry in the UK and Greece. *International Journal of Information Management, 23*(1), 41–53. doi:10.1016/S0268-4012(02)00067-1

Kim, G. S., Oh, J., & Park, S. B. (2008). An examination of factors influencing consumer adoption of short message service (SMS). *Psychology and Marketing, 25*(8), 769–786. doi:10.1002/mar.20238

Kow, M. P. M. (2009). *Feasibility study on sourcing of passive candidates via social networking sites.*

Lee, M. K. O., Cheung, C. M. K., & Chen, Z. H. (2007). Understanding user acceptance of multimedia messaging services: An empirical study. *Journal of the American Society for Information Science and Technology, 58*(13), 2066–2077. doi:10.1002/asi.20670

Liao, C. H., Tsou, C. W., & Huang, M. F. (2007). Factors influencing the usage of 3G mobile services in Taiwan. *Online Information Review, 31*(6), 759–774. doi:10.1108/14684520710841757

Murray, K. E., & Waller, R. (2007). Social networking goes abroad. *International Educator, 16*(3), 56–59.

Norazah, M. S., Ramayah, T., & Norbayah, M. S. (2008). Internet shopping acceptance: Examining the influence of intrinsic versus extrinsic motivations. *Direct Marketing: An International Journal, 2*(2), 97–110. doi:10.1108/17505930810881752

Oh, S., Ahn, J., & Kim, B. (2003). Adoption of broadband Internet in Korea: The role of experience in building attitudes. *Journal of Information Technology, 18*, 267–280. doi:10.1080/0268396032000150807

Ramayah, T., & Bushra, A. (2004). Role of self-efficacy in e-library usage among students of a public university in Malaysia. *Malaysian Journal of Library & Information Science., 9*(1), 39–57.

Ramayah, T., Chin, Y. L., Norazah, M. S., & Amlus, I. (2005). Determinants of intention to use an online bill payment system among MBA students. *E-Business*, *9*, 80–91.

Ramayah, T., & Ignatius, J. (2005). Impact of perceived usefulness, perceived ease of use and perceived enjoyment on intention to shop online. *ICFAI Journal of Systems Management*, *3*(3), 36–51.

Ramayah, T., Ignatius, J., & Aafaqi, B. (in press). PC usage among students in a private institution of higher learning: The moderating role of prior experience. *The Journal of Business Strategy*.

Rouibah, K. (2008). Social usage of instant messaging by individuals outside the workplace in Kuwait. *Information Technology & People*, *21*(1), 34–68. doi:10.1108/09593840810860324

Ruiz-Mafé, C., Sanz-Blas, S., & Aldas-Manzano, J. (2009). Drivers and barriers to online airline ticket purchasing. *Journal of Air Transport Management*, 1–5.

Seyal, A. H., & Rahman, N. A. (2007). The influence of external variables on the executives' use of the Internet. *Business Process Management Journal*, *13*(2), 263–278. doi:10.1108/14637150710740491

Shin, D.-H., & Kim, W. Y. (2008). Applying the technology acceptance model and flow. *Cyberpsychology & Behavior*, *11*(3), 378–382. doi:10.1089/cpb.2007.0117

Teo, T. S. H., Lim, V. K. G., & Lai, R. Y. C. (1999). Intrinsic and extrinsic motivation in Internet usage. *Omega*, *27*(32), 25–37. doi:10.1016/S0305-0483(98)00028-0

Tong, D. Y. K. (2009). A study of e–recruitment technology adoption in Malaysia. *Industrial Management & Data Systems*, *109*(2), 281–300. doi:10.1108/02635570910930145

Trochim, W. M. K. (2005). *Probability and non-probability sampling.* Retrieved from http://socialresearchmethods.net/kb/sampprob.htm

Van der Heijden, H. (2004). User acceptance of hedonic information systems. *Management Information Systems Quarterly*, *28*(4), 695–704.

Venkatesh, V., Morris, M. G., Davis, G. B., & Davis, F. D. (2003). User acceptance of information technology: Toward a unified view. *Management Information Systems Quarterly*, *27*(3), 425–478.

Venkatesh, V., Speier, C., & Morris, M. G. (2002). User acceptance enablers in individual decision making about technology: Toward an integrated model. *Decision Sciences*, *33*(2), 297–316. doi:10.1111/j.1540-5915.2002.tb01646.x

Venkatetsh, V., & Davis, F. D. (2000). A theoretical extension of the technology acceptance model: Four longitudinal field studies. *Management Science*, *46*(2), 186–204. doi:10.1287/mnsc.46.2.186.11926

Wang, Y. S., Wang, Y. M., Lin, H. H., & Tang, T. I. (2003). Determinants of user acceptance of Internet banking: An empirical study. *International Journal of Service Industry Management*, *14*(5), 501–519. doi:10.1108/09564230310500192

Warr, W. A. (2008). Social software: Fun and games, or business tools? *Journal of Information Science*, *34*(4), 591–604. doi:10.1177/0165551508092259

Warshaw, P. R., & Davis, F. D. (1985). Disentangling behavioral intention and behavioral expectation. *Journal of Experimental Social Psychology*, *21*, 213–228. doi:10.1016/0022-1031(85)90017-4

Yi, M., & Hwang, Y. (2003). System self-efficacy, enjoyment, learning goal orientation, and The technology acceptance model. *International Journal of Human-Computer Studies*, *59*, 439–449. doi:10.1016/S1071-5819(03)00114-9

This work was previously published in the International Journal of Technology and Human Interaction, Volume 7, Issue 2, edited by Anabela Mesquita and Chia-Wen Tsai, pp. 38-54, copyright 2011 by IGI Publishing (an imprint of IGI Global).

Chapter 19

IT Managers' Narratives on Subordinates' Motivation at Work:
A Case Study

Lars Göran Wallgren
University of Gothenburg, Sweden

Svante Leijon
University of Gothenburg, Sweden

Kerstin Malm Andersson
University of Gothenburg, Sweden

ABSTRACT

Little is known about managers' perception of their subordinates' motivation, especially how this perception influences managerial behavior. This study, conducted in the growing IT consultancy sector, focuses on how IT consultancy first-line managers construct their subordinates' motivation. Since work motivation is a complex phenomenon, there is variation in how managers reduce this complexity. The empirical data was collected in semi-structured interviews with six team leaders (three female, three male) and are presented as narratives. In their narratives, the female team leaders present a more transformative view of their subordinates while the male managers present a more transactional view. The authors interpret this variation in the narrations as evidence that the issue of subordinate motivation is not seen as strategically important. This interpretation cast doubts on certain assumptions in organizational psychology theory.

INTRODUCTION

When IT consultants introduce new technologies and new work routines to their customers there is the possibility that such changes will, in varying degrees, either succeed or fail. Successful change depends not only on which new technologies and routines are selected, but also on how they are implemented so that the customers accept them. A significant factor in gaining such acceptance relates to the construction of the change agenda – there are numerous possibilities. Some change

DOI: 10.4018/978-1-4666-1954-8.ch019

agendas are based on certain general concepts such as Total Quality Management or New Public Management, while others build on Organizational Development ideas that address the importance of employee participation. In still other agendas, because of need for more dramatic organizational restructuring, organizational culture issues dominate.

However, regardless of the specific change agenda selected, in the IT consultancy environment, IT team leaders need to understand what motivates their subordinates – the IT consultants – who have to convince their customers to accept the proposed changes. This particular work motivation issue, "the knowledge of the other's motivation", has not been deeply researched. The focus of this study is IT team leaders' conceptions of their subordinates' work motivation.

According to Lawson and Shen (1998), managers benefit significantly from a sound theoretical understanding of subordinates' motivation. In addition, as Steers, Mowday, and Shapiro (2004) note, given the radical change in work contexts in recent decades (e.g., globalization, rapidly changing technology, constant renewal of skills, extensive customer interaction and a labor market that is highly sensitive to economic swings) managers increasingly need to realize that subordinates' motivation is an important contributing factor to the overall success of organizations. For that reason, researchers in organizational psychology ask important questions about how such managerial knowledge can be acquired and used.

The key question is: "What are the best ways to motivate subordinates – intrinsic (satisfaction and flow experiences), extrinsic (money and other benefits), or a mix of these rewards systems?" (Lawson & Shen, 1998, p. 12). For managers in an IT consultancy environment this question is especially relevant because of the increase in the number of knowledge workers whose commitment is critical to organizational success. To answer this question, we need to know what conceptions

managers working in these new contexts have of employee motivation.

In basing our research around this question, we note our study's resemblance to McGregor's (1960) investigation of workforce motivation in which he proposed that understanding such motivation was a fundamental requirement for leading and controlling employees. McGregor's study led to his well-known dichotomy in attitudes toward workforce motivation – Theory X and Theory Y. These theories distinguish between two contrasting assumptions on employee motivation: Theory X assumes that lazy employees require strict control and Theory Y assumes that self-motivated employees will exercise self-control. McGregor's use of the narrative form in describing workforce motivation, albeit in a very different context from our study (the factory floor vs. the customer workplace), is an inspiration for this study.

We also recognize the complexities in this type of research. Knowledge is acquired by constructing it from diverse sources and knowledge of complex issues, such as motivation, that change over time. We understand, in narratives, people use sensemaking, which Weick (1995) identifies as the process whereby people understand their experiences. We caution that in sensemaking, which is a complicated activity, temporary truths may appear as conceptions.

THE IT CONSULTANCY FIRM

In an IT consultancy firm there is typically little direct contact between the IT managers (the team leaders) and the IT consultants (the subordinates). After the IT team managers assign the IT consultants to the customers, the IT consultants locate to the customers' place of business where they are under the supervision of the customers. In this increasingly common professional workplace, where consultants tend to work independently from their statutory employers, managers must trust significantly in their subordinates' self-motivation. According to Jackson and Carter (1995), when a workforce is complex, fragmented and physically remote, an understanding of the organization's members is a necessity.

Therefore, despite the conceptual and physical distance between managers and consultants in this work arrangement, the issue of the consultants' motivation is of great importance to the managers. Future customer relationships depend on the successful execution of customer tasks by the consultants, and successful task execution depends on the consultants' work motivation.

There is not a great deal of published research on IT consultants' well-being, including the factors that motivate them to do good work. The subject of IT managers' understanding of, and interest in, their subordinates' well-being is still less investigated. However, some research has been conducted that provides useful background for this study. In his research into management's attitude toward promoting job satisfaction and stimulating motivation, Alvesson (1993, p. 71) writes: "As job satisfaction is considered to be closely related to work motivation and since motivational complexity is of great interest to the management they must, indirectly at least, take into consideration the well-being of the personnel". In a study of a group of IT consultants in United States, Brown (2002) finds that a job that provides autonomy, challenge, feedback and the opportunity to use skills is important in promoting job satisfaction and stimulating work motivation. Moreover, other research proposes that work motivation may predict job performance (Locke & Latham, 2002; Pritchard & Payne, 2003). Steers et al. (2004) argue that in the new economy, as well as in the more traditional manufacturing and service areas, highly motivated employees are frequently cited as a hallmark of competitive advantage. This study is intended to advance this area of research with its focus on motivation in the specific work environment of the IT consultancy firm.

PRODUCING NARRATIVES

The narratives in this study explore the complex link between managers' conceptions of employee motivation and their leadership styles. Our narrative approach is supported by the assumption that managers, like most people, often try to understand complex phenomena through narratives. A "narrative" is a construct presented in an appropriate medium (e.g., oral or written) that describes the sequence of fictional or non-fictional events in a chronological order. Any account, regardless of the genre, is a narrative (Barthes & Duisit, 1975; Kostera, 2006). Moreover, according to Chatman (1975), every narrative has two parts: a story (the narrative's content) and a discourse (the narrative's method of communication). Additionally, narratives are a consequence of a long socialization process that narrators are often not aware of.

In the last two decades narrative theory has become influential in organization studies. The first use of narratives in research studies is generally credited to Vladimir Propp, the Russian folktale researcher. In his 1928 "Morphology of the Folk Tale" (Propp, 1968), Propp's ambition was to identify and describe the underlying structures in all Russian folktales. In taking this structural approach to the narrative form, Propp's (1968) hypothesis was that all such tales, despite their surface variety, essentially tell the same story (Skalin, 2002). Despite various criticisms, Propp's work on narrative structure is seminal in narrative theory.

In their book on storytelling, Fog, Budtz and Yakaboylu (2003) assert that certain ingredients make one story more successful than another and that a good story contains all these ingredients. The ingredients, the so-called basic elements, are: the message, the conflict, the roles and the plot. The message, often called the moral, is an ideological or moral statement that is presented as a fact in stories. The conflict, presented as the fight between good and evil, is the driving and essential force. The roles are the characters who try to resolve the conflict, and the plot is the series of events that describe this attempt. The story, working as a proof of the moral, conveys the message. Hearing the story, listeners understand and accept the message. However, first listeners must identify with the different characters in the story and understand their roles. When the message, the conflict and the roles are in place, the plot of the story begins to unfold.

Substantial parts of stories are based on people's actual experiences. Thus, when we question people on some topic, we hear evidence of what exists in the here and now as well as evidence from prior periods of their socialization (Berger & Luckmann, 1967). These processes of socialization (i.e., the processes of identity formation) may be inherently conflicting. Indeed, research on managerial identities (Alvesson & Sveningsson, 2003) often uses the metaphor of struggle to illustrate tensions between discourse and a turbulent, changing reality. However, struggle exists in and between managers. For example, whereas Alvesson and Sveningsson (2003) studied only one manager, Garcia and Hardy (2007) studied twenty-two managers in three different university positions. As a result of their research, Garcia and Hardy (2007) constructed six subcategories of narratives, two for each position. Consistent with their study, in this research we expect to find subgroups among the IT managers who narrate different stories that are articulated in different voices.

As noted above, we understand that because our self-images are a result of socialization they may be somewhat more limited than self-images derived from deeper self-knowledge. Our images of people whom we seldom see or talk with may be even more limited. The IT consultants in this study, who mainly work at the customers' offices, receive their tasks and directions from the customers. Actual interactions between the IT consultancy managers and the IT consultants are thus quite restricted. Such managers have little opportunity

to get to know their subordinates even though they must evaluate them in order to distribute assignments and assess performance. The inevitable result, and a subject of interest in this research, is that managers in such environments are likely to characterize their subordinates simplistically, even to the point of stereotyping them.

Steers et al. (2004), in their historical review of work motivation research, identify the 1950s to the 1970s as the golden age of motivation theories, while noting the emergence of a renewed interest in such research at the beginning of the twenty-first century in the so-called new economy. We describe the golden age motivation theories as narratives since they were packaged as persuasive messages with greatly reduced complexity. Such theories were developed for the stable work conditions of the time and were aimed at designing work conditions that motivated employees to perform jobs effectively. An example of such motivation research is the study of the Volvo automobile plants in Kalmar and Uddevalla in Sweden (Engström, Johansson, Jonsson, & Medbo, 1995). In this study, the researchers present a narrative of two Swedish factories in which they describe the alternative and team-based methods of automobile manufacturing that signaled the end of Ford assembly line production.

From a narrative perspective, these early motivation theories, despite their own complexities (Gillespie, 1991), were presented in simpler, more persuasive ways than recent motivation theories that are too complex to be easily integrated into basic narratives of good work versus bad work. For example, Scheuer (1999) recognizes that dynamic motivation is variously dependent on human expectations, the existing workplace norms, the individual's private economy and his/her main work tasks. Work motivation thus varies from one situation to another and requires special analysis to identify the mechanisms that stimulate or suppress it. Complexity of contemporary work conditions, including the necessity for continuous change, requires more flexibility than earlier work conditions did. Narratives based on the new motivation theories can capture this complexity more realistically although the complexity is simplified.

According to Maister (1997), the mission of professional firms (e.g., legal, accounting and engineering) is to deliver outstanding client services and to provide fulfilling careers for their employees. In carrying out this mission, these firms must also be profitable enough that they can attract and reward good employees. The management of professional firms, according to this meta-narrative, involves a complex balancing act among competing demands of the client marketplace, the realities of the staff marketplace and the firm's economic goals. The IT consultancy firm, such as the one in this research, is a fairly recent entrant in the world of such professional firms.

Several researchers (Alvesson, 2006, Kärreman, Sveningsson, & Alvesson, 2002) who study the so-called knowledge workplace find that these modern workplaces can be quite bureaucratic with their centralized managements, clear hierarchies and formalized rules structures. Work freedom is often restricted by such bureaucracy as well as by the standards for performance. Alvesson (2006) identifies a duality in management where the general rhetoric of the workplace narrative is about personal coaching and independent vision, but the reality of the everyday work is control and supervision. In short, there is a tendency in the knowledge workplace to adopt McGregor's Theory X values despite the rhetoric of support for Theory Y values. Managers with the "right" values – Theory Y – are not necessarily free to build the organizational structures they want (Giddens, 1991).

IT consultants, no matter how creative and well educated, are often frustrated by their assignments. First, there is a lack of really challenging work available, the so-called dream projects. Second, IT consultants may have to compete with the customers' personnel (Imparato & Harari, 1994). And third, while IT consultants derive job satisfaction from developing new knowledge areas, the market generally demands utilization of existing knowledge because it is perceived as cheaper and more reliable. As a result, customers are seldom willing to pay for the self-fulfillment of the consultant-supplier (Alvesson, 2004).

In sum, many narratives enthusiastically describe the IT sector as a frontier of modern technological and societal change. In accordance with these narratives, IT consultants may view themselves as important change agents. However, research into the actual experience of IT consultants presents another image. Demanding deadlines and strict customer control are not characteristics associated with the work of agents of grand change.

General leadership narratives suggest that a good understanding of employee motivation is essential for effective management. In knowledge work, this understanding is especially important. According to the early motivational models, knowledge workers, who thrive by creating and developing the narratives of their work, are best motivated by interesting tasks and professional growth possibilities. Providing these tasks and possibilities would seem to be a requirement for management, but research casts doubts on how important managers consider this necessity as they supervise their subordinates.

How do managers deal with this problem? While they must work within existing organizational structures, they still must conform to the possibly overly idealistic narratives supplied by management models. Our belief is that as managers continually cope with this problem, the struggle becomes part of their identity formation. Professional identities that rest more on ideals than on realistic models capture the difficulties and ambiguities of daily work (Leijon & Söderbom, 2005). Such ideals are rooted in the general discourse on management.

While ways of talking about these ideals in organizations are culturally embedded (Holmes, 1997), culture is not a homogenous phenomenon. Because of cultural differences in a society on a macro level as well as cultural differences in specific organizations (Müllern, 1994), different leadership narratives may result. For example, Eagly and Johannesen-Schmidt (2007) report that many earlier studies of leadership style focus on tasks and interpersonal style. However, more recent leadership studies deal with gender and ethnicity (Eagly & Johnson, 1990; Veccio, 2003). Thus we may expect various interpretations of management's role in the narratives produced by the team leaders of this research.

To summarize, the fundamental premise of this study is that managers use narratives to explain complex phenomena. These narratives are the result of a long socialization process that the storytellers may not even be aware of. As some aspects of the process are more evident than others, although not necessarily more valid, the narratives may appear fragmentary. Even in small narrative samples, we expect heterogeneity rather than homogeneity because of the great variation in the socialization processes of the narrators.

EMPIRICAL DESIGN OF THE STUDY

We take a hermeneutical approach in the selection and interpretation of the data produced by the team leaders' narratives. The approach is inductive: From this data, we draw theoretical and general conclusions. The team leaders' substantive responses to the research question of what motivates their subordinates are woven into their narratives that reflect their assumptions about the truth. These assumptions, combined with the evidential material, have inspired us to establish a new horizon of truth (Selander & Ödman, 2004) and to contribute to managerial narrative theories.

The firm in our case study is a typical, mid-size IT consultancy firm. We selected all team leaders - three male team leaders and three female team leaders as narrators. These six leaders were the only individuals acting as team leaders at the

firm. The youngest team leader is 42 years old and the oldest is 52 years old. Each team leader supervises approximately 15 to 20 subordinates and is accountable for a profit contribution to the firm. In each team leader's group, 80% of the subordinates are male and 20% are female. Since the firm has no central Human Resources Department for the coordination of personnel and administrative tasks, the team leaders' are responsible for hiring/firing, salary negotiations and personnel development.

When we began our research, we explained the purpose of the study to the team leaders and told them that participation was voluntary. One interviewer conducted the six individual interviews at the IT consultancy firm's offices as informal conversations. The interviews, not time limited, lasted from 45 to 60 minutes. The interviews were conducted in 2004 when the IT sector was in recovery after the severe industry downturn that began in 2001. At the time of the interviews, there was an overcapacity in the IT consultancy sector, and its customers were more demanding than they had been before the downturn.

We used an interview guide with loosely structured questions supplemented with important key words. We based the guide on the team leaders' daily interaction with their subordinates, particularly those interactions that related to work motivation. We encouraged the team leaders to speak freely in responding to these questions, thereby allowing them large discretion in presenting their narratives. As researchers we reflected upon the narrators' answers and introduced supplementary questions to obtain clarification (Murray, 2006). According to Murray (2006), narratives are just not life stories in the most general sense but also stories about everyday experiences.

Our first question was "What do you think motivates the subordinates in the organization?" As the team leaders responded, we asked more spontaneous questions related to their perception of the factors that motivated their subordinates.

These questions were in response to the team leaders' answers to our first question and therefore sometimes varied among the interviews. We taped the interviews and later transcribed them on level III in accordance with the system Linell (1994) describes in order to standardize the transcriptions to the level of written language.

In order to analyze the accounts, we divided the analysis into two broad phases – descriptive and interpretive (Murray, 2006):

1. First, we read the interview documents in their entirety, line by line, in order to reach an overall idea of their content. Then, to find representative material from each of the six narratives, we selected and coded key issues pertaining to motivation. The themes of motivation were coded and noted in the margin of the documents and then checked against the transcript as a whole. In this way, we determined that the selected material fairly represented the full narrative (Leijon & Söderbom, 2008).

2. Second, we analyzed and interpreted the narratives from a narrative perspective (Czarniawska, 1997; Fog et al., 2003) in order to identify the message that the respondents wanted to convey about what motivates their subordinates. Consistent with our frame of reference, we used theories of motivation and theories of leadership and identity formation.

THE RESULT OF THE STUDY

The Narratives

As four of the six narratives served the purpose of our research, we next present only those four narratives. Following each narrative, we present our commentary on the narrator's thoughts on his/her subordinates' motivation.

The Female Team Leader #1

The most important thing is having a fun and stimulating job, and that's the reason that so many people stay at the company. So I think that's a motivator – enjoying your work and feeling you are learning and growing. The worst situation for a consultant is to be without an assignment – for a week, that can be nice, but a long time, it is tough. I think most subordinates think it is good when there are possibilities to grow; when you don't have interesting tasks, after a while it isn't fun. Or if your salary isn't equal to your worth to the company. Many people think it is important that the social aspects of a company are good – that their colleagues are clever and pleasant and always willing to help. What's bad is not having assignments or having uncertainty about your compensation. Not everyone is glad that salaries are somewhat flexible. If they were given an option, probably most people would rather have a fixed salary because of the security. However, I believe that some people think that compensation structure sends certain undesirable signals. At the same time, most people understand, especially for the years when we couldn't increase salaries, that those who brought a lot of money into the company supported others' compensation and were worth their bonuses. Yes, perhaps there are some who work full-time and want certain actions, for example, starting salary discussions before we have even begun salary negotiations. What motivates these people is money. Therefore there are many people who don't come to meetings or take courses outside their jobs. They would just rather go home to their families. Yet while others are active and take courses, I still I don't think many people separate themselves from the others by their motivation.

Person-specific logic of the female team leader #1. Her main message is that motivation depends on the job. She also says that some consultants are mostly interested in their salaries. However, she does not regard money as the main motivator.

THE FEMALE TEAM LEADER #2

For most employees, the main motivational factors are challenging assignments and opportunities for personal development. Because we are a decentralized organization, it is essential to recognize the subordinates as individuals. They need people to notice their work and show appreciation for it. I think knowing that others care about their work is a motivational factor for people.

As far as bonuses, since the same people get the merit bonuses every month, I don't know if bonuses motivate people. People, of course, want a reasonable salary for what they do, and they use a lot of energy wondering if their compensation is unfair. However, I think the link between a salary rise and harder work lasts no more than a week. The bonus system was once a way to do well economically, but now when times are a little tougher, you can wonder if the situation will really continue. Generally we are in a really difficult economic climate now, and people may have dependent family members and children. So they stay with the company. I also believe people stay in part because of social reasons. They have friends at work, and they feel secure here. Collegiality is important in the knowledge network. I think that over the years the people here have experienced more job security than at other consultancy firms.

Those people who are a little more active are rather social. Unless someone has a special interest to pursue in the company, I think the social motivation is more important. In our kind of work, it is important to get along. It is also typical that we IT consultants like change. Thus many of us feel it is really great to know you have colleagues and to understand how everything works, and even, in certain instances, to feel a connection with the manager. Some people, more than others, think it

is very important to participate in something new in a company and to break new ground – to do something innovative you can identify with. As far as organization changes, some subordinates are uninterested so long as there is a head manager, while others are very engaged with such issues. Sometimes it can be useful to get new managers who have new ideas about the employees.

Getting out, meeting a customer for a follow-up meeting, or receiving the highest praise – it's really fun. In these situations, I am happy the whole day. Even when I'm not the one who has made the contribution, still I am really satisfied. When we have understood the customer's need correctly, and the consultant has done a great job, its feels terrific. I tell the consultant that and hope my praise is motivating and pleasing.

Feedback is highly motivating for everyone. I think it is important that the consultants' work be recognized. Taking responsibility is motivating for many of us. Competence development is also important for motivation. You can increase your competence by taking courses or by pushing people in new directions with new assignments and new customers.

Person-specific logic of the female team leader #2. Her main message is that motivation generally depends on the job. She also thinks it is important to convey to her subordinates that she, as a team leader, cares about them and their work. She recognizes that she must understand the individual needs of the consultants. Some are more interested in money while others are more interested in the social companionship at the firm.

THE MALE TEAM LEADER #1

People are very different. Some people are motivated to satisfy the customer while others only look at a job in terms of the money earned by working the required eight-hour day. It is clear that some people who are driven by money and always work for the bonus really need the money because of their economic needs. Then there are those who are motivated by others' expectations, by company loyalty or by the idea that their jobs are fun. Still others don't care about money, which doesn't mean that they have enough money but rather that other factors motivate them. For example, since children are often sick, those people with children may report that they are home with sick children, whether the children are sick or not. This is interesting. There are, of course, a thousand reasons for how you allocate your time and energy between the family and work. The loyalty to the person who gives you the assignment can be as great as that to the family. When there is an expected time frame for completing a job, it is typical that everyone here is loyal to the manager; if you don't feel this way, you don't have the right attitude for a consultant. It is clear that with bonuses it is important to bring in money. We have had such a climate for a couple of years now – prioritizing your assignments helps the company to advance, on an even keel. In such a work atmosphere, it is not fun when you don't have an assignment.

There is one person I know of, an eager beaver, whose economic situation requires him to make as much money as possible. He is driven to work a lot, not because he is greedy but because he needs the money. Then there is another person who is motivated by the desire to be seen and acknowledged in the company as important – so important that the manager will ask him for advice. This person, who has his own agenda where the recognition of his worth is very important, wants to be a mentor to everyone for everything. Such a person tries to be a coach to everyone, regardless of the situation. I have about 20 consultants, which is probably the maximum number you can manage properly. Some of them require very little attention and some require quite a lot. Five consultants is probably a reasonable number since you yourself must work on the outside as well. The

tougher the work, the more some thrive, although that attitude depends on individual life situations. If you have three small children and a house that needs extensive renovation, you have to spend more energy on the family, and you can't spend so much time on work. Several consultants are in that situation.

Those people who leave the company seem to want something new. When you are a little younger and not so hardened by experience, it is easy to think the grass is a little greener on the other side of the fence. It may then seem that another company would value your competence in a way that this company doesn't.

Person-specific logic of the male team leader #1. His main message is that there is a big difference between people and between what motivates them. As a leader, he must be aware of these differences that may change and that may also depend on the life situations of the consultants.

THE MALE TEAM LEADER #2

I must begin by describing how the group was built up and how people tried to contribute to the group. In the beginning, everyone was interested in sharing, in helping each other, in educating ourselves and in acting as mentors and supporting people. People were strongly motivated, and that was how we started. Half the group members now are from that time and still have that attitude. The other half consists of more traditional consultants, neither better nor worse. The first group is more self-motivated and wants to develop the company according to the ideas I have. As the entire group is no longer homogeneous, there are more demands on the leaders than before when the group was first formed and group members were more involved. The new members were hired in a re-organization and weren't motivated by the fact that they were forced to change managers. The goal was that the two groups would be the same size. Clearly the first group makes more demands on the company – that the company does the right thing, both externally and internally. There is also a certain frustration that we haven't always valued that attitude in recent years.

Yet other consultants are really pleased with their assignments. You discover that certain people feel secure in the consultant's role –working for a customer – and aren't likely to change jobs. In a certain sense, salaries, benefits and a company car are more or less important to everyone, but I don't think they are the main motivators although they are more so to some than others. Some people always work for the incentive bonus and make sure they never miss it. Then there are consultants who are very anti-bonus because they think the bonus system has many negative aspects. I think the bonus system is a one-sided measurement. Of course, we need to make a profit, but I also think it is important to have the right colleagues and the right competences. Still, those people who say they don't like the bonus system nevertheless always come to the internal meetings even though they have a lot to do.

There are a number of people who are involved in special issues related to motivation and development in the company. I think it is a matter of personality that they are more active than others. Those of us in management perhaps have a little-understood role in developing and promoting the company. I think it is interesting how we try to involve the consultants. Often the motivation stems from some competence: "I believe in this area", "I want to do something here", "Company X does this so we should also". There are several new hires who are really interested in such matters that are competence-related. It is interesting to make changes for the sake of change without asking the critical question of how we do it. When you have been at the company for a long time, I think it can be fun to do something new. As the world changes, in the future companies will have to respond to new demands. It can be motivating to

search for ways to make the necessary changes. Of course, there is always the risk that the company will grow too large and the difficulties will be too great – in this case, change may not be fun.

Person-specific logic of the male team leader #2. He realizes he has different subgroups that are motivated differently. One important explanation for these differences has to do with when people joined the company and how long they have been employed there. Another explanation has to do with their opinion of the bonus system, pro or con. Thus he sees a dichotomy in the motivating factors for his subordinates.

THE MESSAGE OF THE NARRATIVES

While the narratives provide responses to our research questions on subordinates' motivation, it is also obvious that the team leaders are trying to describe the nature of their leadership situations. In all narratives, they describe their ambitions that for various reasons have not been wholly fulfilled. The tension between the ideal and the reality shapes their managerial identities, as discussed below.

There is one important difference between the female team leaders' narratives and those of the male team leaders. The female team leaders assume their subordinates will be motivated so long as caring leadership is provided. The male team leaders do not present this view of leadership. Instead, they believe merit bonuses are the main motivation for subordinates. Thus they assume the subordinates' motivation depends on circumstances outside their control.

DISCUSSION

From the beginning of our research we recognized that employee motivation is a complex area. As our research revealed, this complexity leaves room for managerial interpretation and thus the construction of ideas about motivation of subordinates. The construction of motivation in general suggests that motivation is more a matter of socialization (Berger & Luckmann, 1967) than an objective process of knowledge accumulation. Classic motivational theory assumes a true and objective reality is identifiable; more modern theory assumes reality is that which is observed and interpreted. In this very complex area, then, a mutual contract between leaders and their followers can be built on their common interpretation of important motivational dimensions (Weick, 1995).

The Two Subgroups - Female and Male Team Leaders' Narratives

We found that, based on their understanding of subordinates' motivation, the narratives can be divided into two subgroups: one for the female team leaders and one for the male team leaders. In general, the female team leaders express much more concern for the IT consultants' well-being than the male team leaders. The female team leaders emphasize job satisfaction and personal fulfillment as motivating factors while the male team leaders emphasize merit bonuses.

The male team leaders narrate a view of transactional leadership in which leaders have little influence over subordinates' motivation. They therefore assign tasks to their subordinates based on their subordinates' capabilities and take few motivational factors into consideration. By contrast, the female team leaders narrate a view of transformational leadership when they describe their role in promoting the professional development of their subordinates. By meeting the emotional needs of their employees, transformational leaders encourage employees to look beyond their own needs in order to focus on the interests of the group (Avolio & Bass, 2002; Bass, 1985). These female team leaders may adopt a transformational leadership style because it is consistent with the

discourse of the helpful and understanding behavior typically associated with women (Eagly, Johannesen-Schmidt, & van Engen, 2003; Yoder, 2001). Several studies on transformational leadership conclude that women are perceived (Kark, 2004), and perceive themselves, as using transformational leadership styles more than men (Bass, Avolio, & Atwater, 1996; Druskat, 1994).

We also considered other explanations of why the narrations divide along gender lines. In addition to gender, we looked at differences in ages and leadership roles/tasks. However, we found no significant differences in either age or in management responsibilities among the team leader groups. Thus, having excluded age and roles/tasks as possible explanations, gender seemed a probable explanation for the transactional/transformational leadership style division.

This conclusion may be supported by a theory on lateral communication. As Mintzberg (1973) observes, a good deal of communication between leaders is lateral, that is, between fellow leaders. Such exchanges reduce uncertainty through the mechanisms of informal and formal collegial talk. We can speculate that the team leaders in this study may have formed a male subgroup and a female subgroup in which the main communications took place. This sub grouping effect might partially explain the similarities of responses in each subgroup as the result of specific communication patterns.

It is noteworthy that while 50% of the leaders in the study are female, only 20% of the IT consultants are female. If the proportions between the team leaders had been the same as the IT consultants, that is, one female team leader for every five male team leaders, we can speculate whether the narratives produced by the team leaders would have shown more uniformity. If a minority has to be large enough to make a difference (Kanter, 1997), would a ratio of one female manager for every five male managers have produced different narratives?

Although we have no direct evidence of the presence of lateral communication in the subgroups and no evidence of the effect of a hypothetical redistribution of team leaders/IT consultants, we are inclined to conclude that the gender differences in these narratives may be produced and maintained as much by the specific contextual circumstances as by the influence of the discourse on female management. The micro situation (the daily interaction between leaders and their subordinates) is influenced by this discourse that implies subordinates also anticipate gender differences (McColl-Kennedy & Anderson, 2005). We add that relationships between leaders are also important contextual dimensions in producing and maintaining narratives.

Stereotyped Narratives of Subordinates' Motivation

The narratives of subordinates' motivation that both subgroups produced may be examples of what Levy, Stroessner, and Dweck (1998) call social stereotyping. Tajfel (1981) suggests that the stereotyping phenomenon is a result of the need for coherence, simplicity and predictability in the context of an inherently complex social environment. Moreover, Bodenhausen and Wyer (1985) conclude that stereotypes are often useful for providing us with a basis for understanding and predicting the behavior of others when demands for processing of information are high. In short, stereotyping is a way for the team leaders in this study to simplify and predict employee behavior with the result that they do not prioritize work motivation. Team leaders in an IT consultancy firm have to provide tasks that motivate their subordinates, but they do not really have lot of opportunities to influence the tasks and work environment at the customers' locations. They cannot choose between motivating or demotivating tasks since they may not know, or even want to know, the nature of the tasks. This implicit contract (Schein, 1978) between the IT consultancy firm

and its consultant defines the effort the consultant makes in exchange for acceptable working conditions. If the contract becomes explicit, as result of a manager-employee discussion about tasks the consultant finds interesting and rewarding, an expectation is created that such tasks will be forthcoming.

Managerial Values vs. Structural Conditions

All six team leaders of this study recognize the disharmonious effects of the inspirational leadership-bureaucratic supervision conflict. However, the female team leaders seem more concerned with fulfilling their leadership roles than about managing the bureaucratic machinery. Sveningsson and Alvesson (2003) note similar struggles in managing identities in their study on organizational fragmentation. They conclude that a crucial element is the struggle that exists between the demands of leadership and the demands of bureaucratic control. The female team leaders of this study express a more balanced identity construction of the real versus the ideal, while the male team leaders are more fantasy-oriented (Alvesson & Empson, 2008; Sveningsson & Larsson, 2006)

Additionally, we found that the team leaders' narratives reflect both McGregor's Theory X and Theory Y on motivation. Again, some findings reflect the gender distribution of the narrators. The male team leaders, who think that subordinates are largely motivated by money and benefits (Theory X), seem to take less interest in promoting their subordinates' well-being. The female team leaders, who think that job challenge and work satisfaction motivates employees (Theory Y), work to create an environment where those interests may be satisfied. However, all team leaders agree that the structure of the organization, with its inhibiting rules and procedures, defeats the autonomy, self-empowerment and ambition of the well-intentioned IT consultants. This view of organizational structure is consistent with Mc-Gregor's observations.

In summary, this study suggests that the IT team leaders do not place a high priority on subordinates' motivation, largely because of structural impediments, contrary to other research finds that management should prioritize subordinates' motivation as a way to promote their well-being and improve their performance (Wallgren & Johansson Hanse, 2007).

Employee motivation is a complex area. As our research reveals, some of its dimensions appear in some narratives while other dimensions appear in other narratives. Hence, since employee motivation is an important and thus strategic topic, it is essential to retain the complexities from the different narratives. Strategic common narratives that are too simple may reduce the complexities too much (Leijon & Söderbom, 2008).

This article presents a case study of six team leaders at one firm. It can be argued that this focus limits the generalization of the findings. However, we emphasize that this firm is representative of other IT consultancy firms among which there is a great similarity in organizational structure, in management responsibility and in work assignments with statutory employees performing tasks at customer companies. However, the particularity of this study, with its equal subgroups of male and female team leaders, limits its generalization to some extent. In one sense, the broad sweep of the study increases our understanding of managers' views on employee motivation in the area of knowledge firms. However, in a more specific sense, the study illuminates the differences men and women have of employee motivation in this area.

CONCLUDING QUESTION

At the beginning of this article we expressed our agreement with Lawson and Shen (1998) that sound knowledge of subordinates' motivation is critical to good management. Based on the responses we received in the interviews of our research, we have not changed our minds, but we now see that successful motivation of subordinates may be made more difficult owing to the structural impediments of rules and procedures in the organization. The team leaders of this study seem to be aware of this complexity. The female team leaders narrate the dimension they can control (subordinates' well-being) while the male team leaders narrate the dimension outside their control (customer-assigned tasks). The key question is: Is this realistic view of the reality in a firm (i.e., the organizational conditions and the interactions with customers) compatible with good strategic management?

This question suggests an area for future research. We believe it would be fruitful to examine the question from the IT consultants' perspective, using their narratives. What is their view of their own motivation? What behavior and action do they expect of their team leaders that will motivate them to do good work? How should team leaders manage IT consultants such that the IT consultants' in-built complexities and dilemmas are taken into account? The answers to these questions may give us pieces we can use to fit together the puzzle of effective and realistic management.

ACKNOWLEDGMENT

The authors express their gratitude to the anonymous reviewers and the journal editor for their helpful comments and suggestions on an earlier version of this paper.

REFERENCES

Alvesson, M. (1993). *Organisationsteori och teknokratiskt medvetande*. Stockholm, Sweden: Nerenius & Santérus Förlag.

Alvesson, M. (2004). *Knowledge work and knowledge-intensive firms*. Oxford, UK: Oxford University Press.

Alvesson, M. (2006). *Tomhetens triumf: Om grandiositet, illusionsnummer & nollsummespel*. Stockholm, Sweden: Bokförlaget Atlas.

Alvesson, M., & Empson, L. (2008). The construction of organizational identity: Comparative case studies of consulting firms. *Scandinavian Journal of Management, 24*(1), 1–16. doi:10.1016/j.scaman.2007.10.001

Alvesson, M., & Sveningsson, S. (2003). Good visions, bad micro-management and ugly ambiguity: Contradictions of (non-) leadership in a knowledge-intensive organization. *Organization Studies, 24*(6), 961–988. doi:10.1177/0170840603024006007

Avolio, B. J., & Bass, B. M. (2002). *Developing potential across a full range of leaderships: Cases on transactional and transformational leadership*. Mahwah, NJ: Lawrence Erlbaum.

Barthes, R., & Duisit, L. (1975). An introduction to the structural analysis of narrative. *New Literary History, 6*(2), 237–272. doi:10.2307/468419

Bass, B. M. (1985). *Leadership and performance beyond expectation*. New York, NY: Free Press.

Bass, B. M., Avolio, B. J., & Atwater, L. (1996). The transformational and transactional leadership of men and women. *Applied Psychology: An International Review, 45*(1), 5–34. doi:10.1111/j.1464-0597.1996.tb00847.x

Berger, P. L., & Luckmann, T. (1967). *The social construction of reality: A treatise in the sociology of knowledge*. New York, NY: Anchor Books.

Bodenhausen, G. V., & Wyer, R. S. (1985). Effects of stereotypes on decision making and information-processing strategies. *Journal of Personality and Social Psychology, 48*(2), 267–282. doi:10.1037/0022-3514.48.2.267

Brown, M. M. (2002). *An exploratory study of job satisfaction and work motivation of a selected group of information technology consultants in the Delaware Valley*. Unpublished doctoral dissertation, Wilmington College, Wilmington, DE.

Chatman, S. (1975). Towards a theory of narrative. *New Literary History, 6*(2), 295–318. doi:10.2307/468421

Czarniawska, B. (1997). *Narrating the organization – dramas of institutional identity*. Chicago, IL: The University of Chicago Press.

Druskat, V. U. (1994). Gender and leadership style: Transformational and transactional leadership in the Roman Catholic Church. *The Leadership Quarterly, 5*(2), 99–199. doi:10.1016/1048-9843(94)90023-X

Eagly, A. H., & Johannesen-Schmidt, M. C. (2007). Leadership style matters: The small, but important, style differences between male and female leaders. In Bilimoria, D., & Piderit, S. K. (Eds.), *Handbook on women in business and management* (pp. 279–303). Cheltenham, UK: Edward Elgar.

Eagly, A. H., Johannesen-Schmidt, M. C., & van Engen, M. (2003). Transformational, transactional, and laissez-faire styles: A meta-analysis comparing women and men. *Psychological Bulletin, 95*(4), 569–591. doi:10.1037/0033-2909.129.4.569

Eagly, A. H., & Johnson, B. T. (1990). Gender and leadership style: A meta-analysis. *Psychological Bulletin, 108*(2), 233–256. doi:10.1037/0033-2909.108.2.233

Engström, T., Johansson, J. Å., Jonsson, D., & Medbo, L. (1995). Empirical evaluation of the reformed assembly work at the Volvo Uddevalla plant: Psychosocial effects and performance aspects. *International Journal of Industrial Ergonomics, 16*(4-6), 293–308. doi:10.1016/0169-8141(95)00014-8

Fog, K., Budtz, C., & Yakaboylu, B. (2003). *Storytelling – branding i praksis*. Fredriksberg, Sweden: Samfundslitteratur.

Garcia, P., & Hardy, C. (2007). Positioning, similarity and difference: Narratives of individual and organizational identities in an Australian university. *Scandinavian Journal of Management, 23*(4), 363–383.

Giddens, A. (1991). *Modernity and self-identity: Self and society in the late modern age*. Cambridge, UK: Polity Press.

Gillespie, R. (1991). *Manufacturing knowledge: A history of Hawthorne experiments*. Cambridge, UK: Cambridge University Press.

Holmes, J. (1997). Storytelling in New Zealand in women's and men's talk. In Wodak, R. (Ed.), *Gender and discourse* (pp. 262–293). London, UK: Sage.

Imparato, N., & Harari, O. (1994). *Jumping the curve: Innovation and strategic choice in an age of transition*. San Francisco, CA: Jossey-Bass.

Jackson, N., & Carter, P. (1995). The 'fact' of management. *Scandinavian Journal of Management, 11*(3), 197–208. doi:10.1016/0956-5221(95)00016-O

Kanter, R. M. (1997). *Men and women of the corporation*. New York, NY: Basic Books.

Kark, R. (2004). The transformational leader: Who is (s)he? A feminist perspective. *Journal of Organizational Change Management, 17*(2), 160–176. doi:10.1108/09534810410530593

Kärreman, D., Sveningsson, S., & Alvesson, M. (2002). The return of machine bureaucracy? Management control in the work settings of professionals. *International Studies of Management & Organization, 32*(2), 70–92.

Kostera, M. (2006). The narrative collage as research method. *Storytelling, Self, Society, 2*(2), 5–27.

Lawson, R. B., & Shen, Z. (1998). *Organizational psychology: Foundations and applications*. New York, NY: Oxford University Press.

Leijon, S., & Söderbom, A. (2005). Rollkombinationer i ekonomi- och personalarbete. *Nordiske Organisasjonsstudier, 3*(7), 87–110.

Leijon, S., & Söderbom, A. (2008). Builders and cleaners – a longitudinal study of strategic narratives. *Journal of Organizational Change Management, 21*(3), 280–299. doi:10.1108/09534810810874787

Levy, S. R., Stroessner, S. J., & Dweck, C. S. (1998). Stereotype formation and endorsement: The role of implicit theories. *Journal of Personality and Social Psychology, 74*(6), 1421–1436. doi:10.1037/0022-3514.74.6.1421

Linell, P. (1994). *Transkription av tal och samtal: Teori och praktik. Arbetsrapport från tema Kommunikation, 1994:9*. Linköping, Sweden: Linköpings universitet.

Locke, E. A., & Latham, G. P. (2002). Building a practically useful theory of goal setting and task motivation: A 35-year odyssey. *The American Psychologist, 57*(9), 705–717. doi:10.1037/0003-066X.57.9.705

Maister, D. (1997). *Managing the professional service firm*. London, UK: Simon and Schuster.

McColl-Kennedy, J. R., & Anderson, R. D. (2005). Subordinate–manager gender combination and perceived leadership style influence on emotions, self-esteem and organizational commitment. *Journal of Business Research, 58*(2), 115–125. doi:10.1016/S0148-2963(03)00112-7

McGregor, D. (1960). *The human side of enterprise*. New York, NY: McGraw-Hill.

Mintzberg, H. (1973). *The nature of managerial work*. New York, NY: Harper and Row.

Müllern, T. (1994). *Den föreställda organisationen: om kulturella processer i och kring organisationer*. Stockholm, Sweden: Nerenius & Santérus.

Murray, M. (2006). Narrative psychology. In Smith, J. (Ed.), *Qualitative psychology: A practical guide to research methods*. London, UK: Sage.

Pritchard, R. D., & Payne, S. C. (2003). Performance management and motivation. In Holman, D., Wall, T. D., Clegg, C. W., Sparrow, P., & Howard, A. (Eds.), *The new workplace: A guide to the human impact of modern working practices* (pp. 219–233). Chichester, UK: John Wiley & Sons.

Propp, V. (1968). *Morphology of the folk tale*. Austin, TX: University of Texas Press.

Schein, E. H. (1978). *Career dynamics: Matching individual and organizational needs*. Reading, MA: Addison-Wesley.

Scheuer, S. (1999). *Social and economic motivation at work, theories of motivation reassessed*. Copenhagen, Denmark: Copenhagen Business School Press.

Selander, S., & Ödman, P.-J. (2004). *Text och existens: Hermeneutik möter samhällsvetenskap*. Göteborg, Sweden: Daidalos.

Skalin, L.-Å. (2002). Narratologi - Studiet av berättandets principer. In Bergsten, S. (Ed.), *Litteraturvetenskap – en inledning* (pp. 173–188). Lund, Sweden: Studentlitteratur.

Steers, R. M., Mowday, R. T., & Shapiro, D. L. (2004). The future of work motivation theory. *Academy of Management Review, 29*(3), 379–387.

Sveningsson, S., & Alvesson, M. (2003). Managing managerial identities: Organizational fragmentation, discourse and identity struggle. *Human Relations, 56*(10), 1163–1193. doi:10.1177/00187267035610001

Sveningsson, S., & Larsson, M. (2006). Fantasies of leadership: Identity work. *Leadership, 2*(2), 203–224. doi:10.1177/1742715006062935

Tajfel, H. (1981). *Human groups and social categories: Studies in social psychology*. Cambridge, UK: Cambridge University Press.

Veccio, R. P. (2003). In search of gender advantage. *The Leadership Quarterly, 14*(6), 835–850. doi:10.1016/j.leaqua.2003.09.005

Wallgren, L. G., & Johansson Hanse, J. (2007). Job characteristics, motivators and stress among information technology consultants: A structural equation modeling approach. *International Journal of Industrial Ergonomics, 37*(1), 51–59. doi:10.1016/j.ergon.2006.10.005

Weick, K. (1995). *Sensemaking in organizations*. London, UK: Sage.

Yoder, J. D. (2001). Making leadership work more effectively for women. *The Journal of Social Issues, 57*(4), 815–828. doi:10.1111/0022-4537.00243

This work was previously published in the International Journal of Technology and Human Interaction, Volume 7, Issue 3, edited by Anabela Mesquita and Chia-Wen Tsai, pp. 35-49, copyright 2011 by IGI Publishing (an imprint of IGI Global).

Chapter 20
Modelling Factors Influencing Early Adopters' Purchase Intention Towards Online Music

Norazah Mohd Suki
Universiti Malaysia Sabah, Malaysia

ABSTRACT

The Internet is an incredible technology, offering users a vast choice of new songs and catalogue that can be browsed, streamed or bought online. This paper aims to provide an explanation of factors influencing purchase intention of early adopters towards online music. An empirical survey was used to test the hypotheses. Data were collected from a total of 200 questionnaires distributed to early adopters of online music and were analysed using Structural Equation Modeling (SEM) via the Analysis of Moment Structure (AMOS 16) computer program. Results enumerate that perceived ease of use emerges as the important factor which affects perceived value among the respondents followed by perceived playfulness. Perceived value has the only significant impact on the purchase intentions towards online music. The paper rounds off with conclusions and an agenda for future research in this area.

INTRODUCTION

The advent of powerful, widely, accessible and financially viable personal computers with network connections on the World Wide Web has lead to exciting possibilities for creating online music. Consumers are getting online to take advantage of the unprecedented convenience of accessing goods and services. In 2009, more than a quarter of the recorded music industry's global revenues (27%) came from digital channels (IFPI, 2010). In the US, the world's largest music market, online and mobile revenues in 2010 account for around 40% of music sales (IFPI, 2010). Consumer choice has been transformed as companies have licensed more than 11 million tracks to around 400 legal music services worldwide. In 2010, iTunes is the biggest music retailer in the US, accounting for 28% of the overall music market, followed by Walmart, Best Buy and Amazon (NPD Group, 2010). Fans can access and pay for music in diverse ways – from buying tracks or albums from download stores,

DOI: 10.4018/978-1-4666-1954-8.ch020

and using subscription services, to using music services that are bundled with devices, buying mobile apps for music, and listening to music through streaming services for free.

In 2010, illegal music downloading continues to rise in the UK. According to Harris Interactive (2010), there were 1.2m single music tracks illegally downloaded from unauthorised sources with 28.8% of the downloader aged 16-54 years old and 23% using peer-to-peer (P2P) sites and software to obtain unauthorised music (as cited in BPI, 2010). £984,000,000 retail value of single tracks downloaded in 2010 from unauthorised sources (BPI, 2010) which has an implication in some lost of revenues to the musicians and songwriters or music companies who invest in them. The total number of people in the UK illegally downloading music on a regular basis is 7.7m across all sources such as e-mail, instant messaging and newsgroups (BPI, 2010). UKOM/Nielsen (2010) (as cited in BPI, 2010) states that visitors to the five most popular hosting sites (Megaupload, Filestube, Rapidshare, Mediafire and Hotfile) have increased by 45% from 1.6m in September 2009 to 2.3m in September 2010.

IFPI (International Federation of the Phonographic Industry) Digital Music Report 2010 stated that in Asia, around a quarter of the music business is now composed of digital revenues, set against a backdrop of sharply falling physical sales (IFPI, 2010). Digital sales in China, Indonesia, South Korea and Thailand now account for more than half of all music sales. South Korea has seen the benefits of a stronger copyright environment and there has been strong growth in MP3 subscription services. Japan, the biggest market in the region, was hit by mobile piracy and economic downturn, seeing CD sales fall by more than 20% in the first half of 2009, while digital sales were flat. According to Technology Adoption Life Cycle (Moore, 1991), the early adopters consist of technology enthusiasts and visionaries. The enthusiast refers to whom feels a great interest in brand-new technologies and hopes to take the lead in obtaining them, and the visionaries refer to whom have inclinations of easily visualizing, understanding and accepting interests of new technologies and whom tend to buy the products in order to realize their dreams. Suki, Ahmand, and Thyagarajan (2007) found that the support and encouragement by friends to purchase the products through the Internet is the most important attribute in discriminating among five categories of online shoppers (Innovators, Early Adopters, Early Majority, Late Majority, and Laggards).

The main reasons for adopters using the online stores were the lower prices compared to traditional stores, the easiness of online buying procedures and the wide variety of available products. Computer hardware/software and travel tickets were the most commonly purchased categories of products, followed by consumer electronics, CDs/DVDs and books (Saprikis, Chouliara, & Vlachopoulou, 2010). Moreover, who buys online and why, are crucial questions for e-commerce managers and consumer researchers if online sales are to continue to grow through increased purchases by current buyers and by converting those who have not yet purchased online (Suki et al., 2007).

Chu and Lu (2007) conducted a study among 302 online Taiwanese early adopters of online music. Data was analysed via LISREL 8.51. The results confirm that Perceived Value of online music is a significant factor in predicting the purchaser intention of buying online music in Taiwan. However, the current study moves toward a broader view of the relationship between Perceived Usefulness, Perceived Playfulness, Perceived Price, and Perceived Ease of Use towards Perceived Value. Next relationship tests between Perceived Value and Purchase Intention in online music. This research tests a more comprehensive model by examining the integrative system of the relationships using Structural Equation Modeling (SEM) technique via the Analysis of Moment Structure (AMOS 16) computer program. Furthermore, the study incorporates marketing perspectives as inputs into the model, thus strengthening and generalizing its findings as well as broadening the theoretical base in online music research and practice within Malaysia context. The study provides online music practitioners and managers with a useful adoption model that demonstrates the significance of perceived value of online music in influencing the adoption decision. This highlights the importance of maximizing the benefits of online music for potential users to facilitate the adoption process.

Subsequently, this paper discusses the value-intention framework. This is followed by a presentation of the methodology and the results of the statistical analysis. The paper rounds off with conclusions and an agenda for future research in this area.

Literature Review

Innovation is the process of creating and doing new things. Innovation involves acting on the creative ideas to make some specific and tangible difference in the domain in which the innovation occurs. A disruptive innovation is an innovation that disrupts an existing market. The term is used in business and technology literature to describe innovations that improve a product or service in ways that the market does not expect, typically by lowering price or designing for a different set of consumers. Online music is an example disruptive innovation. In the 1990s, the music industry phased out the single. This left consumers with no means to purchase individual songs. This market was filled by P2P file sharing technologies, which were initially free, and then by online retailers such as the iTunes music store and Amazon.com. This low end disruption eventually undermined the sales of physical, high-cost CDs (Knopper, 2009).

Value-Intention Framework

Dodds and Monroe (1985) developed the value-intention framework, which assumes that the individual willingness to perform a certain behavior is directly influenced by perceived value, also known as perceived customer value, of behavior consequences. Their framework proposed an overview of the relationships among the concepts of perceived sacrifice, quality, and value. Perceived value is regarded as the core construct. Woodruff (1997, p. 142) defined value as the trade-off between of benefit, i.e., the received component, and sacrifices, i.e., the given component. However, the value is individualistic and personal. It can be considered from various aspects, and such value is evaluated as high or low depending on individual subjective assessment. Zeithaml (1988, p. 14) defined perceived value as the consumer's overall assessment of the utility of a product based on perceptions of what is received and what is given.

Moreover, quality is considered as the received component in the original value-intention framework. Perceived quality can be defined as consumer assessment regarding the global excellence or superiority of a product (Holbrook, 1996). Perceived quality can be inferred as intrinsic and extrinsic cues. Intrinsic cues involve the physical composition of products such as color, flavor, and texture. Meanwhile, extrinsic cues are product-related but not part of the physical product itself, such as brand, advertising, and store image (Teas & Agarwal, 2000).

Sacrifice describes what must be given up or paid to perform a certain behavior. In the hedonic consumption decision process, price is what a customer pays in money term for a product obtaining. Therefore, price is often used as the key measure to represent what customers have to sacrifice to gain a product. Tam (2004) showed that the more monetary cost customers perceived they have to pay in acquiring products, the lower value they have perceived. Hence, the research model (Figure 1) was adapted from the value-intention framework and identifies key factors that influence perceived value and purchase intention of early adopters in an online music setting. The construct relationships among these hypotheses are elaborated below.

Purchase Intention and Perceived Value

Customer-perceived value of downloadable music, in terms of expected value for money, was found to be quite low (Styvén, 2007). Value could, however, be increased by improving the most important benefits. In addition to fundamental functions, such as ease of use and search, a large music catalogue, and good sound quality, flexibility in use is essential. This involves ensuring transferability, compatibility, possibility to duplicate files, and opportunity to sample. The high level of desired flexibility suggests that digital rights management (DRM) restrictions decrease value by making it difficult for consumers to use the product freely. Furthermore, perceived value could be enhanced by decreasing privacy risk, such as concerns about paying with credit card online, and, most importantly, lowering prices.

Consumers, on average, thought that a downloadable song should cost 5–6 SEK, i.e., about half of the current price. However, providing better value in terms of the proposed benefits, combined with lower risk, would improve consumers' willingness to pay (Styvén, 2007). Accordingly, the study hypothesizes that:

H1: Perceived value is positively related to purchase intentions towards online music.

Perceived Benefit

Individuals assess value based on the net gain of utility between what benefits are received and what sacrifices are incurred by performing the behavior. The original value-intention framework considered the perceived quality as the get-component in assessing value. Consequently, this study considers that perceived benefit substitutes for quality to measure the gains from online consumer's view. Consistent with previous literature on consumer behaviors, the research model comprises two benefit dimensions, including functional and recreational benefits (Childers, Carr, Peckc, & Carson, 2001), for predicting the benefits perceived by online consumers. In the online music setting, functional benefit refers to as the perceived usefulness construct, while recreational benefit refers to as the perceived playfulness construct.

Figure 1. Theoretical framework

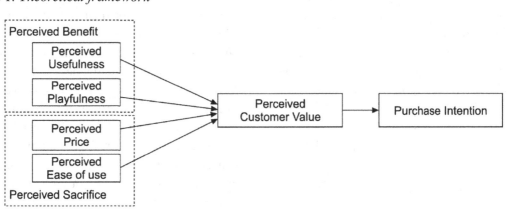

Perceived Usefulness

This study defines perceived usefulness as the degree to which the consumer believes that listening to music online would fulfill the certain purpose. Although online music web sites aim to provide people with an entertaining experience, they also provide functional benefits to them. For example, online music web sites provide more diversiform music works and quicker search service to online users than traditional music stores do. In fact, effectively accessing music and relevant information has become one of the key benefits sought by online music consumers. Perceived usefulness was found to have positively influenced the behavioural intention to use a computer system (Fagan, Wooldridge, & Neill, 2008; Guriting & Ndubisi, 2006; Ha & Stoel, 2009; Hsu, Wang, & Chiu, 2009; Huang, 2008; Suki, Ramayah, & Suki, 2008; Suki, Ramayah, & Kow Pei Min, 2010; Ruiz-Mafé, Sanz-Blas, & Aldas-Manzano, 2009; Seyal & Rahman, 2007; Tong, 2009). Hence, this study believes that perceived value will increase with perceived usefulness of online music. The following hypothesis is proposed:

H2: Perceived usefulness is positively related to perceived value in online music setting.

Perceived Playfulness

Perceived enjoyment (a dimension of perceived playfulness) was found to be positively influenced by behavioural intention to use a computer system (Davis, Bagozzi, & Warshaw, 1992; Lee, Cheung, & Chen, 2007; Suki et al., 2010; Teo, Lim, & Lai, 1999). Perceived playfulness is a significant predictor of perceived value of online music. This finding is consistent with the previous hedonic-oriented IT studies (Hsu & Lu, 2004; Van der Heijden, 2004). Perceived playfulness is defineds as the degree to which the consumer believes that enjoyment could be derived when listening to

online music. Consequently, this study believes that perceived value will increase with perceived playfulness. Therefore, the study posits:

H3: Perceived playfulness is positively related to perceived value in online music setting.

Perceived Sacrifice

Perceived sacrifice is defined as individual feeling regarding giving something up to get something that they intention. When making decisions with regard to online music purchase, online consumers certainly consider both monetary and non-monetary costs. Price is frequently used as the key measure representing what consumers have to pay to obtain a product. Nevertheless, individuals do not always remember actual product prices, and previous studies have revealed that consumers encode prices meaningfully. Consequently, researchers have reached a consensus that monetary costs should be used to measure perceived price encoded by consumers instead of using actual product prices (Monroe, 1973). On the other hand, research on consumer behavior indicates that other costs are relevant to consumers. Therefore, in an online music setting, perceived ease of use captures the non-monetary cost and the associated instrumentality.

Perceived Price

Economically rational shoppers generally see price as an important financial cost component (Zeithaml, 1988). Price had a positive effect on perceived quality, but a negative effect on perceived value and willingness to buy (Dodds, Monroe, & Grewal, 1991). Favorable brand and store information positively influenced perceptions of quality and value, and subjects' willingness to buy. Dodds (1999) pointed out if a price is unacceptable, consumers will then assess the product with little or without net value. Indeed, seeking the best price is a key motivation of online consumers (Swatman, Krueger, & Van der Beek, 2006). Price significantly influences online music purchase decisions (Chu & Lu, 2007). High price is the key inhibitor of purchase willingness. This study defines perceived price as the degree to which the consumer believes that he/she must pay in money to obtain online music. Consequently, the following hypothesis was offered for this study:

H4: Perceived price is negatively related to perceived value in online music setting.

Perceived Ease of Use

Online shopping makes adopters easy to find real bargains or compare shopping across different websites or within a particular website as well (Saprikis et al., 2010). Atkinson and Kydd (1997) found significant effects of ease of use on the Internet usage for entertainment. Van der Heijden (2004) found that perceived ease of use is a significant predictor of adoption intention for hedonic-oriented IT. Perceived ease of use was found to have positively influenced the behavioural intention to use a system where users who believes a system is free of effort, would be more likely to use and accept the system (Fagan et al., 2008; Guriting & Ndubisi, 2006; Hsu et al., 2009; Huang, 2008; Ramayah, Chin, Suki, & Amlus, 2005). However, it is also found in other research that perceived ease of use is found to have not directly influenced the behavioural intention to use a system (Ruiz-Mafé et al., 2009). Generally, when a system is found to be easy to use, users will have the intention to use the system. This study defines perceived ease of use as the degree to which the consumer believes that listening to online music is effortless. Accordingly, this study believes if online consumers perceive that they can reduce effort, namely reduce perceived sacrifice, an increase in value can then be achieved. Thus, the final hypothesis for this study was developed as follows:

H5. Perceived ease of use is positively related to perceived value in online music setting.

Methodology

Questionnaires were completely responded by 200 staffs and students in one of the private higher learning institution in Selangor, Malaysia with 80% response rate following simple random sampling technique; a technique that each element in the population has a known and equal probability of selection. The collected data were analysed using Structural Equation Modeling (SEM) via the Analysis of Moment Structure (AMOS 16) computer program, a second-generation multivariate technique. It is used in confirmatory modeling to evaluate whether the data collected fit the proposed theoretical model. The variables used (Appendix) were adapted as follows: Perceived Usefulness and Perceived Ease of Use (Davis, 1989; Van der Heijden, 2004), Perceived Value and Purchase Intention (Dodds et al., 1991), Perceived Playfulness (Van der Heijden, 2004), and Perceived Price (Sweeney, Soutar, & Johnson, 1997; Tam, 2004). Respondents were asked to express their agreement/disagreement with a statement on a five-point Likert-type scale with anchors ranging from "1=strongly disagree" to "5=strongly agree".

Data Analysis

Personal Characteristics of Respondents

A personal profile of the respondents, summarized in Table 1 indicates that there were more male than female: 60% versus 40%, respectively. The results also show that 80% of the respondents were Malay. Most respondents were 26-31 years of age. More than 70% indicated hold Bachelor, Master and Phd Degree level of educational background. 62% respondent is single, 47% are student and 38% are professionals. The monthly income or allowances indicated by the respondents was more than RM 2001 for over 80% of the respondents.

Structural Equation Modelling

Researchers developed the Structural Equation Modelling (SEM) to evaluate how well a proposed conceptual model containing observed multiple indicators and hypothetical constructs explains or fits the collected data (Yoon & Uysal, 2005). This study used SEM to empirically test the relationships between constructs using the AMOS 16 software. AMOS is more confirmatory in nature and it provides various overall goodness-of-fit indices to assess model fit for convergent validity (Byrne, 2001).

Reliability and Validity

Convergent and discriminant validity were assessed with several tests. Convergent validity was assessed with three tests recommended by Anderson and Gerbing (1988). Table 2 lists the standardized loadings, composite reliabilities, and average variance extracted estimates. Standardized factor loadings are indicative of the degree of association between scale items and a latent variable. The loadings were highly significant. Composite reliabilities, similar to Cronbach's alpha, range from 0.860 to 0.939, all exceeding the minimum limit of 0.70 (Hair, Black, Babin, Anderson, & Tatham, 2010). Thus, suggesting that they are all reliable. Average Variance Extracted (AVE) estimates are measures of the variation explained by the latent variable to random measurement error (Netemeyer, Johnston, & Burton, 1990) and ranged from 0.673 to 0.762, all exceeding the recommended lower limit of 0.50 (Fornell & Larcker, 1981). All tests supported convergent validity of the scales. Thus, all factors in the measurement model had adequate reliability and convergent validity.

To examine discriminant validity, we compared the shared variances between factors with the AVE of the individual factors. Table 3 shows the inter-

Table 1. Demographic characteristics of respondents

	N	%
Gender		
Male	120	60
Female	80	40
Race		
Malay	80	40
Chinese	60	30
Indian	48	24
Others	12	6
Age		
Less than 20 years	34	17
21-25	66	33
26-31	80	40
31 years above	20	10
Educational level		
SPM	5	2.5
STPM/Diploma	40	20
Bachelor Degree	120	60
Master Degree/PhD	35	17.5
Marital Status		
Single	124	62
Married	76	38
Occupation		
Student	94	47
Professional	76	38
Clerical/technical	25	13
Others	5	2
Salary/Allowances		
Less than RM 1000	8	4
RM 1001- RM 2000	30	15
RM 2001-RM 3001	79	40
More than RM 3001	83	41

construct correlations off the diagonal of the matrix. This showed that the shared variance between factors were lower than the average variance extracted of the individual factors, confirming discriminant validity (Fornell & Larcker, 1981). In summary, the measurement model demonstrated discriminant validity.

Model Fit

Bagozzi and Yi (1988) suggested a similar set of fit indices used to examine the structural model. The Comparative Fit Index (CFI), Goodness of Fit Index (GFI), Adjusted Goodness of Fit Index (AGFI), Normed Fit Index (NFI), and Root Mean Square Error of Approximation (RMSEA) were used to judge the model fit.

CFI: The Comparative Fit Index is a recommended index of overall fitness (Gerbing & Anderson, 1993). This index compares a proposed model with the null model assuming that there are no relationships between the measures. CFI values close to 1 are generally accepted as being indications of well-fitting models (Raykov & Marcoulides, 2000). A CFI value greater than 0.90 indicates an acceptable fit to the data (Bentler, 1992).

GFI: The Goodness of Fit Index measures the fitness of a model compared to another model. The index tells what proportion of the variance in the sample variance-covariance matrix is accounted for by the model. This should exceed 0.90 as recommended by Hair et al. (2010) for a good model.

AGFI: Adjusted GFI is an alternate GFI index in which the value of the index is adjusted for the number of parameters in the model. Few number of parameters in the model relative to the number of data points. AGFI value greater

Table 2. Reliability and item loadings

Constructs	Items	Standardized Loadings	CR	AVE
Perceived Usefulness (PU)	PU1	0.55	0.898	0.718
	PU2	0.741		
	PU3	0.802		
	PU4	0.625		
Perceived Ease of Use (PE)	PE1	0.768	0.903	0.729
	PE2	0.788		
	PE3	0.782		
	PE4	0.707		
Perceived Playfulness (PL)	PL1	0.767	0.939	0.747
	PL2	0.935		
	PL3	0.811		
	PL4	0.771		
Perceived Price (PR)	PR1	0.825	0.919	0.673
	PR2	0.879		
	PR3	0.740		
	PR4	0.838		
Perceived Value (PV)	PV1	0.786	0.860	0.762
	PV2	0.818		
	PV3	0.481		
Purchase Intention (PI)	PI1	0.766	0.863	0.694
	PI2	0.912		
	PI3	0.731		

than 0.80 indicates an acceptable fit to the data (Gefen, Karahanna, & Straub, 2003).

NFI: The Normed Fit Index measures the proportion by which a model is improved in terms of fit compared to the base model (Hair et al., 2010). The index is simply the difference between the two models' chi-squares divided by the chi-square for the independence model. NFI values of 0.90 or greater indicate an adequate model fit (Bentler, 1992).

RMSEA: The Root Mean Square Error of Approximation provides information in terms of discrepancy per degree of freedom for a model. This index is used to assess the residuals. It adjusts the parsimony in the model and is relatively insensitive to sample size. According to Hu and Bentler (1999), RMSEA must be equal to or less than 0.08 for an adequate model fit.

To summarise, goodness-of-fit indices for this model were Chi-square/df = 1.257, CFI = 0.951, GFI = 0.924, AGFI = 0.812, NFI = 0.903, and RMSEA = 0.052 (Table 4). All of the model-fit indices exceed the respective common acceptance levels suggested by previous research, demonstrating that the model exhibited a good fit with the data collected. Thus, we could proceed to examine the path coefficients of the structural model.

Hypotheses Testing

The test of structural model was performed using SEM in order to examine the hypothesized conceptual framework by performing a simultaneous test. The test of the structural model includes: (a) estimating the path coefficients, which indicate the strengths of the relationships between the dependent variables and independent variables, and (b) the R-square value, which represents the amount of variance explained by the independent variables. The path coefficients in the SEM model represent standardized regression coefficients.

The structural model reflecting the assumed linear, causal relationships among the constructs was tested with the data collected from the validated measures. The square multiple correlation for the structural equations index connotes that the predictors Perceived Usefulness, Perceived Playfulness, Perceived Price, and Perceived Ease of Use together have explained 45% of the variance in Perceived Value. Next, Perceived Value has explained 23% of the variance in Purchase Intention in online music. In other words, there are other additional variables that are important in explaining Perceived Value and Purchase Intention in online music that have not been considered in this study. Figure 2 depicts the structural model.

Properties of the causal paths for the structural model (standardized regression coefficients (β) with the value above which $p<0.05$, β is con-

Table 3. Correlation Matrix ands Roots of the AVEs (shown as diagonal elements)

	Mean	Standard Deviation	PU	PL	PR	PE	PV	PI
PU	2.141	.569	0.847					
PL	2.289	.784	0.303**	0.864				
PR	2.878	.883	0.091	0.141	0.820			
PE	2.430	.691	0.330**	0.329**	-0.111	0.873		
PV	2.604	.577	0.334**	0.384**	0.028	0.486**	0.833	
PI	2.829	.815	0.237*	0.350**	0.061	0.275**	0.395**	1

** Correlation is significant at the 0.01 level (2-tailed)

* Correlation is significant at the 0.05 level (2-tailed)

Table 4. Goodness-of-fit indices for structural model

Fit Indices	Benchmark	Value
Absolute fit measures		
CMIN (χ^2)		248.882
DF		198
CMIN (χ^2)/DF	< 3	1.257
GFI (Goodness of Fit Index)	> 0.9	0.924
RMSEA (Root Mean Square Error of Approximation)	< 0.10	0.052
Incremental fit measures		
AGFI (Adjusted Goodness of Fit Index)	> 0.80	0.812
NFI (Normed Fit Index)	> 0.90	0.903
CFI (Comparative Fit Index)	> 0.90	0.951
IFI (Incremental Fit Index)	> 0.90	0.952
RFI (Relative Fit Index)	> 0.90	0.932
Parsimony fit measures		
PCFI (Parsimony Comparative of Fit Index)	> 0.50	0.815
PNFI (Parsimony Normed Fit Index)	> 0.50	0.689

sidered significant, standard error, and hypotheses result) are showed in Table 5. Hypothesis 1 points that Perceived Value is positively related to Purchase Intentions towards online music. Findings in Table 5 depict that Perceived Value is directly and positively affects Purchase Intentions towards online music ($\beta_1 = 0.480$, $p<0.05$). Therefore, Hypothesis 1 was verified and accepted. Respondents found that the online music is valuable for them as they consider it to be a good buy. The result is consistent with the empirical research finding by Chu & Lu (2007) where purchase intentions of early adopters of online music can be predicted reasonably well according to perceived value of online music.

Next, Hypothesis 2 postulates that Perceived Usefulness is positively related to Perceived Value in online music setting. Similarly, Hypothesis 2 is also supported by the empirical data in the study ($\beta_2 = 0.262$, $p<0.05$), as noted in Table 5, which appears to correspond to Chu & Lu (2007)'s findings that Usefulness is a significant determinant of Perceived Value for purchasers. Usefulness in online music is clearly seen as the

online music web sites provide a variety of music. Respondent can acquire music information more easily through the online music web sites and can better decide which music they want to listen to than in the past.

Hypothesis 3 proposes Perceived Playfulness is positively related to Perceived Value in online music setting. Results reveal that Perceived Playfulness has positive effect on consumer Perceived Value in online music setting. Therefore, this hypothesis is accepted at $p<0.05$ ($\beta_3 = 0.297$). That is respondents found that listening to online music makes them feel pleasant as they enjoy the course of listening to online music. Thereafter has developed perceived value in online music setting. Buying online has advantages to who's such as too busy or to pack with their schedule but still want to enjoy with music. These findings align with prior studies by Chu and Lu (2007), Hsu and Lu (2004), and Van der Heijden (2004). Playfulness considerations are important for both purchasers and potential purchasers. Early adopters of online music are willing to purchase online music merely when they perceive that online music web sites

Figure 2. Structural model

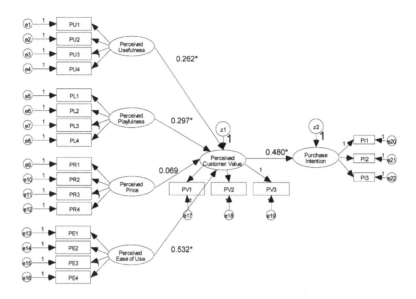

are likely to fulfill their emotional and affective demands either purchasers or potential purchasers.

It was hypothesize in Hypothesis 4 that Perceived Price is negatively related to Perceived Value in online music setting. Result further reports that there is no significant relationship between Perceived Price and Perceived Value in online music setting. Therefore, H4 is rejected by the empirical data in the study at 0.05 level of significance ($\beta_3 = 0.069$). Of the five paths hypothesized in the model, only the influence of Perceived Price was non-significant. Respondents generally found that listening online music would not cost them a lot of money. The price for online music is much less than they expected. If music is

too expensive to explore and enjoy (and there are many ways to measure expense), many will give up on it. The finding is not allied with past studies by Chu and Lu (2007) and not in accordance with research on consumer behavior (Venkatesh & Brown, 2001). They noted that potential purchasers may purchase online music only when they perceive an adequate monetary price; on the other hand, price remains a very important determinant of willingness to make continued purchase decision for purchasers.

The final hypothesis, Hypothesis 5, presumes that Perceived Ease of Use is positively related to Perceived Value in online music setting. Investigation of the findings in Table 5 reveal that

Table 5. Results of hypotheses test

Path			Coefficients	S.E.	C.R.	Finding
Perceived Value	<---	Perceived Usefulness	0.262*	0.069	2.108	Supported
Perceived Value	<---	Perceived Playfulness	0.297*	0.052	2.440	Supported
Perceived Value	<---	Perceived Price	0.069	0.035	0.683	Not Supported
Perceived Value	<---	Perceived Ease of Use	0.532*	0.093	3.182	Supported
Purchase Intention	<---	Perceived Value	0.480*	0.392	3.013	Supported

* $p<0.05$

the hypothesis receives support at 0.05 level of significance ($\beta_5 = 0.532$). It is confirmed that Perceived Ease of Use directly and positively affects Perceived Value in online music setting. Perceived Ease of Use in online music means that learning how to listen to online music would be easy for the respondents. It would be easy for them to become skillful at listening to online music. Interaction with online music web site is clear and understandable. Comparable finding was not found in Chu and Lu (2007) where Perceived Ease of Use did not appear to drive Perceived Value as the study participants have no difficulties in using the online music web sites.

CONCLUSION AND RECOMMENDATIONS

The results show that the proposed model has good explanatory power and confirms its robustness, with a reasonably strong empirical support, in predicting early adopters' intentions to use online music. Pithily, the results evidence for among all the significant variables, and Perceived Ease of Use emerges as the important factor which affects Perceived Value among early adopters of online music, followed by Perceived Playfulness. People unwrap and look to use new music services on their iPods, digital music players, iPads, mobile devices or laptops. Certainly, Perceived Value is the only significant impact on the Purchase Intentions towards online music. However, according to assertion of Technology Acceptance Model, perceived usefulness is more important than perceived ease of use in determining whether or not to use a technology (Cheong & Park, 2005; King & He, 2006). Adopters perceived the positive impact of online shopping to a higher degree compared to non-adopters in terms of that Internet provides them with the ability to shop abroad and purchase at any time of the day (Saprikis et al., 2010). Online music creates the allure of clicking

a link and having the song play instantly either purchasing of downloaded music from iTunes or Amazon or free downloading of songs from peer-to-peer file sharing networks.

Perceived value of downloadable music, in terms of expected value for money relative to other outlets for disposable income should be stressed by the marketers. Giving people mechanisms to audition new music with ease of use and search, a large music catalogue, and good sound quality, flexibility in use is essential and later will let them find the music that they will want to play enough to warrant purchasing it. Online music practitioners should extend their knowledge and insight about this field to creative and innovative, brand new and interesting attractiveness to online music which is easier to purchase without going to the store for it. If practitioners cannot launch the early market smoothly, it is more difficult to make a profit to support the financial issue, and even may withdraw from the market. Thus, music online practitioners should be very up to date with online environment and have a creative idea on how to attract customers.

This study can help online music practitioners to develop better marketing strategies and to create a successful business model. This study also helps practitioners to extend online music market with greater understanding about early adopters' willingness to be involved in online music purchase. In additional, it can help users to be more keen on buying music online with an attractive market strategy. In order to ensure this study to be more accurate and reliable, future research should expand or increase the involvement of respondents. With more geographic areas of research included, the results will be more representative. Besides that, the research should include as variables other factors than the variables the researchers have used. This is because the variables cannot explain the whole factor influence purchase intention of early adopters towards online music.

REFERENCES

Anderson, J. C., & Gerbing, D. W. (1988). Structural equation modeling in practice: A review and recommended two-step approach. *Psychological Bulletin, 103*(3), 411–423. doi:10.1037/0033-2909.103.3.411

Atkinson, M. A., & Kydd, C. (1997). Individual characteristics associated with World Wide Web use: an empirical study of playfulness and motivation. *The Data Base for Advances in Information Systems, 28*(2), 53–61.

Bagozzi, R. P., & Yi, Y. (1988). On the evaluation of structural equation models. *Academic of Marketing Science, 16*, 74–94. doi:10.1007/BF02723327

Bentler, P. M. (1992). On the fit of models to covariances and methodology to the bulletin. *Psychological Bulletin, 112*(3), 400–404. doi:10.1037/0033-2909.112.3.400

BPI. (2010). *Digital Music Nation 2010.* Retrieved from http://bpi.co.uk/assets/files/Digital%20Music%20Nation%202010.pdf

Byrne, B. M. (2001). *Structural Equation Modeling with AMOS.* Hillsdale, NJ: Lawrence Erlbaum.

Cheong, J. H., & Park, M. (2005). Mobile Internet acceptance in Korea. *Internet Research, 15*(2), 125–140. doi:10.1108/10662240510590324

Childers, T. L., Carr, C. L., Peckc, J., & Carson, S. (2001). Hedonic and utilitarian motivations for online retail shopping behavior. *Journal of Retailing, 77*(4), 511–535. doi:10.1016/S0022-4359(01)00056-2

Chu, C. W., & Lu, H. P. (2007). Factors influencing online music purchase intention in Taiwan. An empirical study based on the value-intention framework. *Internet Research, 17*(2), 139–155. doi:10.1108/10662240710737004

Davis, F. D. (1989). Perceived usefulness, perceived ease of use, and user acceptance of information technology. *Management Information Systems Quarterly, 13*(3), 319–340. doi:10.2307/249008

Davis, F. D., Bagozzi, R. P., & Warshaw, P. R. (1992). Extrinsic and intrinsic motivation to use computers in the workplace. *Journal of Applied Social Psychology, 24*(14), 1111–1132. doi:10.1111/j.1559-1816.1992.tb00945.x

Dodds, W. B. (1999). Managing customer value. *Mid-American Journal of Business, 14*(1), 13–22. doi:10.1108/19355181199900001

Dodds, W. B., & Monroe, K. B. (1985). The effect of brand and price information on subjective product evaluations. *Advances in Consumer Research. Association for Consumer Research (U. S.), 12*(1), 85–90.

Dodds, W. B., Monroe, K. B., & Grewal, D. (1991). Effects of price, brand, and store information on buyers' product evaluations. *JMR, Journal of Marketing Research, 28*, 307–319. doi:10.2307/3172866

Fagan, M. H., Wooldridge, B. R., & Neill, S. (2008). Exploring the intention to use computers: An empirical investigation of the role of intrinsic motivation, extrinsic motivation, and perceived ease of use. *Journal of Computer Information Systems, 48*(3), 31–37.

Fornell, C., & Larcker, D. (1981). Structural equation models with unobservable variables and measurement error. *JMR, Journal of Marketing Research, 19*, 39–50. doi:10.2307/3151312

Gefen, D., Karahanna, E., & Straub, D. W. (2003). Trust and TAM in online shopping: An integrated model. *Management Information Systems Quarterly, 27*(1), 51–90.

Gerbing, D. W., & Anderson, J. C. (1993). Monte Carlo evaluations of goodness-of-fit indexes for structural equation models. In Bollen, K. A., & Long, J. S. (Eds.), *Testing structural equation models* (pp. 40–65). Newbury Park, CA: Sage.

Group, N. P. D. (2010). *Amazon Ties Walmart as second-ranked U.S. music retailer, behind industry-Leader iTunes*. Retrieved from http://i486.net/2010/11/28/npd-group-amazon-ties-walmart-as-second-ranked-u-s-music-retailer-behind-industry-leader-itunes/

Guriting, P., & Ndubisi, O. N. (2006). Borneo online banking: Evaluating customer perceptions and behavioural intention. *Management Research News*, *29*(1-2), 6–15. doi:10.1108/01409170610645402

Ha, S., & Stoel, L. (2009). Consumer e-shopping acceptance: Antecedents in a technology acceptance model. *Journal of Business Research*, *62*, 565–571. doi:10.1016/j.jbusres.2008.06.016

Hair, J. F., Black, B., Babin, B., Anderson, R. E., & Tatham, R. L. (2010). *Multivariate Data Analysis: A Global Perspective*. Upper Saddle River, NJ: Pearson Education.

Holbrook, M. B. (1996). Customer value – a framework for analysis and research. *Advances in Consumer Research. Association for Consumer Research (U. S.)*, *23*(1), 138–142.

Hsu, M. H., & Chiu, C. M. (2004). Internet self-efficacy and electronic service acceptance. *Decision Support Systems*, *38*(3), 369–381. doi:10.1016/j.dss.2003.08.001

Hsu, M. K., Wang, S. W., & Chiu, K. K. (2009). Computer attitude, statistics anxiety and self-efficacy on statistical software adoption behavior: An empirical study of online MBA learners. *Computers in Human Behavior*, *25*, 412–420. doi:10.1016/j.chb.2008.10.003

Hu, L., & Bentler, P. M. (1999). Cutoff criteria for fit indexes in covariance structure analysis: conventional criteria versus new alternatives. *Structural Equation Modeling*, *6*(1), 1–55. doi:10.1080/10705519909540118

Huang, E. (2008). Use and gratification in e-consumers. *Internet Research*, *18*(4), 405–426. doi:10.1108/10662240810897817

IFPI. (2010). *IFPI Digital Music Report 2010*. Retrieved from http://www.ifpi.org/content/library/DMR2010.pdf

King, W. R., & He, J. (2006). A meta-analysis of the technology acceptance model. *Information & Management*, *43*, 740–755. doi:10.1016/j.im.2006.05.003

Knopper, S. (2009). *Appetite for self-destruction: The spectacular crash of the record industry in the digital age*. New York, NY: Free Press.

Lee, M. K. O., Cheung, C. M. K., & Chen, Z. H. (2007). Understanding user acceptance of multimedia messaging services: An empirical study. *Journal of the American Society for Information Science and Technology*, *58*(13), 2066–2077. doi:10.1002/asi.20670

Monroe, K. B. (1973). Buyers' subjective perceptions of price. *JMR, Journal of Marketing Research*, *10*, 70–80. doi:10.2307/3149411

Moore, G. A. (1991). *The Chasm: Marketing and Selling High-Tech Products to Mainstream Customer*. Philadelphia, PA: HarperCollins.

Netemeyer, R. G., Johnston, M. W., & Burton, S. (1990). Analysis of role conflict and role ambiguity in a structural equations framework. *The Journal of Applied Psychology*, *75*(2), 148–157. doi:10.1037/0021-9010.75.2.148

Ramayah, T., Chin, Y. L., Suki, N. M., & Amlus, I. (2005). Determinants of intention to use an online bill payment system among MBA students. *E-Business*, *9*, 80–91.

Raykov, T., & Marcoulides, G. A. (2000). *A First Course in Structural Equation Modeling*. Mahwah, NJ: Lawrence Erlbaum.

Ruiz-Mafé, C., Sanz-Blas, S., & Aldas-Manzano, J. (2009). Drivers and barriers to online airline ticket purchasing. *Journal of Air Transport Management, 15*(6), 294–298. doi:10.1016/j.jairtraman.2009.02.001

Saprikis, V., Chouliara, A., & Vlachopoulou, M. (2010). Perceptions towards Online Shopping: Analyzing the Greek University Students' Attitude. *Communications of the IBIMA, 2010*, 1–13.

Seyal, A. H., & Rahman, N. A. (2007). The influence of external variables on the executives' use of the Internet. *Business Process Management Journal, 13*(2), 263–278. doi:10.1108/14637150710740491

Styvén, M. (2007). *Exploring the online music market: Consumer characteristics and value perceptions. Unpublished doctoral dissertations*. Sweden: Lulea University of Technology.

Suki, N. M., Ahmand, M. I., & Thyagarajan, V. (2007). The Influence of Friends, Family and Media in Classifying Online Shopper Innovativeness in Malaysia. *European Journal of Soil Science, 5*(1), 136–143.

Suki, N. M., Ramayah, T., & Kow Pei Ming, M. (2010). Explaining job searching through the social networking sites: A structural equation model approach. *International Journal of Virtual Communities and Social Networking, 2*(3), 1–15. doi:10.4018/jvcsn.2010070101

Suki, N. M., Ramayah, T., & Suki, N. M. (2008). Internet shopping acceptance: examining the influence of intrinsic versus extrinsic motivations. *Direct Marketing: An International Journal, 2*(2), 97–110. doi:10.1108/17505930810881752

Swatman, P. M. C., Krueger, C., & Van der Beek, K. (2006). The changing digital content landscape: an evaluation of e-business model development in European online news and music. *Internet Research, 16*(1), 53–80. doi:10.1108/10662240610642541

Sweeney, J. C., Soutar, G. N., & Johnson, L. W. (1997). Retail service quality and perceived value. *Journal of Retailing and Consumer Services, 4*(1), 39–48. doi:10.1016/S0969-6989(96)00017-3

Tam, J. L. M. (2004). Customer satisfaction, service quality and perceived value: an integrative model. *Journal of Marketing Management, 20*, 897–917. doi:10.1362/0267257041838719

Teas, R. K., & Agarwal, S. (2000). The effects of extrinsic product cues on consumers' perceptions of quality, sacrifice, and value. *Journal of the Academy of Marketing Science, 28*(2), 278–290. doi:10.1177/0092070300282008

Teo, T. S. H., Lim, V. K. G., & Lai, R. Y. C. (1999). Intrinsic and extrinsic motivation in Internet usage. *Omega, 27*(32), 25–37. doi:10.1016/S0305-0483(98)00028-0

Tong, D. Y. K. (2009). A study of e–recruitment technology adoption in Malaysia. *Industrial Management & Data Systems, 109*(2), 281–300. doi:10.1108/02635570910930145

Van der Heijden, H. (2004). User acceptance of hedonic information systems. *Management Information Systems Quarterly, 28*(4), 695–704.

Venkatesh, V., & Brown, S. A. (2001). A longitudinal investigation of personal computers in homes: adoption determinants and emerging challenges. *Management Information Systems Quarterly, 25*(1), 71–102. doi:10.2307/3250959

Woodruff, R. B. (1997). Customer value: The next source for competitive advantage. *Journal of the Academy of Marketing Science, 25*(2), 139–154. doi:10.1007/BF02894350

Yoon, Y., & Uysal, M. (2005). An examination of the effects of motivation and satisfaction on destination loyalty: A structural model. *Tourism Management, 26*(1), 45–56. doi:10.1016/j.tourman.2003.08.016

Zeithaml, V. A. (1988). Consumer perceptions of price, quality, and value: a means-end model and synthesis of evidence. *Journal of Marketing, 52*, 2–22. doi:10.2307/1251446

APPENDIX: MEASUREMENT OF CONSTRUCTS

Perceived Usefulness

PU1 I can better decide which music I want to listen to than in the past.
PU2 I can acquire music information more easily through the online music web sites.
PU3 The online music web sites provide a variety of music.
PU4 Overall, I find online music web sites is useful.

Perceived Playfulness

PL1 I enjoy the course of listening to online music.
PL2 Listening to online music makes me feel pleasant.
PL3 When listening to online music, I feel exciting.
PL4 Overall, I found online music is interesting.

Perceived Price

PR1 The price for online music is a lot of money to spend.
PR2 The price for online music is much more than I expected.
PR3 What I would expect to pay for online music is high.
PR4 In general, I find listening online music would cost me a lot of money.

Perceived Ease of Use

PE1 My interaction with online music web site is clear and understands.
PE2 Learning how to listen to online music would be easy for me.
PE3 It would be easy for me to become skillful at listening to online music.
PE4 In general, I found online music web site is easy to use.

Perceived Value

PV1 The online music is valuable for me.
PV2 I would consider that online music to be a good value.
PV3 The online music service is considered to be a good buy.

Purchase Intention

PI1 The likelihood that I would pay for online music is high.
PI2 My willingness to buy online music is very high.
PI3 In near future, I would consider purchasing online music.

This work was previously published in the International Journal of Technology and Human Interaction, Volume 7, Issue 4, edited by Anabela Mesquita and Chia-Wen Tsai, pp. 46-61, copyright 2011 by IGI Publishing (an imprint of IGI Global).

Compilation of References

Adoghame, P. (2008). *The National Economic and Empowerment and Development Strategy (NEEDS): A critical appraisal of Nigeria's strategy for poverty reduction.* Paper presented at the 49ᵗʰ Annual Convention on Bridging Multiple, San Francisco, CA.

Agarwal, R., & Karahanna, E. (2000). Time flies when you're having fun: Cognitive absorption and beliefs about information technology usage. *Management Information Systems Quarterly, 24*(4), 665–694. doi:10.2307/3250951

Agrawal, A. J., & Chandak, M. B. (2007, April 2-4). Mobile Interface for Domain Specific Machine Translation Using Short Messaging Service. In *Proceedings of the 4th International Conference on Information Technology* (pp. 957-958).

Ahern, D. K. (2007). Challenges and opportunities of ehealth research. *American Journal of Preventive Medicine, 32*(5), 75–82. doi:10.1016/j.amepre.2007.01.016

Ahmed, Z. (2004). *Youth drives India's mobile phone revolution.* Retrieved from http://news.bbc.co.uk/1/hi/business/3585257.stm

Ailon, G. (2008). Mirror, mirror on the wall: Culture's consequences in a value test of its own design. *Academy of Management Review, 33*(4), 885–904.

Ajayi, G. O. (2003). *NITDA and ICT in Nigeria.* Paper presented at the Abdus Salam International Centre for Theoretical Physics Round Table on Developing Countries Access to Scientific Knowledge, Trieste, Italy.

Ajzen, I. (1985). From intentions to actions: A theory of planned behaviour. In Kuhl, J., & Beckman, J. (Eds.), *Action-control: From cognition to behavior* (pp. 11–39). Berlin, Germany: Springer-Verlag.

Ajzen, I. (1991). The theory of planned behavior. *Organizational Behavior and Human Decision Processes, 50*(2), 179–211. doi:10.1016/0749-5978(91)90020-T

Akpan-Obong, P. I. (2009). *Information and communication technologies in Nigeria.* New York, NY: Peter Lang.

Aladwani, A. M. (2001). Online banking: a field study of drivers, development challenges, and expectations. *International Journal of Information Management, 21*(3), 213–225. doi:10.1016/S0268-4012(01)00011-1

Al-Azam, H. (2001). *Electronic government in Jordan, applying possibilities.* Unpublished master's thesis, Yarmouk University, Irbid, Jordan.

Albaum, G. (1997). The Likert scale revisited: An alternate version. *Journal of the Market Research Society. Market Research Society, 39*(2), 331–342.

Alge, B. J. (2001). Effects of computer surveillance on perceptions of privacy and procedural justice. *The Journal of Applied Psychology, 86*(4), 797–804. doi:10.1037/0021-9010.86.4.797

Alge, B. J., Ballinger, G. A., Tangirala, S., & Oakley, J. L. (2006). Information privacy in organizations: Empowering creative and extra role performance. *The Journal of Applied Psychology, 91*(1), 221–232. doi:10.1037/0021-9010.91.1.221

Ali, M., & Brooks, L. (2008). Culture and IS: National cultural dimensions within IS discipline. In *Proceedings of the UK Academy for Information Systems*, Bournemouth, UK.

Al-Kayed, Z., Fayyad, R., & Assaf, M. (1999). *The best practices in the Jordan civil service reforms for sustainable human development in Jordan.* Amman, Jordan: Jordan Institute of Public Administration.

Al-Omari, A., & Al-Omari, H. (2006). E-Government readiness assessment model. *Journal of Computer Science, 2*(11), 841–845. doi:10.3844/jcssp.2006.841.845

Alon, Y. (2007). *The making of Jordan.* London, UK: I.B. Tauris.

Al-Shqairat, Z. (2009). *Understanding the role of public private partnership (PPP) in e-government implementation in developing countries: Case study of Jordan.* Unpublished doctoral dissertation, Leeds Metropolitan University, Leeds, UK.

Alvesson, M. (1993). *Organisationsteori och teknokratiskt medvetande.* Stockholm, Sweden: Nerenius & Santérus Förlag.

Alvesson, M. (2004). *Knowledge work and knowledge-intensive firms.* Oxford, UK: Oxford University Press.

Alvesson, M. (2006). *Tomhetens triumf: Om grandiositet, illusionsnummer & nollsummespel.* Stockholm, Sweden: Bokförlaget Atlas.

Alvesson, M., & Empson, L. (2008). The construction of organizational identity: Comparative case studies of consulting firms. *Scandinavian Journal of Management, 24*(1), 1–16. doi:10.1016/j.scaman.2007.10.001

Alvesson, M., & Sveningsson, S. (2003). Good visions, bad micro-management and ugly ambiguity: Contradictions of (non-) leadership in a knowledge-intensive organization. *Organization Studies, 24*(6), 961–988. doi:10.1177/017 0840603024006007

Alwitt, L. F., & Prabhaker, P. R. (1994). Identifying who dislikes television advertising: Not by demographics alone. *Journal of Advertising Research, 34*(6), 17–29.

Ambrose, M. L., & Alder, G. S. (2000). Designing, implementing, and utilizing computerized performance monitoring: Enhancing organizational justice. *Research in Personnel and Human Resource Management, 18,* 187–219.

Ancona, D., Okhuysen, G., & Perlow, L. (2001). Taking Time to Integrate Temporal Research. *Academy of Management Review, 28*(4), 512–529. doi:10.2307/3560239

Andersen, H., Jakobsen, M. H., & Nilsen, S. (2007). *Mobile-TV usage - customer insights.* Oslo, Norway: Telenor R&I.

Anderson, A. H., Newlands, A., Mullin, J., Fleming, A. M., Doherty-Sneddon, G., & Van der Velden, J. (1996). Impact of video-mediated communication on simulated service encounters. *Interacting with Computers, 8*(2), 193–206. doi:10.1016/0953-5438(96)01025-9

Anderson, A. H., Smallwood, L., MacDonald, R., Mullin, J., & Fleming, A. (2000). Video data and video links in mediated communication: what do users value? *International Journal of Human-Computer Studies, 52,* 165–187. doi:10.1006/ijhc.1999.0335

Anderson, J. C., & Gerbing, D. W. (1988). Structural equation modeling in practice: A review and recommended two step approach. *Psychological Bulletin, 103*(3), 411–423. doi:10.1037/0033-2909.103.3.411

Anderson, J. C., & Gerbing, D. W. (1988). Structural equation modeling in practice: A review and recommended two-step approach. *Psychological Bulletin, 103*(3), 411–423. doi:10.1037/0033-2909.103.3.411

Andersson, J. (2009). SIM cards–the new frontier for biometrics. *Card Technology Today, 21*(4), 10–11. doi:10.1016/S0965-2590(09)70095-7

Andersson, K., Foros, O., & Steen, F. (2006). *Text and voice: complements, substitutes or both? (CEPR Discussion Papers – Industrial Organization No. 5780).* London: CEPR.

Andreassen, H. K., Trondsen, M., Kummervold, P. E., Gammon, D., & Hjortdahl, P. (2006). Patients who use e-mediated communication with their doctor: New constructions of trust in the patient-doctor relationship. *Qualitative Health Research, 16*(2), 238–248. doi:10.1177/1049732305284667

Aoki, K. (2000). *Cultural differences in e-commerce: A comparison between the United States and Japan.* Retrieved from http://www.isoc.org/inet2000/cdproceedings/7d/7d_1.htm

Arasli, H., Bavik, A., & Ekiz, E. H. (2006). The effects of nepotism on human resource management. *The International Journal of Sociology and Social Policy, 26*(7-8), 295–308. doi:10.1108/01443330610680399

Arbaugh, J. B. (2008). Introduction: Blended learning: Research and practice. *Academy of Management Learning & Education, 7*(1), 130–131.

Armitage, R. (2002). *To CCTV or not to CCTV? A review of current research into the effectiveness of CCTV systems in reducing crime.* Retrieved from http://www.nacro.org.uk

Arnold, M. (2003). On the Phenomenology of Technology: The 'Janus-faces' of Mobile Phones. *Information and Organization, 13*(4), 231–256. doi:10.1016/S1471-7727(03)00013-7

Atienza, A. A., Hesse, B. W., Baker, T. B., Abrams, D. B., Rimer, B. K., & Croyle, R. T. (2007). Critical issues in ehealth research. *American Journal of Preventive Medicine, 32*(5), 71–74. doi:10.1016/j.amepre.2007.02.013

Atkinson, M. A., & Kydd, C. (1997). Individual characteristics associated with World Wide Web use: an empirical study of playfulness and motivation. *The Data Base for Advances in Information Systems, 28*(2), 53–61.

Attoh-Okine, N., & Shen, L. (1995). *Security issues of emerging smart cards fare collection application in mass transit.* Paper presented at the Vehicle Navigation and Information Systems Conference.

Avolio, B. J., & Bass, B. M. (2002). *Developing potential across a full range of leaderships: Cases on transactional and transformational leadership.* Mahwah, NJ: Lawrence Erlbaum.

Awad, N. F., & Krishnan, M. S. (2006). The personalization privacy paradox: An empirical evaluation of information transparency and the willingness to be profiled online for personalization. *Management Information Systems Quarterly, 30*(1), 13–28.

Azevedo, R. (2005). Using hypermedia as a metacognitive tool for enhancing student learning? The role of self-regulated learning. *Educational Psychologist, 40*(4), 199–209. doi:10.1207/s15326985ep4004_2

Bagozzi, R. P., & Yi, Y. (1988). On the evaluation of structural equation models. *Academic of Marketing Science, 16*, 74–94. doi:10.1007/BF02723327

Bain, D. (1995). *Smart cards: Implications for privacy.* Sydney, Australia: Australian Privacy Commissioner.

Balakrishnan, V., Yeow, H. P., & Ngo, D. C. L. (2005). An investigation on the ergonomic problems of using mobile phones to send SMS. In P. D. Bust & P. T. McCabe (Eds.), *Proceedings of the Contemporary Ergonomics 2005 Conference* (pp. 195-199). London, UK: Taylor & Francis.

Balakrishnan, V., & Yeow, H. P. (2008). A study of the effect of thumb sizes on mobile phone texting satisfaction. *Journal of Usability Studies, 3*(3), 118–128.

Bandyopadhyay, K., & Fraccastoro, K. A. (2007). The effect of culture on user acceptance of information technology. *Communications of the Association for Information Systems, 19*(23), 522–543.

Banta, T., Black, K., & Kline, K. (2000). PBL 2000 plenary address offers evidence for and against problem-based learning. *PBL Insight, 5*(3), 1–7.

Barley, S. (1988). On Technology, Time, and Social Order: Technologically Induced Change in the Temporal Organization of Radiological Work. In Dubinskas, F. (Ed.), *Making Time: Ethnographies of High-Technology Organizations* (pp. 123–169). Philadelphia: Temple University Press.

Barley, S., & Kunda, G. (2004). Gurus, Hired Guns, and Warm Bodies. In *Itinerant Experts in a Knowledge Economy.* Princeton, NJ: Princeton University Press.

Barrows, H. S. (2000). *Problem-Based learning applied to medical education.* Springfield, IL: Southern Illinois University Press.

Barrows, H. S., & Tamblyn, R. M. (1980). *Problem-based learning: An approach to medical education.* New York: Springer.

Barthes, R., & Duisit, L. (1975). An introduction to the structural analysis of narrative. *New Literary History, 6*(2), 237–272. doi:10.2307/468419

Barwise, P., & Strong, C. (2002). Permission-based mobile advertising. *Journal of Interactive Marketing, 16*(1), 14–24. doi:10.1002/dir.10000

Bassanini, F. (2002). *Delivering services and public: Private partnership in e-government, with a final warning about digital divide, digital opportunity and the danger of a new colonialism.* Paper presented at the 3rd High Level Forum on City Informatization in the Asia-Pacific Region, Shanghai, China.

Bass, B. M. (1985). *Leadership and performance beyond expectation.* New York, NY: Free Press.

Bass, B. M., Avolio, B. J., & Atwater, L. (1996). The transformational and transactional leadership of men and women. *Applied Psychology: An International Review*, *45*(1), 5–34. doi:10.1111/j.1464-0597.1996.tb00847.x

Bauer, H. H., Barnes, S. J., Reichardt, T., & Neumann, M. M. (2005). Driving consumer acceptance of mobile marketing. *Journal of Electronic Commerce Research*, *6*(3), 181–192.

Bell, M., & Pavitt, K. (1993). Technological accumulation and industrial growth: Contrasts between developed and developing countries. *Industrial and Corporate Change*, *2*(1), 157–210. doi:10.1093/icc/2.1.157

Bellotti, V., Ducheneaut, N., Howard, M., Smith, I., & Grinter, R. E. (2005). Quality versus quantity: E-mail-centric task management and its relation with overload. *Human-Computer Interaction*, *20*, 89–138. doi:10.1207/s15327051hci2001&2_4

Bellovin, S. (2005). Security and privacy: Enemies or allies? *IEEE Security & Privacy*, *3*(3), 92. doi:10.1109/MSP.2005.80

Belwal, R., & Al-Zoubi, K. (2008). Public-centric e-governance in Jordan: A field study of people's perception of e-governance awareness, corruption and trust. *Journal of Information. Communication and Ethics in Society*, *6*(4), 317–333. doi:10.1108/14779960810921123

Bentler, P. M. (1992). On the fit of models to covariances and methodology to the bulletin. *Psychological Bulletin*, *112*(3), 400–404. doi:10.1037/0033-2909.112.3.400

Berger, P. L., & Luckmann, T. (1967). *The social construction of reality: A treatise in the sociology of knowledge*. New York, NY: Anchor Books.

Berman, S. J., Abraham, S., Battino, B., Shipnuck, L., & Neus, A. (2007). *Navigating the media divide*. Armonk, NY: IBM Institute for Business Value.

Berman, S. J., Battino, B., Shipnuck, L., & Neus, A. (2007). *The end of advertising as we know it*. Armonk, NY: IBM Institute for Business Value.

Betts, M., & Ouellette, T. (1995, November 6). Taming the email shrew. *Computerworld*, *29*(45), 32–33.

Bies, R. J. (1993). Privacy and procedural justice in organizations. *Social Justice Research*, *6*(1), 69–86. doi:10.1007/BF01048733

Billings, D. M. (2000). A framework for assessing outcomes and practices in web-based courses in nursing. *The Journal of Nursing Education*, *39*(2), 60–67.

Birch, A., & Irvine, V. (2009). Preservice teachers' acceptance of ICT integration in the classroom: Applying the UTAUT model. *Educational Media International*, *46*(4), 295–315. doi:10.1080/09523980903387506

Bisaso, R., Kereteletswe, O., Selwood, I., & Visscher, A. (2008). The use of information technology for educational management in Uganda and Botswana. *International Journal of Educational Development*, *28*(6), 656–668. doi:10.1016/j.ijedudev.2007.09.008

Blundell, J. (2005, July 13). *Linking e-government with efficiency*. Paper presented at the 5th Annual London Connects Conference on Engaging London with Efficient Services, London, UK.

Bly, S. A. (1988, September 26-28). A use of drawing surfaces in different collaborative settings. In *Proceedings of the Conference on Computer-Supported Cooperative Work (CSCW '88)*, Portland, OR (pp. 250-256). New York, NY: ACM Press.

Blythe, M. A., Monk, A. F., & Doughty, K. (2005). Socially dependable design: The challenge of aging populations for HCI. *Interacting with Computers*, *17*, 672–689. doi:10.1016/j.intcom.2005.09.005

Blythe, M. A., Overbeeke, K., Monk, A. F., & Wright, P. C. (Eds.). (2003). *Funology: From Usability to Enjoyment*. Dordrecht, The Netherlands: Kluwer Academic Publishers.

Bodenhausen, G. V., & Wyer, R. S. (1985). Effects of stereotypes on decision making and information-processing strategies. *Journal of Personality and Social Psychology*, *48*(2), 267–282. doi:10.1037/0022-3514.48.2.267

Böhm, G., & Pfister, H.-R. (2000). Action tendencies and characteristics of environmental risks. *Acta Psychologica*, *104*, 317–337. doi:10.1016/S0001-6918(00)00035-4

Böhm, G., & Pfister, H.-R. (2001). Mental representation of global environmental risks. In Böhm, G., Nerb, J., McDaniels, T., & Spada, H. (Eds.), *Environmental Risks: Perception, Evaluation and Management* (pp. 1–30). Amsterdam, The Netherlands: JAI. doi:10.1016/S0196-1152(01)80022-3

Borg, W. R., & Gall, M. D. (1989). *Educational research.* White Plains, NY: Longman.

Bostrom, A., Morgan, M. G., Fischhoff, B., & Read, D. (1994). What do people know about global climate change? 1. Mental models. *Risk Analysis, 14*(6), 959–970. doi:10.1111/j.1539-6924.1994.tb00065.x

Bottge, B. A., Rueda, E., Kwon, J. M., Grant, T., & La-Roque, P. (2009). Assessing and tracking students' problem solving performances in anchored learning environments. *Educational Technology Research and Development, 54*(4), 529–552. doi:10.1007/s11423-007-9069-y

Boudreau, M.-C., & Robey, D. (2005). Enacting Integrated Information Technology: A Human Agency Perspective. *Organization Science, 16*(1), 3–18. doi:10.1287/orsc.1040.0103

Boyle, E. A., Anderson, A. H., & Newlands, A. (1994). The effects of eye contact on dialogue and performance in a co-operative problem solving task. *Language and Speech, 37*(1), 1–20.

BPI. (2010). *Digital Music Nation 2010.* Retrieved from http://bpi.co.uk/assets/files/Digital%20Music%20Nation%202010.pdf

Brey, P. (2006). Surveillance and privacy. *Ethics and Information Technology, 7*, 183–184. doi:10.1007/s10676-006-0015-1

Brooks, L., Davis, C. J., & Lycett, M. (2005). Organisations and information systems: Investigating their dynamic complexities using repetory grids and cognitive mapping. *International Journal of Technology and Human Interaction, 1*(4), 39–55. doi:10.4018/jthi.2005100103

Brown, M. M. (2002). *An exploratory study of job satisfaction and work motivation of a selected group of information technology consultants in the Delaware Valley.* Unpublished doctoral dissertation, Wilmington College, Wilmington, DE.

Brown, G., Anderson, A. H., Yule, G., & Shillcock, R. (1984). *Teaching Talk.* Cambridge, UK: Cambridge University Press.

Brown, I., Cajee, Z., Davies, D., & Stroebel, S. (2003). Cell phone banking: predictors of adoption in South Africa – an exploratory study. *International Journal of Information Management, 23*(5), 381–394. doi:10.1016/S0268-4012(03)00065-3

Brown, J., Shipman, B., & Vetter, R. (2007). SMS: The Short Message Service. *Computer, 40*(12), 106–110. doi:10.1109/MC.2007.440

Brown, S. A., Massey, A. P., Montoya-Weiss, M. M., & Burkman, J. R. (2002). Do I really have to? User acceptance of mandated technology. *European Journal of Information Systems, 11*(4), 283–295. doi:10.1057/palgrave.ejis.3000438

Brown, S., Hine, N., Sixsmith, A., & Garner, P. (2004). Care in the community. *BT Technology Journal, 22*(3), 56–64. doi:10.1023/B:BTTJ.0000047120.60489.7a

Bruce, B. C., Dowd, H., Eastburn, D. M., & D'arcy, C. J. (2005). Plants, pathogens, and people: Extending the classroom to the web. *Teachers College Record, 107*(8), 1730–1753. doi:10.1111/j.1467-9620.2005.00540.x

Bruce, V. (1996). The Role of the face in communication: implications for video-phone design. *Interacting with Computers, 8*(2), 166–176. doi:10.1016/0953-5438(96)01026-0

Bryson, J. M., Ackermann, F., Eden, C., & Finn, C. B. (2004). *Visible thinking. Unlocking causal mapping for practical business results.* Chichester, UK: John Wiley & Sons.

Buchanan, R., & Berman, T. (1992). *Building successful partnerships.* Acquisitions Monthly.

Buckley, K. M. (2003). Evaluation of classroom-based, web-enhanced, and web-based distance learning nutrition courses for undergraduate nursing. *The Journal of Nursing Education, 42*(8), 367–370.

Budé, L., Imbos, T., Wiel, M. W. J. V. D., Broers, N. J., & Berger, M. P. F. (2009). The effect of directive tutor guidance in problem-based learning of statistics on students' perceptions and achievement. *Higher Education, 57*(1), 23–36. doi:10.1007/s10734-008-9130-8

Buellingen, F., & Woerter, M. (2004). Development perspectives, firm strategies and applications in mobile commerce. *Journal of Business Research, 57*(12), 1402–1408. doi:10.1016/S0148-2963(02)00429-0

Burgess, A., Jackson, T. W., & Edwards, J. (2003, May). Measuring electronic communication defects and their impact at 3M. In G. Ross & M. Staples (Eds.), *Proceedings of the Process Improvement and Project Management Issues Conference,* Glasgow, UK (pp. 343-353).

Burgess, A., Jackson, T. W., & Edwards, J. (2004). Email overload: Tolerance levels of employees within the workplace. In Khosrow-Pour, M. (Ed.), *Innovations through Information Technology* (pp. 205–207). Hershey, PA: Idea Group.

Burgess, A., Jackson, T. W., & Edwards, J. (2005). Email training significantly reduces email defects. *International Journal of Information Management, 25*(1), 71–83. doi:10.1016/j.ijinfomgt.2004.10.004

Burgos, D., Tattersall, C., & Koper, R. (2007). How to represent adaptation in e-learning with IMS learning design. *Interactive Learning Environments, 15*(2), 161–170. doi:10.1080/10494820701343736

Buunk, A. P., & Gibbons, F. X. (2007). Social Comparison: The End of A Theory and The Emergence of A Field. *Organizational Behavior and Human Decision Processes, 102*(1), 3–21. doi:10.1016/j.obhdp.2006.09.007

Byrne, B. M. (2001). *Structural equation modeling with AMOS: Basic concepts, applications, and programming.* Mahwah, NJ: Lawrence Erlbaum.

Byrne, R. M. J., & Johnson-Laird, P. N. (2009). 'If' and problems of conditional reasoning. *Trends in Cognitive Sciences, 13*(7), 282–287. doi:10.1016/j.tics.2009.04.003

Byron, K. (2008). Carrying too heavy a load? The communication and miscommunication of emotion by email. *Academy of Management Review, 33*(2), 309–327. doi:10.5465/AMR.2008.31193163

Caloyannides, M. (2003). Society cannot function without privacy. *IEEE Security & Privacy, 1*(3), 84–86. doi:10.1109/MSECP.2003.1203230

Camacho, K. (2006). *Digital divide.* Retrieved from http://vecam.org/article549.html

Campbell, T., & Fuhr, H. (2004). *Leadership and innovation in sub national government: Case studies from Latin America.* Washington, DC: World Bank.

Carroll, A., Barnes, S. J., Scornavacca, E., & Fletcher, K. (2007). Consumer perceptions and attitudes towards SMS advertising: Recent evidence from New Zealand. *International Journal of Advertising, 26*(1), 79–98.

Carter, S. (1999). Anatomy of qualitative management PhD. part two – getting finished. *Management Research News, 22*(12), 1–18. doi:10.1108/01409179910781887

Casey, E. (1993). *Getting Back Into Place: Toward a Renewed Understanding of the Place-world.* Bloomington, IN: Indiana University Press.

Casey, E. (1997). *The Fate of Place: A Philosophical History.* Berkeley, CA: University of California Press.

Castells, M. (1996). The Information Age: Economy, Society and Culture: *Vol. 1. The Rise of the Network Society.* Oxford, UK: Blackwell.

CBORD. (2006). *Client successful story- Deakin University.* Retrieved from http://www.cbord.com/news/success/profile_82.htm

CellBazzar. (2009). *SMS Buy/SMS Sell.* Retrieved from http://corp.cellbazaar.com/sms.html

Cennamo, K. S., Ross, J. D., & Rogers, C. S. (2002). Evolution of a web-enhanced course: Incorporating strategies for self-regulation. *EDUCAUSE Quarterly, 25*(1), 28–33.

Chabrol, J. L., & Périn, P. (1993). *Les pratiques de communication des Français.* Paris, France: Télécom/DPS.

Chace, R. W. (2001). *An overview on the guidelines for closed circuit television (CCTV) for public safety and community policing: CCTV for Public Safety and Community Policing Guidelines and Supplemental Information.* Alexandria, VA: Security Industry Association.

Chandler, P., & Sweller, J. (1991). Cognitive load theory and the format of instruction. *Cognition and Instruction, 8*(4), 293–332. doi:10.1207/s1532690xci0804_2

Chandler, P., & Sweller, J. (1992). The split-attention effect as a factor in the design of instruction. *The British Journal of Educational Psychology, 62*, 233–246. doi:10.1111/j.2044-8279.1992.tb01017.x

Chanlin, L. J., & Chan, K. C. (2004). Assessment of PBL design approach in a dietetic web-based instruction. *Journal of Educational Computing Research*, *31*(4), 437–452. doi:10.2190/UF9Y-92YM-9TUV-RJ78

Chapanis, A. (1975). Interactive human communication. *Scientific American*, *232*, 36–42. doi:10.1038/scientificamerican0375-36

Chapanis, A., Ochsman, R. B., Parrish, R. N., & Weeks, G. D. (1972). Studies in interactive communication: the effect of four communication modes on the behaviour of teams during co-operative problem-solving. *Human Factors*, *14*, 487–509.

Charlin, B., Mann, K., & Hansen, P. (1998). The many faces of problem-based learning: A framework for understanding and comparison. *Medical Teacher*, *20*(4), 323–330. doi:10.1080/01421599880742

Charman-Anderson, S. (2008, September 9). Email becomes a dangerous distraction. *The Sydney Morning Herald*. Retrieved October 31, 2008, from http://www.smh.com.au/news/biztech/youve-got-interruption/2008/09/08/1220857455459.html

Chatman, S. (1975). Towards a theory of narrative. *New Literary History*, *6*(2), 295–318. doi:10.2307/468421

Chauvet, M., & Gallivan, M. (2007). A cross-continent comparison of IS research on IT and culture. In *Proceedings of the 15th Annual Cross-Cultural Research in Information Systems Meeting*.

Chava, V., Smith, M. R., & Dudley, W. H. (2007). *System and method for in-transit SMS language translation* (United States Patent No. 7272406). Washington, DC: U.S. Patent and Trademark Office.

Chen, C. C., Olfman, L., & Harris, A. (2005). Differential Impacts of Social Presence on the Behavior Modeling Approach. *International Journal of Technology and Human Interaction*, *1*(2), 64–84.

Cheng, D., Liu, G., Qian, C., & Song, Y. (2009). User acceptance of internet banking: An extension of the UTAUT model with trust and quality constructs. *International Journal of Services Operations and Informatics*, *4*(4), 378–393. doi:10.1504/IJSOI.2009.029186

Cheong, J. H., & Park, M. (2005). Mobile Internet acceptance in Korea. *Internet Research*, *15*(2), 125–140. doi:10.1108/10662240510590324

Childers, T. L., Carr, C. L., Peckc, J., & Carson, S. (2001). Hedonic and utilitarian motivations for online retail shopping behavior. *Journal of Retailing*, *77*(4), 511–535. doi:10.1016/S0022-4359(01)00056-2

China Mobile. (2009). *2008 Annual Report, page 19*. Retrieved from http://www.chinamobileltd.com/images/pdf/2009/ar/ar_2008_e_full.pdf

Ching, S., Tai, A., Pong, J., & Cheng, M. (2009). Don't let micropayments penalize you—experience from the city University Of Hong Kong. *Journal of Academic Librarianship*, *35*(1), 86–97. doi:10.1016/j.acalib.2008.10.018

Choi, Y. K., Kim, J., & McMillan, S. J. (2009). Motivators for the intention to use mobile TV: A comparison of South-Korean males and females. *International Journal of Advertising*, *28*(1), 147–167. doi:10.2501/S0265048709090477

Choo, C. W., Bergerson, P., Detlor, B., & Heaton, L. (2008). Information culture and information use: An exploratory study of three organizations. *Journal of the American Society for Information Science and Technology*, *59*(5), 792–804. doi:10.1002/asi.20797

Choudrie, J., Weerakkody, V., & Jones, S. (2005). Realizing e-government in the UK: Rural and urban challenges. *The Journal of Enterprise Information Management*, *18*(5), 568–585. doi:10.1108/17410390510624016

Christopher, P. (1999). *Older adults – Special considerations for special people*. Retrieved from http://www.gsu.ed/~mstswh/course/it7000/papers/newpage31.htm

Chu, C. W., & Lu, H. P. (2007). Factors influencing online music purchase intention in Taiwan. An empirical study based on the value-intention framework. *Internet Research*, *17*(2), 139–155. doi:10.1108/10662240710737004

CIA. (2008). *The world factbook*. Retrieved from https://www.cia.gov/library/publications/the-world-factbook/geos/jo.html

Ciborra, C. (2005). Interpreting e-government and development efficiency, transparency or governance at a distance? *Information Technology & People*, *18*(3), 260–279. doi:10.1108/09593840510615879

Ciborra, C. (Ed.). (2000). *From Control to Drift -The Dynamics of Corporate Information Infrastructures.* Oxford, UK: Oxford University Press.

Claisse, G., & Rowe, F. (1993). Téléphone, communications et sociabilité: des pratiques résidentielles différenciées. *Sociétés Contemporaines, 14*(15), 165–189. doi:10.3406/socco.1993.1133

Climent, S., More, J., Oliver, A., Salvatierra, M., Sanchez, I., & Taule, M. (2007). Enhancing the status of Catalan versus Spanish in online Academic Forums. In Danet, B., & Herring, S. C. (Eds.), *The Multilingual Internet* (pp. 87–111). New York: Oxford University Press.

Collie, D. (2005). Tame information overload to increase productivity. *Business Times, 27*(1), 36–37.

Constas, M. (1992). Qualitative Analysis as a Public Event: The Documentation of Category Development Procedures. *American Educational Research Journal, 29*(2), 253–266.

Consulting, C. K. S. (2009). *Teleuse@BOP3: A Qualitative Study, Colombo: LIRNEasia.* Retrieved from http://lirneasia.net/wp-content/uploads/2008/04/qualitativereport.pdf

Cook, S., & Brown, J. (1999). Bridging epistemologies: The generative dance between organizational knowledge and organizational knowing. *Organization Science, 10*(4), 381–400. doi:10.1287/orsc.10.4.381

Corbin, J., & Strauss, A. (1990). Grounded theory research: Procedures, canons, and evaluative criteria. *Qualitative Sociology, 13*(1), 3–21. doi:10.1007/BF00988593

CORDIS. (2010). *Information and communication technologies (ICT).* Retrieved from http://cordis.europa.eu/fp7/ict/

Coroama, V., & Höckl, N. (2004, April). *Pervasive insurance markets and their consequences.* Paper presented at the First International Workshop on Sustainable Pervasive Computing, Vienna, Austria.

Cousins, K., & Robey, D. (2005). Human Agency in a Wireless World: Patterns of Technology Use in Nomadic Computing Environments. *Information and Organization, 15*(2), 151–180. doi:10.1016/j.infoandorg.2005.02.008

Creswell, J. W. (1998). *Qualitative inquiry and research design: Choosing among five traditions.* Thousand Oaks, CA: Sage.

Creswell, J. W. (2003). *Research design: Qualitative, quantitative, and mixed methods approaches* (2nd ed.). Thousand Oaks, CA: Sage.

Creswell, J. W. (2007). *Qualitative inquiry & research design: Choosing among five approaches* (2nd ed.). Thousand Oaks, CA: Sage.

Creswell, J. W. (2009). *Research design: Qualitative, quantitative, and mixed methods approaches* (3rd ed.). Thousand Oaks, CA: Sage.

Creswell, J. W., & Clark, V. L. P. (2007). *Designing and conducting mixed methods research.* Thousand Oaks, CA: Sage.

Creswell, J. W., & Miller, D. L. (2000). Determining validity in qualitative inquiry. *Theory into Practice, 39*(3), 124–130. doi:10.1207/s15430421tip3903_2

Crystal, D. (2008). *Txtng: the Gr8 Db8.* New York: Oxford University Press.

Csíkszentmihályi, M. (1990). *Flow: The Psychology of Optimal Experience.* New York: Harper and Row.

Culnan, M. J., & Armstrong, P. K. (1999). Information privacy concerns, procedural fairness, and impersonal trust: An empirical investigation. *Organization Science, 10*(1), 104–115. doi:10.1287/orsc.10.1.104

Cunningham, R. B., & Sarayrah, Y. K. (1993). *Wasta: The hidden force in Middle Eastern society.* Seattle, WA: Greenwood Publishing.

Cunningham, R. B., & Sarayrah, Y. K. (1994). Taming Wasta to achieve development. *Arab Studies Quarterly, 16*(3), 29–39.

Curran, K., Woods, D., & Riordan, O, B. (2006). Investigating text input methods for mobile phones. *Telematics and Informatics, 23*, 1–21. doi:10.1016/j.tele.2004.12.001

Curry, S. J. (2007). Ehealth research and healthcare delivery: Beyond intervention effectiveness. *American Journal of Preventive Medicine, 32*(5), 127–130. doi:10.1016/j.amepre.2007.01.026

Czarniawska, B. (1997). *Narrating the organization – dramas of institutional identity*. Chicago, IL: The University of Chicago Press.

Dabbagh, N., & Kitsantas, K. (2005). Using web-based pedagogical tools as scaffolds for self-regulated learning. *Instructional Science*, *33*(5-6), 513–540. doi:10.1007/s11251-005-1278-3

Dabbish, L. A., & Kraut, R. E. (2006). Email overload at work: An analysis of factors associated with email strain. In *Proceedings of the 20th Anniversary Conference on Computer Supported Cooperative Work*, Banff, AB, Canada (pp. 431-440).

Daft, R. L., & Lengel, R. H. (1984). Information Richness: A New Approach to Managerial Behavior and Organizational Design. In L. L. C. & B. M. Staw (Eds.), *Research in Organizational Behavior* (pp. 191-233). Homewood, IL: JAI Press.

Damian, D. E., Eberlein, A., Shaw, M. L. G., & Gaines, B. R. (2000). Using different communication media in requirements negotiation. *IEEE Software*, *17*(3), 28–36. doi:10.1109/52.896247

Danet, B., & Herring, S. C. (2007). Language Choice in Europe: Introduction. In Danet, B., & Herring, S. C. (Eds.), *The Multilingual Internet* (p. 18). New York: Oxford University Press.

Darke, P., Graeme, S., & Broadbent, M. (1998). Successfully completing case study research: Combining rigor, relevance and pragmatism. *Information Systems Journal*, *8*(4), 273–289. doi:10.1046/j.1365-2575.1998.00040.x

DARPA. (2009). *Multilingual Automatic Document Classification Analysis and Translation (MADCAT)*. Retrieved from http://www.darpa.mil/ipto/programs/madcat/madcat.asp

Davis, F. D. (1989). Perceived usefulness, perceived ease of use and user acceptance of information technology. *Management Information Systems Quarterly*, *13*(3), 319–340. doi:10.2307/249008

Davis, F. D., Bagozzi, R. P., & Warshaw, P. R. (1989). User acceptance of computer technology: A comparison of two theoretical models. *Management Science*, *35*(8), 982–1003. doi:10.1287/mnsc.35.8.982

Davis, F. D., Bagozzi, R. P., & Warshaw, P. R. (1992). Extrinsic and intrinsic motivation to use computers in the workplace. *Journal of Applied Social Psychology*, *24*(14), 1111–1132. doi:10.1111/j.1559-1816.1992.tb00945.x

Davis, F. D., & Venkatesh, V. (1996). A Critical Assessment of Potential Measurement Biases in the Technology Acceptance Model: Three Experiments. *International Journal of Human-Computer Studies*, *45*(1), 19–45. doi:10.1006/ijhc.1996.0040

Davis, G. (2002). Anytime/anyplace computing and the future of knowledge work. *Communications of the ACM*, *45*(12), 67–73. doi:10.1145/585597.585617

Davison, R., Wagner, C., & Ma, L. (2005). From government to e-government: A transition model. *Information Technology & People*, *18*(3), 280–299. doi:10.1108/09593840510615888

DeBoer, J. (2009). The relationship between environmental factors and usage behaviors at 'Hole-in-the-wall' computers. *International Journal of Educational Development*, *29*(1), 91–98. doi:10.1016/j.ijedudev.2008.02.005

Delone, W. H., & McLean, E. R. (1992). Information systems success: The quest for the dependent variable. *Information Systems Research*, *3*(1), 60–95. doi:10.1287/isre.3.1.60

Demirdjian, Z. (2005). Toward taming the monster in electronic mail. *Journal of American Academy of Business*, *7*(1), i–ii.

Dengler, S., Awad, A., & Dessler, F. (2007, May 21-23). Sensor/actuator networks in smart homes for supporting elderly and handicapped people. In *Proceedings of the 21st International Conference on Advanced Information Networking and Applications,* Niagara Falls, ON, Canada (pp. 863-868).

Denzin, N. K., & Lincoln, Y. S. (2000). Introduction: The discipline and practice of qualitative research. In Denzin, N. K., & Lincoln, Y. S. (Eds.), *Handbook of qualitative research* (pp. 1–28). Thousand Oaks, CA: Sage.

Department of Statistics. (2006). *Employment and unemployment survey (second round)*. Amman, Jordan: Department of Statistics.

Department of Statistics. Jordan (2008). *Population and housing census.* Retrieved from http://www.dos.gov.jo/dos_home_a/main/index.htm

Derrida, J. (1997). *Of Grammatology.* Baltimore, MD: The John Hopkins University Press.

Devadoss, P. R., Pan, S. L., & Huang, J. C. (2002). Structural analysis of e-government initiatives: A case study of SCO. *Decision Support Systems, 34*(3), 253–269. doi:10.1016/S0167-9236(02)00120-3

Devaraj, S., Fan, M., & Kohli, R. (2002). Antecedents of B2C channel satisfaction and preference: Validating e-Commerce metrics. *Information Systems Research, 13*(3), 316–333. doi:10.1287/isre.13.3.316.77

DeZoysa, S. (2002). Mobile advertising needs to get personal. *Telecommunications, 36*, 8.

Dodds, W. B. (1999). Managing customer value. *Mid-American Journal of Business, 14*(1), 13–22. doi:10.1108/19355181199900001

Dodds, W. B., & Monroe, K. B. (1985). The effect of brand and price information on subjective product evaluations. *Advances in Consumer Research. Association for Consumer Research (U. S.), 12*(1), 85–90.

Dodds, W. B., Monroe, K. B., & Grewal, D. (1991). Effects of price, brand, and store information on buyers' product evaluations. *JMR, Journal of Marketing Research, 28*, 307–319. doi:10.2307/3172866

Dordick, H. S., & LaRose, R. (1992, June 14-17). The telephone in daily life. In *Proceedings of the International Conference of the International Telecommunication Society*, Sydney, NSW, Australia.

Dorfman, P. W., & Howell, J. P. (1988). Dimensions of national culture and effective leadership patterns: Hofstede revisited. *Advances in International Comparative Management, 3*, 127–150.

Doyle, J. K., & Ford, D. N. (1998). Mental models concepts for system dynamics research. *System Dynamics Review, 14*(1), 3–29. doi:10.1002/(SICI)1099-1727(199821)14:1<3::AID-SDR140>3.0.CO;2-K

Druskat, V. U. (1994). Gender and leadership style: Transformational and transactional leadership in the Roman Catholic Church. *The Leadership Quarterly, 5*(2), 99–199. doi:10.1016/1048-9843(94)90023-X

du Pre Gauntt, J. (2008). *Mobile advertising: After the growing pains.* New York, NY: eMarketer.

Dubai e- Government. (2008b). *Partner.* Retrieved from http://egov.dubai.ae/?partners_corp,partners_corp,1,&_nfpb=true&_pageLabel=i dex

Dubai e-Government. (2008a). *e-Government core services.* Retrieved from http://egov.dubai.ae/?Services_Corp,Services_Corp,1,&_nfpb=true&_pageLabeCAT-index

Ducheneaut, N., & Watts, L. A. (2005). In search of coherence: A review of e-mail research. *Human-Computer Interaction, 20*, 11–48. doi:10.1207/s15327051hci2001&2_2

Dudman, J. (2003, April 15). Email overload. *Computer Weekly, 36*.

Duhan, D. F., Johnson, S. D., Wilcox, J. B., & Harrell, G. D. (1997). Influences on Consumer Use of Word-of-Mouth Recommendation Sources. *Journal of the Academy of Marketing Science, 25*(4), 283–295. doi:10.1177/0092070397254001

Dunlap, J. C. (2005). Problem-based learning and self-efficacy: How a capstone course prepares students for a profession. *Educational Technology Research and Development, 53*(1), 65–83. doi:10.1007/BF02504858

Duran, R. L., Kelly, L., & Keaten, J. A. (2005). College faculty use and perceptions of electronic mail to communicate with students. *Communication Quarterly, 53*(2), 159–176. doi:10.1080/01463370500090118

Eagly, A. H., & Johannesen-Schmidt, M. C. (2007). Leadership style matters: The small, but important, style differences between male and female leaders. In Bilimoria, D., & Piderit, S. K. (Eds.), *Handbook on women in business and management* (pp. 279–303). Cheltenham, UK: Edward Elgar.

Eagly, A. H., Johannesen-Schmidt, M. C., & van Engen, M. (2003). Transformational, transactional, and laissez-faire styles: A meta-analysis comparing women and men. *Psychological Bulletin, 95*(4), 569–591. doi:10.1037/0033-2909.129.4.569

Eagly, A. H., & Johnson, B. T. (1990). Gender and leadership style: A meta-analysis. *Psychological Bulletin, 108*(2), 233–256. doi:10.1037/0033-2909.108.2.233

Eagly, A., & Chaiken, S. (1993). *Psychology of attitudes.* New York, NY: Harcourt.

Eddy, E. R., Stone, D. L., & Stone-Romero, E. F. (1999). The effects of information management policies on reactions to human resource information systems: An integration of privacy and procedural justice perspectives. *Personnel Psychology, 52*(2), 335–358. doi:10.1111/j.1744-6570.1999.tb00164.x

Eden, C. (1992). On the nature of cognitive maps. *Journal of Management Studies, 29*(3), 261–265. doi:10.1111/j.1467-6486.1992.tb00664.x

Eden, C., & Ackermann, F. (1992). The analysis of cause maps. *Journal of Management Studies, 29*(3), 309–324. doi:10.1111/j.1467-6486.1992.tb00667.x

Eden, C., & Ackermann, F. (1998). Analyzing and comparing idiographic causal maps. In Eden, C., & Spender, J.-C. (Eds.), *Managerial and Organizational Cognition: Theory, Methods and Research* (pp. 192–209). London, UK: Sage.

Eden, C., & Ackermann, F. (2004). *Making strategy: The journey of strategic management.* London, UK: Sage.

Edenius, M. (2006). The function of representation in a 'smart home context'. *International Journal of Technology and Human Interaction, 2*(3), 1–15. doi:10.4018/jthi.2006070101

Elliot, S., & Loebbecke, C. (1998). Smart-card based electronic commerce: Characteristics and roles. In *Proceedings of the IEEE 31st Hawaii International Conference on System Sciences* (Vol. 4, pp. 242-250).

Engström, T., Johansson, J. Å., Jonsson, D., & Medbo, L. (1995). Empirical evaluation of the reformed assembly work at the Volvo Uddevalla plant: Psychosocial effects and performance aspects. *International Journal of Industrial Ergonomics, 16*(4-6), 293–308. doi:10.1016/0169-8141(95)00014-8

Eng, T. R. (2004). Population health technologies: Emerging innovations for the health of the public. *American Journal of Preventive Medicine, 26*(3), 237–242. doi:10.1016/j.amepre.2003.12.004

Eng, T. R., Gustafson, D. H., Henderson, J., Jimison, H., & Patrick, K. (1999). Introduction to evaluation of interactive health communication applications. *American Journal of Preventive Medicine, 16*(1), 10–15. doi:10.1016/S0749-3797(98)00107-X

Eppler, M., & Mengis, J. (2004). The concept of information overload: A review of literature from organization science, accounting, marketing, MIS, and related disciplines. *The Information Society, 20,* 325–344. doi:10.1080/01972240490507974

Ethnologue. (2009). *Languages of the World.* Retrieved from http://www.ethnologue.com/ethno_docs/distribution.asp?by=country#6

European Commission Enterprise and Industry. (2010). *Innovation policy.* Retrieved from http://ec.europa.eu/enterprise/ict/index_en.htm

European Commission. (2006). *Europeans and their languages.* Retrieved from http://ec.europa.eu/public_opinion/archives/ebs/ebs_243_en.pdf

Evans, C., & Wright, W. (2008). To: ALL USERS: Copy: ALL USERS. *Management Services, 52*(1), 24–27.

Evers, K. E., Prochaska, J. O., Driskell, M. M., Cummins, C. O., & Velicer, W. F. (2003). Strengths and weaknesses of health behavior change programs on the Internet. *Journal of Health Psychology, 8*(1), 63–70. doi:10.1177/1359105303008001435

Executive Privatization Commission. (2000). *Privatization law no. 25.* Retrieved from http://www.epc.gov.jo/EPC/Home/PrivateLaw/tabid/86/Default.aspx

Executive Privatization Commission. (2008). *Public private partnership policy for the government of Jordan.* Retrieved from http://www.epc.gov.jo/

Facebook. (2009). *The facebook network.* Retrieved from http://www.facebook.com

Facts, I. T. (2009). *Online consumer spending in 2008.* Retrieved February 18, 2010, from http://www.itfacts.biz/online-consumer-spending-in-2008/12233

Fagan, M. H., Wooldridge, B. R., & Neill, S. (2008). Exploring the intention to use computers: An empirical investigation of the role of intrinsic motivation, extrinsic motivation, and perceived ease of use. *Journal of Computer Information Systems, 48*(3), 31–37.

Faisal, A., & Abdella, M. (1993). A methodological analysis of Wasta: A study in Saudi Arabia. *Journal of King Saud University: Arts, 5*(1).

Fang, X., Chan, S., Brzezinski, J., & Xu, S. (2006). Moderating Effects of Task Type on Wireless Technology Acceptance. *Journal of Management Information Systems, 22*(3), 123–157. doi:10.2753/MIS0742-1222220305

Farhooman, A., & Drury, D. (2002). Managerial information overload. *Communications of the ACM, 45*(10), 127–131. doi:10.1145/570907.570909

Faulkner, X., & Culwin, F. (2005). When fingers do the talking: a study of text messaging. *Interacting with Computers, 17*, 167–185. doi:10.1016/j.intcom.2004.11.002

Feng, L. (2003). Implementing e-government strategy in Scotland: Current situation and emerging issues. *Journal of Electronic Commerce in Organizations, 1*(2), 44–65. doi:10.4018/jeco.2003040104

Ferris, M. (2007). Insights on mobile advertising, promotion, and research. *Journal of Advertising Research, 47*(1), 28–37. doi:10.2501/S0021849907070043

Festinger, L. (1954). A Theory of Social Comparison Processes. *Human Relations, 7*, 117–140. doi:10.1177/001872675400700202

Fetterman, D. M. (2009). Ethnography. In Bickman, L., & Rog, D. J. (Eds.), *The SAGE handbook of applied social research methods* (pp. 543–588). Thousand Oaks, CA: Sage.

Fish, R., Kraut, R., Root, R., & Rice, R. (1992). Evaluating video as a technology for informal communication. In *Proceedings of Conference on Computer Supported Co-operative Work*, Toronto, ON, Canada (pp. 1-12). New York, NY: ACM Press.

Fishbein, M., & Ajzen, I. (1975). *Belief, attitude, intention and behavior: An introduction to theory and research*. Reading, MA: Addison-Wesley.

Fjeldsoe, B. S., Marshall, A. L., & Miller, Y. D. (2009). Behavior Change Interventions Delivered by Mobile Telephone Short-Message Service. *American Journal of Preventive Medicine, 36*(2), 165–173. doi:10.1016/j.amepre.2008.09.040

Fleshman, D., Schweiger, C., Lott, D., & Peirlott, G. (1998). *Multipurpose transit payment media*. Retrieved from http://onlinepubs.trb.org/onlinepubs/tcrp/tcrp_rpt_32.pdf

Fletcher, T. D., & Major, D. A. (2006). The effect of communication modality on performance and self-rating of teamwork components. *Journal of Computer-Mediated Communication, 11*(2), 557–576. doi:10.1111/j.1083-6101.2006.00027.x

Floridi, L. (2005). The ontological interpretation of information privacy. *Ethics and Information Technology, 7*, 185–200. doi:10.1007/s10676-006-0001-7

Fogg, B. J. (2003). *Persuasive technology: Using computers to change what we think and do*. San Francisco, CA: Morgan Kaufmann.

Fog, K., Budtz, C., & Yakaboylu, B. (2003). *Storytelling – branding i praksis*. Fredriksberg, Sweden: Samfundslitteratur.

Ford, M., & Botha, A. (2007, May 9-11). *MobilED - an accessible mobile learning platform for Africa*. Paper presented at the IST Africa 2007 Conference, Maputo, Mozambique.

Fornell, C., Tellis, G., & Zinkhan, G. (1982). Validity assessment: a structural equations approach using partial least squares. In *Proceedings of the American Marketing Association Educator's Conference*, Chicago (pp. 405-409).

Fornell, C., & Larcker, D. (1981). Evaluating structural equation models with unobservable variables and measurement error. *JMR, Journal of Marketing Research, 18*(1), 39–50. doi:10.2307/3151312

Fornell, C., & Larcker, D. (1981). Structural equation models with unobservable variables and measurement error. *JMR, Journal of Marketing Research, 19*, 39–50. doi:10.2307/3151312

Foucault, M. (1983). *This is Not a Pipe*. Berkeley, CA: University of California Press.

Frazee, V. (1996). Is email doing more harm than good? *The Personnel Journal*, 23.

Friedman, Z., Mukherji, S., Roeum, G. K., & Ruchir, R. (2001). *Data input into mobile phones: T9 or keypad?* Retrieved June 10, 2006, from http://www.otal.umd.edu./SHORE2001/mobilePhone/index.html

Friedman, H. H., & Fireworker, R. B. (1977). The Susceptibility of Consumers to Unseen Group Influence. *The Journal of Social Psychology*, *102*(1), 155–156. doi:10.1080/00224545.1977.9713254

Frokjaer, E., Hertzum, M., & Hornbaek, K. (2000). Measuring usability: are effectiveness, efficiency and satisfaction really correlated? *CHI Letters*, *2*(1), 345–352.

Frolick, M. N., & Chen, L. (2004). Assessing m-commerce opportunities. *Information Systems Management*, *21*(2), 53–62. doi:10.1201/1078/44118.21.2.20040301/80422.8

Fulk, J., Steinfield, C. W., Schmitz, J., & Power, J. G. (1987). A Social Information Processing Model of Media Use in Organizations. *Communication Research*, *14*, 529–552. doi:10.1177/009365087014005005

Furnell, S. (2005). Why users cannot use security. *Computers & Security*, *24*, 274–279. doi:10.1016/j.cose.2005.04.003

García-Montes, J., Caballero-Munoz, D., & Pérrz-Álvarez, M. (2006). Changes in the Self Resulting from the Use of Mobile Phones. *Media Culture & Society*, *28*(1), 67–82. doi:10.1177/0163443706059287

Garcia, P., & Hardy, C. (2007). Positioning, similarity and difference: Narratives of individual and organizational identities in an Australian university. *Scandinavian Journal of Management*, *23*(4), 363–383.

Garland, R. (1991). The mid-point on a rating scale: Is it desirable? *Marketing Bulletin*, *2*, 66–70.

Garson, G. D. (2006). *Structural equation modeling.* Retrieved from http://www2.chass.ncsu.edu/garson/pa765/structur.htm

Gaver, W., Sellen, A., Heath, C., & Luff, P. (1993). One is not enough: multiple views in a media space. In *Proceedings of CHI'94: Human factors in Computing Systems (CSCW '00),* Boston, MA (pp. 335-341). New York, NY: ACM Press.

Gefen, D., Karahanna, E., & Straub, D. (2002). *Building Consumer Trust in Online Shopping and TAM: An Integrated Model.* Philadelphia: Drexel University.

Gefen, D., Karahanna, E., & Straub, D. W. (2003). Trust and TAM in online shopping: An integrated model. *Management Information Systems Quarterly*, *27*(1), 51–90.

Gefen, D., & Straub, D. (2003). Managing User Trust in B2C e-Services. *E-Service Journal*, *2*(2), 7–24. doi:10.2979/ESJ.2003.2.2.7

Gelbord, B., & Roelofsen, G. (2002). New surveillance techniques raise privacy concerns. *Communications of the ACM*, *45*(11), 23–24. doi:10.1145/581571.581586

Gentner, D., & Stevens, A. L. (1983). *Mental models.* London, UK: Lawrence Erlbaum.

Gerbing, D. W., & Anderson, J. C. (1993). Monte Carlo evaluations of goodness-of-fit indexes for structural equation models. In Bollen, K. A., & Long, J. S. (Eds.), *Testing structural equation models* (pp. 40–65). Newbury Park, CA: Sage.

Gibbons, F. X., & Buunk, B. P. (1999). Individual Differences in Social Comparison: Development of a Scale of Social Comparison Orientation. *Journal of Personality and Social Psychology*, *76*(1), 129–142. doi:10.1037/0022-3514.76.1.129

Giddens, A. (1990). *The Consequences of Modernity.* Stanford, CA: Stanford University Press.

Giddens, A. (1991). *Modernity and Self-identity: Self and Society in the Late Modern Age.* Stanford, CA: Stanford University Press.

Gieryn, T. (2000). A Space for Place in Sociology. *Annual Review of Sociology*, *26*, 463–496. doi:10.1146/annurev.soc.26.1.463

Gillespie, R. (1991). *Manufacturing knowledge: A history of Hawthorne experiments.* Cambridge, UK: Cambridge University Press.

Girma, D. (2002). Teaching assistant portal in an engineering education: experiences with web-mediated teaching at the University of Strathclyde. In *Proceedings of the 2002 ASEE/SEFI/TUB Colloquium*. Retrieved May 11, 2010, from http://www.asee.org/conferences/international/papers/upload/Teaching-Assistant-Portal-in-Engineering-Education.pdf

Glaser, B. G., & Strauss, A. L. (1967). *The discovery of grounded theory*. Chicago, IL: Aldine.

Glasgow, N. (1997). *New curriculum for new times: A guide to student-centered, problem-based learning*. Thousand Oaks, CA: Corwin.

Glasgow, R. E. (2007). Ehealth evaluation and dissemination research. *American Journal of Preventive Medicine*, *32*(5), 119–126. doi:10.1016/j.amepre.2007.01.023

Goodwin, C. (1991). Privacy: Recognition of a consumer right. *Journal of Public Policy & Marketing*, *10*(1), 149–166.

Goold, B. J. (2004). *CCTV and policing: Public area surveillance and police practices in Britain*. New York, NY: Oxford University Press.

Gordon, J. (2007). The Mobile Phone and the Public Sphere: Mobile Phone Usage in Three Critical Situations. *Convergence: The International Journal of Research into New Media Technologies*, *13*(3), 307–319. doi:10.1177/1354856507079181

Goulding, C. (2005). Grounded theory, ethnography, and phenomenology: A comparative analysis of three qualitative strategies for marketing research. *European Journal of Marketing*, *39*(3-4), 294–308. doi:10.1108/03090560510581782

Grabner-Krauter, S., & Kaluscha, E. A. (2003). Empirical research in on-line trust: a review and critical assessment. *International Journal of Human-Computer Studies*, *58*(6), 783–812. doi:10.1016/S1071-5819(03)00043-0

Grandey, A. A. (2003). When "the show must go on": Surface acting and deep acting as determinants of emotional exhaustion and peer-rated service delivery. *Academy of Management Journal*, *46*(1), 86–96. doi:10.2307/30040678

Grayson, D., & Coventry, L. (1998). The effects of visual proxemic information in video mediated communication. *SIGCHI Bulletin*, *30*(3), 30–39. doi:10.1145/565711.565713

Greene, J. A., & Azevedo, R. (2007). Adolescents' use of self-regulatory processes and their relation to qualitative mental model shifts while using hypermedia. *Journal of Educational Computing Research*, *36*(2), 125–148. doi:10.2190/G7M1-2734-3JRR-8033

Greene, J. A., Moos, D. C., Azevedo, R., & Winters, F. I. (2008). Exploring differences between gifted and grade-level students' use of self-regulatory learning processes with hypermedia. *Computers & Education*, *50*(3), 1069–1083. doi:10.1016/j.compedu.2006.10.004

Green, N. (2002). On the Move: Technology, Mobility and Mediation of Social Time and Space. *The Information Society*, *18*(4), 281–292. doi:10.1080/01972240290075129

Greenspan, S., Goldberg, D., Weimer, D., & Basso, A. (2000, December 2-6). Interpersonal Trust and Common Ground in Electronically Mediated Communication. In *Proceedings of the Conference on Computer Supported Co-operative Work (CSCW '00)*, Philadelphia, PA (pp. 251-260). New York, NY: ACM Press.

Gregoriadis, L. (2007). *Social Commerce Report 2007*. Retrieved from http://econsultancy.com/reports/social-commerce-report-2007

Gregory, D. (1994). *Geographical Imaginations*. Cambridge, UK: Blackwell.

Gribbons, B., & Herman, J. (1997). True and quasi-experimental designs. *Practical Assessment, Research & Evaluation*, *5*(14). Retrieved May 11, 2010, from http://PAREonline.net/getvn.asp?v=5&n=14

Griffin, O. R. (2007). The evolving safety and security challenge. *Pierce Law Review*, *5*(3), 413–432.

Griffiths, G., & Howard, A. (2008). Balancing Clicks and Bricks - Strategies for Multichannel Retailers. *Journal of Global Business Issues*, *2*(1), 69–75.

Group, N. P. D. (2010). *Amazon Ties Walmart as second-ranked U.S. music retailer, behind industry-Leader iTunes*. Retrieved from http://i486.net/2010/11/28/npd-group-amazon-ties-walmart-as-second-ranked-u-s-music-retailer-behind-industry-leader-itunes/

Grunbaum, N. (2007). Identification of ambiguity in the case study research typology: What is a unit of analysis? *Qualitative Market Research: An International Journal*, *10*(1), 78–97. doi:10.1108/13522750710720413

Grzybowski, L., & Pereira, P. (2008). The complementarity between calls and messages in mobile telephony. *Information Economics and Policy*, *20*(3), 279–287. doi:10.1016/j.infoecopol.2008.06.005

Guriting, P., & Ndubisi, O. N. (2006). Borneo online banking: Evaluating customer perceptions and behavioural intention. *Management Research News*, *29*(1-2), 6–15. doi:10.1108/01409170610645402

Haghirian, P., & Madlberger, M. (2005, May 26-28). *Consumer attitude toward advertising via mobile devices - an empirical investigation among Austrian users.* Paper presented at the 13th European Conference on Information Systems, Regensburg, Germany.

Haghirian, P., Madlberger, M., & Tanuskova, A. (2005, January 3-6). Increasing advertising value of mobile marketing - an empirical study of antecedents. In *Proceedings of the 38th Hawaii International Conference on System Sciences*, Big Island, HI (p. 32).

Hair, J. F., Black, B., Babin, B., Anderson, R. E., & Tatham, R. L. (2010). *Multivariate Data Analysis: A Global Perspective*. Upper Saddle River, NJ: Pearson Education.

Halaweh, M., Fidler, C. S., & McRobb, S. (2008, December 14-17). Integrating the grounded theory method and case study research methodology within IS research: A possible "road map". In *Proceedings of the International Conference on Information Systems*, Paris, France.

Hall, H. T. (2004). The standardization of efficiency and its implications for organizations. *Journal of Critical Postmodern Organization Science*, *3*(1), 42–53.

Hammersley, M. (1989). *The dilemma of qualitative method: Herbert Blumer and the Chicago Tradition.* London, UK: Routledge.

Hampden-Turner, C., & Trompenaars, F. (1997). Response to Geert Hofstede. *International Journal of Intercultural Relations*, *21*(1), 49–159. doi:10.1016/S0147-1767(96)00042-9

Hanley, M., Becker, M., & Martinsen, J. (2006). Factor influencing mobile advertising acceptance: Will incentives motivate college students to accept mobile advertisements? *International Journal of Mobile Marketing*, *1*(1), 50–58.

Hann, I., Hui, K., Lee, S., & Png, I. (2007). Overcoming online information privacy concerns: An information-processing theory approach. *Journal of Management Information Systems*, *24*(2), 13–42. doi:10.2753/MIS0742-1222240202

Hanson, N. (1958). *Patterns of Discovery. An Inquiry into the Foundation of Science*. Cambridge, UK: Cambridge University Press.

Hapsari, A. T., Syamsudin, E. Y., & Pramana, I. (2005, January 18-21). *Design of vehicle position tracking system using short message services and its implementation on FPGA.* Paper presented at the Asia and South Pacific Design Automation Conference.

Harvey, D. (1989). *The Condition of Postmodernity*. Oxford, UK: Basil Blackwell.

Ha, S., & Stoel, L. (2009). Consumer e-shopping acceptance: Antecedents in a technology acceptance model. *Journal of Business Research*, *62*, 565–571. doi:10.1016/j.jbusres.2008.06.016

Hassanein, K., & Head, M. (2006). The Impact of Infusing Social Presence in the Web Interface: An Investigation Across Product Types. *International Journal of Electronic Commerce*, *10*(2), 31–55. doi:10.2753/JEC1086-4415100202

Heeks, R. (2003). *Most e-government-for-development projects fail: How can risks be reduced*. Manchester, UK: iGovernment Working Paper Series.

Heidegger, M. (1977). *The question concerning technology and other essays*. New York: Harper and Row.

Heinonen, K., & Strandvik, T. (2003). *Consumer responsiveness to mobile marketing.* Paper presented at the Stockholm Mobility Roundtable, Stockholm, Sweden.

Hemp, P. (2006). Avatar-based Marketing. *Harvard Business Review*, *84*(6), 48–57.

Hennig-Thurau, T., & Walsh, G. (2003). Electronic Word-of-Mouth: Motives for and Consequences of Reading Customer Articulations on the Internet. *International Journal of Electronic Commerce, 8*(2), 51–74.

Hernandez, M. D., Chapa, S., Minor, M. S., Maldonado, C., & Barranzuela, F. (2004). Hispanic attitudes toward advergames: A proposed model of their antecedents. *Journal of Interactive Advertising, 5*(1), 74–83.

Hershkowitz-Coore, S. (2005). Email: Toxic or terrific? *Journal for Quality and Participation, 28*(2), 11–14.

He, Z. (2008). SMS in China: A Major Carrier of the Nonofficial Discourse Universe. *The Information Society, 24*(3), 182–190. doi:10.1080/01972240802020101

Hiller, J. S., & Belanger, F. (2001). *Privacy strategies for electronic government.* Arlington, VA: PricewaterhouseCoopers Endowment for the Business of Government.

Hillestad, R., Bigelow, J., Bower, A., Girosi, F., Meili, R., & Scoville, R. (2005). Can electronic medical record systems transform health care? Potential health benefits, savings, and costs. *Health Affairs, 24*(5), 1103–1117. doi:10.1377/hlthaff.24.5.1103

Hmelo-Silver, C. E. (2004). Problem-based learning: What and how do students learn? *Educational Psychology Review, 16*(3), 235–266. doi:10.1023/B:EDPR.0000034022.16470.f3

Hoecklin, L. (1994). *Managing cultural differences - strategies for competitive advantage.* Reading, MA: Addison-Wesley.

Hoffman, D. L., & Novak, T. P. (1996). Marketing in hypermedia computer-mediated environments: Conceptual foundations. *Journal of Marketing, 60,* 50–68. doi:10.2307/1251841

Hoffman, D. L., Novak, T. P., & Peralta, M. (1999). Building consumer trust online. *Communications of the ACM, 42*(4), 80–85. doi:10.1145/299157.299175

Hofstede, G. (1985). The interaction between national and organisational value systems. *Journal of Management Studies, 23*(4), 347–357. doi:10.1111/j.1467-6486.1985.tb00001.x

Hofstede, G. (2001). *Culture's consequences: Comparing values, behaviors, institutions and organizations across nations.* Thousand Oaks, CA: Sage.

Hofstede, G., & Bond, M. H. (1984). Hofstede's culture dimensions: An independent validation using Rokeach's value survey. *Journal of Cross-Cultural Psychology, 15*(4), 417–433. doi:10.1177/0022002184015004003

Hofstede, G., & Hofstede, G. J. (2005). *Cultures and organisations: Software of the mind* (2nd ed.). New York, NY: McGraw-Hill.

Ho, K. K. W. (2007). The e-government development, IT strategies, and portals of the Hong Kong SAR government. *International Journal of Cases on Electronic Commerce, 3*(2), 71–89.

Holbrook, M. B. (1996). Customer value – a framework for analysis and research. *Advances in Consumer Research. Association for Consumer Research (U. S.), 23*(1), 138–142.

Holland, N. (2006). *Rescuing 3G with mobile TV: Business models and monetizing 3G.* Cambridge, UK: Pyramid Research.

Holmes, J. (1997). Storytelling in New Zealand in women's and men's talk. In Wodak, R. (Ed.), *Gender and discourse* (pp. 262–293). London, UK: Sage.

Hong, J. C., Horng, J. S., & Lin, C. L., & ChanLin, L. J. (2008). Competency disparity between pre-service teacher education and in-service teaching requirements in Taiwan. *International Journal of Educational Development, 28*(1), 4–20. doi:10.1016/j.ijedudev.2006.12.004

Hong, W., Thong, J. Y. L., & Tam, K. Y. (2004). The Effects of Information Format and Shopping Task on Consumers' Online Shopping Behavior: A Cognitive Fit Perspective. *Journal of Management Information Systems, 21*(3), 149–184.

Hooker, J. (2009). Corruption from a cross-cultural perspective. *Cross Cultural Management, 16*(3), 251–267. doi:10.1108/13527600910977346

Hoover, E., & Lipka, S. (2007). Colleges weigh when to alert students to danger. *The Chronicle of Higher Education, 54*(15), 1.

Hourani, H. (2006, December 6-7). *e-Government: Jordan experience.* Paper presented at the Jordan ICT Forum, Dead Sea, Jordan.

House of Representatives. (2008). *Jordanian House of Representatives-formation of the House.* Retrieved from http://www.parliament.jo/english/Fomation.shtm

Hsiao, H. C., Chen, M. N., & Yang, H. S. (2008). Leadership of vocational high school principals in curriculum reform: A case study in Taiwan. *International Journal of Educational Development, 28*(6), 669–686. doi:10.1016/j.ijedudev.2007.12.002

Hsu, C. L., & Lu, H. P. (2004). Why Do People Play Online Games? An Extended TAM with Social Influences and Flow Experience. *Information & Management, 41*(7), 853–868. doi:10.1016/j.im.2003.08.014

Hsu, M. H., & Chiu, C. M. (2004). Internet self-efficacy and electronic service acceptance. *Decision Support Systems, 38*(3), 369–381. doi:10.1016/j.dss.2003.08.001

Hsu, M. K., Wang, S. W., & Chiu, K. K. (2009). Computer attitude, statistics anxiety and self-efficacy on statistical software adoption behavior: An empirical study of on-line MBA learners. *Computers in Human Behavior, 25*, 412–420. doi:10.1016/j.chb.2008.10.003

Huang, W., Olson, J., & Olson, G. (2002, November 16-20). Camera angle affects dominate in video-mediated communication. In *Proceedings of the Conference on Computer Supported Co-operative Work (CSCW '02),* New Orleans, LA. New York, NY: ACM Press.

Huang, E. (2008). Use and gratification in e-consumers. *Internet Research, 18*(4), 405–426. doi:10.1108/10662240810897817

Huang, E. Y., & Lin, S. W. (2009). Do knowledge workers use e-mail wisely? *Journal of Computer Information Systems, 50*(1), 65–73.

Hudson, W. (2002). The lost world of e-banking. *ACM SIGCHI Bulletin, 34*(5).

Hu, L., & Bentler, P. M. (1999). Cutoff criteria for fit indexes in covariance structure analysis: conventional criteria versus new alternatives. *Structural Equation Modeling, 6*(1), 1–55. doi:10.1080/10705519909540118

Hussain, R. M. R., Mamat, W. H. W., Salleh, N., Saat, R. M., & Harland, T. (2007). Problem-based learning in Asian universities. *Studies in Higher Education, 32*(6), 761–772. doi:10.1080/03075070701685171

Hutchings, K., & Weir, D. (2006). Guanxi and Wasta: A comparison. *Thunderbird International Business Review, 48*(1), 141–156. doi:10.1002/tie.20090

Hyvarinen, T., Kaikkonen, A., & Hiltunen, M. (2005). Placing links in mobile banking applications. In *Proceedings of the 7th International Conference on Human Computer Interaction with Mobile Devices and Services,* Salzburg, Austria (pp. 63-68). New York, NY: ACM.

IBM. (2007). *IBM 2007 digital consumer study.* Armonk, NY: IBM.

Idate. (2008a). *DigiWorld yearbook 2008.* Montpellier, VT: Idate.

Idate. (2009). *Mobile 2009: Markets and trends.* Montpellier, VT: Idate.

Idowu, B., Ogunbodede, E., & Idowu, B. (2003). Information and communication technology in Nigeria, the health sector experience. *Journal of Information Technology Impact, 3*(2), 69–76.

IFPI. (2010). *IFPI Digital Music Report 2010.* Retrieved from http://www.ifpi.org/content/library/DMR2010.pdf

Igbaria, M., Parasuraman, S., & Baroudi, J. (1996). A motivational model of microcomputer usage. *Journal of Management Information Systems, 13*(1), 127–143.

Igbaria, M., & Zviran, M. (1996). Comparison of end-user computing characteristics in the U.S., Israel, and Taiwan. *Information & Management, 30*(1), 1–13. doi:10.1016/0378-7206(95)00044-5

Iloanusi, N. O., & Osuagwu, C. C. (2009). *ICT in education: Achievements so far in Nigeria.* Retrieved from http://www.formatex.org/micte2009/book/1331-1335.pdf

Imparato, N., & Harari, O. (1994). *Jumping the curve: Innovation and strategic choice in an age of transition.* San Francisco, CA: Jossey-Bass.

Institute for Alternative Futures (IAF). (2006). *The biomonitoring futures project: Final report and recommendations.* Princeton, NJ: Author.

Isaacs, E., & Tang, J. C. (1994). What video can and cannot do for collaboration: A case study. *Multimedia Systems*, *2*(2), 63–73. doi:10.1007/BF01274181

ITAP. (2005). *The culture in the workplace questionnaire*. Retrieved from www.itapintl.com/ITAPCWQuestionnaire.htm

ITU. (2009). *Measuring the Information Society - The ICT Development Index, 2009 Edition*. Retrieved from http://www.itu.int/ITU-D/ict/publications/idi/2009/index.html

Jackson, T. W., Dawson, R. J., & Wilson, D. (2002). Case study: Evaluating the effect of email interruptions within the workplace. In *Proceedings of the Conference on Empirical Assessment in Software Engineering*, Keele, UK (pp. 3-7).

Jackson, N., & Carter, P. (1995). The 'fact' of management. *Scandinavian Journal of Management*, *11*(3), 197–208. doi:10.1016/0956-5221(95)00016-O

Jackson, T. W., Burgess, A., & Edwards, J. (2006). A simple approach to improving email communication. *Communications of the ACM*, *49*(6), 107–109. doi:10.1145/1132469.1132493

Jackson, T. W., Dawson, R. J., & Wilson, D. (2003a). Reducing the effect of email interruptions on employees. *International Journal of Information Management*, *23*(1), 55–65. doi:10.1016/S0268-4012(02)00068-3

Jackson, T. W., Dawson, R. J., & Wilson, D. (2003b). Understanding email interaction increases organizational productivity. *Communications of the ACM*, *46*(8), 80–84. doi:10.1145/859670.859673

Jacobson, M. J. (2005). From non-adaptive to adaptive educational hypermedia: Theory, research, and design issues. In Chen, S., & Magalas, G. (Eds.), *Advances in Web-based education: Personalized learning environments* (pp. 302–330). Hershey, PA: Idea Group.

Jacussi, E., Hanseth, O., & Lyytinen, K. (2006). Introduction: Taking Complexity Seriously in IS Research. *Information Technology & People*, *19*(1), 5–11. doi:10.1108/09593840610649943

Jagacinski, R. J., Liao, M. J., & Fayyad, E. A. (1995). Generalized slowing in sinusoidal tracking in older adults. *Psychology and Aging*, *9*, 103–112.

Jamali, D., & Olayan, S. (2004). Success and failure mechanisms of public private partnerships (PPPs) in developing countries: Insights from the Lebanese context. *International Journal of Public Sector Management*, *17*(5), 414–430. doi:10.1108/09513550410546598

James, C. L., & Reischel, K. M. (2001, March 31-April 5). Text input for mobile devices: Comparing model prediction to actual performance. In *Proceedings of CHI '01: Human Factors in Computing Systems*, Seattle, WA (pp. 365-371). New York, NY: ACM Press.

Jamil, S., & Mousumi, F. A. (2008, December 24-27). Short messaging service (SMS) based m-banking system in context of Bangladesh. In *Proceedings of the 11th International Conference on Computer and Information Technology*, Khulna, Bangladesh (pp. 599-604).

Janssen, M., & Cresswell, A. (2005). Enterprise architecture integration in e-government. In *Proceedings of the 38th Hawaii International Conference on System Sciences* (p. 118).

Janssen, R., & de Poot, H. (2006, October 14-18). Information overload: Why some people seem to suffer more than others. In *Proceedings of the 4th Nordic Conference on Human-Computer Interaction: Changing Roles*, Oslo, Norway (pp. 397-400).

Järvelä, S., Näykki, P., Laru, J., & Luokkanen, T. (2007). Structuring and regulating collaborative learning in higher education with wireless networks and mobile tools. *Journal of Educational Technology & Society*, *10*(4), 71–79.

Jarvenpaa, S., Lang, K. R., Takeda, Y., & Tuunainen, V. K. (2003). Mobile commerce at crossroads: An international focus group study of users of mobile handheld devices and services. *Communications of the ACM*, *46*(12), 41–44. doi:10.1145/953460.953485

Jayawardhena, C., & Foley, P. (2000). Changes in the Banking Sector - the case of Internet Banking in the UK. *Internet Research: Electronic Networking. Applications and Policy*, *10*(1), 19–30.

Jen, W., Lu, T., & Liu, P. (2009). An integrated analysis of technology acceptance behaviour models: Comparison of three major models. *MIS Review*, *15*(1), 89–121.

Jiang, J., Yan, Z., Shi, J., & Kandachar, P. (2008, May 30-31). Design of wireless mobile monitoring of blood pressure for underserved in China by using short messaging service. In *Proceedings of the International Conference on Technology and Applications in Biomedicine*, Shenzhen, China (pp. 319-322).

Jiao, W., & Zhao, J. (2007, November 23-25). Study on Communication between Home and School System Based on Mobile Education Platform. In *Proceedings of the First IEEE International Symposium on Information Technologies and Applications in Education*, Kunming, China (pp. 478-482).

Johnson-Laird, P. N., & Byrne, R. M. J. (2002). Conditionals: A Theory of Meaning, Pragmatics. and Inference. *Psychological Review, 109*(4), 646–678. doi:10.1037/0033-295X.109.4.646

Johnson, M., & Liber, O. (2008). The personal learning environment and the human condition: from theory to teaching practice. *Interactive Learning Environments, 16*(1), 3–15. doi:10.1080/10494820701772652

Jones, M. L. (2007, June 24-26). *Hofstede - culturally questionable?* Paper presented at the Oxford Business & Economics Conference, Oxford, UK.

Jones, M., & Alony, I. (2007). The cultural impact of information systems – through the eyes of Hofstede – a critical journey. *Issues in Informing Science and Information Technology, 4.*

Jones, B. E. (1970). *Freemasons's guide and compendium* (2nd ed.). London, UK: Harrap.

Jones, D. (2009). Viewpoint a role for the smart card industry in 'social banking'. *Card Technology Today, 21*(5), 16. doi:10.1016/S0965-2590(09)70082-9

Jones, D., & Crowe, B. (2001). *Transformation not automation: The e-government challenge.* London, UK: Demos.

Jordan Times. (2004, November 21). *Meeting discusses future of knowledge stations.* Amman, Jordan: Jordan Times.

Jordan Vision 2020. (1999) *JV2020 Phase I.* Retrieved from http://www.jv2020.com/Default.shtm

Jordan, I. C. T. Forum. (2002, September 30-October 1). *REACH initiative.* Paper presented at the Jordan ICT Forum, Amman, Jordan.

Jordanian, E. -Government. (2008). *e-Government program.* Retrieved from http://www.jordan.gov.jo/wps/portal/General/?New_WCM_Context=/wps/wcm/conect/eGov/Home/&lang=en

Julien, H., & Michels, D. (2000). Source selection among information seekers: Ideals and realities. *Canadian Journal of Information and Library Science-Revue* [Canadienne des Sciences de L 'Information et de Bibliotheconomie], *25*(1), 1-18.

Julien, H., & Michels, D. (2004). Intra-individual information behaviour in daily life. *Information Processing & Management, 40*(3), 547. doi:10.1016/S0306-4573(02)00093-6

Kaikkonen, A., Kallio, T., Kekalainen, A., Kankainen, A., & Cankar, M. (2005). Usability testing of mobile application: A comparison between laboratory and field testing. *Journal of Usability Studies, 1*(1), 4–16.

Kakihara, M., & Sørensen, C. (2002). Post-Modern Professionals' Work and Mobile Technology, New Ways of Working in IS. In *Proceedings of the 25th Information Systems Seminar in Scandinavia (IRIS25).* Copenhagen, Denmark: Copenhagen Business School.

Kakihara, M., Sørensen, C., & Wiberg, M. (2004). Negotiating the Fluidity of Mobile Work. In Wiberg, M. (Ed.), *The Interaction Society: Practice, Theories, and Supportive Technologies.* Hershey, PA: Idea Group.

Kameron, G. (2008). *Freemasonry - the truth.* Retrieved from http://books.google.com/books?id=3GBkhju1XZUC&dq=gordon+kameron&source=gbs_navlinks_s

Kanaan, R. K. (2009). *Making sense of e-government implementation in Jordan: A qualitative investigation.* Unpublished doctoral dissertation, De Montfort University, Leicester, UK.

Kanter, R. M. (1997). *Men and women of the corporation.* New York, NY: Basic Books.

Kanuka, H., Jugdev, K., Heller, R., & West, D. (2008). The rise of the teleworker: false promises and responsive solutions. *Higher Education, 56*(2), 149–165. doi:10.1007/s10734-007-9095-z

Karahanna, E., Evaristo, J. R., & Srite, M. (2005). Levels of culture and individual behavior: An integrative perspective. *Journal of Global Information Management, 13*(2), 1–20. doi:10.4018/jgim.2005040101

Karajaluoto, H. (2002). Selection criteria for a mode of bill payment: empirical investigation among Finnish bank customers. *International Journal of Retail & Distribution Management, 30*(6), 331–339. doi:10.1108/09590550210429540

Kardaras, D., Karakostas, B., & Papathanassiou, E. (2003). The potential of virtual communities in the insurance industry in the UK and Greece. *International Journal of Information Management, 23*(1), 41–53. doi:10.1016/S0268-4012(02)00067-1

Kark, R. (2004). The transformational leader: Who is (s)he? A feminist perspective. *Journal of Organizational Change Management, 17*(2), 160–176. doi:10.1108/09534810410530593

Karlsson, N., Dellgran, P., Klingander, B., & Garling, T. (2004). Household Consumption: Influences of Aspiration Level, Social Comparison, and Money Management. *Journal of Economic Psychology, 25*, 753–769.

Kärreman, D., Sveningsson, S., & Alvesson, M. (2002). The return of machine bureaucracy? Management control in the work settings of professionals. *International Studies of Management & Organization, 32*(2), 70–92.

Kasperson, R. E., Golding, D., & Tuler, S. (2005). Social distrust as a factor in siting hazardous facilities and communicating risks. In Kasperson, J. X., & Kasperson, R. E. (Eds.), *The Social Contours of Risk (Vol. 1*, pp. 29–50). London, UK: Earthscan.

Kasteler, J. (2009). *Why You Should Get Involved With Social Shopping: E-commerce 2.0*. Retrieved from http://searchengineland.com/why-you-should-get-involved-with-social-shopping-e-commerce-20-22995

Kelly, G. A. (1955). *The psychology of personal constructs*. New York, NY: Norton.

Kelman, H. C. (1961). Processes of Opinion Change. *Public Opinion Quarterly, 25*, 57–78. doi:10.1086/266996

Kenny, R. F., Bullen, M., & Loftus, J. (2006). Problem formulation and resolution in online problem-based learning. *International Review of Research in Open and Distance Learning, 7*(3). Retrieved May 11, 2010, from, http://www.irrodl.org/index.php/irrodl/article/view/248/751

Khalilov, M., Fonollosa, J. A. R., Zamora-Martinez, F., Castro-Bleda, M. J., & Espaa-Boquera, S. (2008, November 3-5). Neural Network Language Models for Translation with Limited Data. In *Proceedings of the 20th IEEE International Conference on Tools with Artificial Intelligence*, Dayton. *OH. Osteopathic Hospitals, 2*, 445–451.

Kidwell, R. E., & Bennett, N. (1994). Electronic surveillance as employee control: A procedural justice interpretation. *The Journal of High Technology Management, 5*(1), 39–57. doi:10.1016/1047-8310(94)90013-2

Kilani, S., & Sakijha, B. (2002). *Wasta: The declared secret*. Amman, Jordan: Jordan Press Foundation.

Kim, K., & Prabhakar, B. (2000, December 10-13). Initial trust, perceived risk, and the adoption of internet banking. In *Proceedings of the 21st International Conference on Information Systems*, Brisbane, QLD, Australia (pp. 537-543).

Kim, G. S., Park, S.-B., & Oh, J. (2008). An examination of factors influencing consumer adoption of short message service (SMS). *Psychology and Marketing, 25*(8), 769–786. doi:10.1002/mar.20238

Kim, G., Shin, B., & Lee, H. G. (2008). Understanding dynamics between initial trust and usage intention of mobile banking. *Information Systems Journal, 19*(3), 283–311. doi:10.1111/j.1365-2575.2007.00269.x

Kim, J., & Moon, J. Y. (1998). Designing emotional usability in customer interfaces trustworthiness of cyber-banking system interfaces. *Interacting with Computers, 10*, 1–29. doi:10.1016/S0953-5438(97)00037-4

King, W. R., & He, J. (2006). A meta-analysis of the technology acceptance model. *Information & Management, 43*, 740–755. doi:10.1016/j.im.2006.05.003

Kira, A., Nichols, D. M., & Apperley, M. (2009). Human communication in customer-agent-computer interaction: Face-to-face versus over telephone. *Computers in Human Behavior, 25*, 8–20. doi:10.1016/j.chb.2008.05.013

Kivits, J. (2006). Informed patients and the Internet: A mediated context for consulations with health professionals. *Journal of Health Psychology*, *11*(2), 269–282. doi:10.1177/1359105306061186

Klitgaard, R. (1991). *Controlling corruption*. Berkeley, CA: University of California Press.

Knigths, D., & Murray, F. (1994). *Managers Divided-organizational Politics and Information Technology Management*. London: Wiley.

Knopper, S. (2009). *Appetite for self-destruction: The spectacular crash of the record industry in the digital age*. New York, NY: Free Press.

Knowledge Stations. (2004). *Progress report*. Retrieved from http://www.ks.gov.jo/

Knowledge Stations. (2007a). *Knowledge stations objectives, Jordan*. Retrieved from http://www.ks.jo/objectives.htm

Knowledge Stations. (2007b). *Knowledge stations: Together towards a digital economy & comprehensive development, Jordan*. Retrieved from http://www.ks.jo/default.htm

Knowledge Stations. (2008a). *Statistical data*. Retrieved from http://www.ks.gov.jo/default.htm

Knowledge Stations. (2008b). *Engaging the local community*. Retrieved from http://www.ks.jo/KS_engage.htm

Kogo, C., & Nojima, E. (2004). Student dropout in e-learning and its symptom. In *Proceedings of the 20th Annual Conference of Japan Society for Educational Technology* (pp. 997-998).

Kong, J., & Luo, J. (2006, October 25-27). The Innovative Business Model behind the Rapid Growth of SMS in China. In. *Proceedings of the International Conference on Service Systems and Service Management*, *2*, 1472–1477. doi:10.1109/ICSSSM.2006.320741

Kostera, M. (2006). The narrative collage as research method. *Storytelling, Self, Society*, *2*(2), 5–27.

Kow, M. P. M. (2009). *Feasibility study on sourcing of passive candidates via social networking sites*.

Kramarski, B., & Gutman, M. (2006). How can self-regulated learning be supported in mathematical E-learning environments? *Journal of Computer Assisted Learning*, *22*(1), 24–33. doi:10.1111/j.1365-2729.2006.00157.x

Krampe, R. T., & Ericsson, K. A. (1996). Maintaining excellence: deliberate practice and elite performance in young and older pianists. *Journal of Experimental Psychology. General*, *125*, 331–359. doi:10.1037/0096-3445.125.4.331

Kraut, R., Dumais, D., & Koch, S. (1989). Computerization, productivity, and quality of work-life. *Communications of the ACM*, *32*(2), 220–238. doi:10.1145/63342.63347

Kumar, S. B. R., Raj, A. A. G., & Rabara, S. A. A. (2008, December 12-14). Framework for Mobile Payment Consortia System (MPCS). In *Proceedings of the International Conference on Computer Science and Software Engineering* (pp. 43-47).

Kumar, Y., & Ganesh, S. (2005). Integration of smart card and gabor filter method based fingerprint matching for faster verification. In *Proceedings of the IEEE Annual Indicon Conference* (p. 526).

Kumar, K., & Bjorn-Anderson, N. (1990). A cross-cultural comparison of IS designer values. *Information Systems*, *33*(5), 528–538.

Kumar, N., & Benbasat, I. (2006). The Influence of Recommendations and Consumer Reviews on Evaluations of Websites. *Information Systems Research*, *17*(4), 425–439. doi:10.1287/isre.1060.0107

Kurniawan, S. H., Nugroho, Y., & Mahmud, M. (2006). A study of the use of mobile phones by older persons. In *Proceedings of CHI'06: Human Factors in Computing Systems*, Montreal, QC, Canada (pp. 989-994). New York, NY: ACM Press.

Kurniawan, S. H. (2008). Older people and mobile phones: A multi-method investigation. *International Journal of Human-Computer Studies*, *66*(12), 889–901. doi:10.1016/j.ijhcs.2008.03.002

Kurniawan, S. H., King, A., Evans, D. G., & Blenkhorn, P. L. (2006). Personalising web page presentation for older people. *Interacting with Computers*, *18*(3), 457–477. doi:10.1016/j.intcom.2005.11.006

LaLomia, M. J., & Sidowski, J. B. (1990). Measurements of computer satisfaction, literacy, and aptitudes: A review. *International Journal of Human-Computer Interaction*, *2*(3), 231–253. doi:10.1080/10447319009525982

Lambert, N., Plumb, J., Looise, B., Johnson, I. T., Harvey, I., & Wheeler, C. (2005). Using smart card technology to monitor the eating habits of children in a school cafeteria. *Journal of Human Nutrition and Dietetics*, *18*(4), 243–254. doi:10.1111/j.1365-277X.2005.00617.x

Lambrinoudakis, C., Gritzalis, S., Dridi, F., & Pernul, G. (2003). Security requirements for e-government services: A methodological approach for developing a common PKI-based security policy. *Computer Communications*, *26*(16), 1873–1883. doi:10.1016/S0140-3664(03)00082-3

Lam, W. (2005). Barriers to e-government integration. *The Journal of Enterprise Information Management*, *18*(5), 511–530. doi:10.1108/17410390510623981

Landauer, T. K. (1988). Research methods in human-computer interaction. In Helenander, M. (Ed.), *Handbook of Human-Computer Interaction* (pp. 905–928). Amsterdam, The Netherlands: North-Holland.

Langan-Fox, J., Code, S., & Langfield-Smith, K. (2000). Team mental models: Techniques, methods, and analytic approaches. *Human Factors*, *42*(2), 242–271. doi:10.1518/001872000779656534

Langer, A., Kumar, B., Mittal, A., & Subramaniam, L. V. (2009, March 6-7). Mobile Medicine: Providing Drug Related Information through Natural Language Queries via SMS. In *Proceedings of the IEEE International Advance Computing Conference*.

Laukkanen, T. (2007). Internet vs mobile banking: comparing customer value perceptions. *Business Process Management Journal*, *13*(6), 788–797. doi:10.1108/14637150710834550

Laukkanen, T., & Lauronen, J. (2005). Consumer value creation in mobile banking services. *International Journal of Mobile Communications*, *3*(4), 325–328. doi:10.1504/IJMC.2005.007021

Lavie, A., Pianesi, F., & Levin, L. (2006). The NESPOLE! System for Multilingual Speech Communication Over the Internet. *IEEE Transactions on Audio. Speech and Language Processing*, *14*(5), 1664–1673. doi:10.1109/TSA.2005.858520

Lawson, R. B., & Shen, Z. (1998). *Organizational psychology: Foundations and applications*. New York, NY: Oxford University Press.

Layne, K., & Lee, J. (2001). Developing fully functional e-government: A four stage model. *Government Information Quarterly*, *18*(2), 122–136. doi:10.1016/S0740-624X(01)00066-1

Lazar, J., Jones, A., & Shneiderman, B. (2006). Workplace user frustration with computers: An exploratory investigation of the causes and severity. *Behaviour & Information Technology*, *25*(3), 239–251. doi:10.1080/01449290500196963

Leavitt, W. (2008). The tyranny of email. *Fleet Owner*, *103*(7), 20.

Lee, H. (1999). Time and Information Technology: Monochronicity, Polychronicity and Temporal Symmetry. *European Journal of Information Systems*, *8*(1), 16–26. doi:10.1057/palgrave.ejis.3000318

Lee, H., & Liebenau, J. (2000). Temporal Effects of Information Systems on Business Processes: Focusing on the Dimensions of Temporality. *Accounting. Management & Information Technologies*, *10*(3), 157–185. doi:10.1016/S0959-8022(00)00003-5

Lee, H., & Whitley, E. (2002). Time and Information Technology: Temporal Impacts on Individuals, Organizations, and Society. *The Information Society*, *18*(4), 235–240. doi:10.1080/01972240290075084

Lee, J. K., & Lee, W. K. (2008). The relationship of e-Learner's self-regulatory efficacy and perception of e-Learning environmental quality. *Computers in Human Behavior*, *24*(1), 32–47. doi:10.1016/j.chb.2006.12.001

Lee, J., & Lee, J. N. (2009). Understanding the Product Information Inference Process in Electronic Word-of-Mouth: An Objectivity–Subjectivity Dichotomy Perspective. *Information & Management*, *46*(5), 302–311. doi:10.1016/j.im.2009.05.004

Lee, K. C., & Chung, N. (2009). Understanding factors affecting trust in and satisfaction with mobile banking in Korea: A modified Delone and Mclean's model perspective. *Interacting with Computers*, *21*(5-6), 385–392. doi:10.1016/j.intcom.2009.06.004

Lee, M. K. O., Cheung, C. M. K., & Chen, Z. H. (2007). Understanding user acceptance of multimedia messaging services: An empirical study. *Journal of the American Society for Information Science and Technology*, *58*(13), 2066–2077. doi:10.1002/asi.20670

Lee, M. S. Y., McGoldrick, P. F., Keeling, K. A., & Doherty, J. (2003). Using ZMET to explore barriers to the adoption of 3G mobile banking services. *International Journal of Retail & Distribution Management*, *31*(6), 340–348. doi:10.1108/09590550310476079

Lee, T. H., Shen, P. D., & Tsai, C. W. (2008). Applying web-enabled problem-based learning and self-regulated learning to add value to computing education in Taiwan's vocational schools. *Journal of Educational Technology & Society*, *11*(3), 13–25.

Lee, Y. S., Hong, S. W., Smith-Jackson, T. L., Nussbaum, M. A., & Tomioka, K. (2006). Systematic evaluation methodology for cell phone user interfaces. *Interacting with Computers*, *18*, 304–325. doi:10.1016/j.intcom.2005.04.002

Lee, Y., Kozar, K. A., & Larsen, K. R. T. (2003). The technology acceptance model: Past, present and future. *Communications of the Association for Information Systems*, *12*, 752–780.

Leijon, S., & Söderbom, A. (2005). Rollkombinationer i ekonomi- och personalarbete. *Nordiske Organisasjonsstudier*, *3*(7), 87–110.

Leijon, S., & Söderbom, A. (2008). Builders and cleaners – a longitudinal study of strategic narratives. *Journal of Organizational Change Management*, *21*(3), 280–299. doi:10.1108/09534810810874787

Leppäniemi, M., Karjaluoto, H., & Salo, J. (2004). The success factors of mobile advertising value chain. *E-Business Review*, *4*, 93–97.

Leung, L. (2007). Unwillingness-to-communicate and college students' motives in SMS mobile messaging. *Telematics and Informatics*, *24*(2), 115–129. doi:10.1016/j.tele.2006.01.002

Levy, S. R., Stroessner, S. J., & Dweck, C. S. (1998). Stereotype formation and endorsement: The role of implicit theories. *Journal of Personality and Social Psychology*, *74*(6), 1421–1436. doi:10.1037/0022-3514.74.6.1421

Lewis, J. R., & Sauro, J. (2006). When 100% really isn't 100%: Improving the accuracy of small-sample estimates of completion rates. *Journal of Usability Studies*, *3*(1), 136–150.

Liao, C. H., Tsou, C. W., & Huang, M. F. (2007). Factors influencing the usage of 3G mobile services in Taiwan. *Online Information Review*, *31*(6), 759–774. doi:10.1108/14684520710841757

Liao, Z., & Cheung, M. T. (2002). Internet based e-banking and consumer attitudes: an empirical study. *Information & Management*, *39*, 283–295. doi:10.1016/S0378-7206(01)00097-0

Li, D., Chau, P. Y. K., & Lou, H. (2005). Understanding Individual Adoption of Instant Messaging: An Empirical Investigation. *Journal of the Association for Information Systems*, *6*(4), 102–129.

Li, H., & Stoller, B. (2007). Parameters of mobile advertising: A field experiment. *International Journal of Mobile Marketing*, *2*(1), 4–11.

Likert, R. (1932). A technique for the measurement of attitudes. *Archives de Psychologie*, 140.

Lindback, R., & Fodrey, B. (2009). Using technology in undergraduate admission: Current practices and future plans. *Journal of College Admission*, *204*, 25–30.

Linell, P. (1994). *Transkription av tal och samtal: Teori och praktik. Arbetsrapport från tema Kommunikation, 1994:9*. Linköping, Sweden: Linköpings universitet.

Ling, R. (1999). Traditional and fixed and mobile telephony for social networking among Norwegian parents. In L. Elstrom (Ed.), *Human Factors in Telecommunication: 17th International Symposium* (pp. 209-256).

Ling, R. (2007). SMS og hvordan elder blir utestengt. In Proitz, L., Luders, M., & Rasmussen, T. (Eds.), *Livet I og utenfor skjermene*. Oslo, Norway: Uniersitetetsforlaget.

Lin, J. C.-C., & Hsu, C.-L. (2009). A multi-facet analysis of factors affecting the adoption of multimedia messaging service (MMS). *International Journal of Technology and Human Interaction*, *5*(4), 18–36. doi:10.4018/jthi.2009062502

Lin, M., & Sears, A. (2005). Chinese character entry for mobile phones: a longitudinal investigation. *Interacting with Computers*, *17*(2), 121–146. doi:10.1016/j.intcom.2004.11.003

Lipka, S. (2007). Lessons from a tragedy. *The Chronicle of Higher Education*, *53*(34), 12.

Liu, S., Ma, W., Schalow, D., & Spruill, K. (2004). Improving Web access for visually impaired users. *IT Professional*, *6*(4), 28–33. doi:10.1109/MITP.2004.36

Locke, E. A., & Latham, G. P. (2002). Building a practically useful theory of goal setting and task motivation: A 35-year odyssey. *The American Psychologist*, *57*(9), 705–717. doi:10.1037/0003-066X.57.9.705

Locohee, H., & Anderson, B. (2001). Interacting with the telephone. *International Journal of Human-Computer Studies*, *54*, 665–699. doi:10.1006/ijhc.2000.0439

Lonely Planet. (2008). *Map of Jordan.* Retrieved from http://www.lonelyplanet.com/maps/middle-east/jordan/

Lopez-Nicolas, C., Molina-Castillo, F. J., & Bouwman, H. (2008). An assessment of advanced mobile services acceptance: Contributions from TAM and diffusion theory models. *Information & Management*, *45*(6), 359–364. doi:10.1016/j.im.2008.05.001

Loyens, S. M. M., Magda, J., & Rikers, R. M. J. P. (2008). Self-directed learning in problem-based learning and its relationships with self-regulated learning. *Educational Psychology Review*, *20*(4), 411–427. doi:10.1007/s10648-008-9082-7

Luarn, P., & Lin, H. H. (2005). Toward an understanding of the behavioral intention to use mobile banking. *Computers in Human Behavior*, *21*(6), 873–891. doi:10.1016/j.chb.2004.03.003

Lund-Thomsen, P. (2007). *Assessing the impact of public-private partnerships in the global south: The case of the Kasur Tanneries pollution control project*. New York, NY: United Nations.

Lu, Y., Zhou, T., & Wang, B. (2008). Exploring Chinese Users' Acceptance of Instant Messaging Using the Theory of Planned Behavior, the Technology Acceptance Model, and the Flow Theory. *Computers in Human Behavior*, *6*(2), 1–11.

Lyon, D. (2001). *Surveillance society: Monitoring everyday life*. Buckingham, UK: Open University Press.

Lyon, D. (2002). Surveillance studies: Understanding visibility, mobility and the phenetic fix. *Surveillance & Society*, *1*(1), 1–7.

M'Chirgui, Z. (2003). *An empirical evidence of the electronic purse's adoption: The case of Moneo*. Aix-en-Provence, France: Universite de la Mediterranee.

Maister, D. (1997). *Managing the professional service firm*. London, UK: Simon and Schuster.

Makhoul, J., & Harrison, L. (2004). Intercessory Wasta and village development in Lebanon. *Arab Studies Quarterly*, *26*(3), 25–41.

Ma, L., Banerjee, P., Lai, J., & Shroff, R. (2008). Diffusion of the 'Octopus' smart card e-payment system. *International Journal of Business and Information*, *3*(1), 115–128.

Malhotra, N. K., Kim, S. S., & Agarwal, J. (2004). Internet users' information privacy concerns (IUIPC): The construct, the scale, and a causal model. *Information Systems Research*, *15*(4), 336–355. doi:10.1287/isre.1040.0032

Mantei, M. M., Baecker, R. M., Sellen, A. J., Buxton, W. A. S., Milligan, T., & Wellman, B. (1991, April 28-June 5). Experiences in the use of a media space. In *Proceedings of CHI '91: Conference on Human Factors in Computing Systems*, New Orleans, LA (pp. 203-208). New York, NY: ACM Press.

Mao, E., & Palvia, P. (2006). Testing an Extended Model of IT Acceptance in the Chinese Cultural Context. *ACM SIGMIS Database*, *37*(2-3), 20–32. doi:10.1145/1161345.1161351

Martin, O. (2010). Texting was never actually designed for the consumer market. *The Guardian*. Retrieved from http://www.guardian.co.uk/business/2010/jan/01/texting-never-designed-for-consumers

Masoodian, M., & Apperley, M. (1995). User perceptions of human-to-human communication modes in CSCW environments. In *Proceedings of ED-MEDIA'95: World Conference on Educational Multimedia and Hypermedia*, Graz, Austria (pp. 430-435). Chesapeake, VA: AACE.

Masoodian, M., Apperley, M., & Frederikson, L. (1995). Video support for shared work-space interaction: An empirical study. *Interacting with Computers*, 7(3), 237–253. doi:10.1016/0953-5438(95)93603-3

Massey, D. (1998). *Space, Place and Gender*. Cambridge, UK: Polity Press.

Materka, A., Strzelecki, M., & Debiec, P. (2009). Student's electronic card: A secure Internet database system for university management support. *Internet-Technical Development and Applications*, 64, 59–72. doi:10.1007/978-3-642-05019-0_8

Mathwick, C. (2002). Understanding the Online Consumer: A Typology of Online Relational Norms and Behavior. *Journal of Interactive Marketing*, 16(1), 40–55. doi:10.1002/dir.10003

Mattern, F. (2005). Ubiquitous computing: Scenarios for an informatized world. In Zerdick, A., Picot, A., Schrape, K., Burgelman, J.-C., Silverstone, R., & Feldmann, V., (Eds.), *E-Merging Media - Communication and the Media Economy of the Future* (pp. 145–163). Berlin, Germany: Springer.

Maxwell, J. A. (2009). Designing a qualitative study. In Bickman, L., & Rog, D. J. (Eds.), *The SAGE handbook of applied social research methods* (pp. 214–253). Thousand Oaks, CA: Sage.

Mayes, K., & Markantonakis, K. (2006). On the potential of high density smart cards. *Information Security Technical Report*, 11, 147–154. doi:10.1016/j.istr.2006.05.002

Mazmanian, M., Yates, J., & Orlikowski, W. (2006, July). Ubiquitous Email: Individual Experiences and Organizational Consequences of Blackberry. In *Proceedings of the IFIP 8.2 Working Conference on Ubiquitous Computing*, Cleveland, OH.

McColl-Kennedy, J. R., & Anderson, R. D. (2005). Subordinate–manager gender combination and perceived leadership style influence on emotions, self-esteem and organizational commitment. *Journal of Business Research*, 58(2), 115–125. doi:10.1016/S0148-2963(03)00112-7

McCourt, R. S. (2006). *Smart parking meters take over the west*. Retrieved from http://www.dksassociates.com/admin/paperfile/Smart_Parking_Meters_Take_Over_the_West.pdf

McCoy, S., Galletta, D. F., & King, W. R. (2005). Integrating national culture into IS research: The need for current individual-level measures. *Communications of the Association for Information Systems*, 15, 211–224.

McGill, T., & Bax, S. (2007). From Beliefs to Success: Utilizing an Expanded TAM to Predict Web Page Development Success. *International Journal of Technology and Human Interaction*, 3(3), 36–53.

McGregor, D. (1960). *The human side of enterprise*. New York, NY: McGraw-Hill.

McLean, R. (2008). Pixel chix and digi guys: Exploring the experiences of the 'digital citizen' in two contexts. *International Journal of Technology and Human Interaction*, 4(2), 1–21. doi:10.4018/jthi.2008040101

McSweeney, B. (2002). Hofstede's model of national cultural differences and their consequences: A triumph of faith - a failure of analysis. *Human Relations*, 55(1), 89–118.

MDA. (2009). *Text IT, Mobile Data Association*. Retrieved from http://www.text.it/mediacentre/sms_figures.cfm

Mello, M., & Sahay, S. (2007). "I am Kind of Nomad Where I have to Go Places and Places"… Understanding Mobility, Place and Identity in Global Software Work from India. *Information and Organization*, 17(3), 162–192. doi:10.1016/j.infoandorg.2007.04.001

Merisavo, M., Kajalo, S., Karjaluoto, H., Virtanen, V., Salmenkivi, S., & Raulas, M. (2007). An empirical study of the drivers of consumer acceptance of mobile advertising. *Journal of Interactive Advertising*, 7(2), 1–19.

Merisavo, M., Vesanen, J., Arponen, A., Kajalo, S., & Raulas, M. (2006). The effectiveness of targeted mobile advertising in selling mobile services: an empirical study. *International Journal of Mobile Communications*, *4*(2), 119–127.

Merisavo, M., Vesanen, J., Arponen, A., Kajalo, S., & Raulas, M. (2006). The effectiveness of targeted mobile advertising in selling mobile services: An empirical study. *International Journal of Mobile Communications*, *4*(2), 119–127.

Mermelstein, B., & Tal, E. (2005, November 28-30). Using cellular phones in higher education: mobile access to online course materials. In *Proceedings of the IEEE International Workshop on Wireless and Mobile Technologies in Education*.

Merriam, S. (1988). *Case study research in education: A qualitative approach*. San Francisco, CA: Jossey-Bass.

Mintzberg, H. (1973). *The nature of managerial work*. New York, NY: Harper and Row.

Mitleton-Kelly, E. (2001). *Complexity science and order creation*. Retrieved from http://www2.lse.ac.uk/research-AndExpertise/Experts/e.mitleton-kelly@lse.ac.uk

Mitra, S., Mitra, M., & Chaudhuri, B. B. (2008, November 19-21). Rural cardiac healthcare system-A scheme for developing countries. In *Proceedings of the IEEE Region 10 Conference* (pp. 1-5).

Miyazaki, A. D., & Fernandez, A. (2001). Consumer perceptions of privacy and security risks for online shopping. *The Journal of Consumer Affairs*, *35*(1), 27–44. doi:10.1111/j.1745-6606.2001.tb00101.x

Mobilcom Austria. (2008). *Annual Report Year Ending December 2008*. Retrieved from http://www.telekom-austria.com/ir/annual-reports.php

Mohamed, A. A., & Hamdy, H. (2008). *The stigma of Wasta: The effect of Wasta on perceived competence and morality*. Retrieved from http://mgt.guc.edu.eg/wpapers/005mohamed_hamdy2008.pdf

Mohammad, A.-R., Al-Ali, A. R., & Eberlein, A. (2006). Remote patient monitoring and information system. *International Journal of Electronic Healthcare*, *2*(3), 231–249.

Mohammad, H., Almarabeh, T., & Abu Ali, A. (2009). e-Government in Jordan. *European Journal of Scientific Research*, *35*(2), 188–197.

MOICT. (2000). *e-Government program overview*. Retrieved from http://moict.gov.jo/

MOICT. (2002). *Launching e-government in Jordan: A proposed approach*. Retrieved from http://moict.gov.jo/downloads/Jordan_E-Gov_Ch4.pdf

MOICT. (2003). *e-Government: Status update*. Retrieved from http://www.moict.gov.jo/en_index.aspx

MOICT. (2006). *e-Government program overview*. Retrieved from http://moict.gov.jo/MoICT_program_overview.aspx

MOICT. (2006a). *e-Government strategy document* (06-09). Amman, Jordan: MOICT.

MOICT. (2006b). *New e-government strategy* (2007-2008-2009). Retrieved from http://www.gov.jo/en_index.aspx

MOICT. (2007) *Statement of government policy 2007 on the ICT & postal sectors*. Retrieved from http://www.moict.gov.jo/MoICT/en_index.aspx

Moka, L. L. C. (2009). *Moka Partners with China Mobile for Mobile Chinese to English Language Translation and Language Learning*. Retrieved from http://www.moka.com/en/news/news-1.htm

Mokdad, A. H., Marks, J. S., Stroup, D. F., & Gerberding, J. L. (2004). Actual Causes of Death in the United States, 2000. *Journal of the American Medical Association*, *291*(10), 1238–1246. doi:10.1001/jama.291.10.1238

Mole, E. (2007). *An explanation of freemasonry*. Retrieved from http://www.macclesfieldmasons.org/index.php?option=com_content&task=view&id=31&Itemid=36

Monroe, K. B. (1973). Buyers' subjective perceptions of price. *JMR, Journal of Marketing Research*, *10*, 70–80. doi:10.2307/3149411

Montalvo, F., & Torres, R. (2004). Self-regulated learning: Current and future directions. *Electronic Journal of Research in Educational Psychology*, *2*(1), 1–34.

Moore, G. A. (1991). *The Chasm: Marketing and Selling High-Tech Products to Mainstream Customer*. Philadelphia, PA: HarperCollins.

Moore, G. C., & Benbasat, I. (1996). Integrating Diffusion of Innovations and Theory of Reasoned Action Models to Predict Utilization of Information Technology by End-users. In Kautz, K., & Pries-Heje, J. (Eds.), *Diffusion and Aadoption of Iinformation Technology* (pp. 132–146). London: Chapman and Hall.

Moores, S. (2003). *e-Government in the Middle East.* Paper presented at the Future IT Conference: Keynote Address, Bahrain.

Morgan, G. (2006). *Images of organization*. Thousand Oaks, CA: Sage.

Morgan, M. G., Fischhoff, B., Bostrom, A., & Atman, C. J. (2002). *Risk communication: A mental models approach*. Cambridge, UK: Cambridge University Press.

Moyal, A. (1992). The gendered use of the telephone: an Australian case study. *Media Culture & Society, 14*, 51–72. doi:10.1177/016344392014001004

MTS Ukraine. (2009). *MTS Group financial results for the fourth quarter and full year 2008.*

Mullen, H., & Horner, D. S. (2004). Ethical problems for e-government: An evaluative framework. *Electronic. Journal of E-Government, 2*(3), 187–196.

Muller, M. J., Carr, R., Ashworth, C., Diekmann, B., Wharton, C., Eickstaedt, C., & Clonts, J. (1995). Telephone operators as knowledge workers: consultants who meet customer needs. In *Proceedings of the SIGCHI Conference on Human Factors in Computing System (CHI'95)*, Denver, CO (pp. 130-137). New York, NY: ACM Press/Addison-Wesley Publishing Co.

Müllern, T. (1994). *Den föreställda organisationen: om kulturella processer i och kring organisationer*. Stockholm, Sweden: Nerenius & Santérus.

Murray, K. E., & Waller, R. (2007). Social networking goes abroad. *International Educator, 16*(3), 56–59.

Murray, M. (2006). Narrative psychology. In Smith, J. (Ed.), *Qualitative psychology: A practical guide to research methods*. London, UK: Sage.

Mutshewa, A. (2007). A theoretical exploration of information behaviour: A power perspective. *Aslib Proceedings: New Information Perspectives, 59*, 249–263.

Nagar, K. (2009). Advertising effectiveness in different media: A comparison of web and television advertising. *IIMB Management Review, 21*(3), 245–260.

Nardi, B., Huchinsky, A., Whittaker, S., Leichner, R., & Schwarz, H. (1997). Video-as-data: technical and social aspects of a collaborative multimedia application. In Finn, K., Sellen, S., & Wilbur, S. (Eds.), *Video-Mediated Communication*. Hillsdale, NJ: Lawrence Erlbaum.

National Agenda. (2006). *The Jordan that we want (2006-2015)*. Amman, Jordan: National Agenda.

National Center for Human Resources Development. (2006). *Human resources development information system (Al-Manar)*. Amman, Jordan: National Center for Human Resources Development.

National Information Technology Center. (2005). *The affection of knowledge stations in bridging digital divide*. Amman, Jordan: National Information Technology Center.

National Information Technology Development Agency. (2001). *The national information technology policy.* Retrieved from http://www.fs.nitda.gov.ng/index.php?option=com_content&view=article&id=65&Itemid=87

National Institute of Justice. (2003). *CCTV: Constant cameras track violators.* Retrieved from http://www.cops.usdoj.gov/html/cd_rom/tech_docs/pubs/CCTVConstantCamerasTrackViolators.pdf

Ndou, V. (2004). e-Government for developing countries: Opportunities and challenges. *The Electronic Journal on Information Systems in Developing Countries, 18*(1), 1–24.

Neitzke, H.-P., Behrendt, D., & Osterhoff, J. (2006). *Alltagsszenarien in der AACC-Welt [Scenarios of everyday living in an AACC-world]* (Tech. Rep. No. 1/2006). Hannover, Germany: Ecolog-Institut.

Nelson, E., Kline, H., & Van Dem Dam, R. (2007). *A future in content(ion)*. Armonk, NY: IBM Institute for Business Value.

Netemeyer, R. G., Johnston, M. W., & Burton, S. (1990). Analysis of role conflict and role ambiguity in a structural equations framework. *The Journal of Applied Psychology*, *75*(2), 148–157. doi:10.1037/0021-9010.75.2.148

Neuhauser, L., & Kreps, G. L. (2003). Rethinking communication in the e-health era. *Journal of Health Psychology*, *8*(1), 7–23. doi:10.1177/1359105303008001426

Neustaedter, C., Bernheim Brush, A. J., Smith, M. A., & Fisher, D. (2005, April). Beyond "from" and "received": Exploring the dynamics of email triage. In *Proceedings of the CHI 2005 Conference on Human Factors in Computing Systems.* New York: ACM Press.

Newell, A., & Simon, H. A. (1972). *Human problem solving*. Englewood Cliffs, NJ: Prentice-Hall.

News, B. B. C. (2005a, October 28). *Vodafone buys into India's Bharti*. Retrieved from http://news.bbc.co.uk/1/hi/business/4384258.stm

News, B. B. C. (2005b, May 21). *A back-to-basics mobile launched*. Retrieved from http://news.bbc.co.uk/1/hi/technology/4566809.stm

Niedzwiedzka, B. (2003). Proposed general model of information behaviour. *Information Research, 9*(1).

Nieto, M. (1997). *Public video surveillance: Is it an effective crime prevention tool?* Retrieved from http://www.library.ca.gov/CRB/97/05

Nissenbaum, H. (1998). Protecting privacy in an information age: The problem of privacy in public. *Law and Philosophy*, *17*, 559–596.

Noe, J. (2005). Contactless cards: The next best thing? *ABA Banking Journal*, *97*(9), 42–46.

Nokia Siemens Networks. (2009). *The connectivity scorecard: Call for action to redefine connectivity.* Retrieved from http://www.nokiasiemensnetworks.com/global/Insight/ConnectivityScorecard/?languagecode=en

Noonan, J. T. (1984). *Bribes: The intellectual history of a moral idea*. London, UK: Macmillan.

Norazah, M. S., Ramayah, T., & Norbayah, M. S. (2008). Internet shopping acceptance: Examining the influence of intrinsic versus extrinsic motivations. *Direct Marketing: An International Journal*, *2*(2), 97–110. doi:10.1108/17505930810881752

Normark, D., & Esbjörnsson, M. (2004). The Mobile Workplace – Collaboration in a Vast Setting. In Wiberg, M. (Ed.), *The Interaction Society: Practice, Theories and Supportive Technologies* (pp. 251–270). Hershey, PA: Information Science Publishing.

Novak, T. P., Hoffman, D. L., & Peralta, M. A. (1999). Building consumer trust online. *Communications of the ACM*, *42*(4), 80–85. doi:10.1145/299157.299175

Novak, T. P., Hoffman, D. L., & Yung, Y.-F. (2000). Measuring the Customer Experience in Online Environments: A Structural Modeling Approach. *Marketing Science*, *19*, 22–42. doi:10.1287/mksc.19.1.22.15184

Nunnally, J. (1967). *Psychometric Theory*. New York: McGraw-Hill.

Nye, J. (1967). Corruption and political development: A case-benefit analysis. *The American Political Science Review*, 417–427. doi:10.2307/1953254

Nysveen, H., Pedersen, P. E., & Thorbjørnsen, H. (2005). Intentions to use mobile services: Antecedents and cross-service comparisons. *Journal of the Academy of Marketing Science*, *33*(3), 330–346. doi:10.1177/0092070305276149

O'Gorman, L. (2003). Comparing passwords, tokens and biometrics for user authentication. *Proceedings of the IEEE*, *91*(12), 2021–2040. doi:10.1109/JPROC.2003.819611

O'Malley, C., Langton, S., Anderson, A., Doherty-Sneddon, G., & Bruce, V. (1996). Comparison of face-to-face and video-mediated interaction. *Interacting with Computers*, *8*(2), 177–192. doi:10.1016/0953-5438(96)01027-2

Ocenasek, P. (2008). Modification of Web Content According to the User Requirements. In *Edutainment 2008* (LNCS 5093, pp. 324-327).

Ochsman, R. B., & Chapanis, A. (1974). The effect of 10 communication modes on the behavior of teams during cooperative problems solving. *International Journal of Man-Machine Studies*, *6*(5), 579–619. doi:10.1016/S0020-7373(74)80019-2

OECD. (2003). The e-government imperative. Paris, France: OECD. Retrieved from http://213.253.134.43/oecd/pdfs/browseit/4203071E.pdf

OECD. (2004). *The e-government imperative*. Paris, France: OECD.

Oh, S., Ahn, J., & Kim, B. (2003). Adoption of broadband Internet in Korea: The role of experience in building attitudes. *Journal of Information Technology, 18*, 267–280. doi:10.1080/0268396032000150807

Okazaki, S. (2006). What do we know about mobile internet adopters? A cluster analysis. *Information & Management, 43*(2), 127–141. doi:10.1016/j.im.2005.05.001

Okazaki, S., Katsukura, A., & Nishiyama, M. (2007). How mobile advertising works: The role of trust in improving attitudes and recall. *Journal of Advertising Research, 47*(2), 165–178. doi:10.2501/S0021849907070195

Okazaki, S., & Taylor, C. R. (2008). What is SMS advertising and why do multinationals adopt it? Answers from an empirical study in European markets. *Journal of Business Research, 61*(1), 4–12. doi:10.1016/j.jbusres.2006.05.003

Olie, R. (1994). The culture factor in personnel and organisation policies. In Harzing, A. W., & Van Ruysseveldt, J. (Eds.), *International human resource management: An integrated approach* (pp. 124–143). London, UK: Sage.

Oliver, R. (2008). Engaging first year students using a Web-supported inquiry-based learning setting. *Higher Education, 55*(3), 285–301. doi:10.1007/s10734-007-9055-7

Olubamise, B., & Awe, J. (2007). *NIGERIA: ICT4D annual review: A synopsis of the ICT4D sector in Nigeria incorporating activities of the government, private sector and non-governmental organizations.* Retrieved from http://www.jidaw.com/itsolutions/ict4dreview2007.html

Omar, S., & Djuhari, H. (2004). Multi-purpose student card system using smart card technology. In *Proceedings of the Fifth International Conference of Information Technology Based Higher Education and Training* (pp. 527-532).

Ondrus, J., & Pigneur, Y. (2006). Towards a holistic analysis of mobile payments: A multiple perspectives approach. *Journal Electronic Commerce Research and Applications, 5*, 246–257. doi:10.1016/j.elerap.2005.09.003

Ong, C. S., & Lai, J. Y. (2006). Gender differences in perceptions and relationships among dominants of e-learning acceptance. *Computers in Human Behavior, 22*(1), 816–829. doi:10.1016/j.chb.2004.03.006

Orlikowski, W. (1992). The Duality of Technology: Rethinking the Concept of Technology in Organizations. *Organization Science, 3*(3), 398–427. doi:10.1287/orsc.3.3.398

Orlikowski, W. (1996). Improvising Organizational Transformation over Time: A Situated Change Perspective. *Information Systems Research, 7*(1), 63–92. doi:10.1287/isre.7.1.63

Orlikowski, W. (2000). Using Technology and Constituting Structures: A Practice Lens for Studying Technology in Organizations. *Organization Science, 11*(4), 404–428. doi:10.1287/orsc.11.4.404.14600

Orlikowski, W., & Yates, J. (2002). It's About Time: Temporal Structuring in Organizations. *Organization Science, 13*(6), 684–700. doi:10.1287/orsc.13.6.684.501

Ornella, P., & Stephanie, B. (2006). Universal Designs for Mobile Phones: A Case Study. In *Proceedings of the Computer Human Interaction 2006 Conference*.

Oruame, S. (2008). *Corruption is killing ICT in Nigeria.* Retrieved from http://www.computerworldwestafrica.com/articles/2008/11/20/corruption-killing-ict-nigeria

Orvis, K. L., Wisher, R. A., Bonk, C. J., & Olson, T. M. (2002). Communication patterns during synchronous Web-based military training in problem solving. *Computers in Human Behavior, 18*(6), 782–795. doi:10.1016/S0747-5632(02)00018-3

Osborne, D., & Gaebler, T. (1992). *Reinventing government: How the entrepreneurial spirit is transforming the public sector*. Reading, MA: Addison-Wesley.

Osborne, D., & Plastrik, P. (2000). *The reinventor's field book: Tools for transforming your government*. San Francisco, CA: Jossey-Bass.

Osborne, S. (2000). *Public –private partnership: Theory and practice in international perspective*. London, UK: Routledge.

Paas, F., Tuovinen, J. E., van Merrienboer, J. J. G., & Darabi, A. A. (2005). A motivational perspective on the relation between mental effort and performance: Optimizing learner involvement in instruction. *Educational Technology Research and Development*, *53*(3), 25–34. doi:10.1007/BF02504795

Palmer, R. (2009). Skills development, employment and sustained growth in Ghana: Sustainability challenges. *International Journal of Educational Development*, *29*(2), 133–139. doi:10.1016/j.ijedudev.2008.09.007

Paris, S. G., & Paris, A. H. (2001). Classroom applications of research in self-regulated learning. *Educational Psychologist*, *36*(2), 89–101. doi:10.1207/S15326985EP3602_4

Park, D. H., Lee, J., & Han, I. (2007). The Effect of On-Line Consumer Reviews on Consumer Purchasing Intention: The Moderating Role of Involvement. *International Journal of Electronic Commerce*, *11*(4), 125–148. doi:10.2753/JEC1086-4415110405

Patton, M. (2002). *Qualitative research and evaluation methods* (3rd ed.). Thousand Oaks, CA: Sage.

Patton, M. Q. (1999). Enhancing the quality and credibility of qualitative analysis. *HSR: Health Services Research Part II*, *34*(5), 1189–1208.

Patton, M. Q. (2002). *Qualitative research and evaluation methods* (3rd ed.). Thousand Oaks, CA: Sage.

Peevers, G., Douglas, G., & Jack, M. A. (2008). A usability comparison of three alternative message formats for an SMS banking service. *International Journal of Human-Computer Studies*, *66*(2), 113–123. doi:10.1016/j.ijhcs.2007.09.005

Peevers, G., & McInnes, F. (2009). Laboratory studies. In Love, S. (Ed.), *Handbook of Mobile Technology Research Methods*. Hauppauge, NY: Nova.

Peevers, G., McInnes, F., Morton, H., Matthews, A., & Jack, M. A. (2009). The mediating effects of brand music and waiting time updates on customers' satisfaction with a telephone service when put on-hold. *International Journal of Bank Marketing*, *27*(2-3), 202–217. doi:10.1108/02652320910950196

Peirce, C. S. (1976). *Collected Papers of Charles Sanders Peirce*. Cambridge, MA: Harvard University Press.

Perels, F., Gürtler, T., & Schmitz, B. (2005). Training of self-regulatory and problem-solving competence. *Learning and Instruction*, *15*(2), 123–139. doi:10.1016/j.learninstruc.2005.04.010

Peters, T. J., & Waterman, R. H. J. (1982). *In search of excellence*. New York, NY: Harper & Row.

Pettigrew, K. E., Fidel, R., & Bruce, H. (2001). Conceptual frameworks in information behavior. *Annual Review of Information Science & Technology*, *35*, 43–78.

Pidgeon, N., & Rogers-Hayden, T. (2007). Opening up nanotechnology dialogue with the publics: Risk communication or 'upstream engagement'? *Health Risk & Society*, *9*(2), 191–210. doi:10.1080/13698570701306906

Pitkänen, O., & Niemelä, M. (2009). Humans and emerging RFID systems: Evaluating data protection law on the user scenario basis. *International Journal of Technology and Human Interaction*, *5*(2), 85–95. doi:10.4018/jthi.2009040105

Plant, S. (2002). *On the Mobile: The Effects of Mobile Telephones on Social and Individual*. Retrieved from http://www.motorola.com/mot/doc/0/234_MotDoc.pdf

Plouffe, C. R., Hulland, J. S., & Vandenbosch, M. (2001). Richness versus parsimony in modeling technology adoption decisions--understanding merchant adoption of a smart card-based payment system. *Information Systems Research*, *12*(2), 208–222. doi:10.1287/isre.12.2.208.9697

Plouffe, C. R., Vandenbosch, M., & Hulland, J. S. (2000). Why smart cards have failed: Looking to consumer and merchant reactions to a new payment technology. *International Journal of Bank Marketing*, *18*(3), 112–124. doi:10.1108/02652320010339662

Plouffe, C. R., Vandenbosch, M., & Hulland, J. S. (2001). Intermediating technologies and multi-group adoption: A comparison of consumer and merchant adoption intentions toward a new electronic payment system. *Product Innovation Management*, *18*(2), 65–81. doi:10.1016/S0737-6782(00)00072-2

PM. (2008). *Prime ministry of The Hashemite Kingdom of Jordan*. Retrieved from http://www.pm.gov.jo/arabic/index.php?page_type=pages&part=1&page_id=126

Polanco, R., Calderón, P., & Delgado, F. (2004). Effects of a problem-based learning program on engineering students' academic achievements in a Mexican university. *Innovations in Education and Teaching International, 41*(2), 145–155. doi:10.1080/1470329042000208675

Poole, S. M., & McPhee, R. D. (1994). Methodology in interpersonal communication research. In *Handbook of interpersonal communication* (pp. 42–99). Thousand Oaks, CA: Sage.

Portney, L. G., & Watkins, M. P. (2000). *Foundations of clinical research: Applications to practice*. Upper Saddle River, NJ: Prentice-Hall.

Pousttchi, K., & Schurig, M. (2004, January 5-8). Assessment of today's mobile banking applications from the view of customer requirements. In *Proceedings of the 37th Hawaii International Conference on System Sciences*, Big Island, HI. Washington, DC: IEEE Computer Society.

Prasopoulou, E., Pouloudi, A., & Panteli, N. (2006). Enacting New Temporal Boundaries: The Role of Mobile Phones. *European Journal of Information Systems, 15*(3), 277–284. doi:10.1057/palgrave.ejis.3000617

Pritchard, R. D., & Payne, S. C. (2003). Performance management and motivation. In Holman, D., Wall, T. D., Clegg, C. W., Sparrow, P., & Howard, A. (Eds.), *The new workplace: A guide to the human impact of modern working practices* (pp. 219–233). Chichester, UK: John Wiley & Sons.

Privacy International. (2007). *CCTV frequently asked questions*. Retrieved from https://www.privacyinternational.org/article/cctv-frequently-asked-questions

Propp, V. (1968). *Morphology of the folk tale*. Austin, TX: University of Texas Press.

Radicati Group, Inc. (2008). *Addressing email chaos: The Email-Manager™ solution*. Retrieved February 6, 2010, from http://www.radicati.com/files/emm-final.pdf

Rahman, F., Kumar, A., Shabana, N., & Srinivasan, S. (2007, November 27-29). Design of a wireless physiological parameter measurement and monitoring system. In *Proceedings of the International Conference on Computer Engineering & Systems*, Cairo, Egypt (pp. 401-405).

Raitt, D. (2005). *ICT developments in Nigerian libraries* [electronic resource]. Bingley, UK: Emerald Group.

Raji, M. O., Ayoade, O. B., & Usoro, A. (2006). *The prospects and problems of adopting ICT for poverty eradication in Nigeria*. Retrieved from http://www.ejisdc.org/ojs2/index.php/ejisdc/article/viewFile/346/192

Ramayah, T., & Bushra, A. (2004). Role of self-efficacy in e-library usage among students of a public university in Malaysia. *Malaysian Journal of Library & Information Science., 9*(1), 39–57.

Ramayah, T., Chin, Y. L., Suki, N. M., & Amlus, I. (2005). Determinants of intention to use an online bill payment system among MBA students. *E-Business, 9*, 80–91.

Ramayah, T., & Ignatius, J. (2005). Impact of perceived usefulness, perceived ease of use and perceived enjoyment on intention to shop online. *ICFAI Journal of Systems Management, 3*(3), 36–51.

Ramayah, T., Ignatius, J., & Aafaqi, B. (in press). PC usage among students in a private institution of higher learning: The moderating role of prior experience. *The Journal of Business Strategy.*

Ranchhod, A. (2007). Developing mobile marketing strategies. *International Journal of Mobile Advertising, 2*(1), 76–83.

Randall, D., & Hughes, J. A. (1995). Sociology CSCW and working with customers. In Thomas, P. J. (Ed.), *The Social and Interactional Dimensions of Human-Computer Interfaces*. New York, NY: Cambridge University Press.

Rappaport, S. D. (2007). Lessons from online practice: New advertising models. *Journal of Advertising Research, 2*, 135–141. doi:10.2501/S0021849907070158

Rastogi, L., & Das, P. (2002). *Re-engineering educational institutions through smart cards*. Retrieved from http://www.au-kbc.org/bpmain1/Security/smartcardwp.pdf

Raykov, T., & Marcoulides, G. A. (2000). *A First Course in Structural Equation Modeling*. Mahwah, NJ: Lawrence Erlbaum.

REACH 1.0. (2000). *Launching Jordan's software and IT industry: A strategy and action plan*. Retrieved from http://www.reach.com.jo/

REACH 2.0. (2001). *Launching Jordan's software and IT services industry: An updated strategy and action plan*. Retrieved from http://www.reach.com.jo/

REACH 3.0. (2002). *Launching Jordan's software and ICT services: An updating strategy and action plan.* Retrieved from http://www.reach.com.jo/

REACH 4.0. (2004). *Launching Jordan's software and ICT services: An updating strategy and action plan.* Retrieved from http://www.reach.com.jo/

Recascino, A. (2009). *Email utilization by university employees: Relationship to job satisfaction in higher education.* Saarbrücken, Germany: VDM Verlag.

Redding, S. G., & Baldwin, E. (1991). Managers for Asia/Pacific: Recruitment and development strategies. *Hong Kong Business International*, 74-77.

Reid, A. (1977). Comparing the telephone with face-to-face interaction. In Pool, I. (Ed.), *The Social Impact of the Telephone*. Cambridge, MA: MIT Press.

Renaud, K., Ramsay, J., & Hair, M. (2006). You've got e-mail…shall I deal with it now? Electronic mail from the recipient's perspective. *International Journal of Human-Computer Interaction*, *21*(3), 313–332. doi:10.1207/s15327590ijhc2103_3

Renn, K. A., & Zeligman, D. M. (2005). Learning about Technology and Student Affairs: Outcomes of an Online Immersion. *Journal of College Student Development*, *46*(5), 547–555. doi:10.1353/csd.2005.0055

Repo, P., Hyvonen, K., Pantzar, M., & Timonen, P. (2006). Inventing use for a novel mobile service. *International Journal of Technology and Human Interaction*, *2*(2), 49–64. doi:10.4018/jthi.2006040103

Reyero, M., & Tourón, J. (2003). *El desarrollo del talento: la aceleración como estrategia educativa* [*The Development of Talent: Acceleration as An Educational Strategy*]. Coruña, Spain: Netbiblo.

Richardson, K. P. (2003). Health risks on the internet: Establishing credibility on line. *Health Risk & Society*, *5*(2), 171–184. doi:10.1080/1369857031000123948

Ringle, C. M., Wende, S., & Will, A. (2005). *SmartPLS (Version 2.0 (beta)).* Hamburg, Germany: University of Hamburg.

Risemberg, R., & Zimmerman, B. J. (1992). Self-regulated learning in gifted students. *Roeper Review*, *15*(2), 98–101. doi:10.1080/02783199209553476

Rivis, A., & Sheeran, P. (2003). Descriptive norms as an additional predictor in the theory of planned behaviour: A meta-analysis. *Current Psychology (New Brunswick, N.J.)*, *22*(3), 218–223. doi:10.1007/s12144-003-1018-2

Robey, D., & Bourdreau, M.-C. (1999). Accounting for the Contradictory Organizational Consequences of Information Technology: Theoretical Directions and Methodological Implication. *Information Systems Research*, *10*(2), 167–185. doi:10.1287/isre.10.2.167

Rochelean, B., & Wu, L. (2005). e-Government and financial transactions: Potential versus reality. *Electronic. Journal of E-Government*, *3*(4), 219–230.

Rochet, J., & Tirole, J. (2003). An economic analysis of the determination of interchange fees in payment card systems. *Review of Network Economics*, *2*(2), 69–79. doi:10.2202/1446-9022.1019

Rogers, E. M. (2003). *Diffusion of innovations* (5th ed.). New York, NY: Free Press.

Root, R. W., & Draper, S. (1983). Questionnaires as a software evaluation tool. In *Proceedings of the CHI 83 Conference*. New York, NY: ACM, New York.

Root, R. W., & Draper, S. (1983, December 12-15). Questionnaires as a software evaluation tool. In *Proceedings of the CHI 83 Conference*, Boston, MA. New York, NY: ACM.

Ross, C. A. (1976). The effects of trial and incentives on repeat purchase behavior. *JMR, Journal of Marketing Research*, *13*(3), 263–269. doi:10.2307/3150736

Rothschild, M. L., & Gaidis, W. C. (1981). Behavioral learning theory: Its relevance to marketing and promotions. *Journal of Marketing*, *45*(2), 70–78. doi:10.2307/1251666

Rouibah, K. (2008). Social usage of instant messaging by individuals outside the workplace in Kuwait. *Information Technology & People*, *21*(1), 34–68. doi:10.1108/09593840810860324

Rouse, W. B., & Morris, N. M. (1986). On looking into the black-box: Prospects and limits in the search for mental models. *Psychological Bulletin*, *100*(3), 349–363. doi:10.1037/0033-2909.100.3.349

Rownok, T., Islam, M. Z., & Khan, M. (2006, December). Bangla Text Input and Rendering Support for Short Message Service on Mobile Devices. In *Proceedings of 9th International Conference on Computer and Information Technology*, Dhaka, Bangladesh.

Ruiz-Mafé, C., Sanz-Blas, S., & Aldas-Manzano, J. (2009). Drivers and barriers to online airline ticket purchasing. *Journal of Air Transport Management, 15*(6), 294–298. doi:10.1016/j.jairtraman.2009.02.001

Ruiz-Mafé, C., Sanz-Blas, S., & Aldas-Manzano, J. (2009). Drivers and barriers to online airline ticket purchasing. *Journal of Air Transport Management*, 1–5.

Rumpa, G. (2005, February 6). Are you banking more on your mobile? *The Times of India.* Retrieved from http://timesofindia.indiatimes.com/articleshow/1013140.cms

Rutter, D. R., Stephenson, G. M., & Dewey, M. E. (1981). Visual communication and the content and style of conversation. *The British Journal of Social Psychology, 20*(1), 41–52. doi:10.1111/j.2044-8309.1981.tb00472.x

Sablonnière, R. D. L., Taylor, D. M., & Sadykova, N. (2009). Challenges of applying a student-centered approach to learning in the context of education in Kyrgyzstan. *International Journal of Educational Development, 29*(6), 628–634. doi:10.1016/j.ijedudev.2009.01.001

Sagahyroon, A., Raddy, M., Ghazy, A., & Suleman, U. (2009). Design and implementation of a wearable healthcare monitoring system. *International Journal of Electronic Healthcare, 5*(1), 68–86. doi:10.1504/IJEH.2009.026273

Sahay, S., & Walshm, G. (1977). Social Structure and Managerial Agency in India. *Organization Studies, 18*(3), 415–444. doi:10.1177/017084069701800304

Salajan, F. D., Schönwetter, D. J., & Cleghorn, B. M. (2010). Student and faculty inter-generational digital divide: Fact or fiction? *Computers & Education, 55*, 1393–1403. doi:10.1016/j.compedu.2010.06.017

Samanta, S. K., Achilleos, A., Moiron, S. R. F., Woods, J., & Ghanbari, M. (2010). Automatic language translation for mobile SMS. *International Journal of Information Communication Technologies and Human Development, 2*(1), 43–58.

Samovar, L. A., Porter, R. E., & Jain, N. C. (1981). *Understanding intercultural communication*. Belmont, CA: Wadsworth.

Saprikis, V., Chouliara, A., & Vlachopoulou, M. (2010). Perceptions towards Online Shopping: Analyzing the Greek University Students' Attitude. *Communications of the IBIMA, 2010*, 1–13.

Saran, M., Cagiltay, K., & Seferoglu, G. (2008, March 23-26). Use of Mobile Phones in Language Learning: Developing Effective Instructional Materials. In *Proceedings of the Fifth IEEE International Conference on Wireless, Mobile, and Ubiquitous Technology in Education*, Beijing, China (pp. 39-43).

Sauro, J., & Lewis, J. R. (2005). Estimating completion rates from small samples using binomial confidence intervals: comparisons and recommendations. In *Proceedings of the Human Factors and Ergonomics Society Annual Meeting (HFES 2005)*, Orlando, FL.

SCA. (2006). *Smart cards and parking*. Princeton, NJ: Smart Card Alliance.

Scanaill, C. N., Ahearne, B., & Lyons, G. M. (2006). Long-term telemonitoring of mobility trends of elderly people using SMS messaging. *IEEE Transactions on Information Technology in Biomedicine, 10*(2), 412–413. doi:10.1109/TITB.2005.859890

Schatzki, T., Knorr-Cetina, K., & von Savigny, E. (Eds.). (2001). *The Practice Turn in Contemporary Theory*. London: Routledge.

Schein, E. H. (1978). *Career dynamics: Matching individual and organizational needs*. Reading, MA: Addison-Wesley.

Scheuer, S. (1999). *Social and economic motivation at work, theories of motivation reassessed*. Copenhagen, Denmark: Copenhagen Business School Press.

Schlosberg, M., & Ozer, N. A. (2007). *Under the watchful eye: The proliferation of video surveillance systems in California.* Retrieved from http://www.aclunc.org/docs/criminal_justice/police_practices/Under_the_Watchful_Eye_The_Proliferation_of_Video_Surveillance_Systems_in_California.pdf

Schlumberger, O. (2002). Transition to development? In Joffe, G. (Ed.), *Jordan in transition* (pp. 225–253). London, UK: Hursy & Co.

Schmidt, H. G. (1983). Problem-based learning: Rationale and description. *Medical Education*, *17*(1), 11–16. doi:10.1111/j.1365-2923.1983.tb01086.x

Schneider, S. C., & Barsoux, J. L. (2003). *Managing across cultures* (2nd ed.). Upper Saddle River, NJ: Prentice Hall.

Schön, D. (1983). *The Reflective Practitioner: How Professionals Think in Action*. London: Temple Smith.

Schultz, E. E., Proctor, R. W., Lien, M. C., & Savendy, G. (2001). Usability and security: an appraisal of usability issues in information security methods. *Computers & Security*, *20*(7), 620–634. doi:10.1016/S0167-4048(01)00712-X

Schultze, U., & Boland, R. (2000). Place, Space and Knowledge Work: A Study of Outsourced Computer Systems Administrators. *Accounting. Management and Information Technologies*, *10*, 187–219. doi:10.1016/S0959-8022(00)00006-0

Schultze, U., & Orlikowski, W. (2004). A Practice Perspective on Technology-mediated Relations: The Use of Internet-based Self-service Technologies. *Information Systems Research*, *15*(1), 87–106. doi:10.1287/isre.1030.0016

Schumacker, R. E., & Lomax, R. G. (2004). *A beginner's guide to structural equation modeling* (2nd ed.). Mahwah, NJ: Lawrence Erlbaum.

Schunk, D. H. (1989). Social cognitive theory and self-regulated learning. In Zimmerman, B. J., & Schunk, D. H. (Eds.), *Self-regulated learning and academic achievement: Theory, research, and practice* (pp. 83–110). New York: Springer-Verlag.

Schware, R. (2000). Information technology and public sector management in developing countries: Present status and future prospects. *The Indian Journal of Public Administration*, *46*(3), 411–416.

Schware, R., & Deane, A. (2003). Deploying e-government programs: The strategic importance of "I" before "E". *Info*, *5*(4), 10–19. doi:10.1108/14636690310495193

Seidman, I. (1998). *Interviewing as qualitative research: a guide for researchers in education and the social sciences* (2nd ed.). New York, NY: Teachers College Press.

Selander, S., & Ödman, P.-J. (2004). *Text och existens: Hermeneutik möter samhällsvetenskap*. Göteborg, Sweden: Daidalos.

Sellen, A. J. (1992, May 3-7). Speech patterns in video-mediated conversations. In *Proceedings of the CHI 92 Conference,* Monterey, CA (pp. 49-59). New York, NY: ACM Press.

Sen, A. (2001). *Development as freedom*. New York, NY: Anchor Books.

Senior, A., Pankanti, S., Hampapur, A., Brown, L., Tian, Y., & Ekin, A. (2005). Enabling video privacy through computer vision. *IEEE Security & Privacy*, *3*(3), 50–57. doi:10.1109/MSP.2005.65

Seyal, A. H., & Rahman, N. A. (2007). The influence of external variables on the executives' use of the Internet. *Business Process Management Journal*, *13*(2), 263–278. doi:10.1108/14637150710740491

Seyal, A. H., & Rahman, N. A. (2007). The influence of external variables on the executives' use of the Internet. *Business Process Management Journal*, *13*(2), 263–278. doi:10.1108/14637150710740491

Shahjahan, M., Nahin, K. M., Uddin, M. M., Ahsan, M. S., & Murase, K. (2008, June 1-8). An implementation of on-line traffic information system via short message service (SMS) for Bangladesh. In *Proceedings of the IEEE International Joint Conference on Neural Networks*, Hong Kong (pp. 2612-2618).

Shang, R., Chen, Y., & Shen, L. (2005). Extrinsic versus intrinsic motivations for consumers to shop on-line. *Information & Management*, *42*(3), 401–413. doi:10.1016/j.im.2004.01.009

Sharma, S. (2007). Exploring best practices in public–private partnership (PPP) in e government through select Asian case studies. *The International Information & Library Review*, *39*, 203–210. doi:10.1016/j.iilr.2007.07.003

Shawwa, N. (2004). *Public officials' attitudes towards the implementation of e- government in Jordan: Field study.* Unpublished master's thesis, Jordan University, Amman, Jordan.

Sheeran, P., & Orbell, S. (1999). Augmenting the theory of planned behavior: Roles for anticipated regret and descriptive norms. *Journal of Applied Social Psychology, 29*(10), 2107–2142. doi:10.1111/j.1559-1816.1999.tb02298.x

Shen, P. D., Lee, T. H., & Tsai, C. W. (2007). Applying web-enabled problem-based learning and self-regulated learning to enhance computing skills of Taiwan's vocational students: a quasi-experimental study of a short-term module. *Electronic Journal of e-Learning, 5*(2), 147-156.

Shen, P. D., Lee, T. H., Tsai, C. W., & Ting, C. J. (2008). Exploring the effects of web-enabled problem-based learning and self-regulated learning on vocational students' involvement in learning. *European Journal of Open, Distance and E-Learning.* Retrieved May 11, 2010, from, http://www.eurodl.org/materials/contrib/2008/Shen_Lee_Tsai_Ting.htm

Shen, P. D., Lee, T. H., & Tsai, C. W. (2008). Enhancing skills of application software via web-enabled problem-based learning and self-regulated learning: An exploratory study. *International Journal of Distance Education Technologies, 6*(3), 69–84.

Shim, J. P., Park, S., & Shim, J. M. (2008). Mobile TV phone: Current usage, issues, and strategic implications. *Industrial Management & Data Systems, 108*(9), 1269–1282. doi:10.1108/02635570810914937

Shin, D.-H., & Kim, W. Y. (2008). Applying the technology acceptance model and flow. *Cyberpsychology & Behavior, 11*(3), 378–382. doi:10.1089/cpb.2007.0117

Short, J. (1974). Effects of medium of communication on experimental negotiation. *Human Relations, 27*, 225–243. doi:10.1177/001872677402700303

Short, J., Williams, E., & Christie, B. (1976). *The Social Psychology of Telecommunications.* New York, NY: Wiley.

Sice, P., & French, I. (2004). Understanding humans and organisation– philosophical implications of autopoiesis. *Journal of Philosophy of Management, 4*(1), 55–66.

Sice, P., & French, I. (2006). A holistic frame of reference for modelling social systems. *Kybernetes, 35*, 5–10. doi:10.1108/03684920610662638

Sillence, E., & Barber, C. (2004). Integrated digital communities: combining and competition. *Interacting with Computers, 16*(1), 93–113. doi:10.1016/j.intcom.2003.11.007

Silverman, D. (2001). *Interpreting qualitative data: Methods for analysing talk, text and interaction* (2nd ed.). Thousand Oaks, CA: Sage.

Singh, J., Goolby, J. R., & Rhoads, G. K. (1994). Behavioral and psychological consequences of boundary spanning burnout for customer service representatives. *Journal of Marketing Research, 31*(4), 558–569. doi:10.2307/3151883

Sitkin, S. B., Sutcliffe, K. M., & Reed, G. L. (1993). Prescriptions for justice: Using social accounts to legitimate the exercise of professional control. *Social Justice Research, 69*(1), 87–111. doi:10.1007/BF01048734

Skalin, L.-Å. (2002). Narratologi - Studiet av berättandets principer. In Bergsten, S. (Ed.), *Litteraturvetenskap – en inledning* (pp. 173–188). Lund, Sweden: Studentlitteratur.

Smith, D. (2008, March 9). Email 'a broken business tool' as staff spend hours wading through inboxes. *The Observer.* Retrieved October 31, 2008, from http://www.guardian.co.uk/technology/2008/mar/09/internet/print

Smith, L. M., & Pohland, P. A. (1969). *Grounded theory and educational ethnography: A methodological analysis and critique.* St. Ann, MO: Central Midwestern Regional Education Library.

Smoreda, Z., & Licoppe, C. (2000). Gender-specific use of the domestic telephone. *Social Psychology Quarterly, 63*(3), 238–252. doi:10.2307/2695871

Song, H. (2006). *e-Government in developing countries: Lessons learned from republic of Korea.* Bangkok, Thailand: UNESCO.

Song, J., & Kim, Y. J. (2006). Social Influence Process in the Acceptance of a Virtual Community Service. *Information Systems Frontiers, 8*(3), 241–252. doi:10.1007/s10796-006-8782-0

Song, Y. (2008). SMS enhanced vocabulary learning for mobile audiences. *International Journal of Mobile Learning and Organisation, 2*(1), 81–98. doi:10.1504/IJMLO.2008.018719

Sørensen, C., & Gibson, D. (2004). Ubiquitous Visions and Opaque Realities: Professional Talking About Mobile Technologies. *Info*, *6*(3), 188–196. doi:10.1108/14636690410549516

Sørensen, C., & Pica, D. (2005). Tales from the Police: Rhythms of Interaction with Mobile Technologies. *Information and Organization*, *15*(2), 125–149. doi:10.1016/j.infoandorg.2005.02.007

Soriano, C., Raikundalia, G. K., & Szajman, J. (2005). A usability study of short message service on middle-aged users. In *Proceedings of the OZCHI 2005 Conferece*, Canberra, ACT, Australia.

Spencer, M. (2000). *CCTV and the protection of privacy: A tale of two cultures.* Retrieved from http://www.worldlii.org/int/journals/PLBIN/2000/43.html

Spradley, J. (1979). *The Ethnographic Interview*. New York: Holt, Rinehart and Winston.

Stacey, R. D. (2001). *Complex responsive processes in organizations - learning and knowledge creation.* London, UK: Routledge.

Stahl, B., & Eke, D. (2009). *Ethical review of ICT projects across UK computing departments: The state of the art.* Paper presented at the 10th Annual Conference of the HEA, Kent, UK.

Stahl, B. (2005). The ethical problem of framing e-government in terms of e-commerce. *Electronic. Journal of E-Government*, *3*(2), 77–86.

Stanton, J. M. (2000). Traditional and electronic monitoring from an organizational justice perspective. *Journal of Business and Psychology*, *15*(1), 129–147. doi:10.1023/A:1007775020214

Steel, E. S. (2007, November 27). Where E-Commerce Meets Chat, Social Retailing Gains Traction. *The Wall Street Journal*, B8.

Steensma, H. K., Marino, L., Weaver, K. M., & Dickson, P. H. (2000). The influence of national culture on the formation of technology alliances by entrepreneurial firms. *Academy of Management Journal*, *43*(5), 951–973. doi:10.2307/1556421

Steers, R. M., Mowday, R. T., & Shapiro, D. L. (2004). The future of work motivation theory. *Academy of Management Review*, *29*(3), 379–387.

Steinbock, D. (2006). The missing link why mobile marketing is different. *International Journal of Mobile Marketing*, *1*(1), 83–94.

Stewart, K. A., & Segars, A. H. (2002). An empirical examination of the concern for information privacy instrument. *Information Systems Research*, *13*(1), 36–49. doi:10.1287/isre.13.1.36.97

Stone, E. F., & Stone, D. L. (1990). Privacy in organizations: Theoretical issues, research findings, and protection mechanisms. *Research in Personnel and Human Resources Management*, *8*, 349–341.

Stone-Romero, E. F., Stone, D. L., & Hyatt, D. (2003). Personnel selection procedures and invasion of privacy. *The Journal of Social Issues*, *59*(2), 343–368. doi:10.1111/1540-4560.00068

Straub, D., Keil, M., & Brenner, W. (1997). Testing the Technology Acceptance Model Across Cultures: A three country study. *Information & Management*, *33*(1), 1–11. doi:10.1016/S0378-7206(97)00026-8

Straub, D., Loch, K., Evaristo, R., Karahanna, E., & Strite, M. (2002). Toward a theory-based measurement of culture. *Journal of Global Information Management*, *10*(1), 13–23. doi:10.4018/jgim.2002010102

Strauss, A. (1987). *Qualitative analysis for social scientists*. Cambridge, UK: Cambridge University Press. doi:10.1017/CBO9780511557842

Strauss, A., & Corbin, J. (1990). *Basics of qualitative research: Grounded theory procedures and techniques.* London, UK: Sage.

Styvén, M. (2007). *Exploring the online music market: Consumer characteristics and value perceptions. Unpublished doctoral dissertations.* Sweden: Lulea University of Technology.

Suh, B., & Han, I. (2002). Effect of Trust on Customer Acceptance of Internet Banking. *Electronic Commerce Research and Applications*, *1*(3-4), 247–263. doi:10.1016/S1567-4223(02)00017-0

Suki, N. M., Ahmand, M. I., & Thyagarajan, V. (2007). The Influence of Friends, Family and Media in Classifying Online Shopper Innovativeness in Malaysia. *European Journal of Soil Science*, *5*(1), 136–143.

Suki, N. M., Ramayah, T., & Kow Pei Ming, M. (2010). Explaining job searching through the social networking sites: A structural equation model approach. *International Journal of Virtual Communities and Social Networking*, *2*(3), 1–15. doi:10.4018/jvcsn.2010070101

Suki, N. M., Ramayah, T., & Suki, N. M. (2008). Internet shopping acceptance: examining the influence of intrinsic versus extrinsic motivations. *Direct Marketing: An International Journal*, *2*(2), 97–110. doi:10.1108/17505930810881752

Suls, J., Martin, R., & Wheeler, L. (2000). Three Kinds of Opinion Comparison: The Triadic Model. *Personality and Social Psychology Review*, *4*(3), 219–237. doi:10.1207/S15327957PSPR0403_2

Sungur, S., & Tekkaya, C. (2006). Effects of problem-based learning and traditional instruction on self-regulated learning. *The Journal of Educational Research*, *99*(5), 307–320. doi:10.3200/JOER.99.5.307-320

Sun, H., & Zhang, P. (2006). The role of moderating factors in user technology acceptance. *International Journal of Human-Computer Studies*, *64*(2), 53–78. doi:10.1016/j.ijhcs.2005.04.013

Suoranta, M. (2003). Adoption of mobile banking in Finland. *Studies in Business and Management, 28.*

Suoranta, M., & Mattila, M. (2004). Mobile banking and consumer behaviour: new insights into the diffusion pattern. *Journal of Financial Services Marketing*, *8*(4), 354–366. doi:10.1057/palgrave.fsm.4770132

Sveningsson, S., & Alvesson, M. (2003). Managing managerial identities: Organizational fragmentation, discourse and identity struggle. *Human Relations*, *56*(10), 1163–1193. doi:10.1177/00187267035610001

Sveningsson, S., & Larsson, M. (2006). Fantasies of leadership: Identity work. *Leadership*, *2*(2), 203–224. doi:10.1177/1742715006062935

Swatman, P. M. C., Krueger, C., & Van der Beek, K. (2006). The changing digital content landscape: an evaluation of e-business model development in European online news and music. *Internet Research*, *16*(1), 53–80. doi:10.1108/10662240610642541

Sweeney, J. C., Soutar, G. N., & Johnson, L. W. (1997). Retail service quality and perceived value. *Journal of Retailing and Consumer Services*, *4*(1), 39–48. doi:10.1016/S0969-6989(96)00017-3

Tahat, A. A. (2009, February 11-13). Body Temperature and Electrocardiogram Monitoring Using an SMS-Based Telemedicine System. In *Proceedings of the 4th International Symposium on Wireless Pervasive Computing*, Melbourne, Australia (pp. 1-5).

Tai, C. F., Chen, R. J., & Lai, J. L. (2003). How technological and vocational education can prosper in the 21st century? *IEEE Circuits & Devices Magazine*, *19*(2), 15–51. doi:10.1109/MCD.2003.1191433

Tajfel, H. (1981). *Human groups and social categories: Studies in social psychology*. Cambridge, UK: Cambridge University Press.

Tam, J. L. M. (2004). Customer satisfaction, service quality and perceived value: an integrative model. *Journal of Marketing Management*, *20*, 897–917. doi:10.1362/0267257041838719

Tang, J., & Isaacs, E. (1993). Why do users like video? Studies of multimedia supported collaboration. *Computer Supported Collaborative Work: An International Journal*, *1*, 163–196. doi:10.1007/BF00752437

Tan, J. (2005). *E-health care information systems. An introduction for students and professionals*. San Francisco, CA: Jossey-Bass.

Tannen, D. (1992). *You Just Don't Understand: Women and Men in Conversation*. London, UK: Virago Press.

Tautz, F. (2002). *E-Health und die Folgen. Wie das Internet die Arzt-Patienten-Beziehung und das Gesundheitssystem verändert* [E-health and its consequences. How the Internet changes the physician-patient relationship and the health system]. Frankfurt, Germany: Campus.

Tavani, H. (2008). Informational privacy: Concepts, theories and controversies. In Hoven, J. V. D., & Weckert, J. (Eds.), *Information technology and moral philosophy* (pp. 131–164). Cambridge, UK: Cambridge University Press.

Taylor, N. (2002). State surveillance and the right to privacy. *Surveillance & Society, 1*(1), 66–85.

Taylor, S., & Bogdan, R. (1984). *Introduction to Qualitative Research Methods: The Search for Meanings*. New York: John Wiley & Sons.

Teas, R. K., & Agarwal, S. (2000). The effects of extrinsic product cues on consumers' perceptions of quality, sacrifice, and value. *Journal of the Academy of Marketing Science, 28*(2), 278–290. doi:10.1177/0092070300282008

Tedeschi, B. (2006, September 11). Like Shopping? Social Networking? Try Social Shopping. *The New York Times*.

TeleAnalytics. (2008). *The quarterly TeleAnalytics mobile TV tracking service 5*. Toronto, ON, Canada: TeleAnalytics.

Teo, T. S. H., Lim, V. K. G., & Lai, R. Y. C. (1999). Intrinsic and extrinsic motivation in Internet usage. *Omega, 27*(32), 25–37. doi:10.1016/S0305-0483(98)00028-0

The Mobile Data Association. (2009). *The Q4 2008 UK mobile report*. Retrieved from http://www.themda.org/mda-press-releases/the-q4-2008-uk-mobile-trends-report.php

The Royal Society. (2006). *Digital healthcare: The impact of information and communication technologies on health and healthcare*. London, UK: The Royal Society.

Thomas, A. (2007, September 12). Plan introduces safety cameras. *The Exponent*, p. A1.

Thulasi Bai, V., & Srivatsa, S. K. (2008). Portable telecardiac system for arrhythmia monitoring and alerting. *International Journal of Healthcare Technology and Management, 9*(5/6), 517–525. doi:10.1504/IJHTM.2008.020202

Thüring, M., & Jungermann, H. (1986). Constructing and running mental models for inferences about the future. In Brehmer, B., Jungermann, H., Lourens, P., & Sevon, G. (Eds.), *New Directions in the Research on Decision Making* (pp. 163–174). Amsterdam, The Netherlands: North-Holand.

Tiwari, R., Buse, S., & Herstatt, C. (2007). Mobile services in banking sector. The role of innovative business solutions in generating competitive advantage. In *Proceedings of the 8th International Research Conference on Quality, Innovation and Knowledge Management*.

TNS. (2008). *Baromètre on-off-mobile*. Paris, France: TNS Sofres.

Tong, D. Y. K. (2009). A study of e–recruitment technology adoption in Malaysia. *Industrial Management & Data Systems, 109*(2), 281–300. doi:10.1108/02635570910930145

Torp, L., & Sage, S. (2002). *Problems as possibilities: Problem-based learning for K–12 education* (2nd ed.). Alexandria, VA: ASCD.

Townley, B. (2002). Managing with Modernity. *Organization, 9*(4), 549–573. doi:10.1177/135050840294003

Townsend, A. (2000). Life in the Real-time City: Mobile Telephones and Urban Metabolism. *Journal of Urban Technology, 7*(2), 85–104. doi:10.1080/713684114

Trappey, R. J. III, & Woodside, A. G. (2005). Consumer responses to interactive advertising campaigns coupling short-message-service direct marketing and TV commercials. *Journal of Advertising Research, 45*(4), 382–401.

Tricker, R. I. (1988). Information resource management: A cross-cultural perspective. *Information & Management, 15*(2), 37–46. doi:10.1016/0378-7206(88)90028-6

Trochim, W. M. K. (2005). *Probability and non-probability sampling*. Retrieved from http://socialresearchmethods.net/kb/sampprob.htm

Trompenaars, F., & Hampden-Turner, C. (1997). *Riding the waves of culture: Understanding cultural diversity in business*. London, UK: Nicholas Brealey Publishing.

Truman, G., Sandow, K., & Rifkin, T. (2003). An empirical study of smart card technology. *Information & Management, 40*, 591–606. doi:10.1016/S0378-7206(02)00046-0

Tsai, C. W., & Shen, P. D. (2009). Applying web-enabled self-regulated learning and problem-based learning with initiation to involve low-achieving students in learning. *Computers in Human Behavior, 25*(6), 1189–1194. doi:10.1016/j.chb.2009.05.013

Tsoukas, H. (1989). The Validity of Ideographic Research Explanations. *Academy of Management Review, 14*(4), 551–561. doi:10.2307/258558

Tuan, Y.-F. (1977). *Space and Place: The Perspective of Experience*. Minneapolis, MN: University of Minnesota Press.

Turban, E., & McElroy, D. (1998). Using smart cards in electronic commerce. In *Proceedings of the 31st Annual Hawaii International Conference on System Sciences* (pp. 62-69).

Turel, O., Serenko, A., & Bontis, N. (2007). User acceptance of wireless short messaging services: Deconstructing perceived value. *Information & Management, 44*(1), 63–73. doi:10.1016/j.im.2006.10.005

Tyler, J. R., & Tang, J. C. (2003, September). When can I expect an e-mail response? A study of rhythms in e-mail usage. In *Proceedings of the 2003 8th European Conference on Computer-Supported Cooperative Work*, Helsinki, Finland (pp. 239-258).

UNIFEM. (2006). *e-Villages project*. Amman, Jordan: UNIFEM.

United Nations Conference on Trade and Development. (2001). *E-commerce and development report*. Retrieved from http://www.unctad.org/Templates/Page.asp?intItemID=2629&lang=1

United Nations Development Programme. (2000). *Information and communications technologies for development*. Retrieved from http://www.undp.org/mlo21

United Nations. (2008a). *e-Government survey, from e-government to connected governance*. Retrieved from http://unpan1.un.org/intradoc/groups/public/documents/un/unpan028607.pdf

United Nations. (2008b). *Handbook on the least developed country category: Inclusion, graduation and special support measures*. Retrieved from http://www.un.org/esa/policy/devplan/cdppublications/2008cdphandbook.pdf

Urry, J. (1985). Social Relations, Space and Time. In Gregory, D., & Urry, J. (Eds.), *Social Relations and Spatial Structures* (pp. 20–45). London: Macmillan.

Urry, J. (1991). Time and Space in Social Theory. In Bryant, C., & Jarry, D. (Eds.), *Theory of Structuration: A Critical Appreciation* (pp. 160–176). London: Routledge.

Vakkari, P. (2008). Trends and approaches in information behaviour research. *Information Research, 13*(4).

Van der Heijden, H. (2004). User acceptance of hedonic information systems. *Management Information Systems Quarterly, 28*(4), 695–704.

Van der Kleij, R., Paashuis, R., & Schraagen, J. M. C. (2005). On the passage of time: temporal differences in video-mediated and face-to-face interaction. *International Journal of Human-Computer Studies, 62*, 521–542. doi:10.1016/j.ijhcs.2005.01.003

Vara, V. (2007). Facebook Rethinks Tracking: Site Apologizes, Makes It Easier To Retain Privacy. *The Wall Street Journal*.

Veccio, R. P. (2003). In search of gender advantage. *The Leadership Quarterly, 14*(6), 835–850. doi:10.1016/j.leaqua.2003.09.005

Venkatesh, V. (2000). Determinants of Perceived Ease of Use: Integrating Control, Intrinsic Motivation, and Emotion into the Technology Acceptance Model. *Information Systems Research, 11*(4), 342–365. doi:10.1287/isre.11.4.342.11872

Venkatesh, V., & Brown, S. A. (2001). A longitudinal investigation of personal computers in homes: adoption determinants and emerging challenges. *Management Information Systems Quarterly, 25*(1), 71–102. doi:10.2307/3250959

Venkatesh, V., Morris, M. G., & Ackerman, P. L. (2000). A longitudinal field investigation of gender differences in individual technology adoption decision-making processes. *Organizational Behavior and Human Decision Processes, 83*, 33–60. doi:10.1006/obhd.2000.2896

Venkatesh, V., Morris, M. G., Davis, G. B., & Davis, F. D. (2003). User acceptance of information technology: Toward a unified view. *Management Information Systems Quarterly, 27*(3), 425–478.

Venkatesh, V., Speier, C., & Morris, M. G. (2002). User acceptance enablers in individual decision making about technology: Toward an integrated model. *Decision Sciences*, *33*(2), 297–316. doi:10.1111/j.1540-5915.2002.tb01646.x

Venkatetsh, V., & Davis, F. D. (2000). A theoretical extension of the technology acceptance model: Four longitudinal field studies. *Management Science*, *46*(2), 186–204. doi:10.1287/mnsc.46.2.186.11926

Vijayasarathy, L. R. (2004). Predicting consumer intentions to use on-line shopping: The case for an augmented technology acceptance model. *Information & Management*, *41*(6), 747–762. doi:10.1016/j.im.2003.08.011

Virilio, P. (1991). *The Aesthetics of Disappearance*. New York: Semiotext(e).

Viswanath, K., & Kreuter, M. W. (2007). Health disparities, communication inequalities, and ehealth. *American Journal of Preventive Medicine*, *32*(5), 131–133. doi:10.1016/j.amepre.2007.02.012

Vollmer, C. (2008). *Always on: Advertising, marketing and media in an era of consumer control*. New York, NY: McGraw-Hill.

Vranica, S. (2008, April 10). Can Dove Promote a Cause and Sell Soap? *The Wall Street Journal*, B6.

Waldeck, J. H., Kearney, P., & Plax, T. G. (2001). Teacher e-mail message strategies and students' willingness to communicate online. *Journal of Applied Communication Research*, *29*(1), 54–70. doi:10.1080/00909880128099

Walker, N., Philbin, D. A., & Fisk, A. D. (1997). Age-related differences in movement control: adjusting submovement structure to optimise performance. *The Journals of Gerontology. Series B, Psychological Sciences and Social Sciences*, *52B*(1), 40–52. doi:10.1093/geronb/52B.1.P40

Wallgren, L. G., & Johansson Hanse, J. (2007). Job characteristics, motivators and stress among information technology consultants: A structural equation modeling approach. *International Journal of Industrial Ergonomics*, *37*(1), 51–59. doi:10.1016/j.ergon.2006.10.005

Wang, Y. S., Wang, Y. M., Lin, H. H., & Tang, T. I. (2003). Determinants of user acceptance of Internet banking: An empirical study. *International Journal of Service Industry Management*, *14*(5), 501–519. doi:10.1108/09564230310500192

Ward, L. (2004, December 23). Texting 'is no bar to literacy'. *Guardian Unlimited*. Retrieved from http://education.guardian.co.uk/schools/story/0,5500,1378951,00.html

Warner, M. (Ed.). (1996a). Management in the United Kingdom. In M. Warner (Ed.), *International Encyclopaedia of Business & Management* (Vol. 4, pp. 3085-3099). London, UK: Thomson Business Press.

Warner, M. (Ed.). (1996b). Management in Indonesia. In M. Warner (Ed.), *International Encyclopaedia of Business & Management* (Vol. 3, pp. 2881-2887). London, UK: Thomson Business Press.

Warr, W. A. (2008). Social software: Fun and games, or business tools? *Journal of Information Science*, *34*(4), 591–604. doi:10.1177/0165551508092259

Warshaw, P. R., & Davis, F. D. (1985). Disentangling behavioral intention and behavioral expectation. *Journal of Experimental Social Psychology*, *21*, 213–228. doi:10.1016/0022-1031(85)90017-4

Watts, L., & Monk, A. (1996). Remote assistance: a view of the work and a view of the face. In M. Tauber (Ed.), *Proceedings of CHI 96: Conference on Human Factors in Computing Systems*, Vancouver, BC, Canada (pp. 101-102). New York, NY: ACM Press.

Weerd, D., & Nederhof, P. C. (2001). Case study research, the case of a PhD research project on organizing and managing new product development systems. *Management Decision*, *39*(7), 513–538. doi:10.1108/EUM0000000005805

Weick, K. (1995). *Sensemaking in organizations*. London, UK: Sage.

Weir, C. S., Douglas, G., Richardson, T., & Jack, M. (2009). Usable Security: User Preferences for authentication methods in eBanking and the effects of experience. *Interacting with Computers*.

Wei, R. (2008). Motivations for using the mobile phone for mass communications and entertainment. *Telematics and Informatics*, *25*(1), 36–46. doi:10.1016/j.tele.2006.03.001

Wei, R., Xiaoming, H., & Pan, J. (2010). Examining user behavioral response to SMS ads: Implications for the evolution of the mobile phone as a bona-fide medium. *Telematics and Informatics, 27*(1), 32–41. doi:10.1016/j.tele.2009.03.005

Weir, C. S., Anderson, J. N., & Jack, M. A. (2006). On the role of metaphor and language in design of third party payment in eBanking: Usability and quality. *International Journal of Human-Computer Studies, 64,* 770–784. doi:10.1016/j.ijhcs.2006.03.003

Weir, C. S., Douglas, G., Carruthers, M., & Jack, M. (2009). User perceptions of security, convenience and usability for eBanking authentication tokens. *Journal of Computers and Security, 28*(1), 47–62. doi:10.1016/j.cose.2008.09.008

Weir, C. S., Douglas, G., Richardson, T., & Jack, M. (2009). Usable Security: User Preferences for authentication methods in eBanking and the effects of experience. *Interacting with Computers, 22*(3), 153–164. doi:10.1016/j.intcom.2009.10.001

Weir, C. S., McKay, I., & Jack, M. A. (2007). Functionality and usability in design for eStatements in eBanking services. *Interacting with Computers, 19*(2), 241–256. doi:10.1016/j.intcom.2006.08.010

Weiser, M. (1991). The computer for the 21st century. *Scientific American, 265*(3), 94–104. doi:10.1038/scientificamerican0991-94

Weiss, M., & Hanson-Baldauf, D. (2008). E-mail in academia: Expectations, use, and instructional impact. *EDUCAUSE Quarterly, 31*(1), 42–50.

Wenger, E. (1998). *Communities of practice: Learning, meaning, and identity*. Cambridge, UK: Cambridge University Press.

Westin, A. F. (1967). *Privacy and Freedom*. New York: Atheneum.

White, C. (2008). *Mobile TV: Strategies, business models & technologies*. London, UK: Informa Telecoms & Media.

White, L. (2001). Internet security is the killer application for campus card. *Card Technology Today, 13*(10), 13–14.

Whiteside, J., Bennett, J., & Holzblatt, K. (1988). Usability engineering: Our experience and evolution. In Helander, M. (Ed.), *Handbook of human computer interaction* (pp. 91–817). New York, NY: North-Holland.

Whittaker, S., & Sidner, C. (1996, April). Email overload: Exploring personal information management of email. In *Proceedings of CHI 96: Conference on Human Factors in Computing Systems,* Vancouver, BC, Canada (pp. 276-283). New York, NY: ACM Press.

Whittaker, S., Brennan, S., & Clark, H. (1991). Coordinating activity: an analysis of computer supported co-operative work. In *Proceedings of CHI'91: Human Factors in Computing Systems,* New Orleans, LA (pp. 361-367). New York, NY: ACM Press.

Whittaker, S. (1995). Rethinking video as a technology for interpersonal communication: theory and design implications. *International Journal of Human-Computer Studies, 42,* 501–529. doi:10.1006/ijhc.1995.1022

Whittaker, S. (2003). Things to talk about when talking about things. *Human-Computer Interaction, 18,* 149–170. doi:10.1207/S15327051HCI1812_6

Whittaker, S., Bellotti, V., & Gwizdka, J. (2006). Email in personal information management. *Communications of the ACM, 49*(1), 68–73. doi:10.1145/1107458.1107494

Whittaker, S., Geelhoed, E., & Robinson, E. (1993). Shared workspaces: how do they work and when are they useful? *International Journal of Man-Machine Studies, 39,* 813–842. doi:10.1006/imms.1993.1085

Wiberg, M., & Ljungberg, F. (2001). Exploring the Vision of "Anytime, Anywhere" in the Context of Mobile Work. In Y. Malhotra (Ed.), *Knowledge Management and Business Model Innovation* (pp. 153-165). Hershey, PA: IGI Publishing.

Wikipedia. (2007). *Closed-circuit television.* Retrieved from http://en.wikipedia.org/wiki/Closed-circuit_television

Wilbur, K. C. (2008). How the digital video recorder (DVR) changes traditional television advertising. *Journal of Advertising, 37*(1), 143–149. doi:10.2753/JOA0091-3367370111

Wilkie, J., Jack, M. A., & Littlewood, P. (2005). System-initiated digressive proposals in automated human-computer telephone dialogues: the use of contrasting politeness strategies. *International Journal of Human-Computer Studies*, *62*, 41–71. doi:10.1016/j.ijhcs.2004.08.001

Wilkinson, D., & Birmingham, P. (2003). *Using research instruments: A guide for researchers*. London, UK: Routledge. doi:10.4324/9780203422991

Williams, E. (1977). Experimental comparisons of face-to-face and video-mediated communication. *Psychological Bulletin*, *84*, 963–976. doi:10.1037/0033-2909.84.5.963

Wilson, T. D. (2000). Recent trends in user studies: action research and qualitative methods. *Information Research, 5*(3).

Wilson, E. V. (2002). Email winners and losers. *Communications of the ACM*, *45*(10), 121–126. doi:10.1145/570907.570908

Wilson, T. D. (2008). The information user: Past, present and future. *Journal of Information Science*, *34*(4), 457–464. doi:10.1177/0165551508091309

Winne, P. H. (2001). Self-regulated learning viewed from models of information processing. In Zimmerman, B. J., & Schunk, D. H. (Eds.), *Self-Regulated Learning and Academic Achievement: Theoretical Perspectives* (pp. 153–189). Mahwah, NJ: Erlbaum.

Winne, P. H., & Hadwin, A. (1998). Studying as self-regulated learning. In Hacker, D. J., Dunlosky, J., & Graesser, A. (Eds.), *Metacognition in Educational Theory and Practice* (pp. 277–304). Hillsdale, NJ: Erlbaum.

Winnips, K. (2000). *Scaffolding-by-Design: A Model for WWW-based Learner Support*. Enschede, The Netherlands: University of Twente Press.

Wiredu, G. (2007). User Appropriation of Mobile Technologies: Motives Condition and Design Properties. *Information and Organization*, *17*(2), 110–129. doi:10.1016/j.infoandorg.2007.03.002

Wixon, B. H., & Todd, P. A. (2005). A theoretical integration of user satisfaction and technology acceptance. *Information Systems Research*, *16*(1), 85–102. doi:10.1287/isre.1050.0042

Wojcik, E. (2005). Full-time stress. *Electric Perspectives*, *30*(4), 50–55.

Wong, L. C., & Kleiner, B. H. (1994). Nepotism. *Work Study*, *43*(5), 10–12. doi:10.1108/EUM0000000004002

Woodman, R. W., Ganster, D. C., Adams, J., McCuddy, M. K., Tolchinsky, P. D., & Fromkin, H. (1982). A survey of employee perceptions of information privacy in organizations. *Academy of Management Journal*, *25*(3), 647–663. doi:10.2307/256087

Woodruff, R. B. (1997). Customer value: The next source for competitive advantage. *Journal of the Academy of Marketing Science*, *25*(2), 139–154. doi:10.1007/BF02894350

World Bank. (2010a). *Data - a short history.* Retrieved from http://go.worldbank.org/U9BK7IA1J0

World Bank. (2010b) *Data – country groups: Lower-middle-income economies.* Retrieved from http://go.worldbank.org/D7SN0B8YU0

Wu, C. C. (2009). Higher education expansion and low-income students in Taiwan. *International Journal of Educational Development*, *29*(4), 399–405. doi:10.1016/j.ijedudev.2009.01.006

Wu, I. L., & Wu, K. W. (2005). A hybrid technology acceptance approach for exploring E-Crm adoption in organisations. *Behaviour & Information Technology*, *24*(4), 303–316. doi:10.1080/0144929042000320027

Xu, D. J., Liao, S. S., & Li, Q. (2007). Combining empirical experimentation and modeling techniques: A design research approach for personalized mobile advertising applications. *Decision Support Systems, 44*(2008), 710-724.

Xu, H., Oh, L.-B., & Teo, H.-H. (2009). Perceived effectiveness of text vs. multimedia Location-Based Advertising messaging. *International Journal of Mobile Communications*, *7*(2), 154–177. doi:10.1504/IJMC.2009.022440

Yan, X., Gong, M., & Thong, J. Y. L. (2006). Two tales of one service: User acceptance of short message service (SMS) in Hong Kong and China. *INFO: The Journal of Policy. Regulation and Strategy*, *8*(1), 16–28.

Yeung, A. S., Jin, P., & Sweller, J. (1998). Cognitive Load and Learner Expertise: Split-Attention and Redundancy Effects in Reading with Explanatory Notes. *Contemporary Educational Psychology*, *23*(1), 1–21. doi:10.1006/ceps.1997.0951

Yi, M., & Hwang, Y. (2003). System self-efficacy, enjoyment, learning goal orientation, and The technology acceptance model. *International Journal of Human-Computer Studies*, *59*, 439–449. doi:10.1016/S1071-5819(03)00114-9

Yin, K. (1994). *Case study research: Design and methods* (2nd ed.). London, UK: Sage.

Yin, K. (2003). *Application of case study research* (2nd ed.). London, UK: Sage.

Yoder, J. D. (2001). Making leadership work more effectively for women. *The Journal of Social Issues*, *57*(4), 815–828. doi:10.1111/0022-4537.00243

Yoon, Y., & Uysal, M. (2005). An examination of the effects of motivation and satisfaction on destination loyalty: A structural model. *Tourism Management*, *26*(1), 45–56. doi:10.1016/j.tourman.2003.08.016

Young, R. M. (1983). Surrogates and mapping: Two kinds of conceptual models for interactive devices. In Gentner, D., & Stevens, A. L. (Eds.), *Mental Models* (pp. 35–52). London, UK: Lawrence Erlbaum.

Yukselturk, E., & Bulut, S. (2007). Predictors for student success in an online course. *Journal of Educational Technology & Society*, *10*(2), 71–83.

Zaino, J. (2008). Tag Sale. *RFID Journal*. Retrieved from http://www.rfidjournal.com/

Zainudeen, A. (2007). *Proof that cost differentials drive SMS usage.* Retrieved from http://blogs.dialogic.com/2007/06/proof-that-cost.html

Zeithaml, V. A. (1988). Consumer perceptions of price, quality, and value: a means-end model and synthesis of evidence. *Journal of Marketing*, *52*, 2–22. doi:10.2307/1251446

Zerubavel, E. (1979). *Patterns of Time in Hospital Life: A Sociological Perspective*. Chicago: University of Chicago Press.

Zhang, J., & Mao, E. (2008). Understanding the acceptance of mobile SMS advertising among young Chinese consumers. *Psychology and Marketing*, *25*(8), 787–805. doi:10.1002/mar.20239

Zhou, N., Zhou, D., & Ouyang, M. (2003). Long-term effects of television advertising on sales of consumer durables and nondurables. *Journal of Advertising*, *32*(2), 45–54.

Zimmerman, B. J. (1998). Developing self-regulation cycles of academic regulation: An analysis of exemplary instructional model. In Schunk, D. H., & Zimmerman, B. J. (Eds.), *Self-regulated learning: From teaching to self-reflective practice* (pp. 1–19). New York: Guilford.

Zimmerman, B. J., Bonner, S., & Kovach, R. (1996). *Developing self-regulated learners: Beyond achievement to self-efficacy*. Washington, DC: American Psychological Association. doi:10.1037/10213-000

Zimmerman, B. J., & Schunk, D. H. (2001). *Self-Regulated learning and academic achievement: Theoretical perspectives*. Mahwah, NJ: Erlbaum.

Zweig, D., & Webster, J. (2002). Where is the line between benign and invasive? An examination of psychological barriers to the acceptance of awareness monitoring systems. *Journal of Organizational Behavior*, *23*(5), 605–633. doi:10.1002/job.157

Zwikael, O., Shimizu, K., & Globerson, S. (2005). Cultural differences in project management capabilities: A field study. *International Journal of Project Management*, *23*(6), 454–462. doi:10.1016/j.ijproman.2005.04.003

About the Contributors

Anabela Mesquita is a professor at the Institute of Administration and Accountancy (ISCAP)/Polytechnic School of Porto (IPP), Portugal. She is also an invited researcher at the Algoritmi R & D Center, Information Systems Group, at the University of Minho (Portugal). She lectures courses related to business communication, information society and digital storytelling. Dr. Mesquita's research interests include knowledge and innovation management, impact of information systems in organization, lifelong learning at higher education levels and e-learning. She also has been involved in several European and national research projects. She has published numerous papers in various international journals and conference proceedings. She has been a member of the programme committee and scientific committee of several national and international conferences, in most cases also serving as referee. She serves as Member of the Editorial Board and referee for IGI Global. She also serves as Associate Editor of the *Information Resources Management Journal*. She serves as referee for the *Journal of Cases of Information Technology*. She has also been evaluator and reviewer for European commission projects.

* * *

Milam Aiken is Professor of Management Information Systems in the School of Business Administration at the University of Mississippi. He holds degrees in business, engineering, and computer science (B.S.), business (M.B.A.), and management information systems (Ph.D.). Milam has published several journal articles in the field of electronic commerce focusing on consumer trust and factors affecting the likelihood of purchase.

Zaid Ibrahim Al-Shqairat is affiliated as an assistance professor of Managing Information System at Al-Hussein Bin Talal University. He received his PhD from UK in 2009, his research interest are in managing information systems issues and e- government.

Ikhlas Ibrahim Altarawneh is affiliated as an assistance professor of human resource management at Al-Hussein Bin Talal University. She received her PhD from UK in 2005. Her research interests are in human resources issues, HRM effectiveness, training and development and strategic HRM approach.

Kerstin Malm Andersson, Master of Science in Business and Economics. After academic studies working as a chief manager in Swedish Health Administration.

Susanne E. Bruppacher is a lecturer in the Education Dept. at the University of Fribourg, and in the Master's Program in Sustainable Development at the University of Basel, Switzerland. She holds a PhD in environmental psychology, and a Master's in developmental psychology, psychopathology and informatics. Her scientific interests are environmentally responsible behavior, education and ecology, and the diffusion of innovations for a sustainable development.

Nancy Chase is currently Associate Professor in Management Information Systems at Gonzaga University in Spokane, Washington. She has taught undergraduate courses in systems analysis and design, Java programming, introduction to MIS, and database management systems, as well as information systems theory and practice at the MBA level. Formerly an Information Technology professional, she worked for over 20 years in the utility, banking, and state government industries. Her specific areas of interest include the effects of IT culture on technology professionals, the tension between quality in IT work and organizational demands, and the impact of electronic communication on workplace environments.

Becky Clegg is a consultant specializing in insurance software projects and user training. She is a seasoned insurance industry specialist and holds a Master's degree in Adult and Organizational Learning from the University of Idaho. Her career spans teaching, insurance agency owner, insurance company district manager, software product director, training director, and regional and corporate sales. Additionally, she is actively involved with the National Association of Insurance Women International. Her specific focus includes the concepts of email overload and impact on the insurance industry workforce.

Frederic de Simoni received his MSc. in computer science from the University of Zurich, Switzerland and followed up by obtaining a Certificate in Advanced Studies (CAS) in Human Computer Interaction Design (HCID) from the University of Applied Sciences, Rapperswil, Switzerland. His main interests are the design of user interfaces and user experience, as well as current and future trends in human-computer interaction.

Gary Douglas graduated in 1996 from the University of Edinburgh with a BSc (Hons) in Mathematical Physics. He completed a PhD in 1999 again at the University of Edinburgh. His work at CCIR includes studies of eBanking web portals, mobile services (including SMS / MMS banking), contact centre technologies, online self-help financial tools, eCRM solutions and 2 factor authentication methods.

Mats Edenius is a professor in Information Systems in the Department of Informatics and Media at Uppsala University, Sweden. His main research interests lie within the areas of Information Technology, Knowledge and Management. Further, his research is also linked with usability issues, ICT and Open Innovation Processes. Edenius research covers both private and public sector.

Lauren Eder is Professor and Chair of the Department of Computer Information Systems at Rider University. She holds a Ph.D. and MBA in Management Information Systems from Drexel University and a BS from Boston University. Her research focuses on the adoption and diffusion of Internet technologies, and has been published in Communications of the ACM, Journal of Electronic Commerce Research, Journal of Information Systems Education, Global Studies Journal, Omega, and others. She is editor of Managing Healthcare Information Systems with Web-Enabled Technologies, Idea Group

Publishing, Hershey, PA (2000). She recently completed a Fulbright Specialist Program assignment at the Universidad de Panama. Prior to joining Rider University, she worked for IBM and Digital Equipment Corporation.

Damian O. Eke is a Nigerian research student at the Centre for Computing and Social Responsibility, De Montfort University, UK. He holds a B.Phil in Philosophy from Pontifical Urban University Rome and MA in Applied Ethics from Norwegian University of Science and Technology under the European Scholarship scheme- Erasmus Mundus. His research interests include; Research ethics in ICT, The Role of ICT in Nigerian Socio-economic Development, The social impact of ICT in Developing countries and Corporate Social Responsibility in Nigeria. Currently, he is working on developing an effective framework for ethical review of ICT research projects within UK university systems. This work is partially sponsored by the UK Higher Education Academy.

Christine Fidler is a principal lecturer in Informatics and research associate of the Centre of Computing and Social Responsibility (CCSR) at De Montfort University. Since gaining her PhD in Management Information Systems from York University, she has been active in research, teaching and publication within several aspects of the IS field, including the impact of culture on IS application, management information systems design and deployment, and customer-relationships management.

Mohammed Ghanbari (M'78-SM'97-F01) is best known for the pioneering work on two-layer video coding for ATM networks, now known as SNR scalability in the standard video codecs, which earned him a Fellowship of IEEE in 2001. He has published more than 450 technical papers and four books on various aspects of video networking. His book on *Video coding: an introduction to standard codecs,* received the Rayleigh prize as the best book of year 2000 by the IET. He is a Fellow of IEEE, Fellow of IET and Charted Engineer (CEng).

Linwu Gu is an Associate Professor of the MIS and Decision Sciences Department of the Eberly College of Business and IT, Indiana University of Pennsylvania, Indiana, Pennsylvania. She received her PhD of Business Administration in MIS, and Master degree in Computer Sciences from the University of Mississippi. She has published a few referred journal papers in e-commerce and decision support systems. She has given numerous presentations in national and international conferences.

Sven Helmer is currently a Senior Lecturer at the Department of Computer Science and Information Systems at Birkbeck, University of London. He obtained a PhD from the University of Mannheim, Germany, and an MSc in Computer Science from the University of Karlsruhe, Germany. He has also held a visiting professorship in databases at the University of Heidelberg, Germany. His research interests include native XML databases, query optimization, multi-user synchronization as well as interdisciplinary research in the areas of information systems, astronomy, physics, and ethnography. He has published more than 45 peer-reviewed papers and book chapters.

Mervyn A. Jack is the Director of CCIR. Research concerns the need to optimise use of new technologies for mass-market access to consumer channels such as telephone and Internet banking where his research on usability engineering is being used to create improved user interface designs for these mass channels. An author of some 240 papers and three textbooks, Professor Jack is a Fellow of the Royal Society of Edinburgh and a Fellow of the Institution of Electrical Engineers.

Raed Kanaan is an assistant Professor in Management Information System at the Arab Academy for Banking and Financial Sciences. He received his PhD in Information systems from the De Montfort University, and MSc in management information systems form the Arab Academy for Banking and Financial Sciences. His research interests include e-government in developing countries, e-commerce, impact of culture on IT adoption and implementations in the Middle East, and Intellectual capital in the Arab universities.

Richard Lee teaches consumer behavior and marketing research courses with the University of South Australia. Prior to academia, Dr Lee spent more than 10 years managing the marketing functions of IT/telecommunication companies in Asia. His research interests are in the areas of consumer behavior, particularly with customer loyalty, social influences, and word-of-mouth.

Svante Leijon, Associate professor, Department of Business Administration, School of Business, Gothenburg University. His research focuses HRM and Organizational Dynamics.

Diarmid Marshall graduated from the University of Edinburgh in 1995 with a MEng (Hons) degree in Electronics. His MEng project with GEC Plessey Semiconductors Ltd. (Swindon) involved looking at demodulation and decoding techniques for digital radios. Diarmid's work has included user trials on automated telephone services, EPGs and interactive television, and alphanumeric data entry techniques.

Andrew McDonald is an independent consultant with extensive experience and knowledge in Project and Programme Management. Over the last 10 years he has worked across all phases of the project life cycle on large-scale implementations in Europe, Asia and Africa. Born in Australia, Andrew began his career in project management through the Australian Army and subsequent deployment as a Combat Engineering Officer. Since then Andrew has worked in various countries with leading telecommunications and consulting companies delivering IT based project management. Most recently Andrew worked as an executive at Accenture specialising in Project/Program Management of OSS and BSS systems. Andrew has a BSc in Information Systems & Management and MSc in Corporate Governance & Ethics (Birkbeck, University of London). He has also researched and written papers on project management.

Michelle Kow Pei Ming graduated with a Masters of Business Administration from the School of Management, Unviersiti Sains Malaysia. Her research focused on the acceptance of users towards social networking sites as a job search tool. Currently she is attached to a multinatinational company in the Bayan Lepas Free Trade Zone in Penang.

Stephanie Moser is senior researcher at the Interdisciplinary Center for General Ecology at the University of Bern, Switzerland. She holds a Master's in social and general psychology and is about to conclude her PhD studies in environmental psychology. Her scientific interests are in individual and societal processes regarding the diffusion of new (environmental-friendly) technologies.

Osemeke Mosindi is PhD researcher in Information Behaviour at Northumbria University. His research interests lie in understanding how organisational behaviour is shaped, in particular how this affects information use. And to identify ways to improve information use, through the identified factors, using complexity theories as a base framework, and social network analysis for graphical representation of behaviour in organisations. He is a member of the British computing society, the UK systems society and has given presentations at UKAIS workshops and consortiums.

Jamie Murphy's industry and academic career spans five continents. His industry experience includes owning hospitality businesses, European Marketing Manager for PowerBar and Greg LeMond Bicycles, and the Google Online Marketing Challenge lead academic. Dr Murphy publishes in academic journals and newspapers such as The New York Times and Wall Street Journal.

Gareth Peevers has a BA (Hons) in Artificial Intelligence and MSc in HCI, both from the University of Sussex, UK. Has been a Research Fellow at Edinburgh University in the Centre for Communication Interface Research (CCIR) since April 2004. Gareth's interests lie in design and research problems that involve a combination of interaction, usability, creativity and learning. His thesis investigated applications of Mobile Banking. Gareth is also a freelance user experience designer.

T. Ramayah has an MBA from Universiti Sains Malaysia (USM). Currently he is an Associate Professor at the School of Management in USM. He teaches mainly courses in Research Methodology and Business Statistics. Apart from teaching, he is an avid researcher, especially in the areas of technology management and adoption in business and education. His publications have appeared in Computers in Human Behavior, Resources, Conservation and Recycling, Turkish Online Journal of Education Technology, Journal of Research in Interactive Marketing, Information Development, Journal of Project Management (JoPM), IJITDM, International Journal of Services and Operations Management (IJSOM), Engineering, Construction and Architectural Management (ECAM) and North American Journal of Psychology. He is constantly invited to serve on the editorial boards and program committees of many international journals and conferences of repute. His full profile can be accessed from http://www.ramayah.com

Hans Rämö is an Associate Professor in Business Administration at Stockholm University. He is a researcher and lecturer in CSR, Organization Theory, and Marketing and Management Communication. Research interests include: temporal and spatial factors of organizations and management; CSR and environmental management; visual communication; organizational trust; philosophy and sociology of science.

Simon Rogerson is Professor in Computer Ethics and Director of the Centre for Computing and Social Responsibility at De Montfort University. Following a successful industrial career where he held managerial posts in the computer field, he now combines research, lecturing and consultancy in the management, organisational and ethical aspects of ICT. He received the 2000 IFIP Namur Award for outstanding contribution to the creation of awareness of the social implications of ICT. In 2005 he became the first non-American to be given the prestigious SIGCAS Making a Difference Award by the ACM.

Swadesh Kumar Samanta is currently working in the rank of Director in Department of Telecommunication, Government of India. He recently completed his PhD from University of Essex, UK under UK-India Education and Research Initiative Scholarships scheme. He was also the recipient of *Chevening Scholarships* awarded by British Council for his MSc study at the UK. He worked (concurrent with PhD) with Network Research Centre, BT, UK where he developed a tool to indentify and account congestion created by the users and their applications in the internet. He has interest on information delivery in next generation network environment, cost analysis, demand modeling and multimedia service pricing. His research has been published in number of international journals and conferences covering both engineering and social science discipline. He is regularly invited to give talks at international conferences.

Jia Shen is an Assistant Professor of the Department of Computer Information Systems at Rider University. She holds a Ph.D. and M.S. in Information Systems from the New Jersey Institute of Technology. She has published in IEEE Transactions on Professional Communication, IEEE Transactions on Systems, Man, and Cybernetics, Journal of Electronic Commerce Research, Journal of Information Systems Education, and Journal of Asynchronous Learning Networks. Her current research interests include Social Computing, E-Commerce, and Human Computer Interaction. Prior to joining Rider University, she was an Assistant Professor at the New York Institute of Technology.

Petia Sice, PhD, is a Reader in Complexity and Organisation at Northumbria University. Her research interests lie in modelling and knowing of social systems from a complexity perspective. This includes first and second order cybernetics, autopoiesis and self-organisation, non-linear dynamics and chaos, and the philosophy of thought and language. She is also a founder of the Complexity and Change Network North.

Norazah Mohd Suki is currently an Associate Professor at the Labuan School of International Business & Finance, Universiti Malaysia Sabah, Labuan International Campus. She has supervised several postgraduate students at MBA and PhD level. Her research interests include Electronic Marketing, E-Commerce, M-Commerce, Consumer Behaviour, Mobile Learning and areas related to Marketing. She actively publishes articles in international journals. She is the editor-in-chief to Labuan e-Journal of Muamalat & Society, a member in the International Advisory Board for GLOBUS An International Journal of Management, and reviewer to many international journals. She has sound experiences as speaker to public and private universities, government bodies on courses related to Structural Equation Modelling (SEM), Statistical Package for Social Sciences (SPSS), Research Methodology. She can be contacted at azahsuki@yahoo.com.

Evan Swinger is a Masters student at the University of Western Australia. His research interests are in the areas of e-commerce and internet marketing.

Chia-Wen Tsai is an assistant professor in the Department of Information Management, Ming Chuan University. Dr. Tsai is one of the Editors-in-Chief of International Journal of Online Pedagogy and Course Design. He is also the Associate Editor of International Journal of Technology and Human Interaction, International Journal of Information Communication Technologies and Human Development, and International Journal of Innovation in the Digital Economy. He is interested in the online teaching methods and knowledge management.

Yann Truong is Assistant Professor of Marketing and Technology Management at ESC Rennes School of Business. He is also Head of the Center for Technology and Innovation Management of the school. His areas of research are digital marketing with a focus on the Internet and mobile phones, management and marketing of innovations, social media marketing, and luxury marketing. He also participates in several funded research and development projects with large and small companies within the telecommunications industry.

Lars Göran Wallgren, Licentiate of Philosophy in Psychology and Master of Science in Business and Economics, is a teacher and a PhD at the Department of Psychology, Gothenburg University, Sweden. His research focuses on work motivation and stress among information technology (IT) consultants. Furthermore, Lars Göran has a long experience as a management consultant in the IT business.

Jianfeng Wang is an Associate Professor of the MIS and Decision Sciences Department of the Eberly College of Business and IT, Indiana University of Pennsylvania, Indiana, Pennsylvania. He received his PhD of Business Administration in MIS from the University of Mississippi. He has published a few referred journal papers in e-commerce and decision support systems and economics of information technology.

Kustim Wibowo is a Professor and Chair of the MIS and Decision Sciences Department of the Eberly College of Business and IT, Indiana University of Pennsylvania, Indiana, Pennsylvania. He received his Ph.D. in MIS from the University of Kentucky. Lexington, Kentucky. Dr. Wibowo also holds an MS in Computer Science from Baylor University, Waco, Texas. His current research interests include: e-commerce and web security, information systems for educational technology, human resource information systems, information for managerial decision support, and business mobile application development. Dr. Wibowo's research articles appeared in such refereed forums as Decision Support Systems, International Journal of Instructional Media, Pennsylvania Journal of Business and Economics, Synergy, and Employee Relations.

John Woods is a senior lecturer and his interests include image processing, autonomous robotics, intelligent power control, networks and network pricing. During his brief career he has accumulated over 60 journal and conference publications accompanied by grants in these areas. He is a member of the IEE and regularly attends and presents at national and international conferences.

Index